16. 95

The world of ISLAM

EDITED BY BERNARD LEWIS

490 illustrations, 160 in colour
330 photographs drawings and maps

The world of ISLAM

FAITH · PEOPLE · CULTURE

TEXTS BY

Bernard Lewis
Richard Ettinghausen
Oleg Grabar
Fritz Meier
Charles Pellat
A. Shiloah
A. I. Sabra
Edmund Bosworth
Emilio García Gómez
Roger M. Savory
Norman Itzkowitz
S. A. A. Rizvi
Elie Kedourie

THAMES AND HUDSON

HANIM SULTAN'A
MAZİNİN ŞANI ÂTİNİN VAADİ

Designed and produced by THAMES AND HUDSON LTD, LONDON
MANAGING EDITOR: Ian Sutton BA
DESIGN: Pauline Baines MSIA
EDITORIAL: Susan Moore BA
                    Rosemary Northcote
PICTURE RESEARCH: Georgina Bruckner MA
MAPS: Shalom Schotten MSIA
DRAWINGS: Peter Bridgewater DIP.A.D.
FILMSET by Keyspools Ltd, Golborne, Lancashire

© 1976 THAMES AND HUDSON LTD, LONDON
First paperback edition with corrections 1992
Reprinted 1994

ISBN 0-500-27624-2

Printed and bound in Slovenia by Mladinska Knjiga

CONTENTS

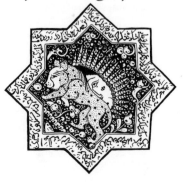

FOREWORD AND ACKNOWLEDGMENTS

IT WAS A LONG TIME before Christendom was ready to recognize Islam as an independent religious and historical fact. For centuries Christians were content to refer to Muslims simply as unbelievers or, if some more specific designation was required, by the ethnic names of the various Muslim peoples whom they encountered, as Saracens, Moors or Turks. Even a convert to Islam was said to have 'turned Turk'. When finally Christian Europe consented to give its great neighbour a religious appellation, it invented one by false analogy, calling the people Muhammadans and their faith Muhammadanism, in the mistaken belief that Muhammad was for Muslims what Christ was for Christians.

From the Renaissance onwards, however, European scholars made a serious attempt to learn the languages of the Muslims, and to understand and interpret their religion and civilization. By the present time there is an impressive body of scholarly literature on the different aspects of Islamic belief, history and culture. In the following pages the reader is introduced to some of these aspects, and to some of the distinctive qualities and achievements of the world of Islam.

The book begins with an introductory chapter, presenting the faith of Islam and the peoples who accepted it. This leads to a group of chapters primarily but not exclusively concerned with the central area and period of Islamic greatness—i.e. with the Middle East and North Africa from the advent of Islam in the 7th century to the aftermath of the Mongol conquests in the 13th. Successive chapters deal with government, art, the Sūfīs, literature, music, science and warfare. The next four chapters deal with specific major areas—Spain, the Iranian world, the Ottoman world and India (the last three being mainly concerned with the post-Mongol period). A final chapter discusses the impact of the West on Islam from the 18th century, and the reactions and responses of the Islamic peoples to that impact.

One of the most remarkable achievements of Islamic civilization is in the arts, through which the outsider may obtain insights which would otherwise be attainable only after a long and difficult philological apprenticeship. Much use has therefore been made of pictorial evidence to present and explain the different topics dealt with in this book.

BERNARD LEWIS

A note on dates

Dates are given first according to the Muslim calendar and then according to the Christian, e.g. 548/1153. The year 1 of the Muslim era is regarded as beginning on 16 July AD 622. According to the former Arab calendar this was the first day of the year in which Muhammad and his first followers undertook the *hijra*, or their migration from Mecca, to establish the first centre of the new faith in Medina. Since the Muslim year is shorter than the Christian, the two never completely coincide. Where the precise date of an event in either calendar is known, the conversion can be exact. Where it is not known we have given the nearest single equivalent. The result, it is true, may be inaccurate by up to one year, but in the present context this seemed preferable to the cumbersome citation of two Christian years for every Muslim one, as is sometimes done.

In the case of the centuries, the correspondence is close enough to make it reasonable to equate them as a rough guide, e.g. VI/12th century. They begin by being out of step by about twenty years (81/700) but the Muslim 700 exactly corresponds to the Christian 1300. After that they begin to get out of step in the opposite direction (see Chronological Table on p. 348).

Following a generally accepted convention, 19th- and 20th-century dates are given only according to the Christian calendar.

This book would have been impossible to produce without the generous assistance of many individuals and institutions. The Editor and publishers wish especially to thank Dr Yolande Crowe, who gave invaluable help with the illustrations, and Professor Edmund Bosworth, who has been responsible for the transcription and styling of Arabic words. The picture sections have been the responsibility of the publishers, but all the authors have been unstinting in their help and advice. Professor Ettinghausen, in particular, provided guidance on many other chapters besides his own. We also wish to record our thanks to Professor Nurhan Atasoy, Istanbul; Manijeh Bayani, London; Dr Kemal Cig, Istanbul; Dr Colin Heywood, London; Madame M. Hirschkopf, Paris; Professor M. S. Ipsiroglu, Istanbul; and Miss Norah Titley, London.

OUTLINE OF ISLAMIC HISTORY

The Prophet Muhammad died in 11/632. At the time of his death, he had already established a Muslim state in a large part of Arabia. His successors were known as the caliphs; but after thirty years the state became split between the followers of ʿUthmān, the third caliph, and those of ʿAlī, the fourth, Muhammad's son-in-law. This division led to the two great religious parties which still exist – the Sunnī (who go back to ʿUthmān's followers) and the Shīʿī (who go back to ʿAlī's).

The dynastic caliphates
In 41/661, the orthodox or patriarchal caliphs, ruling from western Arabia, were succeeded by the first dynastic caliphate, that of the **Umayyads**. These had their main base in Syria, and under their rule the Islamic empire extended eastwards as far as the borders of India and China, westwards to the Atlantic and the Pyrenees. The Umayyad caliphate was overthrown by a successful revolution in the year 132/750 and succeeded by the House of ʿAbbās. The **ʿAbbāsids** transferred the capital from Syria to Iraq, and established their seat of government in the city of Baghdad. The ʿAbbāsid caliphs reigned until the year 656/1258. They were, however, effective rulers only for the first century or so of this period. In the east, local dynasties appeared in Persia, notably the Tāhirids, the Saffārids, and the Sāmānids, who succeeded in establishing an extensive domain in Central Asia, where they greatly extended the borders of the Islamic empire. In the west, the first country to become independent of Baghdad was Spain, where an Umayyad prince fleeing from the east established an independent amirate in 138/756. This was followed by the rise of other independent dynasties in Morocco, in Tunisia and in Egypt.

In the early period effective control of the caliphate remained in the hands of the Arab conquerors and their descendants. Later they were compelled to share power with non-Arab converts to Islam and notably with Persians in the east and Berbers in the west. During the IV/10th and V/11th centuries Persian and Persianized dynasties became the centres of a Persian cultural renaissance.

At about the same time a third ethnic element entered Middle Eastern Islam – the Turks. By the V/11th century they were migrating westwards both north and south of the Caspian and the Black Sea. In the central Islamic lands they were led by the family of **Seljuq**, which established a new institution, the universal sultanate claiming authority over the whole of Sunnī Islam, and co-existing with the caliphate, which it recognized. During the period of Turkish domination, Islam was extended to new areas – in Central Asia, where the Turkish converts to Islam carried the new faith, by conquest and by preaching, to their still unconverted brethren; in India, where Turkish invaders from Iran and Central Asia created a new Islamic empire in the sub-continent; and in Asia Minor, which was successfully invaded by Turkish tribesmen and armies in the V/11th century. A new Muslim principality was set up here, governed by a branch of the House of Seljuq.

The Fātimids and Spanish Umayyads
The independent dynasties which had arisen within the ʿAbbāsid caliphate, while exercising effective independence, were content to recognize the supremacy of the ʿAbbāsid caliph as the single legitimate head of all Islam. In the IV/10th century this was challenged in the west by the rise of the **Fātimid** dynasty, first in Tunisia, where it arose in 297/909, and then in Egypt, which the Fātimids conquered in 358/969. The Fātimids were not Sunnīs but followers of Shīʿism, and denied the right of the ʿAbbāsid caliphs, whom they regarded as usurpers. Instead they established their own caliphate which for a while ruled over large areas of North Africa, Egypt, Syria and western and southern Arabia. The establishment of the Fātimid caliphate in North Africa provoked the Umayyad Amīr of Cordoba in Spain, in self-protection, to proclaim himself as caliph; and there were thus for a time three caliphs in the Islamic world.

The **Umayyad caliphate of Cordoba** foundered in 422/1031, giving way to a number of small local dynasties. The Fātimid caliphate in Egypt was finally suppressed, after a long decline, by a Kurdish officer from the east, Saladin, in 566/1171. He set up a new dynasty, the **Ayyūbids**, which ruled in Egypt, Palestine and Syria until the VII/13th century, when it gradually merged into a new institution, the **sultanate of the Mamlūks** or military slaves.

The Mongols
The migration of the steppe peoples of Central and eastern Asia into the Middle East, which began during the IV/10th and V/11th centuries, reached its climax with the coming in the VII/13th century of the heathen Mongols, who conquered the whole of South-West Asia and incorporated it for the first time in an empire which had its capital in the East, first in Mongolia and later in Peking. The Mongols ruled over Central Asia, Iran and Iraq, extended their suzerainty to Anatolia, and several times invaded Syria. Later they were themselves converted to Islam, as a result of which several new Islamic states, with a strong Turko-Mongol character, appeared in the Middle East.

After the Mongols: five centres of the Islamic world
In the period following the Mongol invasion there were five main political centres in the Islamic world. The first of these was that of the **Ottomans**. With their capture of Constantinople in 857/1453, this became the greatest of all the Islamic empires.

The second was the **Mamlūk** sultanate of Egypt, Palestine and Syria, which survived the Mongol invasion, and was for a while the main citadel of the surviving older Arabo-Islam culture. It was conquered and its territories incorporated in the Ottoman empire in 922–3/1516–17.

The third Islamic state was based on Iran. At the beginning of the XI/17th century a new and powerful monarchy embracing the whole country was created by the **Safavids**, a dynasty originating in the north-west. The Safavids were Shīʿites, and made Shīʿism the state religion of Iran, which it has remained to the present day.

The fourth centre was in India, where a succession of Turkish Muslim dynasties ruled over most of the north. In the X/16th century these were succeeded by the **Mughul** house, founded by Bābur, a descendant of Tamerlane who came to India from Central Asia. The empire he founded lasted until its final overthrow by the British.

The fifth and last centre of Islamic power in this period was in the Eurasian steppes, in what is now southern Russia and Soviet Central Asia. Here there were two large states of Islamicized Mongols, the **khanate of the Golden Horde** based on southern Russia, and the **Chaghatay khanate** based on Central Asia. Both states were later incorporated in the Russian empire.

During this period Islam had both advanced and retreated in various areas. In South-West Europe the Muslims were driven out of Spain, Portugal and Sicily, and even North Africa was for a while invaded by the victorious Spaniards and Portuguese. In Eastern Europe the Ottoman Turks brought Islam to the walls of Vienna but were in due course compelled to relinquish most of their conquests. In Eastern Europe, too, the Golden Horde for a while managed to extend its sovereignty over the princes of Moscow.

The most important area of Islamic colonization was in South-East Asia, to which Islam was brought by traders and others from Arabia and above all from India. By the X/16th century a large part of the Malay lands had already become Muslim.

The last five hundred years
From the X/16th century onwards, Islam was in retreat, and falling under the domination of a Europe which was expanding at both ends. The process began with the reconquest of Russia and Spain. Western Europeans circumnavigated the African continent and began to establish a growing hegemony in South-East, southern and ultimately South-West Asia. Islam was so to speak caught in a pincers movement between Russia from the north and the Western European peoples from the south. These changes were for a while disguised or delayed by the imposing military might of the Ottoman, Persian and Mughul empires; but in time these also weakened and ceased to be able to resist the European advance.

Western domination continued until the aftermath of World War II, when the colonial empires of Britain, France, Holland and Italy were dismantled and their former territories became independent. The resulting national states, whose boundaries largely ignored ethnic division, produced a volatile situation which is still unresolved.

INTRODUCTION

Bernard Lewis

THE CALL FIRST CAME TO MUHAMMAD when he was approaching his fortieth year. The traditional Muslim biography of the Prophet tells that on a night in the month of Ramadān, the Angel Gabriel came to him as he slept in solitude on Mount Hirā' and said, 'Recite!' Muhammad hesitated, and three times the Angel nearly stifled him, until Muhammad asked, 'What shall I recite?' Then the Angel said: 'Recite in the name of thy Lord who created all things, who created man from clots of blood. Recite, for thy Lord is the most generous, Who taught by the pen, Who taught man what he did not know.'

These words form the first four verses of the ninety-sixth chapter of the Qur'ān. This is an Arabic word meaning 'reading' or 'recitation', and is used to describe the book containing the revelations which Muslims believe were vouchsafed by God to Muhammad. After this first message, Muhammad received many more, which he brought to the people of his birthplace, urging them to abandon their idolatrous beliefs and practices and to believe in one, single, universal God.

Muhammad was born in the small oasis town of Mecca, in the region known as the Hijāz, in western Arabia, in about AD 571. The peninsula at that time lay on the margins of the civilized world, in touch with both the Byzantine and Persian empires, but subject to neither. In the south-west were well-watered valleys, where agriculture and cities had flourished since ancient times; but the greater part of Arabia consisted of arid steppe and desert, relieved by scattered oases and crossed by a few caravan tracks. Most of the population were nomads, who lived by tending their herds and by raiding rival tribes and the peoples of the oases and of the borderlands. Some lived by tilling the soil, in the few areas where this was possible; some by commerce, during periods when events in the outside world led to a revival of interest in the trans-Arabian trade routes. The resumption of conflict between Byzantium and Persia, the rival imperial powers that confronted each other in the Middle East, after more than a century of peace, was such a time, and both empires became very active in and near Arabia during the 6th century. A few small towns lived on a share in the traffic that passed through Arabia, between the Mediterranean world and the East. One of these towns was Mecca, originally a southern Arabian settlement, later inhabited by the Arab tribe of Quraysh.

The people of the peninsula, the Arabs, had a common literary language and a rich poetic literature, which helped greatly to give them a common sense of identity. But they had no common political order, and in their religious beliefs they were still pagans, worshipping various gods whom they believed to be under the authority of one supreme god called Allah. They were acquainted with other religions; there were colonies of Christians and Jews in Arabia, and some Arabs were converted by them to Christianity or Judaism. Others became dissatisfied with the idol-worship of their people but were unable to find satisfaction in either the Christian or Jewish faiths. They are known in the Arab tradition as *hanīfs*.

Muhammad's preaching in Mecca began to win converts, first in his own family and then in wider circles. After a while, it aroused opposition among the leading families of Mecca, who regarded the new preaching as a threat both to their faith and to their interests. Pressures of various kinds, and perhaps even physical violence, were used to detach his followers from him. Relations between the Prophet and his compatriots became worse and worse, until some of his converts were impelled to take refuge in Ethiopia.

Then, in the year AD 622 – about thirteen years after his first call – Muhammad made an agreement with emissaries from Yathrib, another town in the Hijāz some 280 miles north of Mecca. The people of Yathrib agreed to welcome him among them, to make him their arbitrator and to defend him and those converts who came with him from Mecca, as they would defend themselves. Muhammad sent the sixty-odd families in Mecca who had joined him, a few at a time, to Yathrib. He himself finally followed them, probably in September 622.

Yathrib now became the centre of the new faith and community and came to be known simply as Medina (al-Madīna) – the City. The migration of Muhammad and his followers from Mecca to Medina, called in Arabic the *hijra*, is regarded by Muslims as the decisive moment in the mission of their Prophet. It is from the year in which it took place that the Muslim calendar is reckoned, so that year 1 of the *hijra* began in 622.

In Mecca, Muhammad had been a private person preaching a new faith, against the indifference or hostility of the ruling powers; in Medina he was first a chief and then a ruler, wielding political and military as well as religious authority.

This new role is reflected in the teachings and activities of Muhammad himself, and in the kind of revelations required for the guidance of his community. Whereas the Meccan chapters of the Qur'ān are concerned chiefly with questions of doctrine and ethics, the Medina chapters deal with many legal and political matters, with problems that arose in the day-to-day life of the Muslim community which had, after the migration, become a Muslim polity.

For ten years after the *hijra*, the Prophet presided over the Muslim community in both war and peace and instructed them in the Islamic faith. His influence was extended by persuasion and by arms, and in the year

9/630 Mecca itself was conquered and brought into the Muslim fold.

On 8 June 632, the Prophet died, after a short illness. He had achieved great things. To the peoples of western Arabia he had brought a religion which, with its monotheism and its ethical doctrines, stood on an incomparably higher level than the paganism that it had replaced. He had brought the believers a book of revelations which was to become in the centuries to follow the guide to thought, faith and conduct of countless millions. And that is not all. He had established a new community and a new state, well organized and well armed, the power and prestige of which made it a dominant factor in Arabia.

The nature of the Islamic state
The word Islam is commonly understood by Muslims and others to mean surrender; that is, of the believer to God. The active participle of the same verb, Muslim, means one who performs the act of surrender. It is likely that the word originally conveyed a somewhat different notion – that of entirety. The Muslim in this sense was one who gave himself entirely to God alone to the exclusion of others, i.e. a monotheist as contrasted with the polytheists among whom the Prophet appeared in 1/7th-century Arabia.

It is no doubt in this sense that Islam was perceived, by Muhammad himself and by the first Muslims, not as an innovation but as a continuation – as a new and this time final phase in the long struggle between monotheism and polytheism. In this struggle, the many monotheist prophets who had preceded Muhammad, and their followers, were also Muslims, and the word Islam denoted the true faith taught by all God's appointed apostles. In this sense, both Judaism and Christianity had been at the time of their advent true religions, earlier phases in the same sequence of divine revelations. In the Muslim view, they were however superseded by the mission of Muhammad. What they contained which was true was incorporated in his message; what was not so incorporated was not true and was the result of a subsequent distortion.

Religiously, Islam is seen as a completion. Historically, it may be seen as a new beginning; the foundation of a new religion, a new empire and a new civilization. There is one important respect in which Muhammad's career differed markedly from that of Jesus and his other predecessors in the sequence of prophets – in that he succeeded in a worldly sense in his own lifetime. At first Muhammad too, like God's earlier apostles, was a humble and persecuted teacher. But instead of martyrdom, he achieved sovereignty.

Through the activities of its founder-prophet, Islam was involved from its very beginnings with political power. The Muslim community of Medina was not just a community, but also a state; subsequent events made it the nucleus of an empire. In the Muslim view the ultimate repository of sovereignty was God, from whom the Prophet derived both his authority and his law. The Prophet was the bearer of God's revelation, the messenger of God's purpose, the ruler, on God's behalf, of God's community of believers. Jesus had instructed the Christians to render unto Caesar the things which are Caesar's and unto God the things which are God's. During three centuries of struggle and persecution, this distinction was firmly established in Christian doctrine and practice, and the Christian religion created its own institutional structure, separate from that of the state – the Christian Church, law and hierarchy. The great change came with the conversion to Christianity of the Roman Emperor Constantine and the beginning of the uneasy linkage in Christendom between Church and state.

This dichotomy between the two powers does not exist in Islam at all; and indeed, such pairs of words as 'secular and religious', 'spiritual and temporal', have no equivalents in classical Arabic. In Rome, Caesar was God; in Christendom, God and Caesar shared power. In Islam, God is Caesar, and the head of the Muslim community is His vicegerent on earth.

When Muhammad died, his spiritual and prophetic mission was completed. His God-given task had been to restore the true monotheism taught by earlier prophets and then distorted and subverted; to abolish idolatry; to make known God's revelation embodying the true religion and the divine law. This he did during his lifetime. In Muslim belief, he was the last of the prophets. When he died, in 11/632, the revelation of God's will to mankind had been completed. There would be no more prophets and no further revelations.

However, though the spiritual function was at an end, the religious function remained; that of maintaining and defending the divine law and bringing it to the rest of mankind. The effective discharge of this religious function also required the exercise of political and military power – in a word, of sovereignty – in a state.

The first crisis: the caliphate
The death of the Prophet brought the first crisis in Islam. Muhammad had never claimed to be more than a mortal man, distinguished above others because he was the bearer of God's Word and the leader of God's people, but himself neither divine nor immortal. 'Muhammad,' says the Qur'ān (iii, 138), 'is no more than an Apostle, and Apostles before him have passed away. If then he dies or is killed, will you turn back upon your heels?' Muhammad had however left no clear instructions as to who was to succeed him in the leadership of the Islamic community and in the headship of the Islamic state, and the Muslims had only the meagre political experience of pre-Islamic Arabia to guide them.

The Prophet was dead and there would be no more. The leader of the community was dead and had to be replaced. In this emergency, the ablest and most active among the inner group of his disciples chose Abū Bakr, one of the first and most respected of the Muslims, and hailed him as leader with the title *khalīfa*, an Arabic word which by a fortunate ambiguity combined the notions of successor and deputy. From this act of improvisation grew the great institution of the caliphate and, in time, the principle of the universal elective caliphal office.

The hereditary principle was not unknown to the Arabs of that time. Beyond the northern borders of Arabia, the two great empires of Byzantium and Persia, representing the world of advanced civilization on the Arab horizon, were ruled by dynastic monarchies. In the south, too, the sedentarized states of south-western Arabia had, until not long before, been governed by lines of local, hereditary kings. Even among the northern Arabs, who provided the main initial support of the new order, a form of legitimism existed, and the chief of a tribe was usually chosen, albeit by no fixed rule of succession, from among the members of a single noble family. Often this family was holy as well as noble, and the descendants of a santon might enjoy the right to the hereditary custodianship of a shrine or sacred object. Judaism and Christianity, both represented in pre-Islamic Arabia, shared a belief in the sanctity and ultimate triumph of the royal house of David, through the anointed Messiah; Zoroastrianism too offered a parallel in the belief in a *saoshyans*, a saviour who would arise at the end of time from the holy seed of Zoroaster.

But if the Arabs knew monarchy, they did not like it, and references to kingship in pre-Islamic times are usually hostile. Prestige is not the same as authority, and the choice of a new tribal chief, even if in practice limited to the members of one family, was not bound by any rule of succession. The choice was personal, and was made for personal qualities – the ability to evoke and retain loyalty. With the advent of Islam, the already existing anti-dynasticism was reinforced by an anti-aristocratic sentiment, expressed in the Islamic belief in the brotherhood and equality of the believers, and rejection of any primacy save that of religious or personal merit. Through all the many subsequent changes in the caliphate as it actually existed, the doctrine of elective succession remained enshrined in Muslim theory and jurisprudence, and the fiction of election was preserved throughout the later caliphal dynasties.

Abū Bakr and 'Umar, the first and second caliphs, both came from clans of minor importance in the society of pre-Islamic Mecca. The third caliph was a man of a different stamp. 'Uthmān ibn 'Affān was a member of the house of Umayya, one of the great clans of Mecca, the only such among the senior companions of the Prophet. His succession was a victory and an opportunity for the Meccan aristocracy, from which they did not fail to profit.

A temporary cessation of warfare on the frontiers gave the tribesmen leisure to reflect on their grievances; the many strains and stresses of a vast new empire gave them matter for reflection. These conflicts and rivalries exploded into a devastating series of civil wars.

The first of these began in 36/656 with the murder of 'Uthmān and his replacement by 'Alī, the son-in-law and cousin of the Prophet. For the first time, a Muslim ruler was murdered by the Muslims and Muslim armies fought against one another. In the ensuing struggle 'Alī too was murdered, the elective caliphate came to an end, and a new caliphate, that of the house of Umayya, emerged, more definitely monarchical in principle. Significantly, they shifted the seat of the caliphate from Arabia to Syria, a newly conquered province, and one deeply marked by the political and administrative traditions of the ancient Middle Eastern empires.

In this complex and many-sided struggle, one group soon acquired special importance – the followers of 'Alī ibn Abī Tālib, the cousin and son-in-law of the Prophet. As husband of the Prophet's daughter Fātima he would have had no special claim to attention – such relationships counted for little in a polygamous society. As Muhammad's kinsman, however, he might, according to the notions of pre-Islamic Arabia, pose his candidature as successor to some part of both the political and religious authority of the Prophet. Already a strong candidate on grounds of personal merit and prestige, he was in addition able to attract the support of many who felt that since the elective caliphate had failed, a return to the kin of the Prophet might bring a restoration of the true, original message of Islam. They were known as the party of 'Alī, *Shī'at 'Alī*, and then simply as the Shī'a.

The Umayyad caliphate maintained itself for almost a century through a series of compromises and interim arrangements which preserved the unity of Islam and Islamic society, but at the cost of establishing and maintaining an Arab aristocratic domination over non-Arabs, including Muslim non-Arabs, and a system of imperial government and administration that came to borrow more and more of the structure, the methods and even the personnel of the empires which Islam had superseded.

There were many who resisted this process. A group of 'Alī's supporters, known as the Khārijīs – 'those who go out' – had withdrawn from his forces and turned against him during his lifetime; they continued to oppose the Umayyads and their successors. Theirs was the most extreme form of tribal anarchism, rejecting any authority not deriving from their own freely given and always revocable consent, and insisting that any believer of whatever origin could be caliph if the choice of the believers fell upon him. The Shī'a of 'Alī gave their allegiance to various members of the Prophet's family and followed a series of leaders who tried to overthrow the Umayyad caliphate and establish a new one in its place.

The second civil war began with a minor rising – minor, that is, in its immediate military and political effects; but of major religious and historical significance. In 61/680 Husayn, the son of 'Alī and grandson of the Prophet, led an insurrection against the Umayyad power. On the tenth day of the month of Muharram, at Karbalā in Iraq, Husayn, his family, and his followers met an Umayyad army and were defeated and killed. According to the tradition, some seventy perished in the battle and its aftermath, the only survivor being a sick child, 'Alī, the son of Husayn, who was left lying in a tent and lived to tell the story. This dramatic martyrdom of the Prophet's descendants, and the wave of anguish and penitence which it inspired, gave a new fervour to the Shī'ī movement, now inspired by the potent themes of sacrifice, guilt and expiation.

The blood of the victims of Karbalā transformed Shī'ism from a party to a sect, from a faction to a religion. In the course of the second civil war, the caliphate was once again plunged into years of struggle, ending only with the accession of another Umayyad, 'Abd al-Malik, who succeeded in restoring and reaffirming the monarchical principle.

The respite which he had won was of brief duration. A third civil war resulted in the overthrow of the Umayyads and their supersession by another branch of the Prophet's family, the 'Abbāsids, in what has often been described as a major revolution. It brought many changes, the most obvious of which was that of the dynasty. Other visible changes were the transfer of the capital from Syria to Iraq, where the city of Baghdad was adopted as the imperial capital, the gradual ending of Arab racial supremacy within the empire, and the emergence, in place of the Arabs, of a new cosmopolitan ruling group of Muslims of many races but with Arabic as their medium of communication and Islam as their common bond and mark of identity.

A fourth civil war occurred after the death of the 'Abbāsid Caliph Hārūn ar-Rashīd in 194/809, between his sons al-Amīn and al-Ma'mūn, in which social, national and regional interests are again clearly discernible.

The Arabs relinquish power

During these early centuries, certain major changes can be observed. One was the cessation of conquest. By the early III/9th century the great wave of Arabic expansion had reached its uttermost limits; in the east on the borders of India and China, in the west on the Atlantic coast and in Spain. For a while it must have seemed that the advance of Islam would continue rapidly and indefinitely until the whole world was brought under Arab rule and to the Islamic faith. By the early III/9th century this was clearly not so; and the final conquest and Islamicization of the world were postponed in the Muslim view to messianic times. The 'Abbāsid caliphs accepted the virtual ending of the war of conquest and settled down to more or less permanent frontiers and coexistence with the non-Muslim states beyond them. The religious duty of *jihād* – the perpetual and obligatory Holy War conducted by the Muslim state and community for the advancement of Islam – remained enshrined in Muslim law and tradition, but was given a more defensive and less military interpretation.

Another change was the fragmentation of the caliphal power, both territorially and politically. Where once all the lands of Islam had been effectively under the rule of a single caliph, the provinces were now governed by *de facto* independent rulers, often hereditary. In time, even in the capital, the caliphs ceased to be their own masters and fell under the rule of their military commanders and eventually of a separate political institution, more openly military in origin and method – the sultanate.

The theoretical unity of Islam was, however, maintained, and expressed a growing unity of language, culture, religion, institutions and the arts. The institution of the caliphate exercised a unifying influence even during the time of its weakness and decadence.

It has sometimes been said that the Islamic religion was imposed by force. This is not true, though the spread of both Islam and Arabism was to a large extent made possible by the parallel processes of conquest and colonization. When the Prophet died in 11/632, his faith, Islam, was known only in Arabia; the Arab people to whom he had brought it and the Arabic language in which his revelation was expressed – 'We have revealed an Arabic Qur'ān, so that you may understand' (Qur'ān, xii, 2) – were still confined to the Arabian peninsula and the desert borderlands of the Fertile Crescent. A century later the Muslim Arabs governed a vast empire, of many lands and peoples. In this empire, ruled by the heirs of Muhammad, Islam was the dominant religion and Arabic was rapidly replacing other languages to become, in time, the principal medium of government, commerce and education. With the inspiration of the Muslim faith, under the protection of the Islamic state and through the richness of the Arabic language, a vital and original culture evolved, created by men and women of many races and religions, but bearing the distinctive stamp of Arab tradition and modes of expression, and of Islamic values and standards.

The prestige of the speech of an aristocracy of conquerors, the practical usefulness of the language of administration and business; the diversity and opportunities of an imperial civilization; and most of all, the reverence accorded to the sacred idiom in which the Islamic revelation was preserved and explained; all helped in their different ways to further the processes of assimilation and Arabization.

In the course of the centuries, the Arab dominion of the caliphate passed away; and the Arabs were compelled first to share and then to relinquish control of the empire which they had created. But though other peoples succeeded them in political and military power, their language, their faith and their law remained as an enduring monument of their rule and achievement.

The ending of Arab political supremacy did not halt this process of Arabization, which continued to such effect that in most of the provinces of the Arab empire little remains of their previous languages and identities. Of the lands which the Arabs conquered in the 1/7th and 11/8th centuries, only their European acquisitions, Spain, Portugal and Sicily, are no longer Muslim, but have reverted to their Christian faith and Latin civilization; and even in these the period of Muslim rule has left many traces.

Iran: the exception

There was one country, however, which, though conquered by the Arabs and converted to Islam, nevertheless retained its own distinctive national identity. That exception is Iran. Like the other subject peoples of the Arab empire, the Persians had an ancient language and civilization of their own. Unlike the others, they also had a state and empire of their own, which lasted until they were destroyed by the advancing Arabs. Iraq under Persian rule, Syria, Palestine, Egypt and North Africa under Byzantine rule, had long since lost and forgotten their ancient glories, and were merely exchanging one imperial master for another. The Byzantines abandoned a number of provinces, but kept their heartlands and their capital, Constantinople, to which many of the Byzantine magnates fled from the lands lost to the Arabs. Iran was wholly overrun, and ceased to exist as a separate polity. Its capital passed into Arab hands, and its ruling classes, apart from some who found refuge in India, stayed where they were and earned themselves a place in the new order. The great reserves of skill and experience which they brought with them enabled them to make an immense contribution to the development of Islamic civilization – of society and culture, government and opposition, and even of the Muslim religion, in which Persians, in increasing numbers, found a refuge from defeat and despair.

Persian Muslims played some part in the further expansion of Islam in Central Asia. They played a much greater part in the flowering of Muslim culture, and in the international literature of Islam in the Arabic language. But they also preserved their own language, which after an interval reappeared in a new form, written in the Arabic script and with a large admixture of Arabic loan-words, yet still unmistakably Iranian – as Iranian as English is English and not French, despite the trauma and changes resulting from the Norman conquest of England.

The decline of caliphal power offered new opportunities; and, during the III/9th and IV/10th centuries, Iran re-emerged on the political scene. Persian dynasties ruled in many parts of the country, and a new, Persian culture evolved, responsive to the tastes of Persian courts and patrons, and reflecting an awakened sense of Persian cultural identity within Islam. From this time onwards, Persian joined Arabic as the second major language of Islam. Until then, Arabic had been the universal literary language of Islam, as was Latin in medieval Europe. It remained so for certain religious and legal purposes, and more generally in the countries where Arabic was spoken. Farther east, in Iran and in the whole wide area of Iranian cultural radiation, Persian became the dominant language, and the Persian classics provided the basis of education and the model of literary excellence.

Crusaders and Mongols

By the V/11th century the whole Islamic world was in a state of crisis. Its weakness was revealed by a series of invasions – Turks from the east, Caucasians from the north, Bedouins and Berbers from the south and Franks from the west. It is in this context that the Christian re-conquest of Spain and the arrival of the Crusaders in Palestine was perceived by Muslim historians.

The coming of the Crusaders to the East had several permanent effects. The most important of these was the growth of trade between the Islamic world and the West, across the Mediterranean. This trade had already begun, in small way, before the Crusaders arrived. It flourished greatly in the Levant ports under the Crusaders' rule, and survived their departure, as the Muslim leaders of the reconquest discovered the many advantages which this traffic brought them.

Another result of the Crusades was a permanent deterioration in the situation of the non-Muslim minorities under Muslim rule. At a time when the Crusaders had established a series of principalities in Syria and Palestine, the native Christians of these territories were suspected – often with good reason – of collaboration or at least sympathy with the enemies of Islam. Though persecution remained rare, there was a hardening of attitudes and a worsening of relations between the Muslims and those whom they regarded as disaffected subjects and as potential allies of a dangerous foreign enemy.

The Crusaders are the best known of the various invaders who entered the Islamic world in the Middle Ages. Far more important, however, from the Islamic point of view was the coming of the steppe peoples from the north. The first and greatest of these were the Turks, who established a new hegemony and inaugurated the second great age of Islamic power and expansion, renewing the *jihād*, and carrying the processes of conquest, conversion and colonization into vast new lands in Asia and Europe. At first they came as individuals, as slaves caught or bought beyond the Central Asian frontiers of Islam, imported at an early age, trained, educated and converted, and then enrolled in the armies of Islam, which they soon came to dominate. Such military slaves are known as *mamlūks*, an Arabic word meaning 'owned'. They were followed by free Turkish tribes, under their own chiefs, who migrated into the Islamic world, adopted Islam and became its most effective champions.

In the east, in the early V/11th century, the Turkish general Mahmūd of Ghazna led an army of frontiersmen and settlers into India, where the seeds they planted flowered into the great and rich Islamic civilizations of the sub-continent. In the west, later the same century, the Seljuq Turks won new lands from the Byzantines in Asia Minor and began the processes of migration, settlement and assimilation which in time gave that country the name of Turkey. Later, under the Ottoman successors of the Seljuqs, the Turks continued their advance far into Europe and set up an empire which endured for half a millennium – the last and greatest of the Islamic monarchies. At the same time, other Turkic peoples were colonizing in the areas of the great Eurasian steppe, north of the Caspian and Black Seas, reaching northward and westward as far as Finland and Poland.

An entirely new phase began with the conquest of the Middle East by the Mongols, a heathen people of eastern Asian origin who invaded and devastated the Islamic lands in the VII/13th century, destroying the Baghdad caliphate in 651/1258. This was a great shock and was seen by contemporary Muslims as a turning-point in Islamic history. The Mongols set up new states in the Middle East, for a while under the supremacy of the great Khān in the Far East, at first in Mongolia and later in Peking. But in time the Mongols, too, were assimilated. They were converted to Islam, their armies and followers Turkicized and the states established by them assimilated, though with many important changes, to the Muslim pattern.

The next stage in the domination of the steppe peoples was the campaigns undertaken by the great conqueror Tīmūr-i Lang, also known in the West as Tamerlane, whose dramatic career during the VIII/14th century created a huge and ephemeral empire. In the X/16th century the Uzbeks conquered new ground; thereafter, the invasion of the settled lands of the Middle East by tribes from the northern steppe ended, though the seepage of those already in the area into villages and towns and into the apparatus of government continued.

The coming of the Mongols represents a dramatic climax, marked by catastrophic defeats for Islam and the subjection of the Muslim heartlands, for the first time since the days of the Prophet, to non-Muslim domination. But, though the Mongol invasions marked the peak, they are only part of a larger process extending over centuries, one which transformed Middle Eastern civilization and turned it to new paths.

After the Mongols

There are several distinctive elements in this new pattern. One is the universal political and military domination of the Turks. Everywhere from Egypt to India and Central

Asia, the rulers, the military, the governors, the dominant caste were Turks; so much so that it came to be accepted as the normal and natural thing for Turks to fight and rule, often to the exclusion of others.

Related to this change was a new stability both of territorial entities and of institutional structures. The steppe peoples created new forms, notable among them the sultanate, a political and military sovereign authority distinct from but complementary to the caliphate, now restricted, in the main, to religious and legal matters.

The coming of the Turks brought new vigour into Islam, enabling it to resist and finally repel the Crusaders, and to launch a new Muslim advance into the heart of Europe. Turkish, in various forms, followed Arabic and Persian as the third major language of Islam in order of appearance, and the first in political importance.

In the post-Mongol period, there were four main centres of power in the Islamic world. One was the so-called Mamlūk sultanate, based on Egypt and including most of Syria. The Mamlūk sultanate, though governed by Turks and Circassians, with the native Arabic-speaking population in a subordinate role, nevertheless remained the stronghold of the older Arab culture. Neither Persian nor Turkish was extensively used, Arabic remaining the sole language of government, commerce, education and authorship. In the history of Arabic culture, Mamlūk Egypt represents a silver age – an age of compilation and commentary. In a sense, the Mamlūk sultanate was a kind of Arab Byzantium – a bastion of the older culture holding out against the new wave represented by the Turks, Mongols and their successors in the north.

The second centre was in Persia, ruled first by the Il-Khāns, the successors of the Mongol conquerors of the Middle East, and then by a number of Mongol and Turkish dynasties, the most notable among which was the line of Tamerlane. This in turn broke down, and a period of anarchy followed, ended by the emergence, at the turn of the IX/15th and X/16th centuries, of a new dynasty, that of the Safavids, with a strong religious character derived from their espousal of Shī'ism, from this time onward the state religion of Iran. The Safavids were the creators of the realm of Iran in the form in which, with some modifications, it has survived to the present day.

Farther west, the Turks in Anatolia, after the break-up of the Seljuq sultanate, split into a number of small states, the most important of which was that of the Ottomans. The small Ottoman principality in western Anatolia gradually grew by conquest on both sides of the Dardanelles Straits in Asia and in Europe into a vast empire.

The Ottoman state went through several stages. It began as a principality of march warriors. Then it became an Islamic monarchy and a successor to the Seljuq Sultanate of Rūm. Finally, its rulers saw it as a new Islamic universal monarchy, the successor of the caliphs of Islam and the emperors of Rome. Masters of both Greece and Anatolia, they needed a new capital for their empire, a coping stone for the arch which they had built. On 29 May 1453, two years after his accession, the Ottoman Sultan Mehmed II captured the city of Constantinople. In doing so, he sealed the union of two continents and two traditions which made up his inheritance. The last segment was fitted into place. For Europe this marked the end of the Middle Ages, according to the traditional view. In Islam it inaugurated a new Ottoman Imperial Age.

For a while the Ottoman sultans of Turkey and the Safavid shāhs of Iran confronted one another for the supremacy of the Middle East. Eventually, the Ottomans succeeded in defeating but not overwhelming Iran and then turned their attention to the surviving sultanate of Egypt, which they were able to overthrow without difficulty, incorporating its domains, Egypt, Syria and western Arabia, in the Ottoman realm. From 924/1517 onwards there were only two states of any significance in the Middle East, Turkey and Iran; and this remained the position until the present century.

The fourth major Turkish monarchy was that of northern India. After the conquests of Mahmūd of Ghazna, a Muslim state in India was ruled by Turkish sultans, known as the Slave Kings of Delhi. Their monarchy crumbled in due course and was replaced by a greater and more powerful empire founded by Babur, a descendant of Tīmūr-i Lang, who conquered India at the beginning of the X/16th century and established the so-called Mughul empire.

Apart from the four great monarchies, other Muslim states arose in both the old and the newly acquired territories of Islam – in North and tropical Africa, in Central Asia and in the vast new areas opened to Islam by peaceful penetration in South-East Asia. Only in one area was the advance of Islam decisively halted and reversed – in southern Europe, where after a long and bitter struggle the Muslims were finally evicted from the Iberian peninsula and from the islands of the central and western Mediterranean. And even this seemed to be more than compensated by the Ottoman advance as far as the walls of Vienna, the domination of Islamicized Mongols over the princes of Muscovy, and the steady Muslim advance into Hindu India.

But the might of the four great Muslim empires was deceptive, and concealed a fundamental change in the relationship between Islam and Christendom. From the end of the IX/15th century Europe embarked on the great movement of discovery and conquest which eventually brought almost the whole world within the orbit of European power and European civilization. The expansion of Europe began at both ends – the maritime peoples of the west by sea, the Russians in the east by land, both advancing into the Islamic world, from the north and the south. While the Muslim states of the Crimea, the Don and Volga basins and Central Asia passed under Russian rule, those of South and South-East Asia and of the Middle East were successively penetrated, influenced and dominated by newcomers from Western Europe.

For the second time, the first since the Mongol conquests, the Islamic heartlands were again subject to non-Muslim rule; the resulting shock, the responses and reactions of the Muslim peoples to this challenge, and the gradual transformation of Muslim society that followed, are the dominant themes of Muslim history in the modern age.

Mecca, the centre of the world: the frontispiece of an Arabic atlas of 958/1551. Round the edge of the circle are the names of all the Islamic countries, with lines showing their orientation relative to the Ka'ba. Mecca ceased to be of political importance within a few years of Muhammad's death, but it remained the spiritual centre of Islam, the focus of devotion and goal of pilgrimage. (1)

The historic lands of Islam stretch from Morocco to South-East Asia, forming a belt roughly 20°N to 40°N. Over most of this area rainfall is sparse and agriculture – and hence civilization – has to huddle round the oases and the great rivers. Above: a Moroccan village, a sudden patch of green amid barren mountains. Right: landscape near Mecca. Desert does not necessarily mean sand. Over much of the Islamic territories it is simply land without water. (2, 3)

Water brings life. Here the Tigris near Baghdad supports a rich agriculture. The best land was that made fertile by silting and flooding. Failing that, elaborate irrigation schemes brought fields along the banks into cultivation. Both the Tigris and the Euphrates rise in Anatolia. Fed by mountain snows, they remain abundant throughout their thousand-mile journey to the Persian Gulf. (4)

With the Umayyads the character of Islamic civilization began to change radically. It became less Arab and more Persian and Byzantine. Early Umayyad art was at first inclined to adopt the Hellenistic conventions common to the whole eastern Mediterranean. Above: stucco head from Khirbat al-Mafjar, near Jericho, first half of the II/8th century. Below: dancing girl from a painted glass bowl from Syria of about the same date. (5, 6)

The desert palaces of Qasr Amra, Mshatta, Khirbat al-Mafjar and 'Anjar (above) bear witness to the luxurious style of living enjoyed by the Umayyad caliphs. 'Anjar, which dates from the II/8th to III/9th century, and which has been partially reconstructed, employs the same architectural vocabulary as contemporary Early Christian and Byzantine buildings. (7)

Chess came to Islam from India. This ivory chessman in the form of an armed horseman is Persian, II/8th to III/9th century. (8)

The symbolism of power and of pleasure was taken over by the caliphs from their Byzantine and Sāsānid predecessors. The lions on the base of a stucco figure of a caliph from Khirbat al-Mafjar (left) go back to ancient Persia. The female figure (below left) is from the same palace; both date from the time of Caliph al-Walīd II, 125–6/743–4. (9, 10)

Fragments of paintings (above) from the ʿAbbāsid palace of Samarra (mid III/9th century) show that it was richly decorated in a style that owed more to Central Asia than to the classical world. The frescoes must have depicted scenes from court life. (11)

Under the Fātimids of Egypt the classical tradition still lingered. A carved ivory plaque (right) of the v/11th to vi/12th century contains scenes of hawking, harvesting and feasting. (12)

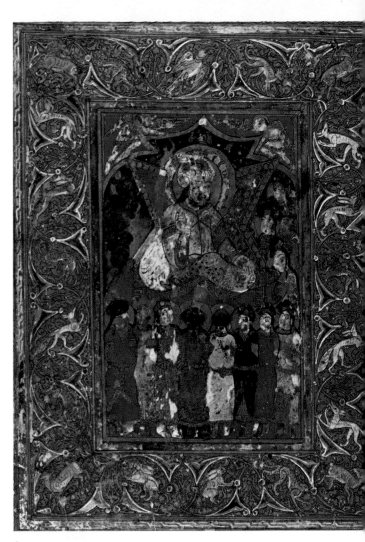

Every race was equal under Islam, and the only discriminations recognized in the Qur'ān were between believer and unbeliever and between man and woman and master and slave. But in practice things were not always so simple. In the early days all influential positions were held by Arabs; and even when this ceased to be so, the possession of Arab blood carried social prestige. The Arab prince and his court (above left), from al-Harīrī's *Maqāmāt*, was painted in the mid vii/13th century. (13)

Turks entered Islam at an early date, first as soldiers and then as rulers. The Turkish military official (above) comes from the same double frontispiece to the *Maqāmāt* as his Arab companion. (14)

In a ship sailing from Basra to Oman, the crew are apparently Indian, the passengers Arab. Apart from this glimpse into social roles, this *Maqāmāt* picture is also a reminder of the scope of Arab operations. Marco Polo found an Arab community flourishing in the China of Kubilai Khān. (15)

Men of learning in distant places were commonly Arab. Another *Maqāmāt* illustration shows a prince of the 'Eastern Isles' of the Indian Ocean. Two Arab astrologers, left and right, calculate the horoscope of his newly born son. (16)

'A tremendous disaster such as had never happened before, and which struck all the world, though the Muslims above all' is how Ibn al-Athīr described the Mongol invasions of the early VII/13th century. Rashīd ad-Dīn's *Universal History* (late VIII/14th century),

from which this miniature comes, takes the same point of view. But in the longer perspective of history it can be seen that the caliphate was already moribund and that the new *pax Mongolica* was in many ways an improvement on the old order. (17)

The Mongols accepted Islam, and although theoretically subject to the Great Khān in China were in fact independent by the end of the VII/13th century. Their internationalist approach opened a new era in Islamic history. But at the beginning of the IX/15th century a new conqueror appeared in the person of the Turko-Mongol Tamerlane (Tīmūr-i Lang), whose dynasty, the Tīmūrids, for a while dominated the empires of Turkey, Persia and India. Above left: the mausoleum of Tamerlane at Samarqand, originally planned as the burial place of his nephew. Below: the Mongol ruler Tahmaras, the 'fully armed', with an Arab scribe. The Mongols found themselves in much the same position as the Arabs at the beginning of their expansion, dependent for the machinery of government upon the more advanced peoples they had conquered. (18, 19)

Chapter One

THE FAITH
AND THE FAITHFUL

Bernard Lewis

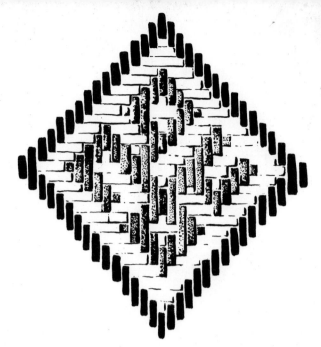

The name 'Muhammad' in stylized Arabic script, forming a pattern of bricks on the wall of a mausoleum. See opposite. (1)

THE WORD ISLAM has several different meanings. In the traditional sense, as used by Muslims, it connotes the one true divine religion, taught to mankind by a series of prophets, each of whom brought a revealed book. Such were the Torah, the Psalms and the Gospel, brought by the prophets Moses, David and Jesus. Muhammad was the last and greatest of the prophets; and the book he brought, the Qur'ān, completes and supersedes all previous revelations.

In this sense, the Jewish prophets and heroes before Christ, and the Christians before Muhammad, were all Muslims – apart from those who had corrupted the revelations vouchsafed to them and gone astray. More commonly, the term Islam is restricted to the final phase of the sequence of revelations – that of Muhammad and the Qur'ān. Here again there is a range of meanings, which should be, but are not always, distinguished. In the first instance Islam means the religion taught by Muhammad himself, through the Qur'ān and through his own precept and practice. By extension, it is used of the whole complex system of dogma, law and custom, which was elaborated, on the basis of his teachings and of others ascribed to him, during the centuries after his death.

In a still wider sense the word Islam is often used by historians, and especially non-Muslim historians, as the equivalent not of Christianity but of Christendom, and denotes the whole rich civilization which grew up under the aegis of the Muslim empires.

The basic religious precepts of the Qur'ān are already contained in the early chapters, those revealed at Mecca before the migration of the Prophet and his followers to Medina. They teach that there is one God, omnipotent and omniscient, creator of all that exists; that it is the duty of men to submit themselves completely to the will of God; that those who rebel against the prophets sent by God to guide them and who persist in their unbelief are punished both in this world and the next; that after death there is a heaven and a hell where the good are rewarded and the wicked chastised; that at the end of time and the end of the world, there will be a resurrection of bodies and a universal judgment.

The Qur'ān may be supplemented as a source of guidance by *hadīth* ('Sayings'), the technical name for reports concerning the actions and utterances of the Prophet, who is believed by Muslims to have been divinely inspired in all that he did and said. These were therefore handed down by oral tradition and later committed to writing in collections which have an authority among Muslims second only to that of the Qur'ān itself. Already in medieval times, Muslim scholarship questioned the authenticity of many of these traditions. Western scholarship has done so in a much more radical form without, however, seriously shaking the authority which the traditions still hold among Muslims.

Qur'ān and *hadīth* form the basis of the *sharī'a*, the Holy Law. This great corpus, lovingly elaborated by successive generations of jurists and theologians – where the law is seen as enacted by God and promulgated by a prophet, the two are not clearly distinguished – is one of the major intellectual achievements of Islam, and in many ways the fullest and richest expression of the character and genius of Islamic civilization. Unlike other systems of law, it does not rest primarily on the legislative acts of governments, though the decisions of the Prophet and of those who governed the Islamic community after him, as transmitted by tradition, contributed significantly to its development. Its source, for Muslims, is revelation, manifested through the Qur'ān and *hadīth*, and then amplified and interpreted through the work of the jurists. In this work, they relied on tried and tested methods of reasoning and interpretation. Since the doctors of the Holy Law were not state officials but private citizens, their rulings were not formally binding, nor were they unanimous.

The *sharī'a* covers all aspects of the public and private, communal and personal lives of the Muslims. In some of its provisions, especially those relating to property, marriage, inheritance and other matters of personal status, it is a normative code of law, which men were expected to obey and society to enforce; in others, more especially in its political prescriptions, it is rather a system of ideals towards which men and society were presumed to aspire and strive. Muslim scholars divided the law into

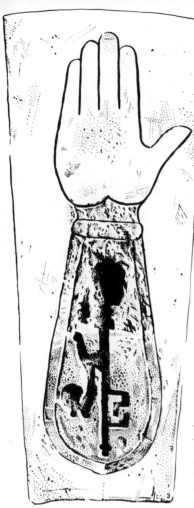

*The five precepts of Islam –
profession of faith, prayer,
pilgrimage, fasting and
charity – can be symbol-
ized by an open hand. This
one is carved on the key-
stone of a doorway in the
Alhambra, Granada. (2)*

two main parts, one concerned with the minds and hearts of the believers; that is, with dogmatics and individual morality; the other with external acts in relation to God and to man; that is, with worship and with civil, criminal and constitutional law. The purpose of both was to define a system of duties fulfilment of which would enable the believer to live a righteous life in this world and prepare himself for the next.

The five pillars of Islam

Of the body of Islamic observances, five are regarded as central and fundamental. The first of these is the *shahāda* or Testimony, the profession of faith, in which the Muslim testifies that there is no God but God and that Muhammad is the Prophet of God. This assertion of the unity and uniqueness of God and of the mission of Muhammad is the basic creed of Islam, and most Muslim theologians agree that any man who subscribes to it may be regarded as a Muslim. At different times and in differ- ent places, learned men have drawn up longer creeds with more dogma and with greater philosophical and theolo- gical subtlety. This simple formula, however, remains the irreducible minimum of belief to which all who would call themselves Muslims must subscribe.

The second of the five pillars of Islam is prayer. This is of two kinds. One, *duʿāʾ*, is a personal, spontaneous prayer, not bound by any rules or rituals. The other, *salāt*, is the set ritual prayer to be offered with prescribed words and motions five times every day at sunrise, mid- day, afternoon, sunset and evening. This is a religious obligation of all adult Muslims, both men and women, except those incapacitated by illness. The worshipper

must be in a state of ritual purity, in a ritually clean place and facing in the direction of Mecca, the birthplace of the Prophet. The prayer itself consists of the profession of faith and some passages from the Qur'ān. The times for the prayer are indicated by the *adhān*, or call to prayer, usually given from the top of the minaret of the mosque.

Communal prayer takes place at midday on Friday in the mosque, the Muslim place of worship. The word mosque comes from the Arabic *masjid*, literally a place of prostration. The primary purpose of the building was indeed communal prayer. But it would be misleading to describe the mosque as the Islamic equivalent of the Christian church or the Jewish synagogue. As a place of worship, of weekly public prayer, the mosque is indeed the equivalent of these. But, in another sense, it is the successor of the Roman forum and of the Greek agora. The mosque was not only a place of public prayer but also the centre of Muslim society, especially in the new towns created by the Muslims after the conquests. The pulpit, *minbar*, of the mosque was the platform from which im- portant decisions and announcements were proclaimed, such as the appointment and dismissal of officials, the first appearance of new rulers or governors, statements of policy, important news of war and conquest and other major events. In the earliest cities, the mosque, the government offices and the military cantonments were all grouped together in a sort of central citadel, and it was the ruler or governor in person who made important pronouncements from the pulpit. It was customary for the speaker in the pulpit to hold a sword, staff or bow, symbolizing the sovereignty and supremacy of Islam.

As the state authority increased and became more complex, the political role of the mosque diminished but never quite disappeared. Appointments, including the accession of a new caliph, were still proclaimed from the pulpit, and the weekly *khutba* or address from the pulpit was still politically significant, especially that part of it consisting of the bidding prayer in which the names of the ruler and governor were mentioned. This was one of the recognized tokens of sovereignty in Islam.

The mosque is not open only at official prayer times. It is always open for meditation, study and spontaneous prayer and also for other business of various kinds. In early times it often served as a court of justice, since the law of Islam was the holy law, and law and religion were inseparably intermingled. The mosque also served as a place of study, a school, and later was frequently linked with a seminary in which not only the Qur'ān but the rest of Muslim learning was taught. From the earliest times, many mosques had schools attached to them and the practice arose of maintaining these by pious endow- ments called *waqf*.

The interior of the mosque is simple and austere. There is no sanctuary and no altar, since the Islamic religion has no sacraments, no mysteries, no priestly office. The imam is a leader in prayer, and any Muslim knowing the prayers and the ritual may act in this way. If one may speak of the mosque as the equivalent of the church in the sense of a building and a place of worship, there is in Islam no equivalent of the Church as an institution.

The third pillar of Islam according to the traditional reckoning is pilgrimage – the *hajj*. At least once in his lifetime every Muslim is required to go on pilgrimage to

Two drawings from a X/16th-century poem on the rites of pilgrimage. The first shows pilgrims' tents ranged before Mount 'Arafāt; in the top right-hand corner are the three mahmals, or ceremonial litters. The second page is a schematized representation of the valley of Mīna with the Jamrat al-'Aqaba, the place of ritual stoning. (3, 4)

the two holy cities in Arabia, and to re-enact the migration of the Prophet from Mecca to Medina. Women may go with the permission of their husbands and with a safe escort. Those who are unable to go may entrust this duty to others on their behalf, even by testament. The pilgrimage takes place between the seventh and tenth days of the month of Dhu'l-Hijja and culminates in the Festival of Sacrifices known as the Greater Festival.

This annual pilgrimage, which brings together Muslims from many different lands in a single act of devotion, is one of the most potent unifying factors in the world of Islam. To comply with this requirement of their faith, every year vast numbers of Muslims from every part of the Muslim world, men and women of many races and of different social strata, leave their homes and undertake a long and frequently arduous journey to participate in a single, joint act of devotion. These journeys are quite different from the mindless, aimless collective migrations of Antiquity and the Middle Ages, in that each such journey is voluntary and individual – a personal act following a personal decision and resulting in a series of wide-ranging personal experiences.

This form of physical mobility, unparalleled in premodern societies, had important social, intellectual and economic consequences in medieval Islam. If the pilgrim was rich, he might be accompanied by a number of slaves, some of whom were sold in the course of the journey, as a kind of traveller's cheques, to pay expenses. If the pilgrim was a merchant, he might combine his pilgrimage with a business trip, buying and selling goods in the various regions through which he passed and thus learning something of the markets, products, merchants, customs and usages of different countries. If he was a scholar, he might take advantage of the opportunity to attend courses, meet colleagues and buy books, thus contributing also to the interchange and diffusion of knowledge and ideas. In order to facilitate the pilgrimage – and in this the duties of the Faith reinforce the needs of government and trade – it was necessary to maintain a

suitable network of communications between Muslim countries, often far away from one another. The pilgrimage gave rise to a rich travel literature full of useful information about distant places. All this helped to develop among Muslims the feeling of belonging to a single, vast whole. This awareness was reinforced by the participation in the ritual and ceremony of the pilgrimage at Mecca and Medina.

The fourth pillar is fasting. This refers to the fast of Ramadān, the ninth month of the Muslim year, which all adult Muslims, men and women, are required to observe with the exception of the aged and the sick. Those on a journey may postpone the fast. For the whole of the month of Ramadān, believers must abstain from sunrise till dusk from food, drink and sexual relations. During the night, special prayers are recited. When the new moon appears and the month of fasting is ended, there is a festival called 'Īd al-Fitr which lasts for three days. This is sometimes called the Lesser Festival.

The fifth and last of the five pillars is the *zakāt*, a financial contribution paid by Muslims to the community or to the state. Originally a charitable levy collected from the believers for pious purposes, it was transformed into a kind of tribute or tax whereby converts to Islam gave formal expression to their acceptance of the authority of Islam and their allegiance to the Muslim state.

Belief, opinion and toleration

Modern writers on Islam often use such words as orthodoxy and heresy to denote the mainstream of Islamic belief and deviations from it. Such terms are, however, inappropriate to the Islamic situation. They derive from Christian history and institutions, and reflect conditions which have no parallel or equivalent in Islam. Islam in its classical form had no priestly hierarchy and no ecclesiastical authority. There were no councils or synods to hammer out an agreed formula, no equivalent of the Church to promulgate it as official truth. Where there was no orthodoxy, there could be no heresy, since heresy

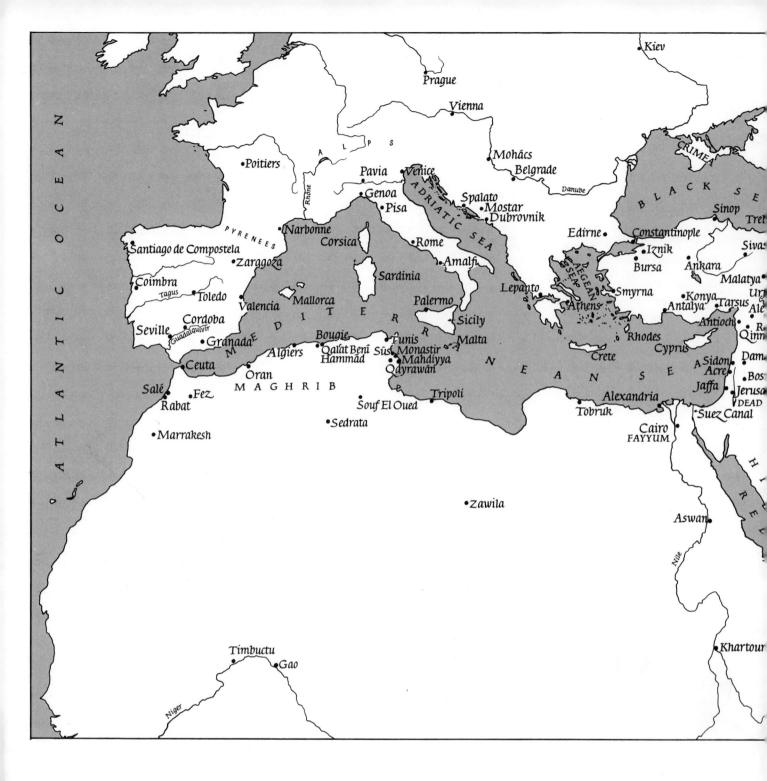

means an error, a deviation from the truth as authoritatively defined.

The nearest approach to a clergy in Islam are the ulema (from Arabic *'ulamā'*, plural of *'ālim*; one who knows, possesses knowledge); these are theologians and jurists who may as individuals or in schools formulate dogma and interpret scripture, but form no constituted ecclesiastical authority to lay down a single orthodox dogma and interpretation, deviation from which is heresy. There is thus no Church or other body to impose dogma; and attempts by the state to do so were very rare and almost always unsuccessful.

The sole universally accepted test of right belief is the *ijmā'*, the consensus of the believers, which in modern terms might be translated as the climate of opinion among the learned and the powerful. Such a consensus may seem intangible and inconstant, varying from time to time and from place to place. In the earliest Islamic times this was indeed so, and wide scope was left to human reasoning and individual opinion. In time, however, the range of variation was greatly reduced and ultimately limited in effect to questions that were minor, marginal, local or new. A great body of rules for correct behaviour and belief – the nuclei of Islamic law and theology – came into being, and gained almost universal acceptance. The guiding principle in its formation was respect for tradition – that is, for the *Sunna*. In ancient Arabia this word meant ancestral precedent, the custom of the tribe. In the earliest Islamic times the *Sunna* was still the living, growing tradition of the community, developed by the actions

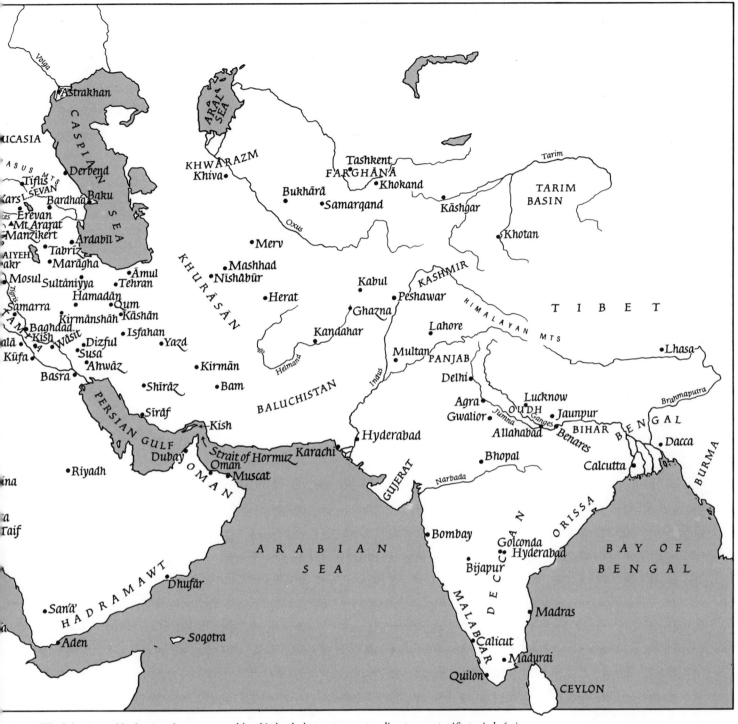

The Islamic world, showing the area covered by this book, but not corresponding to any specific period. (5)

and policies of the Prophet and of the first caliphs. In the II/8th century, a more rigorously traditionalist point of view prevailed. The *Sunna* was equated with the practice and precept of the Prophet as transmitted, so it was believed, by the relators of authentic tradition, and was held to override all but the Qur'ān itself. With the general acceptance of this view and of an agreed corpus of traditions that were put forward as recording the legislation of the Prophet, the role of opinion and therefore of consensus was much reduced, though never entirely eliminated; and the basis was laid for an Islamic orthodoxy in the sense of a generally accepted central core of traditional practice and doctrine, departure or deviation from which might be condemned, according to circumstances, as error, crime or sin.

Those who accepted this orthodoxy were called Sunnīs, a term which implied loyalty to the community and acceptance of its traditions rather than the Christian concept of orthodoxy, belief in a creed and submission to ecclesiastical authority. The same communal, traditional implications can be discerned in the various technical terms used by Muslims to denote deviation from the *Sunna*.

Probably the nearest Muslim approach to an equivalent of the Christian concept of heresy is the term *bid'a*, innovation. Observance of tradition is good and it is by this that Sunnī Islam is defined; departure from it is *bid'a* and is bad unless specifically shown to be good. The extreme traditionalist view is well summed up in a saying attributed to the Prophet: 'The worst things are those that

29

are novelties. Every novelty is an innovation, every innovation is an error and every error leads to hell-fire.' To condemn a doctrine as *bid'a* meant, in the first instance, not that it was false, but that it was new – a breach of tradition, respect for which is reinforced by the Muslim belief in the finality of Muhammad's revelation.

There is thus an important distinction between the Christian notion of heresy and the Muslim notion of *bid'a*. Heresy is a theological transgression – a wrong choice or wrong stress in doctrine. Innovation is a social more than a theological offence. So too is excess, the reproach implied in another technical term – *ghuluww*, from an Arabic root meaning to overshoot, to go beyond the limit. Some diversity of opinion within the community was accepted as harmless and even beneficial. There are four different schools of Holy Law, each with its own principles, its own law books and its own judiciary, yet living in mutual toleration. There are differences even on important matters of doctrine within the community. But there must be limits. Those who carry their divergences to excess (*ghuluww*) are known as *ghulāt* (singular, *ghālī*), and in the view of the majority of theologians may not be considered as Muslims.

Characteristically, the Sunnī theologians differ on where to draw the line; but there was a line, and those beyond it were not heretics but infidels.

Muslim theologians were ready enough to hurl charges of innovation or deviation or extremism against doctrines with which they disagreed, but were usually reluctant to pursue these charges to their logical conclusion. Since heresy and heretics are not recognized categories in Muslim theology or in Muslim law, to denounce a doctrine as non-Islamic meant that those persons, nominally Muslim, who professed that doctrine were apostates and therefore subject to the utmost penalty of the law. The sectarian, though some of his beliefs might in time be excluded by the consensus from the mainstream of Islam, remained a Muslim, still entitled before the law to the status and privileges of the Muslim in society – in property, marriage, inheritance, testimony and the holding of public office. If captured in war or even in rebellion, he was to be treated as a Muslim. He was not subject to summary despatch or enslavement, and his family and property were protected by the law. Though a sinner, he was not an unbeliever and might even aspire to salvation in the life to come. The vital barrier lay not between Sunnī and sectarian but between sectarian and apostate. Apostasy was a crime as well as a sin, and the apostate was damned in this world as well as the next. His crime was treason – desertion and betrayal of the community to which he belonged and to which he owed loyalty. His life and property were forfeit; he was a dead limb to be excised.

Charges of apostasy were not unusual, and in early times the terms unbeliever and apostate were commonly used in religious polemics. 'The piety of theologians,' says al-Jāhiz (d. 256/869), 'consists of hastening to denounce dissidents as unbelievers.' Al-Ghazālī (d. 505/1111) speaks with contempt of those 'who would constrict the vast mercy of God to his servants and make paradise the preserve of a small clique of theologians'. In fact, such accusations have little practical effect. The victims for the most part suffered no inconvenience and many held high office in the Muslim state. In later times,

as the rules and penalties of Muslim law were systematized, charges of apostasy became rarer. Few theologians were both willing and able to invoke the penalties for apostasy against those whose beliefs differed from their own. Only where dissent was extreme, persistent and aggressive were its followers to be put beyond the pale of the community of Islam.

The absence of a single obligatory dogmatic orthodoxy in Islam was not due to an omission but to a rejection – the rejection of an attitude which was felt by Sunnī Muslims to be alien to the genius of their faith and dangerous to the interests of their community. 'There is no compulsion in religion,' says the Qur'ān (ii, 257). A saying attributed to the Prophet goes even further: 'Difference of opinion in my community is a manifestation of divine mercy.'

Ultimately, membership of Islam was a matter of allegiance, not creed; its test was loyalty rather than belief. Only persistent and militant deviation and misconduct were to be condemned as unbelief. The offender was to be summoned to recant and repent; and, if he refused, be put to death.

This does not mean that the repression of religious dissent was unknown in Islam. From time to time, holders of unpopular beliefs were arrested and tried and sentenced to imprisonment, physical punishment or death. Inquisitions were rare and atypical; but the ordinary Islamic judiciary could undertake the discovery, punishment and suppression of religious error. The one constant criterion for intervention and action was subversion. Whenever the doctrines and practices of a sect threatened the state, the dynasty, the fabric of society or accepted standards of common decency, they were outlawed and repressed; while others, however remote from the central tradition, were accorded tolerance and even allowed the name and status of Muslims.

In the course of the centuries, many religious groups grew up within Islam, to which it would not be inappropriate to apply the Christian term sects. Some of these differ from the main Islamic consensus only on minor points of belief and ritual; others embraced beliefs of extraneous origin often very remote from the mainstream. The significant divisions between religious groups in Islamic history were not, however, over questions of belief nor even over questions of usage and ritual, though these last could often give rise to conflict and recrimination. The most important divisions, those which provoked the greatest struggles and the most sustained animosities, were concerned with the issue of the headship of the community, of the caliphate – in other words with an issue which was basically political rather than religious.

The majority of Muslims belonged, and, at the present time, still belong, to the mainstream, that of the *Sunna*, and are known as Sunnīs. The largest dissident group is the Shī'a, which is, in turn, subdivided into several smaller groups, the most important of which is the Twelver Shī'a, so called because they believe that there were twelve Imams – 'Alī and his descendants – after the Prophet, and that the twelfth did not die but disappeared, and will return at the end of time. Since the x/16th century, Twelver Shī'ism has been the state religion of Iran. It also commands the support of significant minori-

The first four caliphs were Muhammad's companions. They were succeeded by two dynasties, the Umayyad and the ʿAbbāsid. The first presided over the astonishing conquest by Islam of the whole of North Africa and western Asia from Morocco to Persia. The second stabilized and administered this territory, though faced by increasing threats. Two outstanding caliphs were the Umayyad ʿAbd al-Malik (left) (65–86/685–705) – this coin is thought to be the first showing the Sword of Islam – and the ʿAbbāsid al-Muqtadir (295–320/908–32. (6, 7)

ties in Iraq, India, Pakistan and elsewhere. A smaller Shīʿī group is that of the Ismāʿīlīs, famous in the Middle Ages as having given rise to the schismatic Fātimid caliphate in Egypt and to the notorious order of Assassins, from whom the practice of political murder takes its name in most of the languages of the West.

The rule of law

The Islamic state as conceived by pious Muslims is a religious polity established under divine law. The source of its sovereignty is God; its sovereign, the caliph, has as his primary task to maintain and spread Islam. Its law is the Holy Law revealed by God and elaborated by the recognized interpreters of the Faith. This law is not limited to matters of belief, ritual and religious practice; it deals also with criminal and constitutional matters, with family and inheritance and with much else that in other societies would be regarded as the concern of the secular, not the religious, authorities. In classical Muslim theory there is no secular authority, and no secular law. 'Church' and state are one and the same, with the caliph as head; the Holy Law, which he exists to uphold, regulates the whole range of human activities. Where the basic tie between subject and sovereign is conceived as a religious one, political and religious attitudes coalesce. Political protest, itself perhaps socially determined, finds religious expression; religious dissent acquires political implications. In such a society, adherence and resistance to the existing order both tend to manifest themselves in religious terms – in attitudes and ideologies which may be characterized in Western parlance as orthodoxy and heresy. Some critics are moderate in their dissent and passive in their opposition; others are more radical in their divergence from accepted beliefs, and more violent in their methods, seeking to overthrow the existing order by means which may be described as revolutionary.

There were many such movements of religious dissent and revolt in Islam. The coming of Islam was itself a revolutionary change, with a new state, a new social order and a new doctrine to replace or transform existing institutions and ideas. In Islam as conceived by the first Muslims, there was to be no church and no priests, no kings and no aristocrats, no castes and no estates, and no privileges other than the natural and rightful superiority of those who accept the new dispensation over those who wilfully reject it.

In fact, however, the revolutionary change was less than complete. Some inequalities inherited from the old order – such as those of women and of slaves – were maintained in the new dispensation. True, these were softened by Islam. A slave was no longer a mere chattel but a human soul with definite legal and moral rights. Woman, though still subject to polygamy and concubinage, was given substantial protection in property and some other matters. By the moral and social standards of the time, neither slavery nor the inferiority of women was in any way objectionable. By recognizing and therefore regulating these institutions, Islam was able to bring some improvement in the situation of both groups.

As well as women and slaves, the tolerated non-Muslim subjects of the Muslim state also derived some advantages, in terms of acceptance and security, from their status of limited and regulated inferiority.

The tensions and conflicts which shook medieval Islamic society resulted not from those forms of inequality and discrimination which were sanctioned by Islam and regulated by Islamic law, but rather from those which survived in spite of Islam and in violation of its principles. Even though, in the early centuries of the Islamic empires, the Muslims constituted only a small dominant minority, it was not from the non-Muslim subject masses that opposition came, but rather from groups within the Muslim community who felt that they were being denied the rights and status accorded to them by Islam and that, in consequence, the true principles of Islam were being violated and abandoned by the state. In social terms, criticism and rebellion came not from slaves but from freedmen disappointed with their new status. Non-Arab converts to Islam were disappointed when they found that conversion to the ruling faith did not win them acceptance as the equals of the rulers. And even among the Arab conquerors themselves there were inequalities and conflicts of interest which gave rise to bitter struggles.

In the Western world of late Antiquity and the early Middle Ages, neither the spread of Christianity nor the invasions of the Germanic peoples brought any sudden revolutionary change in state and society comparable with those resulting from the Arab conquests and the

31

advent of Islam. For one thing, both the Arab conquests and the spread of Islam were far more rapid and sudden than the processes of migration and conversion in the West. Christianity endured more than three centuries of oppression before it became the official doctrine of the Roman empire. The Germanic invaders came in gradual stages and in the course of their migrations adopted the Christian faith and the Roman state, both of which they adapted to their own needs and ways. The Arab conquerors who came out of Arabia in the 1/7th century brought their own religion and created their own state. Much of the conflict and tension in the early centuries of Islamic history arises from the clash between the two.

In principle, the Islamic state was created to serve and spread the Islamic religion. Instead, in the view of many contemporary critics, it served the interests of small groups of ambitious men who ran it by methods that increasingly resembled those of the Persian and Roman empires which the Islamic state had superseded. Pious Arabs, joined by resentful non-Arabs, denounced the caliphs as perverters of the true faith and as the creators of a secular tyranny. Others, both Arab and non-Arab, pursuing a variety of grievances and ambitions, joined them in rebelling against this alleged tyranny, and by their actions gave rise to a series of civil wars which convulsed and disrupted the community and the government of Islam.

The ostensible issue was the caliphate itself. Who was the rightful caliph? How should he come to power and how should he exercise it? The claim of the rebels was that they were seeking to overthrow the usurpers and tyrants and to restore the authentic Islam. In fact, each struggle, whether won by the rebels or by the defenders, ended with a reinforcement of the state power and a further step towards the creation of a centralized autocratic empire of the old Middle Eastern type.

The Muslim community was caught in a paradox. The identity and cohesion of the community could be maintained only by the strengthening of the state, and yet, as the state grew stronger, it was even further estranged from the social and ethical ideals incorporated in the first Islamic revelation. This process was seen and resisted, but the resistance, even when militarily and politically successful, was unavailing, since even rebels in victory found themselves obliged to follow much the same path.

Out of these struggles there emerged a series of religious groups differing from one another in their doctrines and in the nature of their support, but having as their common purpose to restore the radical dynamism of what they saw as the authentic and original Islam. In early days, when Arab and Muslim meant more or less the same thing, the religious struggle was a civil war between Arabs. Later, as the process of conversion brought increasing numbers of non-Arabs into the Islamic fold, converts, and especially Persians, began to play a growing role. This could be no better proof of the appeal and power of the Islamic message than the fact that all the great opposition movements in the Islamic empire were movements within Islam and not against Islam, having as their purpose not to overthrow the Faith but to purify, restore and enforce it.

The religion of the ulema, with its austere worship and its scholastic teachings, had left a gap in the religious life

During the VI/12th and VII/13th centuries the Islamic world was under attack first from one side and then from the other; from the Crusaders and from the Mongols. Most famous of all the Crusaders' adversaries was Salāh ad-Dīn, known in the West as Saladin, ruler of Egypt and Syria from 564/1169 to 589/1193. He was the real founder of the Ayyūbid dynasty, which replaced the Fātimids. Significantly, he was not an Arab, but a Kurd, stemming originally from northern Mesopotamia. (8)

of many Muslims, particularly among the common people. This was aggravated when, in later medieval times, the ulema moved nearer to the state and in consequence away from the people. Often, the resulting dissatisfaction found expression in Shī'ism and other deviations from the consensus. By the time of the great Mongol invasions in the VII/13th century Shī'ism had ceased to be a major force in the Islamic world. Here and there small groups of Shī'īs continued to practise and even to propagate their religion; but in the main Islamic centres of the Middle East the theologians and the people, suffering a common fate under the double shock of Crusader and Mongol invasions, henceforth professed the same Sunnī faith – the same in its essential and central doctrines, though varying in detail, in practice and in organization from region to region and from group to group.

General acceptance of the Sunnī consensus did not however mean that the old dichotomy between formal and popular religion had ended. Since the VII/13th century that division has mainly been expressed through the interplay between legal and dogmatic religion, and mysticism. Despite a series of attempts to bring the two into communion, they have always remained distinct, sometimes in alliance, sometimes in conflict, sometimes in uneasy association, influencing and modifying one another in various ways. Increasingly, men turned to Sūfism, a form of mysticism with many local variants. Their characteristic form of expression was the brotherhood, offering a mystical and ecstatic faith, local saints and leaders and a latent criticism of the established order in religion and politics. Though the Sūfis were technically Sunnī and politically quietist, many of them remained suspect in the eyes of the state and the ulema, and occasionally joined in open revolt.

Free men, freedmen and 'people of the pact'

Muslim society, like most or all others known to history, was divided into two main groups, which might be loosely described as the upper and the lower. The first consisted of those elements in society which enjoyed education, position, authority and – though these did not always coincide – wealth and property, and with whose acts, needs and thoughts documents and books, history and literature are mainly concerned. The second consisted of the faceless, nameless, voiceless mass of the remainder. The Islamic terms are *khāssa* and *ʿāmma*, meaning special and general.

The distinction was not a legal one, though the law, departing from its egalitarian principles, recognized some forms of privilege and differences of status. It was not primarily economic, for the themes of the poor gentlemen and the rich vulgarian are as common in classical Islamic society as in others – though the difference between those who possess property and control resources and those who do not is obviously relevant. Origin, birth, birthplace, education, status, occupation and wealth all have their part, though their relative importance may vary with time and place. And as in other societies, social distinctions may outlast the economic and political realities that gave rise to them. When power and wealth have gone, snobbery is what remains.

There are certain common characteristics among these upper-class groups. They are on the whole cosmopolitan, or to use a different term, imperial. The Islamic *khāssa* is a group which extends with a common membership and self-awareness over the whole area – much like the upper classes of Europe before the French Revolution. In the Islamic world of the Middle East, North Africa, India and Central Asia there were only two or three languages which mattered – Arabic, Persian and later Turkish. Whatever the local dialect, whatever the local languages, the *khāssa* had its own limited number of common languages and possessed a common culture expressed in them.

There are several ways in which Islamic society may be subdivided. Muslim law in both theory and practice classified the population of the Muslim empire into four main groups, forming legally defined categories with different rights and obligations. The first consists of the Muslim freemen (*hurr*), the word 'free' having a legal, not a political, connotation. These were the full members of the society. In the earliest days they were very few in number and were almost all Arabs, constituting an aristocracy formed and defined by conquest. They monopolized all high offices, provided the armies of the state and paid few taxes, on the contrary drawing pay and pensions from the central registry. In course of time their position suffered a steady decline. The number of Muslims, by natural increase and above all by conversion, grew rapidly. Many functions previously reserved to Muslim freemen were delegated to freedmen and then even to slaves, notably that of military service, so that in time the armies and hence the governments of Islam came to be dominated by slaves and former slaves. The prestige of freemen suffered accordingly, though their legal status remained unchanged.

The second group, the *mawālī* (singular *mawlā*), is that of the freedmen or clients. The status of *mawlā* in medieval Islam represents the confluence of two different traditions – on the one hand that of the freedman in Roman law, who becomes a dependant or client of his former master; on the other that of the adopted member of an Arabian tribe. So closely was Islam identified with Arabism in the early days of the caliphate that for a non-Muslim to become a Muslim it was considered necessary for him to become a *mawlā* – a kind of naturalized or adoptive Arab.

The status of the non-Arab converts to Islam was thus socially and legally inferior to that of the Arabs; and this gave rise to serious problems and tensions. In old Arabia, *mawālī* were of two kinds – those who were such by birth, as the sons of slave mothers and free fathers, and those who became clients by protection of the tribe. The *mawālī* could not intermarry freely with full members of the tribe and their membership was subject to various other restrictions. Before the great Arab conquests virtually all the *mawālī* were Arabs. There were still Arab *mawālī* even during the Umayyad period, but their number was decreasing and instead the term came to apply most commonly to the manumitted non-Arab slaves of the conquerors, and denoted a special relationship to their former masters. This relationship approximated in many respects to the blood-tie. The *mawlā* became a member of the tribe to which his former master belonged and this membership continued from generation to generation. Some legal authorities even allowed a *mawlā* to inherit from his patron, but most jurists denied that right in practice. The *mawlā* was subject to certain economic, fiscal and social disabilities, as for example in the use of personal names and in intermarriage. Eventually the *mawālī* did achieve complete equality, mainly because of two major developments; the rise of slave power, which made the differences between freemen and freedmen unimportant; and the establishment of alien dominations, under which the distinction between Arabs and Arabized non-Arabs ceased to signify. Eventually the term itself passed out of use together with the status which it denoted.

The third legal category is that of the *dhimmīs* or *ahl al-dhimma*, the people of the pact, a legal term for the protected non-Muslim subjects of the Muslim state. These were the Christians, Jews, and in the east Zoroastrians, who were accorded tolerance and a definite legal status in the Muslim community and under the authority and the Muslim state. This status was determined by a pact or *dhimma* deemed to exist between the Muslim community and the non-Muslim communities and to be essentially contractual in character. The basis of the *dhimma* was that the non-Muslim communities accepted the supremacy of Islam and the dominance of the Muslim state, and agreed to a position of subordination, symbolized by the imposition of certain social restrictions and by the payment of a poll-tax not collected from Muslims. In return for this they enjoyed security of life and property, protection against their enemies, freedom of worship and a very large measure of internal autonomy in their communal affairs. The *dhimmīs* had greater rights than slaves and less rights than free Muslims, from whom they were marked off in two important respects – by the payment of heavier taxes and by their legal inability to bear arms.

Pilgrimage certificates – this fragment dates from the VI/12th century – were issued at Mecca and Medina to bear witness that the pilgrim had indeed made the long and often arduous journey. (9)

The social situation was in fact different from the legal situation, and the status and position of the *dhimmīs* better than would have been the result of a strict enforcement of the law. The frequent re-enactment of the edicts against the *dhimmīs* shows that the laws imposing restrictions on them were not regularly or strictly enforced. In early days the *dhimmīs* constituted the overwhelming majority of the inhabitants of all the Muslim lands except the Arabian peninsula. Provided that they were followers of a recognized and tolerated religion, such as Judaism or Christianity, they were not subject – apart from occasional and exceptional outbursts of fanaticism – to any pressure to adopt Islam, and indeed in earlier times were sometimes discouraged from taking a step which would have decreased the revenues and increased the expenditure of the state. Despite this, however, the movement of conversion continued steadily and, at a date which it is impossible to determine precisely, and which varied from place to place, the majority of the population in the countries of the Middle East and North Africa came to be Muslim, while the earlier religions declined and in some areas disappeared. In the eastern lands important Christian minorities survived, especially in Egypt, Palestine, Syria and to a lesser extent in Iraq, where rather smaller Jewish minorities also remained. In the Arab West, in North Africa, Christianity died out, though Judaism survived in some strength. Zoroastrianism had dwindled to insignificance in Iran by the v/11th or vi/12th century.

Throughout, Jews and Christians continued to play an important part in the government of the Islamic empires and particularly in the administrative services of the state. There seems to have been no strong general feeling against the employment of *dhimmīs* among the governing and administering groups. Outbreaks of violence against them are very rare, and are usually the result of what was seen as an undue and unreasonable increase and exercise of power by members of one or other of the *dhimmī* communities.

Though the *dhimmīs* in general enjoyed a high degree of tolerance, they were never allowed to forget their lower status. Their evidence was not admitted before Muslim courts, and they counted as less than Muslims in questions of compensation for injury. They were not free to marry Muslim women; they were subject to certain restrictions on their dress, their homes and their movements, and though these were not usually strictly enforced they could always be invoked. While the *dhimmīs* often acquired considerable financial and economic power, their debarment from the social and political advantages which normally accompany such power forced them to exercise influence, if at all, by intrigue, with harmful effects both on the *dhimmīs* themselves and on the Muslim society and polity.

Slaves

The fourth and last category is that of slaves. The institution of slavery already existed in pre-Islamic Arabia, where slaves were either captured on the battlefield or imported from Africa, mostly from Ethiopia and the adjoining territories. In pre-Islamic Arabia there were no laws to protect slaves, who were entirely at the disposal of their masters. The Islamic dispensation recognizes the institution of slavery but regulates and limits it. The master retains his right of ownership over the slave but is enjoined to treat him kindly and when possible to enfranchise him either by manumission or by allowing him to purchase his freedom. Though legally the slave is inferior, he is, if a Muslim, the brother and religious equal of the freeman. The enslavement of Muslims was discouraged by the early caliphs and made impossible by the jurists, though the conversion of a slave to Islam did not thereby terminate his slavery. It was not permitted, as in some other societies, to enslave a defaulting debtor, or to sell oneself or one's child into slavery. The presumption of the Muslim jurists was that the natural state of man is freedom and that the condition of slavery was limited to those born of a slave mother and infidels captured in war.

The humanizing tendency of the Islamic approach to slavery was to some extent offset by two other developments; the influence in the conquered provinces of the Roman law and practice which the Arabs found there, and the great increase in the number of slaves by conquest and purchase. Slaves were subject to legal disabilities. They were excluded from any office involving jurisdiction; they could not give evidence; they were valued less than freemen in that the penalty for an offence against a slave is half the penalty for the same offence against a freeman. The slave had few civil rights in matters of property, inheritance or bequest. He was however entitled to medical attention, food, and assistance when old, and a *qādī*, or religious judge, could order an owner to manumit his slave for failure to carry out these obligations. The owner was forbidden to overwork his slave and was enjoined to treat him humanely. A slave could marry with the consent of his master; in theory he could even marry a free woman, though this in fact seems not to have happened. A master could not marry a slave-girl unless he freed her. Slaves could be manumitted by a whole variety of procedures laid down by law.

According to the theory of the law, there were two ways in which the number of slaves could be recruited – by birth and capture. In practice two other methods were extensively used – tribute and purchase, both of them from territories outside the direct jurisdiction of the Muslim state and of the Muslim law.

During the early centuries of Islam, at the time of the great conquests, capture was the most important single source of recruitment. Later it accounted for a smaller and smaller proportion of slaves. As the frontiers were stabilized, the Holy War no longer provided enough to meet the demand. Frontier raids still yielded a certain number, but most of these were ransomed or exchanged for Muslim prisoners of war. The activities of Muslim corsairs in the Mediterranean, and wars and raids on the African, Indian and Central Asian frontiers of Islam still brought in a supply, but with the spread of the Islamic faith more and more of the enemies captured in war were Muslim and therefore could not be enslaved.

In the year 31 of the *hijra* (651–2), according to Muslim tradition, the Arab armies in Egypt fought against the Nubians and made an armistice with them by which the Muslims and Nubians agreed that each would not raid the other. In return for this, the Nubians undertook to pay a certain number of slaves every year to the Muslims who in turn would deliver quantities of meat and lentils to the Nubians. The treaty is said to have provided for the delivery by the Nubians of 360 slaves a year or, according to some authorities, 360 for the common booty of the Muslims and an additional forty for the governor. Although the authenticity of this treaty is dubious, it was accepted by most jurists and served as the basis of a very convenient arrangement whereby Nubia remained outside the Muslim empire but in fact tributary to it. Muslim law limited enslavement and prohibited mutilation, and thus restricted the supply of slaves and eunuchs. Both however could be imported from outside the Muslim lands, and Nubia served as a convenient channel.

Later the most important method by which the slave population of the Islamic empire was recruited was purchase. Slaves were bought on the frontiers of the empire from merchants who had brought them from distant lands. They were then moved by well-recognized routes from the frontiers to the major slave distribution centres within the empire. These were in North Africa, Egypt and southern Arabia for African slaves; in Derbend, Aleppo, Mosul, Bukhārā and Samarqand for slaves coming from Europe and the steppe lands.

The slaves were of very diverse origin, imported across all the frontiers of the Muslim empire. Slav and other white slaves were brought from Europe via the Volga, Black Sea and Caspian routes, through the Byzantine empire, and across the Mediterranean. Others came from the Caucasian lands and from India. By far the most important groups of slaves, however, were those who came from the north and the south – the Turkish peoples of the Eurasian steppe, and the black peoples of Africa south of the Sahara. Both of these were outside the Islamic oecumene, and were therefore legally subject to enslavement when captured. Between them they provided the great bulk of the slave population of the Islamic empire.

The slaves were employed for a variety of functions. Unlike the Greco-Roman world, the Islamic world was not primarily a slave-based economy. Its agriculture rested largely on free or semi-free peasants; its industries were mainly manned by free artisans. There were, however, important exceptions to these rules. Slaves, mostly blacks from Africa, were extensively employed in certain areas in large-scale economic projects. From quite an early date we hear of gangs of black slaves employed in clearing the salt-flats of southern Iraq. Their conditions were very bad and resulted in a series of slave risings, one of which, in the III/9th century, for a time offered a serious threat to the imperial capital itself. Other black slaves were employed in the gold mines of upper Egypt and the Sudan, in the salt mines of the Sahara, and elsewhere.

In the main, however, slaves were employed either for domestic or military purposes. The former were used in homes, in shops and in mosques and were mainly of African origin. The latter came increasingly to provide the manpower of the armies of Islam and so ultimately its commanders and rulers. The military slaves were predominantly Turkish, occasionally Circassian, though black military slaves are sometimes found, especially in Egypt and North Africa.

Slave-women of many ethnic origins were recruited in enormous numbers to staff the harems of the Islamic world – as concubines or as menials, the two functions not being clearly differentiated. Sometimes slave-girls received education, and some famous ones figure in the history of Arabic literature. Slaves were often trained and used as performers – as dancers, singers or musicians, and some were even able to achieve fame and fortune – fortune, that is, for their masters and sometimes even for themselves after emancipation.

Women of course constitute a juridical category as such, represented in all four groups, with significant differences of status. These were most important for free Muslim women. The advent of Islam marked an enormous improvement in the position of women in pre-Islamic Arabia, endowing them with property and other rights, and giving them some measure of protection against marital ill-treatment. The killing of female infants, sanctioned by custom in pagan Arabia, was forbidden. But their position remained poor, and worsened when in this, as in so many other matters, the original Islamic dispensation lost its impetus and was modified under the influence of existing attitudes and customs. Polygamy remained lawful, though in practice it seems not to have been widespread outside ruling circles; it was however commonly supplemented by concubinage. An unmarried slave-woman was lawfully at the disposal of her owner; a free woman slave-owner had of course no such rights over her male slaves. The position of woman in society was defined primarily by her function in the family – as daughter, sister, wife or mother, rather than as a person in her own right. She had some compensations; in some property matters she was equal to a man, while for religious offences she was subject to lesser penalties – for example, to imprisonment and flogging instead of execution for the crime of apostasy. But this was a mark of inferiority rather than a privilege. Like the other disadvantaged groups, such as *dhimmīs* or slaves, she was subject to certain formal marks of inferior status in the law. In inheritance, testimony in a lawsuit, and bloodwit, she was valued as half a man.

Besides the formal, legal classification into free, freed, *dhimmī* and slave, there were of course other categories, determined by social, economic and functional differences, which were no less important, and were even to some extent recognized by the law, notably in the rules relating to the principle of *kafāʾa*, equality of birth and status in marriage. A free, responsible Muslim woman could give herself in marriage, but her husband was expected to be her social equal. This rule did not prohibit unequal marriages; it did however enable a father or other legal guardian to prevent or, in certain circumstances, annul an unsuitable marriage contracted without his permission. The jurists discuss at some length the various considerations involved in determining a man's status for this purpose. They include piety, moral character, wealth, freedom, Islam, descent and occupation. The last four clearly involve questions of status. A Muslim slave may in law marry a free Muslim woman, though this seems to have been very rare in practice; a *dhimmī* may never marry a Muslim woman, though the reverse is permitted and common. The requirements of 'freedom' and 'Islam' under the rules of *kafāʾa* refer to the freedman and the convert, and to their descendants up to three generations, after which all are deemed equally free and equally Muslim. Before that, however, the question of *kafāʾa* could be affected by the number of generations between the bridegroom and the act of enfranchisement or conversion which brought him into the fold. Descent and occupation are more obviously social, and may vary in status and acceptability. There is also an ethnic order of preference: first members of Quraysh (the tribe to which the Prophet belonged), then other Arabs, then non-Arabs. These classes are in turn subdivided.

Men of the pen

Medieval writers frequently divide the dominant elements in society into two main groups, the men of the pen and the men of the sword. The latter consisted of the military in all its different branches; the former included both the civilian bureaucracy and the men of religion.

It is paradoxical that while medieval Islam, unlike medieval Christendom, recognized no distinction between Church and state, it nevertheless developed something which the medieval West failed to produce – a secular literate class, separate and distinct from the men of religion. The bureaucracy was an inheritance to the Islamic state from its Byzantine and Iranian predecessors. Under the early caliphs this was true in the most literal sense. The same government offices staffed by the same officials, Persians in the east, Christians in the west, continued to function in the old way, assessing and collecting taxes by the old rules, but remitting them to Arab instead of to Iranian or Byzantine masters. Even the language of administration continued as before – Persian in the east, Greek in the western parts of the empire acquired from Byzantium. In time, however, the older languages fell into disuse; Arabic was adopted in their place, and a unified administrative system was gradually introduced all over the empire. *Dhimmīs* of various origins continued to play an important part in the bureaucracy, and even later, when Muslims came to predominate, many of these were of Persian, Coptic and other non-Arab origin. Even in much later centuries, Christians and occasionally Jews continued to play an important role in the public service.

The term generally used for members of the bureaucratic class is *kātib*, a scribe. The scribes formed a numerous and powerful group in Islamic society, of vital significance. Their external sign was the *darrāʿa*, a kind of cloak. Their chief was the vizier, the supreme civilian official under the sovereign. They formed an important non-clerical learned class, with a distinctive education of their own, predominantly literary. A large proportion of classical Arabic literature is the product of the scribal class. reflecting their outlook, needs and ideals. Scribes were paid salaries in money, sometimes reaching very considerable sums in the higher ranks. In later times, with the decline of the monetary economy, they were often paid in grants of land or assignments of revenue.

The rise of the military regimes in the high Middle Ages reduced the status of the civilian bureaucrats. They remained, however, essential to the conduct of government, and made a vital contribution to the stability and continuity of the medieval Islamic states. The long survival, for example, of the Mamlūk sultanate in Egypt, from the mid-VII/13th to the early X/16th century, is due as much to the Egyptian and Syrian civil service as to the Turkish and Circassian Mamlūk soldiery. This civil service was partly of native origin, partly recruited from the Islamicized and Arabized descendants of the Mamlūk amīrs, who by the necessity of the Mamlūk system were themselves excluded from the military governing élite. Many of these founded great bureaucratic families, which continued from generation to generation.

There is no priesthood in Islam in the sense that there is no sacerdotal interposition between the worshipper and his God, no sacraments requiring an ordained priest for their performance, no organized clergy forming a separate corporation or caste in society or the state. But if there is no priesthood in the theological sense, there is certainly a professional religious class in a sociological sense. The men of learning, the ulema, formed a definite and distinct order in society, including religious teachers, imams who officiate at local mosques, professional theologians and jurists – the doctors of the Holy Law.

Since there was neither ordination nor hierarchy, the usage of the term *ʿālim* was fluctuating and indefinite. In the earliest times it seems to have been given by a kind of popular recognition. Later it was conferred by *ijāza*, a licence granted by an established *ʿālim* to a pupil who had studied under him to his satisfaction. Finally it was accorded only to graduates of the *madrasas*, the theological seminaries which spread across the Islamic world from the IV/10th and V/11th centuries onwards.

Like the scribes, the ulema too had their external symbol, the turban. Already in the Umayyad period they appeared to have enjoyed a high social status. The Umayyad caliphs concerned themselves principally with the political aspects of their office, leaving religion in the stricter and narrower sense to the dogmatists and traditionalists of the Ḥijāz and of Iraq and thus fostering an unintended separation of religious and political authority, which came to be recognized as normal. The accession of the ʿAbbāsids failed to change this system, despite the attempt made by the ʿAbbāsid caliphs to integrate the ulema into the service of the state and to establish an official orthodoxy. These attempts came to nothing and if anything the ulema became even more isolated from the state, the service of which was regarded as demeaning.

In the unofficial separation of powers which evolved between the state and the ulema, the exclusive competence of the men of religion was recognized in the sphere of Holy Law. This coupled with their aloofness from the state, gave them immense moral authority, and marked them off, in effect though not in theory, as a separate clerical class. Law in Islam means far more than in the Western world; and the Holy Law regulated most social and personal relations, thus giving its authorized exponents a pervasive role in society. The mass of the people were dependent on the ulema for guidance and even for decision on such matters as property, marriage, divorce, inheritance and the like; and their influence in consequence grew steadily.

In theory there was an important distinction between the Sunnī and the Shīʿī ulema. According to the Sunnī view, the use of reasoning by analogy and personal judgment for the interpretation of the Holy Law was permissible for approximately the first two and a half centuries of Islam. This process, known technically as *ijtihād*, was used to supplement and interpret the teachings of the Qurʾān and the traditions, and to answer the questions for which they provided no explicit guidance. By the beginning of the 4th century of the *hijra*, approximately AD 900, Sunnī jurists of all schools seem to have agreed that all the important questions had already been answered and a consensus established. In the juridical phrase, therefore, the gate of *ijtihād* was closed; and thereafter jurists, and after them all Muslims, were bound to practise *taqlīd*, that is to say, unquestioning conformity to the doctrines established by the authorized schools. The Shīʿa did not accept this Sunnī doctrine of the closing of the gate of *ijtihād*, but instead claimed the right to continue the practice. Indeed, Shīʿa men of religion are usually known not as ʿālim but as *mujtahid*, i.e., one who practises *ijtihād*. In reality, however, the distinction between Sunnī and Shīʿa usage was more theoretical than real. The Shīʿa *mujtahids*, though claiming the right to innovate, were usually as conservative as the Sunnīs; the Sunnī ulema, while theoretically bound by precedent and able only to follow established rules, in fact used independent judgment as often as the Shīʿa. The main theoretical distinction between them was that the Sunnī ulema were bound by the doctrine of consensus to accept the prevailing political order; the Shīʿa were similarly bound by their teachings to reject it as a usurpation. In fact, even on this point, there was little practical difference between the two.

The relationship between the men of religion, whether Sunnī or Shīʿī, and the state raises interesting questions. The posture of non-cooperation of the early pietists of Arabia was hopelessly theoretical. The ulema laid down a politically impracticable doctrine of rights and duties;

rulers anxious to win their support were asked, as a condition of that support, to apply an ideal system based on a sanctified and mythologized past. The resulting impasse led to a tendency on the part of the ulema to abstain from political life. In fact, of course, a *modus vivendi* was found and a kind of truce established between the state and the ulema. The civil authorities recognized the Holy Law in principle, avoided open contravention of its precepts, particularly in matters of ritual and of social morality, and from time to time consulted ulema and elevated them to positions of authority. The ulema on their part tried to avoid too close an involvement with the state. When they accepted office they did so with becoming reluctance – and it is indeed a common theme of pious biography that an ʿālim either accepted with misgiving, or, better still, refused, an appointment of profit under the state. One of the greatest of the men of religion, al-Ghazālī, explained this. The revenues of the state are obtained by oppression and extortion, which are sinful. Anyone therefore who accepts a paid position under the state becomes a participant in oppression and extortion and thus a sinner. The general feeling of the more pious ulema was that the state was a contamination which they should avoid. *Qāḍīs*, religious judges, were appointed by the state and in consequence regarded by the ulema with some mistrust. Indeed, there is a rich folklore of proverb and anecdote indicating contempt for *qāḍīs* and mistrust of both their learning and their integrity. The counterpart of this is the support sometimes given by ulema to rebellions against the state.

A result of this relationship is that the ulema tended to be split into two groups. One consisted of the strict pietists, regarded by their colleagues and by the mass of the people as the upright and pious custodians of the truth, at least detached from the state and often in opposition to it; the other group, which might be described as compliant or realistic, comprised those ulema who accepted service under the state and by accepting power lost their moral authority. A system such as this, whereby the less conscientious and less scrupulous of the ulema entered the public service while the more pious and conscientious avoided it, had harmful effects both on the state and on religion. Popular sympathy was undoubtedly with the abstainers, and many of the recommendations of pious writers amount to a demand for a virtual boycott of the state service.

In time the ulema gradually and imperceptibly developed into a separate corps with hierarchy and ranks. The process was completed in Ottoman times when, no doubt partly as a result of the Byzantine example, they became part of the apparatus of government. Inevitably, as they moved nearer to the state, they moved away from the people and lost much of their influence to another class of men of religion.

Those of the ulema who were in the service of the state were of course paid in the normal way – by salaries in some periods, by grants and assignments in others. The larger and more important group of ulema, and in particular those who abstained from the service of the state, subsisted by other means. Some engaged in various crafts or in trade; and indeed many of them seemed to have belonged to the merchant class, the outlook and ethics of which they frequently reflect. But increasingly they seem

This horseshoe-shaped disc from Kāshān is a unique record of early Shī'ī piety. The inscription tells how in 711/1312, a citizen of that city had a dream in which he saw a tent, with a horse and dromedary tethered next to it. Out of the tent came a young man of wonderful beauty, who drew back the flap revealing an even more splendid figure seated inside, dressed in armour and wearing a sword at his belt. This was 'Alī, Commander of the Faithful, who commanded the dreamer to build a magnificent chapel for pilgrims. On awakening he saw in the ground the print of an enormous horseshoe, over 11 inches across, the form and dimensions of which are reproduced in the raised rim of the disc. The importance of 'Alī in the story, as well as its Persian provenance, makes it certain that this pious foundation has a Shī'ī background. (10)

to have relied for their subsistence on *waqf*; that is to say, endowments of land or other revenue-producing properties established in mortmain for pious purposes such as the maintenance of mosques and seminaries. Members of the ulema were frequently the beneficiaries and almost always the administrators of these endowments, which eventually came to comprise a considerable body of property and became an economic factor of prime importance.

Who owned the land?

The men of the pen and the men of the sword are both defined in relation to function and relied principally for their livelihood on stipends, grants or endowments of various kinds. It is more difficult to arrive at any classification of a more strictly economic nature in relation to ownership or occupation, the more so in a society in which the state was so powerful and individual property so insecure. Clearly, in an overwhelmingly agricultural society, the ownership or control of land was of major significance. Landowners do indeed form a vitally important group in classical Islamic society. The word is however in need of rather closer definition. The independent small-holder, of a kind known in other societies, exists in the Islamic Middle East; but he is rare and exceptional. This type of tenure does not easily flourish in societies dependent largely on artificial irrgation and therefore in need of central direction and easily subjected to central control. Far more common is the pattern of large landowning, in which again there are

several different types. Modern discussions of the economic history of the Middle East frequently use such terms as feudal and fief. These are specific to the history of Western Europe and have meanings derived from the local history of Western Europe; the use of such words to denote the social and economic phenomena of the Islamic Middle East is at best a loose analogy and can be extremely misleading.

There are several ways in which a large landowner could own or hold his land. One was *milk*, a term roughly equivalent to the English freehold. This is found principally in cities; it consisted mainly of building land and of vineyards, orchards, vegetable gardens and the like, and is unusual in the countryside or in villages.

Most agricultural land was held by the large landowners on some form of grant from the state. The earliest kind, given by the first caliphs, was a cession to an individual Muslim, normally one of the Arab conquerors, of lands from the property of the state; that is to say, from publicly owned lands which at that time in effect meant lands acquired by the state as a result of conquest. These were of two main types – domain lands of the previous state, i.e., lands which were state property under the Persian or Byzantine regimes, and lands abandoned by their former owners. When Arabs conquered Syria, Palestine, Egypt and North Africa, many of the great Byzantine magnates fled, abandoning their property. This became state property and was assimilated to the former state property. The so called dead lands, i.e., uncultivated, unused lands, could also be granted in this way.

Lands of these types, all of them at the disposal of the state, were ceded or granted to individuals with what was in effect a permanent, irrevocable grant. Once such a grant was given it was for life, and was alienable, heritable and not conditional on any service or status. The recipient of such a grant was required to pay a tithe to the public treasury on his land, where he himself collected taxes from the inhabitants. His profit from his grant was the difference between what he collected from the cultivators and what he paid to the state.

This system continued for a while and then gradually died out with the cessation of conquest. It was replaced by another and more common type in which the grant was not of land but rather a delegation of the fiscal rights of the state over land. The state granted the right to collect taxes to an individual, usually in lieu of pay from the public treasury in return for services, most commonly military services. In principle officers and other servants of the state were paid salaries in money; but it became increasingly frequent for money to be lacking and for officers to be paid instead by grants. Often the person to whom an assignment of taxes was given also had to go and collect it himself. Such a grantee did not of course pay taxes to the state; he was receiving the taxes himself in lieu of the pay which the state owed him for his service.

A grant of this kind was primarily functional, given in return for a service. If the grantee ceased to render this service the delegation of fiscal rights was terminated. This type of grant was not, like the earlier one, irrevocable and permanent. It was in principle temporary, limited and revocable if the condition on which it was given ceased to operate. It was neither alienable or heritable but was personal to the grantee. By abuse, however, it frequently became permanent, alienable and heritable and likewise by abuse was retained even when the services were no longer rendered. It was at this point that it begins to resemble in some respects the feudal system of medieval Europe. It did not however carry with it anything like the seigneurial rights of a European feudal magnate of the Middle Ages. The holder of such a grant had no rights over the inhabitants of the area to which his grant applied other than the right to collect taxes and of course to use such force as might be necessary for that purpose. But unlike the lord of the manor in the West, he did not dispense justice, or grant smaller fiefs within his fief, or maintain a private army of his own retainers. Nor did he usually reside in the area of his grant, like the Western feudal lord, or rule it as an independent principality.

In another type of arrangement, more of a contract than a grant, the state commuted the taxes due from a region or an estate or a group of some kind, in return for an agreed fixed sum. By such an arrangement the state withdrew its fiscal agents or tax-collectors, and no longer concerned itself either with the assessment or with the collection of taxes. This was delegated by contract to an intermediary who might be a tribal chief, the head of a religious community, or simply an entrepreneur, buying a tax-farm for profit. The contractor, having entered into such an agreement with the treasury, was bound to pay the agreed annual amount. What he then collected and how he collected it was his own concern.

There was always a tendency for the unit of the grant to grow larger. This happened in several ways. It would happen, for example, when a large and powerful landowner extended his protection to smaller and weaker neighbours less able to look after themselves in times of trouble. This protection gradually solidified into a virtual takeover of the smaller landowners' holdings. This sometimes even happened voluntarily, when a smaller landowner found that he could not defend himself in periods of civil war, invasion and the breakdown of order; he therefore sought the help of a powerful neighbour, and, in return for a guaranteed income, assigned his rights to him. From time to time, when a regime was overthrown and a new regime established, whether by conquest or by successful rebellion, the old landowners were ousted and a new group of landowners installed in their place. Sometimes this happened with the existing territorial and fiscal units maintained. More frequently the units were all brought under the control of the state and then redistributed in a different way to new beneficiaries.

Like 'feudalism', such words as gentry, nobility and aristocracy are of dubious value when applied to classical Muslim society. We can however observe the crystallization of a hereditary landowning class which held property in one form or another, whether freehold, lease, or grant, and managed to pass it from father to son. The general tendency of Muslim rulers was to try to prevent, interrupt or reverse this process, preferring a situation in which all power, all wealth and all authority derived directly from the state rather than from inheritance or assured and accepted position. There is a recurring tendency to seek to destroy or uproot such elements as do not depend on the state, but rather on inherited wealth, like landowners, or on public acclaim and recognition, like the ulema and the provincial gentry. Such hereditary groups tend to form and persist when the central authority is for one reason or another weak; they are undermined and often destroyed or replaced when the central authority is strong, particularly after a new conquest. This is a continuing struggle which can be traced through Islamic history. It was finally decided in favour of an autocratic state and against the limiting factors by the introduction of modern technology and in particular of modern communications and modern weapons. With these, the intermediate powers which had previously restricted the autocracy of the state were doomed.

The rest of the *khāssa* was made up of the merchants and industrialists, the upper segments of whom formed a kind of urban patriciate, and the remaining learned professions. The most important of these were the physicians and oculists, some in the service of the rulers and of high officials, others private practitioners. To these may be added the scientists, astronomers, teachers, engineers, agronomists and architects, all of whom played a role in the Muslim city, most of them in one form or another maintained by the state by salaries or by patronage.

Of the *'āmma*, the common people, we know very little. The great majority of the population were of course peasants. Their views, their feelings, are for the most part not reflected in the sources from which alone we derive our information about the history of medieval Islam. From time to time, men of peasant background emerged from that background and found their way into the higher strata of society, becoming merchants, ulema, landowners, ministers or soldiers. But when that happened they usually ceased to be peasants and to reflect a peasant point of view. Even today, with populist ideologies to inspire and modern communications to facilitate such enquiries, it is still extraordinarily difficult to find out what the peasant is really thinking in these countries.

We hear more about the slaves, who lived mostly in cities, and, through their daily contact with the *khāssa*, sometimes escape from the anonymity of the mass. Such were the military slaves who battered their way into history; the harem slaves, who as the favourites or mothers of monarchs might, from their place of concealment, influence the course of public affairs; and the domestic slaves, who by serving in the houses of the great could attain an occasional description or mention in literature.

We know more about the craftsmen, who also lived in cities, and in villages large enough to have a specialization of labour, providing shelter, clothing and utensils, luxuries and works of art. We perceive them in the tracts and manuals of the guilds in which they were organized;

in the literature of mysticism, through which so many of them found expression for their religious and social needs; and perhaps most of all in their handiwork, rarely signed but often personal, which forms one of the most typical and most universal creations of Islamic civilization.

A distinguished Islamicist, S. D. Goitein, has called Islam the intermediate civilization. The term is apt. In time, the golden age of Islam lies between the pioneering civilizations of antiquity, Middle Eastern and Hellenistic, and the dawn of the modern age, marking an essential transition from the one to the other. In space, Islam extends from the Mediterranean world to the remoter cultures of Asia and Africa, tied to the former by innumerable threads of common inheritance and achievement, to the latter by the efforts of generations of soldiers and traders, artists and artisans, scholars, teachers, and saints. Drawing on many traditions, sustaining and sustained by many peoples, Islam stamped its own distinctive mark on all of them, and provided the setting and the inspiration for a profoundly original and significant contribution to the arts and sciences of mankind.

'Recite!' said the Angel Gabriel to Muhammad. 'Recite in the name of thy Lord who created all things, who created man from clots of blood.' The word for 'recitation' or 'reading' is *qur'ān*, which became the name for the collected revelations accorded to Muhammad. To-

gether they form the basis of Islam, the authority to which Muslims refer for the solution of every problem – doctrinal, ethical, legal and political. This vivid miniature of the Archangel was painted in Egypt or Syria in the early VIII/14th century. (1)

وَمِنْهُمْ جَبْرَئِيلُ

قَابِذُنَا امِيرُ الْوَحِى وَخَازِنُ الْقُدُسِ وَيُقَالُ لَهُ ايْضًا الرُّوحُ الاَمِينُ وَالرُّوحُ الْقُدُسِ
وَالنَّامُوسُ الاَكْبَرُ وَطَاوُسُ الْمَلَائِكَةِ جَاءَ فِى الْقُرْآنِ انَّ اللهَ تَعَالَى اذَا انْتَكُمْ بِالَّذِى
سَمِعَ اهْلُ السَّمَاءِ صَلْصَلَةً كَجَرِّ السِّلْسِلَةِ عَلَى الصَّفَا فَيُصْعَقُونَ وَلَا يَزَالُ وَنَ كَذَلِكَ
حَتَّى يَاتِيَهُمْ جِبْرَئِيلُ فَاِذَا جَاءَهُمْ فُزِعَ عَنْ قُلُوبِهِمْ فَقَالُوا يَا جِبْرَئِيلُ مَا ذَا مَا لَدْ رَبَّكَ
فَيَقُولُ الْحَقَّ فَنَادَوْنَ الْحَقَّ الْحَقَّ وَجَاءَ بِالْجُثْمَانِ النَّبِى صَلَّى اللهُ عَلَيْهِ وَآلِهِ وَسَلَّمَ
قَالَ لِجَبْرَئِيلُ انِّى احِبُّ انْ ارَاكَ عَلَى صُورَتِكَ فَقَالَ انَّكَ لَا تُطِيقُ ذَلِكَ

There was no 'Church' and 'state' in Islam, and no distinction was made between secular and spiritual authority. The mosque was the meeting place both for prayer and for public announcements of all kinds. This VIII/14th-century miniature shows Chingiz Khān, though not a Muslim, availing himself of the pulpit or *minbar* to proclaim to the people of Bukhārā that he had been sent by God to punish them. (2)

Prayer is to be offered five times a day, at sunrise, midday, afternoon, sunset and evening. The worshipper must be ritually clean and facing towards Mecca, but need not necessarily be in a mosque. Communal prayer takes place at midday on Friday. The scene shown here, from al-Harīrī's *Maqāmāt*, illustrates most of the standard features of the mosque – *mihrāb*, *minbar*, mosque lamps and minaret. (3)

To find the direction of Mecca from any given spot calls for a certain scientific expertise. This XII/18th-century disc from Turkey has a movable pointer fixed at Mecca on the map; by aligning the pointer with the appropriate place, the required direction of the *qibla* wall (in which was built the *mihrāb* niche, indicating the direction to face) could be worked out. The back of the disc (on the right) depicts Mecca itself, with the Ka'ba in the centre of an arcaded courtyard. (5, 6)

The spacious courtyards (left) of the mosques, going back originally to the courtyard of Muhammad's house, are used for meeting together and often for ritual washing. This photograph of the courtyard of the Great Mosque at Aleppo was taken over eighty years ago (Max van Berchem Foundation). Two rows of worshippers are lined up facing the *qibla* wall. In the background is the unmistakable silhouette of the Aleppo Citadel. (4)

Those who made the pilgrimage to Mecca, which is one of the five requirements of Islam, still decorate their houses with traditional patterns. A doorway in Jerusalem (right) carries a naïve picture of the Ka'ba and a minaret. (7)

The goal of pilgrimage was Mecca, Medina and their neighbourhood. Mecca is represented in countless miniatures, rugs and tiles, such as this Ottoman example of 1077/1666. The other buildings shown are also connected with the pilgrimage, which involves several days of prayer and ritual observances in Mecca and its neighbourhood. (8)

'**There is no God but God** and Muhammad is his Prophet': the profession of faith which is the first of the five essential requirements of Islam. A typical Turkish pulpit tile of the xi/17th century (below) bears the words of the creed surrounded by a lively floral pattern. (9)

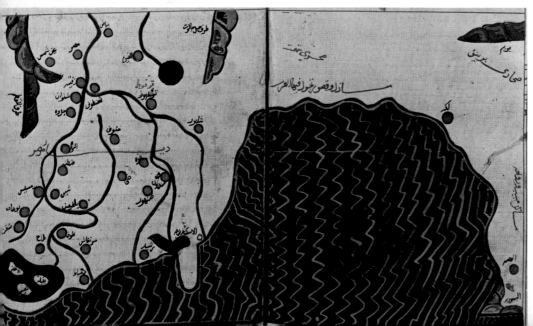

The needs of pilgrims acted as a spur to map-making and other attendant sciences. One of the main transit points for the North African pilgrims was Cairo. This map of the Nile delta is from Idrīsī's atlas of 549/1154. (10)

Majnūn visits the Ka'ba: an episode from the most popular of all Muslim romances, *Laylā and Majnūn* (miniature from a IX/15th-century manuscript). Majnūn was taken by his father to the Ka'ba in order to pray that he should be cured of his love for Laylā; instead he prayed that it should increase. The Ka'ba itself is a gaunt windowless cube traditionally believed to have been built by Abraham. Before Muhammad it was filled with idols, and particularly venerated because of the Black Stone (probably a meteorite), embedded in one of its corners and said to have been given to Abraham by Gabriel. Muhammad purged it of its idols and it became the holiest shrine of Islam. (11)

'Men of the pen' included the scribes. This miniature of *notarii Saraceni* is from a Christian manuscript produced in Sicily, where all cultures met, in 1195. (12)

'Men of the sword': a warrior from the brass basin known as the Baptistère de St Louis, first half of the VIII/14th century. (13)

The qādī – judge or magistrate – settled all practical disputes in the community. In the *Maqāmāt* illustrations (VII/13th century) he is always shown as a member of the bourgeoisie, not socially superior to the people he is judging. Here (left) he settles an argument between a father and daughter. (14)

Society was divided by medieval writers into free men (the nobility and upper classes); freedmen, or clients; 'people of the pact' – non-Muslims; and slaves. Political writers divided the ruling élite into 'men of the sword', 'men of the pen', merchants and husbandmen.

'People of the pact' meant primarily Christians and Jews. They enjoyed freedom of worship and the protection of the law, suffering only certain social restrictions and the payment of a special tax. Right above: Virgin and Child from a Gospel Book copied in Mosul between 1216 and 1220. Below: the Passover service, from a Hebrew manuscript made in Spain under Muslim rule. (15, 16)

'Men of affairs' included the businessmen who were often key figures in town life and among the stabilizing elements in Islamic society: the 'merchants' who appear in so many popular stories. Here again, al-Harīrī's *Maqāmāt* offers a unique series of early illustrations (below and left). Foodstuffs were often transported long distances and occasionally exported to Christian Europe. Sicily, Thrace and Egypt were the great granaries of the Mediterranean world, as they had been in Roman times. (17, 18)

Money hardly existed in the Arabia of Muhammad. Like so much else, it was taken over by the Arabs from their more sophisticated subjects. The silver dirham (left) has a Byzantine prototype, while the Syrian dinar (far left) of before 71/690 is a literal copy of a Sāsānid coin with an Arabic inscription added. 'Dirham' derives from the Greek *drachma*, 'dinar' from the Latin *denarius*. (19)

Slaves also had rights, though they were limited. They were entitled to medical attention, food and upkeep when old, and could own a certain amount of property. Legally, a man could only be a slave by birth or capture; but in practice they were also acquired as tribute, or simply bought – mostly from Central Asia and Africa. Above: the slave-market at Zabīd in the Yemen, another illustration from the *Maqāmāt* dated 635/1237. Right: a Fātimid glass weight, used in commercial transactions. (20, 21)

Long trains of camels were a familiar sight in most Islamic countries, which consisted, to a greater extent than those of the West, of towns and cultivated areas separated by tracts of mountain and desert. An early VII/13th-century plate from Iran has a realistic line of camels with their attendants plodding round the rim. In the centre sits an enthroned figure, one of the many local rulers who governed the country before the Mongols. (22)

The caravanserais were necessary staging posts in the long journeys, both in the deserts and in the midst of towns, where they would be built close to the bazaars. Some of them still fulfil their traditional purpose. Right: the caravanserai of As'ad Pasha in Damascus, dating from the XI/17th century, a photograph (Max van Berchem Foundation) taken before 1900. Below right: the caravanserai of Mahyar, in Iran; tribesmen and their cattle in the foreground. (25, 26)

The world of travellers is the setting for many of the stories in al-Harīrī's *Maqāmāt*. Below: a tale of misfortune on the Euphrates. The boat uses both sail and oars, and also has a rudder, something which did not reach the Christian Mediterranean for several centuries. Right: scene in the caravanserai of Wāsit, with arcade below and gallery above. (23, 24)

The life of common people is described at more length in Chapter III. The miniatures on these two pages are from a Persian dictionary dating from the early x/16th century. Left: **ploughing** with buffalo. The ploughman carries a goad in his right hand. (27)

Centre left: **pounding grain.** (28)
Above: **churning.** (29)
Left: **shaping a millstone** with hammer and chisel. (30)

Processing cotton for various uses is shown in these four miniatures. First, sifting the flowers. Second, carding the strands. Third, combing. Fourth (right), spinning; one hand turns the handle, the other holds the bobbin of thread. (31–34)

Dyeing the cloth (below). Vats very like these are still to be seen in Muslim towns (see p. 105). (35)

Manufacturing gold wire (below right) by pulling with pincers on to a spindle. In all these miniatures the technical operations are accurately portrayed, but the idyllic rural setting is a convention. (36)

The minting of coins began with the Umayyad caliphs. At first, as we have seen, they were based on Persian or Byzantine models, and these often bear figural designs that are alien to Islamic ways of thought. Later coins tend to have inscriptions only; but that soon became an art form in itself.

From Khurāsān, a silver dirham (right) of the Umayyad governor 'Abdallāh ibn Khāzim; a close copy of a Sāsānid coin. (37)

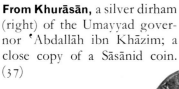

The 'Abbāsids replaced the Umayyads in 132/750; but for some years before that they had been building up a power centred on Nīshābūr, where this silver dirham was minted in 128/746. (38)

The Baghdad caliphate saw the full flowering of Islamic civilization, II/8th to V/11th century. Reproduced here are coins of two III/9th-century caliphs, al-Mu'tasim and al-Mutawakkil; the dromedary on the reverse perhaps can be seen as a nostalgic memory of their Bedouin origins. (39, 40)

The Būyids ruled in Persia and Iraq before the arrival of the Seljuqs. Left: gold dinar minted by Majd ad-Dawla of Ray between 387/997 and 420/1029. (41)

The Fātimids seized control of Egypt and Syria in the early IV/10th century. This quarter dinar was minted in Sicily by al-Mustansir (427–87/1036–94). (42)

Artuqids and Zangids were two of the dynasties, Turkish in origin, who took over parts of the old Seljuq empire in the VI/12th century. Shown here are bronze coins of the Artuqid Najm ad-Dīn Alpi, of Mārdīn, with a profile head that is astonishingly Greek, and the Zangid Mas'ūd I of Mosul. (43, 44)

Chingiz Khān (silver dirham, left) had, by 625/1227, gained a vast Asian empire. In 651/1258 Baghdad fell to his grandson Hülegü. **Christian kingdoms** still existed under the Mongols. At Tiflis, in Georgia, the Queen Regent Turakina issued her own silver dirhams with a design derived from the Hellenistic *sagittarius*. (45, 46)

Retail selling in Islamic countries still follows the pattern of a thousand years ago. A bazaar, or *sūq*, is a large covered market, protected from the glare of the sun, with shops grouped together according to the commodity being sold. The whole complex is like a giant department store under multiple and competing managements, in a setting provided by the civic authority or community. A scene such as this, the cloth section of the Bazaar at Aleppo, has probably not changed in essentials since the Middle Ages. (47)

55

Peasants who worked the land were ultimately the foundation of Islamic life; but as with most civilizations their role is largely unsung and unillustrated. This scene from the Arabic version of the Pseudo-Galen's *Book of Antidotes* (595/1199) shows grain being harvested, threshed and winnowed – with the labourers' lunch arriving top left. Islamic agriculture was generally more intensive than that of medieval Europe because there was relatively less cultivable land and because water was scarcer. In irrigation techniques and the variety of plants grown, Muslim farmers could give lessons to their Christian counterparts. They also specialized in dried fruits – apricots, pimentoes, figs, grapes – which lasted the winter and could be transported any distance. (48)

Chapter Two

THE MAN-MADE SETTING

Richard Ettinghausen

Horseman with a banner: an Iraqi lustre plate of the IV/10th century. It is typical of Islamic figural art that the subject is stylized and often reduced to a silhouette. (1)

A PRESENTATION OF ISLAMIC ART has to begin with a basic question: is there such a phenomenon as Islamic art, that is to say, an art which is characteristic of the civilization in its totality? It seems at first a near-insurmountable task to offer relevant remarks about the nature of Islamic art *as a whole* and the causes for its unique and universal quality.

Such an enterprise appears difficult for a whole range of reasons. This artistic tradition, with its natural sequence of many styles, extended over an enormous time-span, from the end of late Antiquity in the late I/7th century, throughout the Migration Period into the late XII/18th and early XIII/19th centuries, when it was seriously challenged by European concepts. It was fashioned within an area from Spain and Morocco in the west to Central Asia and the Indian sub-continent in the east. It contained many cultural foci, often of a highly individual nature; and these became more evident when in the III/9th and IV/10th centuries the caliphate began to disintegrate into many separate political entities, often hostile to each other and headed by rulers with diverse artistic attitudes and tastes. This was more so after the disappearance of the caliphate in 656/1258. Furthermore, the inhabitants of this vast area comprised at least five ethnic strands: Arab, Iranian, Berber, Turkish and Indian. Within these races, too, there were contrasts, as, for instance, between the Muslims of northern India, Kashmir, Bengal and the Deccan. From the beginning, moreover, the larger body politic included non-Muslim communities such as the eastern Christian denominations and the Jews.

The artistic life of Islam also had its divisions of social class: the numerous luxury-loving courts; the vast body of the often learned urban middle class, largely trade- or craft-oriented; the ubiquitous nomadic tribes, important as the milieu from which, for instance, in Iran, most of the dynasties originated; and the mass of common folk who in spite of their narrow circumstances still showed not rarely an awareness of the beautiful, by having carved beams on their houses, or owning a simple carpet or a decorated dish. There were also the ever-shifting religious, mystical and legal groups, differing greatly in their attitudes towards those luxuries of life that included the arts. Artistic expression was further diversified by the absence of any wider regulatory directive or code for artists or craftsmen throughout the Muslim world; nor did there develop – although it was a highly literate society – any manner of conceptualizing about the artistic process. This deficiency was accompanied by a derogatory attitude towards even the finer forms of manual work. While artistic products were fully acceptable in the civic body because they constituted the substance of a vital local and world-wide trade, they were nevertheless outranked by far by the higher esteem given to governmental, military, religious, judicial, literary or mercantile activities and their representatives.

The basic conditions of Islamic art, then, would speak for a civilization of loose cohesion and little overall resemblance. Even a cursory survey of buildings and objects from various parts of the Muslim world seems to bear this out: the shape and decoration of a minaret reveals at once the country where it was built, as well as the period. Pottery is different from country to country, even from town to town; and it changes from century to century. Strong regional and chronological differences also appear in the script, be it in one of the monumental hands called Kūfic or in the cursive hands.

The same multi-national and multi-religious factors operated in Islamic civilization as a whole as in the arts. This was explicitly recognized in the second half of the III/9th century by members of the philosophical society Ikhwān as-Safā', when they stated:

> The ideal and morally perfect man should be of East Persian derivation, Arabic in faith, of Iraqi education, a Hebrew in astuteness, a disciple of Christ in conduct, as pious as a Greek monk, a Greek in the individual sciences, an Indian in the interpretation of all mysteries, but lastly and especially a Sūfī in his whole spiritual life.

Yet there were forces that mitigated unfavourable separatistic tendencies and that helped, in one way or another, to create a noble art of a universal and generally unified character.

Universal aspects

In architecture, a prime example of how the integrating forces worked is shown by the use of the eyvan (or *liwan* in Arabic). This consisted of a high vaulted hall, usually within the centre of a building tract and whose whole front opened to the adjoining courtyard. This architectural form was western Parthian and Sāsānid in origin. It became prevalent in medieval and post-medieval Iran and Iraq, and subsequently in Syria, Anatolia, Egypt and Morocco; and remained in use into the XIII/19th century. Similarly, a style of VIII/14th- and IX/15th-century necropolis with loosely grouped cubic structures covered by melon-shaped domes is found as far apart as Samarqand and Cairo; another, originally domed, group of mausoleums is met with in Chella near Rabat in Morocco. Or, if one considers the artistic production of artisans, the output of carpets was enormous throughout the Muslim world. This was particularly so in regions between Turkey and Central Asia; but applied also to Egypt, North Africa, Spain and even the Balkans. So pervasive was this industry that it persisted in Spain and the Balkans as a Muslim bequest after the Christian reconquests. A more technical example is the *shādirvān* (called *chadar* in India), a water slide, for wall fountains or formal gardens, made of marble carved with chevron patterns. This feature, too, had a long tradition and a wide geographical distribution. The earliest known is found in an Algerian palace of the V/11th century; but it undoubtedly goes back to an earlier origin, borrowed perhaps from Spain or Morocco. It is then traceable in a Sicilian Arab villa of the VI/12th century. Later on it formed an attractive aspect of XI/17th-century Mughul gardens, and is finally found in the XIII/19th-century gardens of Iran.

Much apparent homogeneity was due to an absence of division between the sacred and the profane. Thus the eyvaned buildings, in a quadruple arrangement around a central courtyard, served not only as mosques and theological schools *(madrasas)*, but also as palaces, caravanserais or hospitals. In the same way, it is difficult to decide whether certain candlesticks were made for a sacred shrine or for a royal audience hall – just as a prayer carpet may be decorated with the characteristic symbolic arch of the prayer niche *(mihrāb)* found in a mosque; or it may be just an ordinary carpet or mat of the proper small size, but woven for any number of different purposes. Besides this one modest requirement and the *mihrāb* and pulpit, no liturgical or ritual objects were needed for the proper functioning of the mosque, and because of this lack of prescribed requirements, Islam – unlike Christianity – developed no exclusively sacred art of an applied or decorative nature.

Another unifying factor was the ready transfer of a technique or pattern – whether appropriate or not – from one medium to another. Thus three-dimensional abstract designs composed of bevelled curved lines were first used in III/9th-century Iraq to carve stones, stucco and wood; it was then also employed in Egypt, Iran and Central Asia. This working mode was, however, also adapted in Iran for achieving repoussé patterns in silverwork; for impressing moulded ornaments in plaster, by cutting them in glass; or, in two dimensions, by painting them on pottery. The range of this all-purpose patterning was applied not only to abstract designs, for which it was eminently suitable, but also – less adequately – to represent animals. Similarly, all-over star and cross patterns as well as hexagons developed for dadoes of plaster were then used on pottery or metal vessels for whose bulbous surface they were quite inappropriate; or illustrative conventions worked out for manuscripts were transferred to pottery, tiles, glass, pen-boxes, book-bindings, painted chests and even carpets and textiles.

The basically anonymous character of the arts was another equalizing factor. Although there are signatures of executing artists, their names on the whole mean little and the production remains generally non-individualistic. But the quality of the production was dynamic enough to counteract and absorb the artistic capabilities even of non-Muslims within the community. Religious or ethnic minorities contributed actively to the body of Islamic art without changing its actual fabric. For instance, the excavations of the early II/8th-century mansion of Khirbat al-Mafjar near Jericho revealed a marble slab with Hebrew lettering; yet nothing in the rich decoration or the structure of the palace strikes a Jewish note. There exist Persian and Turkish ceramic vessels of the X/16th and XI/17th centuries which have Armenian inscriptions; but they betray no visible Armenian character. The same could be said about carpets from Anatolia and the Caucasus which show Hebrew or Armenian inscriptions.

On the other hand, the arts of these non-Muslim religious communities bear all the hallmarks of the Muslim environment. Thus a manuscript of the Prophets written in Tiberias in 890 has several purely non-figural carpet pages which in their general character are like those of the contemporary Qur'ān frontispieces. And the woodcarvings of the Coptic convent Dayr al-Banāt near al-Fustāt or the wooden doors of the Synagogue of Ben Ezra in Cairo are identical in character with those preserved from the palace of the Fātimid caliphs in the same city. Only when it came to the ritual requirements, and especially the established religious iconography to illustrate sacred books, did the congregations of the 'People of the Book' insist on the continuation of their own tradition; but even here one notices the stylistic impact of the surrounding Muslim world.

Due to these levelling tendencies a number of monuments and other artefacts which lack identifying inscriptions cannot be specifically dated or localized. Thus a spectacular mausoleum (alleged to be that of the great theologian al-Ghazālī) at Tūs in north-eastern Iran has been variously dated between the V/11th and the VIII/14th centuries. Even when two media – such as calligraphy and illumination – are involved, as in the case of several III/9th- to IV/10th-century Qur'ān MSS. with 'carpet pages', it has not been possible to date any of them more precisely or to attribute them to a specific country. Another example is the fashioning of rock crystals. It is known from al-Bīrūnī that the craft of carving this hard and rare semi-precious stone was current both in Egypt and Iraq in the IV/10th and V/11th centuries. Yet no one has so far been able to isolate the Iraqi pieces, even though political hostility between the two countries would have suggested two distinct styles. Finally, a group of carpets, thought until recently to be Iranian and of the X/16th century, are now considered to be Turkish and of the xIII/19th century, their re-attribution being based on technical considerations and not on stylistic features.

What, then, were the powerful and pervasive forces, which led to this inner consistency throughout the Muslim world?

The forces of unity

Three major interacting conditions can, perhaps, be identified. The first was, of course, the normative force of Islam itself as the basis of the whole civilization. The Muslim faith influenced art not through official concern – which was minimal – but by creating a way of life and general attitudes that were to become universally accepted. There was on the one hand a strong consciousness of belonging to the *umma* or whole Muslim community, and on the other, a common purpose through shared rituals and beliefs. These included a deep faith in the revealed message of the Qur'ān; acceptance of the essential duties of a Muslim; and a common image of the whole cosmos. This in turn affected religious architecture; the paramount use of the Arabic language and script as the vehicle of the divine revelation; the range and character of iconography; and the treatment of ornament.

The Muslims furthermore belonged to a system in which both religion and government had, ideally if not in practice, a monolithic character, a fact which led to a general coordination of beliefs and practices. In religion this was due to the general principle of *ijmāʿ*, that is, of considering the consensus of theological opinion as the acceptable norm. Uniformity was similarly promoted by the principle that 'the people follow the religion of their kings'.

A second unifying factor was that the heartlands of the Islamic sphere – excepting Arabia – had for centuries formed part of a large political and cultural entity, the Roman empire; or, in more general terms, the Mediterranean world. More distant countries like Iran or India and even southern Arabia had at least felt its impact. This heritage influenced the arts in a limited fashion and often only indirectly; it did, however, create a common psychological climate, and engendered attitudes propitious for the generalizing tendencies of the arts.

This leaves us to consider the high mobility of Muslim civilization, the third factor which was particularly important for the levelling of the arts. Quite apart from the nomadic tribes still found throughout most of the Muslim world, large and small population groups, as well as courts and individuals of significance, were on the move and creative in regions far from their original home. Among migrations of whole population groups, the most momentous was that of the Seljuqs in the v/11th century, which affected not only Iran and the Fertile Crescent, but also Anatolia which, through it, was all at once transformed into a Muslim land with a very rich art; it also created the historical base for the future Ottoman empire. Other migrants included the Moroccan Almoravids and the Almohads with their Berber followers in Spain and, throughout south-west Asia east of Syria and Palestine, the Mongols.

In addition to such mass migrations, the rulers of many countries were alien. From the II/8th to the IV/10th century the Maghrib was governed by many foreign rulers: by the Umayyads, the Idrīsids, the Rustamids, the Aghlabids, the Tūlūnids, the Ikhshīdids and the Fātimids. Iran was so consistently ruled by non-Iranians that the late III/9th and the IV/10th centuries, which were an exception to that rule, have been called the 'Iranian intermezzo'. Egypt and India likewise both came early under foreign rule and remained so. Indeed it was not unusual for kings and sultans not to speak the language of their subjects, or at least to prefer their own tongue. Yet at their courts the arts often flourished to a very high degree, not least on account of interaction between traditional native influences and imported styles.

The middle classes, too, were often geographically mobile. According to the Geniza documents, Egypt and North Africa witnessed an influx, shortly before the year 391/1000, mostly of merchants, from Iran, Iraq and Syria; after that date, however, economic and political pressures started a counter-movement to the east. The artistic effect of this urban, middle-class migration is traceable from the existence of an Iranian house type in Egypt, or the fact that large amounts of IV/10th-century Iraqi (and possibly Iranian) pottery were found in Fustāt and eventually influenced Fātimid wares. Further aesthetic evidence of this east-west movement is furnished by the lustre tiles in the Great Mosque of Qayrawān of about 248/862 which were apparently imported from Baghdad, or of the Mosque of Ibn Tūlūn in Cairo, the building technique and decoration of which are decidedly Iraqi in character.

The migrations of architects or artisans helped to disseminate artistic ideas, regardless of whether they sought work in an economically more prosperous place, or had been invited by an artistically inclined ruler. Building inscriptions, texts on metal objects, pottery vessels or tiles, and colophons in manuscripts all provide evidence for this cross-fertilization. From countless examples it may suffice to refer to just three monuments in Cairo: there the Nilometer of 247/861 was designed by a mathematician and astronomer from Farghānā in Central Asia; the city gates of 480/1087 by a fortification specialist from Urfa (Edessa) on the upper Euphrates; and the two minarets of the Mosque of the Amīr Qūsūn of 730/1329 by an architect from Tabrīz. Often such an artistic transfer is apparent only from the results; for instance, Spain's flourishing silk industry was probably promoted by immigrant craftsmen from the East; in particular from Greater Syria. Such developments were, however, occasionally recognized by contemporary writers, at least by implication. In the VIII/14th century Ibn Khaldūn stated:

> When the realm of a dynasty is large and far flung with many provinces and subjects, workers are very plentiful and can be brought together from all sides and regions and superior social organization and engineering skill [are present].

Involuntary migrations of artists also contributed to the dissemination of ideas, whether they were refugees, conscripts, or craftsmen brought to an alien capital by coercion. Forced labour already existed in Umayyad times: Greek and Coptic craftsmen from Syria and Egypt were sent in 88-90/707-9 by the Caliph al-Walīd to help reconstruct the Mosque of Medina, while skilled workmen from Egypt were compulsorily enlisted between

87/706 and 96/714 for the building of the Mosque of Damascus. A similar arrangement enabled the extensive new 'Abbāsid capital of Samarra to be built and equipped in record time. An outstanding example of obtaining master craftsmen by force is shown by Tamerlane (Tīmūr-i Lang), who, according to the Spanish Ambassador Clavijo, provided for his capital city of Samarqand by carrying off weavers, bow-makers, armourers, makers of glass and porcelain, gun-makers and silversmiths, as well as masons from Syria and Turkey.

Sometimes it was not the artisan who was displaced, but the ruler who had to go into exile, incidentally diffusing artistic predilections. Thus, in the middle of the 11/8th century the Umayyad 'Abd ar-Rahmān carried with him to Spain his partiality for Syrian art, resulting in a considerable influence on Moorish architecture, especially its greatest monument, the Great Mosque of Cordoba – for example in the use of the horseshoe arch, the combination of red and white stones, roofing with parallel gables and so on. In the 1540s, during his enforced stay in Iran, the Mughul Emperor Humāyūn developed a special liking for Persian miniatures, which resulted in pronounced borrowings from the Iranian canon in the developing art of Indo-Muslim painting.

However far-reaching these influences, the widest artistic interaction was probably due to extensive commercial activities. Here S. D. Goitein's studies of the Geniza documents have been particularly revealing. A trader in Cairo, for example, would easily and often travel by sea or land to distant countries: to North Africa, Sicily and Spain in the west or to Syria, Palestine, Aden and India in the east. Political frontiers seem to have been hardly any impediment; nor, despite the horrors of shipwreck and piracy, did distances hold any terror.

Four other factors further increased this mobility. First, there was in the bazaar no strict separation between the manufacture and the sale of merchandise. This produced more immediate results. Secondly, it was an established trading principle to take goods abroad, and to return not with cash but with other merchandise to sell at home. Thirdly, through its vast and far-reaching influence, the merchant class often exerted great political power. Indeed, great merchants were at times thought to be more powerful than viziers. The fourth factor applies to all Muslims: the basic requirement of Islam to perform the pilgrimage to Mecca at least once (Sūra iii, 97).

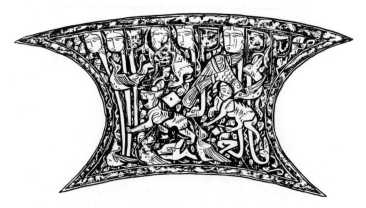

Detail from a bronze bowl with silver inlay of the late VII/13th century showing Arabic script with human heads and animals prowling between the letters. (2)

The local copying of fashionable but expensive imports was a further step in the blending of foreign and native strains. It applied particularly to textiles, these being easily shipped over large distances and highly subject to the whims and fashions of an international clientele. Men from Qayrawān in Tunisia wore fabrics from Iran; Iraqi silk was traded in Alexandria; and exports from Sicily to Egypt included Tustarī gowns, so named after a town in south-western Iran. Rūmī kerchiefs, a fabric in the style of Sicily, were manufactured in Tinnīs in the Nile delta. The export and subsequent local copying of fabrics eventually lowered prices and extended their use. An example is the use of a particular cloth from Tabaristān in northern Iran. At first only the 'Abbāsid caliphs, such as al-Mahdī (158-69/775-85), could afford this product. Around 391/1000 its fame had so increased that traders were said to come in search of it to Āmul, the main city of Tabaristān, from Iraq, Syria, Khurāsān, the borderlands of India and Central Asia. The same fabric also must have reached Egypt in quantity, because in the IV/10th century it became a favourite item in Cairo in the trousseau lists of well-to-do brides; and eventually this Tabarī cloth was locally imitated.

The internationally traded products of other crafts are also numerous. Square ready-made bookbindings were sent from the Maghrib to Egypt, while pottery from Tinnīs in the Nile delta was shipped to Ramla, in Palestine. Trading links between the Near East and India were particularly extensive and lucrative. According to the Geniza documents, India exported bronze and brass vessels, silks, cottons and leatherwork, while its imports included textiles, clothing, silver vessels and ornaments, brass, glass, carpets and mats. Archaeological discoveries have, in a limited fashion, confirmed such written records. Excavations in Egypt have yielded many medieval Indian cotton fragments, while Iraqi painting of the first half of the VII/13th century revealed a very odd, borrowed feature – the so-called protruding further eye – which was a typical Indian motif of the period. The same source of influence is disclosed by Egyptian renditions of Indian-type demons. In the extreme west of Islam transshipment also occurred. Here the most striking and excellent example of copying in a distant Muslim country is provided by a silk fabric of the first half of the VI/12th century, featuring two addorsed sphinxes in roundels. Its inscription states that it was made in Baghdad; and naturally it was at first believed to have come from there. Subsequently, however, on the basis of the technique, the colouring and the Maghribī spelling of a common word in the inscription, it was proved instead to be a Spanish copy.

The unity of symbolism: Arabic script

Probably the most typical and widespread art form of Muslim character is calligraphically rendered Arabic script. It is found throughout the Islamic world from Spain to India and from the earliest to the most recent times. At first it was executed in simple ways, but from the III/9th century onward in a progressively ornate, yet usually abstract manner. The reason for this development lies in the nature of the Prophet of Islam and his prophecy. Muhammad claimed to be an ordinary human being who had been appointed only as a messenger

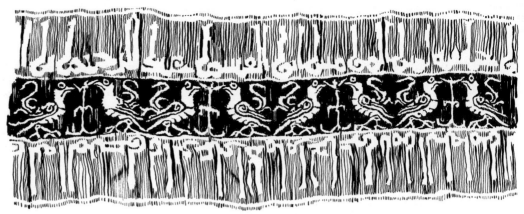

between God and the Muslims. Islam, therefore, unlike Christianity, was not founded on the exceptional life experiences and martyrdom of a miracle-performing prophet. Instead, the divine book – the Qur'ān – and its message were of paramount importance. Inscriptions – and primarily those containing pertinent passages of the Qur'ān – replaced the figural iconography used by other religions.

Significantly, Arabic writing is already used extensively in the earliest surviving Islamic building, the Dome of the Rock in Jerusalem. This monument had been planned by the Caliph ʿAbd al-Malik in 72/691 as a symbol of the new supremacy of Islam and its unitarian beliefs; and at the same time was meant to be a victory monument to commemorate the defeat of the Byzantines and Iranians. Soon, however, it was interpreted as a memorial of Muhammad's ascension to heaven, which traditionally is connected with this site. The monumental inscription 240 metres long, in gold mosaic cubes on blue ground, is conspicuous and must accordingly have been deemed important; and its appearance indicates that it must also have had a decorative function. The guiding principles of this epigraphic decoration are evident both in this early monument and in countless later inscriptions. It renders various Qur'ānic passages indicating the building's function; and closes with the name of the Caliph (later replaced by that of the ʿAbbāsid al-Ma'mūn) and the date. Most later inscriptions indicate the purpose of the building to which they were applied, either by appropriate Qur'ānic passages or, in the case of secular buildings, by means of prose or verse; they too added the name of the ruler (or whatever patron); the date; possibly also that of the official immediately responsible for the structure; and that of the architect, decorator or scribe. The specific nature of the Jerusalem inscription thus prefigures the pragmatic nature of the civilization to which it belonged – one in which the scribe with his documents and the merchant with his accounts played such dominant roles. As in the Dome of the Rock, such inscriptions were given an important place, usually below the dome, the crowning architectural element, around the *mihrāb*, the focal point of any sanctuary, or as a frame of the monumental entrance gate.

It is significant that the Jerusalem inscription is in the hieratic form of Kūfic writing with a minimum of diacritical points to distinguish the various letters. It was therefore difficult to read, especially as the not-too-large letters were placed high up on the walls. This was even more so when in other buildings inscriptions became more and more ornamented with floral and braided features, and were combined with other inscriptions or set against a background decoration. The difficulties of reading an often complex script in Arabic became compounded when the building of which it was a part was located in one of the many countries where Arabic was not the generally spoken language. It becomes clear, in fact, that after its first application, the pious inscription was primarily meant as a symbol, addressed to God rather than men. Its function became that of a beautiful affirmation of the Faith, no longer intended to be deciphered by worshippers or passers-by word by word.

The symbolic character of Arabic writing can be also deduced from a more specific situation. On the many large Iranian VII/13th- and VIII/14th-century tiles whose arches mark them as prayer niches *(mihrāb)* for the decoration of the mosque walls facing Mecca, the inscriptions – mainly religious and often Qur'ānic verses – are invariably in cobalt-blue letters rendered in relief. These are firmly visible from whichever angle one looks. By contrast, the inscription's rich background design of scrollwork and arabesques is always executed in lustre painting, often with the patterns reserved in white from the golden background. In contrast to the solid blue, lustre has an evanescent quality so that certain limited parts can only be seen from certain angles; when the viewer changes his position or just moves his eye, the visible part of the design disappears and another section becomes noticeable. To the reflective Muslim mind, especially one nurtured by the symbolism of mystic writers such as Jalāl ad-Dīn Rūmī, this could only mean that the Word of God was forever enduring, while man and his handiwork had at best only a fleeting existence.

The symbolic purpose of writing is borne out by the fact that after 79/698-9 Muslim coinage is with very few exceptions purely epigraphic. Like the inscriptions in the Dome of the Rock, it presents Qur'ānic and other pious texts, combined with pertinent information about the ruling caliph, the minting lord and the date and place of minting. Equally revealing is the Muslim custom of honouring a distinguished person by giving him a fine robe of honour *(khilʿa)*, in which the name and titles of the caliph, the nature of the workshop and the names of its director, place of manufacture and date are woven in formal Kūfic or in the later cursive script. A special expertise was required to decipher them. Indeed some are so arcane or interspersed with decorative elements that reading them presents a challenge even to a skilled epigraphist. Even the original owners must have found them indecipherable; nonetheless, since the garments that bore them comprised practically the only mark of governmental appreciation, their symbolic function remains undoubted.

The rejection of sculpture

Another aesthetic feature – albeit a negative one – common to all Islam is at once obvious in any museum of Muslim art: namely, the almost total absence of sculpture. True, there exist from the Umayyad period rather heavy-set, at times even clumsy, free-standing human and animal figures in stone and stucco. These were, however, a legacy from earlier times, Eastern versions of Hellenistic art. Chinese influence is also evident in the form of stucco figures, with strong Far Eastern physiognomies, from the late Seljuq, or, more likely, Mongol, periods. Figural stone reliefs also survive from a few other periods and from marginal regions, particularly Seljuq Anatolia and the Caucasus; but these too are atypical of Muslim civilization as a whole.

Related to this almost total lack of sculpture is the broader question of the use of representational art in Islam. In this context the extensive range of figural designs seen in European and American museums is, in a way, misleading. For the West representation is the touchstone for the evaluation of art; hence Western collectors of Islamic art have all along sought primarily this genre, despite its minor part in the whole body of artistic creation.

There are no specific early pronouncements on the figural arts as such, but the general attitude towards them can be construed from the Qur'ān and the monuments themselves, especially those from the first centuries. From a few passages in the Qur'ān (Sūra v, 92; vi, 74), it is apparent that Muhammad linked statues with pagan idols. Allah is the true 'fashioner' (*musawwir*, Sūra lix, 24); He alone – unlike the human *musawwir*, usually a painter – is able to apply the breath of life to His creation (Sūra iii, 43). The II/8th-century *hadīth* elaborated this concept by stating that on the Day of Judgment the human artist, who, in his hubris, has dared to make images, will be called upon to instill life into them; naturally he will be found wanting and be condemned. This rejection of figural designs extended to manuscripts of the Qur'ān, although certain stories involving the Prophet and Biblical figures would have lent themselves to such an undertaking. Only from the VIII/14th century onwards were such sacred personages depicted pictorially, and then they were treated more as historical or poetic than as religious figures. Figural representation was similarly excluded from wall decorations, murals and mosaics of mosques. Thus, while animals are depicted on, for instance, the façade of the secular parts of the Umayyad desert castle of Mshatta, they are absent in the section in front of the mosque. This way of thinking also governed the social status of artists engaged in figural work; theologically they stood on the lowest level, otherwise reserved for usurers, tatooers and buyers of common, non-hunting, dogs. Alone of Istanbul's XI/17th-century guilds, that of the figural painters could not boast a patron saint.

The result of this approach was that for centuries – from the III/9th century till the arrival of three-dimensional European art – artists in those countries and periods which favoured figural designs endeavoured to devise animals in silhouette style, without a viable corporeal quality, and appearing as mere shadows or symbols of the real creature. Later, when on carpets, animals and human beings were realistically rendered, they were usually skilfully hidden in a dense landscape scenery. In addition, the concepts of the *hadīth* and *fiqh* meant that being sat and trodden upon reduced their esteem.

Orthodox disapproval of figural designs naturally brought other more innocuous patterns to the fore. Hence Muslim art, especially in the public and religious sector, is prolific in vegetal, geometric, epigraphic decorations, and even non-figural landscapes. All the creative potential that in other cultures was more widely spread was channelled in the case of Islam into the so-called 'minor arts' of decoration. And the very small ritual requirements of mosques made it inevitable that art was predominantly secular. Even objects made for a religious use are not different in kind, as they would be to a large extent in the West.

In spite of all these considerations, however, a limited range of figural wall paintings and a much larger body of manuscript illuminations was produced. How was this possible? Two factors can be adduced. Firstly, pre-Islamic pictorial traditions were still intermittently active. One of them was the classical heritage, both the lively Hellenistic genre and the severely stylized forms of Byzantine tradition; another the arts of Sāsānid Iran, especially in the rendition of royal themes; also those of Central Asia and India. So strong were these traditions that they not only lasted a long time – the classical, for instance, into the VIII/14th century – but could also be exported, to kindle new forms and activities. From Syria, Arab painting of the Byzantine type spread to the Maghrib, while in Sicily there appeared a mixed classical-Iranian style. The Iranian strain in its later developed form, being very potent and readily applicable, was easily transferred to both Turkey and India, where it then adjusted to local propensities. The first strong outside influence on Iranian painting itself was from the Far East. As such, it was an after-effect of the Mongol invasion of the VII/13th century, later supplemented by trading and diplomacy. In Turkish painting European influence began to appear in the late IX/15th century. It became particularly incisive in Mughul India in the late X/16th century and, from the middle of the next century, in Iran.

The second factor tending to promote figural painting arose from the subject matter of the works to be illustrated. Scientific texts are greatly helped by miniatures. Inspired by pictures in Greek manuscripts which had been translated, Arabic and Persian books on astronomy, botany, zoology, medicine and mechanical devices as well as cosmological treatises from the V/11th to the XI/17th century were furnished with explanatory illustrations; and these at times included renderings of persons and animals. And once the taste for representational art had taken root it could be indulged in spite of clerical disapproval. Patrons could conceal illustrated manuscripts in the private rooms of their houses, while rulers could own or commission such works without challenge from anyone. Rulers were indeed the main patrons of the arts. Following an Iranian tradition, paintings – especially murals, but also war records in book form – became demonstrations of the sovereign's power and glory. In the same way, lions, eagles and certain fabulous birds were employed as symbols of royalty.

While figural painting always remained non-acceptable to the official religious establishment, this strict attitude weakened noticeably in the course of time. A writer like Saʿdī no longer saw figural designs of animals as blasphemous acts, but regarded them as creations which like everything else had God as their source and inspiration. The great mystic Jalāl ad-Dīn Rūmī went still further. Not only did he not disapprove of representations of such religious subjects as Joseph of Qurʾānic fame and the houris of paradise and of demons and devils; he believed them to have didactic value and to be worthy of spiritual contemplation. At length, indeed, the brush, as the tool of the painter, came to be esteemed on the same artistic and spiritual level as the reed pen *(qalam)*, the tool of the scribe and as such a transmitter of divine knowledge and even the subject of a Qurʾānic oath (Sura lxviii, 1; xcvi, 3–4).

The mosque: origins and meaning

The centre of religious life throughout the Muslim world was the mosque, called *masjid* or place of prostration; in the capitals major ones were designated *jāmiʿ*, gathering, or *masjid al-jumʿa*, Friday mosque. There is, however, no universally used structure, no 'Islamic mosque' as such, only various regional types – an Arab type, an Iranian type and a Turkish type (or types), to which major categories one could add the Mughul-Indian, Kashmiri and Chinese varieties and so on. At first the plan of the Arab-type mosque gained almost general acceptance; but eventually mosque architecture came to reflect the traditional domestic architecture of each ethnic or regional entity. In each case these forms were enriched by concepts derived from local pre-Islamic architecture, and elaborated by specific technical considerations. However, in the evolution of the mosque, religious requirements were minimal, and the structure itself came to differ from pre-Islamic equivalents only by its elaborations. It represents the final form of earlier architectural manifestations.

The prototype of the Arab mosque was the simple urban house of sun-dried bricks, or, more specifically, Muhammad's house in Medina. As reconstructed from historical sources, this consisted of a large courtyard with several entrances. On one side was an open portico which stretched across the full width, but with the depth only of two rows of roof-supporting tree trunks serving as columns. This was the main part of the house, where the Prophet met his followers. Opposite stood a similar portico, though of less than half the width of the courtyard and with only one row of columns. This served as shelter for some of the poorer adherents of the new faith. The private quarters were a mere appendix to this main ensemble and consisted of a series of small square cubicles for each of the Prophet's wives. The public parts of this house became ultimately a mosque and thus established the model of the Muslim house of worship: the main portico took on the function of the sanctuary proper while the smaller shelter was enlarged to surround the whole courtyard and to serve as shady retreat from the sun and as a possible meeting place of the worshippers before or after the services. This spatial arrangement, especially that of the sanctuary, fitted the general requirements of the service, although the many columns formed

Detail from a Persian lustre dish, VI/12th century. The great bird, with its feet breaking through the floral border, characteristically combines formality with vitality. (4)

an encumbrance in the service, and more so in the later vast hypostyle versions. The orientation of all mosques was towards Mecca with its Kaʿba, the central sanctuary of Islam. Directed by the prayer leader, the worshippers were wont to line up in parallel rows like military units, with the aim of being as close as possible to the wall towards Mecca. This naturally made a shallow oblong building the more suitable shape.

While the unsophisticated hypostyle arrangement of Muhammad's house sufficed for prayer meetings, for the spiritual and communal centre of a victorious state a monumental style was needed. The change was facilitated by political and military circumstances. In towns that surrendered to the Arab invaders without resistance, adherents of established faiths – Christians, Jews and Zoroastrians – could keep their houses of worship. However, if the town resisted these were turned into mosques. At first this conversion happened particularly in Syria. In practice this meant that these imposing basilica-like churches of much greater length than width, and oriented eastward, were changed into mosques directed south towards Mecca. Hence the original longitudinal direction became now the width of the building, and its original rather limited width its new depth. In other words, the new very wide but shallow sanctuary structure reflected the general proportions of Muhammad's house. However, the height of the buildings, together with the marble columns and capitals, rendered them more grandiose and more appropriate for the main centres of Islam, especially in cities where the state wanted to impress a large Christian population. When such a ready-made conversion was not possible, these churches were then copied in their general aspects. Old temples and churches were ransacked for suitable columns and capitals, not only as a quarrying procedure, but as a symbol of the triumph of Islam over the old religion. East of Syria, where no marble columns were available, the roof was carried by massive brick piers covered with plaster, which limited the space available for worshippers. In all these cases the many rows of supporting members, especially when viewed from an oblique angle, created a striking though also bewildering impression, especially as there was very little in the way of directional indications.

While the space unit in the mosque was the area between four columns or pillars, the space-creating elements were the rows of roof-supporting members. These could be added length- and/or sideways to extend an existing building – as, for instance, in the Great Mosque of Cordoba. This was the same additive principle that also governed the composition of poetry, particularly of such a genre as the *Maqāmāt*.

Several novel developments made the traditional structure more specifically a mosque and emphasized its orientation. One was the *mihrāb*, a real or simulated niche in the centre of the wall towards Mecca, the so-called *qibla* wall. It designates the part of the mosque to be faced during prayer, more symbolically than practically, however, as it is usually much too small to be seen by most of the worshippers, even in the case of the biggest – actually a small room – in the former Great Mosque of Cordoba. The often highly decorated area near the *mihrāb*, called the *maqsūra*, was reserved for the devotions of princes; it was often covered with a small canopy-like dome or marked by an adjacent royal box of richly carved wood.

For all practical purposes the *mihrāb* is now kept empty. Formerly a lamp, probably of glass, may have been suspended from its apex as commonly represented on the lustre tiles of VII/13th-century Iranian *mihrābs* and IX/15th-century versions from Anatolia. If so, this feature was probably engendered by the Qur'ān in Sūra xxiv, 35:

> Allah is the light of heavens and the earth; a likeness of His light is as a niche in which there is a lamp, the lamp is in a glass and the glass is as it were a brightly shining star lit from a blessed olive tree.

The decoration of the *mihrāb* is for the most part in the manner of its country and period; that is, with carved stone or stucco, ceramic glazed tiles, ornamental painting, mosaics or *opus sectile* work; at times it remains unadorned. In Turkey, *mihrābs* of the XI/17th and XII/18th centuries are at times decorated with plan-like renditions of the Ka'ba in Mecca. The niche may also contain or be flanked by two candlesticks. Without ever being flashy, the niche decoration (and that of the area around it) comprises the mosque's most sumptuous ornamentation.

To stress the significance of the *mihrāb*, a wider and at times higher axial nave leads to it from the central entrance to the sanctuary – as, for example, in the Great Mosque of Damascus. The T-plan mosque, developed in the temporary III/9th-century 'Abbāsid capital of Samarra, was formed by widening the nave running along the *qibla* wall, whose importance was thus emphasized.

Another feature found in the Friday mosques is the pulpit or *minbar*. This is placed to the right of the prayer niche, and from it the leader of the congregation pronounces the Friday sermon and allegiance to the caliph. It consists basically of two richly ornamented triangles of wood or stone enclosing a series of steps; these lead to a small platform often covered with a small dome-like or pyramidal canopy.

The function of the courtyard *(sahn)* is both practical and aesthetic. Usually it contains a large water basin for the strict washing procedure obligatory before prayer. It constitutes an open-air space – which must have been welcome in the crowded cities and towns – and an area of communication. In certain mosques, primarily, for example, in the al-Azhar Mosque in Cairo, this function was extended to include that of instruction, which was given in the porticoes. Some courtyards, too, were ornamented with a fine geometrically patterned pavement of coloured marbles in the *opus sectile* technique. Well-known examples include the Great Mosque in Aleppo and the Madrasa of Sultan Hasan in Cairo. The proportions of the courtyard varied. In the Maghrib and Spain they were small in relation to the sanctuary. On the other hand, the very large, now ruined, mosque of Rabat showed, besides, the regular *sahn* in front of the sanctuary, two lateral courtyards within the columns of the large hypostyle hall. In Anatolia during the VII/13th century the courtyard of Arab-type mosques became internalized, together with its fountain, under an open roof or, more usually, a dome with an open oculus. Another Turkish practice, after the example of Christian churches, was to dispense with the courtyard altogether, as in the hypostyle mosques with tall wooden columns of the VII/13th and VIII/14th centuries.

For the stranger or traveller, the feature that first marked a building as a religious structure and more specifically as a mosque was the tower known in English as a minaret (Turkish-Arabic *mināre*). From its top the muezzin summoned the faithful to the five daily prayers. In Syria, Spain and North Africa, and in early times also in Iraq and Iran, it was originally square, following the towers of Christian churches. But in Samarra and Fustāt, a spiral minaret developed from Sāsānid structures; while in Iran, Iraq, Anatolia and the Ottoman empire a tapering cylindrical type was established. Mamlūk Egypt, on the other hand, favoured a composite variety. No tower as such is in fact obligatory; in Anatolia, Egypt and Iran, the same purpose has been answered by little baldachined platforms on the roof. Nor is the position of the tower definitely fixed in relation to the mosque proper. It can be connected with the mosque as it is in Damascus, Qayrawān and Cordoba, or it can be free-standing, in close proximity to the building, as is the case at Samarra, at Fustāt and in the Seljuq mosques of Iran.

In Seljuq times (second half of the VII/13th century) two minarets flanked the entrance gate, first of a Konya mosque and then of several *madrasas* in Anatolia. This monumentalizing feature was possibly inspired by Iranian prototypes. In any event, in Iran itself, the double minaret was widely used in Mongol, Tīmūrid and Safavid times for both entrance gates and sanctuary eyvans. In Ottoman times three, four and even six minarets were used for more important mosques.

In view of its physical prominence and liturgical function, it was only natural that the minaret acquired a specific Muslim significance which made it practically a symbol. This is borne out by a quatrain attributed to 'Umar Khayyām which begins by contrasting characteristic Christian and Muslim features:

> *How long the incense and the cross*
> *The mosque lamp and minaret?*
> *How long the balance-striking yet*
> *Of Heav'n for profit, Hell for loss?*

[A. J. Arberry's translation]

In addition, the minaret had a demonstrative quality, especially in larger and caliphal mosques. When Sultan Ahmad I decided to provide six minarets for his mosque in Istanbul (1018-25/1609-16), the six minarets of the shrine in Mecca had to be increased to seven.

The characteristic shape of the mosque was a novelty in architecture, and can be significantly paralleled in other art forms. Early Qur'ānic manuscripts for instance were horizontal in format, contrasting sharply with the vertical columns of Greek papyrus scrolls, codices and consular diptychs. There was also no common Christian equivalent to a place of worship with a large interior courtyard. Finally, early mosques were (like most Near Eastern houses) kept outwardly in a low key. Their height did usually not dominate, and the architects concentrated on the interior rather than the outside walls. Only occasionally, as in Cordoba, do the gateways have a richer framework. Façades appear rather late, starting only in the v/11th and vi/12th centuries, with mosques such as those in Cairo of al-Hākim and al-Aqmar.

What seems significant is that, in spite of their pagan and Christian prototypes, these buildings also had Arab roots. The house of Allah was still reminiscent of an Arab house with all its essential public parts, even if now built on a grand scale. The *mihrāb* was a term used in pre-Islamic Arab literature and in Arab territory there even existed representations of it. The *minbar* reflected the stoop from which the tribal judge or leader had made pronouncements. To an historically minded Arab, moreover, even the dome *(qubba)* before the *mihrāb* – as exemplified for instance in the Great Mosques of Damascus, Qayrawān, Cairo and Cordoba – might, according to some authors, have had a meaning. In pre-Islamic times the *qubba* was a small domed leather tent, carried by a camel, in which certain tribes kept sacred stones. The tribal leader – 'the Lord of the *qubba*' – used this betyl both in war and in peace to obtain auguries. Hence both before and after the establishment of Islam the domed tabernacle was associated with a sacred object and with leadership.

The Iranian mosque

In Iran the Arab-type hypostyle mosque was at first widely used as shown by the still standing mosques in Dāmghān (ii/8th century) and Nāyin (iv/10th century), and the excavated one in Susa. It continued into fairly modern times – witness the xiii/19th-century version recently discovered in Marāgha, in north-west Iran. But another specifically Iranian pattern of mosque, called the kiosk mosque, was used concurrently with the Arab type. It continued the form of the *chahār tāq* fire temple, which consisted of a square building with four wide arched openings covered by a high dome. These often courtyardless buildings were of rather limited size, and accordingly served primarily small towns and villages. To offset this handicap hypostyle halls were sometimes added to the side of the dome structure. The latter part alone,

being solidly constructed from baked bricks, was likely to survive the ravages of time.

The main further development, in the Seljuq period, consisted in combining the dome and hypostyle group with a courtyard, each of whose four sides has a high eyvan in its centre; the first eyvan was the entrance, the second and third were in the centre of the side wings, while the rather shallow fourth eyvan opposite the entrance opened into the imposing dome chamber in front of the *mihrāb*, which served as a kind of *maqsūra*. The first such combination probably dates from the late v/11th century; but the earliest surviving four-eyvaned mosque constructed as a whole, is in the little town of Zavareh, and dates from 530/1135. The largest and most imposing building of the type is the Masjid-i Jum'a in Isfahan, a composite structure begun in the Būyid period and added to in the late v/11th and early vi/12th centuries, with many subsequent alterations. Other splendid, unified examples are found in Varāmīn (viii/14th century), Mashhad (ix/15th century), Isfahan (early xi/17th century) and elsewhere up to the xiii/19th century.

The model for the eyvaned structure is the Iranian house, of which simple one-, two- and four-eyvaned versions exist. Archaeologically the type is as early as the Parthian period, though in the form of larger mansions, probably as enlarged versions of the basic home. In the Seljuq period this large four-eyvaned variety was most likely used for the newly established theological school or *madrasa*, which under the state fostered instruction in the canonical Sunnī faith. This form of building was, therefore, very influential and spread widely. In the *madrasa* the large eyvans served as lecture halls, while students were housed in the one- or two-storey section in between. The combination of sanctuary eyvan and domed *mihrāb* chamber was inspired by another Iranian archetype, namely the palace, which, as Sāsānid examples show, had likewise used a shallow entrance eyvan leading to the domed throne-chamber. This royal association is still occasionally clear; in Isfahan an inscription indicates this below the south-west dome. Two facts demonstrate the prevalence of the *madrasa* scheme: all geographical handbooks and travellers of the first half of the viii/14th century in Iran speak of *madrasas* rather than mosques; and secondly, specifically established *madrasas*, like that built on the Chahār Bāgh in Isfahan by Sultan Husayn in 1118-26/1706-14, is typologically no different from the large mosques of the Seljuq and later periods.

The dramatic appearance of the Iranian mosque became accentuated by two flanking minarets on either side of the gateways, and, subsequently, the sanctuary eyvans as well. Another highly decorative feature was the *muqarnas*, inaptly translated as honeycomb vault. This was at first inserted, perhaps as a strengthening element, in the four squinches of the intermediary zone placed between the square *mihrāb* chamber and its covering cupola; it consisted of staggered rows of half niches, in which the second, higher, row was on the level of the projecting points of the first, the third row on that of the second and so on in diminishing number. Its first documented occurrence is in a mausoleum known as Arab Ata in Tim, Uzbek SSR (dated 367/977-8), and it spread not only to Iran, but throughout the Muslim world, becoming a feature of architecture both sacred and secular. The voids of other arched structures, such as the tops of the eyvans, were filled in the same way; *muqarnas* could be used to form mouldings or cover any curved surface. Impressive opportunities were provided by the high niches in the richly ornamented entrances to Syrian and Anatolian *madrasas*, by the pendentives of Egyptian mausoleums, and, most spectacularly, in the Maghrib – for instance in the VI/12th-century Mosque of the Qarawiyyīn of Fez, or in the VIII/14th-century Palace of the Alhambra in Granada, which boasts an even more exuberant variation known as the stalactite vault, a vertical element descending from the tip of each individual niche.

The novel and composite character of the Iranian mosque is unfailingly impressive. The greatly enlarged eyvans created rhythmic accents and the large dome chamber clearly marked the direction of the *qibla* wall. In this way the monotony of the porticoes and the lack of direction in the Arab hypostyle mosque were overcome. But there was a price to pay. The side eyvans were used only temporarily, for overflow crowds of worshippers when this particular side of the mosque was in the shade. The cell-like units on the two lateral and entrance sides of the courtyard served as lodgings and had therefore no ritual function in a mosque; and the *mihrāb* area was separated from the bulk of the faithful in the lateral wings by the massive supports of the huge dome. The accretion of still other units for prayer, meditation, instruction or receptions meant a further segmentation of space. However, the dramatic aspect of the whole, together with its multi-purpose qualities, appealed to the Iranians; and it became the standard mosque and *madrasa* type. And being based on the Iranian house, it was only natural that its layout was used also for caravanserais and, at least in Anatolia and Syria, for hospitals.

In India it led to a sub-type, the Mughul mosque of the XI/17th century, in which the entrance eyvan was developed into a high, impressive gateway on top of a flight of steps, while the hypostyle sanctuary became crowned by three large onion-shaped domes. As *madrasa*, the Iranian plan was faithfully copied throughout Islam.

The Turkish mosques

While the Arab hypostyle mosque and the Iranian four-eyvaned mosque soon became largely standardized, mosque architecture in Anatolia, and later in Istanbul (VI/12th to IX/15th century), showed a great many typological variations. Only in the X/16th century did a basic concept become more prevalent throughout the Ottoman empire.

After the conquest of Anatolia in 463/1071, the hypostyle mosque plan was widely used, with both heavy pillared roof supports and slender wooden columns. The eyvaned mosque was also known but little favoured. Two other varieties were typically Turkish: the single-domed mosque over a square base, and the mosque modelled on the longitudinal nave and aisles arrangement of Christian churches. Common to all these was the conspicuous use of domes, both before the *mihrāb*, and elsewhere. A single dome, at times of large proportions, might be used, or alternatively a series of domes in alignment. Two particular instances demonstrate the novel use of the dome in Anatolia. In the VII/13th century

the courtyard of some Seljuq four-eyvaned *madrasas* was covered by a large dome which centralized the building. Later in Ottoman times a mosque type was evolved in the VIII/14th century which was based on the *madrasa* scheme and which evolved in Bursa in the first half of the following century: a dome covered the cubic sanctuary area, and a second dome the outer square courtyard.

The initial stimulus to use a dome, especially in a technical sense, came undoubtedly from Byzantine architecture. But within the Turkish tradition there must have been also a psychological readiness to accept this feature. As with other ethnic mosque types, the Turkish mosque may go back ultimately to domestic architecture, in this case the *yurt*, the domed ancestral tent.

After the Ottomans' conquest of Constantinople in 857/1453, the prominence given to domes increased. One stimulus was the great Imperial church of Hagia Sophia. Immediately after the conquest it was converted into a mosque, according to custom, under the name of Aya Sofya, and endowed with *mihrāb* and minarets. Its immense size, its soaring dome with its two aligned half domes, and the beauty of its parts greatly impressed the conquerors. A contemporary official and writer, Tursūn Beg, expressed this sentiment first in this couplet:

If you seek Paradise, oh you Sūfī
The topmost heaven is Aya Sofya

and he explained it further:

What a dome, that vies in rank with the nine spheres of heaven! In this work a perfect master displayed the whole of the architectural science. With half domes one upon the other, with angles both acute and obtuse, with peerless vaults like the arched brows of heart-ravished girls, with stalactite ornaments, he made the interior so vast that it can hold 50,000 persons. [Bernard Lewis's translation]

This vastness not only accommodated large numbers of the faithful – the enormous hypostyle mosques of Samarra and Cordoba had already achieved this – but it did so in an interior without obstructing columns or pillars; for the first time all could worship in sight of the directional symbol of the *mihrāb*, which, like the *minbar*, was correspondingly enormous.

The development of the Imperial Turkish mosque from 907/1501 to 983/1575 represents only variations on a mighty theme. The object became to equal, if not surpass, Aya Sofya's diameter of 101½ feet; to integrate the lateral parts, under smaller domes and half domes, into the main sanctuary area; and if possible to create the traditional Muslim breadth instead of the longitudinal emphasis of the Byzantine model – and to present all as a balanced composition culminating in the upward thrust of the large central dome. The architect Sinān (d. 996/1588) attempted this in the great but still deficient Shehzade and Süleymaniye mosques of 955/1548 and 963/1556, and triumphantly succeeded in his Mosque of Selīm II in Edirne (977-83/1569-75). From the exterior, these Ottoman buildings of unadorned grey stone strike one with the sheer mass of their compact units. Domes, half domes and buttresses surround the mountainlike central dome, whose heavy earth-hugging forms are skilfully juxtaposed with slender pointed minarets which, like darts, seem to be pointed towards heaven. No wonder that these vast domed structures were imitated, though never equalled, throughout the empire. It is the Ottoman mosques of Konya, Damascus and Cairo which dominate the skyline of these cities and not the buildings constructed in the local tradition, splendid and extensive as they might be.

In their construction of domes the Turkish architects followed Byzantine models. Eschewing the Iranian squinch, they chose the curved triangular pendentive used in Santa Sophia and elsewhere. Characteristically, however, this feature was not slavishly copied by the Seljuqs but broken down into a series of large triangles set on their points. Or the transitional zone between the square chamber and the cupola might become a sequence of triangles which alternatively changed direction. These and the many other variations made Turkish architecture a constant source of surprise and delight.

The Iranian mosque had already served a double purpose, as both *masjid* and *madrasa*; and sometimes as a hostel for travellers. Another dual purpose was provided by the *madrasas* of medieval Syria and Anatolia, which served both for instruction and as burial place of the founder and his family. The idea of communal commitment was taken up in the mosques of VIII/14th-century Iznik and further developed in the following century in Bursa. The mosque of Murād I Khudāvendigār (767-87/1366-85) in that city was built specifically for the triple function of *masjid*, *madrasa* and hostel or hermitage (*zāwiya*). With growing social demands, however, both on towns and their communal centres, the inclusion of every function under one roof became increasingly difficult. The response to this was the now common *külliyye*, or complex of public buildings, of which examples date from the early VIII/14th to the XII/18th century. A very extensive though not yet organized grouping of different buildings was realized by Bāyazīd I in Bursa in 802/1399 though finished only after his death in 806/1403. Its walled-in area had two gates and included a mosque, a *madrasa*, a royal mausoleum, a fountain, a kitchen for the poor (*ʿimāret*), a public bath (*hammām*), an aqueduct, and a royal palace. Nearby stood a hospital (following the *madrasa* scheme), a dervish monastery and a caravanserai. The whole comprised a social pattern that was followed by all the great mosques in Bursa and Istanbul.

From the time of Mehmed II Fātih (867-75/1462-70), however, the *külliyyes* were symmetrically organized. The Conqueror's mosque occupied the centre of a large plaza, with four *madrasas* on each of its two sides, while the *külliyye* of Bāyazīd II in Edirne of 892/1486 placed a large hospital and medical school to the one side of the mosque, and a soup kitchen, a bakery and a refectory on the other.

Non-canonical aspects

There are certain Muslim attitudes and observances which run counter to the orthodox creed and yet have found universal acceptance throughout Islam. Clearly they have satisfied deeply felt religious needs, and at times go back to pre-Islamic forms of piety. In architecture, the most conspicuous example of such processes is the development of the mausoleum.

The Prophet regarded himself as an ordinary human being unable to perform miracles; and the veneration of saints was denounced in the Qurʾān (Sūra ix, 31). And just as no individual enjoyed preferential positioning in communal prayer (except the prince, to ensure his physical safety), there was in early Islam no special embellishment of funerary sites; as a poet quoted about 66/685 by al-Balādhurī stated: 'the tombs of the rich and poor are alike'. Yet on all these beliefs and practices Islam in time followed a contrary practice.

The first changes occurred through veneration of the tombs of holy persons. Oleg Grabar has shown how this led in the late III/9th and the IV/10th centuries to the building of commemorative buildings over certain burial places, especially those of Shīʿī saints. Before long memorials were also erected particularly in Iran and Central Asia, to rulers of marginal or semi-independent regions, who often followed non-Sunnī beliefs. As status symbols and demonstrations of secular power, these buildings were outspokenly ambitious, whereas those of holy men of more local significance were simpler – although they fully satisfied the devotional needs of the population. Mausoleums were also built to commemorate Biblical persons, companions of the Prophet and scholars, together with popular heroes and *ghāzīs* (fighters for the Faith) in the frontier provinces. The names of many of the saintly figures so honoured later became forgotten, so that now their mausoleums are anonymous or attributed to legendary or obscure persons. From the VI/12th century these structures proliferated as secular mausoleums. From the IV/10th and V/11th centuries, they were particularly numerous in Egypt and Central Asia; then in northern and north-eastern Iran and Anatolia; and also in India and North Africa. Mausoleums continue to be built, both for spiritual and secular leaders. Modern memorials of this kind include those to Firdawsī, Avicenna, ʿUmar Khayyām, the late Āghā Khān and the poet-philosopher Iqbāl, as well as the particularly imposing structures for Riżā Shāh Pahlavī, Atatürk and Muhammad ʿAlī Jinnāh.

There are basically two types of mausoleum: the circular, tower-like form, and the often more grandiose square or polygonal type. Both can be covered either by a circular dome or a conical or pyramidal roof. Often, complex ensembles grew up around the tombs of certain saints, such as that of the mystic poet Jalāl ad-Dīn Rūmī, in Konya, or of Bāyazīd, in Bistām (713/1313). Another feature of princely mausoleums was their proliferation in one locality. Typical examples are the Tīmūrid Shāh-i Zinda group in Samarqand of the late VIII/14th and IX/15th centuries, the Mamlūk tombs of Cairo and the VII/13th- and VIII/14th-century Marīnid mausoleums in Chella near Rabat.

The earliest surviving tombs of saintly persons, both of them Shīʿī, are the mausoleum of Fātima, the sister of the Imam ʿAlī ar-Riḍā in Qum, and that of the Caliph ʿAlī in Najaf; these probably date from the late III/9th and early IV/10th centuries. The earliest princely tombs are better preserved and therefore reveal their original character more clearly. The first is that of the ʿAbbāsid Caliph al-Muntasir, who was buried in Samarra in 248/862 together with his successors, the Caliphs al-Muʿtazz and al-Muhtadī; it was built as a domed square building surrounded by an octagonal ambulatory. The mausoleum of the Sāmānids in Bukhārā, commonly referred to as the Tomb of Ismāʿīl, was constructed before 332/943 and consists of a square structure with a large central dome and four small corner ones set over a gallery. Especially noteworthy is the use of bricks to create different patterns in its various parts.

Thousands of mausoleums survive throughout the Muslim world. The most remarkable of the early structures is the mausoleum of the well-known Ziyārid Shams al-Maʿālī Qābūs, whose court in Gurgān had included such Iranian luminaries as Avicenna, al-Bīrūnī and ath-Thaʿālibī. This austere monument of baked brick was built in 397/1006-7 and consists of a slightly tapering tower, ten engaged buttresses and a conical roof. Its only decorative features are two inscriptions in simple Kūfic naming the builder, the purpose of the structure and its date.

Undoubtedly the most grandiose of all the self-glorifying mausoleums is that of the Il-Khānid Sultan Öljeytu. Originally it was planned by him as a final resting place for the remains of the Caliph ʿAlī and of the Imam Husayn, and for this reason conceived as a spacious place of pilgrimage. Begun in 710/1310, it comprises a huge octagon topped by a gallery below a *muqarnas* cornice, from which springs a huge pointed dome, eighty feet in diameter, ringed by a crown of eight minarets, one in each angle of the octagon. Inside and out the building displays a lavish variety of richly decorated features: bricks glazed in various colours, combinations of faience strips, carved and painted stuccoes, ornamental wall paintings, epigraphic units and, for the first time in Iran, faience mosaics covering complete surfaces both inside and on the exterior. Another striking princely mausoleum is that of Tamerlane in Samarqand. Built after 806/1403, its main feature is a high melon-shaped dome whose ribbed outer shell rises over an inner ceiling seventy-three feet high to a total height of over 111 feet. The ensemble of decorated ribs makes a gentle inward turn before joining the high circular drum, where a repeat in large Kūfic letters declares to the mortal onlooker that 'Allah (alone) is permanent'.

In a quite different tradition four imperial Mughul mausoleums should be mentioned, all of them set in formal gardens. Two are crowned with a huge dome: that of Humāyūn (d. 963/1556) in Delhi, built of red sandstone and white marble; and the celebrated Tāj Mahal, built from 1042/1632 in Agra by Shāh Jahān for his favourite wife Mumtāz Mahal, in white marble with inlaid decorations of semi-precious stones *(pietra dura)*. The tomb of Mumtāz Mahal forms part of an ensemble, together with a small mosque and an assembly hall of red sandstone, the whole, in its garden setting, being entered by a large gateway. The mausoleum of Akbar (d. 1014/1605), in Sikandra, is, by contrast, three storeys in red sandstone diminishing in width, and a fourth enclosing the cenotaph of white marble. That of his son Jahāngīr (1037/1627), near Lahore, consists of a low building with four tall, massive minarets in the corners and likewise combining red sandstone with white marble.

Just as non-canonical as the cult of tombs was the ordinary Muslim's faith in astrology. Both were contrary to the doctrines of the Qurʾān, but both were equally widespread and fundamental. The general aspects of astronomy are being covered in more detail by Professor Sabra in Chapter VII, on Islamic science. In the present context we can only refer briefly to the most common forms in which astrology appeared in the arts.

Representations of the seven planets and the figures of the zodiac occur frequently. The earliest examples of the latter are found on a metal bowl of the Ghaznavid period (v/11th century); and there are countless others on objects of bronze and brass, in manuscripts and occasionally in pottery. In the Seljuq and Mughul periods figures of the zodiac appear even on coinage. A mercantile society like that of medieval Islam, trading over enormous distances, threatened by brigands, extortion, unfavourable winds, shipwreck and piracy, was naturally predisposed to enlist astrological help. The earliest representation of the planets exercising their maximum power by standing in exaltation in their respective signs of the zodiac is to be found on an important point of international transit trade, the great vi/12th-century Tigris bridge of Jazīrat ibn ʿUmar.

Astrolabes, for measuring the elevation of a star or to cast a horoscope, began to be made in the ii/8th century, if not earlier. The oldest dated instrument is from 348/959. Making astrolabes was an established and well-recognized skill, the artisans in question having a specific designation *(astūrlābī)*.

Colour: the response to environment
Though the area of Islam is immense, stretching from the Atlantic to the China Sea, certain characteristics are prevalent everywhere. A great deal of the landscape is barren, of a single dull colour and usually devoid of striking features. The main elements of nearly every region are deserts, treeless mountains and the unrelieved monotony of infinite vistas, in which fierce sun and hot winds punish man by day, while at night the harshness of existence is increased by piercing cold. Man could not escape these conditions, but by submissive acceptance or successful adaptation he could adjust himself to them.

The most elemental proof of environmental factors is the outwardly monotonous character of villages, towns and cities. They had to be built with the prevailing building material: sun-dried mud bricks for simpler houses, and baked bricks for those of more demanding functions; and grey or red sandstone for buildings of importance in the community. The wealthy and old-established city of Damascus produced this typical reaction from a 19th-century European traveller:

> The street is formed by the palaces of the principal *agas* of Damascus; they are the nobility of the country; the façades of the palaces on to the street resemble the long walls of prisons or hospitals, walls of grey mud . . .
> [Lamartine, 1865]

The same could be said of cities in Iran or North Africa, though in the latter case the walls would have been uniformly whitewashed.

The unrelieved monotony of both the surrounding landscape and the urban setting demanded at least psychological relief. This was provided in the first place, by colour in clothing, in the objects of daily use or in the decoration of the houses and other buildings.

Some idea of contemporary costumes and other

textiles can be gathered from this passage of S. D. Goitein, based on study of Egyptian Geniza documents of the v/11th and vi/12th centuries:

> While men today are normally satisfied with various shades of gray, brown, blue, black or white, the medieval man, like tropical singing birds, liked in addition to these colors green, red and intensive yellow, and above all, intricate nuances with all kinds of 'glitter', 'gloss', iridescence, stripes and waves and patterns. The carpets, couches, and draperies decorating the rooms showed the same variety in coloring and treatment as the clothing.

Goitein refers to an order for covers: 'one [of the colour of] gazelle blood, one pure violet, one musk coloured [i.e. reddish brown], one silvery, one intense yellow, two others pure clean white inclining to yellow'. He states also that even such usually inconspicuous items as shoes had to match the rest of the costume. This is borne out by the clothing of both sexes in miniatures from Arab countries from the vii/13th and viii/14th centuries. No wonder that Goitein speaks of the 'colour intoxication' of this age.

Evidence for the high degree of colour sensitivity is provided by a handbook attributed to the Tunisian Zīrid ruler al-Muʿizz ibn Bādīs (406-53/1016-61), which deals with the manufacture of books. Its recipes for the making of writing inks describe a range far surpassing our own usual supply of black, blue or red, and extending to the colour of peacocks, of the rose, pistachio and apricot; also ruby red, purple, green, yellow and white, in addition to many mysterious inks of special qualities whose colours cannot be easily surmised.

The medieval Egyptian carpets to which Goitein has drawn attention are primarily known to us from literary sources, but his conclusions are borne out by the evidence of Turkish carpets from the vii/13th century, and later types from other regions of the Muslim world, that have in fact survived. Again the customers were not satisfied with the natural colours of fur-bearing animals – white, black and browns – but demanded the richest possible range of hues, and patterns of great contrast.

The same colour-consciousness is found in pottery. From the iii/9th century, the limited colour range of the classical and Sāsānid period was succeeded by a highly varied series of decorated glazed vessels. In the ceramic medium the 'glitter' and 'gloss' noted in medieval Egyptian textiles had its counterpart in the form of lustre vessels and tiles decorated with a thin shiny metal film which was deposited on the usually white glaze in a second firing. This technique was widely used, extending to Egypt, Iraq, Iran, Syria and Spain. The various ceramic traditions of the Muslim world represent a technical and artistic climax; and it was only natural that the influence of this craft should go beyond Islam, to Byzantium and Italy.

Other craft media, too, injected a strong colouristic emphasis. By the v/11th century, the glass industry had developed intaglio and relief cutting to a very high standard. Glass had apparently first been regarded as a form of artificial rock crystal, of which the very skilful but colourless manner of decoration had accordingly been copied. In the iii/9th century the first colour appeared, in cameo-cut glasses. Finally in the vii/13th and viii/14th centuries, ornamentation with gilding and coloured enamels was fully mastered in Syria and Egypt. It was especially this aspect of decorating glass which inspired the artisans of Venice, so that they were eventually able to successfully emulate it.

Metal was less suited to embellishment with colour, though a duality of colours and textures had occasionally been introduced in the preceding Byzantine period by inlaying silver into bronze; and Sāsānid craftsmen had likewise infrequently applied niello into silver pieces. Both techniques were subsequently taken up in the Islamic period. Niello on silver was used in a limited fashion in Iran from about the ii/8th century to the xi/17th, while the craft of inlaywork in brass and bronze experienced a real flowering from the mid-vi/12th to the viii/14th century in Iran, Mosul, Syria and Egypt. By adding a black material (which is so far unidentified and may be either a paste or niello) to copper, silver or gold inlay a range of up to four colours was achieved. The most colourful of metal techniques, however – that of cloisonné enamelling – was apparently practised only on a minor scale in making jewellery during the Fātimid period in Egypt and in Spain under the Umayyads; and in the Nasrid period in Spain, for trinkets, horse trappings and weapons. Perhaps, like the composition of mosaics with tesserae, enamelling was a craft too closely associated with rival Byzantium to attract Muslim patrons.

Miniature painting, and in particular that practised in Iran in the ix/15th and x/16th centuries and to a lesser degree that of Turkey in the x/16th to the xii/18th century, provides another proof of this high degree of colour susceptibility. The intensity of many pure and of a few mixed colours in the limited space available on the pages of manuscripts can hardly be surpassed. By contrast, line drawings and delicately shaded paintings were hardly fostered in the early periods and then only under Chinese influence or as a form of 'chinoiserie'. When they finally make their more general appearance in Iran in the mid-x/16th century, as a new artistic expression, and especially so in the xi/17th century, this development led to a decline of the art.

The use of colour in architecture represents a special Islamic achievement, and one that strongly contrasts with the chromatic restraint in Western buildings. Every weary traveller in Iran will have had the experience, on approaching a mud-coloured town or sometimes even a village, of being cheered by the turquoise or blue tiles on the dome or conical roof of the tomb of a saint or of the local mosque. The architectural standards of an Iranian capital demanded more spectacular efforts. This visual excitement was provided by the most brilliant ceramic revetments for the outside or the inside of buildings ever devised by man. Each coloured glazed tile for this purpose was fired in a kiln to maximum brightness; the patterns were then hammered out and the various elements assembled into complex 'faience mosaics'. After hesitant partial experiments in Iran in the vi/12th and vii/13th centuries, the first complete covering of a building with this type of decoration was accomplished in 640/1242 by a master from Tūs in Khurāsān, who in this fashion decorated the Sircalı Madrasa in Konya, the Seljuq capital of Anatolia. In the viii/14th and ix/15th centuries the technique was refined in Iran for the decoration of great buildings both inside and out. Consummate designs in this technique, dating from the early IX/15th century, are to be found in the Tīmūrid buildings of Herat. In the Tīmūrid buildings of Transoxiana, especially the late VIII/14th- and IX/15th-century mausoleums of Samarqand, colourful faience revetments in different techniques are used at their most varied. The last flowering of faience mosaic and of other forms of tile work dates from late X/16th- and early XI/17th-century Isfahan, then serving as the capital of Shāh ʿAbbās. The Masjid-i Shāh and the Masjid-i Shaykh Lutf Allāh are the finest of these buildings; and the so-called Madrasa-yi Mādar-i Shāh of Isfahan of 1118-26/1706-14, and even later structures, show that these techniques of clothing a whole building in colour extended over a long period.

Imperial Turkey, in its heyday in the X/16th and XI/17th centuries, witnessed a second flowering of tile production. In Jerusalem, the upper part of the exterior of the Dome of the Rock's main octagonal structure was sheathed with a polychrome revetment, while on the Rüstem Pasha Mosque in Istanbul colourfully patterned tiles were used in smaller amounts externally and more lavishly on the inside.

Although the exuberance of this exterior architectural style was never matched outside Iran, Turkey and Central Asia, a predilection for colour in architecture did show itself elsewhere. Mamlūk Egypt tried out the use of glazed tiles – but rejected it for other chromatic effects. In Mughul mosques, palaces and mausoleums it led to the combination of white marble and red sandstone, and the inlay of differently coloured semi-precious stones into the white marble walls.

In other countries it was the interior to which richly coloured decorations were applied. From the III/9th century on, Iraq and Iran used carved and painted stucco panels as a form of wainscot. In Spain and North Africa polychrome-patterned glazed tiles were used for the same purpose, while the practice developed there of using complex carved and painted *muqarnas* configurations as a decoration for ceilings. From the VI/12th to the VII/13th century craftsmen in Iran also employed colourful tile combinations, usually in the form of lustre-decorated eight-pointed stars and dark blue or turquoise crosses. On floors and fountains of palaces, baths, private houses and *madrasas* in Mamlūk Egypt, as well as on the *qibla* walls of mosques and mausoleums, variously coloured marbles were used to form geometric designs in the *opus sectile* technique. Floors and fountains continued to be made in this fashion in patrician houses in Syria till the XIII/19th century. By contrast, the floors of the noble houses of Morocco were composed of polychrome-glazed tiles. Colour was also introduced into interiors by the use in windows of stained-glass units in plaster mountings, a technique used from the early Middle Ages till the XIII/19th century.

The decorative urge

The artistic endeavours of many ethnic or religious groups show a strong tendency to decorate surfaces. In traditional societies the themes are usually symbolic or representational; and in the West, until the arrival of the Renaissance, they were less frequently of a merely ornamental nature. In Islamic art (that is, primarily in the minor arts) the decorative urge is much more pronounced than elsewhere, and purely ornamental motifs predominate.

There are various reasons for this striking aspect of Islamic art. The major cause was most probably another psychological reaction to the vast, featureless and barren landscape around towns and villages. A plain surface on an object of daily life subconsciously evoked the bare, surrounding world, its unpleasantness and its dangers due to lack of water, food and comforts and the presence of ever-lurking robbers and jinns. By being ornamented the object lost this bothersome association and the mirror image of a fearful and primitive world became so to say tamed and cultivated and was also made enjoyable.

Three factors reinforced this attitude. First, a vocabulary of abstract decoration had been created which was accepted by everybody everywhere and which could be easily applied. As most artistic endeavour was gauged to this general artistic language, there was comparatively little specific representational art (other than wall paintings and illustrations of texts) and rarely any influence from local folklore. Secondly, the cost of artisan labour was extremely low; most of the price to be paid was for the raw material. In the bazaar a more highly decorated piece of approximately the same value as a simpler one was therefore more attractive and more readily saleable. Thirdly, a richly ornamented object offered more opportunities for social pretension (see also Chapter III).

The consequent high standard of decoration was naturally, therefore, influential in a religious context. In the mosques, the *mihrāb* and surrounding area were generally richly ornamented – although, with the exception of the calligraphically rendered inscriptions and the renditions of lamps, it was not of a specifically religious nature.

It is a puzzling aspect of Islamic art that while the vessels, implements and interior wall surfaces – in other words, the inside world – were highly decorated, most of the exteriors of buildings were often not. The plainness of the outside walls of the Great Mosques in Qayrawān and Cordoba, of the Madrasa of Sultan Hasan in Cairo and the large Imperial mosques of Istanbul, all corroborate this point. It may very well be that the restrained, frugal streak in Islam as well as the sheer mass and height of these monuments and the religious associations of their domes, minarets and gateways created a sense of awe adequate in itself. Where decorative features – notably inscriptions – were deemed necessary they were applied accordingly to the significant components (domes, minarets and gates) rather than over the main structure.

Dust, heat and gardens

The hostile environment and the harsh climate engendered still another artistic expression: the garden. It was envisaged, through religious inspiration, as the earthly reflection of paradise. The fact that the high points of garden development appear as early as the V/11th century, to continue till the XIII/19th, and are found in similar forms in Spain, Iran, Central Asia and India, speaks not only for an identical reaction to the environment, but underlines the universality of Islamic art. As a response to an arid, endlessly extended landscape of featureless monotony, the garden was formally planned, with geometrically laid out paths, and water courses that nurtured a rich vegetation, especially of trees but also of flowers, in precisely laid out beds. The earliest medieval gardens are those excavated and reconstituted in Spain. A number of xı/17th- and xıı/18th-century gardens still exist in Morocco as well as in India in the capitals of the Mughul empire and the residences of rajahs. The few that have been preserved in Iran date from the xı/17th to the xııı/19th century.

All these expansive gardens with their lavish use of valuable water were set in inclined areas outside the cities. They represented the wealth and privilege of the rulers and leading members of society. Yet the less prosperous, too, established some minimal connection with nature. In the courtyards of their houses small trees, bushes, vines and flower pots were grouped around a central water basin or fountain. Small as these cellular mini-gardens were, they nevertheless form the breathing core of the residences and one of their delights. Like the gardens of the nobility, they are a pan-Islamic feature.

The cult of the garden also had an influence on the decorative arts. Even earlier and more elaborate than the oldest surviving Persian gardens are the copies of their design on x/16th-century carpets. Such formal recreations of landscape architecture continued, moreover, for two centuries, even in the provincial regions of northwest Iran. For the middle class this tradition offered a happy surrogate of the real thing, the representation of an indoor garden to be enjoyed in all seasons, day and night.

When the arts of Turkey became more realistic in the middle of the x/16th century and those of Iran and India in the xı/17th, they incorporated a richly varied series of recognizable flowers in their pottery, tiles, textiles, carpets and in the marginal decorations of manuscripts and albums, thus extending yet further the spirit of the garden.

Besides their more spectacular features, both domestic and sacred architecture made other, mundane endeavours to overcome the severities of setting and climate. Water was introduced as much as possible, even, in Anatolia, as early as the vıı/13th century, as fountains within the mosques. Private houses, *madrasas* and monasteries in Egypt and Syria had special ventilation arrangements, such as the movable roofs depicted in vıı/13th-century miniatures from Iraq; and in near-tropical regions, high funnel-like wind-towers were installed. Interiors were high-ceilinged, with floorings of stone, if not marble. In Egypt or Palestine people used cool woven mats for seats, while in cooler areas and in winter wool carpets were used.

Drinking, washing and bathing were, of course, important factors in the daily battle against heat and dust. In every house water was kept in jugs unglazed to keep their contents cool by evaporation. These sometimes sizable pieces of pottery, and especially those from vı/12th- and vıı/13th-century Iraq, often had characteristic rich decorations – epigraphic, ornamental and figural – of which the most elaborate were created by stamps or soft clay applications in the *barbotine* technique – much in the manner of icing on a cake. Most of these jars were made for the middle classes, and provide important clues to the taste and iconographic requirements of this stratum of society. Drinking vessels were of a more varied and at times fanciful shape, especially those made for the court and for the drinking of wine. The finest, from vı/12th-

and vıı/13th-century Iran, were of overglaze painted pottery; while those from the same period in Syria took the form of enamelled glass beakers and had a wide distribution both in the Muslim world and beyond. Probably the most precious drinking vessels, however, were those made of jade in ıx/15th-century Iran and xı/17th-century India.

Washing was done with the help of ewers, basins and buckets; the finest of these displayed chased decoration and inlay work. The ubiquitous *hammām* (public bath-house) derived in its heating technique and fourfold organization (disrobing chamber, cold, tepid and hot rooms) from the Roman bath, though its decoration was strictly Islamic. With their glass inserts in the domes serving as miniature skylights, these *hammāms* were characteristic of the Islamic city-scape.

The Islamic interior: textiles

There was almost no wooden furniture in the Muslim world: no wardrobes, bedsteads, tables or chairs existed; we only know of small chests, from the remains of Egyptian examples of the ıı/8th to ııı/9th century with rich inlays of various woods and bone, and representations in vıı/13th-century Iraqi miniatures. People sat on stools or low settees or sofas covered with textiles, and ate and slept on the floor, making themselves comfortable with carpets, bolsters and mattresses. Books and other objects were stored in niches, of which many forms are known, from the ııı/9th-century stuccoed examples in the excavated houses of Samarra to the recesses in the xıı/18th-century wood-panelled interiors of Damascus. Clothing and bedding were stored in cupboards and chests or just piled up in a corner of the room. The finer work of the carpenter comprised doors, shutters, ceiling beams and panelling.

For these reasons, the textile industry was crucial to the Muslim world, very much as the steel industry is today; it provided not only clothing, but also curtains, bedding, couches, pillows, carpets, tents and, as we learn from miniatures, canopies and garden enclosures as well. No wonder, then, that the Geniza documents and other sources indicate that 'a very great proportion, perhaps the majority of the working population and certainly of the distributing classes were engaged in this branch of the economy'. The textile industry was pre-eminent not only in large urban centres, but also in many smaller ones and even in tribal areas as well, which produced particularly the tapestry-woven *kelims*.

Aesthetic attitudes were consequently much affected. Textiles were unbreakable, and easily transported. Their extensive trading brought about a steady cross-fertilization of patterns throughout the Islamic world, a process which can be closely observed wherever carpet production still continues. Secondly, familiarity with textiles prompted ready acceptance of flat, infinite patterns in other media as well. For instance, much decoration of architecture was regarded as 'clothing', applied to the body of the structure. This explains the 'textile' quality of much architectural design, whether as straightforward copying of carpet patterns or as textured decoration on one or two levels – as seen in Iranian brickwork of the v/11th century – somewhat like the raised designs created in knitting or matting. A tendency to a mere surface treatment existed already in Byzantine architecture, consequently appearing in the earliest Muslim building still standing, the Dome of the Rock in Jerusalem of 72/691. As Muslim arts developed, this textile character came to be both widespread and more marked, becoming particularly evident in later periods. In the same way, metalwork was hardly ever rendered in a three-dimensional style, but covered with a design which is only skin deep. Inlaid Iranian pieces of the VI/12th and VII/13th centuries often feature a series of figural roundels, in the textile tradition of the Sāsānid to the Seljuq periods. Spanish and Turkish tile revetments are also reminiscent of textiles, while the frontispieces of IX/15th- to XI/17th-century Persian manuscripts resemble contemporary carpets. Designs in the non-textile media, however, are on the whole conceptually more complex and more sumptuous in execution. This indicates that the textile character is rarely based on specific models, but rather reflects a similar aesthetic approach.

Influences between cultures

Many features which are regarded as typically Islamic go back to a time before Muhammad. Just as the Qur'ān and Muslim theology abound in references to earlier religions, so in the arts, the burgeoning Islamic civilization, lacking its own tradition, was ready to borrow from its predecessors. Mosque plans, as we have seen, were based on pre-Islamic concepts, while the *hammām* followed a Roman prototype. In the decorative arts, the vine and grape design, the bevelled style and the circular units on textiles all have had a pre-Islamic history. The same applies to certain techniques, such as silver inlay in bronze and of niello in silver. Even such a typically Islamic craft as carpet weaving, which is based on the continuous knotting of coloured wool threads into two neighbouring warp strings, followed Iranian precedents antedating the arrival of Islam by about a thousand years. Simple as this technique is, it still continues in use.

In painting, the modes of the first seven Muslim centuries, especially in Arab countries, derive from, or at least were inspired by, orientalized late classical or Byzantine prototypes. Here, however, a change often occurred in the iconographic interpretation. Thus Biblical scenes were adapted and re-used with a new meaning, so as to serve, for instance, as illustrations for Syrian VII/13th-century *Maqāmāt* manuscripts. On the other hand, constellation pictures remained basically unchanged in manuscripts from the early V/11th to the XII/18th century; but, as the old mythological significance ceased to be understood, they received new names. Heracles became 'the Dancer', Cassiopeia 'the woman with a seat', Andromeda 'the woman who never had a husband', and so on.

Despite the direct aesthetic influences exercised on other civilizations by Islam, few of its techniques in the arts were invented in the Near East in Islamic times. Two of them were over-glaze painting in pottery and faience mosaic. Others, such as lustre painting on pottery, came to be imitated in Europe. The same applies to certain designs, in particular to the graceful arabesque displayed to cover surfaces. Although this most typical Islamic design had become highly developed and used thousands of times from the IV/10th century on, it went nevertheless back to seminal prototypes in Byzantine art. Eventually this motif had become so perfect that it was, in turn, able to create a widely spread fashion in X/16th-century Europe.

These given examples should suffice to demonstrate that a cultural interdependence existed, and that it brought Islamic civilization close to the mainstream of Western history. It is this kinship that has made its art appreciated in the West, from the earliest gifts to medieval cathedrals, up to the present museum departments of Islamic art.

One question remains: was there in Islam a phenomenon similar to the Renaissance in Europe, which revitalized the arts at a critical point in its history? The answer for the greater part of the Islamic world has to be negative.

The exception was Iran, where from the IV/10th century a strong national self-awareness prompted a return to artistic ideals from the pre-Islamic past. In particular it found expression in Firdawsī's epic, the *Shahinshāh-nāma* which dealt with the pre-Islamic Iranian history in the purest Persian language. Very shortly after this political and literary resurgence, Parthian and Sāsānid architectural prototypes were used for the mosques, and old Iranian motifs, especially scenes of kingship, reappeared. This cultural reorientation initiated a period – from the V/11th to the VII/13th century – of great imaginative versatility and expert workmanship: a high-water mark in the arts of the Islamic world.

From the VII/13th to the XI/17th century Egypt, Spain, Iran, Turkey and India witnessed periods of high artistic achievement; yet after 1650 artistic standards in these countries were slowly declining; and in the XII/18th and XIII/19th centuries the rate of deterioration increased. With the possible exception of painting in the Qājār period of Iran, the strong European influence on much Islamic art in the late XII/18th and XIII/19th centuries proved unfortunate. More recently, however, the blending of traditional forms with new concepts and techniques seems to demonstrate – especially in architecture – that age-old creative forces are active and may still be able to produce remarkable monuments and other works of art.

The creation of pattern lies at the heart of Islamic art. Religious orthodoxy spurned images, and this operated against the growth of a rich figural tradition; but even without it the natural instinct of the Islamic artist seems to have been towards abstraction rather than representation. Even elements which have naturalistic origins, such as leaves, are so stylized as to be barely recognizable. At its most typical, the geometry of the pattern is such that it can go on multiplying itself for ever; the border introduces an arbitrary break in a potentially infinite extension. This frontispiece from a volume of the Qur'ān was painted about 803/1400 in Egypt. Its dense covering of the surface, its division into separate panels and its combination of rectilinear and curvilinear forms are characteristics which recur again and again in almost all Islamic art. (1)

Arabic script is among the earliest and most widespread of Islamic decorative motifs. Originally revered because it was the medium in which the Prophet's teachings were recorded, it quickly became esteemed in its own right, a highly sophisticated discipline, often in fact so ornate that it is practically impossible to read. The examples on this double page are chosen from widely different regions and periods. For Muslims, inscriptions occupy the place of a sacred, figural iconography in Western art – the word instead of the image.

Round the Dome of the Rock (left) in Jerusalem, inside and outside the arcade, runs a band of lettering which is the first monumental example of Islamic writing. It is 240 metres long, of gold mosaic cubes on a blue ground, and celebrates the building of the mosque in 72/691 with appropriate Qur'ānic verses. (2)

On a minaret (right): turquoise glazed bricks on the minaret of Jam, Central Asia, VI/12th century. The whole tower is covered with verses from the Qur'ān. Kūfic lettering has by now assumed a different form from four or five centuries earlier; turquoise was the first and most popular colour used for glazing in Islam. (5)

On a mosque lamp (far left) from Syria, of the VIII/14th century. The lotus pattern round the middle section shows the influence of Chinese textiles, which began to be imported in the preceding century. (3)

On a mihrāb niche it was normal to place a Qur'ānic inscription round three sides of the frame (see, for instance, that at Cordoba, shown on p. 239). This moulded tile (left) comes from Kāshān and dates from the VII/13th century. It shows the *mihrāb* with a lamp hanging in the centre, the original arrangement, symbolic of the divine light. (4)

On a monastery (right): the façade of the monastery of Natanz in Persia shows two types of writing side by side: a cursive script at the top and rectangular Kūfic below. Natanz was built in 725/1324–5. (6)

75

The simultaneous appearance of the same pattern in region after region and one material after another is a striking proof of the unity of Islamic culture, but often makes it difficult to allocate a work of art to a specific time and place. The same interlinking line forming a star, for instance, occurs throughout Islam in different guises.

On brass (top left): a VIII/14th-century basin made in Iran. The ornament is a combination of figures, sitting, standing and on horseback, with the star pattern which seems to culminate in the scallops of the edge. (7)

On leather (above): a gold-tooled binding from Morocco; 655/1256. The flap on the left folds over the manuscript and tucks under the upper cover. (8)

In stone (below left): detail from the Seljuq caravanserai of Sultan Han, east of Konya, Anatolia (see p. 286), first half of the VII/13th century. (9)

On tiles (below): four *mudéjar* tiles, in imitation of ceramic mosaic, from Spain; VII/13th century. (10)

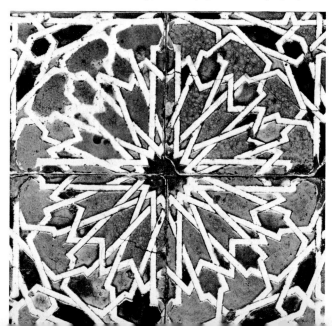

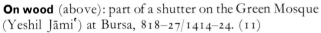

On wood (above): part of a shutter on the Green Mosque (Yeshil Jāmiʿ) at Bursa, 818–27/1414–24. (11)

In wood and bronze (top right): door-knocker on the Puerta del Perdón, Seville Cathedral, VI/12th century. Here the curving forms of the knocker contrast with, but do not threaten, the rigid pattern of the door. Both contain ingeniously rendered texts. (12)

In bronze (below right): part of the door of the Sultan Hasan Madrasa, Cairo, 757/1356. (14)

On paper (below): page from a Qurʾān in Maghribī script; VI/12th–VII/13th century. More classical than the other examples, this pattern is self-contained. (13)

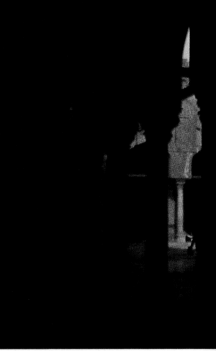

The 'gathering place' of the Muslim community is the *jāmi'*, the mosque. Islam has nothing corresponding to the liturgy of the Christian religion, and the design of mosques has therefore been free from the requirements of ritual that have governed the layout of churches.

The traditional elements are the *mihrāb*, the niche indicating the direction of Mecca; and next to it the *minbar*, the pulpit; illustrated here in the Sultan Hasan Mosque

in Cairo (right). The mosque interior was basically an ordinary
room enlarged; the early ones,
such as that of Qayrawān, Tunisia
(above left), are hypostyle halls
using capitals from classical buildings, a tradition that was still alive
in Seljuq times, e.g. at the Alaeddin
Mosque at Konya (below left).
Integrated into every major mosque is a spacious courtyard where
the faithful can congregate, and
where the ablutions fountain is
placed. Above: the courtyard of
the al-Azhar Mosque, Cairo.
(15–18)

The Iranian mosque is characterized by a spectacular development of the courtyard. Each side is given a high eyvan in its centre – a deep hallway which was eventually decorated with elaborate honeycomb vaults (*muqarnas*). One eyvan is the entrance to the courtyard, one leads into the prayer-hall itself, the other two into the side halls. The courtyard of the Masjid-i Jum'a (the 'Friday mosque') of Isfahan (left) is perhaps the most magnificent of all. (19)

The Turkish mosque evolved from the earlier Anatolian domed prayer-hall. After the Ottoman capture of Constantinople, its development was further encouraged by the church of Aya Sofya, and in the x/16th century the architect Sinān perfected a type of symmetrical mosque covered by a single great dome on pendentives, flanked by four semi-domes (not two, as in Aya Sofya), with the aim of creating an unobstructed central interior. Illustrated here (above) is his Iskele Jāmi' at Üsküdar. (21)

The Arab mosque goes back to Muhammad's own house in Medina. All mosques are orientated towards Mecca, and worshippers normally line up facing the wall (the *qibla* wall) in this direction. Early mosques were therefore wide but usually not very deep. That of Cordoba (left) has been successively enlarged, the *qibla* wall and its *mihrāb* being pushed back each time, resulting in a forest of columns. (20)

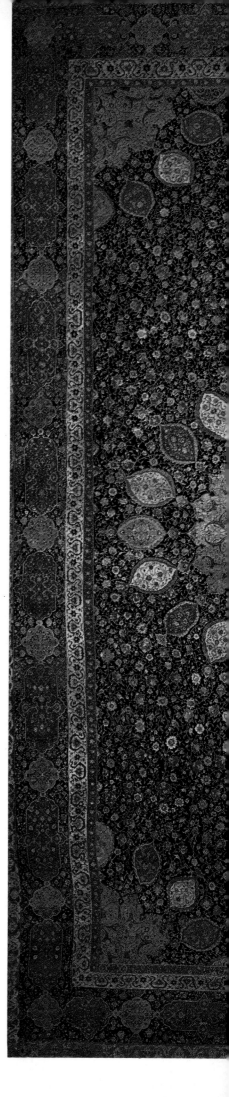

Fields of flowers – patterns based ultimately on the idea of the garden and then taken up in book illustration and textiles – cover walls and vaults in a profusion of brilliance and colour. The splendid Ardabīl carpet (right), over thirty-six feet long, was made in Tabrīz in 946/1539. Its floral design belongs to a type copied in many other materials, some at first sight quite inappropriate to it. Above: tile decoration from the portal of the Masjid-i Shāh (1010–28/1601–18), Isfahan. The panel on the left reproduces various features of carpet design, including the border. (22, 23)

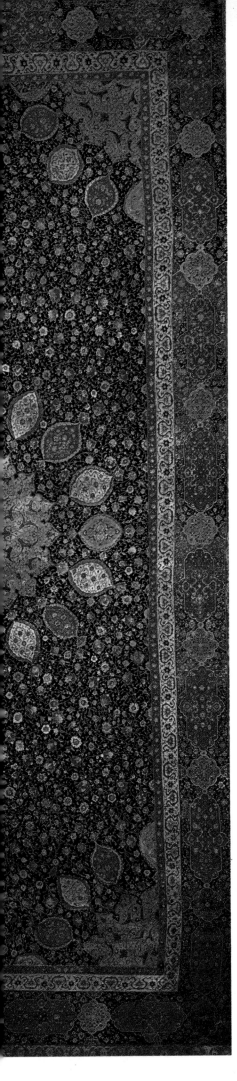

Textiles exploited the floral style. A Persian-type miniature, copied in Istanbul in 964/1557, shows a Safavid monarch in his tent. Both the tent itself and the costumes of his attendants show the same overall flower pattern. The prayer-hall of the Masjid-i Shāh at Isfahan (below) seems almost to reproduce such a tent, in the more durable material of glazed tiles. (24, 25)

In the art of metalwork the Islamic decorative genius finds full expression, and metal objects are often amongst the best preserved of all periods.

The mosque lamp (left) of bronze was probably made as early as the IV/10th or V/11th century. Against a perforated background is silhouetted Kūfic lettering. (26)

A writing box (below left) from Mosul, early VII/13th century, is of bronze, with copper and silver inlay. The compartments are for pens, ink and a damp pad. Inside the lid a Qur'ānic inscription is superimposed on an all-over field of tendrils; at the sides are roundels with signs of the zodiac. (27)

Writing and painting lent their techniques to the alien medium of metalwork. Opposite below left: brass ewer from Iran, VI/12th century, the sides ornamented with knot patterns. But around the top runs a row of birds. Opposite right: the so-called 'Bobrinski bucket', made in 559/1163 in Herat, Khurāsān. Here, along with court scenes, 'knotted' Kūfic and abstract patterns, one finds 'animated script'. In the top row men seem to grow out of the upright strokes of the letters; in the bottom animals prowl between them. (30, 31)

The animals of Islamic art have a fierce appearance in spite of being severely stylized. Right: a large bronze griffin, now at Pisa. This has been attributed to a variety of places, from Spain to Persia, and a variety of dates – a proof of the ease with which a style could be assimilated in all parts of the Islamic world. Below: bronze incense-burner in the shape of a lion, from VI/12th-century Iran. (28, 29)

In the midst of dust and heat the garden became for Islam one of the most expressive of art forms. It was lush where the rest of the environment was arid; colourful where that was drab and monotonous; formal where that was formless. Few real gardens have survived; but their character can still be felt in miniatures and in the carpet designs which they inspired. Right: a Mughul painting showing Bābur supervising a garden. Its cruciform water channel is typical. Below: the only garden of classical Islam to have survived practically intact, the Court of the Myrtles in the Alhambra at Granada, probably made in the VIII/14th century. (32, 33)

A garden paradise is re-created in the finest of Persian Safavid carpets. In this example, which is over seventeen feet long and fourteen feet wide, the garden is crossed by an H-shaped channel, swarming with fish, with a pool in the centre where ducks swim. From the banks grow a variety of trees, shrubs and flowers (always at right angles to the water) and through the undergrowth run animals and birds of many kinds. The carpet was woven in the XI/17th century. (34)

In Anatolia the domed burial chambers are covered with pyramidal roofs – probably reflecting the neighbouring Anatolian architecture which surrounds Lake Van. This mausoleum (left) is at Ahlāt, on the western shore, one of many built during the VIII/14th century. Its square base is reduced to an octagon by chamfering and the final shape is dodecagonal. The actual tomb is under the main chamber, which contains only a cenotaph. (35)

Groups of tombs formed cemeteries, which are still a conspicuous part of Islamic towns. Above: three tombs in the Southern cemetery outside Cairo – dating respectively from 736/1335, 910/1504 and 834/1430. (37)

Rich tombs for the dead had no warrant in the Qur'ān, but became almost universal throughout Islam. The earliest were raised over the bodies of saints, but before long they were being erected by ruling families. The mausoleum of the Sāmānids, Bukhārā (left), belongs to a widespread type, a square structure surmounted by a dome; but it is unusual in the elaboration of its brick patterning. (36)

Chapter Three

CITIES AND CITIZENS

Oleg Grabar

IN THE MUSEUM OF ISLAMIC AND ARAB ART in Cairo there is an inscription dated 402/1011–12 which begins with an invocation to God and a quotation from the Qur'ān and then continues as follows:

> this blessed mosque was built by al-Husayn ibn 'Abdallah ibn Muhammad ibn Silsila, the cloth merchant, in his desire to seek the satisfaction of God and of the other world. May God have mercy upon whomever recites a [pious] formula for him, during his lifetime or after his death. The palm tree which is in this mosque is food for Muslims; it can neither be bought nor sold.

No one knows whence this inscription came, where the mosque it mentions stood, and who the cloth merchant may have been. Yet with its simple piety embodied in a single palm tree probably in the courtyard of a small mosque, this document introduces us into another world from that of princes or of soldiers conquering and governing lands, building palaces, distributing gold coins and robes of honour to deserving or sycophantic subordinates. Nor is it a world of austere thinkers who weigh reason and revelation or of mystics contemplating some other, more profound reality. Even if all these worlds were by physical and spiritual necessity interlocked, the inscription makes it possible to isolate a practical, earthbound but God-fearing level of classical Muslim society. Whether it was in a small Egyptian town or in a quarter of Cairo, the mosque was hardly likely to be meaningful beyond the furthest place from which its minaret could be seen. At the same time our merchant was no doubt a 'man of property', different from the poor for whose nourishment the palm tree was kept, different from those who made the cloth.

The Cairo inscription is not the only glimpse we have of men like al-Husayn ibn 'Abdallah. The Hanbalī scholar Ibn al-Bannā', who lived in Baghdad, has left a fragment of his diary covering a little over a year, from August 461/1068 to September 462/1069. It contains an extraordinary picture of the daily activities of a 'citizen' of the imperial capital, recording births, interpreting dreams, praying over the dead, observing what happened around him and listening to others. He relates that there was a riot on 31 January 462/1069, after an incident between Turkish soldiers and people praying in a mosque. In order to settle matters a delegation was sent to the *Dīwān* or government centre. It comprised legal scholars *(fuqahā')*, noblemen *(sharaf)*, merchants *(tujjār)* and notables *(amāthil)*. Several meetings ensued, some devoted to complete recitations of the Qur'ān, others to fund-raising, while garments and provisions were distributed to pacify the mass of the population. In this, as in so many other passages from the diary, it is not a single individual but a whole class of notables which appears, active politically and in matters of faith, a class which neither held formal power nor participated in urban riots.

Finally, recently published sale contracts and endowments *(waqf)* from the IV/10th and V/11th centuries in Damascus introduce another cloth merchant, al-Husayn ibn 'Ubayd, who bought from a Jew and from the two daughters of a presumably wealthy man huge country estates with considerable agricultural income.

It would be fairly easy to multiply such examples of the lives and activities of a class of men and women who did not rule the Muslim world although they controlled much of its wealth and activities, and who tended to be consumers rather than creators of ideas and of culture. They have been called notables, and more recently patricians, but it is perhaps most appropriate to refer to them as a bourgeoisie, for the very vagueness of the term and the multiplicity of its connotations reflect the many facets of this class of people.

Three features stand out at first glance as typical of the Muslim bourgeoisie. One is the overwhelming presence of merchants, especially cloth merchants, among them. The geographical position of the Middle East, and the socio-ideological origins of early Islamic leaders from the mercantile community of Mecca and Medina are obvious explanations of the privileged position of the merchant in Muslim society. The second feature is the consistent relationship between the bourgeoisie and sectarian or heterodox movements within Islam and/or merely changes in the nature and direction of orthodox piety. As a general rule, the growth of such diverse religious and pietistic movements as Shī'ism, Hanbalism and Sūfism,

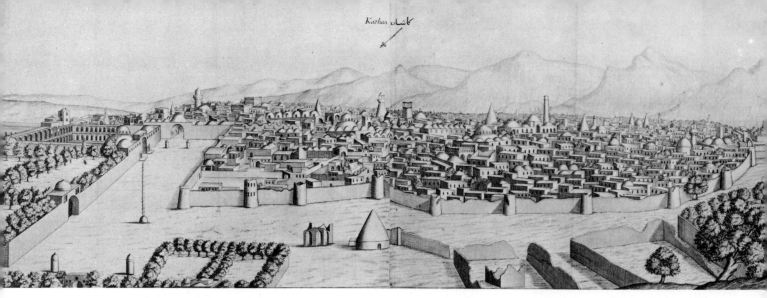

Kāshān كاشان

View of Kāshān, in Iran, in the early XII/18th century. The engraving is from a book of travels published in Amsterdam in 1123/1711. Though not to be relied upon in detail, it gives a good impression of *the walled town, closely packed with houses and dominated by the domes and minarets of mosques. On the left is a large caravanserai. Kāshān was one of the centres for Persian ceramics. (2)*

would not have been possible without the active encouragement and participation of the bourgeoisie.

The third feature involves the relationship of a given social layer to the world around it and to physical possessions or power. On the one hand, as S. D. Goitein puts it, 'early Islam as a whole took a positive, or at least lenient, view of economic activities, luxury and the amassing of capital'. On the other hand, many mystics and even a rather typical *honnête homme* like Ibn Miskawayh in the IV/10th century, argued against the acquisitions of undue wealth and especially against expensive private possessions. It is true that their reasons were different. The mystic saw wealth as evil, whereas Ibn Miskawayh merely considered it as a demeaning and weakening passion, but the practical result can be construed as an ambivalent attitude toward possessions. Equally important, although much more frequently discussed in recent years, is the institutional side of mercantile Islam, its guilds and organizations, and its well-known failure, unwillingness or inability to create urban institutions comparable to Western ones. All these questions can best be explained within the context of an essential but elusive aspect of the Islamic bourgeoisie: its intimate physical relationship to the city, to the urban order.

Beyond the very broad community of the Faithful – the *dār al-Islām* ruled by the caliph as successor of the Prophet – there was no coherent and consistent dynastic or regional allegiance for most Muslims except their city. As a result, medieval history is based either on oecumenical histories or on histories of cities. Although called histories *(ta'rīkh)* in Arabic, the latter are not accounts of the chronological development of a city. Although a topographical description at the time of the author is frequently included, they mainly consist of lengthy lists and biographies of the learned and important citizens. These lives, of which there are literally thousands, have never yet been processed in a systematic manner, but they do form the main written record of the bourgeoisie. Their implication is that a city was less a physical setting than the sum of the lives and activities of the most successful members of its major families.

From the VI/12th century onwards we do have sources dealing with cities as such rather than with men in cities or with special restricted characteristics of cities.

The *Khitat Misr* of al-Maqrīzī, for instance, composed by the middle of the IX/15th century, is a uniquely detailed description of one of Islam's greatest metropolises. Unfortunately nothing like it exists for any other city and the *Khitat* are poorly edited and for the most part not translated.

Another reason for considering the bourgeoisie within the city is the simple fact of the immense concern of Islam, especially during the first centuries of its existence, to build urban centres and maintain and develop older ones. Few activities required a more continuous investment of money and effort than cities. Texts alone make it quite difficult to move away from broad generalization into the details of a given settlement or of urban life. Occasionally incidents related in chronicles or in literature do illuminate certain aspects of an individual city. But otherwise it is less from literary sources than from archaeology that we should be able to reconstruct medieval Islamic towns. Excavations of actual or presumed towns have been carried out in Fustāt, in Sīrāf in southern Iran and at Qasr al-Hayr East in Syria, but the last two examples – and especially Qasr al-Hayr – are perhaps a little too remote from the main centres of Islamic power to be as useful as archaeological information should be.

There are two additional aspects to archaeological and visual sources to define the bourgeoisie. One is the objects, in whatever technique, which can be assumed to have surrounded the bourgeoisie. Their investigation requires a large number of very different methods of analysis, from statistics to art history. The other aspect lies in images. Until the Ottoman period few maps, plans or images of cities were made, but a fascinating document about the bourgeoisie exists in the VII/13th century illustrations of the *Maqāmāt* of al-Harīrī – as yet not published in their entirety – which depict most of its activities.

My main concern will be to integrate the physical character of the city with the lives, activities and institutions of its urban élite. Throughout, the emphasis will be on the period between 800 and 1300, acknowledged to have been the heyday of an Islamic mercantile bourgeoisie, although on a number of occasions information from later times will be used as well.

Time, place and status

Three variables must always be kept in mind as one assesses and describes the Muslim city. They are the size and importance of the city, the precise time under consideration and the geographical area involved. All three variables require brief comments.

The IV/10th-century geographer al-Maqdisī tried to develop a hierarchy from metropolis *(misr)* to capital *(qasaba)*, city *(madīna)*, and plain town *(balad)*. Other, more legalistically inclined geographers rate urban centres as possessors or not of a *minbar*, a chair in the mosque from which the *khutba* of allegiance to the prince was pronounced. Neither distinction is entirely valid. Too much inconsistency can easily be detected in the actual use of the terms given by al-Maqdisī, while an inflation of *minbars* made this particular criterion for a hierarchy quite useless. In the absence of a coherent, internally developed ranking or typology of cities (like the bishoprics of the West, for instance or the Roman military settlements), a hierarchy can be determined from the point of view of the involvement in any one city of what I will call the 'state', i.e. a combination of social, political or other forces which, actually or in theory, tended to unify the parts of the Muslim world.

This involvement took many forms. One is that, from the beginning of Islam, a certain number of towns became administrative capitals and, regardless of size, the character of these *préfectures* was affected by governmental presence. Another form may be called a catalytic involvement. For instance, the town of Isfahan was formed out of a number of villages and small urban centres. At a few key moments these separate entities were unified through externally appointed authorities, for instance, an 'Abbāsid governor in the late II/8th century and the Būyid dynasty in the IV/10th. The city was born out of the product of local developments and external actions. Other cities were entirely official creations and belong to a broad group which has recently been called 'fiat' towns. These could be purely imperial creations like Samarra in which a bourgeoisie hardly played any role at all, or dynastic cities like Baghdad in Iraq, Tinmal in Morocco, Sultāniyya in Iran or Cairo in Egypt which could develop into large urban centres; or frontier cities like Tarsus or Massīsa in Cilicia, Rabat in Morocco, or else organized settlements of newly arrived Muslims like Kūfa and Basra in Iraq, Qayrawān in Tunisia, Gurgān in Iran. While the ultimate character and the development of these 'fiat' cities has varied enormously, they all owe their beginnings to the state.

The variable of time can best be defined through three very general periods. One covers the early years of Islam to about 900: this was a time of reasonably centralized authority: new urban settlements or major changes in older ones were for the most part sponsored and probably paid for by the caliphs themselves or by their immediately appointed governors. From 900 to 1300 the growth of local dynasties, usually supported by soldiers from an ethnic stock different from the local population, transformed almost every town into a centre of power. This development led to an increase in the importance and wealth of many cities and, in spite of apparent political instability, it was a time of prosperity and growth for the bourgeoisie. In the third period, after the Mongol invasions, it is no longer possible to talk of a unified pattern in the Muslim world. The successive empires of Iran had a different effect on cities from that of Anatolian *beyliks*, small dynasties of North Africa and Spain or the complex system of Syria and Egypt.

The regional variable in the development of cities is the most complex one to describe, because it involves so many different features. Two of these may be singled out. One is the sources and distribution of water. Mesopotamian or Egyptian cities along major rivers with regular or irregular floods necessarily acquired a different physical pattern from Iranian cities based on *qanāts* (see p. 249), or from a Jerusalem with its cisterns. Another feature is the presence and nature of pre-Islamic settlements. Damascus or Aleppo, with their ancient stone masonries, shifted their main centres far less frequently than Samarqand or Nīshābur, where successive occupations tended to be next to rather than over each other. The definition of such historical, hydrographic and geographic factors for any one urban centre has only been made in a few instances and it is not yet possible to generalize on them in any meaningful way, although it is obvious to any traveller or historian that considerable differences in looks and in mood separate almost every segment of the Muslim world.

Keeping all these variables in mind, we can only try to outline a profile of the physical city with its inhabitants. The most recent historian of the Islamic city, while agreeing that every town was different and unique, identified in every one of them a number of consistent institutions which he described, at least by the V/11th century, as 'the slave army state, the quarters, and the religious communities in the form of the schools of law'. At the same time this is hardly the way in which a medieval writer described the very same cities. Al-Jāhiz, the great *littérateur* of the III/9th century, when asked about cities, replied: 'There are ten major metropolises [*amsār*]: Baghdad for noble virtue, Kūfa for elegance, Basra for industry, Misr [Fustāt in Egypt] for trade, Ray for perfidy, Nīshābur for tyranny, Merv for avarice, Balkh for boasting, Samarqand for craftsmanship.' The geographer al-Maqdisī, who reports these words, then proceeds to his own series of judgments of the same type, as meaningless to the understanding of a city as they were probably appreciated by his contemporaries. Al-Jāhiz or al-Maqdisī were writers of *adab* (see p. 141); their objective was both to instruct and to please or amuse. And while it is today difficult to be affected by this particular component of contemporary judgment on cities, the point of the examples is that, beyond the three components of the social historian, there is a component of value about a Muslim city, a judgment about its quality. In part it is a component which hardly lends itself to scientific analysis, especially in the terms of moral quality used by al-Jāhiz. But in another way it implies the existence of an urban taste which can perhaps be isolated with some precision. Finally medieval sources as well as archaeological observations deal with the wealth of a city. At times expressed in coldly factual terms of tax rolls, wealth is frequently discussed through the description of characteristic products or activities, as in celebrated references about the manufacture of inlaid metalwork in Herat and in Mosul, or in Ibn Hawqal's description of the agricultural potential of the cities of the middle Euphrates region.

In attempting our portrait of the classical Islamic city we shall pick up these five themes: the quarters, the religious community, the wealth, the state and the taste. In conclusion we shall try to tie them up into broader considerations about the characteristics of an 'Islamic' city and bourgeoisie.

The quarters

Any contemporary visitor to the Near East, at least before World War II, was aware of the Muslim city's division into quarters united by real or imaginary tribal, confessional or other bonds. It has generally been assumed that the patterns of pre-modern times can be transferred to an older past, but this is still problematic.

The norm of bourgeois existence was the family house, the *dār*. In most instances, whether large or small, it had a central open area – a courtyard, or in a few instances, near Merv for example, a domed space – and then single rooms or apartments *(bayt)* reached from the centre. Differences between houses involved size, number of rooms or apartments, presence or absence of fountains and fancy waterworks, decoration of painting or of stucco, and private facilities. A simple cesspool always existed, but a few houses had a private bath and the gossipy *littérateur* of the IV/10th century, at-Tanūkhi, reports that a rich merchant in Baghdad kept his money in his own private latrine. Few of the houses had an elaborate doorway to the outside. The earliest house of some distinction which has survived so far – one of the six units found in the early Islamic settlement at Qasr al-Hayr East – had an entrance leading into a long and dark hall opening into the central courtyard.

There are many reasons for this lack of external ostentatiousness. One is certainly an attempt to protect the private world of wives, children, servants and slaves; the *Thousand and One Nights* are full of adventures which can only be understood in the context of an intensely closed family life. Another reason was the practical one of avoiding the directing of attention to wealth for fear of taxation and confiscation.

Only glimpses can be gathered of the life of the bourgeoisie inside their houses. Some business was transacted there, as well as a lot of gossip. From VII/13th-century miniatures a few details of interiors can be reconstructed: curtains hanging between rooms or as internal partitions, simple ceilings with elaborate ventilation systems, a jar of cool water under a stairway, beds or couches, a few chairs. Spinning was done in the house, and eating could be a major event, with large trays covered with bread, meats and fruit around which men gathered in a circle; the food was generally prepared outside and kitchens seem unknown until Ottoman times. In some houses there were many books and education, especially of small children, took place there in part. Visitors came and went, at times other merchants and men of property, at other times total strangers, real or fake holy men, story-tellers, travellers from far away. The stories of al-Harīrī's *Maqāmāt* often utilize the setting of a *majlis* or gathering of urban notables, just as it is the setting of many political intrigues in early Islamic times, religious and intellectual discussions later on, amorous adventures or practical jokes at all times. It is in such private houses that in III/9th-century Nīshābūr we first hear of *madrasas*, the institution of religious learning which was later to become embodied in monumental architecture.

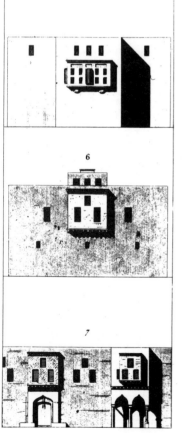

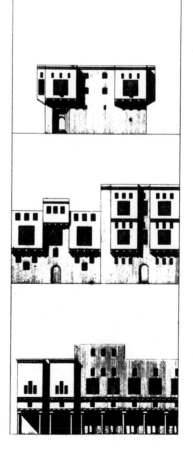

House-types in Egypt in the early XIII/19th century. Islamic private houses remained essentially inward looking, though they might have fairly large windows to the outside world. These, however, were normally screened, so that the women of the household might see without being seen. (3)

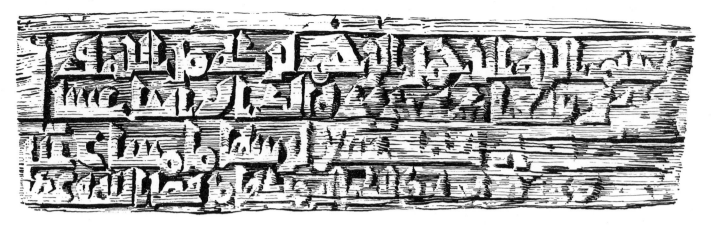

A rare fragment of carved wood from the III/9th or IV/10th century found in Egypt records the ownership of a house in Fustāt. It was probably a pious foundation. The text reads: 'In the name of the good and merciful God. Blessing of God. Success and happiness. Of this house twelve parts out of twenty-four belong to N . . . who received them by God's mercy and generosity.' (4)

Relations between owners of individual houses were not always idyllic. Legal texts and the Geniza fragments are replete with disputes about property rights and about repairs. The main bones of contention were the ownership of walls between houses and about the uses of streets and lanes. The latter is particularly important for an understanding of the city, for there seems to have been a constant tension between the need for a public policy which demanded free movement in thoroughfares and privately owned buildings which crept into the street. Islamic law provided that the open space around or along a building was part of the property to an extent about which medieval legal specialists argued endlessly. Problems also arose about water, at times about rights to the clean water usually brought in at the expense of the state, at times about sewage (or lack thereof). The presence of animals and mills also led frequently to disputes. *De facto* if not *de jure* the Muslim world was moving towards zoning regulations.

Living quarters were affected by such variables as the sources of water or the predominant material of construction. Jerusalem, dependent on cisterns and on expensive aqueducts, could not develop the appearance of Damascus or Fez with abundant waters easily accessible through canalizations, and all three were different from Yazd and Kirmān with their underground *qanāts* bringing water from far away. In Iran, richer houses tended to be nearer the source of water, while in Syria proximity to the centre of town or to some important monument was a favoured location. Then also, Iranian houses in mud brick could easily be abandoned and rebuilt elsewhere, whereas the stone constructions of Syria and Palestine were far more permanent and tended to be constantly repaired. The greater permanence of family ownership of city land in Syria and Palestine led to a greater power of the urban bourgeoisie and restricted, among other things, the showy monumental constructions of princes so typical of Iran. Yet, with all the physical differences which can be demonstrated, there was an internal consistency within the Muslim quarter. Its key lies in what has been called the predominance of a 'familial obligation'. The house of a family was the main cellular unit of the city; it was a closed unit, developing within itself, secretive and interiorized.

Few Muslim cities are understandable without their suburbs, the *rabad* of texts. Damascus and Aleppo evolved and grew as suburbs were incorporated into the city. In many Iranian cities, in Baghdad or Raqqa, there occurred an alternation in importance between early city and suburb, the rhythms and reasons of the alternation varying from place to place.

Whether in the old city or in the suburbs, whether for living alone or for living and manufacturing, the quarter with its individual houses of varying quality, its neighbourhood problems of sewer repairs and balconies over streets, and its gossipy or intellectual meetings, was the core of the bourgeois city. It did not have a formal and consistent administration, although obviously enough a natural or hereditary selection of notables served to defend the interests of the quarter and to communicate to it decisions or demands from the state. The *sharīf* and the *ra'īs* (or *muqaddam*) are perhaps the most consistent terms for leaders of quarters. One of them implied a sort of blood nobility before it became specifically and more uniquely associated with the descendants of the Prophet, while the other one reflects an appointed or elected office, but in both cases there were evolutions in meaning and variations from area to area. Formalized or not, the bourgeois institution had at its disposal several means of pressure. The most important one consisted of a sort of para-military force, the *'ayyārūn*, *ahdāth*, or *fityān*, part rabble and part militia, who occasionally controlled the activities and life of the city and who policed it against thieves and brigands. Instances exist of governors actually removed by the local bourgeois establishment. For practical purposes, however, consistent authority over the affairs of the quarter was in the hands of the *qādī*, the judge, for it is through him that all practical problems were settled, from the uses of water to all-important inheritances. It is interesting to note that the illustrations of the *Maqāmāt* always show the *qādī* as a bourgeois Arab different from the people with whom he deals only by the long veil or *taylasān* over his head and shoulders; he is never shown as the alien prince. It is indeed within this private world of the bourgeoisie that Islamic law developed in the immense complexity of its practical details, and therein lies one of its most significant characteristics and contributions to Islamic culture.

The religious community

The theoretical focus and locus of the Muslim community was the mosque, the congregational *masjid al-jāmi'* which in the past, as today, was the most obvious, largest monument in the city accessible to all Muslims. But this *masjid al-jāmi'*, or simply *jāmi'* as it became known from the IV/10th or V/11th centuries onwards, was in many ways less a reflection of the concrete community of a given town than the symbol and the instrument of a broader authority, that of the caliph and his representatives. In the large metropolises it had become too remote and possibly too anonymous to be the true expression of the local *umma*. There was another monument or institution which was possibly better attuned to the character and needs of the city's own inhabitants. This was the *musallā*, literally place of prayer. There was usually one for every town and it was located outside of the city's walls, frequently, especially in Iran, in or near one of the main cemeteries. It was generally used only for religious and popular festivals and does not seem to have acquired the typological consistency of the congregational mosque. Its practical urban function is still quite unclear but it is curious that in Morocco and in a few Spanish cities it was known as the *sharī'a*: the Law.

Next to the congregational mosque and to the more elusive *musallā*, there were, almost from the beginning, smaller *masjids* for specific quarters or tribes. In later times the number and character of these private restricted places of gathering and prayer changed considerably. By the end of the VII/13th century in Aleppo, there were 208 *masjids* in the city, 10 on the walls and nearly 300 in the suburbs. Comparable figures occur in Damascus, Cairo and Fez, where there were 785 holy places around 1300; numbers are not of the same order of magnitude in Iraq or Iran, and it is possible that there were significant regional variants in the development of the *masjid*. In the Arab core of the Muslim world it tended to become restricted to fairly specific social groups defined by quarter or family as well as by trade or occupation. From one early instance in Baghdad where an old woman's dream led to the development of a mosque all the way to VII/13th-century Aleppo or Damascus where a Mosque of Repentance *(Tawba)* replaced places for drinking and prostitution, it was local needs and local aspirations which led to the creation of most of these monuments. At times, as in the Aqmar mosque in Cairo, they were very impressive works of architecture and decoration, adapted in their shape to pre-existing exigencies of the city's life. Others, such as a small mosque recently excavated in Sīrāf, were quite humble affairs. In contradistinction to what was said about private houses, the *masjids* were frequently provided with external projections in the shape of gates, outside ornament and, especially in Iranian cities of the V/11th and VI/12th centuries, high and fancy minarets. It is curious to note that several of the celebrated minarets in and around Isfahan whose mosques have disappeared were sponsored by the local establishment and not by princes and one of them even has a reference to the title of a *ra'īs*.

A very similar conclusion can be drawn about the second most common religious monument of the medieval city, the *madrasa*. It seems clear that by the V/11th century a private and local patrician institution serving to strengthen the learning and the scholarship of the Sunnī establishment was wilfully transformed into an instrument of the Muslim state. It is only after this change that the first monumental *madrasas* begin to appear, but their number (some forty in Aleppo around 700/1300 and seventy-four in Cairo in the IX/15th century) can be explained only by the fact that they fulfilled an internal urban need. In part it was simply the technical need to provide legal and spiritual leaders, but in another sense it was the place where the aspirations of the local bourgeoisie which endowed these establishments found their legal justification. *Madrasas* began to decline when the urban bourgeoisie lost its power, but for several centuries they were the major foci of urban complexes; the majestic examples so well represented in Cairo by the *madrasa* of Sultan Hasan are generally princely creations but typologically and functionally they derive from humbler bourgeois sources and needs.

A far more complex problem is posed by the third group of a city's religious monuments, the holy sanctuary, variously called *mashhad* – martyrium, *mazār* – place of pilgrimage, *qubba*, *turba* or *imāmzad* – mausoleum. Two cultural strands with early Islamic and even pre-Islamic roots were involved in the development of sanctuaries around tombs of holy men or the commemoration of holy events. One is the Islamic inheritance of thousands of holy places which had maintained their attraction at the level of folk piety and therefore were sooner or later Islamicized. The second strand is the development within Islam itself of a tendency to focus activities or to define legitimacy around specific individuals. This phenomenon took many forms. Shī'ism, for instance, transformed the places where the descendants of 'Alī were buried – Karbalā, Najaf, Qum, Mashhad – into major monuments and centres for pilgrimage. The Sunnī reaction tended to emphasize Old Testament prophets, although the burial place of the traditionalist ash-Shāfi'i in Cairo did become a major sanctuary. The tombs of Sūfī masters also became venerated, although probably not before the V/11th or VI/12th centuries. Even the puritanical Hanbalīs liked to gather in the cemetery where the founder of the *madhhab* was buried. Slowly and in ways which are particularly difficult to unravel, the cemetery became one of the most important parts of the city, with pilgrimages, meetings, revivals, at times even orgies, exemplifying a whole range of relations to the dead. Some of these sanctuaries were Islam-wide in meaning, others only regional, but the vast majority were restricted to local inhabitants. Some eventually became built up and developed by princes and by the military aristocracy, like the great Cairene cemeteries, the Shī'ī centres of Iraq and Iran, or the Shāh-i Zinda in Samarqand. But in many instances, for example Jonas's sanctuary in Nineveh, it is a mass of simple, locally sponsored accretions and modifications which made up the sanctuaries as we can observe them. Even in the great monumental examples princes may have been responsible for the building, but local piety created and used the holy places. A whole system of hostels, retreats, free kitchens, libraries, hospitals, grew around many of them. Many of these were endowed by a city's inhabitants, at times for specific mystical orders, and they formed a link between different cities; travellers like Ibn Battūta could go from one to the other all over the Muslim world. Cities of the dead became cities of God.

Private *masjids*, *madrasas*, sanctuaries, cemeteries were much more than monuments and areas in which inhabitants congregated on certain occasions or for purposes which could be snobbish (to hear a muezzin with a good voice), learned, mystic, or practical (as in seeking cures for sickness). These were the places where political, social and intellectual groupings were made, where the citizenry of a town divided itself into factions, the opposite in a way to the pilgrimage to Mecca which was the greatest unifying factor in the *umma*. It is perhaps because this factionalism took place within or around institutions of piety that so much of classical Islamic factionalism took on a religious or at least pietistic form and why central authorities sought so frequently to build up and to manipulate institutions which had sprung out of the needs of the urban population.

While the confessional building was the main centre of public activities and the source of a bourgeois' allegiances and beliefs, it was not the only one. Baths were remarkably numerous in all medieval cities and served as important social centres. Many have been preserved from Central Asia to Granada. They are usually quite small and their exact uses still merit investigation. There were also organizations which were not tied to specific locales like the *futuwwa* for instance, to which we shall return in another context.

In short, next to quarters centred on the single family house, the urban landscape of traditional Islamic civilization possessed a network of city-wide foci in the form of confessionally restricted centres through which the city's bourgeoisie acquired its allegiances and developed the physical forms of its beliefs. Within the Muslim community, these forms varied from century to century. They were tribal and ethnic in early times, orthodox *madhhabs* from the iii/9th century onwards, Sunnī and Shī'ī from the iv/10th century, frequently Sūfī after the vi/12th. Yet behind the forms there always lay a very deep piety which, as behooves Islam, expressed itself in works as much as in buildings or in professions of faith. This concern for the good of others appears in the humble palm tree with which this chapter began, or in the Baghdad merchant who had made arrangements to have blankets and garments distributed to the Muslim prisoners taken by the Byzantines, or in another wealthy citizen of Baghdad who used to buy up the time of prisoners in jails who had confessed their misdeeds. Most instances like these have not been preserved in written records nor do they appear in monuments, yet they form the most socially and humanely meaningful dimension of the traditional religious community.

Wealth

The ownership of land was the major source of wealth in classical Islam. A town like Raqqa may have had any number of functions and purposes, but one of them was to be the capital of a rich and newly irrigated agricultural area. Estates and entire villages were owned not by the people who lived in them but by city dwellers, and their revenues seemed to embellish the city, at least after the vi/12th century.

The sūq, *a covered street housing shops, is one of the most characteristic features of Islamic towns. This one, designed and built as a sophisticated architectural unit, is at Isfahan. (5)*

Wealth gained from manufacturing also had a crucial influence on the life of towns. Some of the work may have taken place inside the quarters, but for many activities, especially the polluting work of tanners, butchers, brickmakers and so on, there were specialized quarters, on the outskirts of the town. How systematically specialization was divided inside towns is still a moot question, but a bazaar of metalworkers was recently discovered at Sīrāf, and the pre-modern pattern of Aleppo's wonderful *sūq* or that of Kāshān may have early roots.

The visible expression of trade – the third most important source of wealth in the Islamic city – took several forms. On the outskirts of the city there were large caravanserais, usually surrounded by an empty area for the parking of animals. Superb examples of this type have been preserved from x/16th- and xi/17th-century Iran and a similar caravanserai was found recently in Sīrāf. A neighbouring bath probably served the function of our own health inspection at frontiers.

Inside the city there were warehouses, called variously *khān*, *funduq*, *qaysāriyya*, *wakāla*. Each of these terms has its own history and background and there were differences in meaning and possibly in legal and functional uses between them, but the main point is that the centre of the city – and at times several centres in it – was occupied by large storage buildings, at times, as in Aleppo, truly monumental ones. These warehouses were usually built into a system of covered streets with shops, the *sūq*. Plans tend to be either radial from one or more polygonal nodes or consisting of parallel streets with occasional large interior piazzas. Shops are simple but warehouses are frequently monumental. The bazaar is dotted with monuments of practical piety, fountains, small *masjids*, *madrasas*, baths, hospitals. Few people lived there in classical times, but the commercial hub of the city is rarely far removed from the congregational mosque and from the offices and dwellings of princes and governors. Proximity to the bazaar, while not necessarily desirable for living, was obviously a source of much prestige, and could be afforded by the very wealthy, as is suggested by the admittedly late Azem palace in Damascus. Earlier in Cairo pious monuments celebrating the conspicuous consumption of the rulers were all erected near each other, almost always on the same street adjoining bazaars and between two main mosques.

It is not very difficult to imagine the life and activities of a city's commercial centre, its endless movements of people, goods and animals. At certain places, as is shown in an illustration from the *Maqāmāt*, a dentist-barber would set himself up and a host of services sprang up everywhere; water-carrying, cooking and so forth. Law and authority were in the hands of the *muhtasib*, an official specially appointed to supervise weights and measures, fineness of coinage, honesty in merchandising. Punishments of mercantile impropriety seem on the whole to have been far more frequent and more severe than of private immorality.

Any account of the legal and professional organizations common to Islamic commercial life requires the mention of an allied topic, the *futuwwa*. This was a strictly urban movement with elaborate initiation rites, a partly secret code of behaviour and mystical doctrines. It was both a means to formulate and defend local needs and a loose pan-Islamic system of social and political contacts. Frequently it became undistinguishable from Sūfī movements and we shall see later that it may have had some impact on the arts. The relationship between the official world of the *muhtasib* and the locally developed one of the *futuwwa* is difficult to determine properly, but the duality of allegiances and of obligations suggested by the existence of both leads to a major point to which I shall return in conclusion.

Trade, altogether, was much more than the main source of wealth in the city. It was its cultural mix, its source of ideas and adventures, and in many ways the means by which almost everything from a Chinese ceramic to an absurd story could penetrate across social classes and from one end of the Muslim world to another.

The 'state'

Few urban centres could escape the presence of what has been called earlier the 'state', i.e., the complex of administrative, military and ideological forces which tended to reflect a broader entity than the city itself or which consisted of individuals and groups different from the city-born but ruling over them.

Several types of monuments made the state's presence visible. In early times the most common one was the *dar al-imāra*: 'house of government'. Two of these are known archaeologically, both from Umayyad times. One in Kūfa is a sort of castle within the city, with a central court from which one penetrates into a formal audience hall or into a group of small units, either administrative offices or living quarters. The other one, at Qasr al-Hayr ash-Sharqī in Syria, is distinguishable from more common houses only by its ease of access and by a greater concentration of decoration. From literary sources we know that other *dar al-imāras* were quite elaborate, such as the one Abū Muslim built in Merv. But on the whole, as its name indicates, it was not really meant to be more than a 'house' serving the community by harbouring the officials appointed by the central government and the offices, mostly financial, needed for the exercise of their functions.

It is not very clear from sources when the term *dar al-imāra* and presumably the functions associated with it disappeared, but a definite change both in terminology and in type occurs after the foundation of Baghdad in 139/756. Administrative offices became separated from formal and living areas, and at least in the case of Baghdad, they were located along the inner wall of the town. Next to the formal imperial palace was the private palace, often called a *qasr*, castle, inside the city. Fancy names were given to these establishments found in most capital cities: the Palace of the Crown, of the Pleiades, or of Eternity. Often surrounded by gardens, they may not have been more than pleasure pavilions like the later Safavid and Ottoman ones in Isfahan or Istanbul. To the bourgeoisie and to other city dwellers the imperial palace became a myth, the imaginative myth of the mysterious succession of magnificent palaces found in the *Thousand and One Nights*, the romantic myth of Hārūn ar-Rashīd escaping his gilded cage to mix with commoners, the frightening myth of a world from which one could not escape and into which, when called, one brought one's shroud.

Little of day-to-day administration was carried out in these palaces. Instead there were *dīwāns*. Their forms are not known, but one building in Sīrāf has tentatively been interpreted as an office building. It is curious, however, that the illustrations of the *Maqāmāt* of al-Harīrī represent a royal living place as an unusual building, while a *dīwān* or a *dar al-nizāra* is shown in the same manner as regular houses.

The evidence of these illustrations is of course rather late and limited to Iraq. In the meantime a new type of place of government has appeared: the citadel, *qal'a* or *arg*. All citadels were not as striking as that in Aleppo, which dominates the city from the height of a partly natural and partly artificial mound. But in most known instances they were the largest and most impressive monuments in town, as in the striking citadel in Bosra, built entirely around a Roman theatre. Citadels are as ancient as towns, yet they were relatively rare in early Islamic times except in frontier areas. They began to proliferate in the IV/10th century and the earliest evidence known so far is, accidentally or not, from the northeastern frontiers of Islam. Ibn Hawqal describes at

The Talisman gate of Baghdad was one of the last additions to the city made by the ʿAbbāsid caliphate. It was built in 618/1221. Less than forty years later, in 657/1258, Baghdad fell to the Mongols and the caliphate came to an end. The gate was destroyed in 1917. Its decoration was of terracotta; two dragons with convoluted tails flank a human figure at the top of the arch. (6)

Bukhārā a citadel which was outside the city but contiguous to it, a pattern which was to occur in Aleppo, Damascus, Cairo and Granada. It was not simply a fortified enclosure for the military but often a sort of mini-city with a mosque, palaces, cisterns, houses, etc. The creation of a separate and restricted urban entity controlling but different from the main city occurs also in the first Cairo built at the end of the IV/10th century and most spectacularly in the Alhambra in Granada. As has been shown for Aleppo, the evolution of the physical relationship between citadel and city reflects the evolution of the relationship between the local bourgeoisie and the military aristocracy.

Closely related to the citadel were fortifications. Early Islamic towns, with a few exceptions, did not have defensive walls, but in the IV/10th century city walls appear in a systematic manner, totally new ones or, especially in very old cities, refurbished antique ones. Epigraphic information for cities like Diyārbakr, Jerusalem, Cairo and Aleppo clearly indicates that these constructions were almost always the responsibility of local princes and in earlier times of the caliphate.

An interesting aspect of fortifications lies in their gates. Their location usually reflects the existing terrain, internal features of the city like its markets and quarters, some significant suburban feature like a sanctuary, or an activity like tanning which usually took place outside the city walls. The names of gates often indicate the peculiar symbiosis between the world of the prince and that of the city. The former appears in secret gates, the *bāb as-sirr* so often mentioned in sources, or in the symbolic transfers of gates from one city to another, as happened to the gates of Baghdad and is alleged to have happened in one instance in Aleppo. Gates were symbols of princely possession and were frequently decorated with sculptures, most often lions and snakes. It is curious that the Muslim world, which generally avoided an official art of sculptured representation, made quite consistent exceptions for gates, from Bukhārā to Cairo. We know very little about the actual sources of these representations or the specific associations which were made with them. In some instances, especially in Anatolia, there is little doubt that Central Asian, non-Islamic, Turkish pagan or Buddhist explanations can be proposed, but quite frequently local talismans, cults and superstitions were involved, as in the lion gate built in Hamadān by a Daylamī prince, the Aleppo gates with snakes, or pre-Islamic gates with solar symbols re-used in Isfahan. It has been suggested that the now vanished Talisman gate in Baghdad, with a small figure strangling two symmetrically arranged dragons, is an attempt at a precise symbolism of the Caliph an-Nāsir defeating heterodoxies. For the most part, however, the names of gates refer to the people and activities which surrounded them and through their lists, as for instance in VI/12th-century Marrakesh, the tribal and economic organization of the city can be reconstructed. In Jerusalem, on the other hand, the names of gates and their changes reflect the complicated religious associations of the city.

Palace, citadel, fortifications, gates, mosque: such are the most obvious and most important aspects of the state's visibility in the city. Others were the jail, and at times the mint, but these have not been clearly isolated as characteristic forms. An example about which more is known is the large open space found inside the city walls or at its edges. The *maydān* or the *rahba* (the latter, limited, it seems, to the interior of towns) were used for military parades and practice as well as for polo-playing. These are clearly princely activities; the *maydān* built by Ibn Tūlūn in his quarter near Fustāt was within the city and has elaborate units with fancy gates that were used in specific ceremonies. All Central Asian cities are supposed to have had a large open space in front of the citadel. While one must concede that most of these areas were used primarily for the state, they did also serve as market places, especially for animals, and in many cities, Damascus for instance, the *maydān* became an essential part of the physical development of the town. In later Iran, it was a centre for almost all urban activities and acquired striking architectural forms, but it is difficult to know how far back such formalization can legitimately be pushed.

The immediate, daily extension of the state's authority into the city took place through a police force, the *shurta*, and through tax collection, whose practical mechanisms are not very clear. But there were also major state responsibilities inside the city. Water, for instance, was often gathered and distributed through its auspices and thoroughfares were maintained by it, large enough for the horses of the princes, the camels of merchants and the donkeys of individuals. Many caravanserais were built and maintained by princes or the military establishment as well.

Taste

One aspect of the city's taste has been brought out as we discussed other components of the urban complex. The interiorized house off a narrow lane or the private sanctuary emerging in the midst of living quarters or of a bazaar are characteristic elements of an urban taste, for they are the result of uniquely urban needs and affect the modes of behaviour and the habits of the city. Other examples are the mythology formed around princes and in tales about remote lands or about the deeds and misdeeds of the city's bourgeoisie. Much of *adab* literature, from at-Tanūkhī's gossips to al-Harīrī's verbal pyrotechnics, grew out of the world of merchants and artisans. But, beyond these features, a peculiarly medieval Islamic development is the way in which its visual arts also reflected the city and its bourgeoisie. This is most evident in the art of objects, especially ceramics and metalwork, of which so many examples have been preserved.

Three aspects of the art of the object are particularly pertinent for our purposes. One is the development of new techniques – in ceramics, lustre, polychrome glazes and all sorts of means to improve the precision and colour of designs; in metalwork, the rediscovery of silver inlays on bronze objects, as well as similar modifications in glass making and in book decorating, are techniques which share two characteristics. One is that they seek to give brilliant and expensive effects as economically as possible and the other is that they all exhibit interest in visual ostentatiousness for generally very humble objects – a pitcher, a bowl, a mortar, a pen case. The motifs found on them, and especially on ceramics, are amazing in their variety. The recent publication of the objects found in Nīshābūr, one of the great metropolises of medieval Islam, has brought to light thousands of different subjects, from simple proverbs or expressions of good wishes on undecorated backgrounds to personages, animals, floral and other motifs. Metalwork objects tended to be less varied in their subjects of decoration. Most of their themes came from what has been called the princely cycle, hunting, drinking, polo-playing, astrology, the life of

Clay stamps used for loaves of bread have been unearthed in Egypt. They have a variety of simple patterns, many of them representational, and date from the V/11th to the VII/13th century. (7)

pleasure. Yet occasional anomalies suggest that these were not simply illustrations of princely life. Some objects show scenes of daily life in a very specific and literal sense. A particularly extraordinary group shows Christian scenes in the midst of royal pastimes. And then inscriptions indicate that the celebrated Bobrinski kettle, or bucket, in the Hermitage, dated in 559/1163, as well as a strange aquamanile in the shape of a cow made in 600/1203 and from the same museum were specifically made for merchants, while a pen case dated to 543/1148 (also in the Hermitage, and the earliest remaining object with complete inlaid decoration) was made by a city dweller for his brother returning from the *hajj*. What is suggested by these and many other similar examples is that most objects played a role in a very complex system of personal and social relations within the urban bourgeoisie. They were gifts or simply the objects which surrounded life, which made the regular activities of life more attractive and more pleasurable. The very variety of the motifs and techniques found on them argues for an urban origin, for, whereas the art of princes tended to be interchangeable from area to area and less immediately affected by new tastes and new ideas, urban middle classes were more conscious of differences between cities and provinces as well as between individuals.

Finally the iconography of these objects, insofar as we are able to unravel it, confirms the close relationship between the urban bourgeoisie and especially ceramic art. A magnificent plate of the III/9th century from northeastern Iran simply has a decoration of writing consisting of homespun and prosaic proverbs or of standardized greetings. In its prosaically aphoristic character, it illustrates the world of the sanctimonious and pious merchants and artisans who belonged to early Sunnī *madhhabs*. It is their own lives or the world which surrounded them which appear so frequently on contemporary ceramics from Egypt. A celebrated plate in the Freer Gallery in Washington has been shown to be an illustration of mystical literary metaphors, showing a young man who has abandoned his earthly desires (represented on the plate by a riderless horse) contemplating a soul, perhaps his own, which has reached union with the divine and lives in the divine like a fish in water. And, as a final example, a ewer of the late VI/12th century in the Tiflis Museum has a long poem which, in partly naively personal and partly in mystical terms, expresses an artisan's or owner's love for his object and appreciation for its uses. It is certainly not an accident that these last two objects coincide in time with the appearance of the *futuwwa* and of mysticism in urban culture. Even the personal and private character of some of the inscriptions from VIII/13th-century objects, as opposed to the more generalized nature of earlier ones, illustrates the more individualistic type of piety which preceded the Mongol invasions.

It is more difficult to decide whether the existence of a bourgeois art of the city can be extended to architecture. The practical means of building major monuments were most of the time in the hands of the state and most dedicatory inscriptions identify princes or their retinue as the major patrons of architecture. Yet there are two areas in which the taste of the bourgeoisie may have permanently affected architecture, at least until 1300. One is the function of monuments. With the exception of palaces and military architecture, almost all major functions from the caravanserai to the *madrasa* were first developed within the bourgeois world or served its purposes, even if the ostentatiousness of monuments like the *madrasa* of Sultan Hasan in Cairo or some of the Anatolian princely caravanserais is probably royal in nature. The other area of urban bourgeois impact lies in specific forms, or rather in the ways in which forms were treated. As one walks in traditional sections of Muslim towns or contemplates and uses so many of their objects, consistently striking impressions are, first of all, the ubiquitous presence of inscriptions, and then the way in which the rhythm of living activities in the streets is broken up by a doorway to a sanctuary or by a fountain. In all instances the viewer is less affected by the entrance itself or by the fountain than by its decoration. It compels the visitor to stop, to enter into the monument or to use it, and thus to escape from the city's continuous activities, to work out the details of the design, at times to read the inscription. The point of the doorway, of the fountain (or of the minaret) is to remind one of formulas so often found on inscriptions: *al-mulk lillāh* or *al-bāqī lillāh*, 'power is to God' or 'the remainder is to God'. These are not standardized, meaningless phrases, but reminders of the ultimate statement of Islam that there is no one and no thing but God. Inasmuch as piety in its manifold forms was so much a local phenomenon, it can be suggested that there was a bourgeois mode in architectural forms just as much as in objects, and that it consisted in developing designs which required the viewer to stop and to think of God and of things other than the immediately perceptible and immediately compelling life.

The Islamic city: tension and resilience

From this impressionistic and essentially descriptive survey of the urban landscape in classical Islamic times, a number of conclusions emerge, of which two seem to me particularly significant.

The first is that the Muslim city can be defined less as a willed, conscious, so to speak 'programmed' social and physical entity than as a series of tensions between contradictory and at times downright incompatible poles, always subject to the variables of time and area. The city is commercial and artisanal, but much of its wealth derives from agriculture, and the physical separation between urban living and the cultivation of land is never very clear. The city is defined by a single congregational mosque, but it also contains hundreds of private sanctuaries and places of worship. It is the world of a local bourgeoisie, although a military aristocracy of governors from the outside tends to have most of the power. Quarters are divided according to tribal, religious or ethnic groupings, but the hub of the city is its centre of trade, in which many faiths and men of many origins are present. Walls are built to protect it and immediately suburbs grow. Purposes and functions of monuments derive from the needs of the city but only the state has the funds and the power to build major ones. Within the bourgeoisie itself similar tensions occur, between family and professional allegiances, between orthodox legalism and mystical movements, between strictly local pride and more worldwide concerns, between individualism and group interests. All these tensions were translated into institutional and formal terms. The *qādī* and the *muhtasib*, the *shurta* of the state and the *ʿayyārun* or *ahdāth* of the city, the *amīr* and the *raʾīs*, the *jāmiʿ* and the *mashhad*, the *qasr* and the *dīwān*, the *madīna* and the *rabad*, all these pairs of terms illustrate generally unresolved oppositions between parallel sets of institutions.

It would be convenient if one could further conclude that all these examples of binary tension are but illustrations of one or two basic structural tensions within the Muslim world affecting, in this instance, the urban order. And no doubt tensions between military and bourgeoisie, between legalism and Sūfism, between local particularism and pan-Islamic needs can be detected at almost all times.

Should we then argue that there was no 'Islamic' city or bourgeoisie, only a number of local developments and occurrences whose tension took on an Islamic mould? To a degree this is indeed so, and some recent scholarship has sought to emphasize local particularities at the expense of very broad cultural generalizations. Yet even the brief outline given in this chapter suggests a second conclusion, which is the remarkable permanence of so many Muslim cities – almost all of them in fact, except for those like Sīrāf which had from the very beginning a single and limited focus. If, in spite of conflicts, invasions, destructions and tensions, the Muslim world is so frequently defined by its urban life, and if so many of the cities preserved their wealth for so many centuries without abandoning their allegiance to the *umma*, we must assume that they held something in common, something which would have been absent, for instance, from Russian cities, so many of which did not survive the Mongol invasions, or from Languedoc cities which required centuries to revive from the destructive crusades of the vii/13th century. It is in part the very looseness of the Muslim city's institutional system which gave it resilience. For, just as it did not acquire the urban institutions of antiquity or of the medieval West, it did not acquire

sclerotic organisms which could stifle it. Based as it was on a series of bonds between individuals and between units of very different kinds, bonds which were rarely written down but carried on from generation to generation, the Muslim city could define itself, as in the passage of al-Jāhiz cited earlier, in ethical or spiritual terms, for it was based on a relationship between men and not between institutions. This human side explains so much of the city's physical aspects, handsome new houses and monuments next to dilapidated ones originally fulfilling the same purposes, constantly refurbished bazaars, constant relationship to men of the past through large cemeteries and easy abandonment of burial places of forgotten men. This was all possible because it was men rather than formal institutions that remained and men could adapt themselves to new circumstances. Furthermore the Muslim mould, which was given to whatever institution or problem arose, made it possible for Andalusians to move to Morocco, for Moroccans to come to Iran and for more than half the Muslim world to be governed by Ottoman Turks. It is Islam which gave its resilience to the Muslim city and to its bourgeoisie, not because it was necessarily aware of all urban problems but because it had the abstract forms in which all of them could be resolved.

For this reason it is difficult and dangerous to interpret original physical features of a few Muslim cities – the brilliantly symbolic plan of Baghdad, the complex compositions of bazaars in Kāshān and Isfahan, the square patterns of Herat – as expressions of the culture's own unique qualities. In many of these instances, most remarkably in Baghdad, the theoretical pattern hardly survived a generation. And, while abstract urban plans may have developed occasionally within the Muslim world, they tended, more often than not, to be the whims of princes and of the state, not typical expressions of the culture. The latter occurred in the unique character of Islamic life and attitudes, whose shadows only have been preserved in the bourgeois city.

Two great Islamic cities are illustrated opposite and overleaf: Aleppo and Jerusalem. Both were far older than Islam; both became key cities of the new faith. **Aleppo** was a Hittite, Assyrian and Hellenistic site before it was occupied by Muslim armies in 15/636. For the next thousand years it was fought over, won and lost by the Byzantines, the Fātimids, the Seljuqs, the Crusaders, the Mongols, the Mamlūks and the Ottoman Turks. Its citadel, illustrated more fully in the chapter on Warfare (p. 218–19), was one of the strongest fortresses in the world, built on a vast mound in the centre of the city. This miniature (opposite) is from a x/16th-century manuscript, Nāsūh al-Matrakī's *Itinerary*, a description of the campaigns of Sultan Sulaymān the Magnificent, 941-3/1534-6. In spite of its schematic style, the shape of the city is accurate: roughly square, with the citadel in the middle, entered by a bridge across the moat. Like all

Islamic cities, it is crowded with mosques, whose minarets dominate the sky-line. (1)

Overleaf: **Jerusalem,** an air view of the old city, looking east. Standing out clearly (upper right) is the Haram (Temple Mount), a rectangular platform once the substructure of Herod's Temple. In its centre is the Dome of the Rock and to the right the Aqsā Mosque, both among the holiest places of Islam. The old city is traditionally divided into 'quarters', reflecting its long history of religious coexistence. To the north (i.e. left) of the Haram is the Muslim quarter, with to the west (foreground in the photograph) the Christian. On the right are the Jewish (nearest to the Temple) and Armenian quarters. Outside the wall at the top runs the Kidron Valley with, beyond that (out of sight), the Mount of Olives. (2)

The living city formed a dense and organic unity – public and private, sacred and profane, intermingling with no sense of strain. The two poles of middle-class life were the mosque and the bazaar, often built in close proximity,

Inside the bazaar every commodity was for sale under the same roof – an idea that has only recently percolated to the West. An early VII/13th-century illustration (below

for in Islam there is nothing reprehensible in the desire to make money. This panorama of a Turkish town, Ankara (above), was painted by a French artist in the XII/18th century. The square is lined with merchants'

left) to a romance shows a jeweller, an apothecary, a butcher and a baker. Each shop would open into the covered street, or *sūq*. (4)

booths. Women, though veiled, mix freely with the men. At the back, near the centre, can be seen the upstairs room of a private house. Beneath it a money-changer or jeweller weighs his wares on scales. Next to him is the

mosque. On the right are more domestic scenes, with people cooking, smoking and weaving at a loom. Outside the town sheep-shearing is in progress, and in the distance a caravan sets out on a trading journey. (3)

Tanneries, like other trades involving pollution or unpleasant by-products, tended to be assigned special quarters or put on the outskirts of towns. This one exists

today at Fez, in Morocco. The elements of Islamic town life, in spite of modernization, have remained remarkably constant. (5)

Bourgeois patronage of the arts led to the creation of many exquisite objects reflecting a taste which was specifically urban and middle-class, as distinct from that of the court.

A lustre dish from Ray, Iran (left), is painted with a scene possibly showing Laylā and Majnūn at school (their love story is illustrated again more fully on pp. 154–5). The teacher is in the middle; each little scholar has a tablet with the same writing exercise repeated. It dates from the end of the vi/12th century. (6)

From Mosul, in Mesopotamia, comes an unglazed water-jar (below) of earthenware, decorated with moulded reliefs of elaborate floral and animal patterns. Date: vi/12th–vii/13th century. (8)

A water buffalo suckling her calf (below), apparently oblivious of a lion attacking her hump, was made for a merchant. It is more than an ornament – an acquamanile (water-jug) – and is dated 603/1206. (7)

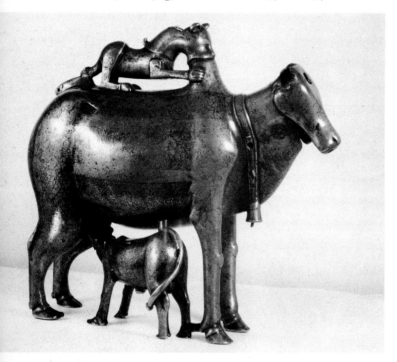

Inlaid metalwork such as this brass ewer (below) often carried a repertory of 'courtly' scenes – hunting, hawking, music-making – for the delectation of their bourgeois owners. The inlay is silver and copper; it comes from Mosul and is signed and dated 630/1232. (11)

The 'Freer Canteen' (above) contains an extraordinary mixture of scenes, some Christian, including the Entry into Jerusalem and the Nativity. But its technique and motifs are entirely Islamic, illustrating the integration of non-Muslims within the Islamic city. (9)

An endearing donkey – or is it a dromedary? – in glass forming a flask (below) comes from Aleppo; II/8th–III/9th century. (10)

Patterns of townscape vary throughout the Islamic world, though all show certain common qualities. The basic unit is the family house, the *dār*. At San'ā', in the Yemen (above), the tendency is to height, giving it a vertical emphasis that is highly distinctive. More commonly the *dār* expanded at ground level, with rooms grouped round a central courtyard. Right: Yazd, in Iran. In the foreground is the courtyard of a mosque. Beyond it stretches the densely packed mass of house-units, each insulated from its neighbour by sheer, windowless walls. (12, 13)

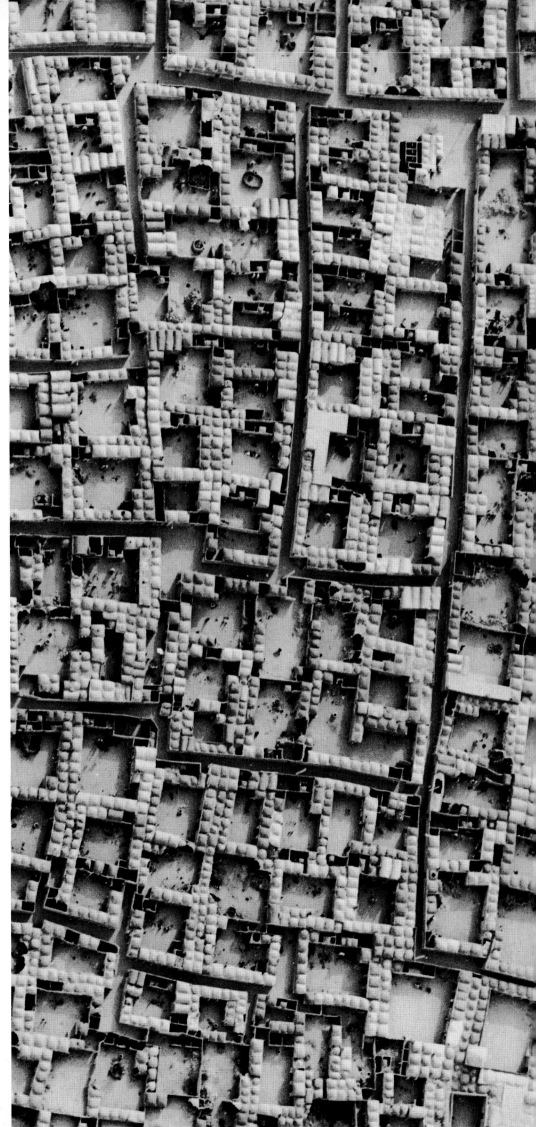

A maze of narrow streets bound the separate properties into a community that was close but not always harmonious. Disputes over access rights, repairs, water supplies, the ownership of boundary walls and the management of animals were constant and acrimonious. An air view such as this of Souk El Oued, in Algeria (right), makes the situation easy enough to understand. (14)

Water has always been a preoccupation of Islamic civilization. Most Muslim countries are arid. The availability of water, methods of collecting, retaining and distributing it – these have often been the determining factors in settlement, and have much to do with the differing characters of the regions of Islam. It has played a crucial role in agriculture, in social life (the baths), in culture (the garden) and in religion (the ablutions fountain).

Huge water-wheels (*nāʿūrā* in Arabic) lined the banks of the Nahr al-ʿĀsī, the ancient Orontes, in Syria. Driven by the force of the stream, they raised water in small troughs, emptying it at the top into channels where it flowed out to irrigate the land. Wheels like this were certainly in use in the VI/12th century. (15)

Street fountains were often provided by private donors. Right above: the fountain of ʿAbd ar-Rahmān Katkhudā, Cairo. Lower right: the Najjārīn fountain in Fez. (16, 17)

Caravanserais, lodgings for travelling merchants and their trains of animals, were the most prominent urban monuments to trade. They were built mostly on the outskirts of cities, and like the fountains were the result of private benefactions. This one (right) is the al-Ghūrī caravanserai, Cairo. (19)

The bath was more than a relaxation – it was a social institution, the direct descendant of the Roman bath. We know it as the 'Turkish' bath. This miniature of 935/1528 shows the Caliph al-Ma'mūn enjoying its luxuries. He is seated in the centre having a haircut. On the left water is drawn up by means of a pulley worked by an ox. At the bottom a man is being massaged. (18)

Hospitals, like schools and almshouses, grew up in the shadow of mosques and were part of their administration. A fine VII/13th-century example (right) is that of Divrigi, Turkey, built in 626/1228. (20)

A glimpse into the past is provided by the early illustrations to al-Harīrī's *Maqāmāt*, where the daily round of a VII/13th-century city comes to life in vivid detail. Above left: inside a mosque, with the imam preaching from the top of the *minbar*; one can see the *mihrāb* at the back and an old woman walking among the assembled listeners. Above right: incident in a barber's shop, with razor and scissors in the rack at the right. Below left: the public library of Hulwān, near Baghdad; the books are laid flat in recesses behind. Below right: in an elementary school, the masters dispute, the students listen, one of them literally 'fanning' the discussion. Opposite: travellers arrive at a village, depicted with every rustic detail (note the chicken on roof); but it too has its mosque with minaret. In all these images there is a fascinating mixture of precision of detail and amused caricature. (21–25)

The heart of the city was the mosque – not set apart from ordinary life but integrated into it, the visible symbol of Islamic civilization's essential unity. This page shows the congregational courtyards of four great mosques in different parts of the Islamic world. Above: the Bādshāhī Mosque, Lahore. Below left: the Mosque of al-Azhar, Cairo. Below right: the Umayyad Mosque, Damascus. Opposite: the Golden Mosque of Baghdad; beneath the two domes lie the tombs of two of the Twelve Imams, the nucleus from which the whole complex grew. (26–29).

Reverence for the dead, though by no means enjoined in the Qur'ān, led to the creation of a whole class of urban monuments – the tombs of rulers or holy men. If they did not generate mosques themselves, as at Baghdad, they became the nuclei of cemeteries, which in turn became meeting places, settings for pilgrimages and ceremonies, leading to the building of hostels, kitchens, libraries and hospitals. Above: the early Tīmūrid mausoleums at Samarqand (now USSR), which include that of Tīmūr-i Lang (Tamerlane). Left: a burial service from the *Maqāmāt*, VII/13th century; the cemetery is typical, with its domed tombs and decorative evergreen trees. (30, 31)

Chapter Four

THE MYSTIC PATH

Fritz Meier

The Sīmurgh, the fabulous bird which symbolizes God in one of the great Sūfī allegories: a detail from pl. 18. (1)

EVEN IN MUHAMMAD'S LIFETIME (he died in 11/632) some of his followers were not content with merely obeying his precepts, but wished to enter into a closer relationship with God. The path they took was similar to that of Christian monks, though they were not necessarily celibate. They tried to loosen their ties with the flesh and with the world, to purge the soul of qualities that had been declared evil or that seemed to them to be concerned only with earthly well-being. This movement grew in numbers as Islam spread in the 1/7th and 11/8th centuries; either the Arab ascetics found imitators in the new territories, or newly-converted, non-Arab Muslims were already acquainted with a similar world-renouncing piety from their earlier faiths. With some, this search for God took the form of isolating themselves from other people; but others merely led a more devout religious life within the framework of human society. If the intensification and introspective trend of this search seemed to be overstepping the limits prescribed by orthodoxy it was not unanimously accepted. The representatives of the movement paid less attention to the legal and philological aspects of the Qur'ān and the *hadīth* (Sayings of the Prophet), and more to their significance for the conduct of the soul. Questions of dogma and metaphysics were also relatively neglected. And so a new theology – if that is the right expression – came into existence, a science of pious self-examination and religious psychology, assisted by study of the Islamic scriptures with that particular end in view. Two of its principal representatives were al-Hasan al-Basrī (d. 110/728) and al-Muhāsibī (d. 243/857). The movement was wide in its scope, reaching from lugubrious asceticism to profound abstract speculation, and its adherents ranged from quite simple souls to men of great intellectual powers. For convenience we will call these adherents 'religious' (rather in the medieval sense of *religiosi*), a rough and ready translation of the Arabic *nussāk* (sing. *nāsik*). The discipline they created received different names at later dates, including the ambiguous 'inner science' and 'teaching of the workings of the heart'.

Preclassical Sūfism

In the 11/8th century, more especially in the latter part of it, these religious included the group known as *sūfiyya*, *sūfiyyūn* (sing. *sūfī*) or *mutasawwifa* (sing. *mutasawwif*). In all probability they were so called because of the woollen habits (*sūf*, 'wool') that they, or some of them at least, wore, and which, intentionally or not, set them apart from other people. The woollen shirt was a garment associated with penitence, worn for centuries by those, including Christian monks, who had adopted poverty for reasons of piety. The notion of poverty did not necessarily entail that of piety, but the word 'pauper' (Arabic *faqīr*, Persian *darwēsh*, later *darwīsh*, hence 'dervish') did come to have these associations. It is not quite clear what else distinguished the Sūfiyya from the other kinds of religious ascetics. Some seem to have displayed a certain contempt for existing social institutions and their theological apologists, asking themselves how far it was possible to go on living in such a society and working to uphold it. Some were indifferent to the customs and standards of society; some believed themselves called upon to oppose them; and all adopted their own life style, singly or in groups. Without doubt they set more store by their personal religious experience than by the traditional forms, and believed themselves to be better attuned to the meaning and purpose of religion than the leaders of established piety, let alone those of secular life. It is possible, though the evidence is extremely tenuous, that the Sūfī practice of listening to poetry and music *(samā')* as a means of intensifying their sensation of love for God and of transporting themselves into states of ecstasy, in which they believed they experienced a direct contact with God, dates from as early as the 11/8th century. The Qur'ānic injunction to remember God *(dhikr allāh)* as often as possible had led, even in the Prophet's lifetime, to the holding of meetings at which questions concerning religion, including the law, were debated. These were continued, in modified forms, in the circles of the various kinds of religious. With the Sūfiyya, perhaps already in the 11/8th century, such meetings came to take the form of collective repetition of certain formulas, notably the first clause of the Islamic creed, 'There is no God but God' *(lā ilāha illā llāh)*, a process which also induced ecstatic states. Both practices, *samā'* and *dhikr*, could be combined at one and the same meeting. The Sūfiyya certainly did not see themselves as disregarding religious laws, but for them observance of the law was no more than a preliminary stage, and many of them overstepped it in their ardour.

Where this early Sūfism originated is still a mystery. Such evidence as exists points, though by no means conclusively, to the civilizations outside Arabia proper, to Mesopotamia, Syria, Palestine, Egypt and especially to northern Syria. But by the year 200/815 it was also known in Mecca, the Yemen and the Oxus region.

Classical Sūfism

Learned theologians did not rate early Sūfism as equal with their own doctrine and some of them had reservations, too, about the 'inner science' practised by the religious. But by the beginning of the III/9th century at the latest, the concept of Sūfism had found approval even among non-Sūfī religious, and many were their attempted definitions. Clearly, the men of the 'inner science' recognized that Sūfism embraced an admirable ideal, just as they found inspiration in the ideal of selfless generosity pursued by the 'associations of young men' *(fityān)*. We do not know what influenced them more strongly: a desire to humble themselves to the level of the vagrant and ignorant, or a desire to lead these people along the right path; admiration for their somewhat odd way of life or the realization that their methods, too, had meaning. At all events, during the III/9th century the term Sūfism came to apply, no longer merely to the rather disreputable revolutionary wing, but to the centre and finally to almost the entire battalion of the 'inner science', usually implying the strictest asceticism as well. The term never became completely general, and some who might on account of their utterances have been called Sūfiyya in the new broader sense refused to accept the designation. It was moreover challenged from the opposite side by a quite different, very exalted concept, that of *gnosis*, higher knowledge.

Thus Sūfism, originally a marginal phenomenon, came during the III/9th century to be the name for the whole movement of religious asceticism and of the 'inner science', and was in turn subsumed in the movement. Throughout the III/9th and IV/10th centuries great masters of the 'inner science', now generally called Sūfiyya, such as Dhū n-Nūn al-Misrī in Egypt, Abū Sa'īd al-Kharrāz, Ibn 'Atā' and al-Junayd in Mesopotamia, Abū Yazīd al-Bastāmī, Abū Hafs an-Naysābūrī and Abū Bakr al-Wāsitī in Iran, and many others, worked at these basic techniques of religious search and religious ecstasy, that were sometimes too lazy and sometimes too violent, until classical Sūfism emerged, an Islamic mysticism which continued to develop variant forms in certain detailed aspects, but seen as a whole gained in homogeneity. The recognized authorities attempted to prune its more exuberant offshoots. They distinguished between the praiseworthy and the blameworthy, separated virtues from emotions, drew up a scale of inner demeanour, ascribed inner functions to specific non-physical organs (heart, spirit, etc.), established a scheme of ethical and epistemological principles and mapped the boundaries of what was permitted in the way of spiritual adventuring;

in short, they evolved an intricate moral psychology, not concerned with the exploration of man, but intended to guide the initiate in his pilgrimage towards purification of the soul. Over all, repeated in variant forms, always stood the tenet of monism *(tawhīd)*, the belief that God is One and that He alone wills, permits and makes possible everything, man's fate and suffering on the one hand, the principle of good and the commandments on the other, in other words that the human subject is a phantom and that apart from God there are only objects created and directed by God himself. This teaching was intended to demonstrate that for man to resist the twofold will of God, expressed in destiny on the one hand, and in the commandments on the other, was senseless and that his natural purpose should be to surrender himself sincerely and unreservedly. In undertaking the path towards purification the mystic could be sure that God was not only the goal ahead of him but was also the force that urged him on from behind.

With its doctrine of God as the only creative and active subject, classical Sūfism occupied the same ground as the traditionalism of someone like Ibn Qutayba (d. 276/889), and promoted the revival of 'orthodoxy' by Ash'arī (d. 323/935). Ash'arī's Sūfī contemporary Abū Bakr al-Wāsitī went so far in monism that he condemned prayers of supplication as an offence against the commandment of subjection to the irreversible will of God.

Mysticism differed from orthodoxy by its advocacy of practices leading to purification of the self, and by its endeavour to direct human spiritual life exclusively into that channel, and to annihilate the pseudo-subject. Philosophers commended Sūfism's efforts to purify the soul, but felt that it lacked the striving for understanding that should follow from it, and also deprecated its relegation of the self to nothingness.

There was some justice in the later designation of classical Sūfism, by the Andalusian scholar Lisān ad-Dīn ibn al-Khatīb (d. 777/1375), as 'the mysticism of ethical behaviour' *(at-tasawwuf al-khuluqī)*.

Textbooks and transition

In the early IV/10th century, al-Hallāj, a native of southern Iran who had travelled widely, stirred up antagonism by his barbed observations on traditional Islam and his criticism of Sūfism as it had by then developed. His thesis was that God was ontologically present in man's every fibre. But he came to grief on the hopeless attempt to merge his own consciousness with God and to achieve union between God and the self. His longing was also expressed in love poems (not all of which he actually wrote) which employ the terminology of secular love lyrics. But they should not be taken dogmatically and the greatest caution should be exercised in making deductions about al-Hallāj's theology from them. If some of the expressions of longing for death are genuine, then he himself saw death as the only help for him. Circumstances, including political intrigue, combined to lead to his execution in Baghdad in 310/922. This was not intended as an attack on Sūfism as such, and did not harm it. But it underlined the need to regulate mysticism and to lay down certain norms for it. Consequently several Sūfī textbooks were composed in the IV/10th and V/11th centuries, which selected commendable texts from the oral tradition handed down from the classical and earlier exponents of the 'inner science' and, where necessary, cited non-commendable ones for their cautionary value.

Significantly al-Hallāj is seldom quoted in these books. An opponent of al-Hallāj, al-Khuldī (d. 349/959), took care to bypass al-Hallāj in tracing his spiritual genealogy back almost to the time of the Prophet, naming al-Junayd as his ghostly father instead. In so doing he created the first pedigree of mystical teachers, a procedure that became usual among later generations of Sūfīyya.

More stringently regulated methods of education of neophytes were introduced at the same time, with the dual purpose of ensuring more effective instruction and of instituting more reliable precautions against error. The earlier practice had been for the pupil to serve a relatively free academic apprenticeship with a master, but that gave way gradually to the establishment of residential schools, in which the novice was more strictly supervised by his teacher, and received instruction from him regulating all his actions. The novice was obliged to reveal his every thought and to submit himself completely to his master (Arabic *shaykh*, Persian *pīr*), until his education was complete.

Post-classical Sūfism

The predominant characteristic of Sūfism from about the end of the v/11th century was the higher value placed upon visionary and occult experiences. The ground was prepared for full acceptance of these attendant phenomena by the theologian Muhammad al-Ghazālī (d. 505/1111), who saw mystical perceptions, such as heightened auditory and visual powers, as evidence for the possibility and reality of prophethood, and thus of the credibility of the Islamic religion; in other words, the 'minor tradition' of mysticism as a proof of the rightness of the 'major tradition' of religion. Visionary experiences, relegated to the background, indeed in many respects disowned altogether under classical Sūfism, were not overvalued, let alone regarded as self-justifying, in post-classical Sūfism; but they gained in importance as symptoms of the student's inner state and of his psychic progress. The teacher interpreted his dreams and visions for him, and the first steps were taken towards a system of interpretation. For although it was acknowledged that there could be direct perception of higher worlds, still one's own psychic characteristics, too, could be manifested, for instance, in the form of animals, and this kind of symbolic image could not be interpreted but by a system of correspondences. But the essential goal was only to be reached after passing through these intervening stages and setting aside their phenomena.

The theory of a divine spark in man also occasionally crops up in the post-classical period, probably as the result of contact with philosophy and perhaps too with Shī'ī thought, deriving for its part from Gnosticism. From this angle, mystical endeavour appears as the liberation of a light and its return to its source.

This 'liberation' was frequently placed in a context derived from philosophical and non-Qur'ānic systems. A favoured doctrine posited the emanation of the world from God descending by various stages to inorganic matter. But the way to know God was not, according to this doctrine, simply a matter of re-tracing the path that

A Sūfī holy man warming his feet. The manuscript is Persian, X/16th century, but details such as the facial type and the clouds point to a Mongol source. (2)

the world took in its genesis, for man does not occupy a position at the lowest point, the most remote from God, but is placed asymmetrically, on an upward-reaching branch, on the tip of the natural world. That is the starting-point for his higher development towards the stage of 'Perfect Man', to use the Sūfī expression, by means of the inner purification already mentioned. Yahyā as-Suhrawardī (d. 587/1191) equated God with absolute light and non-being with darkness, and arranged everything in between according to a scale of steadily diminishing light and steadily encroaching shadow; he also conceived, in addition to this cosmogonic radiance pouring out from the single source, the idea of a second radiance, of 'illumination' *(ishrāq)*, by means of which the already existing levels of light lit each other spiritually, as it were, in manifold ways, but always from above downwards, or at least sideways, never from below. Only with this supplementary radiance does the light incorporated in man acquire the strength and the desire to resist the attractions of the material world, and gain a chance of avoiding, after sloughing off the body in death, the fall into an even lower state, into the body of an animal, from which there would be no further hope of escape. Ibn al-'Arabī (d. 638/1240) substituted for this monism of light a monism of being, in which all phenomena are nothing but manifestations of being, which is one with God. In both systems mysticism occupies the ground between abstract knowledge and experiential perception of this ultimate unity in the original, primordial material, whether light or being. Both theosophers had their followers throughout the ensuing centuries, but Ibn al-'Arabī proved much more influential than as-Suhrawardī, and his teaching spread to the furthest bounds of Islam, proving an apple of discord even in parts of Indonesia in the xi/17th century and later.

If Sūfism in its classical periods was so marginal a phenomenon in Islamic society that it was hardly ever mentioned in non-mystical literature, in the post-classical epoch it advanced steadily into the forefront of people's minds, both rulers and subjects. It managed to gain a place beside official religion and took on some of its attributes. Many Sūfī shaykhs allowed themselves to be praised in odes like other mighty men, married into noble families, owned and administered property, often of considerable extent. The question whether or not the possession of worldly goods was morally right had receded into the background, as something that could be of interest only to those who clung to externals. What mattered was the inner demeanour: patience in poverty and gratitude in wealth. There was a steady increase, especially from the vii/13th century onwards, in propaganda for – if not the worship – at least the veneration of shaykhs. Their claim to dispense divine wisdom became more and more generally accepted; indeed a growing demand compelled them to assume that role. Sūfism in fact underwent a transformation similar to that experienced by the Prophet in his lifetime, between the Mecca period and the Medina period: Sūfism had arrived.

Up to some time in the iv/10th century Sūfiyya used to meet in the houses of their masters or in mosques for spiritual exercises and teaching. From the iv/10th century onwards, however, they had their own conventual houses, which often also served as lodgings for both resident and travelling members of the movement, and where food and drink, too, were dispensed both to them and to the poor, for spiritual welfare and charitable works were activities with which many Sūfiyya concerned themselves, fulfilling a need often neglected by traditional Islamic benevolence. These convents often belonged to a shaykh and his family, but often, too, they were the property or foundation of a rich donor, who placed them at the disposal of the Sūfiyya; from the vi/12th century onwards, again, it was not uncommon for them to belong to a ruler or the pious wife of a ruler. The costs of maintenance and staff were as a rule defrayed from endowments, consisting of estates and villages, and from voluntary or regular contributions. In the year 656/1258 Mosul had a total of twenty-seven convents, and in the second half of the xii/18th century there were still ten in the city.

Very often the convent remained the shaykh's abode even after his death, since he and his successors were buried in or near it. But the convent might also be erected near or over an existing tomb or be founded by a non-Sūfī as his future monument. At all events the Sūfiyya were frequently the pious occupants of a necropolis, which were visited by the people in order to obtain the benediction attaching to it; and potentates won honour by making gifts to the devout guardians of the tombs and by restoring crumbling masonry. Sometimes, like many mosques, the convent or the tomb replaced an older, pre-

Islamic sanctuary and the saints, dead Sūfiyya, venerated there were often the heirs of earlier divine or semi-divine beings. But the Islamic cult of saints was governed by the belief that the dead man was a Friend of God, and able, thanks to the regard in which God held him, to render direct or indirect help, where other help failed.

The orders

Schools (*tarā'iq*, sing. *tarīqa*), in one sense of the word, had already started to evolve during the classical epoch, in as much as certain Sūfiyya inclined more strongly to follow the teachings and the life of one shaykh rather than another. This tendency is to be distinguished from the groups of pupils who lived with their chosen shaykh (*tawā'if*, sing. *tā'ifa*). But the two terms intermingle, and both can be applied to Sūfism as a whole and later to separate orders within it. However, it is only possible to speak of 'orders' when groups see themselves in that light and adopt the name of a patron or a founder. Jullābī, the v/11th-century compiler of the first Persian Sūfī textbook, knew only schools, not orders. His contemporary Ansārī (d. 482/1089), in what is now Afghanistan, mentioned *chishtiyān*, that is, the disciples of a man from Chisht, or inhabitants of Chisht, near Herat, who made up an integrated group, and there are occasional earlier instances of Sūfiyya forming local associations. The charitable work among the poor, which Abū Ishāq-i Kāzarūnī (d. 426/1035) set up in southern Iran, and in the furtherance of which he and his pupils built hospices, undoubtedly required a minimal amount of organization, and after his death the administration was carried on by his kinsmen in the mother-house at Kāzarūn. The transition from a family undertaking to an order was probably effected when the followers started to name themselves after the family.

There were certainly many cases where that step was taken from the vii/13th century onwards, perhaps even already before the end of the vi/12th. One vii/13th-century example which is fully authenticated is the order of the Rifā'iyya, the antecedents of which can be traced from an initial foundation by the uncle of Ahmad ar-Rifā'ī (d. 578/1182), through the work of ar-Rifā'ī himself, to that of *his* nephew. Descendants of the nephew thereafter formed the main line, directing the association from the mother-house in Umm 'Abīda in Mesopotamia. Shaykhs who had completed their education were called 'successors' (*khulafā*, sing. *khalīfa*) or 'deputies' (*nuwwāb*, sing. *nā'ib*), and were often given charge of daughter-houses, where they attracted new members to the order. There were two stages in the climb from novice to 'successor', and each preferment had to be approved by the central house in Umm 'Abīda. There were various periods of retreat, the number and nature of which were laid down in regulations. The successful candidate had to swear loyalty to the founder's family. Similar procedures were followed from the late vii/13th century onwards by the heads of houses of the Mawlawiyya, especially in Anatolia, placing their pupils under a duty to the family who directed the order from Konya. But not every order owed or retained a family affiliation of that kind. Many acknowledged their original founder or patron but beyond that branched off fairly freely, often adding new names. The teachings of the orders were by

no means fixed or constant. Supporters and opponents of Ibn al-'Arabī were found in one and the same order. But a doctrinal breach could lead to a change in the conditions of affiliation. When, in about the year 1500, the mother-house of the Ardabīliyya proclaimed a Shī'ī revolution, many of the disciples, being in foreign countries, were unable to follow suit, and the order in the diaspora was transformed into a network of independent offshoots and new main lines, connected only by the thread of their historical, spiritual descent from Ardabīl. A line of spiritual descent could be broken up by distance, insubordination and objection to a successor. Many convents were houses only for members of the order.

At the same time Sūfism persisted independently of the orders. As such, its adherents included the majority of the 'holy fools', distinguished by their eccentric behaviour, often at odds with the norms of Islamic religion, who were tolerated in all kinds of liberties against high and low alike.

A fundamental distinction must be made between the orders and the descendants of a shaykh. The latter often formed a line of aristocrats, but individual members might belong to an order or not, or be found scattered among various different orders, or be the founders of new orders or branches. North African clans of this kind are called *marabout* families and *marabout* tribes, from the Arabic *murābit*, 'recluse' or 'saint'.

There were no female orders, though there were apparently convents reserved for women. Female Sūfiyya either belonged to one of the existing orders or led a religious life of their own. When associated with men, as pupils or teachers of mysticism, they generally sit segregated from them and separated by veils and curtains. In the VII/13th century the daughter of Awhad ad-Dīn al-Kirmānī was shaykha in seventeen convents in Damascus.

The Sūfī life was governed by many regulations in the post-classical period, which differed in their details from shaykh to shaykh and from order to order. The initiation ceremony included investiture with the woollen habit, which was given at the beginning of the novitiate in some orders, and at the end in others, or both at the beginning and the end. This ceremonial presentation of the old Sūfī garment to the neophyte is believed to date from the time of the Shīrāz shaykh Ibn-i Khafīf (d. 371/981). Later the ceremony came to include cutting the candidate's hair. The regulations covered the food the novice might eat during his compulsory retreat, usually lasting forty days; the formulas and the physical demeanour he was to adopt in the rite of remembering God in that period; the conditions in which musical rituals might be performed; the instruments to be played; the proper apportioning of garments thrown off in dancing; conventions to be observed in receiving invitations, and in entering and leaving a convent; the settlement of disputes; means of earning a living; and so on. A highly regarded shaykh in Baghdad, Abū Hafs as-Suhrawardī (d. 632/1234) – not to be confused with Yahyā as-Suhrawardī, mentioned above – attempted to lay down general guidelines, drawing on the practices and principles of classical Sūfism as a basis, but also taking into account subsequent developments like the evolution of the convents. His work was widely known and respected, but it proved impossible to institute uniformity of practice.

The detailed rules drawn up by the Rifā'iyya in the VII/13th century already differ and make similar claims to supreme validity. They illustrate another of the characteristics of post-classical Sūfism: formularization. Prayers and litanies were already familiar elements of Sūfī worship in the classical period, especially the act of remembrance of God. But it now became customary to compose litanies with an abundant artificial vocabulary and frequently with their own titles, which had to be read at specific times and with the intention of producing closely delimited results. The *opus operatum* of prayer, which al-Qushayrī in the V/11th century had wanted to see confined within narrow limits, now filled the entire day and dominated the novice's course of instruction, and its varying wording often formed one of the distinguishing features between different orders.

The masters of orders and the Sūfiyya regarded themselves as the pacemakers of Islam and by this belief justified their public religious practices, such as collective remembrance of God *(dhikr)* and listening to music *(samā')*. Some orders performed only the act of remembrance of God, others only music, others practised both, but separately, yet others undertook both simultaneously, in which case the ritual was usually called 'remembrance' *(dhikr)* after its less reprehensible part, but was also known by other names. Music played a truly spectacular role among the Mawlawiyya in Anatolia. Mawlānā Jalāl ad-Dīn-i Rūmī (d. 672/1273), after whom the movement

Dervishes dancing in a tekke (dervish monastery) at Constantinople. XII/*18th century.* (4)

Right: a Persian dervish of the X/*16th century, his limbs covered with so-called 'stigmata'. Mystical wounds might be variously caused: the mark of the Prophet's finger on the holy man's body, or a flow of blood when visiting Muhammad's tomb at Medina.* (5)

is named, already seems to have adopted dancing to intensify the effect of the music, probably under the influence of his mentor Shams-i Tabrīzī, and in the course of time music and dance intermingled to create so indivisible a unity that the dances were performed as rituals, in praise of God and as stimulants to an exalted experience of inner harmony. The sympathetic movement of the body *(tawājud)* while listening to songs, which the usual rule books permitted only within certain limits, was thus elevated among the Mawlawiyya to the status of a religious act. According to traditional theory any 'miraculous acts' that might be vouchsafed to a 'friend of God' or 'saint' among the Sūfiyya had to be kept as secret as possible, in contrast with the miracles of a prophet, for whom they were a necessary part of his credentials. One has to reconcile this theory, however, with the fact that the lives of Sūfiyya are packed with tales of miracles and that many of them did not acknowledge the principle. Some orders, indeed, recommended public demonstration of miracles, and their members drank poison, stabbed themselves, entered ovens, threw themselves from heights, in order to show the power of God working in them. The Rifāʿiyya were of this persuasion. Their eponymous patron Ahmad ar-Rifāʿī may not have performed such acts: but the claim made even by some Arabic writers that they derived from extraneous Mongol influences is invalidated by the fact that this kind of thaumaturgy is known to have been practised by one of Rifāʿī's immediate 'successors' in Syria, before the first Mongol invasion took place.

Neo-classical tendencies

There were other voices to be heard here and there, in the VII/13th and VIII/14th centuries, advocating a revival of the more restrained practices and ambitions of the classical era, and a return to the fundamental principles of Islam. Two of them were leading figures in the new order of the Shādhiliyya: Ibn ʿAtāʾ Allāh as-Sikandarī (d. 709/1309) in Egypt, and Ibn ʿAbbād ar-Rundī (d. 793/1390) in Morocco. They wanted to prune the excrescences of

ritualism, and to place the pious seeker once more in direct confrontation with God. They preached simple obedience to God, the uselessness of works not commanded by God, the worthlessness of all 'means' of approaching God, the 'abandonment of human planning' *(isqāt at-tadbīr)*, and gratitude to God. These subtle interpreters of the 'docile religion' (as Islam is often called) may have succeeded in subduing the more frenetic side of Sūfism, but the Shādhiliyya as a whole were by no means a neo-classical order.

Ibn ʿAtāʾ Allāh's opponent, the dogmatic theologian Ibn Taymiyya (d. 729/1328), and his pupil Ibn Qayyim al-Jawziyya (d. 751/1350), also sought some means of purging religious practices. Ibn Taymiyya, the leader of a reformist movement which hoped to restore the whole of Islam to its original primary form, had to denounce Sūfism, since it had not existed at all in Muhammad's time. He did not condemn it wholesale, however, allowing that a large number of well-known Sūfiyya of the classical and post-classical eras occupied the same ground as the early religious. Others, such as al-Ghazālī and thinkers of the stamp of Ibn al-ʿArabī and al-Hallāj, he criticized very strongly, interpreting their views forcefully though not always fairly. He admitted the possibility of suprasensual knowledge, but required in every case that it should be tested against the criterion of the holy tradition. His own observation of thaumaturgical powers compelled him to concede them too, but he regarded them as the work of the devil, for Ibn Taymiyya was no more 'enlightened' than the leaders of the Protestant Reformation in Europe. The measure of all things for him was the authentic religious tradition of the first three generations of Islam, stripped of all later accretions. The state of ecstasy valued so highly by the Sūfiyya for its higher experiences was discounted as a valid criterion for deciding what was or was not acceptable and replaced by the word of the scriptures. Sūfī institutions such as listening to music, the cult of saints and shrines, even the tomb of the Prophet at Medina, were proscribed. The purifying tempest died away

conciliatorily in a commentary by Ibn Qayyim al-Jawziyya on a much-read book by al-Anṣārī (d. 482/1089) on the mystical stations.

Bahā' ad-Dīni Naqshband (d. 702/1380) in Bukhārā also believed that he was restoring the old order when he swept away the ritual of remembering God aloud, periods of retreat and listening to music, and recommended simple adherence to the word of the Prophet as the best path. But the shaykhs of his order by no means followed him in everything.

The mystical cult of Muhammad and the imams

While Christianity did everything it could to emphasize Jesus's proximity, indeed his identity, with God, Islam has always been at pains to separate Muhammad from God. Muhammad himself accused the Christians of deifying Jesus, while laying stress on his own ordinary humanity. The Christian prays to Jesus; the Muslim, by contradistinction, was not supposed to pray to Muhammad or to any other prophet. Ibn Taymiyya wanted to reinstate this principle.

The Prophet had been placed on a higher pedestal by various circumstances and considerations, which had already started to operate while Sūfism was in its classical period. Love of the Prophet, enjoined on the believer by long-established commandments, was part of the love of God, lightened the burden of fulfilling religious duties and increased the prospect of his intercession at the last judgment. It was believed, moreover, that his soul lived, though his body lay buried at Medina. The tendency was further motivated by the dispute, never settled among the Sūfiyya, over the superiority of prophethood or sainthood. The prevailing view was that sainthood, as the more general concept and the soil from which prophethood sprang, was subordinate to it. It followed that the higher saints were honoured, the higher the prophethood had to be raised, to preserve the differential. There was an increase, too, in the spread of a scholastic 'realism', which objectified abstractions, and which encouraged identification of the office with the holder, as of prophecy with the prophet, and since Muhammad was the acme of all prophets, he easily slipped into being the epitome of all prophecy and prophethood, the platonic idea of prophecy in the world scheme. According to the Qur'ān, God is 'the first and the last'. For a Muslim the Prophet was necessarily the door leading to God, one way or another, and so he was the 'second-first' and the 'second-last'. Cosmogonic theory thought up a 'Muhammad-reality', a 'Muhammad-light', which was in the position of the Johannine *logos* immediately next to God, and from which everything, even Paradise and the angels, was created.

These and similar ideas – the wish to cite the Prophet's authority for suprasensual perceptions in the same way as he was cited for religious prescriptions, and surely, too, man's love for the builder of the boat in which he sits – in the post-classical era all this was reflected in the yearning to make direct contact, not only with God, but also with the Prophet. The means of effecting such contact included repeating as often as possible the benediction to the Prophet *(as-salāt' alā n-nabī)* recommended in Sūra xxxiii, 56 and in the Sayings of Muhammad, which grew to become a ritual similar to the remembrance of God. The basic formula, 'God bless our Prophet and lend him salvation', could be varied and expanded in numerous ways, was often spoken in litanies, and repeated a specified or unspecified number of times with the purpose of focusing the attention as exclusively upon the Prophet as upon God in the other ritual. A famous collection of such formulas, much read and recited, was the *Dalā'il al-khayrāt* of the Berber al-Jazūlī (ix/15th century). In 897/1492, his younger contemporary, ash-Shūnī, inaugurated, in Cairo, a weekly session for collective recital of such prayer formulas, lasting through Thursday night till Friday, called *mahyā*, 'vigil'. At a later date, in Central Asia, al-Jazūlī's breviary was learned by heart in *dalā' il-khānas* or *salawāt-khānas* founded specially for the purpose. Another method of concentrating thoughts and feelings upon the Prophet was reading hymns in his praise. The *Burda* of al-Būsīrī (viii/13th century) was particularly popular among such hymns. But it was also possible to sense the Prophet close within oneself by pondering his holy words, and by making the pilgrimage to his sepulchre at Medina, or even by the mere poetic fiction of such pilgrimage. Some pilgrims to the shrine believed that they heard the Prophet reply to their greetings. But the mystic's ultimate longing was for union *(ijtimā')* with the Prophet, for the sight of the Prophet, not only in dreams, not only after death, but awake and in life.

This longing was not confined to North Africa, but it was particularly prevalent there. The charisma of Medina, both as the burial place of Muhammad and as the home of the Mālikī legal school, had always threatened to outshine Mecca, and the learned text in praise of the Prophet, *ash-Shifā'*, by the Qādī 'Iyād (d. 544/1149), was greatly venerated even by common people there. The cult of the Prophet in the west was further promoted by the 'Alids, who in turn were highly regarded on account of their descent from the Prophet. The mystical cult of Muhammad in the west begins as early as Ibn Mashīsh (d. c. 625/1228) and reaches a climax in 'Abd al-'Azīz ad-Dabbāgh (d. early xii/18th century). For the Sanūsiyya order founded in the xiii/19th century, union with the Prophet is the goal of the religious quest.

The feasts celebrating the Prophet's birthday *(mawālid,* sing. *mawlid)* found their ritual form in northern Mesopotamia around the year 1200, and were soon adopted all over Islam, in the farthest west by the VII/13th century, and were part and parcel of the growing cult.

Doctrinal authority was given to 'Alī and some of his descendants by the Twelver Shī'a, who set them up as a kind of pontifical caliphs and called them imams. Sūfī textbooks of the IV/10th and V/11th centuries already represented them as great teachers. For the Twelver Shī'a the imams are actually exponents of the 'inner science' (that is, of the inner side of revelation and of man) and are called 'friends of God' or 'saints', but they form an exclusive clique among the descendants of the Prophet, beginning with his son-in-law 'Alī. Here, for many, prophethood and sainthood (identical with imamate) are the exterior and interior functions of one and the same office of leader, prophethood being the proclamation of the revelation – point; sainthood being knowledge of the meaning of the revelation – continuum. Interpolated in the scheme in this way, the degree of sainthood can be seen as widening further the gateway leading to God, but also as assuming guardianship of man. There was, and there still is, a Shī'ī Sūfism which, much like the Sunnī, simply takes the imams, along with the great shaykhs, as models. But the abundance of grace with which Shī'ī doctrine cloaks the imams was bound to attract the Shī'ī Sūfiyya from the start. The extremist Rajab al-Bursī (VIII/14th to IX/15th centuries) goes so far as to claim that love of the family of the Prophet exonerates all sin. And thus there developed, as a counterpart to the Sunnī cult of Muhammad, a Shī'ī mystical cult of the imams, in addition to that of Muhammad. The objectives of this sort of mysticism are to draw close to 'Alī and the other imams, to enlist their aid and induce them to reveal themselves. During the month of fasting men claimed to receive directions from 'Alī. Even Sunnī Kurds were said to fall into a state of religious emotion as a result of hearing hymns to the imams. The proposition is sometimes made that 'Alī forms a single entity with the Prophet and God. The twelfth imam, however, is believed by the Shī'a not to have died but to have been carried away and to be hidden somewhere on earth; they expect him to return in

his earthly body, in which form they also pray to him to emerge from his invisibility as soon as possible and inaugurate the promised era of justice, a wish that has nothing directly to do with mysticism. The head of the Gunābādī order in Iran claims to act in the name of this hidden imam and even accepts pledges of allegiance on his behalf.

In these cults there is also the idea of a telescoping process of surrender of being *(fanā')*. The mystic loses his being in his shaykh, in an imam, especially 'Alī, in Muhammad, in God.

Membership of more than one order

During the classical period it was still fairly common for aspirant Sūfiyya to change their teachers freely and often to study under quite a large number. In the period of transition leading to the post-classical era, in the IV/10th century, it gradually became customary for a pupil to receive the whole of his basic instruction from a single teacher, and only then perhaps move on to other shaykhs to perfect his learning. The woollen habit soon ceased to be merely a symbol of adherence to Sūfism, as it still was at the beginning of the post-classical era, but became the sign of a pupil's acceptance by a particular shaykh and later, too, of membership of a particular order. Habits associated with the separate orders, differing in shape, colour and other details, appeared as the orders themselves came into existence, from the VII/13th century onwards. Since the recipients placed a value on having as wide an experience and possessing as many different qualifications as possible, while the donors liked to have as large a number of pupils to boast of as possible, one person often accumulated habits and memberships of orders in great quantities. A Persian Sūfī who died in the VII/13th century acquired 124 patched frocks, 113 of which were still among his belongings at his death. The x/16th-century Egyptian Sūfī ash-Sha'rānī was a member of 26 orders. That this was possible illustrates the limitations there must sometimes have been on the authority of a shaykh or head of an order, for nobody could show obedience to so many fathers.

The signs that Sūfism had become a regular theological discipline, which had to be studied if one was to be recognized as a fully-fledged theologian, start to accumulate in the VII/13th century and have become legion by the IX/15th. Once those qualifications had been earned, the student then specialized according to his inclination, devoting himself to Sūfism or to something else, and was recorded in the annals as a Sūfī, a grammarian, a doctor of law or whatever was appropriate. Sūfī orders had many associate members, so to speak, who belonged primarily to some other branch of the religious life, or indeed pursued secular occupations.

Governments attempted to solve the problems posed by the numerous and bewildering varieties of Sūfism by coordinating them. In large cities like Baghdad, Damascus and Cairo, over-shaykhs were appointed *(shaykh ash-shuyūkh)*, whose nominal function was to oversee and represent all the others. The office was usually associated with headship of a particular convent. If circumstances permitted, the over-shaykh sometimes managed to acquire a degree of hereditary local power. But he did not necessarily belong to the professional class of the

This lion (symbolizing the strength of 'Alī) is made up calligraphically from words meaning 'In the name of the lion of God, the face of God, the victorious 'Alī.' It comes from a XIII/19th-century dervish wall-hanging from Turkey. (6)

Sūfiyya. Although in theory this office created a means whereby the orders were placed under the control of the temporal government, the undesirable influence of distant mother-houses was weakened, and the daughter-houses alienated from them, in practice its authority stretched no further than the arm of the state itself, and was liable to be ignored by the more powerful orders. In Egypt the Grand Shaykh set over all the Sūfiyya was, from the beginning of the XIII/19th century, always a descendant of the Caliph Abū Bakr, and known for that reason as *ash-Shaykh al-Bakrī*.

Sūfī pluralism was never endangered by the over-shaykhs. Certain orders posed far more of a threat, in that each claimed to have the best shaykhs and to offer the best methods of attaining salvation in this life and the next. It was in part retrospective propaganda by the orders, exaggerating patrons' or founders' estimates of themselves, or bestowing exaggerated honorific titles on them. 'Abd al-Qādir al-Jīlānī (d. 562/1166), for instance, the patron of the Qādiriyya, is supposed to have claimed to place his foot on the necks of all the saints. And amongst the Rifā'iyya, Ahmad ar-Rifā'ī (d. 578/1182) was called the Seal of the Saints and the possessor of all the attributes of Muhammad. Anyone entering that order, they maintained, must renounce entry to any others, since this would inevitably cause him to stray from the true path of the Prophet. But there were some founders of orders who made inflated claims on their own behalves. The Moroccan Ahmad at-Tijānī (d. 1230/1815), for instance, also claimed to be the Seal of the Saints, appointed by Muhammad himself, and forbade his followers to sustain any previous ties with other orders, or to join another order at any subsequent date.

Not everyone was able to resist the temptation to take the last small step and openly declare himself to be the promised restorer of all good, the *Mahdī*. Everywhere, from sub-Saharan Africa to India and Central Asia, notwithstanding all the differences of epoch and race, Sūfism produced men who succumbed to this delusion and believed themselves chosen to undertake the revolution foretold by the religion of Islam itself. The list is a long one and we shall mention only three here: in the IX/15th century, in the region of Afghanistan and Persia, Muhammad-i Nūrbakhsh, a Kubrawī and an 'Alid, rose up as Mahdī, on the authority of pseudo-Shī'ī ideas originally conceived by the Kubrawī 'Alā' ad-Dawla as-Simnānī (d. 737/1336). The reigning Tīmūrid sovereign rendered him quite ineffectual by bloodless means. Around 1500, in India, another 'Alid, Muhammad of Jaunpur, made the same claim, and to this day there are followers of his who believe that the promised Mahdī has already visited the earth, and await only the resurrection. In the eastern Sudan in the late XIII/19th century the Sammānī and Khalwatī shaykh Muhammad Ahmad proclaimed the end of time, made war on the Egyptians and the British, and won an empire for himself, which was finally lost only by his successor in 1316/1898.

Sūfism and the state

The idea of mysticism creates expectations of a religious outlook remote from wordly concerns, unrelated to the passage of time and reaching out towards the permanencies of eternity. One thinks of the mystic as aloof from temporary phenomena. The call to forsake the world and mankind had rung out often enough in the history of Sūfism and found hearers in plenty, but in the year 370/980 hermits residing in the district of Nīshābūr surprised visitors by expressing curiosity about the latest events. Other Sūfiyya were becoming famous for their readiness to help the poor and suffering among their fellow men. An early fundamental principle warned against any kind of contact with temporal potentates, yet Sūfiyya were frequently found close to princes and men of high position, addressing themselves directly to their consciences, or interceding with them on behalf of the oppressed.

Many Sūfiyya voluntarily fulfilled the community duty to wage the holy war, though they regarded the struggle against the self as the 'greater holy war'. Perhaps they were more inclined to missionary work, converting non-believers and the worldly-minded within the Islamic world itself, following in the train of the advancing armies as spiritual advisers to the soldiery and as colonizers of the new territories, in some cases settling in the areas beyond the frontier. They were active as missionaries in India in the wake of the Ghūrids in the VI/12th century and under their successors, and in the Balkans following up the Ottomans from the VIII/14th century onwards. The Bektāshī order, which deserves much of the credit for the conversion of Albania to Islam, were the chaplains of the Janissaries.

There is some evidence of Sūfiyya playing an active part in politico-military affairs even in the first half of the III/9th century, in Mosul, Alexandria and Cairo, allegedly acting only in the interests of law and justice. Round about 236/850 a large number of 'Sūfiyya' are supposed to have been 'mobilized' in the desert around Qayrawān, to assist the judge Sahnūn in proceedings against an Aghlabid officer. In the year 251/865 Zaydī Sūfiyya took part in a Shī'ī insurrection in Kūfa. During the transference of power from the Almoravids to the Almohads in the VI/12th century the Sūfī Ibn Qasī seized lands in Portugal for himself by force of arms, as did the convent of ad-Dilā' in Morocco in the XI/17th century, during the transition from the Sa'dī line to the Filālī line of the Shurafā'. In the VII/13th century, when the decline of the 'Abbāsids in Baghdad was well advanced, a scion of the Umayyads, a shaykh of the 'Adawiyya order in Syria, dreamed of reviving long-dead glories. In the IX/15th century descendants of the shaykh Safī ad-Dīn al-Ardabīlī (d. 735/1334) established a regime in western Iran, declared a holy war on behalf of the Shī'a in 906/1500 and founded the Safavid dynasty. Its first king, Ismā'īl 'the Sūfī', transferred the leadership of the order to a Grand Deputy. Members of the order of the Ni'matullāhiyya allied themselves by marriage with the Safavids and held office as provincial governors. The Naqshbandiyya order gained strength in large areas of India, Afghanistan and Central Asia in the IX/15th century, making themselves indispensable to some of the Tīmūrid rulers, and, at a later date, threw their weight on the side of those who were resisting attempts to blur the distinctions between Islam and Hinduism. Two lines of descendants of a Naqshbandī shaykh disputed the temporal rule in a part of Central Asia in a feud lasting over three centuries, and before and after 1800 Bukhārā was ruled by amīrs who were also dervishes.

The Sūfiyya reacted to colonialist powers in a variety of ways. In North Africa the Ottomans met resistance from the Darqāwa and the Tijāniyya. The French, on the other hand, had a certain measure of support from the Tijāniyya of Algeria, but were opposed by the Tijāniyya of Morocco and Tunisia. The Tijānī Shaykh al-Hājj ʿUmar established his own state on the upper reaches of the Senegal and the Niger from 1268/1852 to 1280/1864, in defiance of the French and of other orders, but after his death it split into three and finally came under French rule after all. In the present century the industrious 'Mourids' of Amadu Bamba, if anything, constituted a stabilizing factor under the French in Senegal and then also played a formative role in the construction of the republic after independence. Muhammad as-Sanūsī (d. 1276/1859) and the order he founded, on the other hand, were in the forefront of resistance to colonialism. His influence in Libya grew so great that almost unperceived he ruled in place of the Ottomans, like a kind of marcher earl. His successors took arms against the French in the south and then, after the Ottomans had abandoned Libya to its own devices in 1330/1912, had to cope with Italian encroachment in the north. After the Italian annexation came to an end in 1951, a descendant of the order's founder acceded to the throne. On the Arabian peninsula, for a short time up to 1342/1923, the province of ʿAsīr was ruled by a descendant of as-Sanūsī's teacher, Ahmad ibn Idrīs.

It is impossible to categorize the Sūfiyya either as customarily opposed to secular powers, or as cooperating with them. They were sometimes the one and at other times the other. It is equally impossible to describe secular rulers as generally hostile or as generally well-disposed towards the Sūfiyya. There were some princes who believed that they could not hold sway without the blessing of a dervish or other holy man. Persecution of Sūfiyya generally originated in envy and intrigue, sometimes, too, in genuine concern for the 'true faith' on the part of other Sūfiyya factions or of theologians. In recent centuries Sufism has been the object of violent attacks from the Shīʿī *mujtahids* in Persia, the Wahhābīs in Arabia and, in the present century, the reformist movement in Turkey. Another threat is the modern 'enlightenment', which seems to want to turn the Oriental tendency towards mystical fervour inside out, making it extrovert and diverting it towards materialism. But forces are once again at work which are reluctant to see the old values abandoned without a struggle.

Marginal groups

In the course of its history Sufism developed or adopted a number of doctrines which were foreign to primitive Islam. Discriminating Sūfiyya distinguished between good and bad among these 'innovations'. As regards details, differences developed among both Sūfiyya and the orders, but on the whole the classical model continued to provide standards even for those who had no particular wish to revert to that stage of development. There are groups, however, whose relationship to the classical standard is so remote that they qualify as purely marginal. They came within the compass of Sufism's influence, but were never fully assimilated to it. Their origins are obscure for the most part. Their adherence to Islam is only recognizable when they themselves claim it.

The Moroccan community of the Hamādisha (sing. Hamdūshī) remain on the fringe both of Islam and of Sufism. In rituals resembling the Egyptian *zār* or the Tunisian *būrī*. they induce trances or fits in themselves and in the sick in order to clear a path for certain spirits to pass through the soul and depart from it, that is, to release psychic blockages. They are a community of exorcists linked to Islam by the superstructure of God, Muhammad and so on, and to Sufism by their ritual use of music and 'states'. Negro brotherhoods of this kind in North Africa have placed themselves under the patronage of Bilāl, the Prophet's black muezzin. The Haddāwa (sing. Haddāwī) in northern Morocco practise the cult of the saint Ibn Mashīsh (d. 622/1225), love cats because *mashīsh* is the Berber word for cat, wander from place to place as ragged mendicants, smoke and consume narcotics and venerate a gigantic pipe reputed to have belonged to their patron saint. They subscribe to a religious nomadism, in association with an unshakable trust in God (*tawakkul*), for which the Qur'ān can be cited as authority.

The itinerant Qalandar dervishes have been known since the v/11th century. The meaning and origin of their name (*qalandariyya*, sing. *qalandarī*) are unknown. They shared with the even earlier Malāmatiyya, who can be traced back to the III/9th century, the characteristic of making no public show of piety, rather, on the contrary, displaying their bad sides. But while the Malāmatiyya did this in order to combat vanity (thereby perversely cultivating it), the Qalandars did it because they had no interest whatever in works of piety but only in being 'joyful in God' and probably also in demonstrating against conventional standards of good behaviour. In the case of some of the Malāmatiyya, however, the apparent indifference to society's norms of behaviour concealed, or rather revealed, genuine indifference, even contempt. It is thus possible to speak of two kinds of Malāmatiyya, the more disreputable of the two being virtually identical with the Qalandars. At first both kinds were represented by schools but not by orders, but just as Ömer Dede took Malāmatiyya as the name of an order in Anatolia in the IX/15th century, so, shortly after 1200, that is, at the time when the first orders were springing up among the Sūfiyya, a group of Persians in Syria produced a new kind of Qalandariyya, an order whose members caused renewed offence by shaving all the hair off their heads, including their eyebrows. This practice falls in with a custom observed by pilgrims to the sanctuary of the *dea Syria* in Hierapolis in antiquity, but was also a punishment occasionally meted out in Arab countries to delinquents, in order to expose them to public shame. The order of sackcloth Qalandariyya (*juwālaqiyya*), so named after their rough clothing, which was founded then, spread over the area from Egypt to Anatolia, and the practice of shaving the beard and eyebrows spread with it to Iran and farther east. It was forbidden by one of the Mamlūks in the VIII/14th century, and again by one of the Tīmūrid sovereigns late in the IX/15th. There was already an offshoot in what is now Pakistan, in the VII/13th century, called Jalāliyān after its founder, of which the Persian Khāksār order is probably another branch. The Khāksār retain the tonsure only as part of the rite of initiation. The Qalandars since the VII/13th century were alleged to take opium and various forms of hemp and to have little concern with Islamic forms of worship. Some considered women taboo. Just as the very earliest Sūfiyya had flouted the forms of piety current in Islam in their day, so there now arose against them in the persons of the Qalandars (and the Malāmatiyya) adversaries in whose eyes they themselves now appeared as the miserable slaves of sorry delusions.

Contact between Sūfism and Kurdish traditions produced two curious religious hybrids. The Ahl-i Haqq ('Men of God' or 'Truth-worshippers'), also known as the ʿAlī-Allāhī ('Worshippers of ʿAlī'), in the mountains of western Iran, formally acknowledged the Twelver Shīʿa as 'law' *(sharīʿat)*, but superimposed on it a doctrinal system of Sūfī or semi-Sūfī character. This combined cultivation of the inner way *(tarīqat)* and higher understanding with the worship of spiritual beings and the belief that these beings or the great seers are mirrors or manifestations of God. In the other case, that of the Yazīdiyya ('followers of Yazīd'), found principally in the mountains of northern Mesopotamia, what was originally an extreme anti-Shīʿī Umayyad movement was allied to remnants of the structure and the views of a Sūfī order, the ʿAdawiyya. The worship of local saints, placed on an equal footing with angels, is common to both cases. The Caliph ʿAlī is numbered with the angels by the Ahl-i Haqq, and the Caliph Yazīd (61-4/680-83) by the Yazīdiyya. Both sects are monotheistic, but the Sūfī elements are so closely interwoven with the concerns and popular conceptions of the community, that the basic Islamic pattern is barely, if at all, visible. The Ahl-i Haqq lay stress on Shīʿism and show it in their veneration of ʿAlī. The Yazīdiyya, on the other hand, do not regard themselves as Muslims. Since they worship the Peacock Angel, a being who corresponds to the Islamic (and Judaeo-Christian) devil, they are reviled as devil-worshippers; but they have excised the word 'Satan' from their vocabulary. This may be an instance of an indigenous cult cross-fertilized by a Sūfī concept, for some Sūfiyya held the devil in very special esteem as the prototype of monotheism, since according to the Qurʾān he defied God's command to fall down before Adam.

Sūfism and literature

A movement like Sūfism, aspiring to a life of dedication to God and involving itself in social works on a broad front, should not necessarily be judged by the literature it produces.

Narratives known as *hikāyāt* (sing. *hikāya*), comprising both sayings and events from the lives of Sūfiyya and earlier holy men, were already in circulation among the Sūfiyya in the classical period. They began to be written down in the III/9th century, and served as *exempla* in Sūfī teaching. They covered the ground of the 'inner science', between the Qurʾān and the prophetic *dicta* on the one hand, and religious experience and meditation on the other. They provided a third literary tradition in Sūfism, alongside the Qurʾān and the Sayings of the Prophet, but were only advisory or instructional in character, but not mandatory. Abū Turāb an-Nakhshabī (d. 245/859) and al-Junayd (d. 298/910) referred to this corpus as 'God's auxiliaries', strengthening the heart. In the IV/10th century there were specialists who knew hundreds and

This XI/17th-century carpet from Iran is full of objects belonging to the Shīʿī dervish – the cap with twelve panels, the tiger-skin, the begging bowls hanging from hooks at the top, the battle-axes, the knotty stick and the multicoloured cloth bags suspended from the branches of the trees. (7)

thousands of the tales by heart. Writing them down created a direct link with the early masters for posterity, and the question was even raised as to whether, and to what extent, the book might replace the personal teacher. Many students began with the book. But in general personal tuition was considered indispensable. It was in accordance with this rule that the shaykh Awhad al-Dīn-i Kirmānī (d. 636/1238) once had a perfectly good well filled in for no other reason than that the builder had not learnt his skill from a master; the story is quite possibly a fiction, intended to point the moral. The natural interaction of life and literature often makes it hard to distinguish between biography and fiction in the tales. There may well be many instances where what was originally poetic invention was enacted in life and vice versa.

The III/9th century also saw the start of a series of Sūfī treatises on particular subjects and general aspects of mysticism. The majority of the early ones have been lost, but the literary testament of the following centuries has been better preserved. Until the IV/10th century everything was in Arabic. Later Persian, various Turkish languages and other tongues of Asia and Africa came into use too. Some works were 'snatched' from their authors, that is, taken down by pupils from the teachers' oral discourses. The 'ecstatic confessions', comprising accounts of occult experiences, sometimes in the form of letters exchanged between teachers and pupils, are closer to real life than the majority of Sūfī texts. The growing interest in visionary experiences in the post-classical period tempted many beginners to describe even their first experiences in writing, some going so far as to want to write books on the subject, a proceeding they were cautioned against. But Simnānī's dervishes all had a note-book *(majmūʿa)*, in which they took down the instructions and even the discourses of their shaykh. It is to the diligence and authorial ambition of many pupils that we owe not only the numerous biographies and collections of *dicta* of their teachers, but also the hagiographic distortions of historical events.

The Sūfiyya were insatiable in their use of verse: in their schools, in personal conversation, and in their musical rituals. The verses were often not of their own composition, indeed they were not necessarily even mystical in content. They were interpreted mystically, or in whatever other way was appropriate to the occasion. Two of the most famous and most popular mystical poets in the Arabic language were Ibn al-Fārid (d. 633/1235), an Egyptian of Syrian descent, and the Andalusian Abū l-Hasan ash-Shushtarī (d. 668/1269). In his long odes Ibn al-Fārid combined Bedouin themes with mystical love, especially for the Prophet. Ash-Shushtarī favoured strophic forms and often coloured his language with dialect.

The Sūfī didactic poem made its bow in Persian in the vi/12th century, represented principally in the works of Sanāʾī (vi/12th century), ʿAttār (vi/12th to vii/13th centuries) and Mawlānā (d. 672/1273). The *exempla* appear in new splendour in these expansive poems written in an epic style: they embody the poets' abstract ideas in specific stories. Some Sūfiyya became more widely known outside Sūfism as a consequence of these poems and imitations of them.

However, it must be repeated that mysticism and literature are two quite separate pursuits. Ibn al-ʿArabī wrote hundreds of pieces, Ibn Mashīsh almost nothing. Mawlānā wrote thousands of verses, Shams-i Tabrīzī none. Many renounced poetry when they were converted to Sūfism; others left behind them odes which have the standing of holy writ for their followers.

Influence and impact

There are two misconceptions that the modern Western observer must avoid: he must not expect Sūfism to have made any contribution to research in the fields of literary and philological history or the natural sciences. It may be regrettable that al-Bīrūnī and Ibn Khaldūn had no successors, but Sūfism is not to blame. In its inflated form, Sūfism may have had a paralyzing effect on the intellectual development of Central Asia from the x/16th century onwards: the fault lies in the union of Sūfism with the political authorities in a restricted sector and in the lack of challenge. Secondly the Western observer should not necessarily judge an alien culture by whether that culture had or has anything to give to his own. Usually it is precisely the most valuable things that cannot be transplanted, and often those who might have learned something lacked the capacity to learn it. The piety of the early Islamic religious ascetics was influenced in some instances by Christianity; in the late classical and in the post-classical periods Sūfism adopted some concepts from Neo-platonist philosophy, and later assimilated some Indian ideas. But the only influences worthy of the name that Sūfism exercised outside the borders of Islam all proceeded eastwards, to the sphere of Indian culture, where it also assisted certain attempts to reconcile different religions to each other on a higher plane. Sūfism had no perceptible influence on Christian mysticism in the Middle Ages, and none in modern times until very recently. Only in the present century has Sūfism been lauded in the West, at various intellectual and spiritual levels, by Europeans and Orientals, as the allegedly deepest wisdom, the kernel of all religions.

Sūfī mysticism existed side by side with orthodox Islam, providing a direct means of contact with God through solitude, prayer and other techniques. The dance was usually an expression of emotion and ecstasy produced by verse or music. Physical movement served as a help towards psychic illumination. The illustration opposite is from a Persian Tīmūrid manuscript and is dated 896/1490. Like all Islamic art, it is a combination of conceptual truth to nature and a high degree of stylization. The setting is made picturesquely pastoral, but would actually have been inside a *takiyya (tekke)*, a building devoted to dervish ritual. Of the four men dancing, only one is shown with his hands in the 'correct' position. Others in the foreground appear to have succumbed to vertigo. To the right are the musicians. Behind the dancers flows a stream, once painted silver, now tarnished. But the circular composition of the whole picture and the undulating horizon convey something of the ecstatic whirling which was to withdraw the dancers from themselves. (1)

Preaching (left) was a Sūfī usage, and the visit of a famous teacher was an eagerly awaited event. Here, in a mid-x/16th-century Persian manuscript, the Sūfī sits at the top of a *minbar*. Older men sit nearest to him, younger at the side. Women and children occupy a gallery on their own. (2)

Wandering Sūfīs were a familiar sight throughout Islamic history, and stories about them run through the literature. This Persian drawing of the xi/17th century shows two of them deep in meditation. The Sūfī life attracted many young adherents (above), setting out with the few possessions necessary for a life of contemplation – a book of prayers, a pouch and begging bowl. (3, 4)

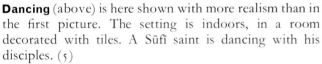

Dancing (above) is here shown with more realism than in the first picture. The setting is indoors, in a room decorated with tiles. A Sūfī saint is dancing with his disciples. (5)

Travelling (far right): the Sūfī poet Fakhr ad-Dīn 'Irāqī is preceded by a troop of *Qalandariyya*. Some wear animal skins. The leader carries a book, others a banner, bowl, bag, candlestick and staves. (6)

Begging: many Sūfīs were mendicants. The impressive image of the *kalandar* (far right) is Tīmūrid, late ıx/15th century. He wears an animal skin and in front of him lie his stick and bowl. The bowl illustrated (below), made from a coconut, bears a Qur'ānic inscription. (7, 8)

131

The techniques of mysticism were made the subject of regulations in Sūfī writings – the way the music was to be played and how the garments, thrown off during dancing, were to be disposed. This Mughul miniature of the XI/17th century shows a scene of dervish ritual in India. The dancers, who include members of several races, line up on the right. On the left are onlookers; among them – on the extreme left – two Europeans. The buildings in the background show Italian influence. (9)

To the tombs of great poets pilgrims came as to the shrines of saints. Sa'dī, one of the most profound of Persian poets, lived in the VII/13th century in Shīrāz. Although he was not a Sūfī, he knew Sūfism well and was deeply influenced by it. In his main works, *Gulistān* and *Bustān*, he used many stories to expound Sūfī feeling and Sūfī wisdom. This miniature (right) of his tomb near Shīrāz is largely imaginary. The tomb itself is immediately behind the main door. On the roof is a mixed party of women and children. In the foreground dervishes dance to the usual musical accompaniment. (11)

The story of Rūmī, the founder of the Mawlawī order of dervishes, and one of the most powerful Islamic poets, goes back to the early VII/13th century, when his father, Bahā' Walad, emigrated from Balkh. After visiting Mecca he reached Asia Minor and settled in Konya. This detail from a Turkish manuscript of the late X/16th century illustrates a miraculous story in which a cow bowed down to the ground at the sight of him. (10)

Medina was the centre of the cult of Muhammad whose mystical goal was union with the Prophet. This Mamlūk tile shows a schematic view of the city in the x/16th century. (13)

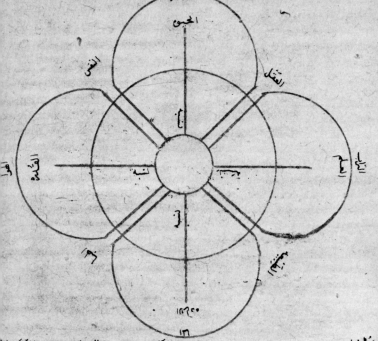

All phenomena, said Ibn al-'Arabī (d. 638/1240), are nothing but manifestations of Being, which is one with God. Mysticism occupies the ground between abstract knowledge and experiential perception of ultimate unity. A diagram from a x/16th-century manuscript of Ibn al-'Arabī tries to show the many emanating from the One. (12)

'There is no God but God, and Muhammad is the Messenger of God.' The conventional Muslim credo is here made into a quadrangular pattern inscribed in stylized script on a IX/15th-century mosque in Cairo. One of the methods of attaining a mystical state was by the endless repetition of such phrases. (14)

The soul lives in the Divine like a fish in water. Such is the image used on this plate from Iran, dated 607/1210. The young man has abandoned his earthly desires (represented by the riderless horse), and in a state of mystical exaltation contemplates his own soul in the form of the small female figure below. (15)

The Travellers and the Elephant
(right) is a story from Rūmī's
great didactic poem, the *Mathnawī*. A party of travellers, ignoring the advice of a wise man,
kill and eat a calf elephant. The
mother attacks them, sparing
only those whom she can tell by
smelling have not eaten her offspring. Allegorical meaning:
the young elephant was
righteousness, the travellers'
greed sin, the mother elephant
Judgment. (16)

When Sa'dī (left) was on his way
to Mecca with pilgrims, they met a
black boy whose singing charmed
everyone except one devotee who
despised dervishes. But even the
man's horse was affected and began
to prance, throwing his rider.
Sa'dī said: 'those strains made an
impression on an animal. Could
they not move *you*?' (17)

The Conference of the Birds (right)
is an allegorical poem by Farīd
ad-Dīn 'Attār (d. 618/1221). The
birds go on a pilgrimage to the
court of Sīmurgh, their king.
Thirty of them endure the fatigues
of the travel and finally they discover that they are Sīmurgh themselves (*sī murgh* means thirty birds).
The poem began to be illustrated
in the IX/15th century: this is one
of the earliest. (18)

The Shī'ī Twelve Imams are invoked in the twelve segments of the domed ceiling of a Sūfī shrine. It is part of a complex of buildings round the tomb of the Sūfī poet Shāh Ni'matullāh Walī (d. 835/1431; the shrine built from the ix/15th century onwards) at Māhān, near Kirmān. (19)

The dervish dance fascinated European observers, who left many illustrations of it. This painting shows a *tekke* at Istanbul in the xii/18th century. (20)

The tombs remain places of pilgrimage. Above left: tomb of Sūfī al-Ansārī at Gāzurgāh, near Herat (d. 482/1089, tomb late IX/15th century), which became the burial place of many members of the Tīmūrid dynasty. Above right: the tomb of Rūmī at Konya, within the dervish convent that he founded. Below left: mausoleum of Baba Rukn ad-Dīn (d. 769/1367) at Isfahan, with later burials clustering round it. (21–23)

Dervish convents have qualities of beauty and seclusion comparable to many in the West. At Māhān, in Persia, an outstanding group of buildings dating from the ix/15th century onwards houses the community founded by Shāh Ni'matullāh Walī, a Sūfī poet and mystic who settled there in 809/1406. His tomb is under the blue dome, built by Shāh 'Abbās in 1010/1601. Māhān is a green oasis surrounded by desert and mountains, an image of the paradise garden. Four open courts flank the shrine. The 'spiral' roof illustrated earlier covers one of the rooms. Left: part of the ceramic decoration of the tomb of al-Ansārī at Gāzurgāh, near Herat. (24, 25)

Chapter Five

JEWELLERS WITH WORDS

Charles Pellat

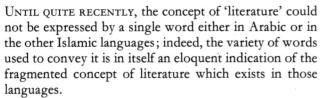

A scribe at work: illustration from an VII/13th-century manuscript of al-Harīrī's Maqāmāt. *(1)*

UNTIL QUITE RECENTLY, the concept of 'literature' could not be expressed by a single word either in Arabic or in the other Islamic languages; indeed, the variety of words used to convey it is in itself an eloquent indication of the fragmented concept of literature which exists in those languages.

However, the Arabs recognized at an early stage that some exceptional beings among them possessed the gift of arranging their words in an expressive and artistic manner, and raising the act of communication above the level of ordinary speech. Among them was the *shāʿir*, the poet, who in the act of poetic expression assembled words like rare jewels and fitted them together *(nazm)* with as much art as a jeweller mounting a necklace. Another type was the *khatīb*, the orator or spokesman of the tribe, who chose his words carefully but, so to speak, scattered them *(nathr)* without respecting the order imposed on the poet by his metre. A third type was the *kāhin*, the sooth-sayer, who expressed himself in rhyming, oracular language, and was distinguished from the orator by the deliberately enigmatic nature of his utterances. Thus the whole to which we now give the name 'literature' was referred to in the Middle Ages by the expression *manzūm wa-manthūr*, 'ordered and scattered', or as we would say now, 'verse and prose'. The complete man of letters was called *shāʿir khatīb*, even though by this time the written word was more dominant than the spoken, and artistic prose was no longer oratorical but truly literary in form.

In the last century the Turks found themselves obliged to find a specific term to designate literature as it is conceived in the West, and they had recourse to an Arab word, *adab*, to which they neatly added a suffix, also Arabic, and used to form abstract nouns. The result, which is written *edebiyat* in Turkish, perfectly expresses the concept of literature, applying to *belles lettres* in general and also to 'letters' as in the expression 'faculty of letters'.

The original meaning of *adab* is a 'way of acting, of behaving' according to a traditional norm, and even today it has retained the sense of 'good education, politeness, good manners' which it has always implied, since education tends to inculcate a fixed form of conduct. Once these rules of conduct are put down in writing, they inevitably produce a literary genre. If these rules are no longer applied to a moral attitude but to a stereotyped,

professional mode of behaviour, they can give rise to another literary genre which is different from the first. And finally, a compilation of such rules addressed to the educated public easily assumes the appearance of a manual of general culture. This is what happened with the Arabs, and as a result we find the word *adab* used to refer to literature in general, even though good intentions do not necessarily produce good literature, and morality, professional behaviour and general culture have little relation to contemporary literary productions.

From the moment that the Arabs started to write in prose, they certainly attached a major importance to religious knowledge and produced works which historians of Arabic literature are compelled to take into account, even though they are for the most part devoid of any real literary value. From the II/8th century, however, they were able to write books designed essentially to instruct without boring the reader, to educate while providing entertainment. The oldest of these writings is a translation of a Pahlavī version of the *Panchatantra*, known in Arabic as *Kalīla wa-Dimna*. The book consists of a collection of animal fables designed chiefly for the moral education of its readers. The translator, Ibn al-Muqaffaʿ (executed *c.* 139/757), was also the author of a number of treatises on ethics which still appear in school syllabuses today, and of other translations from Pahlavī which introduced a substantial part of the Iranian literary tradition into Arabian Islamic culture. Even, and perhaps especially, when they recount the lives and exalt the virtues of the kings of the past, these works have an undoubted moralizing value, and it is this secular *adab* which may be considered as the first appearance of Arabic prose literature.

A contemporary of Ibn al-Muqaffaʿ, ʿAbd al-Hamīd al-Kātib (d. 132/750), founded the epistolary tradition which soon became a speciality of those authors who, like him, were scribes of the official administration. His works include a sort of *Fürstenspiegel* dedicated to an Umayyad prince, and in particular an epistle addressed to secretaries which is probably the first trace of that 'professional' *adab* which was to have such a successful career.

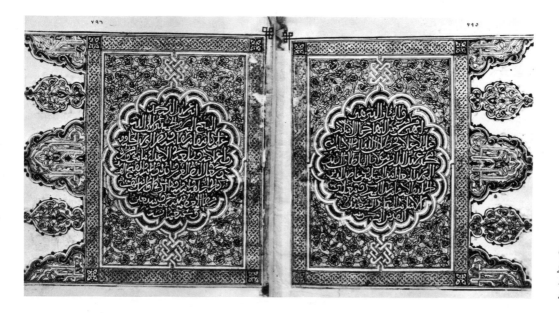

Above literature: the Qur'ān

It may seem a little bold to state that the writings of Ibn al-Muqaffaʿ and ʿAbd al-Hamīd are in fact the first manifestations of Arab literature, especially to the reader who knows that the Arabs started to compose verses well before Islam and that the first great literary monument in prose is the Qur'ān. But for the Arabs, the Holy Book of the Muslims, being a divine revelation, can hardly be placed on the same footing as human productions. The Qur'ān could never serve as a model to men of letters since the slightest attempt at imitation was regarded as sacrilege, and critics and commentators on the Arabic language considered it inimitable in both form and content. In studying the Islamic literary tradition, one can therefore only take the Qur'ān into account insofar as it had an inner influence on literary thought and style.

One of the characteristic features of early Islamic prose literature was indeed the frequent echoes of the Qur'ān which inevitably appeared in the works of writers who had learned to read from it and committed many of its texts to memory. At the same time the Holy Book contains numerous moral principles which writers after Ibn al-Muqaffaʿ incorporated in ethical treatises. These works had a strong Islamic flavour, with quotations from the Qur'ān and accompanying commentaries. Indeed, such quotations were frequently found in works which had little to do with religious or moral considerations.

The necessity of explaining the obscure passages of the Qur'ān and the prophetic traditions gave rise to the activities of the philologists, who undertook extensive researches among the Arab tribes. Their aim was firstly to collect the elements of vocabulary which would enable them to restore Arabic – itself considered as a language of divine origin – to its pristine form. Secondly they collected narrative verses, proverbs, historical or legendary traditions which must have originally served to explain the Qur'ānic texts, but which by force of circumstance became the foundation of the Arabic 'humanities' or 'classics' when they were pressed into service against the opponents, if not of Islam, at least of the supremacy of Arab culture. The documentation thus collected, particularly from the II/8th century onwards, was initially presented piecemeal, most often orally by researchers who

also did what would now be called their own field-work. From this their disciples built up a vast body of material by putting into order the data supplied by their masters and presenting monographs devoted to, for instance, the human body, the horse or camel, or to such and such a tribe or person. Now all that was lacking were artists who were capable of making use of the information which they had at their disposal and giving it a literary treatment. Artists were few and far between, but they were able to give *adab* a more eclectic character by mixing together the original Arab traditions, the by then widespread importations of Indo-Iranian culture, and elements of Hellenism made available through translations of Plato and Aristotle. The latter provided a leavening for the existing material and became to some extent authorities, encouraging writers not merely to make a choice of sources, but to reflect upon the teachings of the past.

Thus the animal fables, the ethical treatises composed of quotations borrowed from various sources which had now become available, were joined after ʿAbd al-Hamīd al-Kātib by a type of manual still conceived on the same principle, but containing practical advice directed at the members of various social categories: viziers, schoolteachers, scholars, judges, officials of the administration. However, the majority of these people needed not only adequate professional training but also a modicum of general culture in order to be able to maintain their position honourably in a society where fine language and elegant speech were among the most highly appreciated qualities a man could have. This resulted in the appearance of a third type of *adab*, which can in fact be termed the '*adab* of general culture'. This third class of works is easily assimilated to our sense of 'literature'. They were anthologies containing pieces of prose, extracts from speeches, memorable sayings of the great names of Islamic thought, quotations from Greek or Iranian works translated into Arabic, anecdotes and above all poems and fragments of verse. The whole was intended to be memorized and used when the occasion arose in distinguished conversation. From the III/9th century onwards, the technique of *adab* was extended into new fields, so that this genre includes, for instance, a manual of general history such as the *Kitāb al-Maʿārif* ('Book of

Profane Knowledge') by Ibn Qutayba (d. 276/889), and the geographical work entitled *Kitāb al-Buldān* ('Book of the Countries') by Ibn al-Faqīh (written around 290/903). Most outstanding is the famous *Murūj adh-dhahab* ('Golden Meadows') by al-Masʿūdī (written in 332/943), in which geography and general history were combined so as to make a work which was relatively handy and agreeable to read and also provide educated circles with a compendium containing the essential facts of worldly culture.

In the various types of writing which have been mentioned, the part played by personal creation was minimal, being generally reduced to the choice and arrangement of traditional material. This principle of avoiding personal observations and relying on precedent, whether the product is a simple digest or has some pretensions to literary style, is a characteristic feature of Arabic prose literature throughout its history.

A man possessing a wide knowledge of the 'Arabic humanities', some smattering of the Hellenic heritage and a reasonable grounding in the Iranian tradition was termed an *adīb*, a word which is generally translated as 'man of letters'. But the *adīb* was also one who composed works aimed at the secular education and entertainment of his readers – who for their part were growing tired of the serious religious writings which had hitherto formed their staple diet.

Poetry of the desert
When a biographer said of a person that he was *shāʿir adīb*, he was placing him at the very top of the literary hierarchy, since this meant that he possessed both the general culture which enabled him to write prose with reasonable facility, and more especially the ability to compose verse, since poetry, in the Arabic literary tradition, was the only creative activity worth consideration.

In their search for the 'Arabic humanities', the philologists of the 11/8th century found among the tribes, or in the towns where they stayed periodically, men known as *ruwāt*, endowed with a prodigious memory, who were able to recite thousands of verses attributed to various ancient poets dating from before or slightly after the birth of Islam. This large body of verse is divided by the specialists into two fundamental categories of composition, the earlier and simpler *rajaz*, probably used in composing small unpretentious pieces such as chants or insults to be hurled at the enemy of the battlefield, and the more sophisticated *qasīda*.

The *qasīda* has an elaborately metrical scheme and a tripartite structure, consisting of:
(a) A prologue in which the poet sheds tears over the abandoned encampment of his loved one's tribe and recalls the happy days he passed in her company. This is probably a survival from an ancient custom of temporary marriage and seems to prove that the *qasīda* dates back to very early times.
(b) An account of a journey in the desert with a description of the poet's mount, the dangers he has encountered and the merit he has acquired in undertaking such a perilous excursion to visit a person or a tribe who is mentioned in (c).
(c) A eulogy of the tribe or person in question, or the contrary if they are an enemy.

This is the general form of the *qasīda*, an artificial composition which is susceptible of a number of variations. The lover's prologue is omitted, for example, when the final and most important part is an elegy on the death of the person mentioned, and the panegyric can easily turn into personal glorification or contain a few moralizing maxims. Thus the general framework is not rigid. Many of the pieces which appear truncated may in fact be complete; the extent of the different parts varies and although common themes recur in different poems, the poets do strive for a certain degree of originality in both form and content. For all that, one of the oldest of them exclaims: 'Have the poets left a single spot for a patch to be sewn?', thus giving the impression that everything had already been said in this remote Islamic period when, admittedly, the conditions of life did not change and the most fertile imagination was prevented from innovation by the fetters of tradition.

The most remarkable of the ancient *qasīdas* were collected in the 11/8th century and seven of them, which were given the name of *Muʿallaqāt* ('suspended'), met with great success in the Muslim world, where they are still taught as prime examples of the poetic genius of the Arabs. Even the West, since serious study of Oriental literature, art and scholarship began, has acknowledged these eloquent relics of a consummate art, to judge by the number of translations which have been published. Historians and critics attribute the seven *Muʿallaqāt* to the following authors: Imruʼ al-Qays, the wandering King; Tarafa, whom the Gods loved; Zuhayr ibn Abī Sulmā, the Moralist; Labīd ibn Rabīʿa, the Centenarian; ʿAntara, the black Knight; ʿAmr ibn Kulthūm, the Regicide; al-Hārith ibn Hilliza, the Leper; the epithets given are those of A. J. Arberry.

The clouds cast their burden down on the broad plain of al-Ghabit,
*   as a trader from al-Yaman unfolds from the bales his store;*
And the topmost crest on the morrow of al-Mujaimir's cairn
*   was heaped with the flood-borne wrack like wool on a distaff wound.*
At earliest dawn on the morrow the birds were chirping blithe,
*   as though they had drunken draughts of riot in fiery wine;*
And at even the drowned beasts lay where the torrent had borne them, dead,
*   high up on the valley sides, like earth-stained roots of quill.*

(From the *Muʿallaqāt* of Imruʼ al-Qays, translated by C. J. Lyall.)

Paradoxically, the Prophet pronounced anathema on poets, although this did not prevent him from using the services of the poet Hasan ibn Thābit (d. c. 40/660), who was a Muslim. He even accepted the homage in verse of the pagan Kaʿb ibn Zuhayr, and threw his own coat round the latter's shoulders as a sign of approbation, a symbolic gesture which subsequently inspired many a poem in praise of Muhammad. The condemnation of poetry may have placed a brake on the activities of the versifiers, judging by the relatively small number of poems from the beginnings of Islam collected by the philologists. However, it seems unlikely that the bards of the desert abandoned their habitual occupation overnight, and no doubt much of their production was forgotten, neglected or rejected, especially when it was directed against the

Prophet. Judging by what remains, however, the poets writing about Muhammad described him in similar terms to those which were used in praising or abusing the tribal chief, according to whether the poets were favourable or hostile to him. In fact the new religion does not seem to have been a source of inspiration for those who witnessed its birth, and indeed Islam itself is not such a very frequent theme in the poetry of later centuries, or even among current apologists, who tend to extol the Prophet himself rather than the details of his work. Otherwise, religious poetry in Arabic, Persian, Turkish or Urdu is essentially mystical, that is to say it transcends Islam in the strictest sense of the word.

Both critics and historians state that the early poetry was primarily Bedouin, or at least of the Bedouin type, the towns of the Arabian peninsula having produced only a limited number of gifted poets. After the birth of Islam and the subsequent conquests the old habits persisted, and in the 1/7th century the most celebrated poets were still the Bedouins. And the latter, while frequenting the newly found cities in Mesopotamia or the Umayyad capital, Damascus, still maintained the life style of desert-dwellers and composed quite classical *qasīdas*. The Christian al-Akhtal (d. *c*. 92/710), al-Farazdaq (d. 110/728) and Jarīr (d. 110/728) are the most outstanding figures of this period, both for their ability to produce compositions worthy of the ancient poets and for their debates in verse which recall the contests of the pre-Islamic period.

Nevertheless, the impact of the Islamic conquests on the existence of so many early Bedouins was bound to have repercussions, not so much on the structure of poetry as on its content. Carried far from their native country by the Muslim battles for the conquest of the world, the soldiers expressed, in generally simple poems, their feelings of homesickness, their pride as victorious warriors or their exultation at the rich booty they had found. Poets such as these could hardly take the time to write long *qasīdas*, and most of their surviving works are fragments of a few lines. During the same century, conflicts within the Islamic community and the formation of dissident and antagonistic groups gave rise to poetry with a political and religious flavour. Its chief exponents were the intransigent Khārijīs, who used their poetic talents to stir up their supporters against their opponents and vilify the government. But if we examine it closely, this poetry remains basically traditional in character, recalling the magical verses which the pre-Islamic poet improvised in his role as tribal bard to encourage his companions and cool the enemy's ardour. If there is a difference, it undoubtedly lies in the sincerity of the earlier fighters, who were fired by an ardent faith in the righteousness of their actions. The poems were not always properly speaking *qasīdas*, and the surviving works often show an original development of the characteristic themes of the pre-Islamic poem. While the 'classical' poets faithfully followed tradition and respected the tripartite form of the *qasīda*, others took a part of it and developed it as they pleased, concentrating on one or two chosen themes.

The poetry of wine and love

Another striking example of this development is provided by bacchic poetry. Before Islam, there were many poets – some of them famous even if they could not compete with

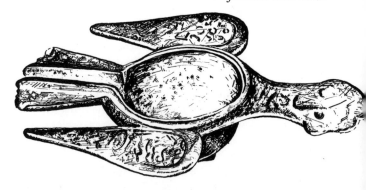

Bronze Persian vessel for preparing ink. Shaped like a human-headed bird, it dates from the VI/12th century. (3)

the authors of the *Mu'allaqāt* – whose *qasīda* included a passage glorifying the joys of drinking wine, consuming the wares of the sherbert seller and leading a riotous life in the company of singing slave girls. This was a frequent theme in poems of self-eulogy, and from it a tradition of bacchic poetry arose in the towns of Mesopotamia and in Damascus. Its exponents included al-Akhtal, who being a Christian had every right to drink wine, and more especially an Umayyad prince, al-Walīd ibn Yazīd (d. 124/743). Originally Bedouin, the theme became an urban one, for it was only natural for the city-dwellers to make allusion in their verses to the pleasures of this new manner of existence in ancient centres of civilization. We shall soon see that bacchic poetry, however paradoxical it may seem in a society where the consumption of alcohol was forbidden, developed to the point of becoming one of the characteristics of 'modernism'.

An even more paradoxical development took place in the holy cities of the Hijāz, Mecca and Medina. Whereas one might expect the places where the Prophet had lived to produce a form of religious poetry paralleling the pious activities of their inhabitants, what literature brings us is the celebration of a life of pleasure. In fact, from the late 1/7th century onwards, music and song developed extensively in the Hijāz, producing schools which retained their reputation even after the development of those of Basra, Baghdad and later Seville. The profession of entertainer also came into being, for the amusement of an idle aristocracy enriched by the booty from the Muslim conquests. While the Bedouin women celebrated at the beginning of the *qasīdas* had always enjoyed great freedom, the women of the cities had hitherto been more reserved. Now they felt emancipated to a degree and without perhaps indulging in a life of debauchery at least mixed freely with the opposite sex. So it was that Mecca and Medina witnessed the birth of a frivolous form of poetry which probably took its roots from the prologue of the *qasīda*, but developed this to the point of making love the sole theme in an unashamed celebration of the poet's adventures and pleasures. 'Umar ibn Abī Rabī'a (d. between 93 and 101/712–19) was a master of this genre and his works are still admired by even the least historically minded among cultured men. Just as the various schools for training musicians, singers, singing slaves, humorists and jesters were to emigrate to Iraq, so this frivolous but still respected form of poetry was imitated in Basra, Kūfa and Baghdad. A large number of poets flourished in these places, and a few fragments of their verse have been preserved by anthologists, but largely neglected by the critics. Nevertheless, far from being mere versifiers they often possessed a real poetic talent, genuine originality and a sincerity of expression which stand out against the mediocrity of more conventional poems, which can be appreciated more for their form than their content.

Convention and creation

We should not forget that both in the pre-Islamic period and later the poet who wished to make a name for himself had a heavy task in front of him. Far from being free to compose as he wished, he first of all had to conform to more or less inviolable technical and aesthetic rules. The metre imposed restrictions on his use of vocabulary so that he was unable to employ many no doubt poetic expressions. And however rich the language in general terms, the principle of monorhyme obliged him to choose words which rhymed as expected by the reader and thereby controlled the whole structure of the line. The line had to be a self-sufficient unit; a complete statement rarely spread over more than one line. As a result the poem does not form a homogeneous whole as demanded by modern criticism and it is quite easy to construct a *qasīda* from fragments having the same metre and the same rhyme, taken from pieces written by different authors. No doubt the authors who relayed the early poetry to us made use of this fact, and in the absence of firm criteria the critic must be constantly on his guard.

In addition to these technical restrictions, there were also social constraints. Before Islam, the poet was the spokesman of his tribe; he was therefore an integral part of it, without any individual identity. The form of his works could be varied, but the content had to remain faithful to the common opinion.

After the coming of Islam, the poet acquired a degree of autonomy which enabled him to express his own feelings or ideas. But to compose poetry as one pleased was a luxury which only the economically independent could afford; most of the poets were obliged to please powerful patrons, who expected them to write eulogies conforming to tradition but expressed in original terms.

And so one looks in vain for sincerity in the great poets who, even in their attacks and all the more inevitably in their panegyrics, try not to surprise the listener and merely to say what is expected better than others. There are some fine panegyrics composed in the hope of gaining favours from some particular person, but which for one reason or another were eventually addressed to another, only the name having been changed. This poetry is all the more impersonal in that the Arabs tend to be somewhat reserved; they are discreet in their private lives and in expressing their feelings, and the stock of clichés and figures of speech available enables them to remain on the surface, without revealing themselves even in the poems of self-eulogy.

Challenge from Persia

From the ii/8th century onwards we find a new form of poetry developing, in the hands of men who were generally not of Arab origin but had mastered the language of their conquerors. In particular the Persians now felt sufficiently well armed to challenge a cultural hegemony which they must have found particularly irksome in view of their own glorious past. Their activities took place within the context of the Shuʿūbī movement, whose supporters were Arabized Persians using the Arabic language because they no longer had any other at their disposal but struggling with what means they possessed against the developing Islamic tradition. The most famous of these writers were compelled to practise two different techniques in order to exist – panegyrics in the traditional, classical style, and freer pieces of a rather different nature. In the poetic field, the *Kitāb al-Aghānī* ('Book of Songs'), compiled in the iv/10th century by Abū 'l-Faraj al-Isfahānī, provides numerous examples of this attempt at literary emancipation and the desire to break free of both Islam and the Arabs. Among the Shuʿūbīs, one thinks immediately of Bashshār ibn Burd (executed in 167 or 168/784–5), a blind poet from Basra who combined a number of conflicting tendencies and indeed marks a transition. His panegyrics of the great figures of the time are classical and even archaic, while he was an innovator in his amorous pieces, which are often sensual or licentious. He excelled, however, in the genre of epigram and parody, and his discreet allusions to the religion of his Mazdean or Manichaean ancestors mark the beginning of what has been called 'modernist' poetry. In the second half of the same century even Abū Nuwās (d. *c.* 200/815), who was also of Persian origin, felt obliged to prove that he was capable of writing classical poetry in his panegyrics and even used archaic forms in his hunting poems, but he owes his fame to his erotic and bacchic pieces. As we have seen, many poets, including Bashshār himself, have more or less successfully sung the praises of wine, but Abū Nuwās broke new ground by composing entire poems on this theme, replacing the amorous prologue of the *qasīda* by lines celebrating wine. Moreover his bacchic and erotic poems were composed with the deliberate intention of making a stand against tradition and committing an act of sacrilege. In the poetry of Abū Nuwās's predecessors wine and love seem a natural part of their exaltation of sensual pleasures, but his own work clearly aims to scandalize his audience by celebrating male love and the liquor which was forbidden by Islam. After Abū Nuwās, these two themes became conventional. The most pious and pedestrian of writers judged them an indispensable part of their verse, but used them as an artificial device, almost always addressing the object of their passion in the masculine, even if the latter was a woman. The bacchic genre, the *khamriyyāt*, was much cultivated in later centuries, but no poet ever matched Abū Nuwās, and his true successors were the Sūfīs, who glorified the intoxication caused by the 'wine' of mystical love.

> *Seest thou not that I*
> *have pawned my soul for liquor,*
> *Kissed the mouth of fair*
> *gazelle and foaming beaker?*
> *'Tis because I know,*
> *full well I know and fear it,*
> *Far apart shall be*
> *my body and my spirit.*

(Lyric by Abū Nuwās, translated by R. A. Nicholson.)

The work of his contemporary Abū l-'Atāhiya (d. 210 or 211/825–26) was treated by posterity in quite a different fashion. Admittedly less talented, the latter followed many of his contemporaries in composing light verse celebrating his love and expressing his griefs, but most of this output is now neglected in favour of his *zuhdiyyāt* ('ascetic' poems), on which his reputation is based. These poems are dominated by the idea of death and the preparation which is necessary for it. They are simple, almost popular in conception, and well suited to a large and evidently religious public – though there are many indications of religious indifference in the historical sources.

Thus we come to the end of the II/8th century, and by this time the literary tradition was well established, at least as far as poetry was concerned.

Historians of Arabic literature generally term the poetry which we have been talking about 'modernist', and that which flourished from the III/9th century onwards as 'neo-classical'. In fact it is difficult to make such a clear-cut distinction, for all the features of the latter were already present to a greater or lesser extent during the II/8th century. Also, our point of view is somewhat distorted by the judgments of posterity, which have tended to be based on specific personalities rather than on groups. The work of poets such as Bashshār or Abū Nuwās did not die with them; it continued to be cultivated by poets of a lesser calibre, but these were overshadowed by two poets who were not 'modernist'. One of them is Abū Tammām (d. 231 or 232/845–46), a provincial with Bedouin leanings whose work is traditional in the sense that it consists of panegyrics which are written in the classical style but nevertheless contain allusions to contemporary events. The other is al-Buhturī (d. 284/897), who respects the tripartite *qasīda*, composing poems of self-eulogy to start with and then passing on to the panegyric. In fact the term 'neo-classical' is only justified by the existence of the intervening 'modernist' period, and the fact that the work of such poets no longer refers to an exclusively Bedouin world.

In the following century, the outstanding representative of 'neo-classicism' was al-Mutanabbī (d. 354/965), who revived echoes of pre-Islamic poetry in his panegyrics, the most memorable being that of the ruler of Aleppo, Sayf ad-Dawla; a writer of amazing virtuosity, al-Mutanabbī left a body of work which has been held up as a model for a thousand years, and has provided inspiration for a number of contemporary writers. In the same period, a cousin of Sayf ad-Dawla, Abū Firās (320–57/932–68), won a lasting reputation with the more personal note of the poetry which he wrote during his captivity in Constantinople; self-eulogy, which is by no means absent from the work of al-Mutanabbī, occupies a substantial place in that of Abū Firās, who could in any case afford not to compose panegyrics, except when he needed the aid of his cousin while he was a prisoner. There was also a constellation of minor poets gathered round Sayf ad-Dawla who were noted for their tendency to intersperse their panegyrics with descriptions of nature, gardens and flowers. This form quickly became stereotyped and was widely imitated throughout the empire.

After Sayf ad-Dawla we must mention another Syrian poet of lasting fame, Abū l-'Alā' al-Ma'arrī (363–449/979–1058), who was blind like Bashshār. He refused to become a professional panegyrist, preferring to retain his independence and compose philosophical works meditating on the problems of human existence. His work is that of a sceptic and lies outside the classical, modernist or neo-classical traditions, both in its content and in its form, relating neither to the true philosophers nor to the mystics. He is also the author of a masterpiece, the *Risālat al-Ghufrān* ('The Epistle of Pardon'), which has been compared to the *Divina Commedia*, and which is in prose – a medium to which we shall now return.

The catalogue of a Baghdad bookseller, Ibn an-Nadīm (d. 387/895), not only gives an idea of the number and volume of poetical collections circulating at the time but also reveals the existence of a considerable number of works in prose, or prose and verse mixed. In particular it mentions a series of romantic novels, the most famous of which is that of Qays, known as al-Majnūn ('the Madman'), and his beloved Laylā. Many other unhappy lovers, inevitably frustrated by social or family pressures, became the heroes of similar compilations. None of these romances has survived in its entirety and we only know them from extracts preserved by the anthologists, who merely quoted the passages which they themselves found interesting. The general theme was taken up again later by the mystics, and by a number of Persian poets who were probably more receptive than the Arabs to the romanticism of the subject. The latter only took up the general theme comparatively recently, though it is one which seems to the contemporary reader singularly out of date.

> *My songs gave eyes to the blind, ears to the deaf,*
> *Set the critics flapping like nightbirds,*
> *Set me at rest all night in my bed.*
> *And pay me well if I write you a eulogy.*
> *The flatterers will come to you mouthing it.*
> *And desert every voice but mine, for I*
> *Am the singing lark, the rest are echo.*
> *Time is my scribe and my register;*
> *It follows me singing the words I drop.*

(Lyric by al-Mutanabbī, translated by Herbert Howarth and Ibrāhīm Shukrallah.)

Literature for the people

Many legends were collected at an early date in Arabia and elsewhere, but they were never given a proper literary treatment. Successive compilers restricted themselves to reproducing the text and sometimes adding a detail or two of their own invention. Moreover the public storytellers who still make use of them seem to rely on a version which was written down at some particular date rather than on an uninterrupted oral tradition. A repertoire of humorous anecdotes, on the other hand, was committed to writing at an early stage, before once again falling into the oral domain. This can be seen in the stories of Joha, the original collection of which is almost contemporaneous with the hero, and the now forgotten anecdotes which figured in the *adab* of the Middle Ages. The same can be said of the *Thousand and One Nights*; the Indo-Persian nucleus of this was introduced into written Arabic literature in the IV/10th century, or perhaps even a little earlier, but it quickly became the point of departure for a collection which was subsequently added to by the story-tellers. It is significant that the Arab critics do not consider these famous stories as literature, even though they too underwent some literary elaboration and revision. Indeed it is only now that writers are beginning to take notice of them and exploit their themes in their own work, following the interest shown by the Western public during the past few centuries.

This taste for works of entertainment, be they romances, collections of humorous stories or fairytales and legends, seems to have set off a reaction in religious circles which considered jokes as incompatible with Islam. This was true to such an extent that the great prose-writer of the III/9th century, al-Jāhiz (d. 255/868), felt obliged to include an apologia for laughter in the introduction to his *Kitāb al-Bukhalā*' ('Book of the Misers'). This work is on a far more sophisticated level than the collections of anecdotes, for al-Jāhiz not only reproduces amusing stories but also carries out an analysis of avarice – though without being able to construct a 'type' which would have synthesized his findings. Al-Jāhiz is also known for his encyclopaedic *Kitāb al-Hayawān* ('Book of the Animals') and an anthology, *Kitāb al-Bayān* ('Book of Expression'), which lays the foundations of literary criticism. His portraits and essays, in particular, mark a great step forward for Arabic literature, raising *adab* to a new artistic level in its depiction of society and psychological analysis. Unfortunately, he had no successors in his achievement; received with sarcasm by narrow-minded critics, it was long neglected and is only now beginning to be rehabilitated. It was more than a century before an admirer of al-Jāhiz, Abū Hayyān at-Tawhīdī (d. 414/1023), produced an appreciable number of personal works in plain prose, in a milieu otherwise dominated by rhyming prose. These included a satirical portrait of the two viziers Ibn al-ʿAmīd and Ibn ʿAbbād, and accounts of political or scientific salons which reflect the intense intellectual activity of the time.

The work of at-Tawhīdī was also neglected until fairly recently, and later generations have generally preferred a more classical type of *adab*, usually anthologies and encyclopaedic compilations of general culture, if a somewhat narrow one. A notable example is *al-ʿIqd* ('The Necklace') by the Andalusian Ibn ʿAbd Rabbihi (d. 328/940).

The subject of the literature of Muslim Spain is treated in more detail in Chapter IX. At the risk of repetition, however, we must here mention the type of poem called the *muwashshah*, a strophic poem which does not respect the classical metres and ends in a sort of *envoi*, the *kharja*, which has to contain foreign words – in this case Romance ones. It was basically an original combination of two lyric poems, one Arabic, the other Romance or Spanish. The latter probably originated with slave singers whose native language was Romance, and who gave the creator of the genre the idea of using some popular refrain, perhaps already bilingual in itself, to give his compositions more life and originality. A whole book could be written on the role of slave singers in Islamic civilization. In the East and later in Spain, astute businessmen bought young female slaves, gave them an advanced artistic and literary education and then sold them, often at very high prices.

These singers had the right to mix with men and would participate in the salons of the aristocracy and the bourgeoisie. Here they would not only sing verses set to music, but also improvise on light and frivolous subjects, inspiring the poets present to spirited and witty rejoinders. The *Kitāb al-Aghānī* mentioned above contains some remarkable specimens of these improvisations, but the later anthologists did not generally see fit to collect new ones and some potentially interesting material has been lost.

The *muwashshah* was considered a popular genre although the language used in its composition was classical Arabic. It nevertheless spread to the Arab countries of the East, changing as it went, and here the *kharja* might be presumed to have contained Persian or dialect words. In most cases, however, it was in classical Arabic like the rest of the piece, and did not always run to the form laid down by an Oriental theorist – alert, lively, high-spirited, and if not obscene at least highly frivolous. The Eastern form has persisted and contemporary Arab poets still use it on occasion.

Written and spoken language

It is important to be clear about the difference between vernacular and so-called 'classical' Arabic. The latter, which, with changes more in vocabulary than in phonetics, morphology or syntax, is still used in present-day literature, was formed on the basis of a *koine* or common language superimposed by the pre-Islamic poets on the archaic dialects. Consecrated by its use in the Qurʾān, it was added to over the centuries without undergoing profound alterations. The dialects, on the other hand, evolved naturally both in Arabia and in the rest of the Arabic-speaking world, and became considerably differentiated from one another. Nowadays the development of the press, radio and television and the spread of popular education tend to attenuate the differences among the various dialects themselves and between the dialects and the classical language. The result is a kind of intermediate language which is used by educated people. At the same time the dialects retain their individual characteristics and it is they which are used spontaneously by Arabic speakers, above all when they have received only a rudimentary education. This double language presents a problem to present-day novelists and playwrights, who naturally hesitate to make characters from the common people speak in the language of scholars; recently a famous Lebanese poet even went so far as to compose a series of poems in dialectal Arabic and then transcribe them into Latin characters.

The growing divorce between written and spoken Arabic led to a situation in which scholars and men of letters were obliged to learn a special language which they hardly ever used in speech, so that it gradually lost its spontaneity and expressiveness. As long as the differences were not too great, an unlettered poet could still speak verse while respecting the classical metre. But when the dialectal language had lost its flexional endings and the syllabic structure had been disturbed by the loss of certain short vowels, one had to be educated in order to follow the poetic tradition inherited from antiquity. It therefore seems likely that, from the moment when the divorce between the two was complete, uneducated but

147

naturally talented poets began to compose pieces which were somewhat different in structure and metre from the classical *qasīda*.

At the same time as the appearance of dialectal verse forms, new poetic forms in written Arabic, which were distinguished from classical poetry by their metre, made their appearance in the East. Among them is the *dūbayt* which, as is indicated by its name – hybrid of Persian (*dū* = two) and Arabic (*bayt* = line) – is a couplet (or counting the hemistichs separately, a quatrain) which lends itself to various rhythmic combinations. The most notable of these is the *rubā'ī*, the plural of which, *rubā'iyyāt*, inevitably evokes the name of 'Umar Khayyām (d. 517/1123). This form, which is based on a combination of lyric poems like the *muwashshah*, has had less success than the latter in Arabic but occupies a substantial position in Persian literature.

Neo-Persian

By the time the Arabs conquered Iran, Pahlavī, the language of the sacred books of ancient Iran, was in a state of complete decadence, and it does not seem to have produced any notable literature in the first centuries which followed the conquest. But these centuries did see the formation of neo-Persian, a version of Pahlavī revivified by the addition of some 50 per cent Arabic vocabulary. We have seen how poets of Persian origin had injected new blood into the ancient traditions of Arabic poetry during the II/8th century. The literary renaissance in Persia also mainly took the form of poetry, as soon as the language had become sufficiently rich and the political circumstances favoured an indigenous reaction against the cultural domination of the Arabs. The formation of states which were more or less independent of the 'Abbāsids in the III/9th century hastened this awakening of literary consciousness which was expressed in the creation of new poetical forms. At the same time the Arabic model was followed in Persian, particularly in the panegyric, and some Iranian poets still composed their verses in the language of their conquerors. It was a poet of Balkh, Abū Shukūr, who is credited with having created the *rubā'ī*, as well as the *mathnawī*, after 335/947. The latter resembles some of the compositions in the *rajaz* metres in that the two hemistichs rhyme with one another and the rhythm changes with each line, but it differs from the *rajaz* in the use of some of the other metres of the *qasīda*. Applied to ethical, romantic, epic or didactic subjects, this form met with widespread success, but was not imitated by the Arab versifiers.

In the III/9th century Mahmūd of Ghazna gathered around him a group of poets who composed *dīwāns* filled with pastoral panegyrics. Most outstanding was Firdawsī (d. 410/1020), whose work marked the beginning of a new and rapid stage of evolution. His work, the *Shahinshāh-nāma* 'The Book of Kings'), is considered a masterpiece unique in the Islamic literatures; consisting of the history of the mythical sovereigns of ancient Iran and the successive dynasties, it is no less than a national epic in verse. The elements it contains had been known to the Arabs for at least two centuries through translations of the original Pahlavī texts. Thus the material to which Firdawsī applied his genius was already freely available, although only Arab historians had hitherto made use of it.

The *Shahinshāh-nāma* is a sort of historical encyclopaedia, a collection of myths, legends and traditions which are supposed to give a poetic picture of the history of Iran since the Creation up to the Arab conquest. It is openly anti-Arab, and Firdawsī's attitude is emphasized by his reaction against the Arabic language and his desire to achieve a pure 'Iranism'. But he was none the less a Muslim and he is credited, perhaps wrongly, with a religious poem inspired by the Qur'ān, the story of Joseph and the wife of Potiphar, *Yūsuf ū Zulaykhā*. While the stories contained in the Qur'ān inspired a series of Arabic works in prose entitled *Qisas al-anbiyā'* ('Edifying Tales of the Prophets'), only a few of them have been exploited in a literary form, chiefly by modern playwrights, whereas the mystics made extensive use of the theme of Joseph and Zulaykhā both in Persian and in Arabic. Any discussion of Islamic literature must of course include that of mysticism, but as this is the subject of a separate chapter it is omitted here.

> *They lighted, tied their chargers to a rock,*
> *And cautiously advanced in mail and casque*
> *With troubled hearts. They wrestled like two lions*
> *Until their bodies ran with sweat and blood.*
> *From sunrise till the shadows grew they strove*
> *Until Suhrāb, that maddened Elephant,*
> *Reached out, up-leaping with a lion's spring,*
> *Caught Rustum's girdle, tugged amain as though,*
> *Thou wouldst have said, to rend the earth, and shouting*
> *With rage and vengeance hurled him to the ground.*

(From Firdawsī's *Shahinshāh-nāma*, translated by Arthur and Edmond Warner.)

Arabic rhyming prose

Whereas Persian poetry had begun to flourish before the time of Firdawsī, prose had still not really achieved any status. In Arabic, on the other hand, it had undergone a revolutionary change which also somewhat influenced the Persians, and this was the transition from simple prose to rhyming prose.

A number of more or less genuine examples of pre-Islamic prose collected by philologists in early Islam consisted of rhyming phrases. The Qur'ān itself contains many passages in plain prose, particularly in the sūras revealed at Medina. More often, however, the verses rhyme with one another, although the principle on which this is done remains to be analyzed and it is not yet known whether rhyming prose obeys definite rules, like poetry. The Qur'ān is thus merely following an ancient tradition, and the opponents of Muhammad did not fail to draw attention to the fact that he expressed himself like the old-fashioned soothsayers, above all in the passages designed for rhetorical effect. During the first three centuries of Islam, the authors of religious, juridical, historical and other works did not seek to give their production an artistic character. Those whose possessed a real literary talent, like al-Jāhiz, were not above including a few rhymes in their prose, but the latter drew its aesthetic value essentially from its simplicity and the richness and vigour of its language, rather than the use of artistic devices. In fact this kind of prose style has never been analyzed with a view to discovering the basis of its artistic merit, since for the Arabs, as for the peoples who underwent their influence,

Royal patronage of literature is amply illustrated in the manuscripts. This miniature of a poet reading to a prince was painted in Bukhārā in 968/1560. (4)

poetry is the means of expression par excellence and is the only one worthy of study. Prose – apart from that of the Qur'ān, which has given rise to a series of works on its inimitability *(i'jāz)* – is sometimes admired but never subjected to critical examination.

Nevertheless, in the context of *adab*, the kind of prose literature which began with the translation of *Kalīla wa-Dimna* soon gained ground, chiefly in the form of the epistle *(risāla)*. By the III/9th century it had even begun to compete with poetry on its own ground, that of the panegyric, the elegy and the satire – albeit only in exceptional cases and with individual writers. We should not forget that from the II/8th century onwards the ideal of the poet with a growing reputation was to have access to the court, while that of the scholar who had received the necessary education was to obtain employment in the administration of the caliphate. As a result, the official scribes tended to have a monopoly of secular culture, and took an active part in the development of prose. This they not only did through writing books of *adab* and, like 'Abd al-Hamīd, giving advice to their future colleagues, but also in composing administrative letters. Indeed, writers outside the administration soon used the epistle as a means of justifying their own activities, claiming modestly, and hypocritically, that they were writing on

such and such a subject at the urgent entreaty of a friend, whose name they took care not to mention. One also finds treatises on law, theology or philosophy, presented in this form, although in many cases they have not been commissioned and are the spontaneous work of the author.

However, if simple prose was a means of expression which anybody could use, the nature of Arabic made it difficult to give the former a literary character without using the devices associated with poetry. So as prose writings became more numerous, authors, and more particularly the scribes, tended to embellish them with poetic ornament, first by introducing rhymes between phrases of varying length and then by having recourse to the tropes which are so abundant in Arabic rhetoric. From the IV/10th century, rhyming and ornamented prose invaded all literary domains and apart from a few outstanding exceptions – notably at-Tawḥīdī and Ibn Hazm – a writer would have felt himself put to shame if he had used a simpler style. Even technological works did not escape the contagion and it is rarely that the preamble at least is not entirely rhymed. The scribes of the Būyid administration (during the IV/10th century, before the arrival of the Seljuqs) distinguished themselves particularly in this respect, and while it is difficult to estimate the part played by the Persians here, it seems significant that the majority of officials at this period were bilingual. A writer who frequented the Būyid court, though not one of its officials, can be considered the creator of a genre which had its roots in *adab* and was to become a characteristic form of Arabic prose literature, the *maqāma* or 'session'. This was Badī' az-Zamān al-Hamadhānī (358-98/968-1008), who was both a poet and a writer of epistles and other forms of prose. The *maqāma* is a work of imagination, probably the first in the history of Arabic literature, which features two principal characters, a hero and a narrator who recounts the adventures of the former in rhyming prose. In fact al-Jāhiz had introduced some highly coloured characters into *adab* in the III/9th century – vagabonds and beggars whose caperings loosed the purse-strings of an admiring audience – but in this case it is difficult to judge what is fact and what is fiction; the author may simply have been presenting real happenings, whereas the *maqāma* is quite palpably invented. Almost at the same time a picture of the life of city dwellers written in simple prose, the *Hikāya* ('Representation [of reality]'), might have given birth to the novel as we know it; but it seems to have been eclipsed by the *Maqāmāt* of Badī' az-Zamān and not to have been followed up. It is interesting to note that the vagabonds of al-Jāhiz and the adventurer of the *Maqāmāt* are two links in the chain which leads from the Arabic story-telling tradition to the picaresque novel. In the famous Spanish original of that genre, *Lazarillo de Tormes*, the central tale is obviously borrowed from a collection by a later compiler who was inspired by al-Jāhiz and whose work was evidently known in Spain.

Instead of perfecting the *maqāma* as a work of imagination, the philologists were not slow in seeing that picaresque narrative might also be an effective means of teaching the most out-of-the-way Arabic vocabulary. Thus it was that al-Harīrī (446-516/1054-1122) in his turn composed *Maqāmāt* which abounded in verbal acrobatics, to the detriment of the originality of the subject-matter and the interest of the adventures recounted. The immense popularity that these still enjoy is a crucial indication of the decline of literary taste among the Arabs. The technique invented by Badī' az-Zamān was soon widely employed to serve various ends, even literary criticism, for example; it became an artificial convention which authors no doubt felt would help to hold their readers' attention. The 19th century saw an attempt to give new life to this authentic Arabic genre and with it to the classical language, and this produced a *maqāma* of great literary and sociological interest which was the swan-song of medieval literature. Its title is the *Hadīth 'Īsā ibn Hishām* ('Sayings of 'Īsā ibn Hishām', from the name of the narrator of the 'sessions' of Badī' az-Zamān) and the author Muhammad al-Muwaylihī (1285-1349/1868-1930). The work brings to life a pasha of the olden days in order to show in a humorous but quite untranslatable form the changes that had taken place in the life of the Egyptians over the last century.

These days rhyming prose is considered heavy and pedantic and writers have completely abandoned it, but not so long ago it was in favour in chancellories which followed the tradition started by the Būyid scribes and brought to its peak by al-Qādī al-Fādil (529-96/1135-1200), one of Saladin's collaborators, whose letters are models of epistolary style. The systematic use of rhyming prose, with the numerous make-rhymes which it involves, makes the interpretation of these texts particularly laborious. A disciple of al-Qādī al-Fādil, the Persian 'Imād ad-Dīn al-Isfahānī (519-97/1125-1201), who was also Saladin's secretary, left a biography of the Sultan in Arabic and an account of his last years, with the capture of Jerusalem. It is written in a bombastic style full of endless verbal ingenuities, from which any author of a manual of rhetoric could easily draw all his examples.

Although held in great esteem in Iranian circles, rhyming prose was for a long time peculiar to Arabic. In Persian literature secular prose offered little competition to poetry, for it usually had no literary character. One might make an exception of the *Siyāsat-nāma* by Nizām al-Mulk (d. 485/1092), which possesses some aesthetic value thanks to its simplicity of style, appearing as it did exactly at the moment when rhyming prose had invaded Arabic literature; also a re-working of *Kalīla wa-Dimna* (VI/12th century); the *Jawāmi' al-hikāyāt* by 'Awfī (d. after 670/1232); and naturally the works of Sa'dī (580-691/1184-1291), who used artistic prose to treat ethical subjects. Stylistically, his works are the acme of formal perfection, while their content represents the spirit of non-Arabian Islam. The author of erotic and mystical poems, he also left us the *Bustān* ('Garden'), a moral treatise in the tradition of the moralizing *adab* which had already been cultivated in Persian by several authors; and the *Gulistān* ('The Rose Garden'), which is the same type of work as the *Bustān*, but written in a mixture of prose and verse. Mysticism, for its own part, as we have seen in Chapter IV, began to make use of prose; and one of the most remarkable examples in this respect is the *Mantiq at-tayr* ('The Conference of the Birds') by Farīd ad-Dīn 'Attār (d. 627/1230), which relates the allegorical journey of thirty birds *(sī murgh)* in search of the Sīmurgh, the mythical bird which represents God.

Then they gave themselves up to meditation, and after a little they asked the Simurgh, without the use of tongues, to reveal to them the secret of the mystery of the unity and plurality of beings. The Simurgh, also without speaking, made this reply: 'The sun of my majesty is a mirror. He who sees himself therein sees his soul and his body, and sees them completely. Since you have come as thirty birds, *si-murgh*, you will see thirty birds in this mirror. If forty or fifty were to come, it would be the same. Although you are now completely changed you see yourselves as you were before.

'Can the sight of an ant reach to the far-off Pleiades? And can this insect lift an anvil? Have you ever seen a gnat seize an elephant in its teeth? All that you have known, all that you have seen, all that you have said or heard – all this is no longer that. When you crossed the valleys of the Spiritual Way and when you performed good tasks, you did all this by my action; and you were able to see the valleys of my essence and my perfections. You, who are only thirty birds, did well to be astonished, impatient and wondering. But I am more than thirty birds. I am the very essence of the true Simurgh. Annihilate then yourselves gloriously and joyfully in me, and in me you shall find yourselves.'

Thereupon, the birds at last lost themselves for ever in the Simurgh – the shadow was lost in the sun, and that is all.

(From Farīd ad-Dīn 'Attār's *Conference of the Birds*, translated by C. S. Nott.)

However, it is Persian poetry again which serves most successfully to express the mystical ideas of Jalāl ad-Dīn Rūmī (d. 672/1273), the founder of a dervish brotherhood and author of the famous *Mathnawī*, which is a treatise on mystical theology.

> *As salt resolved in the ocean*
> *I was swallowed in God's sea,*
> *Past faith, past unbelieving,*
> *Past doubt, past certainty.*
>
> *Suddenly in my bosom*
> *A star shone clear and bright;*
> *All the suns of heaven*
> *Vanished in that star's light.*

(Quatrains by Jalāl ad-Dīn Rūmī, translated by A. J. Arberry.)

There is not enough room to mention here all the Persian poets who gained a reputation in genres unknown to their Arab colleagues or little practised by them. It would be impossible, however, to omit mention of Nizāmī (d. 600/1203), who wrote magnificent romantic poems on Arabic-Persian themes such as *Laylā ū Majnūn*, which revived a forgotten theme of the Arabic romances, or *Khusraw ū Shīrīn*, which hymns the love of Parvīz and the beautiful Shīrīn. Nizāmī appears as a master of Persian language and rhetoric at a time when Arabic literature was beginning seriously to decline.

The end of greatness

With Rūmī, Sa'dī and a few others, we reach the period of the Mongol conquest, which accounts for a great many things. Intellectual activity in the Arabic-speaking regions had begun to decline long before the arrival of Hülegü, the first Mongol sovereign of Persia. But with his capture of Baghdad (656/1258), the centre of the Arab world became displaced towards the west and the Muslims were thrown back upon themselves, feeling clearly that their mainspring had been broken. From that moment, while literary tradition was respected in all its aspects, poets and prose writers seemed to take a refuge in a faithful imitation of the past and showed little taste for innovation. This was the period of the great encyclopaedias, the great dictionaries which tried to survey the Arabic language before it disappeared in the cataclysms which were shaking the Muslim world, the great universal histories which were the first the West was to know because they were easy to handle. It was the period, too, of Ibn Khaldūn (732-808/1332-1406) in whom one can see the founder of historical sociology, and in Spain of thinkers and philosophers who were studied in medieval Europe through Latin translations. In a word, intellectual activity remained intense, but it was charged with a feeling of anxiety. In some authors one can sense a desire to react against the general apathy, to take refuge in frivolity by contrast with the sombre atmosphere which prevailed everywhere, but their efforts rapidly descended into obscenity.

And yet, while we can confidently apply the term 'decadent' to this period, which is generally known as the 'Dark Ages' and came to an end with the modern Islamic renaissance, the fact remains that it has not been very closely studied and may contain unsuspected talents which have yet to be revealed. Moreover, although historical and geographical works have so far been counted as technical and therefore left out of account, we cannot ignore a genre which is usually classed within geography but really belongs to prose literature, namely the travelogue *(rihla)*. While geographers, even when travelling, confined themselves to describing towns and noting distances, the Western style of travelogue often contained graphic narratives of the vicissitudes of a pilgrimage to Mecca or the exploration of a little-known region. The first Arabian traveller to leave us a detailed account with a completely modern flavour is Ibn Jubayr (540-614/1145-1217); but the most famous is undoubtedly Ibn Battūta (703-79/1304-77), who not only journeyed to the Hijāz but went on to visit India and China and then Africa. The genre continued to be practised in later centuries with varying success, for very often a *rihla* was simply a means for the author to mention the religious men and mystics he had met, and he did not bother to embellish his narrative with the picturesque details which constituted the charm of earlier accounts. In more recent times, and especially in the 19th century, travellers from the East made for Europe; and some of them followed the pattern of the early travelogues, leaving us narratives which have both a documentary interest and a literary value.

In Persia during the decline of Arabic literature, poetry remained the principal mode of expression and some very eminent figures appeared. Once the initial crisis had passed, secular poetry reasserted itself in a reaction against the situation and we see even Zakānī (d. 772/1370) exercising his satirical gifts against the decadence of society and opposing the moralizing *adab* with ironically humorous maxims. However, the most famous poet of the period is certainly Hāfiz (719-91 or 93/1319-8989 or 90), the author of a *Dīwān* containing erotic poems with a

The most prominent Persian poet of the VIII/14th century was Hāfiz, seen here in a Mughul manuscript of about 1019/1610, pointing out a poem in his Dīwān. *(5)*

mystical interpretation; the formal perfection of his work shows his total mastery of the language. After him, the decadence becomes more marked up to Jāmī (d. 898/1492), whom one can consider the last of the great classical poets.

Decline and revival

The decade in which Jāmī died was marked by events with universal repercussions. Two of them, the end of Islamic domination in Spain and the discovery of the route round the Cape, reacted upon the Muslim world, which found itself cut off from Western civilization and benefited only very late from the progress achieved by the latter after the Renaissance. Thus we can reasonably make a jump of three centuries, in the course of which the medieval tradition was maintained without any marked changes, despite the efforts of a few individuals to draw the Muslim world out of its isolation. It was only in the 19th century that the rediscovery of the West led to what the Arabs call the *Nahda*, the revival which has continued up to the present day.

Like the Greek works translated into Arabic in the Middle Ages, it was technical treatises which were initially the subject of translation, and then European literature, particularly French, spread into Oriental circles. There were timid attempts at imitation; the creation of drama, which was unknown up to that time, at least in its modern form; and the introduction of the novel and the short story, ignoring the medieval precedents but trying all the same to Arabize the imported genres. Poetry of the 19th century remained neo-classical in the style of al-Mutanabbī and continued to be widely cultivated, proving the vitality of the indigenous literary tradition.

At present it may be said that the break with the past is complete as far as prose is concerned. The rhyming form has been abandoned in favour of simple prose, sometimes modelled on that used by avant-garde Western writers in search of new forms. The highly original *maqāma* was obviously doomed to disappear, and since the work of al-Muwaylihī at the beginning of this century not a single one has been composed. The supporters of innovation at all costs have carried the day and a uniquely indigenous form has been lost. The literary press has opened its columns to a multitude of writers, chiefly of short stories. The novel, which requires a talent of greater staying power, is not however neglected, and long works are often published in serial form. The novel has even undergone a characteristic evolution: historical at the end of the 19th century, romantic in the first half of the 20th century, it subsequently became realist, then realism was abandoned in favour of symbolism. The theatre has followed a similar course; plays are written to be read rather than to be acted, and the cinema provides fierce competition for those which are put on; but at the same time, playwrights are finding a new outlet in television.

Generally speaking, Western fashions are being adopted with a slight time-lag, and this can be seen even in poetry, which is currently undergoing a kind of revolution both in content and in form. Poets are making an effort to free themselves from the formal constraints of the past, opting for *vers libre* and prose poems, the latter being often more poetic than the verse. The content reflects a feeling of Arab decadence among avant-garde poets, who are seeking to resolve the metaphysical problems which confront them and to promote a new civilization which will arise from the ashes of the old. The stressing of political involvement in all forms of literature robs them of a great deal of their interest, even if contemporary events might be considered to justify the emotional outbursts which readers seem to expect from their authors.

As we have seen, the Islamic literary tradition is one in which verse occupies an infinitely more important place than prose. This is natural enough, for the two main languages of the medieval Muslim world, Arabic and Persian, were eminently poetic, and verse was their most characteristic means of literary expression. The poetic conventions were fixed at an early date; they withstood the attempts to change them in the 11/8th century; and it is quite possible that they will resist the onslaught which they are undergoing today. The attacks led by supporters of Persian culture in the Middle Ages came up against a solidly established tradition, and the innovators were considered as heretical as those who tried to introduce innovations into religious law. Despite the protests of the revolutionaries, the true poets of today are those who compose neo-classical poems, not the authors of obscure and hermetic pieces without rhyme or rhythm, modelled on works coming from the West. The dramatic political events from which the latter take their inspiration are, we hope, a passing phenomenon, so that the kind of poems which are proliferating at present will soon be only of historical interest. At the same time, they are still poems, and one cannot help being struck by the prominence given to poetry in literary journals: the taste for this characteristic mode of expression persists.

Prose has always been written abundantly in the principal languages of the Muslim world, but as we have already pointed out, truly literary works of prose are to be found only in classical *adab*, the epistle form and, from the IV/10th century onwards, in the *maqāma*. All the rest is technical, religious, juridical, philosophical, historical or geographical, even if the authors of such material, having all received a similar education, show a penchant for well-turned phrases. During the centuries of its decadence, *adab* became a literature of compilation, and the widespread adoption of rhyming prose rendered many potentially interesting texts almost unreadable.

The return to original sources in the 19th century gave new life to poetry, but the effect on literary prose was negligible. A few masterpieces have been produced during the course of the present century, including Tāhā Husayn's autobiography *al-Ayyām* ('The Days'), but the number is very small. It is significant that publishers produce rather small editions of contemporary works, while the medieval texts which we have mentioned, and in particular works relating to Islam, its doctrine, civilization and history, are in constant demand. And this is happening at a time when the Islamic world has taken over the printing of Arabic texts and many scientific editions are being satisfactorily published. A lesson, as the Arabs say, for those who wish to learn.

At the root of Arabic literature lies the *adab*, a short pithy saying akin to a proverb, inculcating a fixed rule of conduct applicable at a moral, social or (eventually) cultural level. In this way *adab* becomes equivalent to the Western concept of 'literature', something which at first could not be expressed in Arabic. But it underlines the tendency common to Arabic writing to have a strong didactic purpose. Works were rarely composed for entertainment only, and those that were – such as the *Thousand and One Nights* – were not treated as serious literature. This Khurāsān plate, dating from the IV/10th century, bears a typical precept: 'He who professes the Faith will excel and whatever you accustom yourself to, you will get used to. Blessings on the owner.' (1)

Love stories fell somewhat outside the literary *adab* proper, but were extremely popular from early times. Romances followed a conventional pattern, and episodes could be joined together in a more or less arbitrary way. They invariably end unhappily. Among the earliest manuscript survivals is this III/9th-century fragment (left): the two lovers are dead, but a palm tree grows between their graves, uniting them. (2)

The lover faints on hearing bad news (below): an episode from the tragic story of Bayād and Riyād, from an early VII/13th-century manuscript, written in either Spain or Morocco. This drawing is additionally interesting for its detailed portrayal of the water-wheel. (3)

Laylā and Majnūn was the most widely loved of all the romances and was often illustrated. The poet Qays (known as al-Majnūn, 'the madman') falls in love with Laylā, the daughter of a powerful shaykh. She returns his love but is forced to marry someone else. In despair he wanders in the hills and deserts, writing poems and seeing Laylā at rare intervals until her death. This story of the Arabian desert was transplanted to Persia and then to India, where these two miniatures were painted. Opposite above: Majnūn throws himself on Laylā's tomb. Below: The old woman brings Majnūn to Laylā's tent. (4, 5)

155

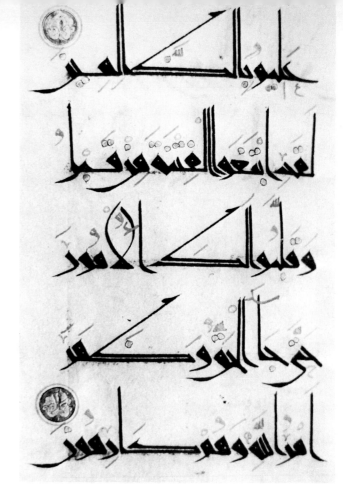

Kūfic, III/9th century (6)

The Qur'ān, the first great work of Arabic prose, occupies a paradoxical position in literary history. The fact that it was a divine revelation meant that it was above both criticism and imitation. Any attempt to use it as a model would have been regarded as sacrilege. Yet it was so basic to the whole of Islamic thought that its style, rhythms and phraseology penetrated the subconscious of every Arabic writer. Echoes of it are everywhere. It was quoted in every context, sometimes – to Western eyes – quite inappropriately. Its influence is therefore all-pervasive but not explicit.

On these pages are shown a selection of extracts from the Qur'ān written in different Arabic scripts to illustrate the history of calligraphy. The early, monumental Kūfic gradually gave way to a more ornamental style which could be combined with varied decorative motifs.

Persian Kūfic, V/11th century (7)

'Bent' Kūfic, IV/10th century (8)

Qur'ān stand of carved wood (9)

Naskhī script from Baghdad, IV/11th century (10)

Maghribī script, VI/12th- VII/13th century (11)

Jalil script: a Mamlūk manuscript, VII/13th century (12)

Jalil script from Mosul, VIII/14th century (13)

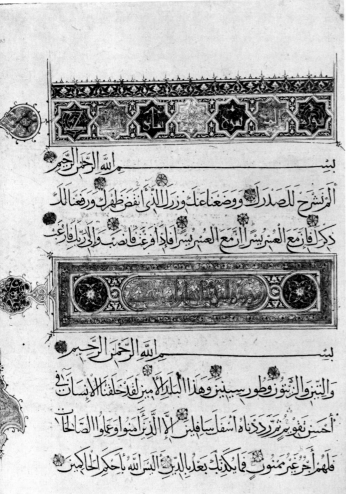

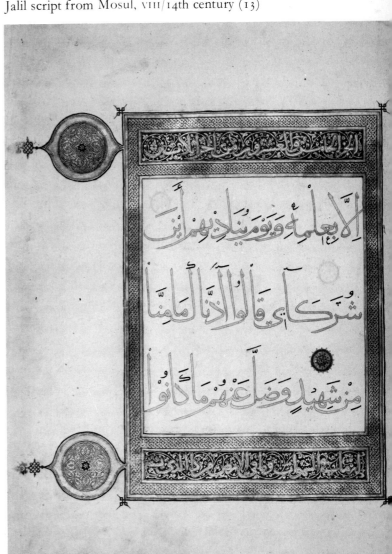

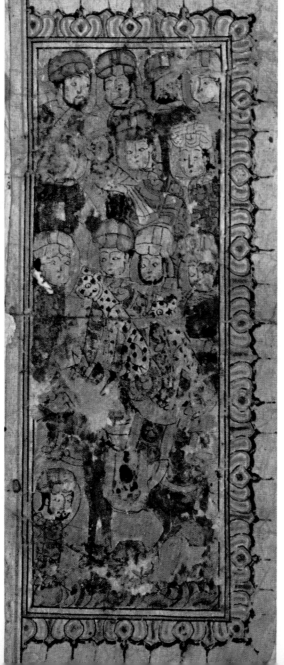

Animal fables, designed to educate in an entertaining way, are among the oldest types of literature in Arabic, going back to an era before Islam. In the II/8th century Ibn al-Muqaffaʿ translated a Pahlavī collection of such stories, *Kalīla wa-Dimna*, which was itself a translation from the Sanskrit. Kalīla and Dimna are two jackals. The 'moral' of these stories is often mere worldly cleverness, but they gained a reputation throughout the whole Islamic world and beyond. The two miniatures above – Dimna talking to the lion, and the stupid fish caught in the net – come from an Arabic manuscript of the VII/13th century. That on the left is the frontispiece to an VIII/14th-century Persian translation. A Turkish translation, called the *Humāyūn-nāma*, was made by ʿAlī Chelebi; a V/11th-century manuscript (below) illustrates the battle between owls and crows, caused by the jealousy of the crows when an owl was elected King of the Birds. (14–17)

الأول النزار وبني الثاني إلى المرام وما أوصف إذا أردف باللون نقص صاحبه
في العيون وقوم باللون وخرج من اللون وعرض للهون فهذه شاعرة مسله

وفق عادكم وزندكم لدكه ولوز دتم ز دنا وان علتم عدنا قال المحبر
هذه الحكايه فورد على نامن لحاجيه اللاتي هانت لما انها لت ماحارف

To read and appreciate literature was one of the essentials of social position. Elegant speech and the ability to handle words cleverly had been highly valued even among the Bedouin. Eventually verbal ingenuity reached such a pitch that only the highly educated could understand it. Spoken and written Arabic diverged, the latter becoming reserved for literary and religious usage. This illustration from al-Harīrī's *Maqāmāt* shows a literary gathering in a garden outside Baghdad. Its members sit amid shady trees, cooled by the water of a fountain. A musician plays. Outside, the working man, excluded from the circle of the literati, urges on his buffalo team. (18)

خادم قذعلته كبره وعرته عبرته وقال ياقوم لاتوسعوا أستأوا ولا يرجعوا

خبا فان الفي جنون ثاملا وشغلا عن الحديث شأنا فقال له ابوزيد بغز خانو ولبس

وأستنشر بوطه وحوله جمع كيف الحواشي ومونش والجاشي لا هلة صوته

'**Assemblies**' or 'meetings' (the Arabic word is *maqāmāt*) was the term for one of the most sophisticated literary genres. It consisted of a series of encounters and conversations between a witty protagonist and a series of characters whose adventures are narrated. The language is elaborate and artificial, using a technique for which there is no Western equivalent, rhymed prose. One of the most famous writers of *maqāmāt* was al-Harīrī (446–516/1054–1122), in whose hands the form became largely an excuse for clever word-juggling. These miniatures are illustrations of his work. Top: the Eastern Isles, a land reached by the boat on the left and peopled with human-headed animals and birds. Bottom: al-Harīrī and his companions meet an old man. (19, 20)

Chapter Six

THE DIMENSION OF SOUND

A. Shiloah

THE MUSIC OF ISLAM'S GOLDEN AGE is extolled and described at length by philosophers and writers, but any attempt to reconstruct what it was actually like encounters immediate difficulties. It was transmitted by ear, not written down, so we have to rely entirely on the interpretation of literary sources. Can we not try to bridge the gap by going to present-day music and using it to clarify these sources? – the music of the Islamic world has, after all, a strong feeling for the continuity of tradition. But there are two main drawbacks. Firstly, music of different regions has tended to acquire strongly local characteristics, and which variant are we to choose as the closest to the original? Secondly, contact with other cultures has radically affected Islamic music throughout its history. Indeed the sound-documents accumulated since the invention of recording demonstrate clearly the deep and significant changes that can occur in less than a century. Certainly the changes in the last few decades under modern pressures have been particularly striking, but this does not mean that similar pressures have necessarily been absent during the previous thirteen centuries of Islamic musical tradition. The musical styles of present-day Muslim countries should therefore be viewed as the varied descendants of the early tradition, but none of them as its exact embodiment.

Islamic music was the fruit of a fortunate encounter between different musical cultures, producing a 'new music' which contained characteristics and concepts from all of them, with the Arabian element acting as a catalyst. This encounter, however, took place only at the level of 'art' music. The various ethnic and regional styles were left virtually untouched, and in fact continue to survive to this day, in the shadow of art music, retaining their distinctive character although occasionally influencing and being influenced by it.

The 'new music' spread rapidly across an immense territory, from the Caucasus to the Persian Gulf and from the Oxus to the Atlantic. Already by the end of the 1/7th century it was universally known and enthusiastically appreciated, and the musicians who performed it were rewarded with fabulous sums. Music had become part of culture, and an important part of social life. Famous performers might spring from a wide variety of origins:

some were Arabs, others were freed slaves of Persian, Turkish, Byzantine or Negro extraction.

During the early years of Islam, the Arabs were evidently prepared to accept the varying musical styles of their subject peoples and not to try to eliminate them or make them conform to their own. Thus, al-Kindī, the 'Philosopher of the Arabs' (d. c. 261/874), writes in his treatise on the lute:

> Know thee that each people possesses with regard to this instrument a musical system of its own which is not shared by any other. The differences between peoples in this respect are of the same nature as their differences in everything. The Arabs, the Rum [the Byzantines], the Persians, the Khazars [a people of the Caspian shores], the Ethiopians and the totality of men differ from each other by their nature, their intelligence, their opinions, their wishes and their behaviour.

The same point of view was expressed even more explicitly a century later in the Ikhwān as-Safā''s *Epistle on Music*:

> Know thee, my brother – may God assist you and us by a spirit emanating from him – that the humours of the body are of many aspects, and the natures of animals are of numerous species. To each humour and to each nature correspond a rhythm and a melody whose number cannot be counted but by God Mighty and Great. You will find the proof of the veracity of what we have said and the rightfulness of what we have described if you take into consideration that every people of humanity possesses melodies and rhythms of its own which bring enjoyment and delight to its children, whilst none except them would find either pleasure or delight in them. This is the case of the music of the Daylamites, the Turks, the Arabs, the Armenians, the Ethiopians, the Rum and other peoples who differ from each other by their language, their nature, their characters and their customs.

How far these passages correspond to the real situation, and to what extent national differences were already distinct when al-Kindī and Ikhwān as-Safā' were writing is difficult to say. Our knowledge has to be based on relatively late sources. One of the most valuable, for instance, the *Kitāb al-Aghānī* ('Book of Songs'), a mine of information on music, musicians and musical life over several centuries, was written by Abū 'l-Faraj al-Isfahānī, who lived from 284/897 to 357/967.

From these and other sources it is possible to deduce that the 'new music' was the result of a successful fusion of elements which were diverse although they had certain traits in common. Nevertheless, it seems that the dominant factor which gave the 'new music' its *raison d'être* was the Arab contribution, namely the Arabic language and Arabic poetry. It is therefore not surprising that vocal music became the preferred type. One finds an intimate alliance between text and music, the music being used to emphasize the meaning of the text. Vocal inflexions and rules of prosody often determine the rhythmic and melodic structure of the music. We know, moreover, how strong a sensibility exists to particular intonations – indeed a term equivalent to 'dialect' or 'pronunciation' is used to indicate the musical and melodic style of a particular region.

It was deviation from this basic approach that led in the III/9th century to various controversies, including the schism between the 'Ancients' and 'Moderns' and the question of the possible independence of instrumental music – an idea that could not have arisen in the original terms of the 'new music'. By the IV/10th century one can see the beginning of those separatist movements that would lead to the rejection of Arabic as a musical *lingua franca*. Present-day Islamic music derives from four distinct national sources: the Near Eastern (the cradle of the whole tradition), the Iranian (extending eastwards to Central Asia), the Maghribī and the Turkish.

Folk music

What we have called art music has so monopolized the interest of musicologists that the various traditions of folk music have remained almost totally unexplored. Yet recent research, as well as scattered information to be found in the literature of the past, proves that folk music can clarify many points in the development of art music, as well as being of considerable value in its own right. At different periods it has fertilized art music and (as in the West) professional musicians have found inspiration in it.

While art music is tied to the entertainment of aristocratic and urban society, requiring a certain professionalism in performance and reference to rules and aesthetic values for its understanding, folk music is closely associated with the ethnic groups of the region. It serves as a means of marking every important event in the life of the individual or the community. Many of its forms are unknown in art music, e.g. epic songs, dances, processions, passion plays such as those of Iran and Iraq and ceremonies of exorcism. Others have made the transition from folk to art (e.g. the music used to accompany the *orta oyunu* and the shadow theatre), and have given birth to sophisticated theatrical forms now in the repertory.

Since both folk and art music have been transmitted orally and have intermingled through many generations,

it is at times difficult to draw the line between them. Even folk music is not homogeneous; we can perhaps best imagine it as a continuum. At one end are songs and dances composed of short, melodic formulae, repeated either identically or according to the principle of 'open' and 'closed' phrases (the latter bringing the melody back to its conclusion). The tonal range is narrow, rarely going beyond a fourth, but the music displays rich rhythmical patterns and is performed antiphonally or responsorially to the accompaniment of hand-clapping and drums. With the exception of the epic songs, performed exclusively by soloists and accompanied on the *rabāb* (a one-stringed fiddle), this type of music is essentially communal, serving a social function. Instruments are rarely used. The words consists of exhortation formulae or improvised verses of various genres. At the opposite end one finds a very different category of songs, essentially solo, fairly melismatic (i.e. several notes being used for one syllable) and much more sophisticated. Their tonal range is wider, sometimes exceeding the octave. With their vague references to modal concepts and their use of vocal improvisation, these songs are closer to art music. Forms which use languages and dialects other than Arabic are particularly difficult to categorize: they always remained completely alien to the 'new music', yet they can be highly sophisticated and share many features of art music, and therefore lie nearer that end of the continuum.

A women's song from a wedding ceremony. (2)

Introduction to a song from the Yemen, of the kind popular among Bedouin fishermen, and sometimes used in exorcism ceremonies. This introduction would be played on a simsimiyya, *a five-stringed lyre plucked with a plectrum. (3)*

Excerpt from a debka, *the best-known dance of a wide region stretching from Sinai to northern Syria. It would be played on a* mugwiz, *a double-reed instrument with two equal pipes. (4)*

Folk music springs from a milieu in which poetry is considered important in social life and is held in profound esteem. Its language ranges from semi-classical to colloquial and comprises a great number of subjects; but all are of significance in the life of the community.

This poetry is exclusively sung. Music and poetry form an indissoluble unity. If a poet is asked to recite a poem without the help of the melody he finds it difficult, and since the structure of the verse is mostly determined by the melody it defies the normal metrical rules of poetry. Author, composer and performer are the same person. Sometimes one finds two such poet-musicians exchanging extempore verses and stanzas. This is a test of their powers of invention but at the same time offers each in turn a respite in the course of long performances.

The bulk of the material used by these bards is drawn from a traditional repertory. They choose formulae appropriate for the occasion, rearranging them as required. New words are composed more readily than new melodies. The same melody or poetic formula can occur in a wedding song, a work song or a religious procession, but the total number of forms and genres is very great, surpassing that of art music.

As we have seen, most of them consist of music fulfilling social functions, in which the public participates in various ways: singing, hand-clapping to lively and occasionally complicated rhythms, processional steps and dancing. Dances are almost always accompanied by songs. The songs themselves fall into two main categories – 'syllabic' songs (one note per syllable), with lively, measured rhythms and restricted range; and 'melismatic' (several notes per syllable) with free rhythms, sung by a soloist. Popular music usually has a single line of melody, but rudimentary forms of polyphony do appear: organum, drone, ostinato, overlapping and heterophony. The bulk of the folk repertory is sung without instruments, though epic songs and certain dances are accompanied by flutes and reed instruments. With the exception of Central Asia, there is practically no purely instrumental tradition.

Art music

In contrast to folk music, art music has been repeatedly analyzed, interpreted and argued over throughout Islamic history. Many of its preoccupations have been cosmological and ethical, but aesthetic considerations have never been absent. Musical criticism, for instance, has tried to define the emotional qualities embodied in the melodies and modes, which can range, according to these theories, from sensual pleasure to purely intellectual enjoyment. In the controversy between 'Ancients' and 'Moderns' in the III/9th century, such aesthetic categories were repeatedly discussed, simplicity and sobriety being contrasted to Baroque exuberance. Delight in playing for its own sake was certainly valued. Prince Ibrāhīm ibn al-Mahdī told his rival, the illustrious musician Ishāq al-Mawsilī: 'You do this professionally, but we do it for entertainment and harmless fun.' On the other hand, brilliance and virtuosity – even exhibitionism – were also highly prized. The beauty of the voice is often mentioned, and voices and vocal qualities are classified with some subtlety.

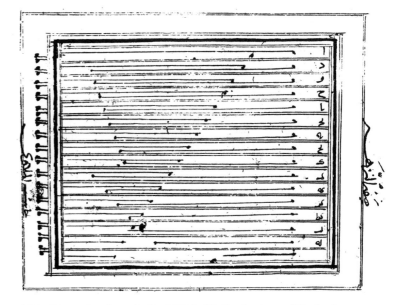

This illustration from Safī ad-Dīn's Kitāb al-adwar *('Book of Musical Modes') uses an alphabetical system to represent the tuning; but this was done only for instruction, not for musical notation. The instrument is a* nuzha, *a square* cithar *invented by Safī ad-Dīn but now obsolete. (5)*

Since all music was transmitted orally, composers were not able to avail themselves of notational devices. It is true that alphabetic systems are found in some treatises, but these seem to have been used only for explanation and instruction. The systems invented in Turkey in the XI/17th century and Western notation introduced in the XIII/19th were not widely adopted, and in the areas where they were, they led to a deterioration in the essential quality of Islamic art music. Oral transmission gave it a particular character of its own; expertise was difficult to acquire, needing both inborn talent and long training.

Training was always individual, based on a master-pupil relationship which began as purely pedagogic but ended as almost paternal. The finished ideal was the *musicus perfectus*, a man with an extraordinary aptitude for music – creative as a composer, practised as an instrumentalist and singer, gifted with a phenomenal memory, able to improvise effortlessly and to write good prose and verse and finally to be a man of wide general culture.

In art music, as in folk music, the singer is pre-eminent. This is true even in those regions where instrumental playing is highly developed, e.g. Persia. Concerts are usually private. The singer, accompanied by one instrument or a small ensemble, performs for a select gathering of connoisseurs. This intimacy, with the singer sitting in the midst of his audience, makes for a perfect rapport between them. All the performers are in their way soloists, and each displays his own talent. When several musicians play the same melodic line together, each slightly varies the tempo and ornamentation. This typical performing practice, known as heterophony, together with the use of drone and parallel intervals (octaves, fifths and fourths), constitutes a form of polyphony, though it is, as it were, grafted on to a type of music that is essentially non-polyphonic. Every detail relates to the linear development, from which spring a whole range of further refinements, both vocal and instrumental, such as nasal tone, vibrato, guttural sounds, *sforzando* and *diminuendo*, *portamento*, *glissando* and numerous other devices.

Technique and expression: the modes

Although both the technique and the style of Islamic music are governed by strict rules, a large measure of freedom is still left to the performer for the display of his creative powers and imagination. This is true not only of improvised pieces but also of fixed compositions. Indeed, much of the art resides in the manner of singing and playing, i.e. in the use of ornament and variation.

In Iranian music ornaments are divided into two kinds: 'usual' and 'personal'. Together these encompass *appoggiaturas*, trills, *grupetti*, quick repetition of notes and the subtle *tabrīr*, vocal embellishments on a single syllable. A given model can be modified in both melody and rhythm; new words can be fitted to an already existing melody, accents can be displaced, tempi changed. Such modifications and variations constitute the most important aspect of music-making in this region. 'Originality' does not mean to create *ex nihilo*, but to improve on a traditional model. In the art of the Iranian *avāz* the freedom allowed in choosing melodic sequences *(gūshés)*, manipulating them and progressing from one to another makes it difficult to distinguish between such variations on a fixed composition and truly improvised pieces.

Because the interest centres on the melodic line, Islamic music employs a far greater and more subtle range of intervals than is normal in the West. There are, for instance, several seconds and thirds of different pitch, including the 'neutral' third fixed by Zalzāl (d. 175/791). There are also intervals of 3/4, 5/4 and 6/4 of a tone. A number of theories were evolved to systematize these intervals and these theoretical structures approximate to the 'modes' of classical music much more closely than to the diatonic keys in use in the West today. A favourite instrument used to demonstrate them was a short-necked lute, the *'ūd*. Thus the first modal theory, that of *asābi'* (fingers), ascribed to Ishāq al-Mawsilī (150-236/767-850), is related to the frets and fingers used in producing notes on the *'ūd*. Its four strings were tuned in fourths, and each one of them had the range of a fourth whose two outer notes were fixed while the others were variable.

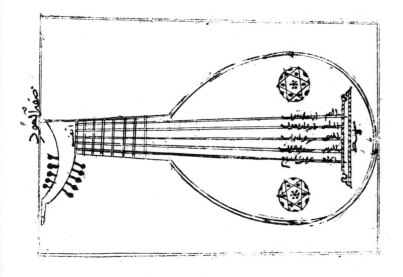

The 'ūd, or short-necked lute, was one of the most popular instruments of Islamic music and was often used to demonstrate and explain musical theory. This drawing is again from Safī ad-Dīn's treatise, a seminal work quoted by almost every subsequent theorist. The 'ūd is shown with frets and five double strings, whose names are given. (6)

When the intervals on one string had been defined, the theorists fixed the intervals on other strings by locating the octaves, fourths and fifths of the fundamentals. Once they had obtained all the intervals they organized them in *genera* and systems. Although in a succession of four notes only one type of second and one type of third can be used, there are still numerous possible combinations of *genera* or tetrachords. So by combining identical or different *genera*, the musician has available a great many systems, some of which constitute the fundamental scales of the modes.

(a)   (b)   (c)

(a) *Tetrachord* rast;
(b) *tetrachord* higaz *transposed on G (normally on D)*;
(c) *combination of (a) and (b) producing the system or modal scale of the* maqām *called* suznak. *Had the upper tetrachord been identical with the lower, then the scale obtained would have been that of* maqām rast, *the scale of the next example.* (7)

In the course of the XIII/19th century new theories were evolved which divided the scale into seventeen intervals (i.e. roughly into thirds of a tone) or twenty-four (i.e. into quarters of a tone). It was the latter which gained more favour and was eventually adopted almost everywhere. In theory, therefore, the intervals of Islamic music are far subtler than Western; but in practice they are subtler still. Musicians are still very sensitive to the variability of movable intervals, and the players of fretted instruments often shift the frets in order to adjust them to the expressive character required.

In addition to constituting the basic scales (like major, minor or modal in Western music), the modes have other devices and an expressive function for which there is no Western equivalent. They affect methods of composition, practices of performance, improvisation and even certain musical forms. Instead of discussing the modal system in the abstract, it may be better understood if we look at some of the most representative of these forms.

The Iranian modal system *(avāz)* is made up of twelve modes, divided into seven principal and five secondary *(dastgāhs)*. Each consists of a variable number of melodic sequences *(gūshés)* which succeed each other in a given order. These *gūshés* are the basic material at the musician's disposal, and each mode has between twenty and forty of them traditionally associated with it. This is one limitation on the performer's freedom. Another is the fact that among the notes of the fundamental scale there are certain ones that are preferential: the *shāhid* or 'witness' note, a central note frequently repeated; the *ist* or 'pausing' note; the *mutaghayyir*, the 'variable' note; and the *furūd-i kamāl*, 'concluding' note. In the course of a piece of this type the *shāhid* systematically rises. Certain *gūshés* can deviate to another fundamental scale; but they have to return in the end to the first one, concluding with the original mode. The series of *gūshés* follows an accepted schema: at first introductory and slow, then lively and full of virtuosity, then a series emphasizing the ascent of the *shāhid*, and usually a lively conclusion. Within this fairly strict framework, both singers and instrumentalists are able to display all their art and improvisatory skill.

The Iraqi *maqām* includes a whole array of special conventions: scales, motifs and melodies, types of singing, literary or dialect texts, nonsense words and characteristic rhythmic instrumental accompaniment, though the accompaniment is always subordinate to the vocal line. (The plural of *maqām* is *maqāmāt*, which we meet elsewhere in this book as a literary form.) Occasional modulatory progressions lead from one *maqām* to another, but the basic idea is to keep the unity intact.

The *nūba* of North Africa is a related form consisting of a suite of instrumental and vocal pieces composed in one mode, with emphasis on rhythmic organization and progression. All *nūbas* begin with an instrumental prelude, followed by other instrumental items leading to a series of accompanied vocal pieces in different forms and rhythms, and using numerous vocal and instrumental embellishments including improvisation. A dozen or so *nūbas* are still performed, each with its own specific instrumental layout; this part is fixed, the vocal open to variations.

The Turkish *fasil* is similarly a suite of instrumental and vocal pieces in different genres, arranged in a certain order. The prelude and conclusion are both instrumental; the rest consists of songs of various kinds interspersed with instrumental improvisations known as *taqsīm*.

The *taqsīm* is an instrumental improvisation, again made up of a series of sections, characterized this time by a 'central' note and opening and concluding motifs. The sections are separated and defined by rests or by recognized concluding motifs functioning as cadences. These cadences, together with the various central notes, largely determine the structure of the *taqsīm*. Each section has its own central note, which is stressed in various ways. The first few sections are generally in the lower range, and the player afterwards modulates into the upper range. At that point the section can become longer and with a wider range. Modulatory progressions play an important part in the development of the *taqsīm*. The complex possibilities available to the player in progressing from one section to the next are a test of his ability, his command over the material and the response he is able to draw from his audience. The rhythm is free, not confined to periodic accents or to fixed formulae. The *taqsīm* is a form that follows a set general plan but offers variation in the details.

Layālī are local improvisations. The name means 'nights', and derives from the words *yā-laylī* ('O night'), which provide the phonetic base; occasionally this is changed to *yā 'aynī* ('O eye'). Upon these words the singer improvises a florid vocal line, sometimes using one note per syllable, sometimes many. Structure and general characteristics resemble the *taqsīm*. Usually the player accompanies himself alone on the *'ūd*, but is sometimes joined by other instruments for short interludes. Both *taqsīm* and *layālī* are usually inserted in suites, though nowadays they are also performed separately.

The *mawwāl* is yet another vocal form, but less dependent on improvisation and occupying a position between the *layālī* and the metrical rhythmic forms. Its text is performed in a free *parlando* style.

Rhythm is as important a part of Islamic music as the modal structures, and a systematic theory of it was evolved as early as the III/9th century. It was conceived as the way in which melody is divided, sounds (or beats) being separated by periods of silence (rests) whose duration could be more or less long. The melodic unit was modelled on the verse used in the *qasīda*, which has been fully described in Professor Pellat's chapter on literature (Chapter V). The single *qasīda* verse consists of two clearly distinct halves. The rhythmical period was seen in the same way, and likewise divided into two equal parts. Each part was made up of smaller, usually asymmetrical elements, and was conditioned by the scansion of the poetry. From prosody the musical theorists borrowed, among other things, the symbol of a circle followed by a point (O.) to indicate the beat and the subsequent rest. Circle and point represent equal lengths of time; but the point can stand for either silence or the prolongation of the preceding sound. Hence a combination like this OO. O.O. O.. can mean either ♩ ♩ ♩ ♩. or ♩ ♩𝄽 ♩𝄽 ♩𝄽 ♩𝄽𝄽. The length of a beat is naturally determined not only by the distance separating it from the following beat but also by the speed of the movement. Besides the principal beats there are secondary ones which differ in timbre and quality; some are used merely as ornaments.

Working along these lines, eight basic rhythmical 'modes' were defined. In the course of time these have been added to and enriched, and musicologists now speak in terms of over a hundred.

Excerpt from a vocal improvisation in maqām rast. *(8)*

The instruments of Islamic music

The instruments described in the literature relating to music are many and varied. Some are still used, others have become obsolete. One serious problem in using these written sources is to decide what instruments are meant by the old terminology. In some cases several different names are used for one instrument; in others one name is applied to several different instruments. The term *mizmār*, for instance, can mean wind instruments in

All the illustrations on this page come from the Kanz al-tuhaf, *an important Persian treatise of the* VIII/*14th century, by an unknown author. Here, the* ʿūd, *a short-necked lute.* (9)

The mizmār, *a reed instrument, and the* nāy, *a flute.* (10)

The saḥīn, *another form of lute, now obsolete.* (11)

The gank, *a small harp held against the chest.* (12)

general, double or single reed instruments, or even a psalm.

The following list is generally confined to instruments still in use, though they obviously derive from models going back into the past. Many more are known from literature and painting, but we cannot be sure how they sounded.

The idiophones (instruments which produce their own sound) include metal castanets; tiny cymbals attached to dancers' thumbs and middle fingers; a larger variety used in military music; wooden spoons; and finally copper plates or oil containers used as drums.

Membranophones (drums) are the richest and most varied family, especially in folk music. Frame drums can be circular or rectangular; some have jingling discs, others strings stretched under the skin. One type of vase-shaped drum *(darbukkah)* was formerly made of earthenware, but is now more usually of metal. The Iranian *ẓarb*, made of wood, is associated only with art music; it is placed either under the left arm or between the legs and

The nuzha, *square* cithar. *(13)*

The qānūn, *trapezoidal* cithar. *(14)*

The nabāb, *a bowed instrument.* *(15)*

The rabāb, *another bowed instrument.* *(16)*

beaten in the middle and near the edge with both hands.

Cylindrical drums *(tabl)* with two skins are hung at an angle from the neck of the player and skins at each end beaten with two flexible sticks. Occasionally one finds ensembles of cylindrical drums of different dimensions, but mostly they are used with double-reed instruments or cymbals at processions, dances and open-air ceremonies.

Kettledrums *(naqqārāt)*, hemispherical with a skin stretched over the top, come in pairs. The larger ones are carried on camels and played during pilgrimages.

Another type is used to accompany one of the Mawlawī ceremonies. Under the late 'Abbāsids and Fāṭimids in Egypt, kettledrums were beaten before the five daily prayers, and small ones form part of present-day orchestral ensembles.

Aerophones (wind instruments). Oblique flutes *(nāy)* without mouthpiece exist in different lengths, usually with five or six finger-holes on the upper side and one on the under side. They can cover a range of two and a half octaves; some of the notes can be modified by blowing

167

harder or softer. Flutes are favourite instruments of some of the mystical orders, and are used in both folk and art music. Simpler varieties made of reed or metal are played by shepherds and at dances.

Double reed instruments (similar to the oboe) *(zurna* or *ghayta)* and single reed (similar to the clarinet) are exclusively associated with popular ceremonies. The former are made of wood and widen at the bottom into a bell shape. The double reed instrument is enclosed in a small brass mouthpiece, the reed being entirely held inside the player's mouth and his lips pressing on a small metal ring; it has seven or eight finger-holes. These flutes are either accompanied by a cylindrical drum or played as an ensemble using instruments of different sizes. One type was included in the military bands of the Janissaries.

There are a great variety of single reed instruments with two pipes, some of equal length, others with one pipe longer than the other. In the latter case the long pipe sounds a more or less continuous drone.

Bagpipes are found in several areas: the Maghrib, Turkey, Egypt and the Persian Gulf. Horns and trumpets were until the last century in use in military bands. One type of trumpet called the *karna*, played in Iran as part of the imperial ensemble, was six feet long.

Chordophones (strings). Most Islamic string instruments are plucked, not bowed. Chief among them are the various types of lute. We have already met the *'ūd*, the short-necked lute used in working out musical theory. Its body is pear-shaped and originally it had four strings and frets. The present-day *'ūd* is fretless and has five double strings tuned in fourths, except for the lowest, which is a second away from the next lowest. If a sixth string is added it is tuned a second higher than the fifth. Plucking is with an eagle's feather or a plectrum. In the Maghrib a variant of the *'ūd* is used which has four double strings tuned E, A, F, B; this overlapping tuning limits the range and makes the fingering awkward.

Long-necked lutes are also widespread and appear under a variety of names. The *sitār* has four strings tuned C, G (or F), C (identical with first) and C (an octave lower). It has twenty-five movable frets, and is plucked with the nail of the index finger. A variant of the *sitār*, the *tār*, has a figure-eight body and is covered with skin. It has three double strings tuned C, G, C (an octave lower), twenty-five frets, and is plucked with a plectrum. Other types used in Iran, Central Asia, Turkey *(tambūr)*, Syria and Lebanon, have two, three or four strings. The Kirghiz *komuz* and Kazakh *dombra* are long-necked with three strings but no frets. In Turkish folk music the number of strings can rise to nine. In the Maghrib, on the other hand, we find a variety with only two, plucked by the fingers.

There are two important types of *cithar*: one (the *qānūn*) is plucked, the other (the *santūr*) struck with two sticks. Both are essentially trapezoidal boxes. The *qānūn* has twenty-four triple strings, under the end of which are placed little movable bridges to allow the player to modify the tuning of the strings. It is held on the player's knees and plucked with a plectrum attached to each index finger. The *santūr* has seventy-two strings grouped in fours supported by eighteen movable bridges in two rows of nine dividing the whole into three registers.

The only bowed instrument is the *rabāb*, which exists in two forms. The simpler is either rectangular or round, covered with skin and strung with a single string. As we have seen, it is played by the popular poets to accompany their recitations. The other kind of *rabāb* is oval or spherical in shape, has two strings tuned a fifth apart and is associated principally with art music. A more complex type, the *kamanja*, has a wooden body ending in a peg, and three or four strings. All these, unlike the violin of the West, are played by holding the bow steady and moving the instrument. In Morocco a violin is often used instead, but it is played in the same manner. A lyre known as *simsimiyya* and strung with five strings is a favourite instrument in the Red Sea area.

Religion and music
The question whether music is permissible at all began to be debated in the first century of Islam and the debate has continued to this day, filling many thousands of pages. Apart from the theological arguments, opposition to music on the part of certain early religious authorities seems to have arisen from the role it had begun to play in society. The 'new music' was associated more and more with a life of pleasure and a taste for luxury. It acquired connotations of frivolity and sensuality, reinforced by the participation of women in music-making and by the dancing (often considered indecent) and the drinking of intoxicating beverages that went with it. Even the two holy cities of Mecca and Medina were not immune from these temptations, and indeed they quickly became veritable centres of entertainment.

There was no clear line of demarcation between sacred and secular music, and sacred music itself has throughout its long history oscillated between art and folk music. According to some of the traditions adduced in the controversy, Muhammad would have approved of the latter but not of the former, and art music was consequently completely banished. Nevertheless, the interpenetration of the two genres has meant that the emphasis has continually fluctuated.

On the theological and philosophical level, the authorities to which the two sides appeal are the Qur'ān, the *hadīth*, the writings of religious leaders, the opinions of mystics and legal precedents. The Qur'ān provides no specific verdict one way or the other, so it was the *hadīth* which was the main source of ammunition. Literal interpretation of texts was reinforced by reasoning by analogy. Al-Ghazālī (d. 505/1111) makes brilliant use of this method and the chapter devoted to music in his *Vivification of the Religious Sciences* is a masterpiece.

The mystics held music in the highest esteem, and made it an essential element in the *dhikr* ceremonies. Closely related to the mystical movement was a genre of literature entitled *samā'* ('listening'), partly description, partly polemical. For the most part it favoured music, but it recognized certain abuses and was occasionally opposed to dancing and the use of instruments. Writers within the same tradition would often disagree, and controversies continued over many generations. Thus, for instance, the treatise of 'Abd al-Ghanī an-Nābulsī (d. 1144/1731), called *Convincing Proofs Concerning the Permissibility of Listening to Musical Instruments*, was attacked by a later writer, who was in his turn attacked by Muhammad ad-Dāmūnī (d. 1215/1800).

Such questions were of concern not only to the religious authorities, spiritual leaders and jurists but to writers in general. The most important of these who contributed to the discussion are Ibn 'Abd Rabbihi (246-329/860-940), al-Ibshīhī (d. 850/1446), an-Nuwayrī (d. 732/1332) and Ibn Khaldūn (d. 808/1406).

But what exactly were the uses of music in religious contexts which gave rise to such passionate disagreements? There were three that were particularly important: the chanting of the Qur'ān, the call to prayer, and a few hymns for special occasions and holy days.

The musical setting of the Qur'ān goes back to the second half of the 1/7th century, but it is not related to either Jewish or Christian musical traditions, and according to literary sources derives from ancient incantations and chants of pre-Islamic poetry. Its purpose is to enhance the meaning of the text and convey it in an effective way. Treatises on the subject codified rules (*tajwīd* – 'embellishment of the reading'), whose aim was to teach the reader how to present the sacred text to the faithful in a comprehensible and moving way, while avoiding any heresy that might result from a misreading. Accentuation, prolongation and assimilation of certain letters, pauses and correct pronunciation were all covered, as well as the three possible speeds – slow and solemn, rapid and intermediate. It is often stressed that such chanting has nothing to do with art music, and is actually in theory not counted as music at all. Nevertheless, in practice it has always absorbed elements from art music. In some countries it is even performed in different modes. But the basic traits are always kept, and ornate style and instrumental accompaniment are avoided.

The call to prayer *(adhān)* was established by Muhammad between 1/622 and 3/624. The first muezzin, who became the patron saint of muezzin guilds in Turkey and Africa, was a freed slave called Bilal, whose martyrdom is a favourite subject of modern plays and films. The structure of the *adhān* is determined by the phrasing of the text; it is composed of twelve musical phrases setting a seven-line text, with repetitions. But the rhythm is relatively free, and the melody varies from region to region and is related to folk music. It is simple in the Maghrib and highly embellished in Near Eastern countries, though always proceeding according to the principle of 'open' and 'closed' phrases which as we have seen is a common characteristic in folk melody. Its general shape is a curve whose high point coincides with the seventh phrase out of the twelve. The *adhān* is intoned five times a day with a powerful and expressive voice. For certain occasions it is augmented by additional lines. Nowadays the *adhān* is often transmitted by microphone and loudspeaker instead of being given vocally from the top of the minaret.

At certain special festivals other musical forms are performed. On the nights of Ramadān one hears a special tune for this occasion, the *fazzāziyyāt*; and on the Anniversary of the Prophet (the *mawlid*), hymns and chanted narratives of his birth and life. Turkey has a special poem for the *mawlid* composed by Sulayman Chelebi (d. 812/1409), a real musical piece in four distinct sections, each in a different *maqām*. In other countries other genres evolved in connection with periodic commemoration of venerated saints. The passion play based on the martyrdom of Hasan and Husayn, celebrated in Iran and Iraq during the first ten days of Muharram, is described in more detail by Professor Savory (Chapter X).

In this context we should also mention Jewish and Christian religious music, which with its rich and distinct liturgical repertoire, ranging from musical settings of the scriptures and prayers to very elaborate hymns, offers many parallels with Islam. Some factors have tended to divide the music of the three faiths (e.g. the special ritual requirements of Judaism and Christianity and the use of different languages); and there are features, such as the Jewish *te'amīm* (a sort of notation system for the *Torah*, part-musical, part-grammatical) or the Christian modal system of *octoechos*, derived from Byzantine tradition, which have no place in Islamic music. But the influence of secular art music is strongly felt in the singing of hymns, and in some cases the musical setting of sacred texts has been affected by it. This is due partly to the fact that some cantors were also active professional musicians.

In the mystical brotherhoods, as distinct from the official religious services, music always had a revered and acknowledged place. The experience of listening, called *samā'*, has already been mentioned. '*Samā'* cannot produce in the heart what is not already there,' said Abū Sulaymān ad-Dārānī, who died about 205/820. '*Samā'* is like the sun, which shines on everything but affects them differently according to their degrees: it burns, or illumines, or dissolves,' said al-Hujwīrī. Sayings like these abound in mystical writings. It is remarkable that the term 'music' is never used, and its elements are rarely discussed. It is always a question of 'listening', which includes attending to dancing as well as music. Voice, gesture and musical instruments are all aids to the devotee in his spiritual exercise, which, as Professor Meier has described, leads him to ecstasy and to supreme union with God. Hence *samā'* is a vital and indispensable element in the mystical search. The founder of the Mawlawī, Jalāl ad-Dīn Rūmī, says: 'The *samā'* is the soul's adornment which helps it to discover love, to feel the shudder of the encounter, to take off the veils and to be in the presence of God.'

The *dhikr* ceremonies common to all the orders have also been mentioned. It is here that the *samā'* finds its fullest expression. The series of 'phases' on the way to supreme existence are marked by a well-articulated musical organization which attains its highest achievement in the Mawlawī ceremony *'Ayn Sharīf*. This constitutes a real composition of art music, and there exist examples by known composers such as Mustafā Dede (1019-86/1610-75), Mustafā 'Itrī (1050-1123/1640-1711) and the Dervish 'Alī Sīrajānī (d. 1126/1714). Besides the singers, it uses a large ensemble including flutes, kettledrums, frame-drums, fiddles *(kamanjas)* and long-necked lutes. The same union of art music and mysticism exists also in Iranian brotherhoods. Many others, however, reject instruments, or content themselves with percussion. In these cases the result is close to folk music, though a rudimentary form of polyphony occurs. The devotees repeat the name of Allah incessantly, shortening it to *lah* and then to *ah* as they go from phase to phase. This forms a kind of *ostinato*, upon which are grafted the chant of the soloist or the responses of the participants.

Excerpt from a Mawlawī ceremony, ʿAyn Sharīf, *played by an instrumental ensemble:* son yürük semai. *(17)*

Excerpt from music played at one of the zikr *ceremonies of the Dassukia brotherhood. (18)*

Theory and practice

By the III/9th century musicians, writers and philosophers began to speculate on the origins and nature of their music. In the absence of historical documents they often had to go to legends and vague traditions (Lamak, for instance, was said to have made the first lute from the leg of his dead son, whose loss he lamented with it). Concern about the origin and evolution of music was only one aspect of musical studies which had voluminous results in the succeeding centuries.

Society was eager for knowledge of all kinds. The study of music became a necessary part of every cultured man's education, part of the encyclopaedic learning he was expected to acquire, and in the intellectual flowering which reached a climax in the IV/10th century music played a role. But, as the greatest of Arabic theorists, al-Fārābī (d. 339/950), wrote in his *Kitāb al-Musīqī al-Kabīr*: 'Theory did not appear until practice had already achieved its highest development.' This was certainly the case by his own time.

Musical theory had been stimulated by the translation of Greek treatises on the subject into Arabic in the second half of the II/8th century. Many Greek manuscripts were acquired by the enlightened Caliph al-Ma'mūn, and were translated by Christians who had mastered both languages. The first to take advantage of these newly discovered treasures was al-Kindī, 'the Philosopher of the Arabs'. He wrote thirteen musical treatises and is considered the first distinguished representative of the Arab *musica speculativa*, a category of writing which presented two major trends – one emphasizing the ethical and cosmological aspects of music, the other mainly its mathematical and acoustic side. Al-Kindī's writings belong predominantly to the first, as does a treatise produced by an order known as the Brotherhood of Purity – Ikwān as-Safā'. This, which is of considerable literary quality, tries to initiate the brethren into the basic doctrines of the order through music. Music, it taught, leads to 'spiritual knowledge'; it helps to untie the knots in the soul by making man aware of the beauty and harmony of the universe and the need to go beyond material existence.

The second trend, which studies music scientifically, as an activity that is strictly mathematical and almost independent of the human ear, is mainly represented by the great philosophers and theorists al-Fārābī (257-339/870-950), Ibn Sīnā (Avicenna) (370-429/980-1037), Ibn Zayla (d. 440/1048) and Safī ad-Dīn al-Urmawī (d. 693/1294), who deal with the theory of sound, intervals and their ratio, harmonies and dissonances, genres, systems, modes, rhythms and rhythmical modes, as well as with the theory of composition and the construction of musical instruments. Both kinds of writing rely heavily on Greek sources, but do not reproduce them mechanically. The Arab theorists expanded and improved their models to correspond with the living music of their own time.

Treatises of this type form one category of the vast quantity of musical writings. Two other categories which must briefly be noticed are the literary, encyclopaedic and anecdotal sources, and books on the theory of the practice of music.

The first comprises chapters, fragments or passages on music to be found in the literature of *adab* (see Chapter V) and in books of medicine, history, geography, religion and Sufism. Here music is either mentioned in the course of a narrative or is discussed incidentally – for its influence on moral conduct, its religious uses, or its role in manners, education and general knowledge. One of the most outstanding books in this last class is *Kitāb al-Aghānī* ('The Book of Songs') by Abū 'l-Faraj al-Isfahānī (284-357/897-967), a fruitful source on music, musical life and aesthetics. Al-Isfahānī collected the songs which were popular in his own time, adding details about their authors and their background which seemed of interest to him, and also included a certain amount of technical information. For instance he goes into the modal theory of *asābiʿ* (fingers), which has already been briefly discussed earlier in this chapter, and prefaces each song with instructions based upon it. He also gives the main note of the mode, the type of third to be used and very often the rhythmical mode.

Books on the theory of the practice of music were written mainly for educational purposes, to provide a comprehensive groundwork in actual music-making for both amateur and professional; though the theoretical aspects are not entirely neglected. Ahmad al-Kātib's *Perfection of Musical Knowledge*, for instance, ranges over a wide field of subjects with observations and advice, from problems of phonetics, breathing and pronunciation to the arranging of musical concerts, audience-reactions,

Shepherd playing a nāy *(flute), from a Persian dictionary of rare words, X/16th century. (19)*

Harp and lute (ʿūd; see fig. 6). The man on the left is clapping his hands to mark the rhythm. (20)

plagiarism, classification of voices and treatment of the voice, while on a more theoretical level he explains current terminology and problems relating to modality. To some extent the *tajwīd al-Qurʾān* ('embellishment of the reading') should be included in this category, since it deals with actual performance and aims to educate the reader.

Six periods of Islamic music

During the first period of Islam, and particularly during the reigns of the last two Orthodox caliphs, ʿUthmān and ʿAlī, Medina became the centre of intense musical activity. Despite frequent campaigns against music by the religious authorities, professional musicians were welcomed in the houses of the rich and noble, and encouraged by lavish rewards. These musicians were mainly freed slaves of Persian origin, such as Tuwais (d. 92/710) and Khathīr (d. 64/683), who is said to have taught Arabic music to Nashīt, the Persian slave who became a famous musician. The vogue for Persian songs during this period may also have been helped by the influx of Persian prisoners to work as masons at Medina. Among the female musicians of Arab origin ʿAzza al-Mayla (d. 86/705) occupies the first place. Her house was a real cultural salon, frequented by the literary and musical élite. Some of the rhythmical modes began to crystallize during this period; its most characteristic type of song is called the *al-ghināʾ al-mutqan*.

Under the Umayyads the centre of musical interest shifts to the new capital, Damascus. Some of the caliphs had a real passion for music; consequently musical activity increased, musicians multiplied and their social status rose. The practice of music also spread among amateurs, and was widely taught by the virtuosi. Ibn Misjah (d. *c.* 169/785) played a leading role in the blossoming of the 'new music'. It was said that he had learned Persian and Byzantine music, rejected what was alien to the spirit of 'Arabian song' and retained the propitious elements, namely 'the most advantageous of the modes'. He was one of the 'four great singers', the other three being Ibn Muhrīz, the son of a Persian freed-man (d. *c.* 97/715), Ibn Surayj, the son of a Turkish slave (13-108/634-726), and al-Gharīd (d. *c.* 106/724), who belonged to

a family of Berber slaves. Two more notable artists were Maʿbad, the son of a black, and Jamīla (d. *c.* 102/720), a famous female singer.

With the ʿAbbāsid dynasty the capital moved to Baghdad. Here, during the next two centuries, Islamic music attained its highest point. This was its golden age. Musicians continued to enjoy favour at the caliphs' court and to play an important part in the country's cultural life. The study of music was now obligatory for every educated man, and equally the musician was expected to be widely cultured. Music itself became highly sophisticated and began to be the subject of learned controversies between thinkers with different artistic conceptions. 'Ancients' and 'Moderns' held public debates. On one side stood Ibrāhīm al-Mawsilī (d. 188/804) and his son Ishāq (150-236/767-850), on the other Ibn Jāmiʿ and Prince Ibrāhīm ibn al-Mahdī (163-225/779-839). It was within this milieu that the first musical literature grew up. The melodic and rhythmic modes were definitively codified. Theories were evolved, practice described. At the same time the instruments themselves were perfected and standards of performance rose even higher. Ancient musical forms became more refined and some new ones came into being. Among the numerous great musicians, besides those already mentioned, are Siyyāt (d. 169/785), Zalzāl (a famous instrumentalist, who fixed the neutral third; d. 175/791), Mukhāriq (d. *c.* 229/845), ʿAllūya and ʿAmr ibn Bānā (d. 278/891). Celebrated female singers were Basbas, ʿUbayda, Shariyya, Danānīr and Mahbūba.

The music of Islamic Spain is to some extent a separate story. Its founder was Ziryāb, a pupil of Ishāq al-Mawsilī. As a rival to his master he was obliged to leave Baghdad, and arrived in Spain in 206/821, where ʿAbd ar-Rahmān II took him into service. A great artist and a man of wide culture and prodigious memory, he added a fifth string to the ʿūd and introduced new methods of musical education. Many members of his family followed in his footsteps and became famous musicians. In the later years of Muslim Spain music continued to play a prominent part in spite of the worsening political situation. Cross-fertilization between the indigenous Visigothic culture, that of the Berbers and the sophisticated Umayyad traditions led to a particular style and special musical forms such as the *muwashshah* and the *zajal*, which were to survive in the Maghrib as well as farther east. These developments are discussed at more length by Señor García Gómez (Chapter IX). Perhaps the most characteristic achievement of the Andalusian tradition was the *nūba*, a suite form which took root in various parts of North Africa after the fall of Granada in 1492.

The fifth period of Islamic music is immensely long – from the v/11th century to the xiii/19th. Politically this is marked by the decline of the caliphate, ending in the Mongol invasion of 657/1258 and the splitting up of the Islamic world into independent states. Musical life, however, continued almost without interruption. Although less fertile and less original than in previous periods, it in some ways benefited from decentralization. At the various smaller courts, music was often encouraged by rulers anxious for prestige, and was able to assimilate new contributions leading to great diversity. Interestingly, it was often the mystical brotherhoods, mainly in Turkey and Iran, who did most for the development of art music, not only by promoting music for their own needs, but also by creating the conditions for a wider musical culture in general.

The contemporary period is marked by two trends – on the one hand the rediscovery and renewal of Islamic traditions, on the other contact with the West. Western music was introduced first in Turkey before 1242/1826, later in Egypt and Iran. Musicians from Europe were invited to instruct local players for such things as military bands. It was the start of a long process which is still continuing, bringing with it Western musical notation, Western instruments and teaching methods and Western forms such as opera and operetta. At the same time much of the Islamic tradition survived intact; folk music was hardly affected, and even in contexts open to Western influence music retained its typically monodic character. Scholars and musicians began investigating the roots of their own musical history, and in 1932 an important conference, the 'Congrès de Musique Arabe', was held in Cairo. Here specialists from both Europe and Near Eastern countries tried to define the most important aspects of Islamic music and to ensure that it survived and continued to develop. Since then the process of change has become even more marked in almost every way – in the type of sound produced, in musical language, in teaching and in performing conventions. The concept of Islamic music nevertheless remains viable, to undergo further transformations in the future.

Aristocratic music-making: these ivory plaques from Fātimid Egypt (v/11th to vi/12th century) show small groups of performers playing to a select gathering in a private house: a dancer, a lute-player and a flautist with a double flute. The lute is the type known as the *ʿūd*, perhaps the most widespread of all Islamic instruments. (1, 2)

The power of music was recognized early in Islam's history – so much so, indeed, that there was for centuries a running controversy over the question whether it was strictly permissible at all. Orthodox minds associated it with dancing and luxurious living. Nevertheless music served religion in some contexts, though never attaining the importance which it enjoyed in the Christian Church.

The call to prayer, repeated five times a day, had been instituted by Muhammad himself. The musical content varied according to the period and the religion, but always consisted of twelve phrases setting a seven-line text; and these phrases were often related to the local folk music. This detail (left) is Persian, from a manuscript of Sa'dī's *Gulistān* copied in Shīrāz in 974/1566. (3)

To the mystical brotherhoods music meant something deeper, and has been considered as an essential element in the *dhikr* ceremonies. The elements of the music itself seem to have been of minor importance. What mattered was concentration upon the actual experience of listening which 'helps the soul to discover love . . . and to be in the presence of God'. This detail from a Mughul miniature of 1004/1595 shows musicians accompanying a dervish dance with long- and short-necked lutes and tambourine. (4)

The road to Mecca was enlivened by music of a semi-military character. Opposite: a scene from al-Harīrī's *Maqāmāt* painted in Baghdad in 635/1237. Note particularly the large kettledrums (*naqqārāt*) carried on the camels. They were made in pairs, and were hemispherical in shape with a skin stretched over the top. (5)

وَكَادَ يَنْزِعُ الجِمَالَ النَّشْرُ وَانْشَدَ

مَا الحَجُّ سَيْرُكَ تَأْوِيبًا وَادْلاجًا وَلا الغَيَامَ جِمَالًا وَاحْدَاجًا

الحَجُّ أَنْ تَقْصِدَ البَيْتَ الحَرَامَ عَلَى تَجْرِيدِكَ الحَجَّ لا تَبْغِي بِهِ حَاجَا

وَتَقْتَضِي كَاهِلَ الإِنْصَافِ مُتَّخِذًا رَدْعَ الهَوَى هَادِيًا وَالحَقَّ مِنْهَاجَا

The lute: an early form from a Seljuq relief; late VI/12th century. (6)

Short-necked lute, tambourine and harp being played in a tavern (above right); Iran, 654/1256. (7)

The harp accompanies a game of chess (right), from a Spanish Christian manuscript of the 13th century. (8)

Harp, flute and lute (below): details from a brass basin inlaid with silver, from Syria or Mesopotamia, dating from the VII/13th century. (9, 10, 11)

The **instruments** of Islamic music are many and varied. Some of them are well known from descriptions and pictures; we know what they looked like, but we cannot be sure how they sounded. It is, of course, possible to use present-day specimens for comparison.

The horn, played by a man who is probably a shepherd. The painting comes from a Persian album of the early XI/17th century. (12)

The oblique flute varied in length and had five or six holes in the upper side and one on the lower; Persian, mid X/16th century. (13)

Trumpets had their expected place in military bands and could be of immense size. Some reached a length of six feet. (14)

Castanets, used by a dancer to mark the rhythm. Both these illustrations are from a Persian dictionary executed in the early X/16th century. (15)

Music was a part of social life. From primitive villages to sophisticated courts, events like weddings, funerals and festivals were marked by music, in which the public could participate by singing, dancing or hand-clapping. The marriage of Akbar's brother (opposite) at Agra in 969/1561 called for the services of many musicians and dancers. Note the long S-shaped trumpet at the back, the castanets held by the dancers, and the drums of different shapes and sizes. The music was never written down, but so well defined were the conventions governing what each man could do that they could combine together in complicated patterns of sound. Even today, when Western methods of notation are available, Islamic music is still essentially improvisatory. (18)

Military music had an important public function and was played by large ensembles, which included, under the Fāṭimids in Egypt, five hundred trumpets and five hundred drums. These ensembles aimed to display royal pomp, splendour and luxury. The Turks employed it on both ceremonial and warlike occasions, and the 'Turkish march' became a recognized style in the Europe of Mozart's day, featuring drums, trumpets and cymbals. Above: Turkish military band in 1001/1592, from a manuscript describing the events of Murād III's reign. Roughly the same combination of instruments must have been common two hundred years earlier, since one of al-Jazarī's *Automata* (right) imitates trumpets and drums on a mechanical water-clock dating from the early VIII/14th century. (16, 17)

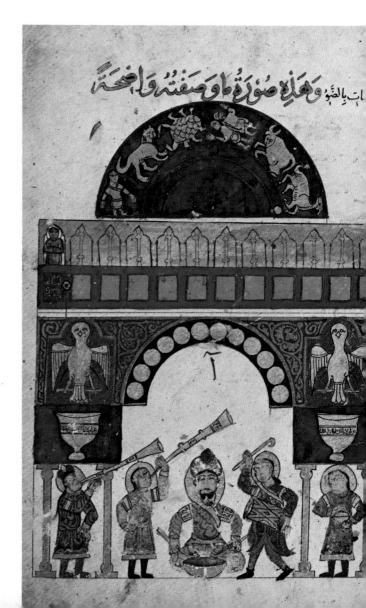

Folk music has almost completely escaped the attention of chroniclers and illustrators, but something of its history can be deduced from present-day survivals. Both instruments and techniques of playing are now being subjected to close study. Above: a large cylindrical drum, beaten at both ends with flexible sticks, about to be used in some village celebration, together with the oboe-like *zurna*. Above right: a double reed instrument, the *urghul*, made of two unequal pipes; it belongs to the clarinet family. (19, 20)

A village procession (below) celebrating the *mawlid*, anniversary of the Prophet, sets out with drums and cymbals. In 1932 an important conference was held in Cairo, the 'Congrès de Musique Arabe'. The two photographs below right were taken on that occasion. The upper one shows an ensemble comprising two types of cithar, the *qānūn*, where the strings are plucked, and the *santūr*, where they are beaten with two sticks; a bowed instrument, the *kamanja*, which has a wooden body ending in a peg and three or four strings; and the *duff*, a tambourine. In the lower one is another ensemble playing on *zurnas*, oboe-like instruments of different sizes, and a drum. (21, 22, 23)

Chapter Seven

THE SCIENTIFIC ENTERPRISE

A. I. Sabra

Islamic science was essentially a development of Greek theory and research. This Persian plate, dated 971/1563, shows the signs of the Zodiac in forms very close to their Greek originals. (1)

A STORY FROM THE IV/10th CENTURY offers an explanation of the rise of science and philosophy in Islam: it all started with a dream which the ʿAbbāsid Caliph al-Maʾmūn (198–218/813–33) had. There appeared to him, sitting on a couch, a man with a fair and ruddy complexion, a broad forehead, joined eyebrows, a bald head, light-blue eyes and a pleasing appearance. Filled with awe, the Commander of the Faithful asked: 'Who are you?' 'Aristotle,' the man replied. Delighted with the answer, and being granted to ask further questions, al-Maʾmūn came out with the all-important question: 'What is good?' 'That which is good in the mind,' replied Aristotle. 'And what comes next?' 'That which is good in the Law.' 'Then what?' 'That which is considered good by the people.' Finally Aristotle advised al-Maʾmūn that he should treat as gold whoever advised him about gold (alchemy) and he should hold to the doctrine of *tawhīd*, or Oneness of God. It was in consequence of this dream, so goes the story of the bibliographer Ibn an-Nadīm, that al-Maʾmūn determined to seek the books of ancient philosophers and have them translated into Arabic.

The appropriation of ancient learning

The story appears to link al-Maʾmūn's official support for the Muʿtazilīs, who insisted on a primary role for reason in matters of religious dogma, with his well-known efforts to disseminate the sciences of the Greeks among Muslims. The Muʿtazilīs were called the *ahl at-tawhīd*, the upholders of the doctrine of the Oneness of God, in consequence of their particular stand on the issue of God's attributes. Their position became epitomized in the doctrine of the createdness of the Qurʾān as the Word of God, which al-Maʾmūn sought to force upon unsympathetic Traditionists and legists, thus initiating the Inquisition which in the time of his successor al-Muʿtasim (218–28/833–42) led to the persecution of Ahmad ibn Hanbal, the highly esteemed Traditionist and founder of a strict legal school that had no use for rational argumentation.

Al-Maʾmūn was probably not the founder of the government-supported Library in Baghdad which quickly became the centre of translation into Arabic; but it was in his reign that the Library, under the name of the Bayt al-Hikma, or Institute of Science, perhaps reached the

highest point in its career. Tradition has it that al-Maʾmūn, like al-Mansūr (138–9/754–5) and ar-Rashīd (170–94/786–809) before him, obtained from Byzantium Greek scientific and philosophical books which he subsequently ordered to be translated. Another collection is said to have come to him from Cyprus. Such collections had in fact been gradually gathered from as far back as the end of the Umayyad period, when the process of translation had already begun. It does appear, however, that translation at Bayt al-Hikma, in the time of al-Maʾmūn, became a well-organized activity of unprecedented scope and vigour. Translators worked in groups, each supervised by an expert and assisted by copyists. Works translated from Syriac were checked against the Greek originals when possible. And Arabic translations from Greek were revised in the light of newly acquired manuscripts. Al-Maʾmūn can truly be said to have given great impetus to the movement which was soon to bring the bulk of Greek science and philosophy within reach of a large number of Arabic-reading scholars. And his personal interest in the translation activity may well have been connected with his sympathy for the rationalizing Muʿtazilīs.

The translation work which began in the second half of the 11/8th century was practically done by the end of the IV/10th, never to be taken up again on any significant scale in the Islamic Middle Ages. A brief look at a few of the translators reveals something of the ethnic and religious variety they displayed and the degree to which the political establishment was involved in promoting their work. Some of them were Persians, like the astrologer Ibn Nawbakht, who was making translations for ar-Rashīd from Pahlavī into Arabic. Al-Fazārī, whom al-Mansūr ordered to work with an Indian from Sind on the translation of the astronomical *Sindhind* from Sanskrit, was of Arab descent. The most active translator of medical works from Greek and Syriac, the celebrated Hunayn ibn Ishāq (d. 260/873), was a Nestorian Christian from al-Hīra. Possibly in connection with Bayt al-Hikma during the reign of al-Maʾmūn, and continuing until the time of al-Mutawakkil, whose personal physician he

Detail from the first page of 'The book of the excellent Galen On Medical Sects for Students', translated by Abū Zayd Hunayn ibn Ishāq the physician. This page is especially interesting because it is annotated by two former owners, one of them none other than Avicenna. His note is on the right, just under the main heading, and reads: '[Came] into the possession of Husayn ibn 'Abdallāh ibn Sīnā the physician in the year 407' (i.e. 1016–17). The second note is bottom right and reads: '[Came] into the possession of Jibrā'īl ibn Bakhtīshū', the Christian physician.' Jibrā'īl is known to have died in 214/828. (2)

became, Hunayn brilliantly led a team of translators who rendered into Arabic the works of Hippocrates and Galen. His son and pupil Ishāq (d. 299/911), who, like his father, knew Greek, translated philosophical works by Aristotle, the *Elements* of Euclid and Ptolemy's *Almagest*. Thābit ibn Qurra (d. 281/901), a member of the pagan community at Harrān, was a distinguished mathematician and astronomer who worked on the translation of mathematical works from the Greek. He was introduced to the court of the Caliph al-Mu'tadid (279–90/892–902) by one of the sons of Mūsā ibn Shākir, 'the Astrologer'. The three sons of Mūsā, Muhammad, Ahmad and al-Hasan, had as young men been protégés of al-Ma'mūn and later became noted for their persistent efforts to obtain books from Byzantium, and for their encouragement and generous financial support of the translation activity, in addition to their own work in mathematics and mechanics.

It is easy to think of reasons why members of the ruling class wanted to surround themselves with future-telling astrologers and health-preserving physicians. It is also true that Muslims in all parts of the Muslim world were in need of mathematically educated persons who would be able to determine the astronomically defined times of prayer and the direction of Mecca. A large mass of literature, much of which is hackneyed – though some of which is quite ingenious – and the apparently wide-scale production of portable instruments (such as astrolabes and quadrants) for the determination of time, can be accounted for in terms of these needs. But the enterprise of Islamic science and philosophy, with its high level of achievement and its marked interest in theoretical and abstract questions, can hardly be explained as the unintended consequence of the practical concerns of a few individuals, however powerful and influential. In Islam, as in other civilizations, nothing less profound than

genuine curiosity, or less complicated than the interplay of social, cultural and deep human needs, can suffice to explain such an impressive and long-lasting enterprise.

To a large extent, Islamic science was a continuation of an already existing though waning Greek tradition: Baghdad was heir to an Alexandrian school which had been drawn to it after journeying through Antioch and Harrān. Another formative influence came from Jundīshāpūr, in south-west Iran, where a medical school had flourished for a long time. Nestorians, who originally sought refuge there after they had been expelled from Urfa (Edessa) in 489, taught Greek medicine in Syriac and Persian translations. A new influx of Greek ideas came with the arrival of Neo-platonic philosophers after the closing of their school at Athens in 529. At the time of Anūshirwān (531–79) the city of Jundīshāpūr became an active centre of learning in which Greek, Persian, Syriac, Jewish and Indian ideas intermingled. All of these elements were to exert a profound influence on Islamic intellectual life from the beginning of the 'Abbāsid period. The head of the medical school at Jundīshāpūr, the Nestorian Jibrā'īl ibn Bakhtīshū', was called to Baghdad in 148/765 where he became court physician to the Caliph al-Mansūr. During the reign of Hārūn ar-Rashīd, Jibrā'īl was charged with building a Bīmaristān or hospital at Baghdad after the Syro-Persian model already established at Jundīshāpūr, and this copy again became the prototype of many hospitals subsequently built at Baghdad and elsewhere. Jibrā'īl returned to Persia a year or two before he died, but other members of the Bakhtīshū' family remained in the service of the 'Abbāsids for a long time.

Arabic scientific geography began with the translation of non-Arabic texts at the beginning of the 'Abbāsid rule. As in the case of Arabic astronomy, the sources of Arabic geography were various: Indian and Persian as well as Greek. But it was again the Greek influence, exerted mainly through the works of Ptolemy and Marinus of Tyre, that became predominant. Following the Greeks the Arabs generally divided the inhabited world into seven climes represented by circles parallel to the equator and to the north of it, and divided the climes longitudinally into ten sections. This became the authoritative framework into which all geographical information, both old and new, had to be fitted.

The work of al-Idrīsī, produced in the vi/12th century under the title *Kitāb Nuzhat al-mushtāq fī ikhtirāq al-āfāq*, is a good illustration of this tendency. As a scholar in the service of Roger II, the Norman King of Sicily, he was commissioned to prepare a geographical survey of the world with separate maps for all the climatic sections. This was a collaborative effort, and with the help of technicians and other scholars at Roger's court a large planispheric silver relief map was constructed which incorporated information derived from travellers as well as from Greek and earlier Arabic sources.

Despite the continuity with earlier traditions in which Greek learning had played a predominant role, historians have rightly emphasized the novelty of the scientific enterprise that was launched at Baghdad. For the first time in history, science became international on a really wide scale; and one language, Arabic, became its vehicle. A large number of scholars belonging to different nations and professing different beliefs collaborated in the process of moulding into this one language materials which had previously existed in Greek, Syriac, Persian or Sanskrit. It is this enduring character of the scientific enterprise in medieval Islam which is being emphasized when the phrase 'Arabic science' is used.

The opposition

The sciences imported mainly from Greece were bound to meet with opposition from various quarters. From the time when the translation movement began to the end of the Islamic Middle Ages, these sciences were either frowned upon or openly attacked by practitioners of the indigenous religious and Arabic disciplines. Grammarians rejected the claim of the teachers of Aristotelian logic that they were the sole arbiters of sound discourse; legists were unwilling to see their newly found forms of argument being refashioned in foreign moulds; and the adherents of the religious science of *kalām*, who were developing a whole world-view of their own, had no use for the peripatetic and Neo-platonic doctrines current among the *falāsifa* (sing. *faylasūf*) or followers of Greek philosophy. The 'foreign sciences', which included not only mathematics, astronomy and medicine, but also magic, alchemy and astrology, were generally felt by pious people to constitute a serious threat to religious beliefs and the values of religious life.

An exaggerated role has often been assigned to al-Ghazālī in the history of this conflict. This greatly influential religious thinker and spokesman for a mystical version of Sunnī (orthodox) Islam (he died in 505/1111) not only wrote a well-argued refutation of philosophy, but repeatedly warned against exposing Muslims to potentially misleading though essentially innocuous rational sciences. Historians have sometimes viewed the conflict simply as an orthodox reaction, and by emphasizing the negative act of rejection, they have turned attention away from what still remains in need of explanation: the fact that science and philosophy continued to exist and develop in Islam for many centuries, despite the uninterrupted opposition.

Rather than being a marginal phenomenon, the enterprise of science and philosophy in Islam presents the historian with a real paradox. It would have been only natural for the self-confident Muslims from Arabia to launch an assault against vestiges of the pagan culture which they encountered in the conquered lands. The legend of the burning of the library of Alexandria by the Arab invaders, which was invented by a zealous Muslim at the time of the Crusades, has largely gained in plausibility from the expectedness of the alleged event. Nor would it have been surprising if the early Muslims had stood aloof from the activities of the Hellenized Christians and the Sabians. What those early Muslims did, however, was quite different and unexpected. Rather than suppress the declining Greek intellectual tradition, they sought out its sources and encouraged its cultivation. Theirs was not primarily an attitude of rejection or even of mere toleration, but of protectiveness and active participation. The foreign sciences of the Greeks could have lived as long and developed as much as they did in Islam only because of continued positive interest and support. To characterize their status in Islamic civilization as marginal would merely serve to relieve us from the task of explaining their existence.

The paradox is heightened by the fact that the philosophical and scientific disciplines were largely kept out of those institutions of learning, the *madrasas*, which were established primarily for religious education and which admitted the linguistic disciplines as a necessary adjunct to the study of the Qur'ān, the Traditions and the Law. Medicine was taught as well as practised in generously endowed Bīmaristāns or hospitals, and students of law were able and often required to learn some mathematics in the *madrasas* and in the mosques. But these observations do not adequately explain the high level of scientific and mathematical sophistication that was achieved in the works of Islamic scientists from the III/9th to the IX/15th century. It is, for example, clear from the output of able mathematicians from that whole period that their education in the mathematical and neighbouring fields, far from being elementary or spotty, was well-organized and wide-ranging. It is as though they had gone through a systematic course of study. A strong tradition of teaching the foreign sciences in Islam must have existed for many centuries, even though we do not know the full details of how it worked. That this tradition existed largely as a private institution does not diminish its importance.

The attitude of orthodox religious thinkers towards the sciences of the ancients was more complex than is usually assumed. Al-Ghazālī, who has often been blamed for the decline of science and philosophy, firmly believed and repeatedly declared that the study of the religious sciences of *kalām* and jurisprudence must be preceded by a sufficient grounding in Greek logic. He understood logic to be no more than a useful instrument for laying down rules of correct definitions and inferences. But by admitting Aristotelian logic into the curriculum of religious learning he opened the door for deeper penetration by other parts of Aristotelian philosophy into the various religious disciplines. The historian Ibn Khaldūn (d. 809/1406) has remarked, for example, that, as a result of the writings of al-Ghazālī and those of Fakhr ad-Dīn ar-Rāzī (d. 606/1209), it had become difficult in his own time to distinguish between a work on *kalām* and a work on philosophy.

Al-Ghazālī's attitude was in sharp contrast to that of the Hanbalī jurist Ibn Taymiyya (d. 729/1328), who launched a vehement and uncompromising attack on Greek logic. Unlike al-Ghazālī, he considered the whole system of Aristotelian logic to be based on a metaphysical doctrine which threatened the Islamic worldview; and he regarded the Aristotelian forms of argument as inimical to Islamic modes of thinking. It would, however, be wrong to conclude that a necessary connection existed between a strict view of Islam and such extremist views as those of Ibn Taymiyya. The Spanish thinker Ibn Hazm, for example, vigorously maintained a literalist view of Islamic law, but he was no enemy of Greek logic and even composed an introductory account of it. In any case, it was al-Ghazālī's view, and not that of Ibn Taymiyya, which has prevailed in important centres of Muslim education, such as the Azhar University in Cairo, where Aristotelian logic has continued to be taught up till now.

On the threshold of Islamic science and philosophy stands the unexpected figure of Yaʿqūb ibn Ishāq al-Kindī (d. *c.* 257/870). A Muslim and a member of the Arab aristocracy (his family descended from the kings of the ancient south Arabian tribe of Kinda and his father had held the high position of governor at Kūfa), he set up himself as a propounder of the Greek scientific and philosophic tradition which in his time was identified mainly with non-Muslims and non-Arabs. 'We should not be ashamed,' he wrote, 'to acknowledge truth and to assimilate it from whatever source it comes to us, even if it is brought to us by former generations and foreign peoples.' And further: 'My principle is first to record in complete quotations all that the Ancients have said on the subject; secondly, to complete what the Ancients have not fully expressed, and this according to the usage of our Arabic language, the custom of our age and our own ability.' Writing as a Muslim who addressed himself to a Muslim audience, he laid the foundations of Islamic philosophy by taking the first significant steps in the direction of reconciling Islamic doctrines with a Neoplatonic version of Greek philosophy. His philosophical system preserved such Islamic beliefs as the createdness of the world and the resurrection of the body, but he had no intention of downgrading the values of Greek philosophical thought to which he remained committed enough to deserve to be called a *faylasūf*, a philosopher in the sense of the Greek tradition. His espousal of Greek thought was uninhibited and all-embracing; he opened up his mind to astrology and alchemy, as well as to metaphysics, meteorology, optics, music and medicine. Al-Kindī depended on translations made by others who were learned in Greek or Syriac, but he was able to play a special role in bringing about the naturalization of the ancient sciences, both linguistically and intellectually. The results of his vigorous and whole-hearted efforts were far-reaching.

Later Islamic philosophers were frequently even more confident of their adopted values than al-Kindī, and sometimes went even further than he in their commitment to the aim and methods of Greek thought. For the most part they were neither meek nor secretive, as one might have expected from a 'marginal' group who felt themselves on the defensive. Al-Fārābī (d. 339/950) openly declared his conviction that the dialectical argumentation of Islamic theology was definitely inferior to the demonstrative methods of the *falāsifa*. Abū Bakr ar-Rāzī (d. *c.* 313/925), the philosopher-physician who aligned himself with Plato and Galen, held heretical views with regard to all revealed religions. And Avicenna's position on fundamental issues concerning God and His relation to the world was such as to bring down upon him the wrath of orthodox religious thinkers. It is true that for a long time philosophy remained on the defensive in the Maghrib and in Spain. And yet it was from the Cordoban Averroes that came the strongest rebuttal to al-Ghazālī's attack on philosophy. And there is evidence to suggest that in Averroes' time something like an alliance between the political establishment and philosophical élitism was being forged against the Mālikī jurists. In general physicians and mathematicians were not readily identified with views which injured the sensitivity of pious people. Frequently astronomers and physicians claimed that their work revealed evidence for the wisdom of God. At the same time, however, they were prone to look down on practitioners of the religious sciences for having substituted authority for genuine knowledge.

Innovation and tradition: mathematics
The finest treatise in Arabic arithmetic was written in the year 830/1427 in Samarqand – a time and a place far removed from ʿAbbāsid Baghdad where, in about 210/825, al-Khwārizmī composed probably the first Arabic compendium of Indian-type arithmetic. The author of that treatise, Jamshīd ibn Masʿūd al-Kāshī, was a Persian from Kāshān who had moved to Samarqand, where he secured a distinguished position among the group of astronomers and mathematicians patronized by the learned Sultan Ulugh Beg. Al-Kāshī's treatise, entitled *The Key to Arithmetic*, was a comprehensive, clearly written and well-arranged handbook intended for the use of merchants, clerks and surveyors, as well as theoretical astronomers. One of its notable contributions was its full and systematic investigation of decimal fractions which had made an appearance in Islam as early as the IV/10th century in the work of a Damascene arithmetician named al-Uqlīdisī. Al-Kāshī's novel treatment of the subject thus anticipated similar developments in Europe by about two hundred years. His *Key to Arithmetic* circulated widely in the Islamic world, its influence already reaching Constantinople in the second half of the IX/15th century. The occasional use of decimal fractions has been noted in a Byzantine document which made its way to Vienna in 970/1562.

Al-Kāshī's achievement in arithmetic was the culminating point in a series of developments in which the power of tradition seems often to have inhibited the will to innovation. The Islamic world had inherited three different systems of numerical calculation which were of different origins and which continued to exist side by side for many centuries. The first, of unknown origin, was called 'finger reckoning' because in performing its operations one retained the results of intermediate steps by holding one's fingers in certain positions. It was also called 'arithmetic of the scribes' (or secretaries). The title of a handbook of this type of arithmetic, written in Baghdad about 370/980 by Abū 'l-Wafā' al-Būzjānī, indicates that it was intended for the use of the government bureaucracy. The system in fact continued to be used by members of the secretarial class despite the existence of the much superior type of reckoning which had come from India in the II/8th century or earlier, and on which many handbooks were available.

In the 'arithmetic of the secretaries', numbers were written out in words. Based on the place-value idea, the Indian system of reckoning was able to express any number, however large, with the help of only ten figures, including a sign for zero (*sifr*) which indicated an empty place. Medieval Arabic authors referred to these figures as 'Indian' or 'dust' numerals, thereby indicating their origin and the fact that the operations effected by their means were performed on a dust-board. In the Islamic world, Indian numerals existed in two forms, one in the east, the other in the west, and it was from the latter that medieval Europe derived its 'Arabic numerals'.

Decimal fractions first appeared in Arabic in the work of the IV/10th-century Damascene arithmetician Abū 'l-Hasan al-Uqlīdisī. This page from the unique manuscript of al-Uqlīdisī's Kitāb al-Fusūl *shows the decimal point as a stroke above the number in the units place in line 10. (3)*

Astronomers simply ignored the advantage of the Indian system of numeration. Continuing the tradition of Greek astronomical works, they adhered to the old Babylonian system in which letters of the alphabet stood for numbers. It was in fact a mixed system in which a non-place-value decimal notation was used for integers and a place-value sexagesimal system for fractions. This meant that in Islam the most sophisticated computations were performed in sexagesimals indicated by alphabetical symbols. Despite the apparent analogy between the decimal and sexagesimal systems, and although decimal fractions had already appeared in the IV/10th century, it was not until al-Kāshī's time that a unified place-value system was formulated for both fractions and integers.

It is impossible to explain the character of Arabic mathematics (let alone Arabic science as a whole) in terms of such entities as the Arab or Islamic 'mind', or even the Arabic language, though attempts have been made in this direction. Not only in arithmetic, but also in geometry and algebra, much of the character of the Islamic products can readily be explained by reference to older traditions. Innovations of varying degrees of importance were bound to occur, and did occur, in all these fields. It may be interesting to view these developments against the background of a pervasive medium, such as the Arabic language, or a supposedly prevalent intellectual attitude, such as 'atomism', but this alone would be a poor substitute for real historical analysis.

The beginning of Arabic algebra may be taken as an example. The first Arabic treatise on this subject was written under al-Ma'mūn by Muhammad ibn Mūsā al-Khwārizmī. The question of his algebraic sources has been much debated. Some of his methods are anticipated in Indian and Babylonian records. His treatise did not use any symbolic notation, but, like all subsequent algebraic treatises in Arabic with the exception of one by al-Qalasādī (d. c. 891/1486), was entirely rhetorical. On the other hand, his geometrical proofs of algebraic procedures are Euclidean in character. The title of his treatise, *al-Jabr wa 'l-muqābala*, referred to the two operations used by him in the process of solving linear and quadratic equations, namely those of eliminating negative quantities and reducing positive quantities of the same power on both sides of the equation. It now appears that these terms, which may be translated as restoring (or completing) and balancing respectively, in fact rendered concepts already present in the work of Diophantus. And yet, no prototype of al-Khwārizmī's book as a whole is known to have existed in any language prior to the III/9th century. Medieval Arabic authors classed al-Khwārizmī's treatise among those compositions which started something new. Its systematic approach, represented by its reduction of the treated problems to canonical forms provided with proofs, can be said to have impressed its character on subsequent algebraic works, even when these (like the treatises of al-Karajī and 'Umar Khayyām) went far beyond it.

No mystery surrounded Arabic geometry; it was Greek in origin, methods and terminology. Basing themselves on Euclid, Archimedes and Apollonius, Islamic mathematicians produced a large number of treatises in which they explained, developed or criticized the works of their Greek masters. Islamic civilization did not produce an Archimedes or a Leibnitz, but its better mathematicians mastered the higher techniques of the Greeks and were sometimes able to use them to formulate and solve new problems.

The *Elements* of Euclid received perhaps more attention than any other mathematical work from Antiquity. It was translated into Arabic under ar-Rashīd and again under al-Ma'mūn. Several versions of the *Elements*, called 'Recensions', were prepared at different times. These were textbooks in the best sense of the word, and often contained rearrangements or extensions of the Euclidean theorems. Investigations of Euclid's concepts of ratio and proportion, which were felt to be unsatisfactory, finally led Islamic mathematicians to a widened concept of number which included the irrational. Much of the credit for this development goes to 'Umar Khayyām and Nasīr ad-Dīn at-Tūsī. The definition of proportion utilized by these mathematicians is not that of Eudoxus and Euclid, but seems nonetheless to be of Greek origin.

Research into Euclid's theory of parallels is another example of the Islamic mathematicians' taste for foundational problems. Attempts to prove Euclid's parallels postulate have been found in Arabic writings dating from the III/9th to the VII/13th century. The problem underlying these investigations had been pointed out in Antiquity. The Arabs inherited the problem; but rather than acquiesce in a ready-made solution, they pursued the search for ever better solutions. They did not finally propose a non-Euclidean system of geometry, but they formulated and proved some non-Euclidean theorems,

The problem of parallel lines, posed by Euclid's parallels postulate, received much attention from Islamic mathematicians throughout the history of medieval Arabic science. Naṣīr ad-Dīn aṭ-Ṭūsī's was probably the most mature treatment of the problem in Arabic, making use of Euclid's definition of parallel lines as non-secant lines and drawing on the results of his predecessors. The page from his ar-Risāla ash-Shāfiya shows Ṭūsī's figure for proving 'Saccheri's hypothesis' of the right angles, which is equivalent to Euclid's postulate. (4)

and one of their attempts to prove the postulate later became known to European mathematicians, who made notable contributions to the history of this problem, such as Wallis and Saccheri.

Applied mathematics

The idea of mechanics as applied mathematics was not foreign to Islamic civilization, being clearly implied in the works of Greek mechanicians, such as Hero of Alexandria and Philo of Byzantium, which became available in Arabic translations. The Greek concept of mechanical technology was often expressed in Arabic by the phrase *ʿilm al-ḥiyal*, or 'science of devices'. In his *Catalogue of the Sciences*, the philosopher al-Fārābī (d. 339/950) explicitly declares that the aim of this science is to determine the means by which those things whose existence is demonstrated in the various mathematical sciences can be applied to physical bodies. Elaborating this important idea, he explains that in order to produce the truths of mathematics artificially in material objects, the latter may have to be subtly altered and adapted. In this sense, the 'science of devices' is a general art which includes algebra (on this account a kind of applied arithmetic that seeks to determine unknown numerical quantities) as well as building, surveying, the manufacture of astronomical,

musical and optical instruments, and the design of wondrous devices. All these and similar arts, says al-Fārābī, are principles of the practical crafts of civilization.

It is therefore worthy of note that many of the writers on mechanics, such as the Banū Mūsā, al-Bīrūnī, al-Karajī, ʿUmar Khayyām, Ibn al-Haytham, were distinguished mathematicians. But these were not entirely armchair mechanicians. The Banū Mūsā, whose work on mechanical devices is largely concerned with trick vessels, supervised various engineering projects for their patrons, the caliphs at Baghdad. Al-Bīrūnī made accurate determinations of specific gravities. Ibn al-Haytham had a scheme for regulating the flow of the Nile water. And so on.

The most important and most informative document on Islamic mechanical technology that has come down to us is a treatise written in the beginning of the VII/13th century by Ibn ar-Razzāz al-Jazarī. Entitled *The Book of Knowledge of Ingenious Mechanical Devices*, it presents itself as the work of a craftsman, not of a theoretical or mathematical mechanician. Written for the Artuqid prince of Diyārbakr Nāṣir ad-Dīn Maḥmūd, whom al-Jazarī served, it describes in great detail the construction of a large number of devices of a wide range which the author divided into five main categories: clocks of various kinds, vessels, measuring basins, fountains and water-raising machines.

Astronomy: theory and observation

The general history of astronomy in medieval Islam exhibits a curious lack of interaction between theory and observation, though both of these were actively pursued. Observations, on the whole, had little impact on theoretical developments; and theoretical innovations were neither inspired by nor did they lead to novel observations. It is as if each of these two activities revolved within a limited sphere of its own.

Translations in astronomy were at first made from a variety of languages – from Sanskrit, Pahlavī and Syriac, as well as from Greek. The result was an eclecticism which marked the early productions of Arabic astronomy, and which also made a later appearance in Muslim Spain. After the translation of the *Almagest*, however, the superiority of Ptolemy's system was quickly recognized, and, from then on, Arabic astronomy remained predominantly Ptolemaic in conception and method.

The Arabs inherited from Ptolemy a concept of testing which they constantly kept before their minds and frequently put into practice. In the beginning of the IV/10th century, the Harrānian astronomer al-Battānī, whose *az-Zīj as-Ṣābī* was modelled after the *Almagest*, ascribed to Ptolemy the 'injunction' that observations be made after him for the purpose of testing his own observations, just as he himself had made tests of the observations of his predecessors. This exhortation, which is in fact implicit in Ptolemy's book, was taken quite seriously by Islamic astronomers, and the words *miḥna* and *iʿtibār*, used by the translators of the *Almagest* to render the Greek concept of testing, can be seen almost everywhere in the medieval Arabic literature on astronomy. The lesson learnt from the example set by Ptolemy was assiduously applied. Throughout the history of Islamic astronomy, observations were made at various places and at various centres of astronomical research. Thus, during the reign of al-Ma'mūn a group of astronomers prepared a new set of tables or *zīj*, known as the *Ma'mūnī* or *Mumtahan* (tested) *zīj*, on the basis of new observations made at Baghdad and Damascus. Also under the ʿAbbāsids, Habash al-Hāsib made observations of solar and lunar eclipses and of planetary position at Baghdad, Samarra and Damascus. Ibn Yūnus (d. 400/1009) conducted observations at Cairo in the IV/10th century. At Shīrāz, beginning in the year 359/969, the famous as-Sūfī made a series of observations to determine the lengths of seasons. Towards the end of the IV/10th century, the great al-Bīrūnī was engaged in observations of lunar eclipses in Khwārazm. In the VII/13th century, astronomical observations were carried out for a continuous period of about twenty years at Marāgha, where Hūlegū had built in 685/1259 an observatory in which a group of astronomers worked, headed by Nasīr ad-Dīn at-Tūsī. This may have been the first observatory in the full sense of the word. It had a staff of about twenty astronomers drawn from various parts of the Islamic world, including one from China; it was equipped with a library and in it instruments (quadrants, armillaries, astrolabes) were designed and constructed. In the first half of the IX/15th century Sultan Ulugh Beg founded an imposing observatory at Samarqand whose remains can still be seen.

Most of these observations had the limited aim of checking values received from different sources or improving the Ptolemaic parameters. They yielded, for example, new values for the inclination of the ecliptic, the rate of equinoctial precession, the mean motions of the sun, the moon and the planets and so on. This limitation cannot be ascribed to the instruments used, some of which (like those constructed by al-ʿUrdī at Marāgha) were sophisticated and capable of producing more significant results than those in fact obtained by their means. One is left with the impression that Islamic astronomers were engaged in correcting and re-correcting previous observations, rather than testing newly imagined hypotheses.

Not that new hypotheses were never invented. The astronomers at Marāgha, and later Ibn ash-Shātir at Damascus, produced non-Ptolemaic planetary models which have recently been compared with their counterparts in Copernicus. But these inventions were independent of observations, whether made at Marāgha or elsewhere, and the story of their coming into being must be told in quite different terms. The story seems to begin in the V/11th century when Ibn al-Haytham, the mathematician from Iraq who lived in Cairo at the time of the Fātimid Caliph al-Hākim (d. 412/1021), wrote an attack on Ptolemy's planetary theory. Ibn al-Haytham accepted

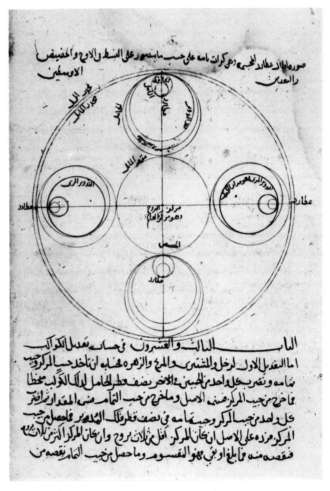

Islamic astronomy limited itself to reforming Ptolemaic planetary theory rather than testing fundamentally new hypotheses. This reform, begun in the VII/13th century by Nasīr ad-Dīn at-Tūsī at Marāgha, reached its culmination in the work of the VIII/14th-century Damascene astronomer Ibn ash-Shātir. These two diagrams from Ibn ash-Shātir's Nihāyat al-sūl *illustrate the first successful representation of the motions of Mercury exclusively in terms of uniform circular rotations. The diagram to the right shows the solid spheres rotating in accordance with the uniformity condition geometrically represented on the left. (5, 6)*

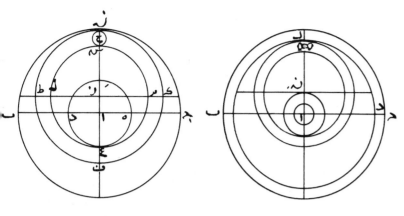

Ptolemy's Planetary Hypotheses *exerted enormous influence on the development of Arabic astronomy. In it Ptolemy presented the motions of the planets in terms of solid spherical bodies corresponding to the geometrical representations in the* Almagest. *The impressive work of the Marāgha school in the VII/13th century and of Ibn ash-Shātir in the VIII/14th century would have been inconceivable without a strong commitment to the programme outlined in the* Planetary Hypotheses. *These diagrams from Part II of Ptolemy's book, of which the Greek original has not survived, illustrate Ptolemy's models for Saturn and the sun, respectively. (7)*

the Ptolemaic explanation of the apparent motions of the planets by means of epicycles and eccentric deferents on which the epicycles revolved. But he charged that Ptolemy's equant hypothesis, according to which the epicycle-centre appeared to move uniformly from a point other than the centre of the deferent or the centre of the world, violated the accepted principle of uniform velocity for all heavenly bodies. Ptolemy, and no doubt other astronomers, had been aware of what was entailed by the equant hypothesis. But while Ptolemy had tried to produce arguments in defence of his procedure, and in contradistinction to the astronomers who, as far as we know, had preferred to be silent on the matter, Ibn al-Haytham insisted that Ptolemy's constructions must be declared false and that new constructions must be found. His criticisms, and those of at-Tūsī and his collaborators at Marāgha, are an indication of the profound influence which Ptolemy's *Planetary Hypotheses* exerted on Islamic astronomers. In this work Ptolemy had conceived of the apparent motions of the planets as produced by the combined motions of corporeal spherical shells in which the planets were embedded. It was the idea that a physical body, the deferent sphere associated with a given planet, should rotate with variable speed, that Ibn al-Haytham and those who shared his views found unacceptable. Unwilling to abandon the physicalist view, the astronomers at Marāgha set out to construct models which would be mathematically equivalent to those of Ptolemy but which would also be in accord with the nature of the heavens. Only such models could possibly be considered true. Observations play no essential part in this story, either as causes or as consequences. The theoretical innovations developed at Marāgha and by Ibn ash-Shātir were imaginative and ingenious attempts to straighten up Ptolemy by bringing him into line with his own principles; but their authors show no desire to break away from his system.

Light and vision

Experiments of various kinds are described in medieval Arabic works on medicine, alchemy, mechanics, specific gravity and music, among other subjects. A certain taste for experimentation has been noted in the writings of so-called theologians or *mutakallimūn*, such as an-Nazzām (d. *c.* 226/840). It was in the field of optics, however, that a concept of experiment clearly emerged as an identifiable method of procedure in empirical enquiry. The sources of Arabic optics were the writings of the mathematicians Euclid, Ptolemy, Archimedes and Anthemius, the medical treatises of Galen and the philosophical works of Aristotle and his commentators. At first, these three traditions remained separate. Al-Kindī in the III/9th century wrote in the manner of Euclid; Hunayn ibn Ishāq in the same century approached the problem of vision from a Galenic point of view; and Avicenna in the v/11th century treated the subject in Aristotelian terms.

Ancient and medieval optics was primarily a theory of vision. In Islam, mathematicians and the followers of Galen held the view that vision occurred through a ray which issued from the eye towards the object, and either by touching the object or compressing the intermediate air conveyed an impression of the object to the brain. Natural philosophers spoke of vision as resulting from the impinging of a 'form' of the object on the eye. The most important student of optics in Islam, Ibn al-Haytham, was convinced that a correct theory of vision must combine the 'mathematical' approach of Euclid and Ptolemy with the 'physical' doctrine favoured by the natural philosophers. The result of his deliberations in his major work on *Optics* was a new theory of vision which was richer and more sophisticated than all preceding theories. He considered that light and colour, two physical properties which existed independently of the perceiving subject and of each other, emanate from every point on the visible object rectilinearly in every direction. With the help of suitable assumptions (some of which concern the geometrical structure of the eye), he set out to show how an entity (called by the Aristotelian name of 'form') capable of representing the visible features of the object first occurs in the eyes, whence it is carried to the brain, where it is apprehended by the faculty of sense. This entity is not an image which can be seen anywhere inside the eye, though it is the means by which a picture of the object is ultimately worked out and made to appear to the sense faculty. The apparently immediate judgment that what is perceived is an object which lies at a distance from the eyes, and which has, for example, a certain size and shape, is, according to Ibn al-Haytham, the result of an 'inference' from the visual material received in the brain and the stored information of past experience. Ibn al-Haytham did not only champion the intromission hypothesis, nor did he merely subject it to mathematical treatment; he incorporated that hypothesis into a highly elaborate theory of perception which has yet to receive sufficient attention from historians.

Arguing for the basic view that vision resulted from an effect of light upon sight, Ibn al-Haytham cited certain experiences such as those of after-images and the pain felt in the eyes when gazing on a strong light. These observations were not in themselves new, but in the *Optics* they illustrate an experimental approach which

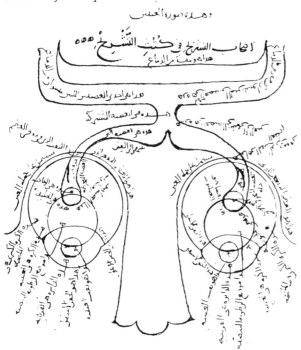

characterizes the whole book. The concept of testing, already found in astronomy, here explicitly appears as a distinct concept of experimental proof, and it is by manipulative experiments that Ibn al-Haytham seeks to establish such properties of light as rectilinear propagation, reflection and refraction. 'Dark chambers' are some of the devices used in these experimental studies.

The Arabic equivalent of the expression *camera obscura* occurs in a chapter of the *Optics* which is missing from known manuscripts of the medieval Latin translation of this book. The expression may have been originally derived from Greek works. But though dark chambers are utilized in the *Optics*, no proper *camera obscura* images are described anywhere in it. This is interesting, because it means that the eye is not considered in this book as a pinhole camera (nor, of course, is it assigned the role of a lens camera).

That Ibn al-Haytham had some, rather advanced, knowledge of the working of the *camera* is, however, clearly revealed elsewhere in his writings. In a treatise on *The Shape of the Eclipse*, he made an attempt to explain the crescent image cast by the partially eclipsed sun through a small round aperture. His experimental study of this phenomenon, which had been of interest to astronomers for many centuries, makes use of two principles. The first stated that light from all points on the shining crescent simultaneously passed through every point in the circular hole, thus producing infinitely many inverted crescent images on the screen behind the hole. The second principle stated that light emanating from each individual point on the crescent sun in the shape of a cone determined by the size and distance of the hole, produced a

Ibn al-Haytham's Optics, *written in Egypt in the first half of the V/11th century, represented a theory of vision that went beyond Galen, Euclid and Ptolemy. This diagram of the two eyes seen from above, showing the principal tunics and humours and the optic nerves connecting the eyeballs to the brain, is from a copy of the First Book executed by the author's son-in-law in 476/1083, i.e. about forty-three years after Ibn al-Haytham's death. Though we may assume that the copyist was probably transcribing an autograph manuscript, the diagram does not adequately represent the geometrical arrangement of the various parts of the eyes, which is meticulously described in Ibn al-Haytham's text. The diagram below is a later and more accurate illustration of the same text; it comes from a 14th-century Latin version of the* Optics, *which had first been translated a century or two earlier. (8, 9)*

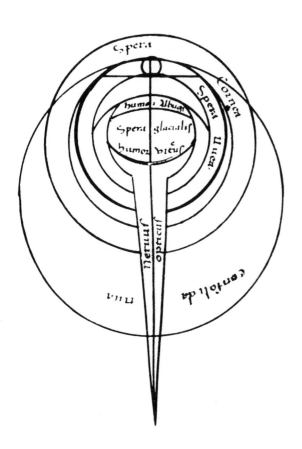

Diagram illustrating two principles of the camera obscura *from a résumé of optics by Kamāl ad-Dīn al-Fārisī (early VIII/14th century). These principles had already been applied three hundred years earlier by Ibn al-Haytham in his explanation of the formation of inverted images through a small circular aperture. The circle at the top is the light source, that in the middle is the aperture. The light emanating from individual points on the circle passes through the hole in the form of a cone. The three intersecting circles at the bottom are the images cast by three such cones. Light from the circle as a whole, on the other hand, converges at the centre of the aperture and diverges on the other side, producing the middle circular image, which is inverted. (10)*

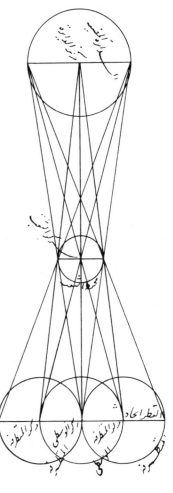

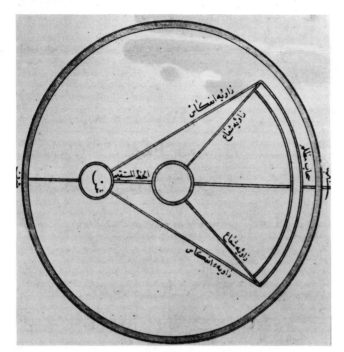

Illustration of Avicenna's (Ibn Sīnā's) explanation of the rainbow. From a late X/16th-century copy of a Turkish version of al-Qazwīnī's popular cosmography Wonders of Creation. *The light from the rising sun (small circle on left) is reflected to the observer from two points on a 'dark cloud' (double arc on right). Avicenna (wrongly) emphasized that a dark background was necessary for the raindrops to act as mirrors. (11)*

circular image on the screen. Ibn al-Haytham considered that the observed image was the combined effect of the images produced in accordance with these two principles. As far as we know, the treatise containing these results was not known to medieval Latin authors.

The rainbow was another phenomenon whose experimental study in Islam was remarkably successful. With regard to this phenomenon, Avicenna declared himself 'unconvinced by what our friends the peripatetics said about it', and he even went as far as to assert that current explanations of the rainbow colours were 'all false and absurd'. In the section of his *ash-Shifā'* dealing with meteorology, he related his own 'repeatedly made' observations of the bow, but failed to produce a satisfactory explanation, admitting that as far as he was concerned the rainbow remained a puzzling phenomenon. He did, however, emphasize the role of water droplets in generating the bow – an idea which had appeared in Aristotle and which was to inspire the Persian Kamāl ad-Dīn more than two hundred and fifty years after Avicenna's death.

Kamāl ad-Dīn, who made a careful study of Ibn al-Haytham's *Optics*, started his investigations from the rules of refraction experimentally determined by his predecessor, and from the latter's study of the behaviour of light as the parallel rays from the sun passed through a burning sphere. The raindrop and the glass sphere had already been mentioned by Avicenna in the same context, and it remained for Kamāl ad-Dīn to explore the analogy between them by means of the geometrical tools at his disposal. The research on which he thus embarked is a remarkable example of experimental science which was only surpassed in modern times. By bringing mathematics to bear on the experimental situation in which a spherical glass vial filled with water stood for the raindrop in the moist air, he was led to the successful explanation

which had defeated all his predecessors since Aristotle. The primary bow, he showed, was produced by the light of the sun that reached the observer after two refractions and one reflection inside the raindrops hanging in the atmosphere. He also showed that the secondary bow was produced by the light that had been reflected twice inside the raindrops, in addition to being refracted upon entering and leaving the drops, before reaching the observer. His explanations accounted for the shape of the rainbow and for the fact that the order of the colours in the secondary bow is the reverse of their order in the primary bow.

The history of experimental science in Islam, as exhibited in optical research, presents us with a few short-lived outbursts of creative activity, separated by long intervals of gestation or stagnation. A period of more than a hundred and fifty years separated the conservative treatises of al-Kindī and Hunayn from the revolutionary work of Ibn al-Haytham. And Ibn al-Haytham's *Optics*, written in Egypt in the first half of the v/11th century, appears to have remained practically unknown to scholars in the Islamic world until Kamāl ad-Dīn applied himself to its study in Persia at the end of the vii/13th century. Already in the same century, however, a Latin translation of Ibn al-Haytham's book had become the subject of intensive study in the West, where it was recognized as the most important source of optical knowledge.

Al-Andalus versus the East
The first notable philosopher in the Muslim East, Ya'qūb ibn Ishāq al-Kindī, died *c.* 257/870. The beginnings of serious interest in philosophical thought in Muslim Spain have been connected with the name of Muhammad ibn Masarra, a Neo-platonizing thinker from Cordoba who died in 319/931. The distance between their dates may be taken as an indication of how far al-Andalus lagged behind the East in the cultivation of the ancient sciences. But this would only be a rough indication. Ibn Masarra is a vague and confused figure compared to that of al-Kindī, and with his interest in Sūfism and the ascetic life it is even doubtful whether he can be called a philosopher in the sense in which this term would apply to al-Kindī. It was not in fact until the v/11th and vi/12th centuries that Muslim Spain produced really forceful figures in the field of science and philosophy, though elements of ancient learning had begun to arrive in al-Andalus from the East in the iii/9th and iv/10th centuries, if not earlier.

The vicissitudes of intellectual life in Muslim Spain show certain parallels with earlier developments in the East. The role of al-Ma'mūn as an enthusiastic patron of the scientific activity at Baghdad is paralleled by the role of al-Hakam II a century later at Cordoba. Already as crown prince under the reign of his father 'Abd ar-Rahmān III (300–50/912–61), and until his death in 366/976, al-Hakam showed real interest in promoting the cause of science and philosophy in his country. He sent emissaries to Egypt and Iraq, among other Muslim countries, in search of books, and gradually built up at Cordoba a library which was said to have almost equalled the great 'Abbāsid collections. He employed copyists to duplicate rare manuscripts and generally encouraged scholars in the secular branches of learning. Thus the

بشبه المفصل من اسنان في الطرف كاترى وقد صنعتم مستطيله

كالكلاليب على هذه الصور كاترى لها اسنان كأسنان المنشار يقطع

بها ويبرضل ن شاء الله تعالى

صورة مذقف ايضًا

صورة صنارة

هذه الضنان فيها غليظ قليلا ليلا عند جذب الجنبين بها

صورة صنان ذات الشوكتين

صورة مبضعين عريضين لقطع الجنين

Probably the first encyclopaedic work of medical instruction and practice to have been written in Muslim Spain was the Kitāb at-Tasrīf *of Abū 'l-Qāsim az-Zahrāwī, the Abulcasis of the Latins, native of Madīnat az-Zahrā' near Cordoba, who died about 404/ 1013. The Tasrīf consists of thirty treaties, of which the last was devoted to the art of surgery. In some manuscripts this treatise displays more than two hundred drawings of surgical instruments designed and originally drawn by the author. The drawing reproduced here illustrates various types of scrapers, scalpels, hooks and forceps, some of which were to be used in obstetric operations. Translated into Latin by Gerard of Cremona in the 12th century, this surgical treatise received more attention in the West than any other part of az-Zahrāwī's book. (12)*

ancient sciences received their first powerful impetus in Spain from the royal court, just as had happened earlier at the beginning of the ʿAbbāsid era.

It was in the reign of ʿAbd ar-Rahmān III, shortly after the year 341/952, that a new Arabic translation of Dioscorides' *Materia medica* was undertaken at Cordoba. The translation was based on an illustrated Greek text received shortly before as a gift from the Byzantine Emperor. A monk from Constantinople who read Greek, Christians knowing Latin, and Arabic scholars collaborated in this work with the help of the Jewish scholar Hasdāy ibn Shaprūt, who was physician to ʿAbd ar-Rahmān. Until this translation was made Dioscorides' fundamental work had been known both in al-Andalus and in the East in a version prepared at Baghdad in the III/9th century by Stephanus, son of Basilius, and revised by Hunayn ibn Ishāq. Many of the Greek names of drugs in the Stephanus–Hunayn version had been simply transliterated, and it was the task of the new translators to identify the corresponding Arabic names with the help of the illustrations contained in the Greek manuscript.

A reaction set in after the death of al-Hakam, comparable to the religious reaction which had taken place under the ʿAbbāsid Caliph al-Mutawakkil (233–47/ 847–61). At the instigation of the powerful *ʿulamāʾ*, books on the rational sciences in al-Hakam's library (excluding those on arithmetic and medicine) were burned, drowned or buried, and the philosophic and scientific movement went underground. After the end of the Umayyad rule in 422/1031, however, a revival took place as a result of the ensuing competition between the petty states which sprang up all over al-Andalus. This again paralleled the efflorescence of learning in the East after the ʿAbbāsid empire broke up towards the middle of the IV/10th century into independent states which vied with one another for cultural prestige as well as political power.

With only a few exceptions, e.g. the astronomer az-Zarqālī, who flourished around 463/1070, the important figures in the history of science and philosophy in Muslim Spain all belonged to the VI/12th century. Not surprisingly, some of them knew and influenced one another. Ibn Tufayl, the author of the famous philosophical romance of *Hayy ibn Yaqzān*, was a court physician of the Almohad ruler Abū Yaʿqūb (559–80/ 1163–84), to whom he introduced the young Averroes. It was on the ruler's advice that Ibn Tufayl urged Averroes to write the commentaries on the works of Aristotle which later earned their author the title of 'The Commentator' in the Latin West. In 565/1169 Averroes was appointed judge of Seville; in 567/1171 he became chief judge at Cordoba; and in 578/1182 he replaced Ibn Tufayl as court physician. He continued to serve the Almohads until he fell into disgrace only four years before he died in 595/1198 during the reign of Abū Yaʿqūb's successor, Abū Yūsuf (580–96/1184–99). Averroes was a friend of the physician Abū Marwān ibn Zuhr, with whom he published a comprehensive medical encyclopaedia consisting of the *Kulliyyāt* (composed by Averroes) and the *Taysīr* (by Ibn Zuhr). The astronomer al-Bitrūjī was a younger associate of Ibn Tufayl; and from the latter he derived the idea of designing a non-Ptolemaic astronomical system more in agreement with Aristotelian principles. The need for such a system was also urgently expressed by Averroes in his large commentary on Aristotle's *Metaphysics*. Maimonides, a product of the same philosophical milieu, though he left Spain relatively young and eventually settled in Cairo, shared this negative attitude towards Ptolemaic astronomy. We seem entitled to talk about a philosophical and scientific movement.

This movement has been viewed as a revival of Aristotelianism initiated by the Andalusian philosopher Ibn Bājja, or Avempace (d. 430/1138), who is said to have fallen under the influence of the Second Teacher, al-Fārābī.

Spanish Aristotelianism exhibits, however, certain peculiar features which, it seems, can best be understood against the background of a growing Spanish attitude of self-assertion towards the Muslim East and its intellectual authorities. In the V/11th century this attitude became crystallized in the thought of Ibn Hazm of Cordoba, one of the most original minds in Andalusian history. Ibn Hazm developed the literalist (*zāhirī*) approach to Islamic law into a whole philosophy of religion. His aim was twofold: to protect the divine law from human encroachment; and, simultaneously, to define the domain of valid rational thought. The whole of religion, he argued, was explicitly stated in the Qur'ān and in the *hadīth*, and he accordingly rejected all forms of inference from these two sources. No human being, he said, had the right to propose the results of his own efforts, no matter what they were and no matter on what basis, in the name of religion. The religious commandments should be obeyed, he declared, not because they were derivable from reasons which could be discovered by human endeavour, but because they issued from divine authority. The Law was grounded in the divine will, not in human wisdom.

Ibn Hazm's view clearly implied a rejection of the authority of all the legal schools which had been founded in the East. His position was paralleled in a remarkable way by the later developments of thought in Muslim Spain both in the field of religion and in the secular sciences. The founder of the Almohad movement, Ibn Tūmart (d. 421/1130), apparently inspired by Ibn Hazm's literalism, accepted the Qur'ān, the *hadīth* and the consensus of the Prophet's Companions as the only sources of law; and he preached against accepting the authority of the Eastern masters of the established schools. The third Almohad ruler, Abū Yūsuf Ya'qūb (580–96/1184–99), who, like Ibn Tūmart, was opposed to the proliferating systems of positive law elaborated by members of the various schools, urged jurists not to imitate the ancient masters and to base their judgments on the Qur'ān and the *hadīth*. Not only the masters of the legal schools but also the authorities of Arabic grammar came under fire from the literalist-inspired camp. Ibn Madā' of Cordoba, who achieved the position of chief judge under the Almohads (he died in 592/1196), wrote a refutation of the theory of 'the agent' which had been at the basis of Arabic grammar since Sībawayh (d. *c.* 179/795). He strongly repudiated the effort to look for grammatical 'causes' (corresponding to the 'reasons' of the legal theory), the only real cause of linguistic phenomena being, in his view, the *individual* speaker, not any hidden 'agent' which it was the task of the expert grammarian to uncover.

It is difficult not to see a parallelism between the literalist trend in Andalusian thought, with its aggressive overtones, and some of the characteristic philosophical and scientific ideas developed in the VI/12th century under the Almohads.

Averroes' 'pure' Aristotelianism, for example, was a kind of literalism in philosophy which implied condemnation of the earlier Muslim interpreters (or corrupters) of Aristotle. His *Incoherence of the Incoherence* was not only an attack on al-Ghazālī's *Incoherence of Philosophy*, but also a repudiation of pretended Aristotelians such as Avicenna and al-Fārābī: one of al-Ghazālī's errors, according to Averroes, was to attribute to the ancients doctrines which were in fact manufactured by Islamic peripatetics.

There is evidence to show that a connection existed between Averroes' nationalism and his vision of himself as the true heir to genuine Aristotelian thought. In his middle 'Commentary' on Aristotle's *Meteorology* he likens the climate of al-Andalus to that of Greece (Cordoba is not too far from the latitude of Athens), and draws the consequence that, like the Greeks, the inhabitants of his country were better disposed for philosophical thought than, for example, the people of Iraq.

Averroes' attitude towards Ptolemaic astronomy (which he shared with Ibn Tufayl and al-Bitrūjī), is a direct consequence of his view of Aristotle as the best and last philosophical authority. Thus whereas Avicenna had included a summary of Ptolemy's *Almagest* in his *summa* of peripatetic philosophy, Averroes concludes from an examination of the Ptolemaic system in the light of Aristotelian cosmology that 'the astronomy of our time agrees with computations, but not with what exists'. Averroes, like Maimonides, was thus aware of the strength of the Ptolemaic system of astronomy: it saved the celestial phenomena. But the system made use of eccentric and epicyclic spheres and thereby violated the Aristotelian conception of the world according to which all celestial bodies must rotate about the unique centre of the world. Since the Aristotelian theory was demonstrably true, Ptolemy's system must be false. Averroes was not himself able to discover an alternative system, but he urged others to continue the search. The theory proposed towards the end of the VI/12th century by al-Bitrūjī was a failure from the astronomical point of view, but it stands as a witness to a unique situation in the history of Islamic science.

Islamic scientists always regarded their Greek mentors with profound respect, often with awe. But the best among them were not slavish followers of their Greek predecessors: they regarded such authorities as Galen and Ptolemy as fallible human beings who made mistakes and who ought to be criticized and corrected. In astronomy, Islamic mathematicians compiled a vast mass of observations, checking Greek and Persian sources and refining Ptolemaic parameters. They devised ingenious methods of computation, and posed and solved numerous problems in spherical trigonometry. They produced non-Ptolemaic models for the planets which have been compared to those of Copernicus, but made no attempt to abandon the Ptolemaic geocentric system of the world. In spite of substantial advances in optics, there were no telescopes, and research was confined to pinpointing the position and movements of heavenly bodies with the naked eye, as indeed was the case with all astronomy up to Galileo. This illustration is from an Ottoman manuscript of the second half of the X/16th century, the *Shahinshāh-nāma*. The instrument is a giant armillary sphere, supported by a wooden frame set up on the ground, apparently in the open air. The five graduated rings correspond to five fundamental circles of the heavens. The man in the centre is adjusting the meridian ring (the large circle seen in the foreshortening) with a plumbline. Above him three astronomers are taking observations. The two on the right seem to be looking along the graduated circles at some planet or star, while an assistant records the results. (1)

A celestial sphere from Iran is dated 684/1285. It incorporates information derived from ʿAbd ar-Rahmān as-Sūfī's *Book of Fixed Stars* (see opposite below). Stars are marked by points of silver. (2)

Spherical astrolabes were rare: this is the only one known to exist, dated 885/1480. The large ecliptic circle bears the names of the signs of the Zodiac. The *rete*, or star map, is attached to the globe with pointers for nineteen fixed stars. (3)

An observatory and centre for astronomical studies was founded at Marāgha in Azerbaijan by the Il-Khānid ruler Hülegü about 657/1259. In charge was the great scientist Nasīr ad-Dīn at-Tūsī, who is depicted with his collaborators (below) in a x/16th-century manuscript. It was here that the tables known as the *Il-Khānid zīj* were drawn up, incorporating the results of new observations. A page giving the ascensions of the signs of the Zodiac for latitude 38° N is reproduced below. (4, 5)

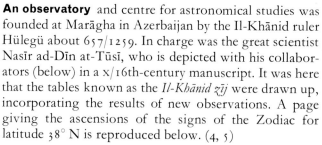

The astrolabe was for measuring the altitude of heavenly bodies above the horizon, and so determining (among other things) the time of day or night. Readings are taken by means of a rotatable alidade, a diametrical rule with sights. This example, the more normal planisphere, dates from the III/9th century. (6)

The Book of Fixed Stars was the main work of ʿAbd ar-Raḥmān as-Ṣūfī (290–376/903–86). In it, following ancient Greek tradition, he represented the constellations by animal or human figures or by objects. Shown here

At Samarqand Sultan Ulugh Beg, the grandson of Tamerlane, founded another great observatory. This trough supported a large arc erected in the meridian plane. Celestial bodies crossing this plane cast light through an opening at the arc's centre onto a graduated cylindrical base, from which their altitudes could be read off. (7)

are Cepheus, wearing a mitre; Sagittarius, represented as a centaur – both as in Ptolemy – and Andromeda, as seen on the celestial globe and in the sky. (8, 9, 10)

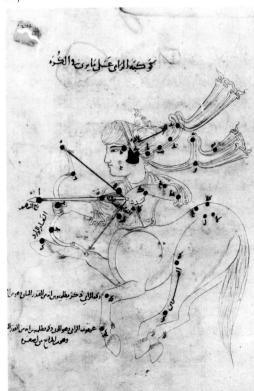

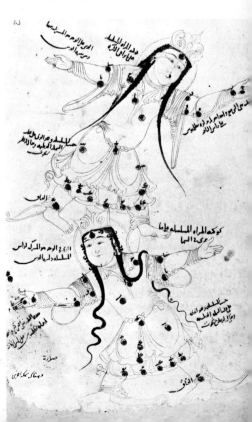

Aristotle was as seminal a figure in the East as in the West. A deliberate policy of translating his works was initiated by the caliphs as early as the II/8th century. He was known both as a philosopher and as a biologist. This portrait of him (left) comes from the *Description of Animals* by Ibn Bakhtīshūʿ, early VII/13th century. (11)

From Galen Islamic scientists inherited an empirical method of enquiry, a body of useful medical knowledge – and some errors. In optics Galen postulated a 'visual spirit'. Hunayn ibn Ishāq's *Book of the Ten Treatises on the Eye* (opposite) in the III/9th century adopted a Galenic theory of vision, but anatomically his work is outstandingly accurate. It was still a standard work in the VII/13th century, when this copy was made, although by that time a far more original treatment of the problem, Ibn al-Haytham's *Optics*, had been in existence for two hundred years. (14)

Dioscorides' treatise on herbs, one of the many Greek texts obtained from Constantinople in 512 (the Greek script shows through from the verso), is annotated with the name of each herb in Arabic. This one is saxifrage. (12)

The Book of Antidotes, attributed to Galen and John the Grammarian, was translated early and widely used in medicine. As on this page (below) the text is decoratively arranged, constituting one of the earliest of all Arabic illuminated manuscripts, 595/1199. (13)

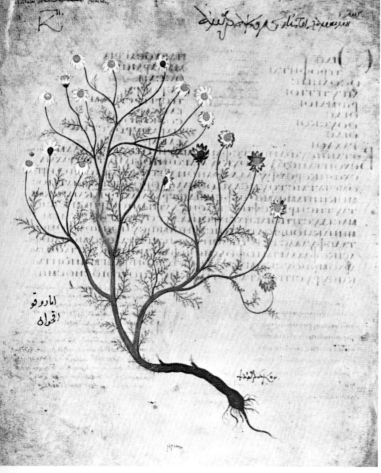

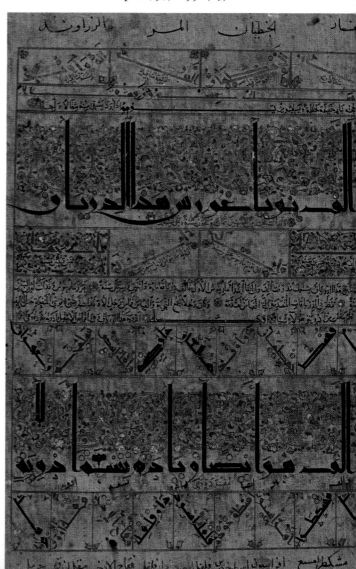

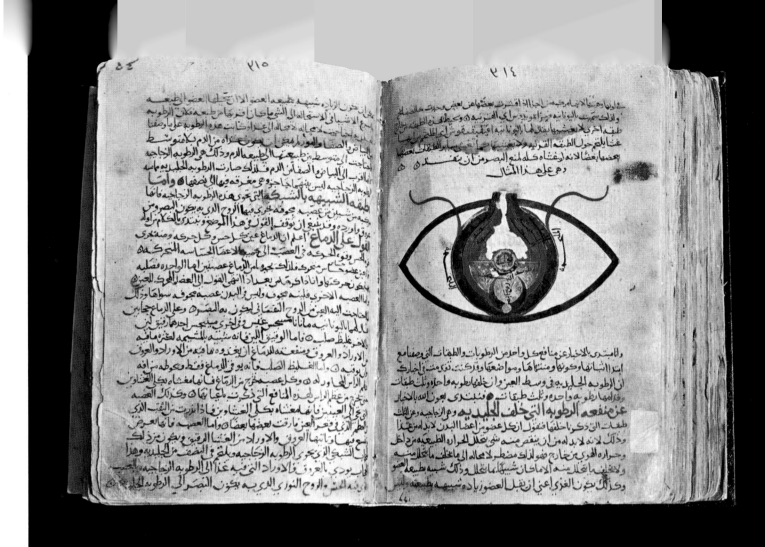

A pharmacist prepares his drugs. The scene comes from a VII/13th-century Arabic version of Dioscorides' *Materia Medica*, a work whose influence lasted until the 19th century. (15)

Arabic medicine was in advance of European throughout the Middle Ages, and from the first medical school of Salerno down to Vesalius, Western doctors learned from their Muslim counterparts. This anatomical plate from a Persian *Medical Treasury* is as late as the XI/17th century. (16)

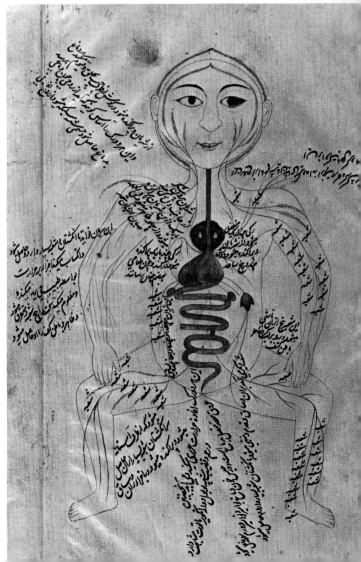

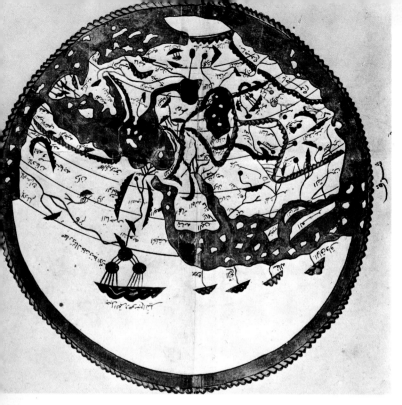

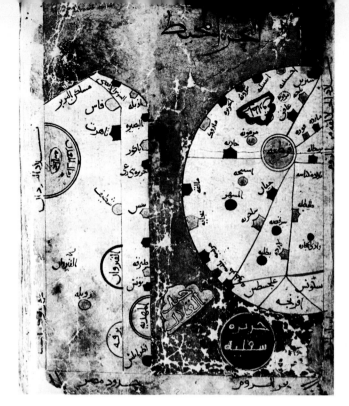

The world takes shape: Arab geographers understood the basic outlines of Asia, Europe and North Africa by the VI/12th century, and their knowledge was summed up in the great atlas of al-Idrīsī of 549/1154 (above). It places south at the top; we have inverted the map to make it recognizable. (17)

A schematic world, analogous to the Christian *mappa-mundi*, was common in Islamic atlases beginning in the III/9th century. A Baghdad example (791/1388) from al-Qazwīnī's *Wonders of Creation* is shown below. The world is surrounded by water, with the Mediterranean cutting into it from the west and the Red Sea from the east. (19)

The Mediterranean is given a more schematized form in this IV/10th-century map from al-Istakhrī's *Book of Countries*. Spain is on the right; the circle near the middle contains the name of Cordoba. The black circle at the bottom is Sicily. On the left, North Africa. (18)

The country round Shīrāz in Iran is shown in this detail from al-Istakhrī's *Book of Countries*. South is top left, north bottom right. Shīrāz itself is marked by the double circle in the middle. Istakhrī's maps are really stylized itineraries showing towns and the roads between them. (20)

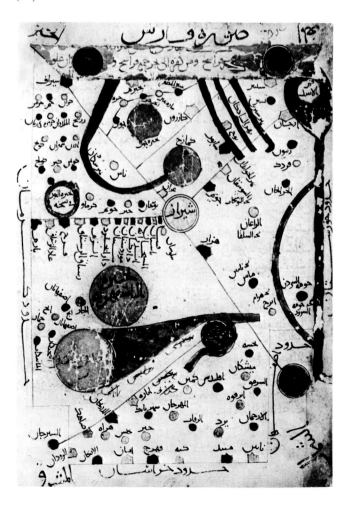

The **toy-like forms** of al-Jazarī's *Automata* should not distract attention from their mechanical ingenuity. His book was written about 603/1206; the illustrations on this page are from manuscripts of a century later. The device on the right is for measuring the amount of blood taken from a patient during blood-letting. The blood runs into the basin in the centre. As this gets heavier it operates a pulley which moves the two scribes sitting at the top. One points to a circle divided into 120 units (one for each dirham, i.e. about three ounces), the other to a tablet similarly divided. (22)

A hydraulic pump: the water flowing into the pool from the right discharges through a pipe in the bottom of the pool, thus causing the scoop wheel (bottom left) to turn. Through the enmeshed toothed wheels (beneath and above the pool) the motion is transferred to a wheel (top left) to which roped jars are attached. The jars scoop the water off the pool, and lift it to the top of the machine where it is discharged into a channel. Halfway up the long vertical shaft an ox revolves, as if providing the motive power. (21)

A mechanical wash-stand (right): water runs from the tank at the top, through the pitcher held by the servant, into a basin. The owner washes his hands and the water is drunk by the duck standing in the basin and runs out into the lower tank. As it rises here it moves the other hand of the servant who holds out a towel and comb. (23)

The study of the heavens was eagerly pursued in almost every Islamic country, partly – as in Europe – because of its relevance to astrology. Here astronomers are working at the short-lived x/16th-century observatory built at Istanbul by Murād III for Taqī ad-Dīn, the clock-maker turned astrologer. On the far side of the large table in the middle of the room an astronomer (Taqī ad-Dīn?) holds an astrolabe; the one to his right looks through an alidade attached to a quadrant; while another, at the far left, looks through a diopter. (24)

The indispensable instrument remained the astrolabe, almost always planispherical and made of bronze or brass. Astronomers and astrologers used it throughout the Islamic world, and many treatises were written on its construction and use. With it the altitudes of celestial bodies could be measured with the help of a rotating alidade. From such information the time of day or night could be determined. As an analogue computer constructed on the principles of stereographic projection, it was used for solving problems in spherical astronomy. Below left: scene with an astrologer holding an astrolabe, from a VII/13th-century *Maqāmāt*. Below: astrolabe made in Cairo in 634/1236, of engraved brass inlaid with silver and copper. (25, 26)

Chapter Eight

ARMIES
OF THE PROPHET

Edmund Bosworth

A mounted archer or fāris *of the Mamlūk army c. 700/1300, from the so-called Baptistère de St Louis. Note the composite bow and bow-case, and the kite-shaped shield on the rider's back. Practice in shooting from horseback was one of the principal features of the* furūsiyya *exercises or trials of skill in the equestrian arts and in weapon handling. (1)*

ONE OF THE POPULAR STEREOTYPES which grew out of the long centuries of Muslim–Christian religious antipathy and warfare over possession of the Mediterranean basin was that of the bellicose and bloodthirsty Saracen, impelled by the fanaticism of his Faith and by a prospect of the Muslim paradise of houris and gardens, the prize of the warrior slain in *jihād*, or battle for the Faith. Certainly, the most spectacular and continuous contact between Islam and Christendom was on the military and naval planes. For some eight centuries, Constantinople lay as the supreme goal of Muslim arms, just as the recovery of the Christian Holy Places in Palestine and the patriarchal seats of Antioch and Alexandria did for the Latin Crusaders. Moreover, when, in regard to the Christian shrines, the Crusaders had resigned themselves to relinquishing their last footholds in the Levant, and when in regard to Constantinople, the Muslims achieved their aim in 857/1453, the sequel to these centuries of accumulated mistrust was a continued clashing by land and sea: the Ottoman Turkish imperial expansion into the Balkans, and the Spanish and Portuguese attacks on Muslim North Africa, although the purely religious motive gave place from the XI/17th century onwards to motives of political, economic and strategic domination.

It must be admitted that there is some truth in the medieval and later stereotypes of the Muslim warrior-fanatic, the *ghāzī* or *mujāhid*; and memories of the religiously inspired desperadoes, the Assassins, in VI/12th- and VII/13th-century Syria and Persia have retained a favourable enough connotation in the modern Islamic world for the Arabic term applied to such a desperado, *fidā'ī*, to be revived in the Persian and Arabic worlds and applied to religiously or politically motivated terrorists, the *fedayeen*: those eager to sacrifice their lives. A good proportion of the successive ruling dynasties of the caliphs and their epigoni in the provinces, and of the great empires in the later medieval period, such as those of the Mongols, the Mamlūks, the Ottomans, the Safavids and the Mughuls, certainly had their origins in military conquest or revolutionary movements, within some of which religious motives were interwoven; and the regime arising from a military coup continues to be the norm over much of the contemporary Arab world. The alarums of war often impinged on the daily lives of

Muslim peoples. Lands were trampled over by invaders or by internal rebels and aspirants to power, and towns were sacked. As the medieval Islamic world evolved, much of its governmental apparatus, and especially its land tenure system, became geared to making war. It is for factors such as these, then, that the topic of warfare and military organization in Islam is worthy of isolation and study.

Within the cultural and social backwater that was Arabia, the basic military feature of tribal life was the *razzia* or raid (from Arabic *ghazw*, *ghazwa*, with the same meaning), aimed at aggression against or revenge upon a rival tribe, and achieved by killing the enemy's fighting men (thereby crippling its power and ability to survive in the harsh environment of the desert) and by carrying off its camels or wealth and captives from it as slaves. These raids were always limited operations for a specific purpose, and the famous so-called 'wars' of pre-Islamic Arabia, such as those of Basūs (late 5th–early 6th centuries) and Dāhis (late 6th century), were in fact strings of small-scale campaigns spread over a period of many years, and not full-scale operations with set battles. Pre-Islamic Arabic poetry is imbued with the spirit of *fakhr*, glorying in the martial exploits of the tribe, and it lauds the heroic virtues of bravery and fortitude in battle. The ability to defend oneself was crucial to survival, for, as the poet Zuhayr ibn Abī Sulmā noted,

Whoever is in terror of the ways Death may come, Death shall yet slay him, though he aspire to mount to heaven on the rungs of a ladder.

Whoever suffers people always to be riding upon him, and never spares himself humiliation, shall come to rue it.

Whoever defends not his water-tank with his goodly weapons will see it broken; whoever assaults not others is himself assaulted.

Yet because these raids were limited operations, economy of men and materials was always observed; endurance in battle did not entail foolhardiness, and the inevitability of reprisals, under the vendetta system, was a powerful deterrent against indiscriminate slaughter.

The actual weapons employed must, by later standards, have been poor. Swords are often described as 'Yemenī' or 'Indian' in origin, but the really indigenous Arab weapons were firstly the lance, for which shafts were obtained from the coastal regions of the Persian Gulf and the marshlands of Lower Iraq, and secondly, the self bow and arrow, which could be fashioned locally. In pre- and early Islamic times, the warrior endeavoured always to have with him his bow, and carrying a bow was the mark of the Bedouin in the town; the poet al-Hārith ibn Hilliza extemporized his great poem, his *Mu'allaqa*, before the Lakhmid king in central Iraq, 'Amr ibn Hind, leaning so heavily on his bow that the string cut into his palm, and the Caliph 'Alī supported himself on his bow during an altercation with the Khārijī schismatics. The only body protections were leather cuirasses and simple mailed shirts, doubtless adequate against the poor weapons of the nomads, but even these were prized enough to be handed down from generation to generation, and raids were undertaken to secure valuable suits of mail, such as the attack on the castle of the warrior-poet Samaw'al ibn 'Ādiyā' at Ablaq in the northern Hijāz in order to obtain possession of the shirts and weapons deposited there by the poet Imru' al-Qays.

The Arab eruption
The bursting forth of the Arabs from their desert fastnesses in the 1/7th century under the inspired leadership of the Prophet Muhammad was a mass movement of their adult fighting men, one which gathered momentum as reports filtered back of the rich plunder to be gained in Syria or Iraq or Persia. Islamic sources naturally stress the religious motivation, the stimulus of such classic Qur'ānic injunctions as:

Fight those who believe not in God and the Last Day, and do not forbid what God and His Messenger have forbidden – such men as practise not the religion of truth, being of those who have been given the Book – until they pay the tribute out of hand and have been humbled [ix, 29].

We today are more inclined to stress secular factors, such as hunger, an upset in the balance of population within Arabia and a sheer love of spoils, all these coinciding with a period when the two great Middle Eastern world-empires of Byzantium and Persia were exhausted from warfare and therefore vulnerable. But religious enthusiasm should not be underestimated as a motive all through Islamic warfare; one can, for instance, trace the spirit of *jihād* in so recent an event as the Kashmiri *jihād* of 1948, when Muslim volunteers from north-west India and Afghanistan poured into Kashmir in an effort to preserve this overwhelmingly Muslim province entirely for Pakistan. The role of the volunteer religious enthusiast remained important all through the Muslim Middle Ages, and these *ghāzīs* often formed a significant element of Islamic armies. Except when full-scale military expeditions were mounted into infidel territory

(such as the various abortive attacks on Constantinople by the Umayyad and early 'Abbāsid caliphs, the campaign of the Caliph al-Mu'tasim against Amorium in central Anatolia in 838, and the Spanish Umayyad viceroy al-Mansūr's expedition against the shrine of St James of Compostela in 997), the brunt of frontier defence in Anatolia, northern Spain, Central Asia and the Indian borderlands devolved on these volunteers, who usually manned the frontier posts or *ribāts* there and along the Mediterranean and Atlantic coasts exposed to Christian or Viking attacks.

The methods of warfare in the first years of the Islamic conquests inevitably followed the limited ideas of pre-Islamic Arab warfare, though even in Muhammad's lifetime there were signs that newer ways would have to be adopted, and here influences from Byzantium and Persia were important. When in 6/627 the Prophet's Meccan enemies besieged him in Medina with a grand coalition of Meccans and Bedouins, the exposed northern side of the town was protected by a defensive trench, whose construction had been advised by a Persian convert, Salmān; feeble though this protection must have been, its novelty seems to have deterred the attackers. Three years later, Muhammad was faced with the problem of reducing the town of Taif, the only one in Arabia with defensive walls; he is said to have sent to the Byzantine frontier for siege weapons, but continued to lose men in a vain attempt to storm the walls, and in the end, Taif surrendered voluntarily. But once outside Arabia, the Muslims soon learnt how to handle the new engines of war; probably those Arabs who lived along the Syrian and Iraqi frontiers and who had served the Greeks and Persians as auxiliary guards were to some extent already familiar with them. Hence the use of mangonels and ballistas for hurling missiles, rams for battering down walls, towers manned by soldiers for pushing up against walls, and the techniques of mining and countermining – all of which had been highly developed in Byzantine military tradition – were gradually adopted. The Arabic term for the larger type of catapult or mangonel, *manjanīq*, stems from Greek *manganikon*, and the use of catapults is mentioned at the siege of Damascus in 14/635 and that of Istakhr in Fārs in 16/637.

The Arab forces at this time comprised numerically small but highly mobile groups mounted on camels or horses, which fanned out through the deserts and steppes of the Near East and North Africa up to the Armenian and Iranian plateaux, often bypassing fortified points or towns and only returning later either to reduce them or to receive their voluntary submission. Unlike the conventional Byzantine and Persian armies, with their heavily mailed cavalrymen and infantry and their encumbering baggage trains, the Arab raiders were largely self-sufficient and could live frugally off what they carried or what they could plunder from the countryside. Hence the problem facing most invading armies, that of increasingly long supply lines, was rarely a problem for them, and we find Arab troops making tremendous leaps, such as along the North African coast to the Moroccan shores of the Atlantic, through the Caucasus to the mouth of the Volga, and along the shores of the Indian Ocean via what is now Baluchistan to the Indus, even though the intervening lands were not always immediately secured.

Consolidating the conquests

For the proper securing of the conquered lands, the Arab leaders, starting with the second Caliph 'Umar (13-23/634-44), founded *amsār* or garrison cities, either using existing centres, such as Damascus, Merv, Qum and Qinnasrīn, or else laying out new encampments, such as Kūfa, Basra and Wāsit in Iraq, Fustāt in Egypt, and Qayrawān in Tunisia. These garrison cities were strategically situated centres of military power, in Bernard Lewis's graphic phrase, 'the Gibraltars and Singapores of the early Arab empire', from which control by an Arab élite was exercised over vast subject populations. The Syrian and Iraqi *amsār*, in particular, stood on the edges of the desert and could therefore act as concentration-points for Bedouin reinforcements. It was from Kūfa that the conquests of Armenia, Azerbaijan and the Caucasus were organized, and from Basra, those of southern and eastern Persia, Transoxiana and Sind. Gradually, these artificial creations became flourishing centres of commercial and intellectual activity, with organic lives of their own; Kūfa declined, but Basra is today the second city of Iraq, and Fustāt was the forerunner of later Cairo. When the Umayyad governor of Iraq, Ziyād ibn Abīhi, took a census of the Arab warriors in Kūfa and Basra less than twenty-five years after their foundation, he found that Kūfa had forty thousand men capable of bearing arms, and Basra sixty thousand, despite the fact that soldiers and colonists were continually going on to the Armenian and Persian fronts. The Arabs settled down in the new camps with their tribal divisions intact, and the tribe as a basis for social and military organization continued to be important for some decades, especially as much of the ninety years of the Umayyad caliphate (41-133/661-750) was racked by internecine Arab tribal warfare. The Umayyads often paid subsidies to tribal chiefs to lead their forces into battle; thus Marwān ibn al-Hakam (65-6/684-5) paid Hasan ibn Mālik, chief of the Yemenī tribesmen in Syria, two million dirhams for a contingent of two thousand men and confirmed the succession of Hasan's son or nephew as tribal leader.

It was the intention that the conquering Arab aristocracy should live as a rentier class off the revenues of the occupied lands. A strict application of Qur'ānic principles would have entailed the dividing-out among the troops of these lands plus any movable plunder captured in war, once the head of the community, the caliph, had extracted his fifth, nominally for God, in effect for the state. The physical division of real property would obviously have caused economic chaos, so the ingenious solution was found of the state's collecting the rent and revenues and then paying out allowances to the Arab warriors and to a few privileged members of the increasing numbers of indigenous converts to Islam, the *mawālī*. The warriors' names were entered in a *dīwān* or register, one of the many administrative innovations of the Caliph 'Umar. The actual cash was paid out by officers called *'arīfs*, who kept lists of the troops in their unit, and the amounts involved came to reflect religious status as much as anything else, with the payment of higher sums corresponding to such significant Islamic facts as earliness of conversion, presence at the Battle of Badr against the pagan Meccans, etc. These pensions were hereditary. In

Metal tip of a Turkish battle standard. (2)

addition, there was always, in this expansionary period, booty to be gained from campaigns, such as weapons, jewels, beasts and, above all, slaves. The Islamic state became increasingly a slave-holding one, though slaves were in this first century or so used for domestic purposes rather than for economic production or for military uses. A prime motive for the North African campaigns was to gain Berber slaves, while the raids through the Caucasus into southern Russia and across the Oxus into Central Asia were aimed at gathering Turkish and other slaves.

It is during the Umayyad period that the classic battle formation of an Arab army seems to emerge; the VIII/14th-century historian Ibn Khaldūn is doubtless correct in attributing it to Byzantine and Persian influence. Previously, the main tactic had been that of a violent charge, followed by a feigned retreat and then a sudden return to battle, the one known as *karr wa-farr*: 'return and flight'. Now there was also adopted the technique of a battle-order *(ta'biya)* in close formation, with even lines 'like rows of worshippers at prayer', for which there was adduced the Qur'ānic verse 'God loves those who fight in His way in ranks, as though they were a building well-compacted' (lxi. 4). The general formation of an army preparing for battle was fivefold (hence the term *khamīs*, sometimes used to mean 'army' in general). There was a centre, where the commanding general was stationed; left and right wings; a vanguard; and a rearguard, where were situated such items as the baggage train, the bazaar of traders supplying the army, any armouries or siege machinery, etc. In front of the army there were scouts and skirmishers, but when two armies came into actual contact there were often single combats between champions from each side, and these might go on for days, as at Siffīn between the Caliph 'Alī and his rival Mu'āwiya in 37/657; these contests had a psychological significance, for an army could become demoralized if its crack warriors were consistently worsted. The signal for general attack was given by a trumpet-blast or the waving of a flag. Some illustrations of the individual tribal banners have recently come to light in an Arabic historical manuscript; these were naturally important rallying points. Within the battle, the old technique of attack and feigned retreat might still be employed; the Muslims in

Spain long used this tactic, and the Arabic expression for it was borrowed by the Christian Spaniards as *torna-fuye*. Although the last Umayyad Caliph Marwān II (127-33/744-50) made some innovations by introducing compact groups of troops into the general line formation, the fivefold deployment of troops long continued as the basic procedure.

By the coming of the ʿAbbāsid caliphs in 133/750, the frontiers of Islam had become largely fixed; indeed, in the III/9th century it was the Byzantines who took the offensive and temporarily recaptured some of their ancient territory in northern Syria, and the beginnings of the Christian Reconquista in Spain can be discerned. After the III/9th century, the unity of the caliphate began to break down and provincial dynasties arose, usually through the successful ambitions of a local governor or commander. Consequently, a more static position was reached along the external frontiers, with much small-scale guerilla warfare but little large-scale campaigning.

The most significant general military trend of the III/9th century onwards is the increased professional nature of armies, as the political dominance of the Arabs declines and other nations come to the fore. The ʿAbbāsids achieved power with the help of troops from Khurāsān or eastern Persia, and very soon the old *dīwān* system of the Arab warriors was in steep decline. These troops had long ceased to be the *levée en masse* of the whole nation, and most of them had become increasingly disinclined to fight. The ʿAbbāsid caliphate was socially a less exclusive institution, with a more cosmopolitan administrative personnel, than the Umayyad caliphate had been; with the victory of al-Maʾmūn, who had been governor of Merv and was half-Persian, over his brother al-Amīn in 198/813, the dominance of the Persian element became more pronounced. Yet the ascendancy of the Khurasanian troops was short-lived, for at this time there began the importation of Turks into the military institutions of the caliphate and its successor-states. Very soon these Turks were able to extend their power from the purely military to the general political sphere, and within a few centuries, Turkish dynasties of military origin could be found ruling from Algiers in the west to Yemen in the south and Bengal in the east; this phase of Islamic history has only really ended in our own time with the deposition in Egypt in 1953 of the young King Fuʾād II, from the Turkish line of Muhammad ʿAlī, and the abolition of the last monarchy of Turkish origin.

The make-up of the armies

Two important features of the new professional armies were, firstly, their multi-racial composition, the exact nationalities of the troops involved being often dependent on geographical accessibility of manpower; and secondly, their being usually composed of, or at least built round, a nucleus of military slaves (*ghulāms* or *mamlūks*, the latter term, literally 'possessed, owned', giving its name to one of the greatest dynasties of later medieval Islamic history). The caliphs and their governors had begun to feel the need for a dependable body of troops brought in from outside as buttresses for increased centralization and for raising the sovereign high above his subjects; the old role of the Patriarchal and early Umayyad caliphs as tribal chiefs, accessible to the

humblest Arab, was now left far behind. Instead, the possession of a standing army and a body of loyal slaves helped to cement a crucial distinction in most Islamic states from the III/9th century onwards, that of the ruling class of soldiers and officials *vis-à-vis* the mass of subjects, whose prime duty was to pay taxes and thus provide the sinews of war; among the Ottomans, this is the division of the *ʿAskerīs* and the *Reʿāyā*.

It was hoped – at least in theory – that slave troops would give unqualified obedience to their masters, since they had no local ties. Hence slaves of any nationality could be brought in from the abode of war, educated in an Islamic environment and then made into an élite force. The Berber Almoravid ruler ʿAlī ibn Yūsuf (500-37/1106-42) is even said to have employed a force of Christian cavalry (presumably Galicians, Basques and others from northern Spain) to collect taxes from the Muslims of the Maghrib, though not, for obvious reasons, to fight in the Holy War against the Spanish Christian monarchs. The Turkish governor and virtually independent ruler of Egypt, Ahmad ibn Tūlūn (254-70/868-84), bought Greek and black Sudanese slaves and recruited free mercenaries, possibly Greeks, Armenians and Balkan Slavs; in the military cantonments which he laid out near Fustāt or Old Cairo, there were special quarters for the various ethnic groups. A Persian observer in Cairo during the v/11th century, Nāsir-i Khusraw, witnessed the ceremonial ride to the Nile on the occasion of the release of the floodgates there, of the Fātimid Caliph al-Mustansir (427-87/1036-94). This ruler was escorted by ten thousand cavalry with richly caparisoned mounts and bejewelled equipment, and the troops included Berbers, Turks, Persians, Negroes, etc. Directly preceding him was a special force of three hundred infantrymen from Daylam, the mountainous and inaccessible region of Persia at the south-western corner of the Caspian Sea, with their characteristic weapons of battle-axes and *zhūpīns*, two-pronged spears or javelins. But more than any other nationality, the Turks, with their hardy steppe background of Central Asia or southern Russia, were prized for their martial qualities.

It is from this period that we have detailed information about the internal organization of the armies from records of periodic musters and reviews of the troops and from accounts of the working of the War Department in the caliphal bureaucracy, the *Dīwān al-Jaysh*. These reviews served as pay parades, the money being disbursed at intervals varying from one to six months, but above all, they were inspections of arms, mounts and equipment, i.e. of the fighting condition of the army. From surviving descriptions of reviews in ʿAbbāsid Baghdad, we learn that the army was drawn up in a square below the palace, and soldiers and mounts carefully checked against the descriptions in the registers of the War Department, with special regard to the facial and physical characteristics of the men and to the colour and brand-marks of the beasts. The fighting qualities and the standard of weapon training of the troops were also tested by field exercises, and a note made in the registers: a *j* (for *jayyid* 'good') if a man were first class, a *t* (for *mutawassit* 'moderate') if he were average, and a *d* (for *dūn* 'inferior') if he were below standard.

It is also from this time that we hear of distinctive

An Egyptian river boat, from the Mamlūk period, IX/15th century, containing three archers with drawn bows. This is a figure, made from painted leather, which was used in the Egyptian shadow-plays of this period. (3)

uniforms for palace guards and other special bodies of troops, who might be used to line a reception hall or throne room on ceremonial occasions. In the 'Abbāsid caliphate of the III/9th and IV/10th centuries, the sovereign's Turkish guards lived in quarters within the palace complex itself and received ceremonial uniforms, arms, equipment and mounts directly from the caliph, whereas the mass of soldiery normally provided these items out of their own resources. Our information about these uniforms and weapons is almost wholly derived from descriptions in literary sources, and virtually no material objects have survived from this period. But there was discovered in the early 1950s in southern Afghanistan, along the banks of the River Helmand, a series of ruined palaces originally built by the Ghaznavids, a dynasty of Turkish military slave origin, who from their centre at Ghazna built up a vast if transient empire in northern India, eastern Persia and Central Asia. The murals surviving fragmentarily in the audience hall of one of these palaces at Lashkar-i Bāzār depict the Turkish *ghulāms* or palace guards of Sultan Mahmūd (388-421/998-1030), and strikingly confirm the information of the literary sources that these troops were splendidly clothed in uniforms of the silk brocades of Baghdad, Isfahan and Shushtar and bore bejewelled weapons with gold and silver mountings, probably maces or battle axes.

Tactics of battle

Provincial dynasties like the Ghaznavids of Afghanistan, and a host of others in such regions as Persia, Syria, southern Arabia, Egypt and the Maghrib, rose out of the ruins of the 'Abbāsid universal caliphate, by the later IV/10th century only a shadow of its former self. Their military practices, like their administrative traditions, were derived largely from 'Abbāsid practice, such was the prestige of Baghdad and the normative value of everything done there, although there were inevitably local modifications and developments, reflecting the strategic needs of border regions or the availability of men and matériel. Thus it was the Ghaznavids again, with their access to the Indus–Ganges plains of northern India, who during the V/11th and VI/12th centuries introduced the use of war elephants into the Islamic world for tactical purposes. These elephants were

supplied with armour plating over their heads and forequarters, and placed in the front line and stampeded towards the enemy; their bulk and the noise of their metal accoutrements struck fear into the hearts of troops, like the Ghaznavids' enemies in Central Asia, unaccustomed to such beasts. However, the use of elephants as tactical weapons of war largely vanishes from the Islamic world, outside India itself, after the Mongol invasions, though they continued to be used, in the Persian world at least, for ceremonial occasions.

The near-ubiquitousness of the Turks in the lands east of the Maghrib brought with it the dominance in this period of the swift-moving cavalryman – even when there were specialist corps of infantrymen, these often rode to the scene of battle and then dismounted to fight – and above all, the dominance of the hand bow, the weapon par excellence of the steppe cavalryman. Already in the III/9th century, the author al-Jāhiz of Basra commented that if one numbered a Turk's days at the end of his life, one would find that he had spent more time in the saddle than on the ground, that the Turks always carry with them two or three bows and their strings, and that they are such expert archers that their arrows shot backwards when retreating are as deadly as those shot forwards. Five centuries later, Ibn Khaldūn wrote:

> We hear that the fighting technique of the contemporary Turkish nations [he is thinking of such powers as the Egyptian and Syrian Mamlūks and the Turcoman epigoni of the Mongols in Iraq and Persia] is the shooting of arrows. Their battle order consists of a line formation. They divide their army into three lines, one placed behind the other. They dismount from their horses, empty their quivers on the ground in front of them, and then shoot from a squatting or kneeling position. Each line protects the one ahead of it against being over-run by the enemy, until victory is assured for one party. This is a very good and remarkable battle order.

Indeed, the skill of the Mamlūk archer became legendary, and in the period of Mamlūk independent rule (648-923/1250-1517), the use of the hand bow reached its apogee; we possess from this period and from the preceding Ayyūbid one several important manuals on the art of war

View of the Cairo Citadel, taken from opposite the Muqattam Hills gate, as it appeared to a European traveller in 1822. The Citadel was begun in the later VI/12th century by the Ayyūbid Sultan Saladin and added to by the Mamlūks; by the artist's time, however, it had lost its serious military value. (4)

which are more practical and down to earth than the theoretical discussions of military organization and deployment of armies found in the earlier 'Mirrors for Princes' genre of literature. One brief but interesting work is a manual of war written in the later VI/12th century by one Mardī ibn 'Alī at-Tarsūsī for the Ayyūbid Sultan Saladin, in which he discusses various weapons and techniques of warfare and siegecraft (see further below). A very detailed work specifically devoted to the technique of archery from horseback and the construction of the composite bow and its arrows was written in *c.* 770/1368 by an obscure Mamlūk soldier living in Syria called Taybughā al-Yūnānī, and this treatise amply demonstrates the extreme refinements of construction and shooting achieved by that time.

The actual conduct of war in this period of dominance by the *fāris*, the cavalryman, can be reconstructed from the manuals of statecraft and administration, tested against the evidence of the histories. Non-Muslim sources may be useful also, such as the information about warfare on the Taurus Mountains frontier in the *Tactica* of the Byzantine Emperor Leo VI (886–912); it is he who stresses the mobility of the Muslim forces and their use on the battlefield of an elongated but solid formation, and who comments that 'the Saracens are bold when hopeful of victory, but easily frightened if they are in despair of it'. As among all civilized people, there evolved in Islam a series of conventions for warfare: that unbelievers should first be summoned to Islam before war was launched against them, that quarter should freely be given, that non-combatants should not be attacked, but that any captured non-Muslims might be enslaved or held to ransom. In strict law, only truces of limited duration, and not a lasting peace, were possible with unbelievers. The exchange and ransoming of prisoners was a constant feature of life along the Islamic–Christian frontiers, and this traffic was at times highly organized.

During these centuries of comparatively static frontiers and compact, professional armies, warfare was often quite a small-scale business. It was not easy, even for the most successful of commanders, to keep an army continuously in the field. Soldiers had to return periodically to their *iqtā's*, or land grants, in order to collect their revenues; the harsh climate of regions like the Anatolian and Iranian plateaux meant that winter campaigns were hardly possible; above all, there were constant difficulties in finding food and fodder supplies and cash for donatives to the troops. Hence the great Saladin himself was often frustrated in his plans to sweep the Latin Crusaders out of the Levant. His cavalry were reluctant to engage the entrenched Frankish infantry in such episodes as the attempt to relieve Acre in 585-6/1189-90; and the extreme weariness of his Turkish and Kurdish troops, exhausted after the unprecedented period of four continuous years in the field, prevented them from holding the town of Jaffa, which they had temporarily captured in 588/1192. Because of considerations like these, whole wars might be decided by a single pitched battle; but on the other hand, wars often consisted rather of a string of sieges and counter-sieges.

The siege

It is not therefore surprising that the techniques of military fortification and siege machinery construction became increasingly sophisticated in the later Middle Ages. The warfare between the Muslims and Byzantines, and then between the Muslims and Latin Crusaders, was frequently one of attrition and small-scale changes of territory – the medieval equivalent of the trench warfare of World War I. Hence under the Ayyūbids and Mamlūks there was a flowering of military architecture in the Syrian region especially (where ample supplies of excellent building stone were at hand), seen in the massive towers and splendid enceintes of the citadels at Damascus, Aleppo and Bosra, and also at Cairo, where the citadel defences comprised extensive quarters for the permanent garrison of troops, with a network of passages to the galleries of the outer walls and to the magazines and store rooms of the interior. Towards the end of the IX/15th century, we find modifications of such structures in an attempt to adapt them for the new age of firearms, in the shape of embrasures for firing arquebuses and cannon and strengthened platforms for mounting heavy ordnance. The Syrian traditions, as developed for these new weapons of war, were also adopted by the early Ottomans in the fortifications which they erected to encircle the Byzantines in their shrinking redoubt of Constantinople and to command the naval passage of the Bosphorus. At Anadolu Hisārı on the Asiatic side (begun in 793/1390), and Rumeli Hisārı on the European one (built in 856/1452, the year before the final onslaught on the Greek capital), the construction was on a colossal scale; the three donjons of Rumeli Hisārı are from 77 to 86 feet in diameter and the thickness of the walls varies from 16½ to 23 feet.

Along the coasts of Muslim North Africa, fortifications against sea attacks by the Christians existed from the beginning of the III/9th century, especially in what is now Algeria, Tunisia and Libya. These North African defences or *ribāts*, among which one may cite as examples Sūs and Monastir in northern Tunisia, faced an enemy whose attacks became more and more pressing with the shrinkage of Muslim Spain in the VII/13th century to the petty kingdom of Granada.

Illustrations in manuscripts of certain Islamic manuals of war and in some Christian sources, together with the rather vaguer literary descriptions of warfare, enable us to form a picture of the siege machinery and techniques in general use throughout the Islamic world from Spain to India. Direct assault could be made by bringing up a mobile tower *(burj)* to the walls of the besieged place and landing men on the ramparts, or by the use of a ram *(kabsh)* or testudo *(dabbāba)*, although these were weapons favoured by the Frankish Crusaders rather than by the Muslims. But more often, it was difficult to approach the walls until intervening earthen ramparts had been stormed and ditches filled in with sacks of earth or such articles as stuffed sheepskins. To obviate the need for such procedures, in which large numbers of men might be killed by the arrows and missiles hurled down upon them by the defenders, the attackers might resort to sappers and miners *(naqqābūn)*, who played an especially notable part in the siege warfare involving the Crusaders, the Ayyūbids and the early Mamlūks. Provided that the ground was not too rocky, tunnels could be driven under the fortifications, and the wood which had been used for shoring them up set alight, causing subsidence of the earth above.

Otherwise, the hurling of rocks, arrows and other projectiles was the main weapon employed against stubborn defences. There evolved many varieties of machines for this purpose, all of them having their ultimate roots in the military practices of the Greco-Roman world, but now refined and brought to a new peak of perfection. The general term for the larger type of mangonel was, as noted above, *manjanīq*. In this heavier engine, the projectile was hurled by the centrifugal force produced by a team of men rocking the shorter end of an unevenly-balanced beam (like the medieval European *trébuchet*). The lighter type of ballista, called *'arrāda* and corresponding to the classical Greek *onagros*, hurled a smaller missile through the impact of a shaft released after the winding and twisting of a rope. In the VI/12th century there appears the great arbalist or *qaws az-ziyār*, a mechanical crossbow worked by a team of men, who wound up the cords with a crank and wheel; some models apparently shot three arrows simultaneously. It seems to have been an Oriental invention, unknown in the West; it is recorded that the Emperor Frederick II of Sicily purchased one at Acre in 637/1239.

A valuable contemporary source on these machines is the treatise by Mardī ibn ʿAlī (see above), the manuscript of which contains several illustrations important for the elucidation of the technical descriptions. As well as describing machines of the types mentioned above,

Mardī cites several ingenious inventions of one Shaykh Abū 'l-Hasan al-Iskandarānī, whom he knew personally; some of these inventions are of a distinctly Heath Robinson-ish nature, such as a dual purpose lance and a shield which contained a bow. On a larger scale, the Shaykh constructed a protective shelter of the *dabbāba* type, useful to protect men manoeuvring a mangonel into position; this had a framework held taut by ropes which would cause a missile landing on it to bounce back. Whether these cunningly contrived weapons were ever used extensively in practice is, of course, a different matter.

It may also be noted here that in eastern Islam certainly, the hand-held crossbow was used, Syrian crossbowmen being particularly famed. In the Muslim west, the crossbow was less favoured by the indigenous Muslims, but rulers there employed either Syrians or Christian Spanish slaves and mercenaries to handle it. Thus the crossbow or *ʿaqqāra* (the medieval European *arbalista ad duos pedes*, so called because the archer pinned it down when winding by placing his two feet on the limbs of the crossbow) played a great part in the defence against the Christians of Ceuta, vital as a bridgehead for communication with Granada, from the VI/12th century onwards. The crossbow could not be aimed accurately over a long distance, hence was of little use in mobile, open warfare, but came into its own for sieges and for close-quarters naval engagements. The mention of defence against fire or fiery missiles reminds us that inflammatory substances hurled against the enemy by various means played a noticeable role in fighting from early ʿAbbāsid times onwards, being in some measure the forerunners of firearms. Oil, bitumen and sulphur were mixed together, as by the Byzantines for their famous 'Greek fire'. Corps of *naffātūn* – 'naphtha-hurlers' – were employed by

The siege of a fortress by mailed cavalrymen, III/9th- or IV/10th-century Iranian workmanship, reminiscent of Sāsānid style. (5)

Hārūn ar-Rashīd while campaigning against the Byzantines in Anatolia and by the Seljuq Sultan Alp Arslan at Ānī in Armenia in 456/1064, when archers and naphtha-throwers operated from platforms and towers. It seems that the Muslim *naffātūn* used pots of naphtha attached to javelins and arrows, or else had special tubes from which the fiery substances were projected, the prototypes of our flame-throwers. The bow was certainly used to fire incendiary materials, and the Mamlūk writer Taybughā has a section in his manual on the firing of heated iron pellets propelled by an incendiary 'egg', the pellet and egg being mounted in a funnel fixed to the tip of the arrow. All these incendiary devices were also adopted in naval warfare, again in imitation of Greek practice.

Slave systems

The Mamlūks have already been frequently cited as a dynasty which developed the techniques of war to a high degree. Their rise is one aspect of the general Turkish takeover in the Islamic world, but the difference between them and the earlier Seljuq Turkish sultanate which had grown up in Persia, Iraq and Anatolia during the v/11th and vi/12th centuries was that the Seljuqs were essentially a tribal dynasty of free origin, migrating into eastern Persia from their Central Asian homeland, whereas the Mamlūks were, as their name implies, of servile status, originally Qipchaq Turkish slaves imported from the South Russian steppes, and later, Circassian slaves from the Caucasus, but always with an admixture of several other races, such as Kurds, Mongols and even Slavs and Armenians. A system of slave troops and officials was to be found in the later Muslim Middle Ages, i.e. the post-Mongol period, in varying degrees across most of the Islamic world east of the Maghrib. The Safavids of Persia, themselves springing from a militant Sūfī religious order in Azerbaijan, employed in the x/16th and xi/17th centuries, in addition to their *Qizil-bash* or 'Red-cap' Turcoman troops, contingents of slaves personally attached to the shāh, including Christians from Georgia and Armenia.

But it was under the Mamlūks of Egypt and Syria and the Ottoman Turks that the system of military slavery attained its apotheosis, and it was the successes gained by the Ottoman troops against Christian Europe, above all by their Janissaries, that instilled Christendom with fear of a new wave of Islamic expansionism in the Balkans, Central Europe and Italy. The slaves who came to compose the Mamlūk ruling institution were brought to Egypt as pagans by Venetian and other carriers, and sold there; the nickname of Sultan Qalā'ūn al-Alfī (679-89/1280-90) is usually explained by the fact that he cost one thousand *(alf)* dinars, whereas the great Sultan Baybars (659-76/1260-77), hammer of the Crusader remnants on the Levantine coast, was bought for only forty dinars because of an eye defect. The young slaves or mamlūks purchased by the sultans were given a thorough Islamic education and military training in special schools at Cairo, and when after several years they passed out, they were enrolled in the corps of royal mamlūks, affranchised, and given their mounts, equipment and a land grant by means of which they might support themselves.

Although we describe the Mamlūk, Ottoman and similar systems as 'slave' ones, we must rid ourselves of

the idea that this entailed any deep stigma of social inferiority. Under the Mamlūks, indeed, it was the slave mamlūks who enjoyed the highest prestige and could aspire to the sultanate; their own children, including the sons even of sultans, being free in status, slipped back into the mass of free, second-class soldiery, which suffered serious discrimination in matters of pay and equipment. Likewise, although supreme power in the Ottoman empire remained in the hands of the house of 'Uthmān down to the early xiv/20th century, the highest offices of the civil and military establishment – at least until the xii/18th century – were attained by slaves; this is why we find among the viziers men of such varied ethnic origins as Greeks, Italians, Albanians and Armenians.

In their heyday, the Mamlūk cavalrymen were outstanding for their equestrian skill and for their handling of weapons, above all, of the bow and lance. At the flight-shooting archery field, the Maydān as-Sibāq, laid out in Cairo by Baybars in 1267, there were marble markers recording a distance of 636 yards attained by a Mamlūk amīr using a long arrow (greater distances were possible with shorter arrows, and in 1213/1798 the Ottoman Sultan Selīm III achieved, in the presence of the British ambassador to the Porte, the phenomenal distance of 972 yards). The Mamlūk troops kept up their high standard of weapon-training by practices and exercises at various training grounds scattered around Cairo, and surviving literature on these *furūsiyya* or 'knightly' exercises gives us detailed descriptions of the procedures involved, together with some useful illustrations of the equipment used. There was training in cavalry teamwork and drill, and polo-playing; fencing, and practice with swords cutting through solid objects, layers of clay and felt, till the mamlūk was able to cut through a bar of lead; wrestling; archery exercises, comprising shooting from the saddle through a wooden circle to a target topped by a metal ring and inserting his spear-point through it as he went past.

Regarding weapons, the norm for Islamic swords from early times to the later Mamlūk period was the straight sword, either single or double-edged, made from iron or steel or else, following the Frankish pattern, of iron with a steel cutting edge; the curved scimitar was early known, but did not become common till the ix/15th century. Swords were often damascened with gold or silver, and blades imported from outside the Islamic world, such as from China, India and Malaysia, continued to be esteemed for their high quality. The ancient Arab fashion was to carry a sword from a shoulder belt, but surviving illustrations or designs on metalwork, etc. show that by the Ayyūbid and Mamlūk periods, scabbards were girded at the waist also. Lances were made from steel or wood, with steel points, while for special purposes, coloured pennants or streamers might be hung from their shafts. Maces were of iron or steel, with spherical or polyhedral heads. The battle-axe was a favoured weapon for troops to hold on ceremonial occasions, although surviving specimens show use in battle; these had semicircular heads, and were all single- and not double-headed. Shields were generally round and slightly convex, and made from wood or metal; the kite-shaped or 'Norman' shield with a rounded top was known, but its use was not widespread. We have, surviving from the early Ayyūbid period on-

Two warriors of Fātimid Egypt, V/11th century. Each carries a spear; the one on the left also has a sword (sayf) and a two-horned helmet. (6)

wards, specimens of armour and mailed coats; these must have been preserved on account of their value to succeeding generations. The plain coat of mail survived in Islamic usage down to the XIII/19th century, lingering longest in peripheral regions like India and sub-Saharan Africa; but there were also to be found splint armour, that is, mailed coats reinforced by rectangular, overlapping splints, and the brigandine or short jerkin, a heavily padded or laminated jacket covered with velvet or satin and heavily studded with nails. Helmets comprised those types protecting the head only, and those protecting the head plus the ears and neck; but although the nasal was known, the Ayyūbids and Mamlūks do not seem to have used face guards, as the Crusaders and Mongols did.

Mention should also be made at this point of the importance of the Ayyūbid and Mamlūk periods in the development of heraldry. During these times, the great amīrs used individual blazons, apparently personally granted by the sultan in the earlier period, but by the IX/15th century assumed unilaterally by the amīrs; the Arabic terms for them were *rank* (from a Persian word meaning 'colour') and *shiʿār*, 'emblem'. These devices seem to have originated in the offices of the sultan's household or administration which were held by these amīrs; thus the royal cup-bearer had a stylized cup as his device, the master of polo had a device of polo-sticks, etc. In so far as the sons of amīrs themselves became amīrs – not a very frequent happening, given the peculiar constitution of Mamlūk military slavery – these devices seem to have been hereditary. However, the whole system of personal blazons never assumed the military and legal importance in the Islamic world which it attained in feudal Christian Europe.

The Ottoman armies

The conquests of the Ottomans in their heyday (down to the XI/17th century) are closely connected with the adoption of a military slave institution which provided an

élite corps within their army, the numerically greater part of which actually consisted of free, feudal cavalrymen, the *sipāhīs*, who lived off the revenues of land grants scattered throughout the empire and who rallied to the colours only when a specific campaign was announced. The Janissaries (Turkish *yeni cheri*: 'new troops') were a body of slave infantrymen eventually recruited, by means of periodic levies (which lasted down to the later XI/17th century, when the Janissaries had lost much of their fighting efficiency), largely from the rural Christian subject population of the Balkans; only in Bosnia were Muslims allowed to form recruits. The system was thus a means of tapping this reservoir of non-Muslim manpower for Ottoman state purposes. Taken off to Istanbul for an intensive Muslim intellectual education and for military training, the young Christian boy speedily forgot his origins and became assimilated to the dominant society and faith. Some of these *qapı qulları* – 'slaves of the Porte' – became officials in the royal household; the remainder formed the corps of Janissaries. This last seems to have been in existence from the later VIII/14th century as a bodyguard for the sultans, and to have been originally recruited from slaves taken in war or simply bought, before the *devshirme*, or formal levies of children, were introduced. It was never a numerous body; it was latterly composed of some 196 companies, of variable size, and in the reign of Sulaymān the Magnificent (927-74/1520-66), the total personnel was 12,000 men, while in the early XI/17th century one Turkish authority puts it as 13,600 men. Notable is the fact that *esprit de corps* was fostered by a distinctive costume, including a cap and trousers, and by the corps' affiliation – with increasing formality in the later stages of its history – to the dervish order of Bektāshīs; popular legend credited the order's founder, the shadowy Hājjī Bektāsh, with a prominent role in the creation of the Janissary corps.

At the zenith of their prowess, in the IX/15th and X/16th centuries, the Janissaries seemed invincible to Christian European observers, who saw Albania, Rumania and the Slav provinces of the Balkans fall to the Turkish armies and, by 933/1526, the greater part of Hungary too. It was not easy for such observers to discern that by 1094/1683, when Qara Mustafā made his attack on Vienna, the prime of the Janissaries, their numbers diluted and swollen by free intruders, was past, as was indeed the prime of the Ottoman empire as a whole. The Flemish ambassador of the Habsburgs, Ogier Ghiselin de Busbecq, was in Istanbul from 1554 to 1562 and commented on the discipline, hardihood and frugality of the Janissaries when out on campaign, compared with the love of luxury prevalent in the Christian camps. He wrote in his letters,

> I tremble when I think of what the future must bring when I compare the Turkish system with our own; one army must prevail and the other be destroyed, for certainly both cannot remain unscathed. On their side are the resources of a mighty empire . . . On our side is public poverty . . . Can we doubt what the result will be?

That the Christians avoided this unhappy outcome was due in the first place more to the corruption of the Janissaries' pristine virtues and the general decline in the administrative and military efficiency of the Ottoman

An Ottoman Janissary, armed with a sword, a long spear and a mace, and bearing a shield. Both these woodcuts are from a book by Melchior Lorich, who was a member of the entourage of Busbecq, the Imperial ambassador to Turkey, and who made detailed studies of the Ottoman military machine between 1554 and 1562 in order to awaken Christian Europe to the dangers of the Turkish peril. (7)

An Ottoman sipāhī or feudal cavalryman. These were free land-owners, receiving land grants from the state (tīmārs, zecʿāmets) on condition of providing military service when summoned to the colours for a campaign. Even as late as the XII/18th century, this element of the Ottoman army was still an important one, although at the end of that century attempts were made to westernize and modernize. (8)

empire, rather than to the greater élan and unity of the Christians; and of course, from the XI/17th century onwards, the growing technological superiority of the West placed Turkey and the other few surviving independent Muslim powers in a position of irremediable inferiority.

A revolution in warfare: firearms
That the Ottomans achieved such a position of military advantage in the centuries of the empire's florescence, in regard to both the Christians and the other Muslim powers like the Egyptian Mamlūks and the Persian Safavids, was in fair measure due to the comparatively enthusiastic and expert way in which they took to the revolutionary new means of waging war: firearms. As mentioned above, it was the technical advances and the economic and commercial power of the West which eventually told against the Islamic rulers, but in the earlier centuries, this was not so apparent. The first effects of the new weapons included a gradual dethronement from primacy of the figure which had long dominated Middle Eastern warfare, the horse or camel cavalryman with his bow, lance and sword, and a concomitant of this process was that the superior position of the steppe nomads of Inner Asia *vis-à-vis* the settled lands of ancient Old World culture, such as China, India and the Middle East, was now reversed.

There is much obscurity about the introduction of firearms into the Islamic world, in considerable measure because of the ambiguity of the terms which begin to appear in Muslim sources to denote the new weapons. There was a natural tendency to use words already in existence in Arabic for the various kinds of incendiary substances of the Greek fire type which had long been used in siege and naval warfare. Hence *naft*, originally white bitumen, was used first for saltpetre when this substance was introduced into the Islamic world (probably from China) in the early VII/13th century, and then for gunpowder. One would expect firearms to appear in the Islamic world through contacts with the Christian Europeans, who began to employ primitive cannon for sieges in the early VIII/14th century, and this is what seems broadly to have happened. Hence Spain was a channel of transmission for Muslim Granada and the Maghrib; Germany, Central Europe and Italy for the Ottomans; and the Venetians and Portuguese for Persia.

Siege artillery inevitably appeared before the technically more complex hand guns. What looks like a very early mention in Muslim sources of a true cannon describes a contrivance used during the siege in 724/1324 of the Christian-held town of Huescar by the Nasrid king of Granada Ismāʿīl I: 'the monstrous engine which functions by means of *naft*'. This hurled a red-hot iron ball against the besieged fortress, landing among the defenders and causing extensive damage. By the last years of independent Granada, towards the end of the ix/15th century, both the Castilians and the Moors were regularly using cannon. The Ottomans learnt the use of artillery from the Christians of the Balkans. These weapons were known in Balkan principalities like Bosnia and Serbia, the main suppliers being Hungary, Venice and, above all, Dubrovnik; this latter city had an important cannon foundry in 813/1410, and arquebuses are mentioned there after 831/1428. Despite papal fulminations, there was much clandestine gun-running and even open sale to the Turks, for the Ottomans were prepared to pay well for these weapons and for the services of operators and gunsmiths. As a result, Sultan Murād II was using siege artillery in the Balkans in the 1420s, and Mehmed the Conqueror employed cannon on a large scale for the sieges of Constantinople in 851/1453 and Belgrade in 860/1456; contemporary reports mention cannon over ten tons in weight and firing cannon balls of two or three hundredweights. Field artillery was also adopted at this time, but field pieces could not really be effectively deployed till later technological advances had made them into reliable weapons; a favoured Ottoman tactic came to be that of the battle lager, in which heavy wagons were chained together and reinforced by field pieces and hand guns so as to form a fortress-like block. As was usual in the early stages of the employment of artillery, among both the Christians and the Muslims, cannon were usually cast on the spot from bronze or iron and for a specific purpose, although the Ottomans had an extensive armoury and arsenal, the *Tophane*, adjacent to the palace complex in Istanbul.

The hand gun appears in the shape of the cumbersome arquebus in the 1440s, the time of Murād's Hungarian wars, but may well have been known two or three decades previously. It was slow to find favour among the Ottoman feudal cavalry, but was gradually adopted by the Janissaries. Successful tactical use of hand guns was nevertheless only really possible once the early forms of the musket and pistol evolved. Cultural conservatism and comparative technical backwardness account for the prominence of Christians, both those becoming renegades and those retaining their faith, in the service of powers like the Ottomans and Safavids. The Ottomans, in particular, recruited Serbian, Bosnian and Hungarian gunners from their own subject populations, but also Germans and Italians, and till well into the xii/18th century, non-Turks predominated in technical arms like the artillery and the engineers. It is clear that both artillery and muskets were perfectly well-known in Safavid Persia before the arrival there in 1007/1598 of the two English adventurers Sir Anthony and Sir Robert Sherley, to whom European sources often erroneously attribute the introduction of firearms into that country. The fame of the Turkish gunners was such throughout the Islamic world that we hear of Turks assisting the Safavids, and the Ottomans supplied technical experts as far afield as to Muslim India, where Turkish-manned guns helped to repel the Portuguese from the shores of Bombay and Gujerat in the x/16th century. They further sent firearms to the Crimean Tatars and to the Muslim leader in Ethiopia against the Christians, Ahmad Grān,

enabling the latter in 949/1542 to win a victory over the Emperor of Ethiopia's Portuguese auxiliaries. Some Ottoman artillerymen even found their way to distant Atcheh in Sumatra, and cannon cast by them were used against the Portuguese at Malacca.

The history of firearms among the Mamlūks illustrates the fact that the Muslims often had an ambivalent attitude towards the new weapons. It has been mentioned that the greater facility with which the Janissaries of the Ottomans, an expanding, confident imperial power, took to firearms helps to explain many of their successes in the Balkans, their decisive victory over the Safavids at Chāldirān in 920/1514, and their defeats of the Mamlūks in Syria and Egypt in 922-3/1516-17. It was not that the Mamlūks had religious or moral objections to firearms; static siege and coastal defence artillery was easily adopted, although the traditional mangonels and ballistas remained in use side by side with cannon almost to the end of their independent rule. It was in the use of mobile field artillery and hand guns that they lagged behind, and this for social-military reasons. The whole Mamlūk ruling institution was based on the predominance of the cavalryman or *fāris*, with his superb horsemanship and weapon training, and on the tactics of open warfare. The use of field artillery implies static defence lines, and the use of hand guns meant the increased importance of the infantryman to handle arquebuses; not until the early musket and pistol developed in the x/16th century could the cavalryman make reasonable use of personal firearms. Hence the Mamlūks soon realized that, outside the sphere of siege warfare, the adoption of firearms would entail the dismantling of their whole military system.

The Mamlūks accordingly employed siege artillery all through the ix/15th century, and one of the last sultans, Qānsawh al-Ghūrī (907-22/1501-16), had large numbers of cannon cast, both for the defence of Cairo and the Mediterranean seaboard and also for mounting on ships in the Red Sea and Indian Ocean to combat the Portuguese and assist the Muslim sultanates in South Arabia and India. Qānsawh was also one of the first sultans to try to create a corps of arquebusiers, following on an earlier, unsuccessful attempt *c.* 896/1490 to recruit such a force. Even then, Qānsawh's unit had to be composed not of mamlūks but of socially inferior personnel like black slaves, the free sons of former mamlūks, and despised tradesmen, and there was pressure from the dominant Mamlūk hierarchy to abolish it. With threats in the east from the Portuguese and the increasingly menacing attitude of the Ottomans on the Syrian borders, the new weapons could not be dispensed with. Yet, in the event, the Mamlūks faced the Ottomans at the decisive battles of Marj Dābiq in Syria and Raydāniyya outside Cairo palpably inferior in firepower to Sultan Selīm's troops; as with the Polish cavalry confronted by Hitler's Panzer divisions in September 1939, they found that sheer bravery was not enough.

War at sea

It only remains briefly to say something about naval warfare among the Muslims. Since from the start possession of the Mediterranean shores, and in later medieval times, those of the Indian Ocean as well, was contested with the Christians, one would expect recognition of the importance of sea-power and an enduring care for the maintenance of a fleet. The Umayyad caliphs in Syria, with their strong sense of *jihād* against the Byzantines, were certainly aware of these considerations. Much of their policy was aimed at securing control of the eastern Mediterranean and at the wresting of strategically situated islands like Cyprus, Rhodes and Crete from the Greeks. The attacks in this period on Constantinople itself were coordinated land and sea operations, but the Muslim ships made no lasting headway against the Byzantine navy, with its technical expertise and its skilful use of weapons like Greek fire for close-quarters fighting. The Muslim ships were at this time sailed by Copts, Syrians and Greeks recruited from the coastlands of the conquered provinces and pressed into service (the Arabic word for 'fleet', *ustūl*, is a loan word from Greek *stolos*); Muslim troops stationed on deck did the actual fighting. The Spanish Umayyads were also in possession of a long coastline; they used their ships to attack the Christian lands to the north and to secure islands like the Balearics, and also to further their policy of securing control or influence over the North African coasts.

In later centuries, interest in the maintenance of a navy fluctuated. On the whole, the Islamic peoples, whether Arabs, Berbers, Persians or Turks, had few traditions of seafaring, and in their society, greater prestige attached to the soldier than to the sailor, for it was land forces which had over-run the Middle East and North Africa for Islam. A fleet was often something of a luxury, and was therefore usually an *ad hoc* affair, constituted for some specific occasion like the invasion of Sicily or the repelling of particularly annoying Christian attacks, but then allowed to lapse. Even the appearance of the Crusaders on the Levant coast, whose lifelines were wholly dependent on control of the seas, did not elicit any overwhelming Muslim reaction of enthusiasm for a permanent, powerfully armed navy. Individual sultans like Saladin and Baybars revived and fitted out new fleets, but after Saladin's death in 589/1193, for instance, the Egyptian fleet fell into total neglect and disregard; sailors had to be press-ganged into manning the remaining ships, and were considered as the lowest riff-raff of society. The Mamlūks, conscious of their maritime inferiority, eventually abandoned altogether the defence of the Syro-Palestinian littoral, scorching the earth there and con-

centrating on the fortification of the Nile delta; and their attempts to launch a fleet in the Indian Ocean were frustrated by the better armed, ocean-going Portuguese warships.

The Ottomans, themselves originally a land-locked *ghāzī* principality in north-western Anatolia, took over the south-western principalities like Aydın and Menteshe which maintained corsair fleets. They also needed control of the Aegean and Marmora seas for the invasion of the Balkans and the investment of Constantinople. The stimulus for the creation of a powerful fleet was therefore present from the start in this instance. From the reign of Murād I (762-92/1360-89), Gallipoli became the chief Ottoman naval base, and Greeks and Italians were employed to sail the oar-propelled Turkish galleys; all through its existence, the Ottoman navy retained a strong Greek and Italian imprint, seen for instance in the Turkish technical vocabulary of seamanship. Under command of the High Admiral, the *Qapudan Pasha*, the Ottoman fleet was used to bring under control the Aegean and Ionian islands, and above all, to combat the Ottomans' principal enemy, the Venetians. The ships lost at the defeat of Lepanto in 979/1571 were soon replaced, although the losses of skilled mariners were a more serious handicap to a revival of Turkish naval power. The conquest of Crete from the Venetians, the last major success of Ottoman imperialism, took twenty-five years (1054-80/1644-69); the fleet was not in top form, and difficulties were experienced during the transition from the oar-propelled galleys to purely sail-driven ships, adopted during the course of the Cretan War in imitation of the Venetians. However, the Ottoman ships always maintained close contact with the Turkish garrisons in North Africa, and a lively corsair activity was carried on from Algiers, Tunis and Salé down to the early XIII/19th century; these 'Barbary pirates' became notorious scourges of the coasts of Christendom, carrying off victims from as far away as Ireland and Iceland. Indeed, the whole Ottoman navy long remained – like most European navies down to the XII/18th century – as much a loose grouping of privateers and individual adventurers as an official, state-directed force. Thus of all the Islamic dynasties, it was the Ottomans who, drawing on indigenous Mediterranean seafaring traditions, made the best use of naval power.

It was by the sword that the empire of Islam was created, and throughout the Middle Ages it is probably true to say that the Christian world thought of the Muslim primarily as a warrior. The conquests took place in two waves. The first, soon after the death of Muhammad, covered Syria, Egypt, Armenia, Persia and North Africa. The second, beginning early in the II/8th century, carried Islam west to Spain and southern France, east to the borders of China. The Arab armies constituted the most powerful military machine that the world had ever seen.

How was it achieved? By a combination of religious fervour and careful planning. As the effects of the first diminished, the second became more vital. The Arabs' use of the desert, which they could understand and use, but their enemies could not, has been compared to a maritime nation's use of the sea. They also welcomed technical innovations, keeping ahead of their rivals in

weaponry and logistics. In the IX/15th century the great tradition of Arab arms was reborn in the Ottomans, who took Constantinople, invaded the Balkans and reached the gates of Vienna.

One of the most vivid pictorial records of an Islamic battle is this dish (opposite), painted in Iran during the early VII/13th century. A fortress, on the left, is under attack. Its lower walls are covered with tiles; the upper part has openings through which the defenders fire arrows. There is also a catapult discharging stones. Empty suits of armour and helmets line the ramparts to deceive the attackers into thinking the city better manned than it really is. The invading army is mounted on horses, with one elephant (at the top). In the foreground the defenders have sallied out in a counter-attack and corpses strew the ground. These stripped bodies are among the very few representations of the nude in Islamic art. (1)

The first armies were essentially the *levée en masse* of the Arab people, groups of Bedouin without discipline or organization. Mobile and lightly armed, they rode horses or camels and lived off plunder. This much later miniature (below left) of a fight between rival clans gives an idea of this pre-professional period. During the 1/7th and 11/8th centuries the Arabs learned siege techniques from the Byzantines and by the v/11th and vi/12th were able to meet the Crusaders on equal terms. A fragment from Egypt (upper left), one of the earliest pictures of Islamic warfare, shows warriors carrying kite-shaped 'Norman' shields. (2, 3)

Catapult (below): the arrow or projectile is placed vertically on the left, a heavy counter-weight on the right. (4)

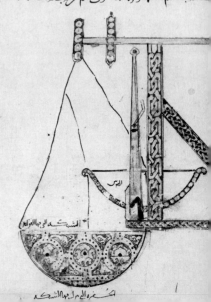

The machinery of war was eagerly studied by Arab leaders. The illustrations on this page come from a treatise compiled for Saladin after the fall of Jerusalem.

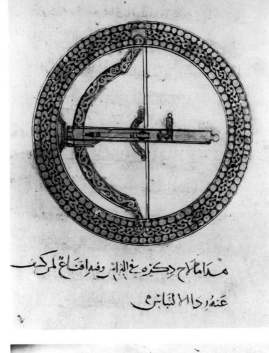

مهما صلاح دكيره في الاذن وفدافقالع لم كسف عنه ورد الا لباس

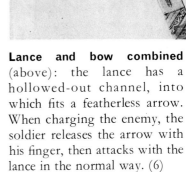

العقرب بالى يسمّى الوتر وأنقلا الوتر والقّ باراضه الضفدره حوف الرمح فدقسمّ شرح السنان عينه وصورته م الرماح والقّ يافه تشره وريه أذكناه منها لقلوب المّراض في جلا لماروس

Shield-cum-bow (right): the string is tautened by winding a key; the arrow emerges from a hole in the shield protected by iron flaps which immediately close up again. (5)

Lance and bow combined (above): the lance has a hollowed-out channel, into which fits a featherless arrow. When charging the enemy, the soldier releases the arrow with his finger, then attacks with the lance in the normal way. (6)

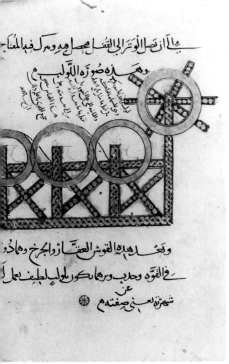

بما ان صل الوتر الى القصا صام واه وكل فيه المنا وهذه صوره التوليم وبعد ما هذه القوير العقّاز والجرح وهاذر في القوّه وحرب وربها كور لولى لبطف بعل عن شهزنه يعنى صفتهم

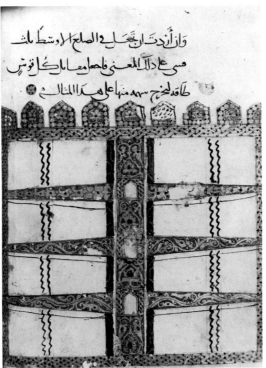

وان أزدت ابجه الصلح الوسط لم مسى عاد لك المعنى فاصما ما كا نوش طاقه لخج سهم منها على مدا لنّاله

A triple bow (left and far left): three sets of cords are linked to a crank and wheel which needs several men to work it. These two drawings show different views of the mechanism. It could have been used only in siege warfare. (7, 8)

نور ان يصح الحربى الحرى الكفه وسّاوحها الخطاف الموضع جرام الكفه خطافم الحرد حراره اسمّا في جلقه ثمتت ى يا عده منا وتره مع الحال الوى ربع النبيكه بخطاف شبى الحال ماد اطلع السله وحرا اما دورى عبام بعوذ سّ ساعده الى الكفه معلها على ما يعم واحد والحال ما لحلت احدها وهذه صون دلكع

Protective shelter (right) for manoeuvring a piece of siege machinery into position. It is basically a wooden framework, bound with iron, over which is stretched a mesh of taut ropes which will send a projectile landing on it bouncing back. It can be covered with straw mattresses and with felt treated to make it fireproof. (9)

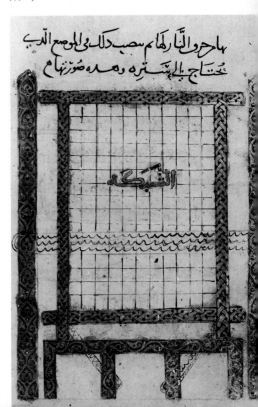

هاحرو الثّار كهام سصب دلك ى الموصع الّى تحتاج بالبشتره وهذه صّورنهام النبيكه

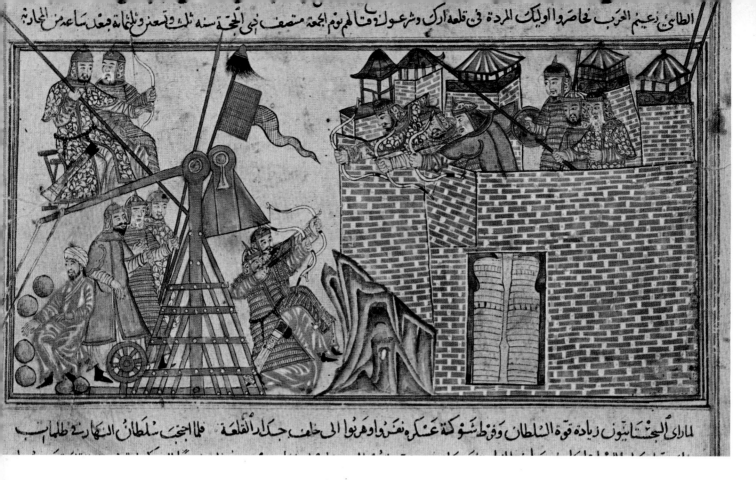

The siege was the major event in Islamic warfare. Battles in the open field were by comparison few and indecisive. Control of cities was the key to victory. Here, in a manuscript of the early VIII/14th century (above), Maḥmūd of Ghazna attacks rebels in the fortress of Arg or Ūq in Sīstān – an incident that occurred in 394/1003 – with a massive catapult, or mangonel. The fortress is made of mud brick, as was normal in that stoneless and treeless region. A subsequent picture (below) shows Maḥmūd receiving the submission of the Ilig Khān, leader of the Turkish

Qarakhanids who had taken over Transoxiana at the beginning of the V/11th century and were attempting to secure Khurāsān. In a battle at Balkh in northern Afghanistan in 399/1008, Maḥmūd of Ghazna's forces included five hundred elephants; and these terrified the Qarakhanids and brought them to rout. Elephants were a powerful psychological factor in warfare. They were virtually indestructible from a distance, though vulnerable if the attackers could get close enough to strike at their soft underbellies. (10, 11)

Tamerlane besieged the Hospitalers' castle at Smyrna in
805/1402. These miniatures (above) were painted some
ninety years later. The drawbridge has been raised, but
the Muslim troops have made another bridge on the
right. Others rush to the wall behind wooden shields. In
the upper right a mine is being dug. Tamerlane himself is
on horseback, lower right. (12, 13)

Burning naphtha was used to set ships and towns on fire
and to scare horses. These 'naphtha men' (right) who
carry lances or javelins with cartridges of naphtha fixed
to them are depicted in a Mamlūk treatise on military
affairs of the IX/15th century. (14)

217

The castles of Islam are among its most impressive building achievements, as well as being central to Islamic military thinking. These examples range from the ii/8th to the xi/17th century.

Qasr al-Kharāna, an Umayyad fortress of the ii/8th century, is built of baked brick over a rubble core. The plan is square, with towers at the corners and half-towers in the centre of the curtain walls. The gatehouse is flanked by quarter-round towers. The building could possibly have been used as a caravanserai as well as a fortress. (15)

Bam (below) in south-eastern Iran, is a huge fortified complex with entrance protected by a barbican. The material is mud brick, and the walls have been rebuilt many times. (17)

The citadel of Aleppo (above) stands on a hill 160 feet high in the centre of the city, which had probably been a fortified site since Hittite times. It was destroyed by the Mongols in 659/1260, and again by Tamerlane at the end of the VIII/14th century, and rebuilt in the early IX/15th by the Mamlūks. The stone walls form an irregular circle punctuated by towers. The entrance (above right), the most heavily defended part, is reached by a narrow causeway exposed to fire from several sides. (16, 19)

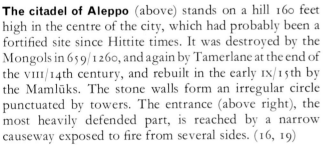

Cairo was defended by massive walls pierced by heavily fortified gates. This one (left), dating from the V/11th century, is the Bāb an-Nasr, the Gate of Victory. (18)

Fez: the New Gate (right). The purpose now is decorative rather than defensive. Horseshoe arches are surmounted by colourful tiles with intricate patterns. (20)

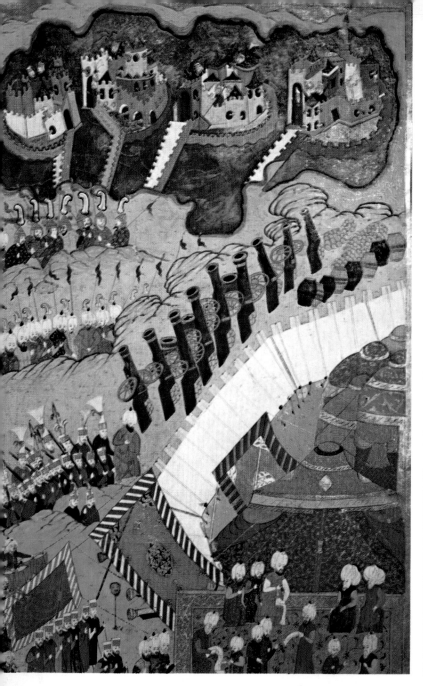

The Ottomans invaded Hungary in 928/1521. At the Battle of Mohács Hungary's army was destroyed and her cities were one by one reduced by siege. Here (above) the new artillery is brought into play. The sultan consults with his advisers in a luxurious tent. (21)

Rhodes, the headquarters of the Knights of St John, fell to the Ottomans in 928/1521, after a prolonged siege. Here (above) Sulaymān directs mining operations. The Knights were allowed to leave, and settled in Malta, where they soon had to endure another siege. (22)

Building a fortress (right): Kars, in eastern Anatolia, was taken by the Ottomans towards the end of the x/16th century, and rebuilt in accordance with Turkish principles of defence. Stylized as it is, this miniature gives much information in its details: the laying of ashlar stone over a rubble core (the top wall) and the placing of cannon in the embrasures of the towers. In the centre is the governor's palace with Muhammad Pasha, the governor of Erzerum, behind it. In the top left corner is the citadel with its mosque and at the bottom the 'outer mosque', i.e. that of the town proper. (24)

The Janissaries (left below) were an élite infantry corps recruited from the children of Balkan Christians and trained at Constantinople. They lived a life of rigorous discipline and, until retirement from active service, were forbidden to marry. This illustration shows their short knives and distinctive styles of hat. The two men at the back are officers wearing the so-called *üsqüf* (literally 'bishop' because it looked like a mitre) surmounted by a plume. The differently coloured coats probably denote the companies to which the soldiers belong. The Janissary caps and trousers derived from earlier groups of the Akhīs, religious enthusiasts who had taken part in the conquest of Anatolia from the Greeks. They were equipped with muskets about 1500 and it was largely through them that Sulaymān was able to penetrate so far into the heart of Europe. (23)

Ceremonial weapons were often adorned with exquisite workmanship. Axes with stylized birds (below left) served as regimental standards. The type of the two-pointed sword (below right) goes back to the days of the Prophet. (27, 28)

The tugh was a pennant or plume of horsehair attached to the lance or flagstaff (below left) of a governor, or a banner incorporating a lattice of ornament and lettering. A **Moorish sword** (below right) from Spain carries a Kūfic inscription and is said to have belonged to the last king of Granada. (29, 30)

The warrior of Islam (far left) in 828/1425 was equipped with sword (worn on the left side), bow (in its case on the right), quiver (at his back), spear (right hand) and shield (left). (25)

Training in swordsmanship included striking into a heap of clay (left) to acquire strength. The illustration comes from the same IX/15th-century Mamlūk manual as that showing the naphtha men. (26)

The curved blade, or scimitar, so closely associated with the popular image of Islam, did not appear until at least the VII/13th century. Its great age was the X/16th and XI/17th centuries, when both quality and decoration reached its most perfect. This sword (right), with its scabbard, must date from about 1036/1626. The jewelled hilt is Persian, the blade made in Eastern Europe. (31)

Armour was always lighter and more flexible than its European counterpart. A suit of the early X/16th century (far right) consists of chain mail with ornamented plates of steel damascened with silver, inscribed as usual with Qur'ānic quotations. (32)

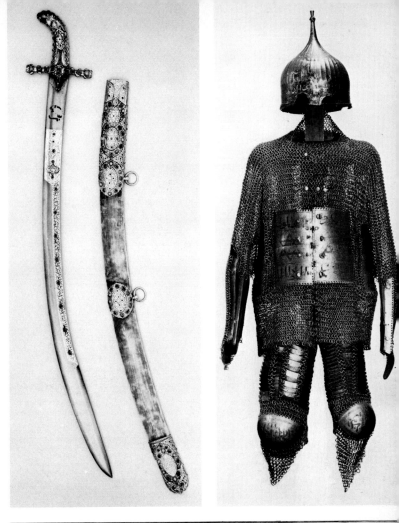

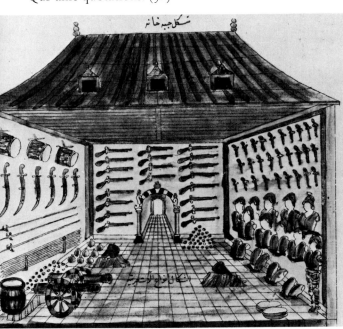

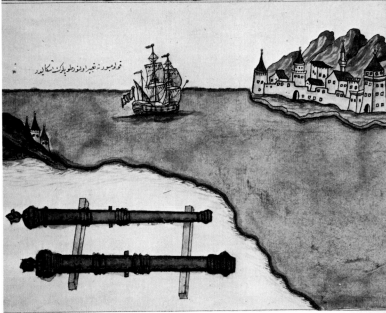

The arsenal (above): a XII/18th-century Turkish illustration to a translated Italian treatise on warfare. Displayed to view are drums, swords, lances, pikes, cannon (with balls and barrel of gunpowder), mortars, bombs, muskets, pistols, helmets and breastplates. (33)

Cannon defending a strait (above), probably the Dardanelles at Gallipoli (Gelibolu): another illustration to the same Italian treatise. The cannon depicted are *kolonburnas* or culverins. (34)

Turkish muskets (below) continued the tradition of fine workmanship in weapons into the XI/17th century and later. (35)

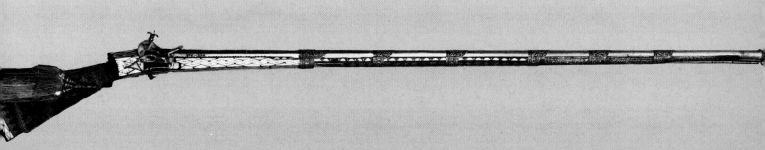

NAVE LORDANA · · LA · NAVE · TVRCESCHA · NAVE · DEL ARMER · L'A PANDORA · · CHMALI ·

Sea warfare was not an Islamic tradition, but when strategy demanded it in the x/16th century the Ottomans created a fleet with their usual speed and efficiency. Their most constant adversaries were the Venetians, who at an engagement at Zonchio (Sapienza) off the Morea in 905/1499 first employed broadsides of cannon against them. In this Venetian woodcut (above) two Turkish ships, flying the crescent, are surrounded by Venetians. The Turks shower balls of fire from the top of their mast. But the battle was indecisive and it was not until Lepanto in 979/1571 that the Turks were seriously checked. Left: the fleet assembled by Khayr ad-Dīn Barbarossa, a Corsair admiral from Algiers who served the sultan from 941/1534 to his death in 953/1546. (36, 37)

Chapter Nine

MOORISH SPAIN

Emilio García Gómez

A gold coin (one third of a dinar) from North Africa, about the year 85/704; that is, a few years before the Arabs started taking control of Spain. The details of that invasion, and even its general outline, will probably always remain a mystery. (1)

SPAIN, LIKE A COIN, HAS AN OBVERSE AND A REVERSE, a dark side and a light side, and the foreigner cannot see both at once. Only the Spaniard, from the inside, can perhaps see both faces simultaneously. And in this duality Islam plays no little part.

The Moorish presence in Spain is a subject of debate. Was Islam beneficial to the Spanish nation, or the opposite? What course would Spanish history have taken without Islam? These questions would require long discussion and in the end lead only to supposition about what might have been.

If there was an element of surprise in the entry of Islam into Spain, then there was also an element of surprise in its departure, for no nation has disengaged itself from Islam so totally. We may also be surprised that the departure took place so gallantly, as if the intermittent conflict between Muslims and Christians throughout the Middle Ages – in the long run a sort of civil war – had been no more than a kind of practice bout. It is somehow symbolic that 898/1492 was both the year of the taking of Granada and the discovery of America.

This gallant departure, unique in history, could not have taken place had the Christians not shown a considerable crusading ardour, which may have aimed theoretically at least at a restoration of the Visigothic monarchy. The whole complex and intermittent movement of restoration and recovery was subsequently given the name of *Reconquista* (Reconquest).

An obvious point, but one often forgotten, is that the movement of reconquest always had a territorial basis from which it took its impetus and which it was constantly expanding and consolidating – Balzac's *'peau de chagrin'* in reverse. It may seem extraordinary in retrospect that the Muslims did not occupy the whole Peninsula from the beginning. Even more extraordinary is the fact that they apparently had no intention of occupying it totally later, even when at the height of their aggressive power. Almanzor, for instance, was bent more on destruction than on occupation. There are many possible reasons for this. One may see it as evidence of the disintegration of an invading force which was already tired and far from its home base. Perhaps it was merely a matter of convenience, the invader only settling those areas which he found agreeable, and neglecting the mountains in favour of the plains. In any case, the

'recovery' took place on two fronts: one beyond the territorial frontiers, and one within them, based on 'fifth columns'. While the first front expanded day by day, the second, initially represented by the Mozarabs, was gradually reduced and became less and less significant, though without ever ceasing completely.

'I do not understand,' José Ortega y Gasset said, 'how something which lasted eight centuries can be called a reconquest.' The obvious reason is that the name was subsequent to the fact. But Ortega y Gasset's comment has other implications which contradict the popular view. The Reconquista cannot be looked upon as the cure for an acute bout of 'Muslim fever' which had suddenly attacked the delicate body of Visigothic Spain – a long-drawn-out fever in which the thermometer shoots up to begin with and then subsides little by little. It was much more complex than that. Its appearance was intermittent, manifesting itself through a long series of events which, though sometimes inconsistent, were interrelated. The fever – to keep the analogy – had many crises, improvements and relapses; at times it seemed incurable, at other times practically non-existent, only to come back as virulently as before.

The conquest and the people of Spain: 93–138/711–55

The question of how and why the Muslims invaded Spain at all remains unanswered. Our only guides are legends and highly partisan historical accounts, which form a very frail basis for theories. Otherwise there is silence, a silence which has been interpreted by some as evidence of a kind of stupor or amazement. The amazement is dubious: but the silence is certain.

We must suppose that Visigothic Spain knew of the Arab campaigns in North Africa. Can we also suppose that there were treaties and agreements between Arabs and Spaniards, not counting the Spanish Jews? Though the evidence is thin, the invasion becomes incomprehensible if this were not the case. There were a few skirmishes and a single great battle (of uncertain location); but otherwise the Arab armies proceeded unchecked along various and apparently predetermined courses through Spain, with only a few towns resisting.

If the expansion of the Muslims from Arabia is insufficiently explained, the success of this expansion is even more so. It seems as if the Arab armies were merely the wind which blew down the already fragile house of cards of many Mediterranean states, amongst them Spain. We must conclude that the Ibero-Roman natives of the Peninsula, not to mention the Jews, could support the weight of the artificial Visigothic oligarchy no longer and were only too pleased at the rapid downfall of a structure that they were finding increasingly repugnant. It seems most plausible that they not only helped it on its way, but to this end made treaties beforehand.

In fact we know very little of Spain under the Visigoths; or rather we only know what the Visigothic oligarchy itself chose to tell us; and even this tends to be seen through the rose-tinted spectacles of the later Gothic revival. It has been stated that one can only speak of a 'Spanish people' from the IV/10th century onwards; but this opinion is probably an exaggeration. We should not take the silence to which the Spanish people were reduced by the Visigothic oligarchy as evidence of their non-existence. In fact the Spanish people were equally reduced to silence by the successive Muslim rulers, although this new oligarchy proved more attractive and congenial than the other, and finally did allow it to speak.

The conquered Hispano-Roman peoples – they were in fact more accomplices than conquered – were undoubtedly there. They were in the countryside and in the old towns and cities (the Arabs created very few *de novo*, even much later). They were there also in the families of the invaders, the vast majority of whom came without wives.

Little by little, scholars have tried to bring to life this native multitude. Julián Ribera discovered a considerable amount of interesting information about the Spanish Goths in the chronicle of Ibn al-Qūtiyya (the name means 'descendant of the Goth-woman'), a Muslim descendant of the Visigothic princes who collaborated with the Arabs. Analysis of place-names is gradually yielding useful information, and recently has proved with near certainty that many of the Berbers who arrived with the Arabs were still Christian. Naturally we know very little about how the Arabs dispossessed the native owners of Spanish territory. It is even less likely that we shall ever know the extent to which the natives renounced their original faith and adopted false Arab genealogies, for since the persons concerned were naturally anxious to hide the truth from their contemporaries, modern historians start at something of a disadvantage. On the other hand, after researching numerous texts (including Khushanī's *History of the Judges of Cordoba*), Ribera was able to throw some light on the diffusion of the Romance language – a derivative from low Latin, which took different forms in different regions and eventually crystallized as Spanish – among the Arabs of al-Andalus. They turn out to have been completely bilingual up to the time of the Almohads and partially so even later.

It was Ribera, too, who first put forward the hypothesis that the Arabs not only spoke in Romance, but also that in al-Andalus they 'wrote poetry and sang' in Romance. This is a subject to which we will return. For the moment

I merely quote the beginning of a famous passage by Tīfāshī (VII/13th century), attributed to Ibn Sa'īd, who had it from Ibn Durayd, who had it in turn from Ibn Hāsib; it runs: 'The singing of the people of al-Andalus was, in former times, either in the manner of the Christians, or in the manner of the Arab camel-drivers [*hudāt*].'

The Umayyads: 138–366/755–976

Singing, then, was in one of two manners, physically united, but of which each went its own way. It is an appropriate symbol for the life of that new Spain, which no doubt gave those who helped to bring about the change food for bitter reflection. It made them see that they had merely changed masters, perhaps for the worse.

Although it is hazardous to talk of what might have been, it seems likely that the Arab adventure in Spain would have ended much sooner, but for a new and sensational factor. This was the arrival in Spain, after a veritable saga of adventures, of an Umayyad prince who had miraculously escaped the atrocious massacre of his kin in the East. 'Abd ar-Rahmān ibn Mu'āwiya, the 'Dākhil' or 'Immigrant', managed to establish a branch of the Umayyad dynasty of Damascus in Spain that was to last more than twice the life-span of its original. (In the East the Umayyad dynasty lasted from 41/661 to 133/750; in the West from 138/755 to 366/976.

The true Umayyad rule in al-Andalus lasted for nine generations, which can be divided into three groups of three generations each. It may have been this that provided the inspiration for Ibn Khaldūn's division of the life of a kingdom into three generations: that of the creator, the preserver and the destroyer. The corresponding kings are as follows:

'Abd ar-Rahmān I	'Abd ar-Rahmān II	'Abd ar-Rahmān III
Hishām I	Muhammad I	al-Hakam II
al-Hakam I	Mundhir and	Hishām II
	'Abdallāh (brothers)	

As this table shows, each group of three generations begins with an 'Abd ar-Rahmān. The first, whom we have mentioned above, was the introducer and consolidator of genius, who renewed the 'Syrian tradition' in Spain. The second, a kind and intelligent man who perhaps needed to forget a terrible childhood, opened al-Andalus to Oriental refinements in the cultural, but not the political, field. The third was another brilliant governor, who after rescuing it from anarchy, raised Muslim power in the Peninsula to its apogee. It was he who proclaimed himself caliph – a gesture aimed at the 'Abbāsids more than the Fātimids – and who built Madīnat az-Zahrā'.

Each of the three 'Abd ar-Rahmāns was succeeded by a weaker ruler: Hishām I, the Meek (though not excessively so, if we are to believe the *Fath al-Andalus*); Muhammad I, whose character remains ill-defined; al-Hakam II, an armchair ruler, a bibliophile. The latter follows the typical pattern one expects after a warlike and glorious monarch; in Spain we may cite Alfonso X – 'the Wise' – following St Ferdinand, and Philip II following the Emperor Charles V.

Finally, each period ends with a monarch whose career was more or less determined by a crisis, which he either overcame or not: al-Hakam I, impetuous and irascible; 'Abdallāh, who skilfully fenced his way through the worst period for the Umayyads in Spain; and Hishām II, a degenerate under whom everything collapsed.

'Abd ar-Rahmān I, the Immigrant, the founder of the Umayyad dynasty in Spain, had learned enough from his terrible journey, and his difficult ascent to power once inside Spain, to know that he could not afford to favour any particular faction. He could trust no one, neither Easterners nor North Africans, neither Arabs nor Berbers, neither his relations, who were always bent on sedition, nor of course the Christians. But he was an intelligent man – the offspring of a princely race used to wielding secular power – and rose naturally to the top, where he could be independent of all others and manipulate them as seemed necessary, establishing modes of government which could be passed on to his successors.

The sovereign's personal guard and the crack army brigades were soon composed of mercenaries, largely slaves of foreign origin (the famous *khurs*, or 'dumb ones', because they did not understand Arabic); and these also formed the royal staff. Internal rebellions were stifled wherever possible with the utmost cruelty; most famous were the 'Day of the Suburb' in Cordoba, a revolt by the malcontents of the capital and the fanatical Mālikī clergy, which was suppressed by the burning of an entire city quarter; and the 'Night of Toledo', which involved the *muladíes* (Spanish converts to Islam) of the old Visigothic capital; both took place in the time of al-Hakam I. A flexible attitude was maintained towards the marches or boundaries, infringements being met with punishment or leniency and compromise as circumstances demanded. Foreign policy was completely uncompromising, both towards 'Abbāsids in the East and towards the Fātimids and their Berber or Arab allies in North Africa. A strong naval force was needed, both to carry out these policies, and to resist Viking incursions. The Christians in the north were subjected to punitive expeditions during the better weather, with varying success. And although the total occupation of the enemy territory was never completely envisaged, an imperialist policy was pursued wherever possible.

The assimilation of native and other mixed elements was of course a long-term process, and the rulers were satisfied if the two groups merely remained in a state of subjection. On more than one occasion they tried to throw off their bonds. Two such conflicts, at different stages of assimilation, furnish examples. The least assimilated natives, the Mozarabs, became increasingly exasperated by the oppression to which they were subjected, and which threatened their own culture. In the time of 'Abd ar-Rahmān II they therefore instituted a suicidal campaign of gratuitous blasphemies against the Prophet. Inevitably these were punished by death. Again, in the time of Mundhir and 'Abdallāh, the most hardened of the *muladíes* (newly converted Muslims) rebelled, rousing almost the whole of Andalusia and leaving the Amīr with only the urban quarter of Cordoba. The rebels comprised not only Muslim converts, but Arabs as well. There was an epidemic of *encastillados*, local chiefs who had grown strong in their feudal castles.

The situation improved considerably in the reign of 'Abd ar-Rahmān III, who proclaimed himself caliph in 317/929. His appearance was something of a historical miracle, like the appearance of Ferdinand and Isabella

Two Umayyad coins. Left: *a silver dirham from Cordoba issued by the first of the Umayyad caliphs of Spain,* 'Abd ar-Rahmān I. *He was one of the few of his family to escape death during the* 'Abbāsid *revolution, making his way to Spain, after a series of dramatic adventures, in 138/756. Right: a golden dinar of* 'Abd ar-Rahmān III *from Madīnat az-Zahrā'. His reign, beginning in 300/912, re-established firm rule after a series of rebellions against a weak government. (2, 3)*

after the disastrous reign of Henry IV. The different ethnic elements of al-Andalus now had to submit to closer contact with one another whether they liked it or not. This is evidenced in a phrase from the *Akhbār majmūʿa*, the chronicle which Ribera contrasts with that of Ibn al-Qūtiyya quoted earlier. The Muslims, says the author, would have been better advised to leave Spain, 'because if God does not take pity on them they will meet a disastrous end'. Written in the glorious days of the caliphate, this seems a paradoxical sentiment indeed, though admittedly it was uttered by an Arab of Quraysh indignant, as Ribera says, 'that the gentlemen of Spanish origin were coming to displace the hereditary Arab nobility' and 'that Spanish families of doubtful pedigree were taking over from the Qurashī nobles in the offices of the Umayyad empire'. A striking symbol of the growing integration of the two races was the invention of the *muwashshah*, a literary form described in the next section.

A multi-racial culture

We can assume that when 'Abd ar-Rahmān I came to power there was little or no Arabic culture in Spain. Everything had to come from the East, then controlled by the Umayyads' mortal enemies, the 'Abbāsids. Consequently the Umayyad regime was obliged not only to import its culture but also to filter out that which was not required. Its criteria included those of politics; the Umayyads' Syrian tradition; and to a large extent Mālikism, the juridical doctrine of Medina, represented by its founder Mālik ibn Anas. Mālikism eventually became the only system of law in al-Andalus and almost always enjoyed official support. This its devotees abused by setting up a form of Inquisition (though they were unable to prevent the birth of heterodox religious circles such as that of Ibn Masarra, whose success we shall mention later). In the political sphere, the Umayyads' good relations with Byzantium formed a useful counterbalance. The two powers exchanged ambassadors, and Cordoba received from the Bosphorus not only mosaic workers to decorate the *mihrāb* of the Great Mosque, but also a codex of Dioscorides with a monk to interpret it, under whose direction one of the great scientific enterprises of Moorish Spain was launched.

The cultural imports were of two kinds: the official, sanctioned by the authorities, and the unofficial, smuggled in by travelling students and pilgrims. Both were facilitated by commerce, and proceeded far more rapidly than one might expect. Twice at least the flow of Arab material reached saturation. One was in the time of ʿAbd ar-Rahmān III with the appearance of Ibn ʿAbd Rabbihi's *al-ʿIqd al-Farīd*, which might be described as Andalusia's doctoral thesis in Eastern culture. 'They're sending us back our own produce!' exclaimed one Eastern Arab, the Sāhib ibn ʿAbbād – though he could not know that this voluminous and famous anthology would preserve things subsequently lost in the East. The other saturation point is represented by the famous library of the Cordoban Caliph al-Hakam II, a collection of some 400,000 volumes which was unrivalled in its time.

The passage by Tīfāshī mentioned earlier speaks of musicians and singers who came to al-Andalus during the time of al-Hakam I, and refers to the arrival of the celebrated Ziryāb, the supremely refined arbiter of taste at the Cordoban court in the time of ʿAbd ar-Rahmān II.

Naturally there had long been poets in al-Andalus, both good and bad. Ghazāl, a curious character, known and named for his good looks, who died in 250/864, at an extremely advanced age, and who was ambassador of ʿAbd ar-Rahmān II to Byzantium, wrote poetry with a remarkably wide range of tone. Ramādī, perhaps of Christian origin, and a highly intelligent poet, produced his best work under Almanzor (d. 413/1022). He started somewhat curiously in the days of al-Hakam II as a kind of bar-room poet in opposition, and appeared as the protagonist of some of the most entertaining Andalusian anecdotes of all time. But apart perhaps from the renegade heretic Spaniard Ibn Hānī (321–63/933–73), a contemporary of al-Mutanabbī who lived in exile in North Africa, these and other poets of the caliphate occupy only a secondary, if distinguished, place in Arabic literature. After this time the most outstanding literary products of Andalusia were works of grammar and philology. The best grammarians of a widely dispersed language are always found on the periphery, for it is here, far from the heartland, that it needs defending most.

Yet the literary culture of al-Andalus was by no means uncreative. Its most interesting feature was indeed the invention of the *muwashshah*. In fact this device is probably more interesting to us Westerners than to the Eastern Arabs, ancient and modern, who, although attracted by its sensuous qualities, regarded it rather slightingly as a cancer on the body of Arabic classicism.

The first critic to probe the merits of Muslim-Spanish strophic poetry was again Julián Ribera. It was he who at the beginning of this century postulated the existence of a 'Romance vernacular literature' in Andalusia and set out to find where it lay. His researches, followed first by those of S. M. Stern, and then by my own, have succeeded in disinterring over fifty examples of the verse form known as the *kharja*. These are short passages in Romance, coming at the end of longer Hebrew or Arab poems called *muwashshahs*. As they are the oldest poetic texts in any vernacular language in Europe, their discovery entirely reorientated the investigation of the origins of lyric poetry in the Romance literatures. The *kharja*'s similarity to the *villancicos* (carols) of the Golden Age and the *coplas* (ballads) still found throughout the vast area of the Spanish-speaking world demonstrates a unique continuity in popular Spanish lyric poetry which has lasted for some ten centuries.

Below are a few examples of *kharjas*; there are three of two lines, one of three, and two of four; the last one of all dates from the first half of the v/11th century.

Ibn Bassām (VI/12th century) and Ibn Sanāʾ al-Mulk, the Egyptian theorist of the genre (VII/13th century), in writings which have only recently been understood, indicate that the *muwashshah* was composed expressly as a setting for one of these fragments of Romance verse. The *muwashshah* is like a glow-worm – a poem with a light in its tail.

The genre itself was invented in the town of Qabra (now Cabra) in Umayyad Spain at the end of the III/9th century or the beginning of the IV/10th, by a blind poet called Muqaddam ibn Muʿāfa. No poems have survived from that time, but there are some from the v/11th and VI/12th centuries and even later. The genre was immediately threatened by the neutralizing effect of Arabic classicism, which tended to absorb and modify alien forms. For this reason, and because of the copyists' difficulty in reproducing foreign texts, not many *kharjas* in Romance have survived. Moreover, they were soon replaced by *kharjas* in colloquial, and later in classical, Arabic. Nevertheless, the non-classical metric framework of the poem remained, and even when this was altered it still retained the isosyllabic character of accentual Romance poetry, at least in Andalusia.

ROMANCE	SPANISH	
Ké faré, mammà?	*¿Qué haré, madre?*	'What shall I do, mother?
me-u l-habīb ešt' ad yana.	*Mi amigo está en la puerta.*	My friend is at the door.'
Benid la Pašqa, ay aún/sin elle,	*Viene la Pascua, ay, aún/sin él,*	'Comes Easter yet/without him
lasrando meu qoragǔn/por elle.	*lacerando mi corazón/por él.*	tearing my heart/for him.'
Komo si filiyólo 'alyēno	*Como si [fueras] hijito ajeno,*	'As if [you were] a stranger's son
non maš adormeš a me-u šēno.	*ya no duermes más en mi seno.*	you no longer sleep on my breast.'
Ké farēyo 'o ké sérad de mībe?	*¿Qué haré o será de mí?*	'What shall I do or what will become of me?
¡Habībe,	*¡Amigo,*	My friend,
non te tolgaš de mībe!	*no te vayas de mi lado!*	do not leave my side!'
Gār ké farēyo,	*Dime qué haré*	'Tell me what I shall do,
kómo bibrēyo:	*como viviré:*	how I shall live:
Ešt' al-habīb ešpēro	*a este amigo espero;*	waiting for this friend;
pōr él morrēyo.	*por él moriré.*	for him I shall die.'
Tant' amāre, tant' amāre	*Tanto amar, tanto amar,*	'So much loving, so much loving,
habīb, tant' amāre,	*amigo, tanto amar,*	friend, so much loving,
enfermīron welyoš nīdioš	*enfermaron ojos bellos*	beautiful eyes fall sick
e dōlen tan māle.	*y duelen tan mal.*	and suffer such pain.'

The *muwashshah* was a marvellous fusion of two literatures and two races in the multi-racial melting pot of Cordoba under the caliphate. It is undoubtedly the most original product of the Umayyad culture, rising far above the provincial level of its other achievements.

We see in Cordoba under the caliphs not only the glory but also the inherent tragedy of Spanish Islam. Foreign to the Christians of the North, who were its half-brothers by blood; foreign also to the peoples of the East, its brothers by race, culture and religion, the great kingdom of the South appears to us as an airy mirage, a blazing sun on a misplaced orbit, which as the poet Ibn Hazm once said of himself, had the fault of rising in the West.

Apart from the *muwashshah*, Spanish Islamic culture is represented far more effectively by its architecture than its literature. We may mention the marvellous palatine city of Madīnat az-Zahrā', built all in stone by 'Abd ar-Rahmān III, which lasted a bare fifty years before being destroyed by the Berbers and is now being restored. Above all we should mention the Great Mosque of Cordoba, a remarkable monument which good fortune has preserved. The building was enlarged three times, each modification more splendid than the last. As the third alteration brought it to the river, a fourth addition carried out by Almanzor had to be continued laterally.

Almanzor and civil war: 366–422/976–1031

Al-Hakam II, the 'majestic, learned and administrative' Caliph al-Mustansir bi-llāh, was physically abnormal, and his son Hishām II al-Mu'ayyad was a degenerate. But Hishām never exercised power. On al-Hakam's death an intelligent and able official named Muhammad ibn Abī 'Āmir, who had worked his way to the top on his own merits and through being the lover of the Caliph's mother, violently disposed of his rivals, and seized absolute power, shutting up the new Caliph in a gilded prison without any means of communication with the outside world.

The usurpation was complete. Ibn Abī 'Āmir, although his official title was that of *hājib*, or prime minister, behaved like a true caliph from the start. He adopted the title of al-Mansūr (Almanzor), 'the Victorious One', by which name he is known to posterity. He built a palatine city, al-Madīna az-Zāhira, which has disappeared without a trace – such are the punishments of usurpation. He set up a court, was more authoritarian than the real sovereigns had been, and started his own dynasty, being succeeded by his two sons, 'Abd al-Malik Muzaffar and 'Abd ar-Rahmān an-Nāsir, known as 'Sanchuelo'.

Almanzor, who came from a noble but penniless family, was by nature as cunning as he was bold. To obtain his people's forgiveness for his usurpation and the violent methods he had used to achieve it he carried out both good works, such as the patronage of writers; and bad ones, which would ingratiate him with the *faqīhs* (doctors of law). The latter actions included an *auto da fé* in which al-Hakam II's fabulous library was expurgated of all its 'impious' books – i.e. all the books on science. But his most celebrated act was to step up the punitive expeditions against the Christians, amid an atmosphere of apocalyptic violence. He directed fifty or more of these expeditions himself and many were undoubtedly successful. He became the 'scourge of God' for his attacks on the Christian strongholds of northern Spain, which included the sacking of the basilica of Santiago de Compostela, the most famous Christian sanctuary in Spain. But it must be admitted that this exalted pose had two major drawbacks.

The first of these was significantly to affect subsequent events in Spain. As a fighting unit, the army of the rulers of Cordoba left much to be desired, and the Andalusian Muslims, either through cowardice or indolence, were generally unwilling to fight. This had already been noted by the geographer and Fātimid spy Ibn Hawqal, who had written a highly uncomplimentary report on the Andalusian army during his trip to al-Andalus in the time of 'Abd ar-Rahmān III. Since the chances of a successful campaign under such conditions were remote, Almanzor decided on a remedy which was worse than the disease: to import mercenaries from North Africa, a region which had been subdued with great difficulty and partially incorporated into the caliphate by al-Hakam II. But to remind the Berbers of the way to Spain was the worst thing that Almanzor could have done. He was unwittingly sharpening a dangerous weapon which would bring about the rapid end of the caliphate and, in the long term, of the whole of Spanish Islam.

The second disadvantage was that these expeditions, though spectacular, were in fact of little use. Being purely punitive rather than aiming at total occupation, they were often counter-productive. Almanzor could have said of the Christians what Horace has Hannibal say of the Roman people (*Odes* IV, 4, 59, 60): '*Per damna, per caedis, ab ipso / ducit opes animumque ferro*'. ('For every loss, for every cut of the knife, from the very edge of the steel it draws fresh power and spirit.') Pruning encourages growth; and furthermore he who lives by the sword dies by the sword and although Almanzor did not actually die in the field, as he had always been convinced that he would, he fell ill on the way back from a campaign against the Christians, and was carried in a litter to die (393/1002) in Medinaceli (Soria). According to poetic legend, a mysterious song was heard along the banks of the Guadalquivir:

En Catalañazor	'In Calatañazor
perdió Almanzor	Almanzor lost
el atambor.	his drum.'

Although Hishām II was still alive, Almanzor's successor was his son 'Abd al-Malik, entitled Muzaffar, a kind and cultured man whose reign seemed to begin as a honeymoon for the people of al-Andalus; but he died soon after, in 399/1008. He was replaced by his half-brother 'Abd ar-Rahmān, entitled an-Nāsir and nicknamed 'Sanchuelo' or 'Sanchol' because through his mother 'Abda he was the grandson of Sancho Abarca, King of Pamplona. Under him the power of the 'Āmirids quickly collapsed. When he foolishly demanded that Hishām II should name him as the heir to the throne, he was assassinated, and civil war broke out.

There is no room here to describe that conflict (known as the *fitna*). It is a complicated tale which has been told many times. The war was devastating, a game of cat and mouse between Berbers of all kinds including the Banū Hammūd (Idrīsids), who were descended from the Prophet, and the Andalusian Arabs and Slavs *Saqāliba* (slaves of Christian origin). Hishām II remained a man of straw in the hands of others. After him came a series of princes, some criminal, others well intentioned, all unsuccessful, together with the incompetent slaves or infamous adventurers who aided and sometimes supplanted them.

The picture is a nightmarish succession of shadowy images, sometimes recurring; a tragic, headlong descent with one or two deceptive pauses. The caliphate was up for auction. Al-Madīna az-Zāhira was swept away. Madīnat az-Zahrā' was likewise destroyed and its columns, capitals and conduit pipes sold off. Everything of al-Hakam's library that had not been burnt was sold off. All was destroyed or debased. The wind of particularism blew once more through the Peninsula.

The curious thing is that what we can see so clearly today as a total collapse was probably not seen as such by the people of the time. They no doubt expected from day to day that fortune would turn in their favour. When, however, the situation became clear to everyone, no one even wanted to be caliph any more. The last Umayyad to bear this title, a cowardly bourgeois, Hishām III al-Muʿtadd, fled from Cordoba, only to be assassinated. And the prominent Cordobans, now with little more than the shell of the city, proclaimed a sort of republic (422/1031).

The cultural climax of a society does not always coincide with its political zenith, and a culture may be on the rise amidst political decline. But here the political earthquake was so abrupt and so devastating that the culture remained as it were suspended. Never had al-Andalus enjoyed a more promising cultural prospect. But then everything went out. The promised harvest was frozen on the vine.

There is a distinction to be made between the royal patronage of literature and a literary court, and although the last Umayyads' patronage was extensive, they did not have literary courts. The one possible exception was Almanzor, who being a usurper needed to ingratiate himself; and his palace consequently swarmed with important poets. There was also Ramādī, and Ibn Darrāj al-Qastallī, whose work continued throughout the civil war. But three major figures must be mentioned above all.

Three writers of the civil war

One is the marvellous historian Ibn Hayyān (377–469/987–1076), the first half of whose life falls into this period. An admirable prose writer, a biting and independent critic, an incorruptible witness to his times, he has left a sweeping though unfortunately fragmentary picture of his period. His masterpiece is the *Matīn*; but before that he published the *Muqtabis*, an edition of chroniclers who had preceded him.

The other two are Ibn Shuhayd (382–426/992–1035) and Ibn Hazm (381–455/991–1063), both sons of high officials. The first came from old Arab stock, the second from a disguised Christian family. Besides being great friends, they were also viziers together at an early age in an ephemeral Umayyad government during the civil war. Together, they form a poetic school which in my opinion represents the highest point of Andalusian Arabic literature. One imagines them as two youths dressed in white, conversing among the white porticos of Cordoba, devotees of swans and lovers of the blonde women who were the erotic ideal of the Umayyads in Spain.

Within the cultural world of the Arabs, they were to an extent revolutionaries: they rejected their teachers, detested current teaching methods, abhorred the bookish tradition and maintained that a poet is born and not made – a thesis which is common enough today but seemed positively scandalous to medieval Islam. On the other hand they formed an aristocratic, 'Arabophile' minority which despised popular literature ('away with the *muwashshah*!'). Yet while their desire for assimilation into the Arab culture was nourished on new things from the East, they paradoxically hated these and aspired to overcome them, giving their work a thoroughly nationalistic flavour. They wrote both poetry and prose, though to us their prose is the more interesting. In any case they failed, for the Umayyad caliphate collapsed on top of them, destroying the best hopes of Andalusian letters.

Ibn Shuhayd, a poet and critic, virtually a pure intellectual, was a better poet than his companion. The prose satires which he let off like squibs against the grammarians and bookish culture in general are worthy of closer study than they have yet received. His most appealing work as far as we are concerned, the *Risālat at-tawābiʿ wa-z̧-z̧awābiʿ*, has only survived in a mutilated form. It is a surprising fictional account of a journey made by the author through the underworld, where he converses with the ghosts or inspiring genii of the major Arabic poets, comparing his works to theirs with typically Spanish pride. It is in fact a sort of *Divina Commedia*, pre-dating Abū l-ʿAlā' al-Maʿarrī and Dante, full of humour and imagination. Persecuted through the reigning princelings' intransigence, Ibn Shuhayd suffered a fatal illness with a stoic fortitude and was buried in al-Khayr, a park in Cordoba. It is interesting to note that his house contained no books.

Ibn Hazm needs little introduction, since his *Tawq al-hamāma* ('The Necklace of the Dove') is today considered one of the few masterpieces of Andalusian Arabic literature as well as the first in time. It has been translated into all the major languages. Basically a treatise on love, it is the best in Arabic on this theme and can be favourably compared with those of Plato, Ovid, Dante, Stendhal and many others. It is a cornerstone of any discussion about the influence of Arabic poetry in Europe. Furthermore it is a poignant elegy for Moorish Andalusia, a remarkable work of autobiography, an incisive evocation of Cordoba under the Umayyads, and the Middle Ages' finest collection of erotic stories. The stories were written directly, almost entirely without reference to books. As the author says in his preface, 'I may have used the innumerable things which one hears about the Bedouins, but I am not in the habit of riding any other mount than my own, nor making a display of borrowed jewels.' And indeed his own jewels shone quite brightly enough, as in these often quoted lines from the *Tawq* (Ch. 20):

Begone, unlucky pearl of China.
I am content with my ruby of Spain! . . .

The *Tawq* is an enchanting book, but a melancholy one. The author (whose many other works include an *Apologetic account of the literature of al-Andalus*, a great *History of Religions* and some penetrating *Confessions* or moral maxims) later abandoned literature and passed from melancholy to anger. Embittered by fierce theological and juridical disputes, estranged from everything and

Spain during the Muslim period, showing towns and sites mentioned in the chapter. (4)

everybody, he spent his last years shut away in the provincial corner from which his family came. He still wrote, but now, in the bitter phrase of Ibn Hayyān, his books did not 'get past the threshold of his door'.

The break-up of the Muslim state: 414–83/1023–91

The new wave of regionalism which overcame the country at the time of the *fitna* or civil war soon became a flood, and led to the establishment of the *taifa* (Arabic *tā'ifa*) states. Once the restraining forces of the Umayyads had been broken, the enmities between all the conflicting elements of the caliphate exploded. There were Arab and *muladí taifas*, naturally; but also Berber ones consisting of Arabized Berbers or recently arrived mercenaries. Even the 'Slavs' considered themselves entitled to political independence. There was a general scramble for power, in which anyone who could *encastillarse* – establish himself in a fortress – did so. At the beginning of this fragmentation, some twenty-eight miniature states were created. This number was later reduced by the inevitable annexations and redistributions of territory, since apart from sporadically uniting against the common Christian enemy, everyone fought everyone else. For the historian, the period is full of difficulties, and modern histories of al-Andalus generally come to grief in the morass.

The *taifas* dispersed the different ethnic groups of the caliphate. But there was no corresponding increase in independence. Political independence was impossible for such small groupings; and instead of cultural independence there was quite the reverse. We have seen how the Umayyad state imported its culture from the ʿAbbāsid East, but that it subjected it to a kind of filter; and in the times of Ibn Shuhayd and Ibn Hazm it was beginning

to despise and rise above them. Now the Andalusian *taifas*, at a time when Eastern culture was least needed, accelerated its importation and not only did not filter it but embarked on a course of frenzied imitation. A host of miniature Baghdads aped the original: in the princelings' ridiculous titles, clothing, protocol, manners, the untimely and unnecessary appearance of Eastern *Shuʿūbiyya* or literary opposition to Arab supremacy. Whereas the caliphate had built a Spanish edifice with Eastern bricks, the *taifas* built an Eastern edifice with Spanish bricks.

The *taifas* were so numerous that between them they had every cultural feature imaginable. Some specialized in prose writing, some in scholarship, others in scientific studies – now openly encouraged – refined behaviour, or music. The one thing in which they all specialized, however, was poetry, including the *muwashshah*, the first surviving examples of which date from this period. Poetry was everywhere; it was the popular vice and the universal instrument, used in everything, from diplomacy to love, from propaganda to satire. The major part of state budgets was spent on it. There were poetic academies in the palaces, with rosters of salaried poets. Kings composed verse on their thrones, ploughmen as they followed their team. A good *qasīda* could not only prove profitable, it might even make the author a vizier.

Pride of place must go to Ibn Zaydūn (394–463/1003–70), who was born in Cordoba, fled to Seville and was the love of the scandalous Umayyad princess Wallāda, to whom he addressed some admirable love poems, including the celebrated *Qasīda nūniyya*. As a poet he was fluent, elegant and extraordinarily human. A little lower on the scale, except for his personal and historical interest, comes Ibn ʿAmmār de Silves, a tortuous and equivocal adventurer who rose from poverty to become vizier to the King of Seville, who had him executed for treason in 479/1086. We must also mention Ibn al-Labbāna of Denia (d. 507/1113), a kind and gentle soul, if only in his disinterested gratitude to the defeated ʿAbbādids – a rare sentiment for the time. All these and others were excellent, but cannot be compared with the great poets of the East.

If we were to single out one figure it would be King Muʿtamid of Seville (reigned 460–84/1068–91), the third and last of his dynasty. He was outstanding not because his poems are technically superior but because they are natural and disinterested. They are the spontaneous emanations of a truly poetic soul, a commentary on the dramatic ups and downs of a life which was almost always poetic in itself, from the moments of triumph to the bitterness of African exile. His last compositions, which we might call the 'Elegies of Aghmāt', are amongst the most bitter testimonies of human pain.

But here we must leave the atmosphere of Moorish-Andalusian romanticism which was the characteristic face of the period, and complete the historical sketch which we began earlier in this section.

The *taifa* states may be likened to the republics of the Italian Renaissance, wearing a turban but lacking a purse, and moreover inclined to betray one another at any moment. Their vulnerability was obvious to the ambitious sovereign of Castile, Alfonso VI, who exploited them unmercifully. He had representatives in all the Muslim courts, and was continually setting them against one another. Alfonso knew Islam at least as well as the Cid, and also had advisers on Islamic matters, who included the Mozarab count Sisnando Davídiz of Coimbra, an émigré from Andalusia. Sisnando advised caution; but unfortunately the King was married to a Frenchwoman and also in contact with the Benedictine monks of Cluny, both of whom, being ignorant of Andalusian politics, recommended violence. It is now impossible to say who was right. Alfonso brought the situation to a head by seizing Toledo (478/1085) and expelling its king. It might perhaps have been better to retain the latter under a protectorate as Sisnando had probably advised. On the other hand, it was obviously tempting to carry the Reconquista as far as the River Tagus and capture the former Visigothic capital itself. The situation was inflamed by violation of a pact whereby the Toledan Muslims could continue using the Mosque, and the Muslims in general lost their tempers.

Al-Muʿtamid, King of Seville – the most powerful and representative of the *taifas* – adopted an extreme attitude; 'Better be a camel-driver in Africa than a swineherd in Castile,' he exclaimed. The King of the Almoravids, Yūsuf ibn Tāshufīn, was summoned from Africa. He crossed the Straits of Gibraltar and a decisive encounter was arranged with Alfonso VI in the traditional way, like a football match. The battle, called Zallāqa by the Muslims and Sagrajas by the Christians, took place in the region of Badajoz (479/1086). Al-Muʿtamid covered himself in glory and Alfonso VI fled, defeated. Yūsuf ibn Tāshufīn returned to Morocco as he had undertaken. But four years later, seeing the disorganization of Andalusia and egged on by the *faqīhs*, he returned and made himself master of southern Spain. The *Memoirs* of ʿAbdallāh, the

last Zīrid king of Granada, give a direct, first-hand account of events. The Andalusian princelings were treated with ruthless cruelty – despoiled, dethroned and exiled or assassinated. Only al-Muʿtamid defended himself bravely, but was betrayed, defeated and exiled.

The Andalusian *taifas* may be likened to the frogs in the fairytale who wanted a king. They did not like the log which Jupiter had sent them, and when they scorned it after Zallāqa Jupiter sent them a serpent (Yūsuf the Almoravid) who devoured them. Only Zaragoza was saved, by its distance from the centre of events.

The domination of the Almoravids: 484–540/1091–1145
The domination of the Almoravids lasted little more than half a century and hardly improved the situation. It merely propped up the crumbling edifice of al-Andalus, without preventing a general deterioration. Despite the ephemeral victory of Uclés (512/1108), Toledo could not be recovered, and in 1118 Islam lost Zaragoza. Valencia was recovered after its occupation by the Cid, but the punitive expeditions of Alfonso I of Aragon were still to be endured in Andalusia itself; and large numbers of Mozarabs fled with him.

Apart from the brief respite enjoyed by the Islamic religion, al-Andalus could now do nothing but decline. Its major loss was to its political pride, since it was not only deprived of its independence, but turned into a mere province subject to a capital which was then uncivilized (Marrakesh). The social structure lost its old ethnic framework with the final dispersion of the Mozarabs by flight or deportation, although bilingualism remained for a while through inertia, as we shall see so clearly in Ibn Quzmān. In a cultural context, the old umbilical cord which linked al-Andalus with the East was almost ruptured. Spain had to fend for itself, and even give lessons to Africa. And emigration of Andalusian authors, such as Abū Salt Umayya and at-Turtūshī, now began.

The Almoravids were merely a brief foretaste of the African invasion of Spain. Their customs produced an initial cultural shock – the veils worn by the men (the *lithām*, still worn by Arabs of the Sahara) and their large-scale use of the camel (Maqqarī, *Analectes*, II, 680). There were three Almoravid rulers in Spain. The first, the great Emperor Yūsuf ibn Tāshufīn, was no doubt uncultured, and naturally spoke little Arabic; while the last, short-lived, ruler, Tāshufīn ibn ʿAlī, was merely insignificant. The intervening monarch, ʿAlī ibn Yūsuf, who ruled for practically the entire period (500–38/1106–43), was reasonably Arabized, reinstated the former officials of the *taifas* and did not differ from the majority of the former Andalusian princes.

Generally speaking, the Almoravids were infinitely closer to the Andalusian way of life than the later Almohads. Granted that they burned the works of al-Ghazālī, but these were soon reinstated by their successors. The Mālikī clergy reigned unchecked in their time, but this was nothing new, and merely represented the swing of the pendulum after the irreligiousness of the *taifas*. Women ruled more than was usual, but this was the Berber custom. Moreover the prevailing ideological intolerance was counterbalanced by considerable license in moral customs. Ibn Quzmān paints a detailed picture of the immoral delights of urban life, and such extraordinary refinements as the practice indulged in by youthful dandies of gilding the calves of their legs.

The Andalusian literati, especially those born under the *taifas*, did not feel very much at home with their new rulers. It was not that they lacked an audience so much as that they no longer received their accustomed lavish remuneration, although it was equally obvious that such prodigious waste of public funds on poetry could not last for ever. When Ibn Bāqī (d. 540/1145), one of the great poets of the period, says:

> The rhymes of poetry weep their fill
> For an Arab lost among barbarians

it is strangely reminiscent of the lines written by Ovid in his exile in Pontus (*Tristium* V, X, v.37):

> *Barbarus hic ego sum, quia non intelligor ulli,*
> *et rident stolidi verba latina Getae*
> ('I am a barbarian here for no one understands me,
> and the boorish Getae jeer at my Latin speech')

but he was obviously exaggerating the situation, having far less reason to complain than Ovid. In any case, if the situation seemed lamentable to the poets, at least it provided them with a new inspiration; and one prefers the unaccustomed tone of their bitter complaints to the stale frigidity of their panegyrics.

There was one curious result. In the work not only of Ibn Bāqī but also of Tutīlī, the blind poet of Tudela (d. 520/1126), and other lesser poets, one theme – perhaps an ancient one – recurs, which I have called 'the hatred of Seville'. This great city, in which poetry was in eclipse, is accused of incomprehension and disdain. This poetic attack on Seville is the more interesting because it shows that the Andalusian Arabs were aware of the decline of their literature (an unaccustomed feeling in an Arab), and realized that after a 'golden age' they were now entering on a 'silver age'. They even came close to this Occidental terminology, for we find a poet asking the author of an anthology (the *Dhakhīra*, 1–2, 391) to include the 'silver verses' which he is sending him after his 'golden verses'.

The appearance of anthologies is significant here, for prompted by this feeling of decadence the writers of Almoravid Andalusia undertook great anthologies so that the glories of the past should not be lost. One such writer was Ibn Bassām of Santaren (d. *c.* 542/1147), author of the enormous *Dhakhīra*, even now not published in its entirety. The work fully deserves its title of 'Treasury', since it is a mine of literary information and texts, including the work of Ibn Shuhayd and Ibn Hayyān. The anthologies of the cynic Ibn Khāqān (d. between 525/1130 and 535/1140) are less lengthy. In his *Matmah al-anfus* and *Qalā'id al-'iqyān* (the famous 'Golden Necklaces') he used a different system, interspersing fictionalized biographies of the authors in coruscating rhymed prose with the actual selections from their work. It might be added that he also collected contemporary poems which were paid for by the proceeds of a publicity agency and by blackmail.

Although even here one finds strains of bitterness, Valencia, the garden of Spain, represents a single oasis of tranquillity and perfection in the poetry of the Almoravid period. This was an area whose fertility had attracted the Arabs since very early times (as a result of which the language was purer than elsewhere), and which with the 'Slavic' *taifas* and the adventure of the Cid had been thrust from its isolation into the foreground of history.

The great poets of this area and period were not the importunate beggars of other places, but well-heeled bourgeois who instead of writing panegyrics for their bread, dedicated poems to local officials who could solve problems for them or get their taxes reduced. We mention only two, uncle and nephew: Ibn Khafāja (450–533/1058–1138) and Ibn az-Zaqqāq (d. 529/1134). The first was a prolific author and an admirable poet who specialized in descriptions of nature, thereby earning himself the sobriquet of *al-Jannān*, 'the Gardener'. The second was a great artist who, coming at the end of his school, renewed and embellished the artificial style of lyric poetry which had preceded him. His exquisite art is a perfect example of how a creative mind can subtly lubricate the creaking machinery of metaphoric invention.

Ibn Quzman, poet of Muslim Spain

The poets of Almoravid Spain weathered the storm in different ways – some by ignoring it, others by airing their injured pride; some changed their technique. Thus it was that the Almoravid period was a golden age for the *muwashshah*, whose form was traditional in some aspects, such as the Romance *kharjas*, but innovatory in others, particularly its refined and exquisite musicality. Many of its poets cultivated classical and strophic poetry with equal facility. They belonged to a group headed by two masters already mentioned, Tutīlī and Ibn Bāqī.

The *zajal*, a genre which first appears about this time, is a variety of the *muwashshah*, its chief characteristic being that it is written entirely in the vernacular. There is some evidence for the belief that it was invented by the famous philosopher and musician of Zaragoza, Ibn Bājja, otherwise known as Avempace (d. 533/1138). During the course of its development it came to have more strophes than the *muwashshah*; it also simplified the structure of the latter, being a more popular form, and finally lost the *kharja*. The Romance words which are characteristic of the genre are no longer contained in the *kharja* but scattered throughout the composition. Whether Avempace was the inventor of the *zajal* or not, there is no doubt that it appeared more or less around his time, and reached its culmination in the work of the Cordoban poet Ibn Quzmān.

Ibn Quzmān was as attractive a personality as he was an outstanding talent. Tall, blond, ugly, possibly with a squint, he has been taken by some for a kind of Gothic throwback, particularly in view of the similarity between his name and the Germanic Guzman. It seems a doubtful thesis, however, since he belonged to an ancient and noble Arab family. Unless they were written with ingenuous sincerity – which is unlikely in view of their content – his poems seem to display the worst kind of moral cynicism, though they are highly sympathetic for all that. In them he reveals himself as conceited, sycophantic, amusing, an importunate joker who did not hesitate to beg for the things which he needed to live and enjoy life. He was a professional Don Juan, a wooer of men as well as of women.

We may well wonder what prompted this rare poet to abandon the classical language he clearly knew so well, and use only the colloquial language of Andalusia. If his motives were purely artistic, then it was a stroke of genius unparalleled in Arabic literature. His style is a curious amalgam of the colloquial language studded with the rarefied terms of cultured speech (*gharīb*) and words and phrases in Romance. This, together with the fact that his work has survived only in a Palestinian manuscript (an indication of his international success), makes his work difficult to approach. Until recently such editions as existed were unsatisfactory and the translations were incomplete and unreliable.

In 1972 I decided to publish a transliterated edition, in three volumes, together with a translation following the original metre and notes and analytical comments. Apart from enabling the reader to enjoy Ibn Quzmān's poetry in itself, my intention was twofold: to discuss the Romance words and phrases included in the *zajals* and to establish a relationship between their characteristic metres – admirably musical – and Spanish metric conventions. I believe that they must conform to the latter, since they cannot be interpreted in terms of Arabic metrics.

The work of Ibn Quzmān represents a major step towards a new concept of poetry. He has an immense gift for vivid story-telling, and for the dramatic use of stylized dialogue. All this is unique in Arabic literature, as is the spontaneity, the novelty of his work. We may note also his gift for making poetry out of whatever comes into his mind, often using parody, playing with different themes and weaving them in and out of the current of his verse. The tone is almost constantly ironic, often tender, only occasionally brutal and always full of good humour. It is 'a voice from the market-place'.

Ibn Quzmān is one of the best poets of the Middle Ages in any language; he is the best poet of Muslim Spain and ranks with any of the Arabs. His work, coming later than Ibn Hazm's 'Necklace of the Dove', is the second master-work of the literature of al-Andalus.

The Almohad domination (540–668/1145–1269)

After an inevitable period of second-generation *taifas*, civil wars and rebellions (such as that of the *murīdūn* in Mertola, who followed the doctrine of the mystic Ibn al-'Arīf of Almeria (d. 536/1141), the Almoravids were replaced by the Almohads, a *nouvelle vague* of African invaders, not without violence and bloodshed.

The Almohad dynasty, more sure of itself than the preceding one, had an organization which may be compared to Italian Fascism. Its manners were pompous and elegant to the point of affectation, as can be seen in the history of the dynasty written by the Spaniard Ibn Sāhib as-Salāt (who was still alive in 630/1232). Al-Andalus continued to be without independence, lacking a direct link with the East, and with few bilingual inhabitants, its racial composition consisting only of Arabs, *muladíes* (Spanish converts) and Berbers. The Almohads even allowed themselves the dangerous game of letting Andalusians and Berbers argue over the pre-eminence of their respective cultures. One of these arguments resulted in the diminutive but none the less piquant *Risālat fī fadl al-Andalus* ('In Praise of Spanish Islam') by ash-Shaqundī, who died in 629/1231 (*Shaqunda* was Secunda, a suburb of Cordoba), which amply demonstrates the hatred of the Andalusian Arabs for the Berbers.

Two coins from later Islamic Spain. Left: a golden dinar of 'Abd al-Mu'min (524–58/1130–63), first of the Almohad 'caliphs'. The Almohads were a Berber people who took over Morocco in the early VI/12th century. In 550/1145 'Abd al-Mu'min established a kingdom in Spain with its capital at Seville. Right: a silver dirham from the last days of the kingdom of Granada, shortly before 898/1492. The rest of Spain had fallen to the Reconquista two centuries before. Only a combination of diplomacy and luck allowed Granada to survive for so long. (5, 6)

The thing which changed least under the Almohads was literature. Poets still kept the same tone to the point of repetition, both in their courtly panegyrics and in the anacreontic verses they composed amid the delights of Seville. Here the eclipse which poetry had suffered under the Almoravids was over and the Guadalquivir was more crowded with pleasure boats than the Nile. It was in the Guadalquivir that the finest poet of the period, a Jewish convert named Ibn Sahl, was drowned in 649/1251 – 'the pearl returning to its source'. Ibn Sahl wrote some fine *muwashshahs* in the classical style; but the genre was dying in Spain as a whole. One of its last representatives was Abū Bakr ibn Zuhr (d. 595/1198). The *zajal* was still being written.

There were much greater changes in art, which was overtaken by what H. Terrasse has described as the *décor large* or decoration with broad mesh. This is seen in many surviving monuments in Africa and Spain, including the Christian parts of the latter where snobbery seems to have inspired palaces in a pure Arab style, such as that subsequently incorporated in the famous Castilian monastery of Las Huelgas in Burgos. The finest of these monuments is the Giralda, the great cathedral tower of Seville, which seems so plain and unadorned that at times one almost forgets its Arab origins.

The sciences tend to be slower in developing than the arts, and this was the period at which they reached their maturity, exemplified by the achievements of Ibn al-Baytār (d. 646/1248) in botany, and Abū Marwān ibn Zuhr (d. 557/1161) in medicine. The latter was the son of another famous doctor, Abū l-'Alā' (Avenzoar), who died in 525/1130. (The achievements of this remarkable family ranged from the scientific to the military and from politics to literature; they were one of the families who gave their patronage to Ibn Quzmān.) A number of disciplines were renewed and developed, as in the grammatical works of Ibn Madā'. By this time Arab science and philosophy were beginning to filter into Europe through various channels, the most important of which was Spain. This activity was first apparent in the emergence of a school of translators in Toledo which enjoyed the patronage of the Archbishop Don Raimundo (525–45/1130–50); but it became more intense at the court of Alfonso X, the Wise (650–83/1252–84).

There were also great philosophers in Almohad Spain, in particular Ibn Rushd, better known as Averroes (520–95/1126–98), so renowned for his commentaries on Aristotle. Muslim philosophy in the West came to an end with Averroes, whose only disciples, and detractors, were in the Christian schools. But his master was the great Ibn Tufayl of Guadix (d. 577/1181), author of the *Risālat Hayy ibn Yaqzān*, known in Europe as *The Autodidact Philosopher*. This famous philosophical novel has been translated into all the European languages and embodies the eternal myth of the 'second Adam' whose modern incarnations include Andrenio in Gracián's *Criticón*, Robinson Crusoe and Bernard Shaw's Admirable Crichton. After the *Tawq al-hamāma* and the *zajals* of Ibn Quzmān, it is the third and last master-work of Andalusian Arabic literature.

The spiritual sciences flourished in Almohad Spain, thanks to a respite of almost a century in which Mālikism was temporarily eclipsed – a reaction against its monopoly in Almoravid times. Al-Ghazālī was reinstated (but attacked by Averroes in his *Tahāfut at-tahāfut*). The climate was favourable to Sūfī mysticism. The old mystical school of Ibn Masarra had already appeared in Ibn al-'Arīf, whom we mentioned at the beginning of this section as the inspiration of the *murīdūn*. Now it reached its full maturity in Spain, which was able to export its own mystics of genius to the East. The major figure is Ibn al-'Arabī (561–638/1165–1240), one of the most important figures in the whole of Islam. Not far behind him are Shushtarī (d. 668/1269), author of many fine *zajals* on mystical themes, and Ibn Sab'īn (d. 669/1270).

The list of émigrés to the East also includes the geographer, poet and anthologist Ibn Sa'īd (d. 673–85/1274–86), author of the *Mughrib*, a great literary archive which all his family contributed to, having inherited it from Hijārī (d. 550/1155). Another famous anthologist, Ibn al-Abbār (assassinated in 659/1260), and the poet Qartājannī (d. 684/1285) went to Tunis, fleeing from the flames of the Reconquista.

For the forces of the Reconquista, having been defeated at Alarcos in the year 591/1195, won the famous battle of Las Navas de Tolosa in 609/1212. It was a victory comparable to the taking of Toledo, and even more important, for it was the decisive one. From now on Andalusia was at the mercy of the Christians. Castile and Aragon divided the work of reconquest between them, and the victories came in rapid succession: Mallorca (627/1229), Cordoba (634/1236), Valencia (636/1238), Seville (646/1248), Murcia (668/1269), to mention only the most important ones. The Almohad period had seen some respite in the decline of Islam in Spain, but from now on the decline was to become a fall in earnest.

The kingdom of Granada: 665–898/1266–1492

The reconquest of lower Andalusia took place quickly because the king of Castile was St Ferdinand and because the geography of the area made it easy. Since neither of the two peoples tolerated religious minorities, those Muslims who did not emigrate to Africa sought refuge in the mountains, with the result that the population of upper Andalusia increased enormously. For a new St Ferdinand, the conquest of this region would have been relatively easy, despite the difficulties imposed by the

Christian and Muslim playing chess, from a Christian manuscript of the 13th century, a period when Muslim power was declining rapidly and catastrophically. There is something symbolic about the game played between two such opponents – each respecting and learning from the other but moving inevitably towards final and absolute confrontation. (7)

terrain. But as no such figure was forthcoming, Alfonso X decided on a belated policy of indirect government by means of a protectorate similar to, but more clearly defined than, that which Alfonso VI had used with the *taifa* states. Thus began the monarchy of the Banū l-Ahmar or Nasrids, who were Arab aristocrats descended from a Companion of the Prophet. The monarch of Granada functioned at first as a vassal and tributary of the Castilian monarch, and the influence of Castile in the small kingdom was then enormous, even extending to dress and armaments.

Yet neither protectors nor protected could have imagined that the situation was to last for two long centuries. During this unexpected stay of execution the Nasrid kingdom fluctuated between the two equally dangerous extremes of continuing under the protectorate of Castile and submitting to annexation by the new North African Berber kingdom of the Banū Marīn or Marīnids, whose customs it ultimately adopted.

While the Granadan monarchy managed to walk the tight-rope between these two extremes, its characteristics were very much those of the old *taifa* states, with vague archaic reminiscences of the caliphate. Equilibrium was maintained by means of a sort of Machiavellianism *avant la lettre* manifest in the Nasrid vizier Ibn al-Khatīb (713–76/1313–74), the Castilian chancellor López de Ayala (733–810/1332–1407) or in the great Tunisian thinker Ibn Khaldūn (733–809/1332–1406), author of the famous *Muqaddima* ('Prolegomena'), who came from Seville and subsequently went to Egypt. These three were contemporaries. And if it could be said that the *taifas* had been a foretaste of the later Western Romanticism, now the times were working only a little ahead of the Italian Renaissance.

The era of the Granadan monarchy in al-Andalus can be divided into three periods. The middle one, which is the most significant, covers roughly the second half of the VIII/14th century and includes the reign of Muhammad V (from 756/1354 to 794/1391, with an interruption of three years, from 761/1359 to 764/1362). It also coincides with the reign of Pedro I (the Cruel), from 751/1350 to 771/1369, and the great change which the enthronement of the Trastámara dynasty implied for Castile. Another significant event was the assassination, in Fez in 776/1374, of Ibn al-Khatīb, who completed the general history of al-Andalus up to his own time. With his death, the final century of Muslim domination in the Peninsula was left entirely unreported, apart from the fragments which can be gleaned from the Castilian chronicles, literature, documents and coins.

Like its politics, the literature of Granada was generally archaic and unoriginal, though always in good taste. No author equals Ibn al-Khatīb in any genre, and it was he who marked the end of the *muwashshah* with his anthology *Jaysh at-tawshīh*. The many-faceted verse writer Ibn Luyūn (d. 750/1349) preceded him, however, and after him came the great thinker Sātibī and the mystic and spiritual teacher Ibn ʿAbbād ar-Rundī, both of whom died in 791/1388. We might also mention Abū Bakr ibn ʿĀsim (761–829/1359–1426), the author of a mnemonic poem on Mālikī law and an amusing anthology which unexpectedly contains a collection of proverbs in the vernacular Arabic.

Outstanding among the poets is Abū l-Baqāʾ ibn Sharīf (d. 684/1285), who lamented the advance of the Reconquista; also the brilliant Ibn Khātima (d. 771/1369); and above all the famous Ibn Zamrak (d. 801/1393). The latter was a renegade disciple of Ibn al-Khatīb, whom he succeeded as vizier, and for whose assassination in Fez he was partly responsible – he himself met a similar fate at the hands of the royal guard. This was the period in which the poems of Ibn Zamrak were inscribed on the walls of the Alhambra, in a fitting funeral to the Arabic poetry of Andalusia – the final 'illuminated edition' of what had always been a highly decorative art form. Little more than a century later, in the time of Charles V, these same walls would witness a talk between the Italian ambassador Navagiero and the poet-knight Garcilaso which was to set Spanish poetry on a new course under Italian influence.

The Alhambra is of course the jewel of the period, perfectly and lovingly preserved by the Spaniards in spite of its extreme fragility. The most brilliant relic of the Nasrid civilization, it is an eternal proof of how art can transfigure the poverty of materials by the subtlety of its invention. No longer the *décor large* of the Almohads, the

style still inspired Christian imitation; the Alcazar of Seville, for example, is built in the same manner.

According to the famous old romance of Abenámar, the Alhambra, dominating the plain of Granada from its red hill-top, captivated King John II of Castile; and it was his daughter, Isabella the Catholic, who with her husband Ferdinand of Aragon finally entered the town and the palace in 898/1492, bringing to an end the lengthy task of reconquest. It was the culmination of a war which according to a modern historian 'lasted ten years like that of Troy and saw deeds as great as those recounted by Homer'.

The conquest of Granada counterbalanced the loss of Constantinople some years previously. King Boabdil left Granada 'sighing', to exile in the Alpujarras, and later in Africa. Meanwhile Spain said farewell to its brilliant medieval past and with the discovery of America in the same year was preparing to rule a vast empire ranging over two continents.

Coda: Spain and Islam

Spain's relationship with Islam had been established once and for all, and clearly did not end with the taking of Granada. Inevitably, the pacts made at that time were not adhered to. The *mudejars* (Muslims living under Christian rule) and *moriscos* (Moors converted to Christianity) continued to make their presence felt, until their final expulsion by Philip III in the beginning of the XI/17th century. There were always wars and treaties with Turks, pirates and Moroccans, and Cervantes was a captive in Algiers. The relationship with North Africa survives to the present day, when Spain continues to be officially and popularly pro-Arab. It could be said that she built a 'silver bridge' for the flight of the enemies she had herself defeated.

Not officially, however, at first. Naturally there was a reaction against Arab influence, revealed in such things as the architectural contrast between the Palace of Charles V and the Alhambra, between the Escorial and the Great Mosque of Cordoba. But although Spain scarcely participated in the pro-Islamic trend of the Enlightenment, the XII/18th century nevertheless saw a whole-hearted relapse into Arabism in popular architecture. If Spain was infected by the Orientalism of the Romantic movement, this was merely a return to the source, for the European taste for Moorish things had first been born in Spain. Then came the 'scientific Arabism' trend, which in Spain culminated in my own teachers Francisco Codera y Zaidín, Julián Ribera and Miguel Asín Palacios. And the argument still rages.

The long sunset of Moorish Spain – the incredible two centuries of the kingdom of Granada (665–898/1266–1492) – saw a brilliant late flowering of Islamic culture which rivalled that of its golden age three hundred years before. Its greatest monument is the Alhambra, the royal palace outside Granada, built for the most part during the VIII/14th century. The Sala de las Dos Hermanas (Hall of the Two Sisters), probably a former apartment of the queen, is decorated with roundels of stucco-work consisting of Arabic script (opposite). They are in fact

poems, written by one of the most outstanding poets of Granada, Ibn Zamrak. The verses reproduced here celebrate the beauty of the Alhambra itself:

'The Twins stretch out a friendly hand to her
And the celestial moon whispers confidentially.'
A statesman as well as a poet, Ibn Zamrak became vizier in 776/1374, succeeding Ibn al-Khatīb (another literary man), whose assassination in Fez he had partly engineered. He himself suffered the same fate in 797/1393 when he was murdered by the royal guard. (1)

Muslim Spain came of age in 139/756 when the last surviving Umayyad prince, ʿAbd ar-Rahmān, founded a dynasty that was to last for nine generations. At his capital of Cordoba he began the Great Mosque, enlarged by his successors. Shown here are the ceiling of the *mihrāb* antechamber (above) and the *mihrāb* itself (opposite), both of which date from the reign of al-Hakam II (350–55/961–6). Together they constitute the finest surviving monument of Umayyad Spain, complex in design and rich in decoration – marble, stucco and mosaic forming floral patterns (the segments of the dome and voussoirs of the arch) and Qurʾānic inscriptions, e.g. the square frame of the *mihrāb* and the octagonal base of the dome above the ribs. (2, 4)

The elegance of Umayyad court life is evoked in the ivory caskets which were one of the specialities of Cordoba (right). In the carved relief flowers and Kūfic lettering are combined with lively animals and birds. (3)

The palace-city of Madīnat az-Zahrā', named by 'Abd ar-Rahmān III in honour of his mistress az-Zahrā' ('the brilliant'), remains as one of the most evocative relics of Umayyad Spain, though in ruins. It is about six miles outside Cordoba. Work began in 324/936 and went on for about twenty-five years. It had spacious apartments for court officials, a harem and gardens. In its heyday it is said to have housed twelve thousand people. On this page are shown architectural details and some of the objects recovered during excavations. Top row: horse-

shoe arches in the Gran Salón; part of a column base; a green and purple dish of glazed earthenware showing a spotted horse; and a stag in bronze forming the spout of a fountain. Bottom row: a marble bowl; bas-relief panel and capital; a glazed earthenware jug with Kūfic decoration; and a glazed pottery well-head. The whole luxurious ensemble lasted fifty years. In 401/1010 the Umayyad dynasty, already displaced by Almanzor, lost all control. A long civil war broke out and Madīnat az-Zahrā' was destroyed. (5–12)

The quality of life in the great days of Moorish Spain is hard to recapture, since so little of its material setting survives. The literature of the period, however, is plentiful, and it celebrates to the full the pleasures of mind and body – wine, music, poetry and love. One of the very rare illuminated manuscripts that have come down to us (upper left) shows a scene in which the lover Bayād sings of his woes while a noble lady and her handmaidens first listen and then tell stories of their own. Left: a fragment of a silk cope, VI/12th century. The peacock motif may be compared to that in the ivory casket shown earlier. (13, 14)

In the Alhambra (from the Arabic *al-Hamrā'*, 'the red') the Moorish tradition reached its climax, a fusion of architecture and landscape garden that had no parallel in contemporary Christian culture. Its sequence of patios and open rooms create a unity of interior and exterior spaces linked by the brightly patterned surfaces of the walls, by the interpenetrating sunlight and by the sound of rippling water. This view shows the Patio de los Leones, with its fountain of twelve lions in the centre. The stilted arches, covered both inside and out with delicate stucco reliefs, support a frieze of cedarwood. (15)

The Christian population, Visigoths who had settled in Spain during the 6th century, continued to live under Muslim rule; and the two civilizations combined to produce a brilliant and unexpected style known as Mozarabic, of which the illustrations to Beatus' *Commentary on the Apocalypse* (left) are the finest examples. Some of the decorative patterns are Arab; other elements are Visigothic or remotely classical. (16)

The Jews too were able to practise their religion, at least at first, without hindrance. Under the Umayyads they occupied high places in the administration, and Jewish poetry, philosophy and science reached a level unequalled anywhere since the Diaspora. Above: a synagogue from a VIII/14th-century manuscript of the Haggada. Here too such details as the lamps and the dress are characteristically Moorish. (18)

Islam and Christianity were not destined to live in peace, though the two cultures had become so intermingled that the Reconquista was in many ways like a civil war. The tide turned against Islam at the Battle of Las Navas de Tolosa (609/1212) when the standard of the Almohad Caliph Abū Yaʿqūb Yūsuf II (left) was captured. (17)

Chapter Ten

LAND OF THE
LION AND THE SUN

Roger M. Savory

The lion and the sun, emblems of Persia, from a VII/13th-century tile. (1)

IN A NUMBER OF IMPORTANT WAYS, Iran is the 'odd man out' in the Middle East. First, it was an imperial power in ancient times: in 1971, Iran celebrated the 2,500th anniversary of the founding of the first Persian empire by Cyrus the Great in 550 BC. Carved in the solid rock of the mountainside at Bisutūn near Kirmānshāh, in cuneiform script in three languages (Elamite, Babylonian and Old Persian), the sonorous words of Darius the Great (522–486 BC) echo down the centuries: 'I am Darius, the great king, the king of kings, the King of Persia... from antiquity are we descended; from antiquity hath our race been kings.' One would expect to find in modern Iran, therefore, and indeed one does find, a strong sense of tradition and a reverence for traditional institutions.

Second, Iran differs ethnically from its immediate neighbours. The Iranians are not Semitic, nor do they belong to the family of Turkic peoples. They are, as the name of their country indicates, of Aryan origin; in other words, they belong to the same family as most of the peoples of Europe and, despite the centuries of intermingling with other ethnic groups, an Iranian 'type' is still clearly distinguishable.

Third, Iranians speak a language which is different from that of most of their immediate neighbours. Indeed, the term 'Aryan' is used more often these days to denote a language family than a family of peoples. Modern Persian and its cognate Iranian languages and dialects, together with the Indian languages like Hindi and Bengali which stem from Sanskrit, derive from a common Indo-Iranian parent language. By contrast, the other principal languages spoken in the Middle East, Arabic and Turkish, belong to quite different language families.

Fourth, although most Iranians are Muslims, they are not Sunnī or 'orthodox' Muslims, but Shī'ī or 'heterodox' Muslims. Iranians constitute by far the largest group of Shī'ī Muslims in the world today, and the difference between Sunnī and Shī'ī is much greater than that between Catholic and Protestant. In other words, Iranians differ from their Middle Eastern neighbours in race, language, religion and historical tradition, and these differences have profoundly influenced the course of Iranian history.

The rebirth of Iran

In this chapter, although we are concerned primarily with the history of the Iranian world during Islamic times, and particularly with Iran in the post-Mongol period, it is impossible to avoid some reference to ancient Iran if we are to have a proper understanding of subsequent developments.

For the Iranian world, the advent of Islam meant not physical or spiritual liberation, but defeat and conquest by an alien people. It changed the whole course of Persian history. First, the religion of the conquerors superseded the ancient Persian faith, Zoroastrianism, and from that day to this Persians have been Muslims – but Muslims with a difference, because the Persians soon adopted the 'heterodox' Shī'ī form of Islam and used it as a weapon against the Arabs. Second, the egalitarian spirit of the conquerors' religion and the more democratic concept of the elective caliphate challenged but failed to eradicate the ancient Persian tradition of absolute monarchy. On the contrary, as time went on, the Arab caliphs began to look suspiciously like Persian kings, at least as far as court ceremonial and bureaucratic organization were concerned. Third, the language of the conquerors, Arabic, for several centuries replaced the Pahlavī, or Middle Persian, language used by Persians during the Sāsānid period, the period of the second great Persian empire. When I say that Arabic 'replaced' Pahlavī, I mean that it became the administrative and cultural language of Iran, in rather the same way that Norman French superseded Anglo-Saxon in 11th-century England. For some five centuries, the majority of the works written by Persians in the fields of theology, philosophy, medicine, astronomy, philology, mathematics and even history, were written in Arabic. The reason is simple. Until the downfall of the caliphate in 657/1258, the Iranian world was part of the Islamic empire, and Arabic was the *lingua franca* of that empire from Spain and Morocco to South-East Asia. To ensure the widest possible circulation of their works, Persians, like

Spaniards and Moroccans, wrote in Arabic. The first branch of literature to break away from dependence on Arabic, after about two centuries, was poetry, and this was due no doubt to the strength of the oral tradition in the transmission of poetry; but when Persian re-emerged as a written language, in the iii/9th century, it was written in the Arabic script. In addition, large numbers of Arabic words had been absorbed into the Persian language and remained a permanent part of it.

For eight and a half centuries, Iran was little more than a geographical abstraction, with no independent existence. How was the Persian identity preserved under a succession of foreign rulers – Arab, Turk, Mongol and Tatar? Through the strength of the Persian historical and cultural tradition and through the flexibility and resilience of the Persian character. Artists, architects and artisans carried on the Persian tradition of the arts and craftsmanship, and the golden age of Persian literature is commonly held to run from about AD 1000 to AD 1500. Moreover, each successive dynasty of foreign conquerors which imposed its rule on Iran needed the expertise of Persian bureaucrats in order to administer its newly won empire. It is no accident that the ʿAbbāsid caliphs called in Persian diplomats and administrators to help them in dealing with the complex problems of a vast empire. The Turkish and Mongol nomads, who erupted from the steppes of Central Asia and suddenly found themselves masters of tracts of territory even vaster than the lands of the caliphate, were in even greater need of the wise counsel, erudition and administrative skill of Persian professional bureaucrats.

The Mongol invasions of the vii/13th century constitute a watershed in the history of Iran. In 654/1256 Hülegü, a grandson of Chingiz Khān, completed the Mongol conquest of Iran and, in 656/1258, captured Baghdad, put to death the ʿAbbāsid Caliph al-Mustaʿsim, and abolished the caliphate. Not unnaturally, Muslim historians took an apocalyptic view of these invasions. The well-known account of Ibn al-Athīr is typical:

For several years I put off reporting this event. I found it terrifying and felt revulsion at recounting it and therefore hesitated again and again. Who would find it easy to describe the ruin of Islam and the Muslims . . . ? O would that my mother had never borne me, that I had died before and that I were forgotten! . . . The report comprises the story of a . . . tremendous disaster such as had never happened before, and which struck all the world, though the Muslims above all. If anyone were to say that at no time since the creation of man by the great God had the world experienced anything like it, he would only be telling the truth . . . It may well be that the world from now until its end . . . will not experience the like of it again. (Quoted from Bertold Spuler's *History of the Mongols.*)

Until recently, Western historians have tended to echo these sentiments. The present generation of historians, however, is prepared to look at the events of the vii/13th century with greater objectivity, and to note the positive benefits which accrued from the *pax Mongolica*, such as law and order and internal security; economic prosperity resulting from the (for the first time in history) uninterrupted flow of trade between Western Europe and the Far East; and the religious tolerance of the Mongol rulers (many of whom, at least initially, continued to adhere to their traditional pagan beliefs), which enabled Christians (of various rites), Jews, Muslims and Buddhists to live together in harmony.

Although it is true, as Bernard Lewis has said, that 'by abolishing the Baghdad caliphate the Mongols did little more than lay the ghost of something that was already dead', nevertheless for six hundred years the caliphate had been the visible symbol of the unity of the Islamic world, and this symbol had now been removed. For Iranians who, as we have seen, had steadfastly preserved their sense of separate identity throughout this long period, this was an event of the utmost importance. When Hülegü established a Mongol dynasty with his capital in Iran, Iran for the first time since late Antiquity ceased to be a mere geographical expression. By creating a state whose boundaries roughly coincided with those of the ancient Persian empires, Hülegü and his successors created, however unwittingly, the pre-conditions for the establishment of an Iranian national state under the Safavids at the beginning of the x/16th century. Moreover, the very religious tolerance (not to say indifference) of the Mongols, to which we have referred, deprived Sunnī or 'orthodox' Islam of its dominant position in Iran and facilitated the development of Shīʿism which became the official religion of the Safavid state.

The disintegration of the Il-Khānid empire after 736/1335 was followed shortly afterwards by the devastating campaigns of Tīmūr-i Lang (Tamerlane) between 783/1381 and 807/1404, campaigns which left a political vacuum in Iran in which various forces fought for supremacy for virtually a century. Finally, in 907/1501, a new dynasty, the Safavids, came to power in Azerbaijan and over the next decade extended its sway over the rest of Iran and Mesopotamia.

The Safavids: founders of modern Iran

The Safavid dynasty had its origins in a Sūfī order known as the Safawiyya from the name of its founder, Shaykh Safī ad-Dīn Ishāq, who died in 735/1334. This order was centred on the town of Ardabīl in Azerbaijan, and under Shaykh Safī's successors extended its proselytizing activities to most parts of Iran. About the middle of the ix/15th century, a new, militant note is to be detected in the utterances of the Safavid leaders as, exchanging the religious title of 'shaykh' for the secular one of 'sultan', they openly aspired to temporal power. Followers of the Safavids were by now to be found outside the borders of Iran; indeed, their strongest military support came from the Shīʿī Turcoman tribes of eastern Anatolia, the Armenian highlands and northern Syria. Known as Qızıl-bash ('Redheads') because of their distinctive scarlet headgear, these tribes constituted the élite troops which swept the Safavids to power in 907/1501.

On the one hand, the promulgation of Shīʿism as the official religion of the Safavid state was a unifying force within the Safavid empire and enabled the Safavids to make use of latent Iranian nationalist sentiment; on the other hand, it brought the Safavids into direct conflict with the Sunnī Ottoman empire, and led to two centuries of intermittent warfare between these two powerful Muslim states. The Safavids restored law and order and

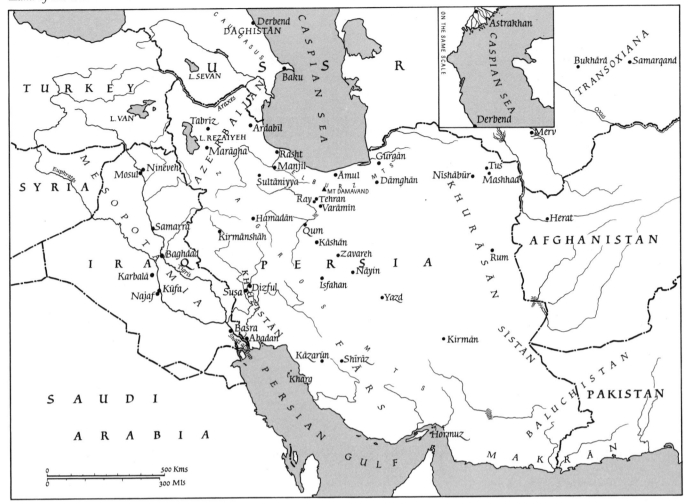

Persia, showing sites and natural features mentioned in the chapter. (2)

stable government, and established the first native dynasty to rule over the whole of Iran since the Arab conquest eight and a half centuries previously; they may therefore with justice be considered the founders of modern Iran.

The Safavids were at the height of their power under Shāh 'Abbās I (996-1038/1588-1629). The formidable Ottomans, who had made substantial inroads into Persian territory during the reigns of his immediate predecessors, were driven back behind their own borders. Shāh 'Abbās inaugurated an unprecedented period of prosperity by abandoning the bigoted attitude adopted by Shāh Tahmāsp (930-84/1524-76) toward commercial operations by foreign merchants in Iran; by permitting various Catholic orders to establish convents in Iran and carry on missionary activity unhindered, Shāh 'Abbās created a climate of religious tolerance which encouraged foreign merchants to live and work in Iran, where the Shāh granted them trading privileges. The court of Shāh 'Abbās was frequented by ambassadors from many European powers, including Spain, Portugal and England, and the Shāh tried in vain to enlist the aid of these powers against their mutual enemy, the Ottomans. The reign of Shāh 'Abbās also marks the culmination of that remarkable flowering of the arts which occurred under the patronage of the Safavid shāhs. In painting and the illumination of manuscripts, the productions of the reign of Shāh Tahmāsp are superior, but in carpet-weaving, textiles and metalwork, those of the period of Shāh

'Abbās are unequalled, and the architectural masterpieces of the latter's capital, Isfahan, are unsurpassed. Shāh 'Abbās was also an indefatigable erector of public buildings of all kinds, and even today, if the traveller enquires who built a certain ruined caravanserai, the inevitable answer is, 'Shāh 'Abbās'.

After Shāh 'Abbās I, Safavid power began to decline, and in 1135/1722 a small Afghan army demonstrated the weakness of the state by invading Iran and starving Isfahan into submission. Seven years later, the intruders were expelled by Nādir Khān Afshār, who made himself shāh in 1148/1736. Nādir Shāh was a brilliant soldier but left the country in administrative and financial chaos, and his assassination in 1160/1747 was followed by half a century of civil war between the Zand and Qājār factions; the Qājārs ultimately emerged victorious and established a dynasty which ruled Iran until the *coup d'état* of Ridā (Rizā) Khān in 1339/1921.

The mystique of the monarchy

Without question, the factor which has contributed most to the preservation of Iranian culture through all the political vicissitudes which Iran has experienced and military disasters which it has suffered, is the institution of the monarchy and the mystical aura surrounding it. The king of Iran is no ordinary king; historically, he is the *Shāhanshāh*, the 'king of kings', the paramount ruler who has subdued other kings and rendered them subject to him; to quote Darius again: 'These are the provinces

247

which are subject to me . . . twenty-three lands in all'. To the Greeks, the Persian monarch was βασιλεύς, 'the Great King', the supreme example of autocracy, and both Greek and Jewish sources bear witness to the existence of the doctrine of the divine right of the Persian kings from the foundation of the Achaemenid empire by Cyrus. In our times, kingship is a 'declining profession', and E. Burke Inlow has pointed out that, 'of the three great imperial rulers of the ancient world to enter the twentieth century – the Emperors of China, the Pharaohs of Egypt, and the Kings of Persia – only the Persian still reigns'. This fact postulates a monarchical tradition of unusual strength and tenacity. And I must emphasize that it is only a *tradition*. We are not dealing with 2,500 years of continuous empire, with king following king in unbroken dynastic succession. On the contrary, as we have seen, for eight and a half centuries no ruler of Iranian origin held political power. This makes the continuance of the tradition the more remarkable. We have to recognize that we are dealing with 'something deep and timeless and gaunt with age', to use Inlow's memorable phrase.

The symbol of this divine right to rule was the 'kingly glory' or 'royal splendour', which was called in Old Persian *hvarnah*, in Avestan *khvarnah*, and in Modern Persian *farr*. The possession of this 'kingly glory' marked the sacred character of Persian kingship. It is depicted as a visible aura surrounding the head of the monarch. The messianic role of the king as the saviour of his people was also inherent in the Persian concept of kingship, and with it was associated an Iranian myth which has analogies with Moses in the bulrushes, Romulus and Remus, and stories associated with the founders of other dynasties. Richard N. Frye puts it thus : —

> The general features of this myth, which then becomes the real history for the Persians, are relationship to the preceding dynasty or possessing royal blood, persecution with flight or exile, and concealment of royal origins, plus a difficult life among nomads or peasants. Finally a son, grandson or later descendant of the exile by manifest signs and qualities receives recognition and the *khvarnah* or imperial glory descends upon him so that he founds a new dynasty.

In Iran today, we see in operation this ancient Persian dogma of the divine right of kings as slightly modified by the Persian Constitution of 1324/1906. Though the Shāh is no longer the 'Shadow of God upon Earth', he still retains the charisma of the *Shāhanshāh* or 'king of kings'. In our egalitarian age, some look askance at such a concept of kingship, but the fact remains that the institution of the monarchy lies at the heart of Persian culture and tradition, and recognition of this fact is of fundamental importance to an understanding of Iran, whether past or present.

The land and the people

The physical geography of Iran has had a marked influence on the course of its history. With the exception of the Caspian littoral, it is a harsh and inhospitable land of barren plains and rugged mountains stripped bare of soil by centuries of erosion often brought about by man's deforestation. Much of the eastern side of the country is made up of salt deserts and stony wastes. The climate is

Painted dish, from the early VII/13th century. It shows one of the petty kings among whom Iran was divided after the period of the Seljuqs and before the main Mongol invasion. (3)

one of extremes: temperatures can rise as high as 140° F in summer near the Persian Gulf, and fall as low as −11° F at Hamadān in winter. As Cyrus the Younger remarked over two thousand years ago, 'My father's empire reaches southwards as far as where it is too hot for men to live, and northwards to where it is too cold.'

The two principal mountain chains form the shape of a V with its apex in north-western Iran; from this apex, the Zagros chain runs south-east towards the Persian Gulf, achieving a maximum height of about 15,000 feet, while the Elburz chain roughly follows the southern shore of the Caspian Sea, reaches its highest point at Mt Damāvand (18,600 ft) north-east of Tehran, and then tapers off in the direction of Gurgān. The Elburz is responsible for the semi-tropical zone of the Caspian littoral, for the prevailing northerly winds pick up moisture from the Caspian Sea which is shed in the form of rainfall when the winds strike the mountain barrier. North of the Elburz the abundant rainfall (26 to 76 in. annually), spread over the four seasons, permits the cultivation of rice, tobacco, tea, oranges and other citrus fruits. South of the Elburz, the contrast is dramatic; the mountain slopes are devoid of vegetation, and the minimal annual rainfall on the plateau (5 in. at Isfahan; 10 in. at Mashhad; 3 in. at Yazd), most of it concentrated between November and April, means that as a general rule agriculture is possible only by means of irrigation. Here, the mountain chains assume a vital role, because they trap the winter precipitation in the form of snow and release it steadily over the spring and summer months as the snow thaws. In the past, lack of snow during the winter meant the certainty of drought during the summer, but the construction of dams during the last fifteen years has improved the situation.

Unfortunately, Iran is not blessed with large rivers and, because the central plateau is a saucer-shaped depression, some of the rivers which do exist do not find their way to the sea but peter out in salt wastes and deserts. Iran is coming to the end of what may be achieved by damming its rivers, and the problem of producing enough water for a rapidly expanding (currently 35 million) population is acute. The production of fresh water by means of desalination would appear to be the only long-term solution. Over much of the country, water is led in underground water-channels called *qanāts*, sometimes over distances of as much as fifty miles, and then distributed through surface channels called *jūbs* to irrigate the fields and orchards. This *qanāt* system is of ancient origin, and is costly and dangerous both to construct and to maintain. But the *qanāts*, the course of which may be traced from the air as a series of crater-like depressions, are Iran's veritable lifelines; these apparent craters are in fact the mouths of the shafts which are dug at regular intervals both to take air down to the *qanāt*-diggers and to enable the excavated material to be brought to the surface. Apart from the Caspian littoral, the rainfall is sufficient for the cultivation of non-irrigated crops only in parts of Azerbaijan and in certain other limited areas. Because of the general aridity of the plateau, the contrast between the desert and the sown areas is startling.

The natural barrier of the southern extension of the Caucasus mountain chains has always protected Iran from the west and north-west, and invaders have been channelled into a number of well-defined and easily defended routes through the mountains. The north-east frontier, however, has always lain at the mercy of nomadic invaders from Central Asia. Across this frontier, over the ages, have poured the White Huns, the Turks and the Mongols. The problem of the defence of this frontier was never solved by any dynasty, because the Oxus River was readily fordable at a number of points, and, once across the river, the invaders could raid deep into Khurāsān, looting and pillaging. Before adequate forces could be mobilized to move against them, the marauders had retired across the Oxus with their booty. Defensive lines of forts proved inadequate, because these could either be

ignored and by-passed by the invaders or surrounded and starved into submission. Even the powerful Safavid dynasty, which ruled Iran from the x/16th to the xII/18th century, failed to solve this problem, though on two occasions the Safavids lured the Özbeg forces into a pitched battle and inflicted a signal defeat on them. Defensive alliances with local Özbeg rulers in the frontier regions worked for a time, but inevitably broke down as the result of treachery, ambition and intrigue. Only twice in Islamic times was the defence of the north-east frontier adequately secured, under the Sāmānid rulers in the III/9th–IV/10th centuries and under the Tīmūrids in the IX/15th century. In each case, the dynasty governed the territory on both sides of the Oxus, that is, the province of Transoxiana as well as that of Khurāsān. For the rest, Persia was unable to maintain control of Transoxiana, and the only answer – had the building material been available – would probably have been a Persian equivalent of the Great Wall of China.

Iran's role in history, dictated by its geography, has been that of a land bridge between Europe, Anatolia and the Mediterranean world on the one hand, and Central Asia and India and South-East Asia on the other. Across Iran in medieval times wound trade caravans, some following the famous silk route to China. With the rise of the Ottoman empire, a formidable obstacle was erected astride Iran's land communications with Europe, since for several centuries Iran was in a state of war, declared or undeclared, with the Ottoman empire. Persian merchants bound for Europe were obliged to take ship from Gilan to Baku or Astrakhan, and then travel overland through Russia or attempt the hazardous northern sea route via Archangel.

The many waves of invasion which have swept across Iran in the course of the centuries have left their mark in the form of racial diversity. Today, this diversity is most clearly seen among the semi-nomadic tribes, who live on the periphery of the plateau and still constitute an important part of Iranian life. Some of these tribes, like

Persian rural life under Sulaymān I, as depicted by a European traveller. The tree in the centre is a date palm. Under it sits a man smoking a hookah. To the left and right are wells, worked by oxen. Various agricultural implements are shown, including plough and harrow, and threshing is in progress. The column of camels at the back seems to be making for the caravanserai, shown right. (4)

the Kurds and the Lurs, are of Aryan origin and speak a dialect of Persian; others, like the various Turcoman tribes of Azerbaijan and Khurāsān, are of Turkic origin, and speak dialects of Turkish. In Fārs, the Qashqā'ī are of mixed Turkish and Persian stock, the Khamseh of mixed Turkish and Arab blood, while the tribes in Khūzistān, on the borders of Iraq, are mainly Arabs. Many of these tribes are transhumant – that is, they migrate twice a year: in late spring they travel from the hot lowlands to the high mountain valleys in search of pasture, and in the late autumn they return to their lower camping grounds. On these migrations, they take with them all their worldly belongings, tents, and flocks of sheep and goats which constitute their means of livelihood. The migrations through rugged mountain country are arduous in the extreme, and involve losses in both men and beasts. The tribesmen of Iran are of an independent nature, and have resisted government attempts, notably under Ridā (Rizā) Shāh, to sedentarize them. They are economically virtually self-sufficient, since their flocks provide them with meat, clothing, material for tents, milk, cheese and yoghurt; they also provide the wool from which the women weave rugs, saddle-bags and many other articles which are not only of practical value in the everyday life of the tribes but find a ready sale in the cities. The income from the sale of rugs and surplus meat and milk products enables the tribesmen to purchase whatever other items they need. Regarded by some as an anachronism, the tribes cling stubbornly to their traditional ways, and of recent years both they and the government have discovered the value of tribal dances, marriage-ceremonies, etc., as tourist attractions.

The Iranian contribution: religion and philosophy

The 'dominant function of the Persian mind has long been recognized as part-solvent, part-catalytic,' wrote G. M. Wickens. These words, it seems to me, form an admirable introduction to a discussion of Iran's contribution to Islamic culture and to world civilization in general. Islam, in its purest, early Arabian, form, was a rather stark and bare type of monotheism. When the Arabs conquered Iran in the I/7th century, Islam came into contact, not only with the ancient Iranian dualist religion, Zoroastrianism, but also with the 'dark, rich flood' of ancient Iranian culture. In Sunnī Islam, the (religious) law soon came to exceed theology in importance, and the subtle, speculative Iranian mind could not be satisfied by the arid disputes of the Islamic jurisprudents. When Islamic theology became involved, for instance, in endless debates on the question of free will versus predestination, the Persian mind grasped the possibility that 'opposites are merely the obverse and reverse of the Divine Mind', to quote Wickens again. In giving this mystical solution to a theological problem, the Persians demonstrated the extent to which mysticism had permeated their understanding and interpretation of the Islamic faith. Islamic mysticism, or Sūfism, has been called the supreme manifestation of the Persian mind in the religious sphere; although it is true that not all Islamic mystics were Persians, it is also true that neither the Arabs, the Turks nor Indian Muslims produced mystics of the stature of the Persians Sanā'ī, Nizāmī, Jalāl ad-Dīn Rūmī, al-Ghazālī, Farīd ad-Dīn 'Attār and Hāfiz. Their place in

the story of Islamic mysticism as a whole has been described by Professor Meier in Chapter IV.

If the development of Sūfism within Islam to the point at which it became virtually a religion within a religion was largely the work of Persians, the divorce of Shī'ism from its purely political, Arab, origins and its development into the official religion of the Iranian state is a purely Persian phenomenon. Initially, Shī'ism provided Persians with a means of expressing their feelings of frustration and discontent under Arab rule. Later, under Turkish and Mongol rule, when official Sunnism was tied closely to the interests of the rulers, Shī'ism became associated with numerous movements directed against the established order.

Iranians adopted the legend that 'Alī's younger son, Husayn, married a daughter of the last Sāsānid king, Yazdigird III. When Husayn was killed at Karbalā by the troops of the Umayyad Caliph Yazīd, Shī'ism acquired a martyr-figure with a powerful and lasting emotive effect. The events connected with the death of Husayn were, and still are, commemorated by mourning processions and by the performance of passion plays called *ta'ziya*. A few lines from a XIII/19th-century threnody on the martyrdom of Husayn may give, even in translation (by E. G. Browne), some idea of the emotive effect of these performances:

> Was he slain unthirsting? No! Did none give him to drink? They did!
> Who? Shimr! From what source? From the source of Death!
> Was he an innocent martyr? Yes! Had he committed any fault? No!
> What was his work? Guidance! Who was his friend? God!
> Who wrought this wrong? Yazīd! Who is this Yazīd? One of the children of Hind! By whom? By bastard origin!

During the periods when Iran was dominated by foreign powers, the performance of the passion plays had a cathartic effect. In 907/1501, when Shāh Ismā'īl I established the Safavid dynasty, he made Shī'ism the official religion of the new state, and so satisfied the latent nationalist aspirations for which Shī'ism had been the medium of expression for eight and a half centuries.

Through the medium of Shī'ism, the Persians introduced into Islam certain theological concepts and dogmas which were absent from Sunnī Islam; of these the most distinctive is the doctrine of the imamate. The function of the Shī'ī imam should not be confused with that of the Sunnī imam, who technically is simply the leader of the Muslim community in the congregational prayers in the mosque. The Shī'ī imams, on the other hand, possess the pre-eminent prerogatives of being the witnesses and interpreters of the revelation, and are the sole repositories of all truth and knowledge. They are distinguished by two special characteristics which have no parallel in Sunnī Islam. The first is the doctrine of intercession, and the redemptive nature of the death and suffering of the imams. The second is the doctrine of the sinlessness, or infallibility of the imams. The latter doctrine, which we find formulated by Shī'ī theologians as early as the IV/10th century, was clearly designed to establish the superiority of the Shi'i imams over the Sunni caliphs, but its implications for Islam were even more fundamental than this: it supplied Islam with an infallible authority in an incarnate form.

The Iranian contribution: literature, science and art
Each of these subjects has a separate chapter devoted to it in this book, and it is therefore unnecessary to give more than a brief outline here. In each case it will be seen that Iran's contribution was of major importance, often clearly dominating the rest of the Islamic world.

As Professor Pellat rightly stresses (Chapter V), there was an intimate alliance between Persian mysticism and Persian literature. The ecstasy of the soul at the moment of reunion with the Creator has never been more beautifully expressed that in the work of Jalāl ad-Dīn Rūmī, and he is but *primus inter pares* in the pantheon of the great Persian mystical poets. Ranking close to him in sublimity are Farīd ad-Dīn 'Attār and Hāfiz of Shīrāz, who brought allegorical mystical expression to its highest pitch of refinement. Hāfiz has never been surpassed. Indeed, after him the symbolism of the mystic (the lover) in search of the Beloved (God), expressed, for example, in the imagery of the nightingale complaining of the cruel indifference of that thorny beauty, the rose, or of the moth hovering round the candle, willing to achieve union with it at the expense of being consumed in its flame, became stereotyped and hackneyed.

Other poets, of whom 'Umar Khayyām is the best known (though his principal claim to fame is as a mathematician, and without the genius of Fitzgerald it is doubtful whether he would have obtained much renown in the West), reveal another strain which is characteristic of the Persian mind; a melancholy pessimism, a sense of the ephemeral and transient nature of earthly power and pomp which is so succinctly expressed in the favourite saying of mystics: 'All else perisheth save His face.'

The part played by Persia in the development of Islamic science again needs no underlining, and is fully treated by Professor Sabra in Chapter VII. Persian mathematics was from the first essentially practical because the caliphs, who extended royal patronage to research in the sciences, wanted mathematics to be used to solve problems in navigation, astronomy, architecture, surveying and the calculation of the calendar, and for such purposes as determining the direction of Mecca. In the pre-Mongol period three names stand out: the III/9th-century al-Khwārizmī, who gave us the words 'logarithm' and 'algebra'; 'Umar Khayyām, who classified the forms of cubic equations; and al-Bīrūnī (363-440/973-1048), one of the greatest geniuses of the medieval world, who reformed the calendar, determined latitudes and longitudes and did pioneering work in empirical physics.

The Persian contribution to medicine consisted of advances in treatment rather than diagnosis. Persia led the world in pharmacy. The III/9th-century pharmacopeia of Sābūr ibn Sahl and the *Antidotary* of Ibn at-Tilmīdh formed the basis of all subsequent works of this kind. Without question, the greatest Persian physician and one of the greatest physicians of the medieval world, was ar-Rāzī, known to the West as Rhazes. His chief work, the encyclopaedic *al-Hāwī*, became a standard textbook in European universities.

It is, however, through her art that the golden age of Iran comes most vividly to life for anyone outside the Islamic world, and although its character and achievement are discussed and illustrated in Professor Ettinghausen's chapter, it cannot be passed over here in complete silence.

Persian art is essentially aristocratic art, in the sense that it was royalty and the upper classes of society which created the demand for works of art and thus stimulated the activity of artists and craftsmen, and also in the sense that these aristocratic patrons frequently dictated what kind of art and what type of objects should be produced. In other words, the patrons were also to a large extent the arbiters of artistic taste, and there was no such thing as 'bourgeois' or 'primitive' art. This is true even of that most characteristic of Persian art forms, the carpet, which originated in the tribal rug, woven by the women and children of the semi-nomadic tribes, using the wool from their own flocks and mainly natural dyes. It was left to the Safavids to develop carpet-weaving from a cottage industry to a fine art on a national scale, and the continuing prestige of Persian carpets derives from the standards achieved at this time; the superior quality and the perfection of colour and design.

The weaving of textiles has an equally long history, going back to Sāsānid times, and here too the Safavid period represents the high point. A taste for Persian fabrics, with their complicated weaves, brilliant colours and apparently unfailing inventiveness of design, spread to Renaissance Europe and Russia. Yazd, Kāshān, Rasht and Isfahan became the great centres of Persian weaving.

Persia never conformed to the general Islamic ban on the representation of the human body in works of art. Basins, dishes, ewers, candlesticks, astrolabes, weapons and many items of household use were decorated with animals and human figures in hunting and other scenes. The Mongol invasions seem to have caused the flight of so many skilled metalworkers to Cairo and other parts of the Islamic world that Persian metalwork suffered a decline until its revival under the Tīmūrids in the IX/15th century. Under the Safavids, designs became smaller and more delicate.

Persia was also supreme in the art of the book. In each of its four main aspects – calligraphy, bookbinding, illumination and illustration – Persian artists reached the peak of perfection. Early Islamic manuscripts were usually written on vellum, later on paper (the manufacture of which the Arabs learned indirectly from the Chinese), in the powerful uncompromising Kūfic or Naskhī script. It was the Persians who invented the more cursive, more delicate Nasta'līq script. Manuscripts were embellished by one or more whole pages of illumination, and the pages of the text were adorned with illuminated and gilded borders and other ornamentation; the chapter headings were frequently contained within panels which were little masterpieces of artistry. The miniature-painter found material most suited to the exercise of his art either in the unending pageant of the Iranian national epic, or in scenes from one of the great romantic epics such as *Laylā and Majnūn*, *Khusrāw and Shīrīn*, *Yūsuf and Zulaykhā* and the like. Those enthusiastic IX/15th-century bibliophiles, the Tīmūrid ruler Shāh Rukh and his son Bāysunqur, commissioned some of the

The Sāsānid inheritance influenced Islamic art both within the confines of Iran and outside. The dragon-peacock, for instance, occurs on Sāsānid textiles and reliefs. This example (left) is on a piece of woven silk made on the eve of the Muslim conquest. On the right is a detail from the façade of the palace of Mshatta of a century later, about 123/740. (5, 6)

finest Islamic manuscripts, and the last Tīmūrid ruler, Sultan Husayn ibn Bāyqarā, bequeathed to the Safavids the brilliant Herat school of painting of which Bihzād was the outstanding member.

The magnificent *The Book of Kings*, which contains over two hundred and fifty miniature paintings, was probably commissioned by Shāh Ismāʿīl for his son Tahmāsp, though the work was not completed until after Ismāʿīl's death. The unique position of this work in the history of Persian painting may be judged by the fact that no other contemporary manuscript contains more than fourteen miniature paintings.

The skills of the miniature-painter were transferred to the tooling and embossing of leather for the covers of manuscripts. The detail of the design of book covers is sometimes as intricate as the design of miniatures themselves, and, by the x/16th century, court painters like Ridā ʿAbbāsī had extended their technique to lacquer paintings which were used as book covers and also on such items as trays, dishes, pen cases, mirror cases and boxes of all kinds.

From early times, Persians had made significant contributions to the development of architecture. The Sāsānids had made great advances in vaulting techniques, and the invention of the squinch, which solved the problem of how to erect a circular dome over a square room, was a major achievement. The contribution of the Seljuqs (v/11th and vi/12th centuries) consisted in the superb use of ornamental brickwork, and this technique was continued in the vii/13th century under the Il-Khāns. At the same time, the use of faience decoration was developed, and stucco was widely used for ornamentation. In Tīmūrid times the double dome was introduced into Iran, and the slightly bulbous shape of the outer dome became a constant feature of Persian domes from then on. The Safavids not only brought the use of

polychrome *(haft-rang)* and mosaic *(muʿarraq)* tile to its highest pitch of perfection, but Shāh ʿAbbās I, when he made Isfahan his capital in 1007/1598, grouped a number of architectural masterpieces round a piazza *(maydān)* seven times the size of the Piazza San Marco to create one of the world's most inspired instances of town planning. Persian architecture developed along entirely different lines from those of Europe. Whereas Gothic architecture did its best to conceal the basic form of the building under a wealth of spires, belfries, gargoyles, pinnacles, flying buttresses and the like, the aim of Persian architects was to clothe the basic structure in the richest possible robe, but without obscuring its lines and fundamental form. It is the unsurpassed mastery of the use of polychrome and mosaic tiles which probably constitutes the greatest Persian contribution to Islamic architecture.

No account of the Iranian world would be complete without some reference to Persian gardens. Those who are familiar with the well-manicured gardens of the West will be disappointed by Persian gardens if they do not understand their essential function, namely, to provide cool shade for the traveller bemused by the merciless sun of the Persian plains, with the sound of running water to delight his ear and trees and flowers to refresh his eye. The Persian insistence on straight rows of trees and regularly planted bushes is explained at least in part by the exigencies of irrigation channels. The Persian love of trees, strong in Achaemenid times, is undiminished today. Xerxes, we are told, so admired a plane tree when he was on his way to Sardis that he hung golden chains and armlets on its branches, and Cyrus the Younger (d. 401 BC) laid out a garden at Sardis and planted some of the trees himself; today, modern Tehranis will water the trees lining the streets in which they live, even though the trees are not on their property. The favourite Persian flower is the rose, and it is no coincidence that Persian poetry is so full of references to it, or that it has come to represent, in Sūfī terminology, the beautiful but cruel Beloved whose thorns keep the languishing lover at bay, and whose fickle behaviour drives him to distraction. Even flowers are not essential to a Persian's concept of a garden, as long as trees are present; 'such beauty as arises from shade and the purling of water', said Lord Curzon, 'is all that the Persian requires'. It is appropriate that our word 'paradise' should derive from an Old Persian word meaning 'enclosed park' or 'hunting preserve'.

Relations between Iran and the West

Throughout the Middle Ages, Islam and Christendom were mutually ignorant the one of the other; but the basis of Muslim and Christian ignorance differed. Muslims were ignorant of the West because they were indifferent to the activities of the 'northern barbarians', as a v/11th-century Muslim judge in Toledo termed most Europeans. The Christian attitude toward Islam was based partly on *odium theologicum*, because Islam, as the only major world religion revealed after Christianity, obviously posed a theological problem to Christians, and partly on fear, because the expansion of the Islamic empire into Sicily and Spain, and Muslim control of the Mediterranean, constituted a military threat to Christendom. On the theological level, the standard Christian answer was that Muhammad was an impostor, and Islam a heresy. On the military level, the Christian response was the Crusades. Neither response was calculated to make the West either better informed as to the nature of the Islamic faith or the political realities of the Muslim world.

What is curious, and irritating to the historian, is the persistence and tenacity of the 'Golden Road to Samarqand' syndrome. Persian carpets have had an obstinate tendency to turn into magic carpets, and Persian gardens into exchanted gardens inhabited by peris, genii and the like. Even Persian cats have retained an indefinably exotic aura, and of course the harem has been a perennial source of interest to overheated imaginations. Fantasies masquerading as serious accounts of Persia, such as the VIII/14th-century publication of that 'undaunted liar', 'Sir John Mandeville', and descriptions of the dream world of the 'Arabian' Nights, which was located in a legendary Persian empire, made matters worse, so much so that in the *British Critic* of 1797 a reviewer doubted whether, amidst 'such a mass of absurdity', 'fictions so romantic and characters so monstrous', the 'vestiges of genuine historic truth' could ever be successfully explored. The truth was, until the XI/17th century, that the Western man-in-the-street had little solid material to bite on; in that century, travellers such as the Huguenot jeweller Chardin for the first time gave the West a picture of the Persian system of government that was largely accurate and penetrating in its insights. But it was not really until the XIII/19th century, that 'vestiges of historic truth' became visible.

Despite the rigours and dangers of the journey, intrepid spirits had travelled between the West and Persia since ancient times. In the 6th century AD the Persian bishop St Ivo had travelled to England, but thereafter the rise of Islam, the Arab conquests both north and south of the Mediterranean and the establishment of the Islamic empire of the caliphate, cut Persia off from Western Europe. It was not until the Mongol invasions of the VII/13th century and the establishment of the *pax Mongolica* from China to Poland, that unhindered, safe travel between Persia and the West again became possible. Reports reached the West that some of the Mongols were Christians, and the rulers of Western Europe saw the Mongols as possible allies in the unending struggle between Christendom and Islam. In 643/1245 King Louis IX of France sent a group of Dominican friars to Persia; and this was the first of a number of diplomatic and missionary missions which yielded no positive result as far as an alliance was concerned, but at least gave the West more accurate information than it hitherto possessed about the geography of Persia and surrounding regions, and about the manners and customs of the inhabitants of Western and Central Asia.

In 659/1260, after the Mongols had suffered a signal defeat at the hands of the Mamlūks in Syria, the Mongol ruler of Persia and Mesopotamia, Hülegü, sent an envoy in his turn to Pope Alexander IV; the envoy informed the Pope of his royal master's desire to be baptized, but his statement was greeted with scepticism. In the event, Hülegü remained a Buddhist, but these diplomatic exchanges opened the way for Western merchants to carry on trade in Persia, and in 663/1264 we find a Venetian merchant established at Tabrīz. Diplomatic missions continued to be exchanged with the West by the Mongol Il-Khāns of Iran until the break-up of the Il-Khānid empire after 736/1335; relations were only briefly interrupted during the reign of Tegüder, who became a convert to Islam. Many of the Il-Khānid rulers, of course, were strongly influenced in state affairs by their Christian wives. The constantly proposed military alliance of the Mongols and the West against the Muslims came nearest to materializing in 690/1291, when the Il-Khān Arghūn proposed to Philip IV of France and Edward I of England a joint attack on Damascus, but once again the plans came to nought, because of the death of Arghūn in 690 March 1291 and the preoccupation of Edward I with his Scottish wars.

The commercial benefits of this century of intercourse between Persia and the West were more solid than were the diplomatic or military results. Tabrīz, the chief town of the province of Azerbaijan, already mentioned as a centre of European commercial activity, became the capital of Iran under the Mongols and a flourishing entrepôt for trade between Europe and Baghdad, the Persian Gulf and India. During the same period, the Dominican order extended its missionary activities in Iran and established a number of bishoprics in the northwest, but its proselytizing efforts fell on stony ground.

The disintegration of the Il-Khānid empire was followed by an unsettled period in Iran during which travel through the country was hazardous; in consequence, trade with the West virtually ceased. By the middle of the VIII/14th century, the rising power of the Ottoman Turks had presented Europe with a new threat, and the West saw in the Tatar conqueror Tamerlane (Tīmūr-i Lang) a possible ally against the Ottomans, a view that was encouraged by the great victory of Tīmūr over the Ottomans at Ankara in 805/1402. The death of Tīmūr in

Shāh Ismāʿīl I, the first of the Safavid kings, spent much of his reign (907–30/1501–24) fighting his enemies abroad – Ottomans to the west, Turcomans to the north and east – and his rivals at home. This coin, dated 913/1507, is an urdu *(literally: 'military camp'), indicating that it was minted while Shāh Ismāʿīl was on campaign. (7)*

807/1405, however, and the renewed expansion of the Ottoman empire culminating in the fall of Constantinople in 857/1453, administered a severe blow to European, particularly Venetian, commercial interests in the East.

In 892/1487, the Portuguese sea-captain Bartolomeu Diaz rounded the Cape of Good Hope and, ten years later, his compatriot Vasco da Gama repeated the feat and reached India. Persia had thus been outflanked as a way-station on the route to India, and yet another major blow had been inflicted on the Venetians, Genoese and others who had relied on the overland route in their trade with India and the Persian Gulf. Ten years after that, the Portuguese signified their intention of consolidating their hold on this valuable trade by occupying the island of Hormuz, and Albuquerque permanently annexed the island in 621/1515 and made the King of Hormuz a Portuguese vassal. This occurred only a year after the Ottomans had decisively defeated Shāh Ismāʿīl I at the Battle of Chāldirān, and the latter was consequently in no position to prevent this Portuguese encroachment on his territory.

With the accession of Shāh ʿAbbās I (996-1038/1588-1629), diplomatic and commercial activity between Persia and the West increased. Shāh ʿAbbās, eager to promote trade, especially the silk trade, with the West, received embassies from Spain, Portugal and England, and, by encouraging the Carmelites, Augustinians and other Catholic orders to establish convents in Iran, he created a favourable atmosphere in which not only foreign missionaries but also merchants could live and work. The Shāh even paid part of the cost of decorating one of the mission churches in Isfahan. In 1032/1622 Shāh ʿAbbās made use of the commercial rivalry among the Western powers and enlisted the assistance of the English in expelling the Portuguese from the island of Hormuz, which they had occupied for over a century.

We have seen that during the VII/13th century diplomatic exchanges occurred between Western rulers and the Mongol Il-Khāns of Persia; these exchanges had as their object joint military action against the Muslim Mamlūk rulers of Egypt, the Holy Land and Syria. During the Safavid period, the idea of a military alliance between Persia and the Western powers was revived in a different form; this time, the Muslim (but Shīʿī) Safavid state tried to enlist the assistance of Christian powers against the Muslim (but Sunnī) Ottoman empire, with which it was locked in deadly struggle for two centuries. The idea was attractive to the West, because the stepping-up of operations against the Ottoman Turks in the East would, it was hoped, force the latter to relax their pressure on Europe. Despite a flurry of diplomatic activity, however, nothing in the way of joint military action was achieved.

In 1026/1617 or shortly afterwards, the English East India Company, having received a *farmān* from Shāh ʿAbbās I, opened factories at Shīrāz and Isfahan, and decided on Jāsk on the Makrān coast as the principal port of entry for their goods. The combined operation with Persian forces which expelled the Portuguese from Hormuz in 1032/1622 meant the end of the influence of the Portuguese in the Persian Gulf, but the Dutch took their place as challengers of England's commercial supremacy there. The growing rivalry between the Levant Company and the East India Company began to have an adverse effect on smooth trade relations between Persia and England.

The Persians had never given up hope of negotiating a military alliance with European powers with the object of joint military action against the Turks, and in 1017/1608 and again in 1024/1615 Shāh ʿAbbās I sent the English gentleman-adventurer, Sir Robert Sherley, to Europe as his personal envoy to try and effect an alliance, but he had no success. In 1090/1679, when the Swedes sent an ambassador to Iran to try and induce the Persians to attack the Turks, the situation was reversed, because the Safavid dynasty was in decline and the Shāh at the time, Sulaymān, not of a martial disposition.

Towards the end of the XII/18th century, Persia was dragged into the arena of Great Power political and commercial rivalry in the Middle East. Napoleon dreamed of invading India by way of Persia, and, after French aspirations in the area had been dispelled, Britain and Russia embarked on a century and a half of political and economic rivalry in the country. The role of Britain, obsessed by the need to protect its Indian empire, was essentially defensive; that of Russia, striving always to attain Peter the Great's goal of a warm-water port on the Persian Gulf, essentially aggressive. During the XIII/19th century, a succession of weak and incompetent rulers burdened Iran with foreign debts, and allowed much of the country's economic resources to fall into the hands of foreign concessionaires. Today, Tehran is once more a centre of diplomatic and commercial activity as Iran, no longer dependent on foreign aid, negotiates on the basis of equality with foreign entrepreneurs.

Modern Iran

On 30 December 1906, when Muzaffar ad-Dīn Shāh signed the *qānūn-i asāsī* or 'fundamental law', Iran acquired a constitution; this was supplemented by an additional constitutional instrument on 7 October 1907. A National Consultative Assembly was established (*Majlis-i Shūrā-yi Millī*, called 'the Majlis' for short), and met for the first time on 7 October 1906. An upper house, termed the Senate, was provided for in the Constitution but not convened until 1950. Subsequent struggles between the Shāh, Muhammad 'Alī, who succeeded his father on 8 January 1907, and the Nationalist parties weakened the country and led to foreign intervention. In 1911 Russian troops marched on Tehran and forced the government to capitulate. Russia remained in complete control of northern Iran until the outbreak of World War I.

Iran officially declared itself neutral in this conflict, but Turkish, Russian and British troops operated on its territory, and German agents were active in many areas. In these circumstances, the central government lost all administrative control of the provinces, and became bankrupt financially. After the Russian Revolution an attempt was made, in 1920, to establish a Soviet Socialist Republic in Iran, but when this failed the Russians finally withdrew.

Iran regained control of its own territory when Ridā (Rizā) Khān seized power in February 1921. In 1925 the Qājār dynasty was officially terminated, and the Majlis voted to confer the monarchy of Ridā Khān, who was duly crowned early in 1926, as the first shāh of the new Pahlavī dynasty. Under Ridā Shāh, who reigned until Anglo-Russian pressure forced him to abdicate in 1941, the need for socio-economic reform was to a large extent subordinated to the over-riding necessity of ridding Iran of foreign political influence and bringing her into the 20th century as an independent nation. The construction of the Trans-Iranian railway was an outstanding achievement, but its alignment and the location of its termini were determined by political and not by economic considerations. In an effort to reduce dependence on foreign, especially Russian, imports, Ridā Shāh embarked on a programme of industrialization, but left untouched the fundamental problem of agrarian reform; by the same token, the achievement of true constitutional democracy had to wait upon the attainment of the primary goal of national independence. Ridā Shāh tended to regard the Majlis solely as an instrument to pass legislation initiated by him, and newspapers which opposed his policies were suppressed. Nevertheless, in sum, Ridā Shāh well deserves the title of the 'architect of independent Iran'.

In 1941, Iran, for a second time, and again against her will, became involved in a world war. As in 1914–18, the uninterrupted flow of Persian oil was vital to the Allied war effort; as in 1914–18, German agents were operating in Iran and one of their objectives was to cut off this flow of oil. In 1941, an additional factor gave Iran even greater strategic importance: this was the urgent need to supply the Soviet Union, then hard pressed by the Germans, with war material. To achieve this end, British and Russian troops jointly occupied Iran in August 1941. Ridā Shāh abdicated, and his twenty-one-year-old son succeeded him as Muhammad Ridā Shāh Pahlavī. Sir Winston Churchill's own comment on the Allied occupation of Persia is perhaps the most apt: '*Inter arma silent leges*' ('In times of war laws are silent').

By the end of 1946, the Allied forces had withdrawn, but the young Shāh faced intractable problems: inflation, shortages of food and materials, and renewed political activity by extremist groups of both Left and Right.

The year 1949 marks a turning-point in the history of modern Iran: the Shāh reacted to an attempt on his life by placing a ban on the Tūdeh (Communist) Party and the Communist-controlled trade unions; convinced that, without increasing his personal authority, he could not control the turbulent forces then threatening to cause a breakdown in government, he brought into being the Senate, or Upper House of the Persian parliament, thirty of whose sixty members were his own nominees. Through the Senate, the Shāh hoped to exert more influence over the Majlis; finally, in 1949, Dr Musaddiq formed the National Front, a coalition of political groups of widely differing political complexions ranging from the fanatical right-wing religious group called the *fidā'iyyān-i islām* to various left-wing splinter groups. The common goal which temporarily united these disparate elements was nationalization of the oil industry, then controlled by the Anglo-Iranian Oil Company in which the British government had a controlling interest. Musaddiq became Prime Minister in 1951, and the bill to nationalize the oil industry was passed. Diplomatic relations with Britain were broken off in October 1951, and in 1952 Musaddiq assumed dictatorial powers to deal with the political crisis generated by his inability to hold the National Front together and by the bankruptcy of the government caused by the cessation of oil revenue. In August 1953, Musaddiq fell from power, and in 1954 the Shāh signed a new oil agreement by which a consortium of foreign oil companies undertook to produce and market Persian oil on behalf of the National Iranian Oil Company (NIOC).

In 1953, the Shāh embarked on what he termed a programme of 'positive nationalism'. He resumed the distribution of crown lands to the peasants, which had been stopped by Musaddiq, and in 1956 he inaugurated the Second Seven-Year Plan for economic development. Many ambitious projects were completed: the Karaj dam (1961), the Farah dam at Manjil (1962) and the Muhammad Ridā Pahlavī dam near Dizful (1963) not only produced hydro-electricity but water to irrigate and bring under cultivation large areas of land.

Between 1957 and 1961, the Shāh attempted to rule as a constitutional monarch and initiate social and economic reforms, but the Majlis, still dominated by the landlords and other vested interests, with the powerful backing of the religious classes, blocked every attempt at reform, particularly in the vital area of land tenure. In 1961, the Shāh, despairing of making progress through the medium of the Majlis, decided to dissolve it and govern by decree in order to get his reform programme implemented. In 1962 a revised and expanded Agrarian Reform Bill became law: no landowner was allowed to own more than one village; all land in excess of this had to be sold to the government at a valuation based on taxes paid by the landlord; this land was to be redistributed to the peasants, who would pay for it in fifteen annual instalments; co-operatives were to be set up to facilitate the marketing of crops and the use of agricultural machinery. The Land Reform Law of 1962, and the supplementary legislation of 1963 and 1964, constituted what Hāfez Farmān-Farmāyān has called 'the greatest single piece of legislation in twenty-five centuries of Persian history'. In January 1963 the Shāh went to the people for endorsement by national referendum of his revised Six-Point Reform Programme: (1) land reform; (2) nationalization of forests; (3) sale of state-owned factories to private ownership; (4) profit-sharing scheme for industry; (5) creation of a Literacy Corps to combat illiteracy; (6) electoral reform, including the enfranchisement of women.

Thus began Iran's 'White Revolution'. The Shāh's programme was opposed by the National Front, the landowners, the religious classes, and the Tūdeh Party. It was supported by the army, the peasants, and a growing body of young technocrats and civil servants. Receiving an overwhelming endorsement for his reform programme in January 1963, the Shāh decided he could return to constitutional rule, and called general elections for September 1963. In June of that year, the National Front and the religious classes organized the worst riots in Tehran's history in a last attempt to challenge the Shāh; but the attempt was crushed. The elections took place as planned, and when the Majlis re-assembled in October 1963, after a lapse of over two years, it wore a new look. Instead of consisting of anything up to 90 per cent landowners, 70 per cent of the new parliament consisted of members of the new professional middle class – civil servants, doctors, businessmen and lawyers. An equally revolutionary feature of the twenty-first parliament was the presence of six women members in the Majlis, and two in the Senate.

In the late 1960s and early 1970s, the 'White Revolution of the Shāh and the people', as the Shāh liked to call it, enabled Iran to make unprecedented progress. Socio-economic development became the primary aim of the government, and the work of the three corps established by the Shāh – the Literacy Corps (1963), the Health Corps (1964) and the Reconstruction and Development Corps (1964) – had a tremendous social and economic impact. All three corps were staffed mainly by conscripts who, after their basic military training, spent the remainder of their service in the rural areas.

During the same period Iran's political stability and economic strength enabled it to play an active part in foreign affairs. In 1967, the formal termination of US economic aid to Iran marked the final stage of Iran's long journey along the path of true self-determination. Detente with the USSR enabled Iran to negotiate a number of major joint-projects: Iran's first, and long-awaited, steel mill, built by Soviet engineers, went into production near Isfahan in 1973; and the NIOC had an agreement to supply the Soviet Union with large quantities of natural gas. Other countries, notably Germany and Japan, signed contracts to build additional petrochemical plants in the south. Oil remained Iran's biggest revenue-earner, but the Shāh, recognizing that oil is a finite source (some estimates put Iran's reserves at no more than thirty-five years' supply), pressed ahead with nuclear power plant to provide an alternative source of energy. In the circumstances, it was not surprising that Iran tried to get the highest possible market price for its oil. Since relations with Iraq were anything but amicable, Iran transferred its main export terminal for petroleum products from Abadan island, only a stone's throw from Iraq across the narrow Shatt al-'Arab, to Bandar Māhshahr, a hundred miles to the south-east. At the same time, to accommodate today's super-tankers, a new deep-water terminal was constructed on Kharg island in the Persian Gulf, and oil was brought to the terminal from the oilfields, over a hundred miles away, by pipeline which is laid across the sea-bed to Kharg.

The Shah left Iran on 16 January 1979, and died in exile in Egypt on 27 July 1980. On 1 February 1979, Āyatullāh Khumaynī returned from Paris, and in March 1979 the new Islamic Republic of Iran was proclaimed. Khumaynī's intention of trying to overthrow those regimes in the Persian Gulf which have not accepted his leadership, were major factors in the outbreak of war between Iran and Iraq on 7 September 1980, a war which was to last for ten years.

One of the most striking features of the Khumaynī regime has been its policy of attempting to destroy the distinctive Iranian culture described in this chapter and to replace its symbols by Islamic ones. The monarchy has been replaced by the mosque as the cultural symbol of Iran. It remains to be seen whether, in the long term, the latter will retain its hold on the hearts and minds of Iranians.

Shī'ism, the national creed, was one of the main factors in the preservation of Persia's identity after the Arab conquest. From the point of view of orthodox Islam, Shī'ism is something of a heresy (it traces its authority to Muhammad's son-in-law 'Alī, and its most distinctive feature is the doctrine of the Twelve Imams – sole repositories of truth, intercessors with Allah, redeemers of mankind). But it was specifically Iranian, setting its adherents apart from the rest of the caliphate. When, under the Safavids, Iran regained her freedom, Shī'ism naturally became the official religion of the new state.

Persian identification with Shī'ism is here portrayed allegorically at the beginning of the most famous of all Persian books, the manuscript prepared for Shāh Tahmāsp (d. 984/1576) of Firdawsī's *Shahinshāh-nāma* ('The Book of Kings'). All the religions of the world (the poet counts seventy) set out across the sea of eternity. Only the Shī'ī one will come safely to land. It bears Muhammad, 'Alī and 'Alī's two sons, Hasan and Husayn. All are shown with flame-like haloes but veiled because of the Muslim ban on figural art – a ban which Iran only partially followed. The turban wound round a baton (*kulāh*) which they are wearing is a Safavid head-dress, especially at the time of Shāh Tahmāsp. (1)

'I, Darius, the great king, the king of kings, the King of Persia . . .' runs the inscription under Darius' monument at Bisutūn. He faces a line of defeated rebels, while his god, Ahūramazda, watches over him. The Sāsānid, **Ardashir II** (left), seven hundred years after Darius, appropriated the Achaemenid tradition, including Ahūramazda. He is the figure facing the King; behind him stands Mithras, the Sun God. **Khusraw I** (below), greatest of all Sāsānid kings, sits enthroned in the centre of the so-called 'Cup of Solomon': the Iranian monarchy personified. (2–4)

Far older than Islam, Persia traced her history back to the Achaemenid dynasty of Darius and Xerxes, and succeeding rulers tried to enhance their power by conveying an impression of unbroken continuity from that time onwards. Achaemenids were followed by Seleucids, Parthians and Sāsānids. In 16/637 Ctesiphon fell to the Arabs and Iran began six hundred years of subservience to an alien power. But after the Mongol invasion, the end of the caliphate and the disintegration of the Tīmūrid empire, she was again free, the first of the Safavids joining hands, as it were, with the last of the Sāsānids. Since then the ruling dynasty has changed many times, but the institution of monarchy has been continuous; and it is this, together with the Shī'ī faith, which binds together the long history of Iran. The recent celebration of the empire's 2,500th anniversary was a spectacular assertion of those traditional claims.

Symbols of royalty, the great horned head-dress, crown this bronze figure of a late Sāsānid king (right). The same attributes occur on coins and reliefs. (5)

As ancient as kingship is the irrigation system of Iran – the network of underground channels called *qanāts*. In the hot desert exposed water would evaporate, so tunnels were dug running for many miles from the foot of the hills to the villages. They are dangerous to make and costly to maintain. On the surface all that can be seen are the crater-like depressions marking the diggers' shafts, sometimes two hundred feet deep. This air view was taken near Isfahan. (6)

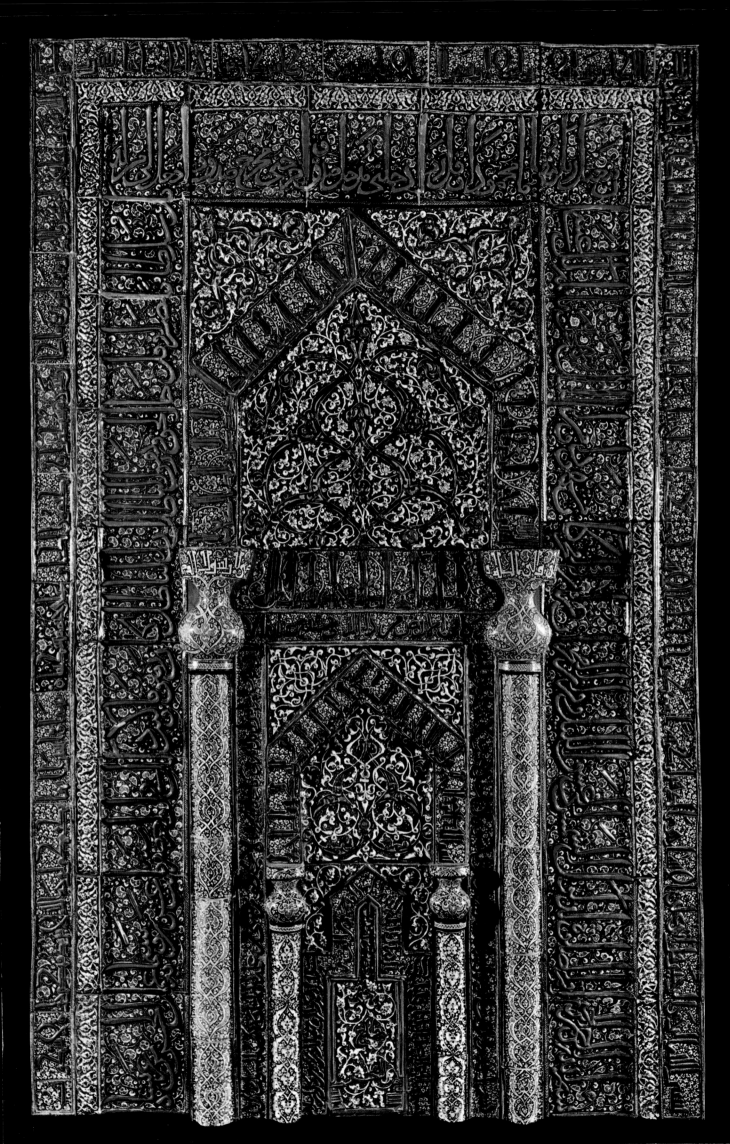

The death of Husayn gave Shi'ism its martyr. Husayn was the younger son of 'Alī. According to legend he married the daughter of the last Sāsānid king, but was killed at Karbalā by troops of the Umayyad Caliph Yazīd. A XII/18th-century school building at Shīrāz (above) displays a series of tile-panels telling his story with the vivid simplicity of folk art. Beginning bottom right, we see Husayn holding his martyred son 'Alī Asghar; then (top) holding his dying eldest son 'Alī Akbar in the field of battle and (bottom) the dying 'Abbās. The next two scenes to the left show Husayn in battle, where he is severely wounded. The whole upper scene shows the last judgment; a woman carrying the severed arms and heads of the martyrs of Karbalā intercedes with Muhammad and 'Alī who sit enthroned with the Twelve Imams. To their left we see hell and its torments. Right: a XIII/19th-century popular woodcut illustrating the life of 'Alī. Here he is slaying Mahrab, leader of the Jews. (8, 9)

The names of the Twelve Imams are found inscribed in the ceramic decoration of Shi'i *mihrābs*. This example from the Maydān Mosque in Kāshān, dated 623/1226, is among the earliest to survive (left). (7)

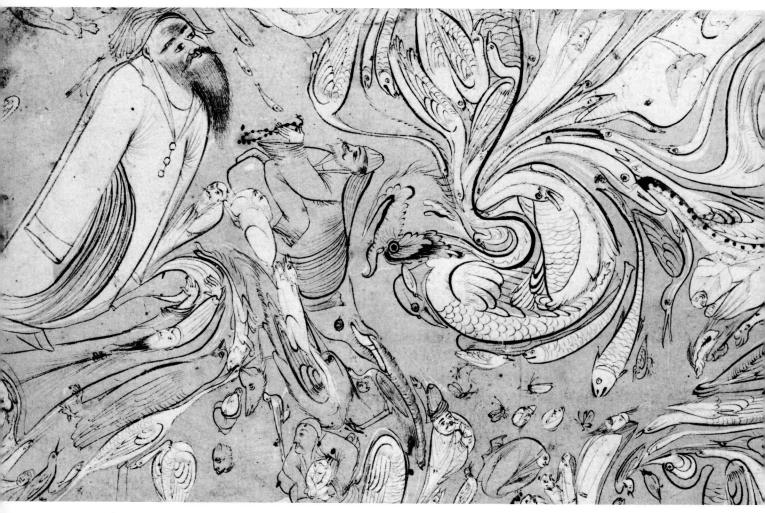

Shī'ism led naturally to mysticism, and it was Persia which produced the most eminent of all Islamic mystical writers. Mystical thought is strictly incommunicable, but poets and artists have striven to find forms to contain it. This fantasy (above) is probably Iranian, of the x/16th or early xi/17th century. Its starting point is the marble-ized borders used by the illuminators of Isfahan, freely expressed rhythms only partially controlled by the con-scious mind. Upon this is grafted a vision of all living things in ecstatic union – dervishes, the Sīmurgh (see Chapter IV), birds, fish, animals and insects, all swept round on the current of a cosmic dance. (10)

Intoxication is the commonest metaphor for ecstasy in mystical poetry, and in fact as a means of attaining illumination alcohol and other drugs were not ruled out. Right: drugged Sūfī in a landscape; an album page from Isfahan, about 1060/1650. (11)

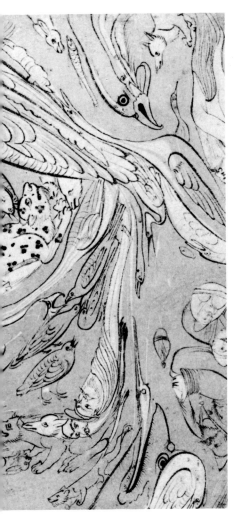

Persian science grew up mainly to solve practical problems, though in the process it contributed notably to pure mathematics (the words 'logarithm' and 'algebra' go back to the Persian-speaking al-Khwārizmī). An engraved metal disc, probably part of an astronomical instrument, made about 1009/1600 (right, above and below) shows craftsmen and scientists in various disciplines engaged in work with instruments. Above: architects with set-square, pick and compass. Below: one man makes observations with an astrolabe while his assistant consults tables in a book. (12, 13)

Poetry emerged from its long eclipse about the year 1000 and the language in which it was written was neither Arabic nor the ancient Pahlavī, but a combination of the two: Persian. Persian became the literary language not only of Iran but of Mughul India; and some of the world's greatest works are written in it.

The Shahinshāh-nāma was composed by Firdawsī in the v/11th century and many illustrated versions of it survive from later times (see pl. 1). This miniature (above) was produced in Tabrīz and dates from 741/1340; the dying Rustam shoots his half-brother while his horse, to the left, lies impaled in a pit. More episodes from the poem are depicted on a soft-paste beaker (left) of the early vii/13th century. On the top register Bizhan overcomes a wild boar. He later falls in love with Marizha, whose father imprisons him in a pit (on the far left an elephant covers the pit with a stone), but he is rescued by Rustam. (14, 15)

'The Treasury of Secrets' by Nizāmī, written about 571/1175, is somewhat like a series of sermons on moral subjects, illustrated by stories. In this miniature (right), made at Bukhārā in 945/1538, Nizāmī reads his work to a prince. The setting is typical of Persian literary gatherings – a garden, with wine and fruit for refreshment and musicians playing. (16)

Shāh Ismāʿīl I (above left), the effective founder of the Safavid dynasty, was of Iranian stock, but came to power with the support of Turcoman tribes. In 907/1501 he seized Azerbaijan and during the next ten years brought the whole of Iran under his rule. **Shāh Tahmāsp I** (above right) succeeded to the throne in 930/1524. A devout

Muslim – he is seen here in meditation – he forbade foreign merchants and missionaries in Iran; his reign lasted fifty-two years. **Shāh ʿAbbās I** (below) reversed this policy, and it was under him that the Safavids rose to the height of their power. Here he sits with his entourage receiving a Turkish embassy in 1018/1609. (17–19)

Shāh ʿAbbās II (above right) reigned from 1052/1642 to 1077/1666. During this period contacts with the West, begun under Shāh ʿAbbās I, were extended. There are several European accounts of the splendour of his court. Above left: a court lady painted by a foreign artist, possibly trained in Turkey. The prince in a slightly later painting (below) is thought to be ʿAbbās II's successor **Sulaymān I** with attendants who include a European and a Mughul. From this time the decline of the Safavid dynasty was becoming clear, and during the early XII/18th century they were no more than puppets, though the family survived until 1200/1786. (20–22)

The high point of Persian culture came under the rule of the early Safavids. In Isfahan Shāh 'Abbās I created a unique synthesis of the arts which ranks it among the world's most perfect cities. Mural painting (above) and textiles (right) both reached a peak of virtuosity and elegance. The scenes portrayed still evoke the life of this sophisticated Safavid court, a life dedicated to the pleasures of this world but – as we have seen – not excluding a mystical awareness of another. (23, 24)

Brilliant tiles clothed the basic structure of the architecture without concealing its lines. The panel (above) comes from Ardabīl, the early centre of the Safawiyya, from whom the Safavids descended. Right: dome of the Masjid-i Shaykh Lutf Allāh, Isfahan, built by Shāh 'Abbās in honour of his father-in-law. (25, 26)

Power passed from the Safavids in 1149/1736 when the great military leader Nādir became shāh. He restored the empire to its ancient limits and even invaded India. After his assassination another dynasty, the Zands, ruled briefly, to be succeeded in 1193/1779 by the sadistic Āghā Muhammad, a member of the Qājār tribe. Qājār rule was stabilized by Fat'h ʿAlī Shāh (below), Āghā Muhammad's nephew. His long reign (1212–50/ 1797–1834) was marked by the growing involvement of Europe in Persian affairs, Persia being eventually reduced to the status of a pawn in the game between France, Britain, Russia and Turkey. The Qājārs, however, remained in power until 1924, when they were ousted by Ridā (Rizā) Khān, the father of the present Shāh. (28)

Conflict with Russia over the Georgian question continued for most of Fat'h ʿAlī Shāh's reign. Persia was twice heavily defeated, in 1812 and 1828, and each time the heir to the throne was killed. Optimistic visions like this one showing Russian soldiers beaten and taken prisoner by the Shāh's armies were unhappily not fulfilled. (27)

Qājār art cannot be compared with the highly sophisticated products of Safavid times, but it has a naïve charm which is now finding admirers. As a historical record, too, it has value, bringing XIII/19th-century Persia to life in vivid and realistic detail. Above: a family taking refreshment on a terrace. Below left: a miniature illustrating the story of *Kalīla wa-Dimna*. A gardener has caged a nightingale which was damaging his roses.

Below right: a tile design with a man in a garden. (29–31)

Overleaf: **A Qājār king**, possibly Fat'h ʿAlī Shāh – looking not unlike Darius or Khusraw – gives audience to delegates from Europe; from a luxurious book-binding. (32)

Chapter Eleven

THE OTTOMAN EMPIRE

Norman Itzkowitz

The glazed ceramic ware of Iznik made Ottoman art valued all over the world. This stylized design of flowers and leaves is from a plate of the late X/16th century. (1)

WORLD HISTORY USED TO BREAK CONVENIENTLY at 1453, the date of the fall of Constantinople. That momentous event was considered to be a significant turning-point, marking the division between medieval and modern times. Every schoolboy and girl used to know that Constantinople fell in 1453, but *to whom* was entirely another matter.

Western sensibilities have long obscured the characteristics of Turkish history with the feeling almost of having achieved a vengeful victory. It is only relatively recently that historical scholarship has rescued much of the Turkish past from its somewhat enforced oblivion. Drawing upon an ever expanding body of knowledge, this chapter presents an overview of Ottoman Turkish history from its earliest beginnings in Anatolia, including the immediate Seljuq background, up to the end of the XII/18th century, when the history of the Ottomans fuses with that of the expansion of Europe. Within a necessarily sparse chronological framework I focus upon Ottoman institutions and thought. The emphasis is on how the Ottomans organized their state, integrated newly conquered areas and peoples and dealt with problems of greatness and decline. We read much about the decline of the Ottoman empire, more so than about its centuries of greatness. It would be salutary at this point to recall the opening sentence of B. H. Sumner's *Peter the Great and the Ottoman Empire*: 'During the half-century of Peter the Great's lifetime (1672–1725) Russia emerged, Austria triumphed, Turkey declined – but from a high point.'

The rise of the Seljuqs

Just how the Ottomans had attained that high point is a fascinating and complicated tale, the beginnings of which go back to the first written mention of Turks in Chinese records of the 6th century. The earliest known Turkish records are the Orkhon inscriptions of the II/8th century. These carvings, found in the Orkhon valley of northern Mongolia in 1889 and deciphered in 1893, date from 732 and 735, when the Turks were still pagans. It was not until the IV/10th century that the Turks of Central Asia were Islamicized in any great number. Islamicization was accomplished largely through missionary efforts supported by the Sāmānids, whose Muslim state of Central Asia straddled the River Oxus. At the end of the IV/10th

century a group of Turks destroyed the hegemony of the Sāmānids. Subsequently, those victors were themselves vanquished by a mighty group of nomadic Turks led by the descendants of a chieftain named Seljuq. Following a significant victory gained in 432/1040, the Seljuqs divided the spoils of war. Seljuq's grandson Tughril received direction of the Seljuq thrust into the Islamic heartland. A combination of sound leadership, military prowess, unbridled energy and zeal, as well as a deteriorating political and economic situation within the Islamic territories in their path, enabled the Seljuqs quickly to make themselves masters of the Iranian plateau, taking Isfahan in 435/1043. Sweeping down from that region into the eastern part of the Fertile Crescent, in 449/1055, Tughril took the caliphal seat of Baghdad.

Ensconced in the religious and administrative capital of the Islamic world, the Seljuqs propped up the caliphate. Using the title of sultan, they exercised power and authority in their own interests. On their journey from paganism to Islam, that took them from the steppes of Central Asia to the urban centres of Islamic civilization, the Seljuqs had embraced Sunnī Islam. Once firmly in control of and responsible for much of the caliphal territories, the Seljuqs themselves came under the powerful influence of High Islamic traditions in government, politics and culture.

Two elements in the inherited High Islamic tradition loomed large for the Seljuqs. One was the on-going struggle against the schismatic Shī'ī who, under the Fāṭimids, controlled Egypt and parts of Syria. The other was the maintenance of the military, bureaucratic and religious aristocracy through land grants (*iqṭā's*) in return for service. Successful management of the offensive against the Fāṭimids required internal tranquillity. The Seljuq military establishment was composed of both a professional army and a nomadic fighting force of turbulent Turcomans. As the Seljuq leadership became politically and culturally more sophisticated, and identified its interests with those of the urban élites it had conquered, the

From a lakeside palace near Konya comes this coloured tile with a design of a fabulous bird – a fragment of the high Seljuq culture which flourished in Anatolia in the V/11th and VI/12th centuries before the rise of the Ottomans. (2)

more it became necessary to keep the predatory Turcomans out of the settled areas. The Turcomans were encouraged to satisfy their thirst for plunder and adventure in the north against Christian kingdoms in Georgia and Armenia. There they joined other Muslim warriors for the Faith (*ghāzīs*) in the holy struggle (*ghazā*) for the greater glory of Islam.

Tughril pressed on with his plan to bring the Fātimid territories under his control and regain them for orthodoxy. His final years, however, saw a great deal of internal strife as various members of the ruling Seljuq family sought to establish personal political hegemony. In 455/1063 Tughril died and was succeeded by his nephew Alp Arslan.

Under Alp Arslan and his vizier Nizām al-Mulk, the Seljuqs attained their apogee. It was a period not only of cultural and administrative achievement, but of military success as well. Alp Arslan waged war on two fronts. In the south he continued the Seljuq policy of confrontation with the Fātimids. In the north he struck against the Armenians; and in 456/1064 his forces gained the Armenian capital of Ānī. Following his example, the Turcomans raided deep into Byzantine territory. They found Byzantium a rich lode worthy of their efforts.

Byzantium's own internal difficulties compounded the threat posed by the Turcomans. Fifty years of strife between the bureaucracy and the army had weakened it. The defences of eastern Anatolia were especially affected, but since Alp Arslan at this juncture wished to maintain a tranquil northern flank while he moved against the Fātimids, the Byzantines and Seljuqs reached an accord in 463/1070 that enabled him to turn his attention southward.

This stalemate on the Byzantine–Islamic frontier was ended the following year, when the Byzantine Emperor Romanus Diogenes gathered a large army and marched eastward across Anatolia. The two armies clashed in August 464/1071 at Manzikert near Lake Van. At first the battle went in favour of the Emperor; but the tide then swung, some sources say through treachery, in favour of the Seljuq sultan. Romanus was captured, and his army fled. Anatolia was now open to permanent Turkish settlement.

The fifty years following Manzikert were marked by confusion. Christians fought Christians, Muslims fought Muslims, Christians and Muslims fought on each other's side and, of course, Muslims and Christians continued to fight each other. But from the tangled welter of events emerge two consistent strands. First, despite a number of attempts at counter-attack, Byzantium steadily lost ground. Second, the sons of Sulaymān ibn Qutalmïsh, descendants of the Seljuq house ruling in the east and representatives of Seljuq sovereignty in Anatolia, gradually gained the ascendancy over the other groups of *ghāzīs* seeking to establish Islam in Anatolia.

The Seljuqs of Rūm

Initially, the Seljuqs of Anatolia, known as the Seljuqs of Rūm (Rūm being the Islamic term for the Roman empire and more especially for the Byzantine territories), looked upon their patrimony there as a base from which to organize a military effort directed at superseding their relatives in Baghdad. Dominion over the Islamic heartland and not glory on the Anatolian frontier had been their major concern. Sulaymān ibn Qutalmïsh himself had died on such a military campaign, in 479/1086 near Aleppo. By the end of the v/11th century, however, Anatolia itself became the focus of their attention and energy.

Both were needed in the maelstrom of Anatolian politics. The Seljuqs found their most formidable Muslim rivals in the *ghāzī* principality of the Dānishmends. Long-time inhabitants of the frontier march against Byzantium, the Dānishmends represented the freer spirit of the frontier. Theirs was a culture amalgamated out of charismatic leadership, tribalism and heterodox religious influences heavily infused with mysticism. The Seljuqs, on the other hand, stood for state control, organization around sound Islamic principles of government and taxation, and religious orthodoxy.

Poles apart on the principles of state and society, therefore, the Seljuqs and the Dānishmends vied for supremacy. In 537/1142 the Dānishmends suffered a severe blow with the death of their leader. Dānishmend unity split asunder into three antagonistic family groupings. On the Seljuq side the same period witnessed the long and stabilizing reign of Qïlïch Arslan II (550–88/1155–92). Pursuing a policy of peace with Byzantium, Qïlïch Arslan devoted himself to the task of securing his position in Anatolia against his rival Muslims. With the death of the last capable Dānishmend leader in 570/1174, the Seljuqs absorbed most of the Dānishmend territory.

Observing this growth in Seljuq power and status, the Byzantine Emperor Manuel decided in 572/1176 to excise the Turkish thorn in his side. At Myriokephalon the battle was joined. Just over a century after Manzikert the Byzantines again suffered a disastrous defeat. Any hope the Byzantines might have had of reconquering Asia Minor perished, along with thousands of their finest fighting men. Manzikert, fought hundreds of miles to the east, had opened Anatolia to Turkish settlement. This new defeat meant that the moribund empire would be helpless to stem the dual tides of Turkicization and Islamicization.

Those dual processes experienced only a temporary set-back as a result of the Fourth Crusade. Deflected from its religious objectives, the crusade eventuated in the Latin occupation of Constantinople (1204). Thrust back into Anatolia as a result, the Byzantines established two strong nuclei, one at Iznik under the Emperor Theodor Lascaris, and the other at Trabzon (Trebizond) under Alexis Comnenus.

Removal of the emperor to Iznik stabilized the Greek–Seljuq frontier in an arc that started west of Sinop on the Black Sea, ran through Kastamonu, which was Muslim, to Fethiye, opposite the island of Rhodes, in south-west Anatolia. Relative quiet prevailed on the frontier. The Seljuqs turned their attention north and southward, taking the major seaports of Sinop, Antalya and Alanya. Some measure of economic prosperity was restored to the Greek side of the border. On their side of the frontier the Seljuqs continued the work of structuring their state along orthodox Islamic lines that included the establishment of a palace school system with its policy of training slaves (*ghulāms*) for state service.

Stability on this frontier was shattered by two occurrences of wide-ranging import. The first was the shockwave caused by the arrival of the Mongols upon the Near Eastern scene. Samarqand and Bukhārā fell to them in 617–18/1220–21. Great movements of people took place as Muslims and non-Muslims, nomads and non-nomads alike, sought to escape the on-rushing invaders. After Chingiz Khān died, in 625/1227, his sons and descendants parcelled out the areas to be conquered. Batu took Russia; and under Bayju the Mongols invaded Anatolia. On 26 June 641/1243, at Köse Dagh near Lake Van, the Mongols routed the Seljuq army. The course of history in Asia Minor was altered practically overnight as the Seljuqs became a vassal state of the Mongols. With the decline of Seljuq authority, the Turcoman *ghāzī* elements on the frontier, which it had previously kept in check, received a new lease on life.

Less than twenty years after Köse Dagh the second crucial event took place. In 1261 the Byzantine emperor returned to Constantinople from Iznik. The combination of a weakened Seljuq state unable to control frontier elements and renewed audacity on the part of the Turcomans spelled doom for what remained of Byzantine authority in Anatolia. Fighting on the frontier and in the mountains rimming the Anatolian plateau broke out again. The revitalized Turcomans nominally recognized Seljuq and Mongol suzerainty: but in fact they were free agents. Organized as *ghāzī* principalities or amirates, they also competed among themselves for a place in the Anatolian sun at the expense of both Byzantium and the crumbling Seljuq state. Foremost among these groups were the Karamanids. In 675/1276 they ousted the Seljuqs from their capital at Konya and claimed inheritance of Seljuq sovereignty in Anatolia. Also noteworthy were the Germiyan amīrs, centred in Kutahya; the Aydın and Sarukhan amirates in the west; and the amirate of Menteshe on the south-west coast.

Bronze coin of the Seljuq chief Ruhn ad-Dīn Sulaymān II, who reigned from 592/1196 to 600/1204. (3)

A new wave: the Ottomans

Closest to the Byzantine frontier, but weaker and smaller than those, was yet another amirate, that of Osman (the Turkish form of the Arabic name 'Uthmān). Capitalizing on his proximity to the Christian adversary, Osman put himself forward as THE *ghāzī*. After his defeat of a Byzantine army at Bapheon in the summer of 701/1301, Osman's fame spread, attracting *ghāzī*s in great number to his banner. *Ghāzī* warfare had as its goal the expansion of Muslim territory, the abode of Islam, at the expense of Christian-held lands, the abode of war. Dedicated to the *ghāzī* ideal, Osman and his warriors, men who had accepted his ascendancy and that of his family, and who were known as Ottomans, that is, followers of Osman, pressed the attack against a retreating Byzantium. Death claimed Osman, but his son Orhan succeeded him. Bursa fell in 726/1326 and became the Ottoman capital. In 746/1345 the Ottomans reached the Anatolian coastline and were separated from Europe only by a narrow waterway, the Dardanelles (the Straits).

Crossing the Straits at the invitation of the Emperor John VI Cantacuzenus, who needed the aid of the Ottomans in his own struggle for power, the Ottomans found the Balkans an arena rich in booty and opportunities for expansion. Cantacuzenus soon regretted his invitation and sought to have the Ottomans relinquish the base they had established on the Gallipoli peninsula. But they refused, and, instead of retreating back into Anatolia, ferried large numbers of *ghāzī*s across the Straits to Europe. The Ottoman occupation of the Balkans had begun.

Moving northward the Ottomans eventually fanned out in a three-pronged attack. Leading *ghāzī* warriors commanded the flanks, while the centre, the traditional place of honour, was reserved for Orhan's son Sulaymān. An accident claimed the life of Sulaymān in 758/1357, but his place was taken by his brother Murād, who in 764/1362 then succeeded Orhan. None of these changes affected the unrelenting Ottoman advance, through the river valleys and along the old Roman route, the Via

Egnatia. Defence against the onrushing Ottomans demanded political unity, or at least a modicum of cooperation. Neither was present.

Competing rivalries and jealousies had replaced the united Serbian empire upon the death in 1355 of its founder, Stephan Dushan. The Ottomans pressured the independent petty Balkan princes and dynasts who, seeing the devastation of which the Ottoman raiders were capable, opted for vassal status. The conditions that they accepted included tribute, contributions of fighting men, and hostage status for their sons at the Ottoman court.

Vassalage enabled the local dynasts to preserve their status and identities; but the Ottomans saw its establishment only as the first step in their own absorption of the Balkans. Once an area had served its purpose as a base from which to initiate the conquest of outlying territory, the vassal dynasties were destroyed and their lands brought under direct Ottoman control. In this way the Ottoman thrust into the Balkans gained them the valley of the River Maritza – Sofia and Nish falling in 787/1385 and 788/1386 respectively – whence they moved into the valley of the River Morava. On the right flank they took the Tundzha river valley, and on the left Salonica fell in 789/1387.

Balkan concerns loomed large for Murād I, but not to the total exclusion of Anatolia, over which he also sought to extend Ottoman dominion. This had to be done judiciously, for two reasons. Given their military organization, which depended, among other things, upon the physical presence of the sultan amidst his troops, the Ottomans had to avoid becoming embroiled simultaneously in the Balkans and in Anatolia. They could only fight in one area at a time. Also, the Ottomans had to tread carefully so as not to outrage Islamic sensibilities by waging war on fellow-Muslims. Reasons of state, however, won out over religious scruples. Murād I, relying heavily upon military contingents sent by his Christian vassals, extended Ottoman control in Anatolia. Ankara, originally gained in 756/1354, was lost and retaken in 764/1362. In 789/1387 the Ottomans defeated their staunchest rivals, the Karamanids, in front of the city of Konya, the former Seljuq capital.

Following this victory, word was received of a revolt raised against Ottoman suzerainty by their Serbian vassals. Murād I wheeled to meet the challenge. He first eliminated the King of Bulgaria, who had sided with the Serbs. Bulgaria was occupied, and the issue was then joined with the Serbs on the plain of Kossovo on 15 June 791/1389. Again victory went to the Ottomans, but it was costly. Murād I was slain. His son Bāyazīd succeeded him.

Bāyazīd I is known in Ottoman history under his sobriquet of 'the Thunderbolt'. First to feel the force of his fury were the amirates of Anatolia who had rejected Ottoman overlordship upon hearing of the death of Murād I. Bāyazīd struck at them, absorbing much of their territory and creating in the east a group of dispossessed and disgruntled Muslim lords who bore him a grudge.

The independent lords of the Balkans fared no better. Bāyazīd moved the Ottoman system of conquest into its second stage, the elimination of vassals and the creation in their place of a centralized state. Newly incorporated areas then became the forward base for the further extension of Ottoman control in the Balkans. Bāyazīd also

cast his eye upon Constantinople, the link between the two halves of his emerging empire.

Bāyazīd's daring did not go unchallenged. A crusading army, representing the flower of Western European chivalry, was formed, and descended the Danube to do battle with this thunderbolt. Bāyazīd was deflected from his preoccupation with Constantinople, but on 25 September 799/1396, outside the city of Nicopolis, enhanced his reputation as a *ghāzī* by thoroughly defeating these new Crusaders.

Invincible against his Christian foes, Bāyazīd again turned to deal with matters in Anatolia. He again defeated the Karamanids in 800/1397, taking Konya. The following year he eliminated the last important centre of opposition in and around Sivas. Having received the title of *Sultān ar-Rūm* in 797/1394 from the caliph living in Cairo under the protection of the Mamlūks, Bāyazīd again embellished his claim to be the inheritor of Seljuq authority by attacking the imperial city of Constantinople.

Besieged by Bāyazīd, Constantinople was rescued from its precarious position by the appearance in the east of another great conqueror. Tamerlane (Tīmūr-i Lang), a fierce Central Asian warrior who claimed to be the rightful heir to the Mongol patrimony, marched into Anatolia against Bāyazīd, whom he considered an upstart. At Ankara (28 July 804/1402), Bāyazīd's army was crushed and he himself taken prisoner.

The defeat at Ankara was a serious blow to the Ottoman process of empire building. Tamerlane reinstated under his protective watchfulness all the amirates dispossessed by Bāyazīd. Ottoman holdings were reduced and parcelled out among Bāyazīd's sons. Necessity forced the Ottomans to act discreetly in their efforts to put the pieces back together. They did not wish to arouse the suspicions and hostility of the amirates, the Byzantines, or Tamerlane and his successors. Gradually, Mehmed (the Turkish form of the Arabic name Muhammad) I and Murād II reunited the Ottoman dominions. They were aided in this enormous task by the groundwork of administrative changes that had been introduced by Bāyazīd himself.

Reorganization of the bases of government was one of Bāyazīd's outstanding contributions. Previously, the Ottomans had been imbued with the *ghāzī* ideal that had as its rationale raiding and the collection of booty. While still extolling the virtues of *ghāzī* warfare, Bāyazīd introduced the traditions of classical High Islam into the Ottoman enterprise, relying heavily upon centralization, land surveys and regular taxation, orthodoxy, bureaucracy, incomes in return for military service (*tīmārs*), and the palace school system designed to produce highly trained state servants owing the sultan undivided allegiance.

Central to Bāyazīd's institutional arrangements, which drew much from Persian concepts of government, were the *tīmār* system and the slave, or *ghulām*, system. The process of integrating conquered lands into the Ottoman domains began with the cadastral survey. A record was made of the population, and of all sources of wealth and tax rates. Shares in the income produced through taxation were distributed to loyal warriors of the sultan in return for military service, primarily as members of the provincial cavalry. These men also performed administrative functions on the local level, representing the sultan's authority. In this manner several important ends were accomplished. Through the surveys the sultans knew the extent of their income and the amount of mounted warriors each area could support. The central government was also able to provide itself, despite a serious shortage of precious metal, with a large fighting cavalry force that was the scourge of Europe.

Alongside the *tīmār* system, at the very core of government, stood the *ghulām* organization. Slaves, procured in a number of ways, including capture in battle, were used in various capacities. Under Bāyazīd I there were some seven thousand slaves in the standing, salaried military establishment, primarily in the famed Janissary corps. The best were educated in the palace school for high-level administrative military positions.

Assured of their status, income and privileges as slaves of the sultan, these men were strongly in favour of a return to a centralized, stable and unitary sultanate under a single representative of the Ottoman ruling family. They supported the efforts of Mehmed I and Murād II to return the Ottoman state to its pre-804/1402 condition.

Murād II restored the fortunes of the Ottomans through a combination of tact, diplomacy and armed might. The leaders of the frontier marches were placated, the *ghulāms* assured of their positions, and when territory was retaken, by fair means or foul, from the rulers who had been reinstated by Tamerlane, those rulers were given rich *tīmārs* in the Balkans. As the healing process proceeded, however, new tensions became apparent.

Chief among these was the rivalry between the older, entrenched Muslim families, most of the ulema (learned professions) class, and the slaves of the Porte (*kapı-kulları*) – that is, the sultan's slaves who represented the military–administrative élite. This tension was epitomized by the grand vizier, Chandarlı Khalīl Pasha, who was himself the scion of an old, distinguished Muslim family, and the advisers around young Mehmed II, Murād II's son and successor. Chandarlı wished to contain the urge for new conquests that set in once the restorative work of Mehmed I and Murād II had been accomplished. He wanted to risk arousing the enmity neither of Europe nor of the Tīmūrids in the east. What had been regained was not to be sacrificed to greed or to the unbridled *ghāzī* zeal of the *ghulāms*. Mehmed II's advisers, themselves slaves of the Porte, advised daring.

Mehmed the Conqueror

Mehmed II was at this period in his second reign. The first had lasted but a short time. He had come to the throne in 848/1444, at the age of twelve, after his father, thinking that he had secured the empire's eastern and western frontiers, had retired to a life of religious contemplation. Europe seized the opportunity and attacked. Murād had to come out of retirement to repulse the invaders, which he did at Varna on 10 November of the same year. In 850/1446 Chandarli Khalīl engineered a Janissary revolt and used it to remove Mehmed from the throne and replace him with the old sultan. Upon Murād II's death in 856/1451 Mehmed II entered upon his second reign, which was destined to become world renowned.

Ottoman tradition called for a new sultan to initiate his reign with a great *ghāzī* conquest. For Mehmed II his *ghāzī* goal was obvious – Constantinople. Speaking to his followers, urging them to press on with the siege of the imperial city, Mehmed II told them that the Holy War was their basic duty as it had been for their fathers. The conquest of Constantinople, he maintained, was essential to the future of the Ottoman state. On 29 May 857/1453 Constantinople fell to the Ottomans. Ever since that momentous event Mehmed II has been known as Mehmed the Conqueror.

Having united the Anatolian and European halves of his empire, Mehmed II set about eliminating any claimants, whether in Trabzon or in the Morea, to Byzantine sovereignty. He also sought to extend Ottoman dominion over all the Balkans through the instrumentality of the Holy War. To carry out his grand designs of conquest, Mehmed II reorganized and expanded the Janissary corps. A stronger Janissary corps also enabled him to erode the power of the frontier commanders and the dominant Muslim families. The Balkans up to the Danube were fully integrated into the empire; and in Anatolia the Karamanid lands were annexed in 873/1468. Where once the Byzantine empire had ruled in competition with a score of Turkish amirates there was now a single state: the Ottomans; one predominant religion: Islam; and one sovereign: Mehmed the Conqueror.

Mehmed II's reign highlights many of the tendencies visible earlier and introduced a number of new elements that would shape the course of Ottoman history for succeeding centuries. *Ghāzī* warfare again took centre stage. Mehmed himself was an incessant campaigner for the thirty years of his reign. The empire was expanded in Europe and in Anatolia, but on one front at a time; in the east, meanwhile, the Ottomans continued to exhibit extreme sensitivity to any rival claims of legitimacy. This time the challenger was Uzun Hasan, head of the Ak-Koyunlu Turcomans. Venice, the Papacy and the Knights of Rhodes entered into an alliance with Uzun Hasan, encouraging him to attack the Ottoman rear. In 878/1473 Mehmed II, leading an army of some hundred thousand men, routed Uzun Hasan; but the idea of a concerted effort against the Ottomans on two fronts would surface again and again in succeeding years.

Under Mehmed II the sultan's slaves assumed new importance in the state's administration. Mehmed II chose his grand viziers from among his *ghulāms*. More and more the authority of the sultan came, in the provinces, to be exercised by his slaves. The laws they enforced, rather than being derived from the *sharīʿa* – the Holy Law of Islam – were promulgated on the basis of the power enjoyed by the sultan. The growing body of administrative law developing outside the *sharīʿa*, and going back to ʿAbbāsid practices, was known as *kānūn*. The complex relationships between administrative law and *sharīʿa* would become a focal point of dispute in future reigns.

Ostensibly unified, strong and on the offensive under Mehmed II, the Ottoman state almost came apart at the seams upon his death in 886/1481. Through the force of his personality and iron determination Mehmed II had ridden roughshod over any objections to his policies, both domestic and external. Many interests had been damaged by his economic policies, which had included the issue of new coins – made possible by the purchase of the old coinage at only five sixths of its face value – the sale of monopolies; interference in properties set aside as pious foundations (*waqf*) by those seeking to safeguard their wealth from the rapacity of the sultan; and the confiscation of private property. Many of those people now stood to gain through the internecine struggle that broke out between Mehmed's two sons, Jem and Bāyazīd.

Jem supported the policies of his father; Bāyazīd sought support by renouncing them. In the end, Bāyazīd won out, and as Bāyazīd II he undid many of the worst depredations of his father's reign. As a result of his need to curry favour his reign was characterized by circumspection both at home and abroad. Much private property was restored to its previous owners, and pious foundations were made more secure. It is important to note, however, that the rights of private property and pious foundations *vis-à-vis* the sultans would continue to be at issue between the sultans and their subjects. Pacific as his reign was in comparison to that of his father, Bāyazīd II is credited with launching the Ottoman empire towards becoming a naval power and a militant contender for supremacy in the Mediterranean.

Ottoman foreign policy took a more bellicose turn with the accession to the throne of Selīm I, who in 918/1512 forced his father to retire in his favour. Selīm I devoted most of his attention to events in the east. In Iran a new threat was posed by the rise of the Safavid house under Shāh Ismāʿīl, who had transformed a Sūfī mystical order into a militant, conquering and expanding state. Breathing new life into the Shīʿī sect, Shāh Ismāʿīl took advantage of the discontent in eastern Anatolia where Turcoman tribesmen complained of Ottoman administrative practices, in particular being registered in Ottoman tax registers. Shīʿī propaganda made serious headway among the inhabitants of eastern Anatolia; and once again the Ottomans were faced with the rise of a strong power on their eastern flank – a threat that Selīm did not shrink from confronting.

Armed with religious opinions (*fetvās*) that denounced Ismāʿīl as a heretic and sanctioned killing him, Selīm set out for Iran with a large army in 920/1514. Subsequent Ottoman campaigns against the Safavids were to be sustained by similar self-serving *fetvās*. On 23 August 920/1514 at Chāldirān, north-west of Lake Van, the Ottomans vanquished Shāh Ismāʿīl's army. For the next two hundred years the Ottomans and the Safavids were locked in a mutually debilitating struggle that would flare up into fierce combat, fuelled by religious differences and economic rivalry – especially in the silk trade.

In the east, yet another threat faced Selīm, in the form of the growing danger represented by the Portuguese, who since their circumnavigation of Africa were threatening Muslim trade and important routes of pilgrimage. The Mamlūks of Egypt, meanwhile, were proving themselves inadequate to the task of defending the Muslim flank against this new Christian danger. At first the Ottomans sought to bolster the Mamlūks by sending them ships, artillery, weapons and gunpowder. Imbued with the knightly virtues, the Mamlūks found gunpowder and firearms altogether detestable, and sea warfare equally abhorrent. After Chāldirān it was only a matter of time before the Ottomans moved against the Mamlūks and assumed responsibility on this new frontier against Christendom. In 922/1516 Selīm defeated the Mamlūks; and by 923–4/1517–18 the Ottomans became masters of Egypt and of the holy cities of Mecca and Medina.

In 926/1520 Selīm died, to be succeeded by his son Sulaymān. Whereas Selīm's enormous energies had been expended in the east, Sulaymān quickly directed the power of the Ottoman state back onto its traditional path of holy war against the Christian West.

True to the Ottoman tradition of inaugurating a reign with a great *ghāzī* conquest, at the end of August 927/1521, Sulaymān fell upon the fortress of Belgrade and added it to his domains. Next, he turned his attention to the island of Rhodes, a prize that had eluded even his grandfather's grasp. Rhodes fell in December 928/1522.

Muslims from Africa to the East Indies now recognized the Ottomans as champions of the Islamic world. Possession of Mecca and Medina imposed heavy responsibilities which the Ottomans could not shirk. Any neglect of their commitments in the east would run the risk of having the Holy Places fall either to the Christians or to the Shīʿī Safavids. Neither case was a prospect that could be entertained. With their centre in Istanbul, which Mehmed the Conqueror had converted into a capital city worthy of the most powerful Islamic monarch and which his successors continued to embellish, the Ottomans also found that their natural area for expansion was being restricted. This was a function not only of geography and logistics, but also of institutions.

The structure of the Ottoman state

Sulaymān's reign, the golden age of the empire, is a convenient point at which to pause and take stock of the state of Ottoman institutions. The empire sprawled from the River Dniester through the Balkans, across Anatolia into the Fertile Crescent, down the Arabian peninsula and across North Africa to Algeria, and contained a population of some twenty to thirty millions. Within that vast expanse a staggering array of languages was spoken and three major religions were professed. What gave cohesion and unity to its splendid variety was the Ottoman system of government and social structure.

Pre-Ottoman Islamic social theorists had posited the existence of four social classes: the men of the sword, the men of the pen, the men of affairs (merchants) and the men of husbandry. In the nascent Ottoman society there was a simpler division into the *Reʿāyā* (subjects) and *ʿAskerī* (military) classes; that is, into the ruled and the rulers. The *Reʿāyā* were the productive element in society, producing the wealth from an agricultural base that supported the military class. Initially, the term *Reʿāyā* covered both Muslims and non-Muslims. Later, however, *Reʿāyā* referred primarily to the non-Muslims.

Military success, with its concomitant expansion of the Ottoman domains, involved extension of the military class and of its functions. Their number grew, and they came increasingly to represent the executive authority of the sultan. Status as a member of the military class carried with it a number of privileges. Exemption from taxation was perhaps the most important; and *ʿAskerīs* also had the benefit of sumptuary laws that served to distinguish them further from the *Reʿāyā*. The division between

'Askerīs and *Re'āyā* was supposed to be maintained in rigid fashion by the sultan, and was a hallmark of Ottoman society.

Secure behind their privileges, *tīmār* holders were the largest constituent element in the *'Askerī* class. Ottoman cadastral registers reveal that in the formative period of the Ottoman state these men were mostly Muslims, with a good sprinkling of slaves belonging to the military leaders on the marches and to the Ottoman rulers. As the Ottomans consolidated their hold on the Balkans, local Christian lords who agreed to function under the Ottoman banner were also granted *tīmārs*. By the early years of the x/16th century, however, those Christian *tīmār* holders drop from sight. They dwindled either through conversion to Islam, or from the Ottomans' unwillingness to continue their former practice, possibly as a consequence of Christian uprisings against the Ottomans in the Balkans. By Sulaymān's time the provincial *tīmār* holders were overwhelmingly, if not totally, Muslim, and numbered some forty thousand.

Tīmārs were allotted on the basis of a land survey, which was carried out upon the initial conquest of a region and then subsequently as required. Cadastral surveys were updated in case of a serious decline in the income from a region; or of the necessity to integrate new sources of wealth into the tax structure; or upon the accession of a new sultan, which usually brought numerous changes in its wake. *Tīmārs* varied considerably in yearly income, and the requirements of service varied with the size of that income. Those who held the more lucrative grants had to contribute more in terms of additional warriors outfitted at the *tīmār* holder's expense; or extra equipment such as armour, tents or field kitchens.

Income from *tīmārs* was stated in terms of the silver coin called an *akcha* (in the ix/15th and early x/16th centuries 50 to 60 *akchas* equalled one gold ducat). Grants with incomes in excess of 100,000 *akchas* a year of a special kind were called *khāss*, and were set aside for the maintenance of particular offices.

Closely intertwined with the *tīmār* system was the provincial organization fashioned by the Ottomans. The basic administrative unit was the *sanjak*; this operated under the command of the *sanjak* bey, who generally resided in the main town of the *sanjak*. He was assisted in his responsibilities, both administrative – including supervision of tax collection and the maintenance of law and order – and military, by his lieutenants, known as *subashis*. Living in the large towns of the *sanjak*, the *subashis* exercised control through the *tīmār* holders resident in the villages that made up the *subashis'* districts. It was a tightly knit chain of command designed to assure maximum military and financial returns to the central government; and to the *Re'āyā*, security, justice and equity in the application of the administrative regulations governing the *sanjak*.

Additional coherence was given to the provincial system by the combination of a number of *sanjaks* into larger administrative divisions known as *beylerbeyiliks*, or provinces. The province was under the command of the *beylerbeyi*, who supervised the province through a number of executive officials forming a miniature replica of the central administration in Istanbul. Those officials kept up to date the registers dealing with *tīmārs*; oversaw the collection and remittance to Istanbul of revenues due to the central treasury; and dealt with correspondence both incoming and outgoing. The *beylerbeyi* represented the executive authority of the sultan, which reached the local level through the *sanjak* beys and *subashis*.

This system of government was primarily concerned with administration and the execution of administrative law. Yet, it must not be forgotten that the Ottoman empire was also an Islamic state resting on the Holy Law of Islam, the *sharī'a*. On the local level administration of religious law was in the hands of the *qādī*, a judge with the authority of religious law. Districts under the watchful eyes of the *qādīs* did not coincide exactly with the administrative subdivisions of the *sanjak*. The *qādīs* were based in the main towns and sent out deputies to the smaller towns and villages. They kept registers of executive decrees from Istanbul, recorded matters of local importance such as guild officials and made record of complaints. If the beys were acting oppressively towards the *Re'āyā*, the *qādīs* could secure redress of grievances by circumventing the provincial administrative structure and petitioning the sultan direct.

The *qādīs* were involved with both religious matters and government. They were paid by the central government and were thus state functionaries – so much so that many capable men of religious bent refused to enter government service as *qādīs*, fearing that in having to execute governmental policy they would run the risk of violating their religious beliefs.

At the court of the sultan

Another large segment of those within the category of *'Askerīs* were the sultan's *ghulāms*, or slaves. The *ghulām* system was another, if not the, central Ottoman institution. Like the *tīmār* system, it too had its antecedents within Islam. Earlier Muslim states had used slaves primarily in the military establishment; and it was in the same tradition that the Ottomans had produced their famous and formidable Janissary corps. An élite infantry corps, the Janissaries were drawn originally from prisoners of war (religious law reserved one in five as the sultan's share of the booty), and subsequently from slaves acquired in other ways. By the end of the viii/14th century the Ottomans had devised another system for the recruitment of slave manpower both for the military and for the select training provided by the palace school. This system was known as the *devshirme* and comprised a levy of Christian youths.

The *devshirme* – the word means to collect or assemble – was conducted as an extraordinary tax levied on the Christian population, grouped in units specially designated for this and similar purposes. Male children were taken, exclusively from rural Christian families engaged in agriculture. In that fashion the local economy was not seriously affected. Moreover, the process yielded recruits who were comparatively unsophisticated and consequently more receptive to the type of education they were to receive.

The number of children levied and the frequency of the collection were determined by governmental needs. Years of heavy military losses would necessitate more frequent and/or larger levies. The children in the area from which the levy would be raised were assembled in each village. Baptismal records were then checked with the priests by the *qādīs* and local *tīmār* holders. The fittest children were selected, and sent in groups of a hundred or so to Janissary headquarters along with one copy of the register giving their names and other vital information. At headquarters they were checked against another copy of the register to prevent children being bought out of the *devshirme* or included in it illegally along the way.

When all the youths were assembled they were again put through a selection process. The best, usually about ten per cent of the levy, were chosen on the basis of physical prowess, comeliness and intelligence (phrenology played a part in determining this quality), and were destined for further training in the palace school. Run-of-the-mill candidates were then hired out to Turkish agriculturists in Anatolia. There they would toughen their bodies and learn the rudiments of the Turkish language and customs, including the Islamic faith, undergoing somewhere in the process conversion to Islam. When ready or needed they would be returned to Istanbul and assigned to Janissary units. As Janissaries they would be entitled to the privileges of *ʿAskerī* status. The *devshirme* was one organized path of movement from the *Reʿāyā* into the military class. Through this process the Janissary corps doubled from six thousand in Mehmed II's reign to twelve thousand during Sulaymān's golden age.

The ten per cent selected for palace school training were soon embarked upon acquisition of the finest education available anywhere in the Islamic world. That education would prepare them for the highest military and administrative positions in the empire. Before the reign of Mehmed the Conqueror those offices had been the special preserve of the scions of leading Muslim families. Mehmed II, however, surrounded himself with men of slave origins, products of the *devshirme* and the palace school. Soon he chose his grand vizier from among them, relegating the traditional Muslim leadership to the back benches. The Conqueror preferred to rely upon men who were totally dependent upon him, loyal and obedient.

Loyalty and obedience, while not specific courses in the palace school curriculum, were absorbed as if by osmosis. Their twin ideals permeated the highly regulated environment in which the youth were trained in the various facets of the High Islamic tradition. They were taught Arabic, Persian and Turkish, the Islamic sciences and mathematics. The manly arts were not neglected, with archery, swordsmanship, horsemanship and wrestling prominent among them.

Designed to turn these Christian youths into loyal Muslim warrior/statesmen willing to give their lives in the sultan's service, this education was hierarchically structured and rigidly controlled. Supervision and discipline was in the hands of palace eunuchs. The initial phase lasted from two to seven years, at the conclusion of which the pages were again subjected to a review. The best were allowed to continue their training in the two chambers of the palace, the Greater and the Lesser. The rest were sent to positions in the household cavalry.

After four years in the Greater or Lesser Chamber the pages were again reviewed. The most able went on to serve in the four chambers directly concerned with the sultan's activities, with the Privy Chamber being the most prestigious. Senior pages left the palace between the ages of twenty-five and thirty. They assumed some of the highest positions in the empire, acting as *sanjak* beys, high-ranking officers in the household cavalry and other units of the military establishment. Those who made it through the Privy Chamber usually went out as provincial governors.

The process by which pages were reviewed, promoted and weeded out was known as *chıkma*. Translatable as 'going out', for many it was a beginning or commencement. The *chıkma* was the bridge between the Inner Service (*Enderūn*), which included the palace and everything that revolved around the sultan's personal life, and the Outer Service (*Bīrūn*), which represented the sultan's relations with the world outside the palace. Depending upon the level at which they were phased out of the palace, these highly trained members of the élite took up positions in the household cavalry, the Janissary corps and guard regiments and were channelled into the provincial administration as provincial governors, *sanjak* beys and *subashıs*. In this way the *chıkma* was also the integrating link between the two core institutions of the empire, the *ghulām* system and the *tīmār* system.

The career of Lutfī Pasha, who served as one of Sulaymān's grand viziers, may serve as an example. He was brought up in the palace in the reign of Bāyazīd II. At the accession of Selīm I in 918/1512 there was a *chıkma* as a result of which Lutfī went from the Inner to the Outer Service. He was given a place in the élite *müteferrika* regiment, and subsequently served in various high-ranking posts in the Outside Service before becoming a *sanjak* bey and then a provincial governor. A man of training, experience and substance, he was ultimately elevated by Sulaymān to the grand vizierate.

By Sulaymān's reign the sultans had removed themselves from the tiring and time-consuming occupation of supervising the day to day conduct of affairs of state. That task was left to the grand vizier, who reported to the sultan directly. The business of the state was conducted in the imperial *Dīwān* by the highest military, financial, administrative and judicial officers of the government. Final decision was in the hands of the grand vizier, who reported to the sultan and obtained approval from him for his actions.

In addition to matters of war, peace, internal security and finances, one of the principal functions of the *Dīwān* was the administration of justice. This was done in the *Dīwān* on behalf of the sultan through the grand vizier and the chief judges of Rumeli and Anatolia. Recognized earlier as the heads of the ulema, the men of the religious profession, these two men were overshadowed in the x/16th century by the *Shaykh ül-Islām*. Although he did not have a seat in the *Dīwān*, the *Shaykh ül-Islām* exercised enormous power, coming to be recognized as the head of the ulema.

Implementation of the *Dīwān*'s decision was facilitated by the efficient Ottoman bureaucracy. The central bureaucracy consisted of the bureaux attached to the *Dīwān* and those that made up the financial administration. They were concerned with in-coming and out-going correspondence, personnel matters and income

The Ottoman empire in Anatolia and Eastern Europe. (4)

and expenditures. Staffing and training within each bureau closely resembled that of the guilds. Each bureau had a bureau chief assisted by senior secretaries and a cadre of scribes. Apprentices were trained by the senior staff. They were taught the scripts employed, and the techniques needed, for the maintenance of the registers kept in the bureau. It was not unusual for a man to spend his entire career within a single bureau, moving from apprentice to scribe to senior secretary. Bureau chiefs, who often had reached that lofty position through a combination of talent and connections, moved from bureau to bureau. They made up the broad upper bracket of the bureaucracy. By Sulaymān's reign the bureaucracy was almost entirely staffed by men who stemmed from Muslim families. In many cases they themselves were the sons of bureaucrats. In all likelihood their sons would follow in their footsteps.

In the expanding, fluid environment of the frontier, the distinction the Ottomans made between ʿAskerīs and Reʿāyā was sufficient. By Sulaymān's reign the ʿAskerī division had stratified along functional lines with the emergence of three core careers, the army, the bureaucracy and the ulema. Each had its own manpower pool and training institutions. One further distinction had arisen. This was the concept of an Ottoman. At the beginning the Ottomans were those who followed Osman and had

thrown in their lot with his. Later, the term acquired a dynastic sense, referring to the House of Osman, his descendants who reigned and ruled as sultans. By the x/16th century the term Ottoman had also a cultural connotation.

Culture had come to be a dividing line within the privileged, ruling ʿAskerī class. It was no longer enough to simply have a position, such as that of tīmār holder or Janissary, that carried with it ʿAskerī status. A new highly educated and culturally refined élite had arisen. They were, and felt themselves to be, the true Ottomans. Three conditions had to be satisfied to qualify as an Ottoman. One had to serve the state, serve the religion and 'know the Ottoman way'. This meant having a position (generally in one of the three core careers) that conveyed the privileged ʿAskerī status; being a Muslim; and being at home in the High Islamic cultural tradition.

Education and religion were now the new dividing lines within the society. The élite Ottomans were culturally differentiated from the vast majority of the ʿAskerī class. The non-Muslims, organized in their religious communities as millets, were separated from the dominant Muslims. Social mobility would depend upon crossing the religious line from non-Muslim to Muslim and the educational barrier from illiteracy to familiarity with the High Islamic tradition. For many the devshirme was the

281

path of mobility; for many, family connections served the same purpose. For most, the end of Ottoman expansion and uninterrupted victories from the middle of the x/16th century brought stagnation and social disorder. With the death of Sulaymān in 974/1566 more than just a golden age had come to an end.

The long decline

It was not immediately apparent to the Ottomans that anything was amiss in their fortunes. Cultural attainments continued at a high level, perhaps in no field more than in literature. Ottoman literature, especially strong in poetry and history, was written in the Arabic script while employing grammatical elements from Arabic, Persian and Turkish. It also had at its disposal the full vocabulary resources of those three languages. In poetry the Persian poetic tradition provided both an inspiration and a model. As in China, the educated élite, most notably the members of the bureaucracy, were both readers and writers of poetry; and classical Ottoman poetry was primarily a pursuit of this élite. But there was another poetical tradition that flourished alongside the classical one. It was more Turkish in vocabulary, grammar and metre, and closer to the people. In the prose field history was the leading genre. Chronicles, court and non-official, extolling the successes and virtues of the sultans, were widely popular. Biographical dictionaries, based on classical Arabic models, also had a large audience. Poetry and prose flourished despite the setbacks in the state's political fortunes. At times those setbacks were reflected in literature, especially in the composition of 'mirrors for princes' and essays of advice to the ruler that increased in the xi/17th and xii/18th centuries.

Literature, especially the chronicles, portrayed the Ottomans as the forceful and successful arm of Islam. Their wide-ranging responsibilities as champions of orthodox Islam continued to demand and receive involvement in traditional areas of concern such as their eastern flank, and brought them into new regions. Still unable to tolerate the existence of a strong state in the east capable of challenging their claim to sovereignty, the Ottomans continued the clash with the Safavids. Sulaymān personally campaigned in Iran, and in 962/1555 the borders were stabilized through the peace of Amasya. In 984/1576 war broke out again. The Ottomans tried to annex the territory between the Black and Caspian seas by means of a series of fortified strongholds. This effort was to engage their attention on and off until 1049/1639, with less than moderate success.

A new region that claimed the Ottoman's concentration was the Volga basin, where they sought to counter the menace posed by Muscovy. During the 1550s the Tatar khanates of Kazan and Astrakhan had fallen to the forces of Ivan IV. Reacting on a grand scale, the Ottomans conceived of a project to construct a canal between the Don and Volga rivers, thus creating an all-water route from the Black Sea to the Caspian which would give them a strategic advantage. They sought to put the plan into effect in 977/1569, but it proved an utter disaster. The project was abandoned and the Ottomans turned their attention to pressing business in North Africa and the Mediterranean.

Here Selīm II, Sulaymān's son and successor, hoped to take advantage of Habsburg internal difficulties with the *moriscos* (Moors converted to Christianity) in Spain and extend Ottoman hegemony in the Mediterranean. In January 978/1570 Tunis fell, followed shortly after by the Ottoman invasion of Cyprus; but the Habsburg fleet met the Ottoman challenge off Lepanto on 7 October 979/1571, and in that last great engagement of galley fleets the Ottomans were thoroughly defeated.

Recovering from Lepanto, but with the myth of their invincibility shattered, the Ottomans pressed the attack in North Africa. They sought to expand into Morocco, but came up against the crusading zeal of Portugal. The Ottomans lost the chance to resolve the issue in their favour when their candidate for the throne was killed at the Battle of Alcazar on 4 August 986/1578. Morocco became the buffer between Christianity and Islam; meanwhile the Iberian peninsula remained Christian; and North Africa, under Ottoman suzerainty, stayed Muslim.

Conquest, which earlier had seemed to be an Ottoman prerogative, was now being gained at increasing cost, and at times even not at all. Nowhere was this more true than on the land frontier with the Habsburgs in Europe. There the nature of warfare was changing. Sweeping invasions, relying heavily on the provincial cavalry, was giving way to fixed-position combat. The fluid frontier was fast becoming a static boundary. The era of relentless Ottoman conquest was coming to an end.

Trouble on the frontier coincided with trouble at home. Sultan Murād IV, a warrior sultan in the older mould, died in 1049/1640. His death ushered in a long period of internal disarray. All of Murād's sons had predeceased him, and he was succeeded by his brother Ibrāhīm, a man who very likely suffered from psychological difficulties. Ibrāhīm's mother, Kösem Sultān, took a leading role in the cabal that removed Ibrāhīm from the sultanate in 1058/1648 and replaced him with his young son Mehmed IV.

Intrigue then ruled the palace; Mehmed IV was only seven years old when he came to the throne, and his grandmother Kösem vied with his mother Turkhān for dominance. Kösem was ultimately put to death by Turkhān's supporters, leaving her the power behind the throne. It was not an easy time in which to exercise power. Anatolia was aflame with social unrest, and Venice, long an enemy of the empire, was mounting a serious threat. After repulsing an Ottoman attack directed against Crete, the Venetians captured the islands of Lemnos and Tenedos at the entrance to the Dardanelles. Istanbul was thrown into a panic. Turkhān Sultān, in this period of Ottoman history known as the 'The Sultanate of the Women' still directing governmental affairs, cast about for a grand vizier capable of rescuing the empire. In mid-September 1066/1656 she gave the seals of office to an octogenarian named Mehmed Köprülü.

Up to the time of his appointment as grand vizier Mehmed Köprülü's career had been undistinguished. He had been educated in the palace and assigned a *tīmār* as the result of a *chikma*. Through the patronage of another grand vizier he prospered somewhat; but in his middle fifties he was again without a patron. He managed to make another connection that brought him a number of posts in Anatolia, but he quarrelled with his new patron and was exiled to his estate.

His had been an undistinguished career, but it had afforded him ample opportunity for observation of the Ottoman system. A thoughtful man, he had diagnosed the ills of the state and had remedies in mind. He was wise, and his wisdom is reflected in the conditions he is said to have set down before assuming office. Decrees were to be issued only upon written communication from Köprülü himself; no one was to act independently of the grand vizier; the grand vizier would make all appointments of office without any interference; and the Sultan (and his mother as well) was not to pay heed to back-biting gossip.

With the ground rules established, Mehmed Köprülü set about to restore the fortunes of the empire. His programme was simple – there was to be an end to corruption and graft. His aim was to have the empire's institutions function as they had in the golden age of Sulaymān. Through a balanced use of force and finesse he rooted out corrupt officials, enforced the body of Ottoman administrative regulations and instilled renewed confidence and vigour into the system.

Having dealt with the state's institutional apparatus, Mehmed Köprülü then turned upon the empire's enemies, both internal and without. Unrest in Anatolia was brought under control, and the Venetian threat averted. Köprülü's reform looked to the past, to the reign of Sulaymān. He demonstrated that the Ottoman empire, possessed of enormous material and human resources, was capable of sustained restorative effort. It was something that would be demonstrated time and time again over the next two and a half centuries.

Recovery having been achieved, the Ottomans soon passed to the attack. Not even Mehmed Köprülü's death in 1072/1661 slowed them up. He was replaced by his son Ahmed Köprülü, an unprecedented move. Already an accomplished administrator at twenty-six, and possessor of the proud Köprülü name, Ahmed pressed the attack in Central Europe. Fear of the Turks, a phenomenon widespread in Luther's time, rose again. Crete was conquered in 1080/1669 and the Ottomans penetrated deep into Poland. Ahmed Köprülü died in 1087/1676; but his brother-in-law Qara Mustafā Pasha kept up the pressure.

Qara Mustafā Pasha saw himself as a conqueror of the old style. He was out to assure his place in the annals of Islamic history with a truly worthy *ghāzī* conquest. He cast his eye upon no less a place than the city of Vienna, besieged for the first time by Sulaymān in 936/1529. Moving out from Belgrade in March 1094/1683, the Ottoman army reached Vienna in mid-July. Two months later it was retreating southward in disarray. Qara Mustafā Pasha hoped to rally his forces at Belgrade for a counter-attack; but on 25 December he was strangled upon the Sultan's order.

The Köprülü interlude was over. The Holy League was formed against the Ottomans, and the Russians joined in with an attack on the Crimea in 1098/1687. The Ottomans were in full retreat. Mustafā II attempted to rally his forces, and for a short time he was successful; but at Zenta on 4 September of that year Eugene of Savoy decimated the Ottoman army. Peace was the only alternative. Another Köprülü, Husayn Amjazāde Köprülü, was brought to the grand vizierate. The magic of his name, it was thought, might make peace more palatable. The treaty of Karlowitz was signed on 26 January 1111/1699;

Silver coin of Sulaymān II (*1099–1102/1687–91*), bearing the name of Constantinople, the city which it was the Ottomans' pride to have conquered. (*5*)

much territory was given up, and for the first time traditionally Muslim lands passed into Christian control.

Ottoman public opinion had to be won over to acceptance of the treaty of Karlowitz. Husayn Amjazāde relied upon the historian Naima to accomplish that task. In the preface to his history Naima put forward the case for the grand vizier's policy. He was not the first Ottoman man of letters to seek to ascertain the nature of the ills afflicting his society and to suggest remedies. Previous Ottoman commentators on Ottoman decline had fastened on the notion of the 'circle of equity'. This view attempted to highlight the inter-relationships between the various segments of society:

1 There can be no royal authority without the military.
2 There can be no military without wealth.
3 Wealth is produced by the *Reʿāyā*.
4 The sultan keeps the *Reʿāyā* through justice.
5 Justice requires harmony.
6 The world is a garden, the walls are the state.
7 The state's prop is the *sharīʿa*.
8 There is no *sharīʿa* without royal authority.

Written in a circle, the parts form an unbreakable chain.

Reduced to its simplest terms, the circle of equity meant that in the Ottoman empire everyone had his place. The function of the sultan was to see that everyone stayed in his assigned place. The sultan who did that, i.e., maintained the division between the *ʿAskerīs* and the *Reʿāyā*, was the just ruler and should be obeyed. In this view Mehmed Köprülü had restored harmony to the Ottoman system by rooting out the factors that had made for disequilibrium. He had returned people to their proper places, restored the sultan's authority and maintained the division between the *ʿAskerīs* and the *Reʿāyā*.

Naima, fully conversant with the politic-ethical literature of High Islam dealing with statecraft, drew upon two additional metaphors: the medical analogy and the cyclical theory of history. In the medical analogy the elements of the state are identified with parts of the body, and the grand vizier with the physician. Naima's argument was that the peace treaty was a necessity in order to give the physician time to determine the nature of the illness and to find and apply remedies. Husayn Amjazāde's peace policy was the correct one, for it was modelled on the actions of the Prophet Muhammad himself. In 5/627 Muhammad had set out to try to take the city of Mecca. He halted at Hudaybiyya, where he had realized that he would not be successful. Not prepared to fight, Muhammad employed 'the means at hand', namely a truce. The correctness of that policy was attested to by his subsequent success. Husayn Amjazāde's policy, therefore, is equally correct.

Turning to the diagnosis, Naima compares the men of the sword to phlegm, men of the pen to blood, men of affairs to yellow bile and men of husbandry to black bile. Of main concern to a state in the Ottoman condition are the black bile and the phlegm, that is, the *Reʿāyā* and the military. It is difficult to control the phlegm, and malnourishment adversely affects the black bile. The body is upset when black bile cannot enter the stomach. In the state the stomach is the treasury. When revenue from the *Reʿāyā* is diverted from the treasury by the military the state suffers. The physician/grand vizier can set things right by maintaining equilibrium among the humours of the body and the four classes of society.

Naima goes on to prescribe a course of treatment. Income and expenditures must be balanced by reducing expenditures. Stipends and salaries should be paid on time to quiet outcries against the government. Abuses in the military are to be purged and the armed forces brought to full strength. Provincial administration should be done justly in order to restore the *Reʿāyā* to prosperity. Finally, the sultan should be cheerful. That way the people will both love and fear him.

In order to dispel any doubts about the future, Naima had recourse to the cyclical theory of history which he took from Ibn Khaldūn. According to that great North African Arab historian of the late VIII/14th and early IX/15th centuries, a dynasty is like an individual. It is born, grows up, ages and atrophies, with about forty years assigned to each phase. Naima discerned five stages in the life of a state: the heroic period of its establishment, consolidation under the dynasty and its slave-servants, security and tranquillity, contentment and surfeit and then disintegration. In 1094/1683, the year of the siege of Vienna, the Ottomans were in the fourth stage, contentment and surfeit. With curious logic, he argued that the Ottomans need have no fear, since they had already lived beyond the number of years assigned a state in their stage of development. Adherence to the grand vizier's policies promised a bright future.

Naima's programme was simple and obviously effective. The years immediately following Karlowitz afford another example of the great recuperative powers of the empire. In 1123/1711 the Ottomans defeated Peter the Great on the banks of the River Pruth. Four years later, in 1127/1715, they retook the Morea from Venice. Between 1149/1736 and 1152/1739 the Ottomans engaged in a hard struggle with two traditional foes, the Austrians and the Russians. The key fortress city of Belgrade was returned to the Ottomans by the treaty with Austria in 1152/1739. Karlowitz certainly seemed to be another Hudaybiyya.

Such thinking was bound to be self-deceptive in the long run. The I/7th century and the XII/18th century were not the same. Sophisticated with reference to the Islamic world, the Ottomans were, outside military and diplomatic concerns, almost totally uninformed about Europe. Extremely few Ottomans had any first-hand knowledge of Europe. Those few tended to be diplomats, travelling on diplomatic missions such as the exchange of treaties, and the announcement of the death and accession of sultans. As long as Ottoman arms had been victorious against Europe there was little need to be informed. Any adjustments made in the society were wholly within the traditional, Islamic framework. The reign of Sulaymān was the model. Experimentation, innovation and openness to change were frowned upon. Success in bouncing back from the humiliation of Karlowitz closed the Ottoman mind to any need to re-evaluate institutional arrangements or seek new ways of doing things. It would take another serious defeat to rouse the Ottomans to the danger of their position.

That defeat came at the hands of Russia in 1188/1774. The treaty of Küchük Kaynarja shattered the Ottoman image of themselves as a vigorous, revitalized, invincible empire. Naima's medications had produced symptomatic relief only. Success had resulted in failure; and there would now have to be a thorough-going examination of the patient. Reform would have to be found that looked not to the past, but to other sources of information and inspiration. In 1204/1789 Selīm III came to the throne. His reign initiated, however tentatively, an era of reform and reorganization that sought to assist the traditional Ottoman empire to transform itself into a more modern entity. His was an era of transition bringing the empire into the XIII/19th century prepared for a programme of forced-draft modernization that would eventually enable the empire to survive right up to its disappearance in the aftermath of World War I.

The Ottoman conquests marked the last wave of that expansion which had begun during the Prophet's lifetime. It was Mehmed II who fulfilled Muhammad's prophecy that one day Constantinople itself would fall to Islam. His successors carried the war deep into Central Europe, and his great-grandson Sulaymān broke the power of one of the major nations of Europe, Hungary, at the Battle of Mohács in 932/1526.

Mohács was a desperate and heroic attempt by King Louis of Hungary to stop the Turkish advance with inadequate forces. This miniature from the *Hüner-name*, 997/1588, shows Sulaymān (upper centre) urging his horse through a pile of dead bodies. Three pieces of artillery precede him. In the lower left-hand corner the defeated Hungarians, wearing European armour, flee on horseback.

Sulaymān did not immediately occupy Hungary, but the way was open, and for 150 years the spectre of Turkish domination haunted the dreams of Europe. During those 150 years, though few realized it, the Ottomans had reached their peak and passed it. At the end of the XI/17th century they made one more bid for Vienna and failed. A period of decline began which was to last until the end of the present century. (1)

The first Turks to found a Muslim empire in Asia Minor were not Ottomans but Seljuqs, who appeared on the scene in the v/11th century and for a time dominated the whole northern Islamic world.

From the Seljuq citadel of Konya come these two sculptured reliefs (above), dated to about 617/1220. One shows a double-headed eagle, the other a winged victory or angel wearing a crown. (2, 3)

The caravanserai of Sultan Han (left), on the road between Konya, the Seljuq capital, and Aksaray, was completed in 634/1236. The complex of buildings includes a mosque as well as accommodation for travellers, and all are elaborately decorated. Through the archway here can be seen one of the gates with a stalactite vault. (4)

After 641/1243 the Seljuqs were ruled by viziers appointed by the Mongols. The characteristically muscular vigour of their early style became qualified by motifs from other parts of the Islamic world. Left: looking up into the portal of the Ince Minaret *madrasa*, Konya, 657/1258. Bands of decorative lettering simulate ribbons crossing each other. Below left: portal of the slightly earlier Karatay *madrasa*, Konya. (5, 6)

Growing refinement but a decline in strength marks Seljuq art a generation after the Mongol conquest. These two details of about 670/1271 (above and below) are from *madrasas* at Sivas, the seat of the Mongol vizier. (7, 8)

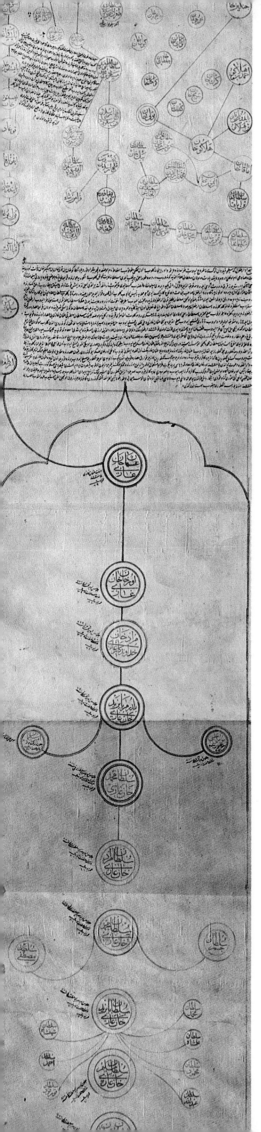

Osman I, 680–724/1281–1324 (10)

Orhan, 724–64/1324–62 (11)

Sulaymān, 806–24/1403–21
(not counted in the line of succession) (15)

Murād II, 824–48/1421–44
and 850–55/1446–51 (16)

The Ottoman dynasty was founded by Osman, who was born in 657/1258. By the time of Sulaymān, when this genealogical tree was drawn up, it had become desirable to give Osman a pedigree going back to Adam. As can be seen, the attempt is not altogether convincing. Osman's name appears in the circle under

Murād I, 764–91/1362–89 (12)   **Bāyazīd I,** 791–804/1389–1402 (13)   **Mehmed I,** 805–6/1403 (14)

Mehmed II, 848–50/1444–6
and 855–86/1451–81 (17)   **Bāyazīd II,** 886–918/1481–1512(18)   **Selīm I,** 918–26/1512–20 (19)

the ogee-headed bracket near the top. After him come Orhan, Murād I, Bāyazīd I, Mehmed I, Sulaymān, Murād II, Mehmed II, Bāyazīd II, Selīm I and Sulaymān. Sulaymān's successors were added by a later compiler in the XI/17th century. (9)

Cadilesquer

Medecin Juif

Jarniffaire, ou Janniffarler Soudart à pied de la garde ordinaire du grand Seigneur

Turque allant au Bain

Religieux Turc

The peoples of the empire comprised a wide array of races and classes. These ten engravings are from a French account of the country published in 1568.

Top row: a *qādī*, a man of law (given the dignity of horseback); a Jewish doctor; a Janissary. (20, 21, 22)

Middle row: a Turkish lady on her way to the *hammām*, accompanied by a servant; a Sūfī; a Christian merchant from Ragusa, in what is now Yugoslavia. (23, 24, 25)

Bottom row: an Arab merchant (Turks, of course, were not Arab); a prostitute; a woman 'in Syrian dress'; a black slave. (26–29)

Marchant Arabe

Fille de Joye Turque

Femme vestue a la Surienne

Sulaymān brought Ottoman power to its peak. In the west his armies drove north to the gates of Vienna; in the east he ruled as far as the frontiers of Persia; at sea his ships dominated the Mediterranean and the Persian Gulf. Sulaymān himself was constantly on the move, and after a reign of forty-six years he died, still on active service, besieging Szigetvár in Hungary. In the West he is known as 'The Magnificent', but in Islam he was called 'The Lawgiver'. A devout Muslim, he is said to have transcribed the entire Qur'ān in his own hand, eight times. Shown here are his ceremonial signature, the *tughra* (right), an elaborate exercise in calligraphy; and a woodcut portrait of him made in 933/1526 by the Dutch artist Jan Swaart. (30, 31)

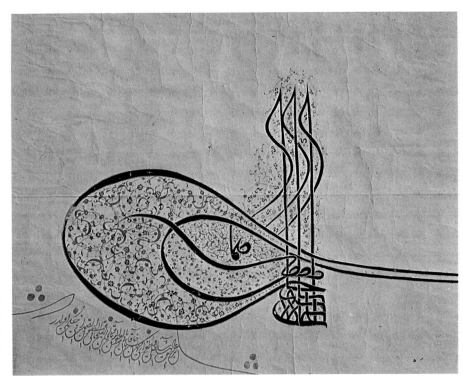

SOLIMANVS IMPERATOR TVRCHARVM, 1526.

The Ottoman army was the dynasty's greatest creation. For three centuries it was the most efficient fighting machine in the world. The Dardanelles was crossed in 758/1357, and although Constantinople itself resisted all attacks, it soon lost its Balkan territories. This miniature from the *Hüner-nāma* (opposite) tells the story of the Christian defeat outside Nicopolis, on the Danube. In 799/1396 a force of Crusaders besieged the city, which was held by the Turks (the Christian camp and artillery are on the right). To the besiegers' surprise, Bāyazīd I and his army (on the left) suddenly appeared in their rear and completely routed them. (32)

Selīm II succeeded the great Sulaymān. Now, behind a façade of impregnability, the Ottomans began a long decline. Selīm had no talent for leadership. He was nicknamed 'the sot'. It was during his reign (974–82/1566–74) that the Turks suffered their first serious naval defeat, at Lepanto. This miniature shows Selīm enthroned, with two unfortunate Christian tax-payers being dragged before him. (33)

At the centre of the empire was the city of Constantinople (Istanbul), conquered in 857/1453; and at the centre of Istanbul was the low, rambling, magnificent collection of buildings known as the Topkapi Saray. It is a series of domestic-scale rooms grouped round courtyards, its splendour depending not on size and symmetry but on richness of decoration and subtlety of design. Right: the Second Courtyard, the Court of the *Dīwān*, surrounded by administrative offices. Here the Janissaries were paid every three months, and at the Festival of Sacrifice a ram was killed in re-enactment of Abraham's token sacrifice of Isaac. (34)

The road to Constantinople led first to Bursa and then to Edirne – successively capitals of the Ottoman state – and as their power grew so did the scale and confidence of their architecture. From the late Seljuqs they inherited an essentially façade style, rich in surface decoration but with little sense of the structure behind it, such as the Gök *madrasa* at **Sivas** of 670/1271 (upper left). But already by the Yeshil Jāmi' at **Iznik** (above), built 780–94/1378–91, the façade is seen as an integral part of the plan, which is expressed in the domes, giving a strong feeling of volume. When the capital moved to **Edirne** (Adrianople, on the European side of the Bosphorus), the style was fully mature; the Üch Sherefeli Jāmi' (below left) dates from 841/1438. (35, 36, 37)

Bursa was the Ottoman capital in the VIII/14th century, and it remained venerated as the burial place of the early sultans. Below: the symbolic tomb of Mehmed II, in the Green Turbe. (38)

It is at Istanbul that one can see the consummation of Ottoman architectural progress in such works as the Sultan Ahmed Jāmiʿ, begun in 1018/1609, known as the Blue Mosque, where exterior volume exactly reflects interior space. The key figure of that progress was the great x/16th-century architect Sinān. (39)

Turk and European knew little of each other, in spite of the fact that the Turks ruled a large part of Europe. The only contact was through Christian communities living within the empire, travellers and diplomats.

Painted panels made for a Christian merchant of Aleppo in about 1009/1600 show the familiar repertory of Turkish ornament (al-Majnūn in the desert, gardens, picnics, etc.), but mingled with specifically Christian subjects like the Madonna and Child. Aleppo was a meeting place of East and West. (40, 41)

An Elizabethan view of Aya Sofya (right): the artist was an Englishman taken prisoner by the Turks and sent to the galleys. His drawing is evidently not meant to be taken literally; indeed with its tiers of windows going right down to the ground it is rather closer to an Ottoman mosque than to its ostensible subject. (42)

Selīm III receives an ambassador at the Gate of Felicity in the Top-kapi Saray. Both the conventions of painting (perspective, use of shading) and the architecture itself show strong European influence. Selīm (1203–22/1789–1807) turned away from the past and sought to bring Turkey into the 19th century as a viable modern state. It was during his reign that printing was established. (43)

VIVAT ELIZABETH REGINA SEMREADEM

The **Turkish 18th century** has much in common with the Rococo of Europe. The greatest painter was Levni. His *Dancing Girl* (far left) catches the spirit of traditional Turkish miniature painting, but with a modern sophistication. His portrait of a European gentleman (left) shows some Western influence in keeping with its subject. (44, 45)

At home the well-to-do Turk created a degree of domestic elegance comparable with his counterpart in Europe. This interior from Damascus (below) dates from 1170/1756. The walls on the left are lined with tiles; the rest with painted wooden panels containing shelves for bottles and vases. Note the honeycomb cornice. Furniture, as always in Islam, is low and unobtrusive – cushions, small tables, trays and an incense-burner. (46)

The Ottoman decline was gradual and – to those who did not look too closely – imperceptible: an era of comfortable living and many pleasures. In this it resembled the decline of Venice. Credit must go largely to the Köprülü family, a dynasty of grand viziers who kept the Ottoman state on an even keel when it became clear that her invincibility was a myth and that the age of conquest was over. During the XII/18th century Turkey aimed at stability, not expansion.

The sultan's entourage lived in rooms that were no grander in scale, though the decoration reflected their dazzling wealth. The Topkapi Saray was added to piecemeal, and never attained the visual symmetry of a European palace (for that, the Ottomans built the 19th-century Dolmabahche Palace on the other side of the Golden Horn). Right: the interior of the Qara Mustafā Pasha Kiosk, near the Baghdad Kiosk. (47)

Fountains play in almost every courtyard of the Topkapi, part of that feeling for water which unites all Islamic landscape from the Alhambra to Delhi. This one (right), next to the Baghdad Kiosk, is again in 'Baroque' style. (48)

OVERLEAF:
Mecca, with the courtyard of the Ka'ba in the centre, seen in a panel of XI/17th-century Turkish tiles. When the power of the Mamlūks collapsed in the early X/16th century, the Turks became the leaders of the Faith, taking most of the sacred treasures from Cairo to the Topkapi, where they still are. The Ottoman Sultan was accepted as the new Caliph, a ruler uniting secular power with religious authority. (49)

Chapter Twelve

MUSLIM INDIA

S. A. A. Rizvi

Detail from the 'pietra dura' decoration of the Tāj Mahal, a high-water mark of this exquisite art in both conception and technique. The stylized foliage design combines Persian and Indian elements. (1)

ISLAM IN THE CONTEXT OF the Indian sub-continent developed along lines quite different from those of other western Asian regions, evolving a culture and civilization which was broadly Islamic but whose principal characteristics were indigenous. Moreover, unlike Muslims in other areas, from the time of their arrival in the sub-continent until the present day, Indian Muslims have never been able to Islamicize the entire country.

Today the majority of Muslims live in the north-west and north-east. Even around their imperial capitals of Delhi and Agra, where Muslims ruled for more than six hundred years, the Muslim population never exceeded ten per cent. A recent census in the sub-continent shows Muslims to non-Muslims proportioned as follows:

	Total Population	Muslims	Percentage of Muslims
Pakistan	64,604,000	62,665,880	about 97
Bangladesh	75,840,000	64,464,000	about 85
India	547,949,809	61,417,934	11·21
TOTAL	688,393,809	188,547,814	

The kaleidoscope of Islamic culture and civilization in India can therefore only really be appreciated through an objective perception of the contacts and conflicts of Islamic India with both western Asia and with indigenous elements, particularly Hinduism.

For present purposes, subsequent references to India will include the whole of the sub-continent.

Before the Mughuls

Even before the time of the Prophet Muhammad, there are reports of Arabs who settled on the Malabar coast; and after their own Islamicization, merchants and sea-farers from the Arabian peninsula probably began converting the local population to their new religion. Legends surrounding the conversion of the sea king of Calicut, known as Sāmurī by the Arabs and Zamorin by the Portuguese, are no more than pious myths; but it can be reasonably assumed that the Calicut rulers welcomed the presence of Arab Muslims in their territory and did nothing to prevent their proselytizing activities. From the II/8th century onwards Arab and Persian settlements on both western and eastern coasts grew in number.

The actual invasion of India by Muslims began as early as 92/711 with an expedition against Sind, and continued for several centuries. But these conquests were neither stable nor lasting. The first Islamic dynasty to exercise permanent rule in India was that of the Ghaznavids, founded by Sebuktigin (in origin a Turkish slave) and extended by his son Mahmūd (388–421/998–1030), whose empire embraced the Panjab, Sind, Khurāsān and Iran as far as Jibāl. Mahmūd invaded India seventeen times, amassing fabulous booty. A far-sighted leader and an orthodox Sunnī, he organized his administration on Iranian lines and adopted Persian as the court language. His patronage of Persian poets and Sunnī theologians immortalized him as a great Islamic hero. His empire building was considered as *jihād* and the Turkish slaves fighting under him came to be known as *mujāhids* ('*jihād* warriors').

The Ghaznavids were succeeded by the Ghūrids, an indigenous dynasty of central Afghanistan. During the later VI/12th century they gained control of most of the old Ghaznavid empire, striking south into Sind and east as far as Benares. Important military outposts were put in charge of ambitious Turkish slaves in return for *iqtāʿs*, or land grants giving them the right to collect land and poll taxes, and thus encouraging them to extend and consolidate the territory under their control. By 599/1203 a Ghūrid slave ruled over most of Bengal.

Why were the Muslims so successful? Although the war equipment of both sides was of a roughly similar quality, thanks to the Indian land and sea trade, the Turks had some advantages. They had been trained in the guerilla warfare of the steppes and were decidedly more mobile and expert in hit-and-run tactics, while the unwieldy forces of the Indian armies, as well as the traditional but immobilizing use of war elephants, were a marked disadvantage. However, the decisive Turkish military victories between the IV/10th and VI/12th centuries stemmed mainly from a high quality of leadership and an appetite for territorial conquest.

Kūfic inscription on the sarcophagus of Maḥmūd, greatest of the Ghaznavid sultans, the founders of Islamic power in India.

The dynasty ruled from the IV/10th to the VI/12th century. (2)

In 607/1210 Delhi, under Shams ad-Dīn Iltutmish, became the capital of the Ghūrid state; and for the next century and a half the Delhi sultanate was the leading power of India. The rise of the Mongols isolated the sultanate from the areas west of the Indus, and with the fall of Baghdad and the caliphate in 656/1258 Delhi became a Muslim refuge and a rendezvous for scholars, theologians and scientists from other parts of the Islamic world which had fallen to the Mongols. Iltutmish was an Ilbarī Turk. His dynasty survived until 689/1290. Of his eight successors, his daughter, Radiyya (634–7/1236–40), was the most colourful.

In 689/1290 the Ilbarī dynasty was replaced by the Khaljī, which provided six rulers under whom the power of Islam began to press southward into the Deccan. But the decline of the Khaljī sultanate brought a period of rebellion and internecine warfare. In the second quarter of the VIII/14th century the powerful Tughluq dynasty attempted to hold the empire together; but in 801/1398 came the irresistible invasion of Tamerlane, and the process of disintegration into independent states accelerated. In Delhi first the Sayyids, then the Lodīs, an Afghan tribe, came to power. In 910/1504 Sultan Sikandar Lodī (894–923/1489–1517), the most successful ruler of the dynasty, made a new capital at Agra in order to be better able to subdue the rebellious Hindu and Muslim chiefs in the neighbouring areas. His administrative measures weakened the tribal spirit of the Afghan *iqtāʿ* holders, and they became a threat to his successor, Ibrāhīm Lodī (923–32/1517–26), who had embarked on a scheme more overtly depriving the old Afghan nobility of what remained of its power.

It was this Afghan civil war which allowed the rise of the first of the Mughul dynasty, Zahīr ad-Dīn Muḥammad Bābur. Bābur, born in 888/1483, was descended on his father's side from Tamerlane and on his mother's from Chingiz Khān. Using his power as ruler of Kabul, he defeated Ibrāhīm Lodī at Panipat, near Delhi, in 932/1526 and the following year routed a further combined Muslim and Rajput force. Bābur then crushed Afghan power in the east as far as the boundaries of Bihar, and laid the foundation of the Mughul state.

The Mughuls: flowering and decline

After his premature death in 937/1530, Bābur was succeeded by his son Humāyūn; but an ambitious Afghan soldier entitled Sher Khān Sūr defeated Humāyūn in two successive battles, forcing him to flee to Persia. The military conquests and administrative achievements of Sher Shāh (945–52/1538–45) were considerable, but the Sūr dynasty was short-lived. In 962/1555 Humāyūn again seized Delhi; but he died the following year.

Humāyūn's son, Akbar, born in 949/1542, was the real founder of the Mughul empire, the last vestiges of which were to remain until their final obliteration by the British after the Indian Mutiny of 1857–8. Akbar proved to be a leader of great foresight, both as a military commander and an administrator.

The new Emperor's first real assertion of imperial power began in 968/1561 when he conquered Mālwa. Early the following year he married a Rajput princess of Amber near Jaipur. At this point he began to show the religious tolerance for which he was to become justly famous. Later he married other Rajput princesses and allowed them to practise Hinduism within the precincts of the palace. Also in 969/1562, Akbar abolished the traditional practice of enslavement of war prisoners. In 970/1563 he remitted the pilgrim tax against Hindus. Ajmer became both a spiritual centre and a base from which Akbar launched his military campaigns. Between 975/1568 and 981/1573 Akbar annexed many Rajput kingdoms, either by force or by conciliation. The conquest of Gujerat in 980/1572 brought him in touch with the Portuguese.

The death of Akbar's half-brother, Mīrzā Hakīm, the Viceroy of Kabul, in August 993/1585 prompted him to proceed to the Panjab to deal with the threat to his northwest frontiers posed by the ambitious ʿAbdallāh Khān Uzbek of Transoxiana. During his long stay in the Panjab region his armies annexed Kashmir in 994/1586, conquered Sind in 999/1590 and seized Kandahar in 1003/1595. It was only after ʿAbdallāh's death in the beginning of 1007/1598 that he left the Panjab, by which time India's north-west frontiers included both Kabul and Kandahar.

After his return to Agra in 1007/1599, Akbar left for the Deccan with the aim of imposing his paramountcy on this region, as he had done so successfully in Rajasthan; and then the Portuguese. However, his plan failed; and although he took Asīrgarh and Ahmadnagar, he never succeeded in subduing the Deccan.

In 1014/1605 Akbar died. The ambitious Prince Salīm, his only surviving son, succeeded to the throne as Jahāngīr. Khusraw, Jahāngīr's son, rebelled in turn against his father, and although unsuccessful, he and his supporters remained a constant threat to Jahāngīr. By 1019/1610 the Deccan guerillas under the Ethiopian Malik Ambar had recovered Ahmadnagar, and in 1031/1621 Shāh 'Abbās Safavī of Persia recovered Kandahar. Jahāngīr's favourite son, Prince Khurram, who had had some success in the Deccan campaigns, killed Khusraw, but himself rebelled against his father when ordered to march against Kandahar. Later he made peace with the Emperor, upon whose death in 1037/1627 he came to power as Emperor Shāhjahān.

Early in his reign Shāhjahān's conquest of Ahmadnagar greatly enhanced his prestige. Bijapur and Golconda, the independent Shī'ī sultanates of the Deccan, adopted a conciliatory attitude which saved them from a similar fate. Shāhjahān's ambition to conquer Balkh and Bukhārā failed; but in 1048/1638 he took Kandahar – although the Persians reconquered it eleven years later.

In September 1067/1657 Shāhjahān fell seriously ill after naming as heir his eldest son, Dārā Shukoh. But the result of the traditional war of succession which followed his decision was that Shāhjahān's third son, Awrangzīb, became emperor. After imprisoning the now recovered Shāhjahān, Awrangzīb had his brothers murdered one after the other. Shāhjahān finally died in captivity in 1076/1666.

From 1068/1658 until 1092/1681 Awrangzīb devoted his personal attention mainly to the problems of northern India, leaving the Deccan in the hands of his senior generals. Although the imperial army was reasonably successful in Assam and eastern Bengal, in the Deccan, Shivaji, the Maratha leader, began amassing extensive power. Meanwhile Awrangzīb introduced several puritanical ordinances, such as discriminatory taxes against Hindus, many of whose temples were demolished. These measures pleased a number of orthodox Sunnīs, but were in general a hindrance to the Emperor's political aims. In 1092/1681 Awrangzīb gave his attention once again to the Deccan. During the next six years he conquered Golconda and Bijapur; and in 1100/1689 Shambhūjī, the successor of Shivaji (d. 1091/1680), was captured and executed.

Awrangzīb's presence in the Deccan now seemed no longer needed. The Mughul empire had reached the apogee of its expansion. But the Emperor's efforts to annihilate the Maratha guerillas by a combination of military pressure and bribery were not successful. The constant Mughul and Maratha troop movements throughout the Deccan ruined its economy, and the Emperor's long absence from the north allowed the Hindu Jāts around Agra and the Sikhs in the Panjab to become formidable powers. The Maratha onslaught against Mālwa and Gujerat was also assuming threatening proportions.

In 1118/1707 Awrangzīb, rosary in hand and a prayer to Allah on his lips, died in the Deccan aged eighty-nine. His death was followed by a struggle for succession amongst his sons. Mu'azzam was the successful candidate and ascended the throne with the title of Bahādur Shāh. Although already sixty-four he attempted to reverse some of the sterner orthodox policies imposed by his father. The real power lay, however, with the leaders of factions within the various racial and ethnic groups, whose shifting alliances were dictated by selfish interests.

The invasion of the Persian conqueror, Nādir Shāh, in 1152/1739, and the sack of Delhi shook the foundations of the tottering Mughul empire. The trans-Indus provinces (Sind, Kabul and the western parts of the Panjab) were ceded to Nādir; and the wealth he removed from Delhi was beyond estimation.

One of the promising Afghan commanders who accompanied Nādir Shāh to Delhi was Ahmad Shāh Durrānī. After the assassination of Nādir Shāh in 1160/1747, Ahmad Shāh built an empire for himself in Afghanistan from which he invaded the Panjab and Kashmir as many as seven times. He sacked Delhi and Mathura in 1170/1757 and gained a resounding victory at Panipat against the Marathas in 1175/1761, seizing what was left of the Mughul treasury.

Maratha power revived again, only to be crushed by the British, who had gained a decisive victory at the Battle of Plassey in 1170/1757 against the Mughul governor of Bengal. The leaders of the various groups in Delhi, losing faith in the Mughuls, had already founded independent kingdoms in Hyderabad Deccan, Arcot, Mysore, Bhopal in central India, Oudh and the Rohilla states between Murādābad and Bareilly. In 1803 the British took the Mughul emperor, Shāh 'Ālam II, under their protection, promising to make 'adequate provision' for the support of the royal family. The phantom of Mughul power nevertheless lingered until the abortive rebellion of 1857–8. Tīpū, the Sultan of Mysore, was killed by the British in 1213/1799, and his state partitioned. In 1801 the administration of Arcot was taken on by the British; in 1856 Oudh was annexed by the East India Company. Only Hyderabad in the Deccan, the northern Rampur state previously ruled by the Rohillas, and Bhopal, Tonk and Junagadh states, survived under British paramountcy. These were merged, after the independence of the sub-continent, in the Indian Union. The predominantly Muslim population in Kashmir was ruled by a Hindu rajah; and after the 1947 partition most of it came under Indian rule, only a part going to Pakistan.

Kings and the court

The court life of the Delhi sultans was largely modelled on that of the Seljuq sultanate of Persia. The sultan was 'God's shadow on earth', who obtained his kingship from God, the 'King of Kings'. Sāsānid kingship, the glory of which is reflected in the *Nasīhat al-Mulūk* of al-Ghazālī, was taken as the Islamic ideal of kingship, but only a few sultans were reckoned as fulfilling this ideal.

In order to overcome any conflict between the different racial groups in his government and military forces, Akbar reorganized both the military and civil services into what was known as the *mansabdārī* system. The word *mansab* means 'rank', and a *mansabdār* was the holder of a position in the administrative hierarchy assigned to him by the emperor himself. The lowest *mansabdār* commanded ten horsemen and the highest, five thousand. There was a definite rate of pay for each level, with salaries paid either in cash or in transferable *jāgīrs* (the assignment of revenues from certain territories). The *mansabs* were both *dhāt* and *sawār*. The *sawār* rank denoted the number of horsemen and horses the *mansabdār* was obliged to maintain. His *dhāt* rank was his position in the hierarchy and salary scale. In subsequent reigns the system was further elaborated; but its essential features remained unaltered.

As well as assimilating newcomers from Central Asia and Persia, the *mansabdārī* system also brought the indigenous élite, both Muslim and non-Muslim, within a coordinated system. Although court rivalries and intrigues did not cease, they were now directed not against the emperor, but against the leaders of the dominant groups. Later, Awrangzīb's offer of *mansabs* as bribes to Maratha and Deccanī Muslims of doubtful loyalty placed the system under such a great strain that a political crisis ensued which became one of the major factors in the disintegration of the Mughul empire.

Although women were not appointed as officials, Iltutmish consulted his daughter, Radiyya, in matters of state, and appointed her his successor over his sons. As a ruler (634–7/1236–40), she took the revolutionary step for a woman of her time of discarding her veil; she also came into close contact with both male officials and the people in general. Ladies in the Ilbarī harem were deeply involved in political intrigue. The mother of Sultan Nāsir ad-Dīn Mahmūd (644–64/1246–66) played a leading role in setting her simple-minded son on the throne and Sultan Muhammad ibn Tughluq (725–52/1325–51) had great respect for his mother's practical advice. The political role of Afghan women is not known; but Humāyūn's mother is recorded as being a woman of intelligence and talent. His sister, Gulbadan Begum, was known to have written an account of the Emperor's reign and to have also worked incessantly to make peace between her brothers. Initially Akbar allowed himself to be used by his former wet-nurse, Māham Anaga, to deprive the regent, Bayram Khān, of any power. The assertion that between 968/1560 and 972/1564 Akbar was under a 'petticoat government' is not correct; but he always looked towards his mother, Hamīda Bānū Begum, for guidance. Akbar married Bayram Khān's charming young widow, Salīma Sultān Begum (whose son was to become Akbar's most talented general, ʿAbd ar-Rahīm Khān-i Khānān). She survived until 1021/1612 and used her influence to alleviate many crises during the reigns of both Akbar and Jahāngīr. Akbar associated his senior queens with the administration by giving them control of the most important imperial seal, the *uzuk*. No imperial document granting high appointments was valid without this seal. Holders of the *uzuk* had their own office in the women's apartments in either the palace or military camps, where all important documents were taken to receive the mark of the seal. Although the offices were occasionally the scene of delays and intrigue, the misuse of power was rare.

In the XII/18th century, a number of Mughul women played an active part in politics, although at times a treacherous and futile one. The women of prominent and well-to-do Mughul courtiers often became scholars, patronized poets and men of letters and founded schools, as well as becoming involved in power politics. They were often expert horsewomen, who played polo; and occasionally they participated in lion hunts.

The stateliness of the court ceremonial and etiquette of the Delhi sultanate, based on Seljuq traditions, was not only for the personal satisfaction of rulers but was intended to impress both foreign ambassadors and the local nobility with the significance of the halo of divine light surrounding the office of kingship. The *Amīr-i Hājib* (Chief Chamberlain) was the second most powerful man at court, as he controlled the royal audiences, even the sultan's ministers being barred from direct access. In order to wipe out the remaining power of the Turkish oligarchy, Balban (664–86/1266–87) first had all his important rivals executed on one pretext or another, and then made court ceremonial unduly harsh and pretentious. He introduced the non-Islamic form of salutation called *sijda* (religious prostration), which was continued into the reigns of his successors. This custom was often euphemistically known as *zamīnbos* (kissing the ground) or *pābos* (kissing the feet). Islām Shāh Sūr (952–60/1545–52) even ordered his nobles to show respect to his slippers in his absence. It is interesting to note that when the Muslims prostrated themselves at the court of Muhammad ibn Tughluq the chamberlains would cry loudly *'Bismillāh'* ('in the name of Allah'), while Hindus performing the same duty were greeted with the cry *'Hadāk Allāh'* ('God guide thee').

Although Humāyūn made many innovations, Mughul court ceremony really originated with Akbar. He added many Tīmūrid customs and ceremonies to existing court etiquette; but the most interesting developments resulted from the concept that both Muslims and Hindus were like brothers and children to the emperor. Although the magnificence and splendour of the court increased, some attempts were made to popularize the mystique surrounding the emperor. Formerly only the élite had been able to see their ruler, but now Akbar introduced the custom of *darshan* (Hindi for 'seeing'); that is, of appearing before the assembled crowd early in the morning either at a window or on a balcony. At a *darshan* petitions could be submitted to the emperor and important state business was often carried on. On occasions 'gladiatorial combats of Mongols' were also organized beneath the *darshan* window. Akbar would greet the sun while his nobles stood on a raised piece of ground, with the commoners gathered in the courtyard below. All of them would then cry *'Pādshāh Salāmat'* ('Long live the King'). Shāhjahān continued this custom; but Awrangzīb abandoned it, believing it to be a form of human worship.

From the time of Akbar, a large drum was beaten to announce the appearance of the emperor to the awaiting crowd. Father Monserrate saw Akbar at Fathpūr-Sīkrī in his hall of audience, dispensing justice sternly and impartially, but without harshness. An executioner would stand by throughout, surrounded by various instruments of torture. Monserrate added that these were not actually used, but were for the purpose of instilling terror. Distinguished ambassadors and visitors were also introduced to the Mughul court in the hall of audience, as well as poets, scholars, musicians and other talented men. Victorious generals would also make their obeisance with great pomp. On festive occasions, particularly on Nawrūz, or New Year's Day according to the Iranian calendar, the hall would be brilliantly decorated and the talented would exhibit their skills.

Sijda (religious prostration) was not permitted in the general audience hall; but Akbar introduced two new forms of salutation called *kornish* and *taslīm*. *Kornish* was performed by placing the palm of the right hand upon the forehead and bending the head downwards; *taslīm* consisted of placing the back of the right hand on the ground, and then raising it gently till the person stood erect.

Court rituals were performed with the same regularity and regard to detail when the emperors were absent from the capital on either military or hunting expeditions. The palace was replaced by a camp of tents; and all around India local people had the opportunity to see their emperor in all his splendour, and to present him with petitions.

The busy routine of administrative duties was broken by such pastimes as listening to music, poetry readings and playing chess and cards. Like his ancestors, Akbar was very fond of pigeon flying, which he called *'ishqbāzī* ('love-making').

The social classes

Muslim urban society in India did not follow the theoretically egalitarian system of Muhammad or his early successors. Nobles and other dignitaries enjoyed a high status; and slaves who were part of the royal household, although ostensibly lower in status than the nobles, were often favourites of the sultans. Frequently they organized their own pressure groups, and on occasion managed to overthrow the sultans and establish dynasties of their own, in turn constituting a new nobility and political élite. The position of domestic slaves and of those employed in factories or imperial supply departments (*kārkhānas*) was not to be envied, however.

By the end of the VII/13th century Turkish predominance had been greatly eroded and the administrative experiments of Sultan 'Alā' ad-Dīn Khaljī (695–715/1296–1316) and Muhammad ibn Tughluq catapulted many members of non-Turkish groups into the ruling élite. Merchants controlling the land and sea trade obtained a dignified position in the upper administrative hierarchy, owing mainly to their wealth and foreign contacts. These advantages generally enabled them to ignore the power struggles and fluctuations in the government.

The *'ulamā'*, Sayyids and Sūfīs were respected, not in their own right but because of their close association with, and influence on, the government, and the revenue-free land grants (*madad-i ma'āsh*) which made them rich. A distinguished VII/13th-century Sūfī told a gathering of leading Sūfīs in Delhi that only money could buy high status in the Sūfī hierarchy. Few members of the *'ulamā'* or Sūfīs starved; and the majority enjoyed the generous patronage either of the state or of wealthy merchants.

Under the Afghan monarchs the power of foreigners revived, and the élite of the earlier Muslim dynasties were shocked to see the Afghans, formerly regarded as rude

and uncultured, suddenly projected into the highest echelons of society and politics. Under Bābur and Humāyūn only the Central Asians and Persians enjoyed a certain degree of power and prestige. Although the introduction of the *mansabdārī* system raised the status of various other groups, the Turks, as descendants of the ruling house, had an intrinsic advantage and could easily enter government service. This prompted the Indian *mansabdārs*, in the reigns of Shāhjahān and Awrangzīb, to wish that their children could 'pass for genuine Mongols' and arrange marriages with fair-skinned Kashmiris. Under both the sultans and the Mughuls, converted or Indian-born Muslims tried to invent foreign parentage; but only the talented managed to achieve prominence.

The best artisans and craftsmen were employed in royal *kārkhānas*. In the VII/13th century some had migrated from neighbouring countries; but non-Indian craftsmen were few. Local artisans and craftsmen were either Islamicized or had been enslaved before being employed in the *kārkhānas*. Some of the skilled artisans worked independently, and these helped to develop urban industries, especially in the provincial urban centres – for during the Mughul period many towns lost their former importance as administrative centres of provincial dynasties and were reduced to the status of manufacturing or commercial towns. The most significant trade in India was in textiles; but as early as the VII/13th century weavers were assigned the lowest position in Muslim society. Partly because of their dependence on the patronage of both the state and high officials, and partly because most of them were Muslim converts, artisans and craftsmen in India failed to organize themselves into powerful guilds and *futuwwa* (chivalric orders) as did the urban craftsmen of Turkey and Iran. Indian Muslim urban artisans and craftsmen were classed like Hindu castes, the only differences being that there was no religious sanction for this; that endogamy was less strict; and that there was a greater degree of mobility according to talent. By the XII/18th and XIII/19th centuries, Muslim artisan groups had also invented a foreign ancestry. The water carriers became 'Abbāsīs, claiming descent from Muhammad's uncle 'Abbās; the barbers became Salmānīs, thus connecting themselves with Salmān Fārsī, a distinguished Companion of the Prophet; and the weavers insisted they be called Ansārīs, or descendants of Muhammad's supporters in Medina. All other artisans and craftsmen followed suit.

Sultan Fīrūz Shāh (752–90/1351–88), in making *iqtā's* hereditary, gave *iqtā'* holders a permanent stake in their villages. The scholars and *'ulamā'* who obtained liberal *madad-i ma'āsh* in Fīrūz's reign also contributed to the rise of a class of absentee rival landlords who mostly lived in towns and formed pressure groups engaged in court intrigue. The Afghan sultans made liberal grants of villages to the Afghan *'ulamā'*. During Akbar's reign all leaders hostile to his regime were deprived of their villages. However, loyal land-grant holders who were not absorbed into the *mansabdārī* system continued to enjoy land rights even though these might be reduced. A large number of land-grant holders, encouraged by Akbar and his successors, started to plant orchards in order to increase their income.

By the XII/18th century, the number of Muslim cultivators and artisans had grown, particularly in Bengal, West Panjab and Sind; but they had no status in the Indian Muslim social structure. The revenue paid by villages was generally used to promote the prosperity of Muslim towns.

The XII/18th and XIII/19th centuries saw a considerable change in the Muslim social structure. Earlier systems gave way to an élite based on the new landlord class, the vast majority of whose members consisted of those of the landlord class who had remained loyal to the British during the Mutiny of 1857–8. Government servants (whether of the British or native states) and influential merchants belonged to this higher stratum of society.

In modern times nostalgia for the past has vanished and wealth, political influence and educational achievements determine social structure and mobility.

The legacy of architecture

None of the monuments built by the Arabs in Sind and the Ghaznavids in the Panjab is still standing. The surviving monuments of the VII/13th century in Delhi and elsewhere indicate that the Muslims wantonly destroyed Hindu and Jain temples and palaces, using the material salvaged to erect their own buildings. From the beginning of the Khaljī dynasty the imperial monuments of the Delhi sultanate were built of quarried stone; but rulers of IX/15th-century provincial dynasties still demolished local temples, replacing them with their own monuments. The most ruthless destroyers were the Sharqī kings of Jaunpur (796–888/1394–1483/4).

To mark the growth of the Ghūrid empire, work was begun on an imposing minaret in Delhi, popularly known as the Qutb Minār, which surpassed the cylindrical minaret (*minār*) of the Ghūrid capital, Firūzkūh, east of Herat. Iltutmish extended the Delhi Jāmiʿ Mosque at its foot and completed the now-famous Qutb Minār arcades around the courtyard of the mosque which still contain the defaced human and animal figures of the earlier Hindu structures. The high arches with their ogee curves were formed by corbelling and smoothing the overlapping stones to form the outline of a false pointed arch. The floral motifs and ornaments are Hindu; and the imposing Qurʾānic verses in Arabic, though based on the work of a Muslim calligrapher, were possibly executed by Hindu sculptors.

Clad in red sandstone, the imposing Qutb Minār circular tower gradually tapers towards the top. The first storey is fluted with alternate angular and rounded ribs on the pattern of Hindu curvilinear towers. The second storey has rounded ribs and the third angular ones. Originally it was some 238 feet high and had four storeys divided by projecting balconies supported by brackets with stalactite ornamentation. Now it has five storeys. At intervals around each storey run bands of inscriptions, mainly of verses from the Qurʾān, interspersed with floral designs. The Qutb Minār has been repaired and renovated many times. Hindu masons in the reigns of ʿAlāʾ ad-Dīn Khaljī and Muhammad ibn Tughluq added inscriptions in Hindi characters. Ibn Battūta considered the minaret had 'no parallel in the lands of Islam'.

The tomb of Balban, otherwise uninteresting, is enlivened by a true arch produced by means of radiations. A shallow domed gateway, the ʿAlāʾī Darwāza, which was added by Sultan ʿAlāʾ ad-Dīn Khaljī to the Delhi Jāmiʿ Mosque, is plain in plan, but its pointed horseshoe-shaped arch with radiating voussoirs suggests that Persian architects were at hand to replace the Hindu structural influence with a lintel across the base of the arch. The white marble and red sandstone have been skilfully used to make a decorative contrast.

The tomb of Ghiyāth ad-Dīn Tughluq is a severe and imposing building with plain battered walls of red sandstone and a pointed white marble dome. The sloping eaves supported on the corbels in the tomb indicate a deliberate amalgamation of the most pleasing features of ancient Indian and Islamic architecture. It stands like a fortress at the entrance to the Sultan's new capital, Tughluqābād. A tomb which the Sultan had built for himself at Multan in the end housed the remains of the celebrated Sūfī, shaykh Rukn ad-Dīn Multānī (d. 735/1334/5). Its inward-sloping walls of chiselled brick, glazed tiles and bands of carved timber combine the imperial and regional styles.

The tomb of Sultan Sikandar Lodī, built in a luxuriant garden, was a precursor of later Mughul tombs. A marked improvement in the construction of domes is an inner one forming the ceiling. The Lodīs abandoned the Tughluq styles, preferring a square plan in place of an octagonal one, although some octagonal Lodī tombs have survived. The greatest examples of the octagonal plan, however, are the remarkable tombs constructed by Sher Shāh at Sahasrām in Bihar. Firstly Sher Shāh experimented with his father's tomb, and later he built his own on an island in a large tank or lake. This splendid structure is about 150 feet high, rising from a square plinth with domed octagonal pavilions at each corner. Two storeys of cupolas adorn the angles, and the building rises to a dome in three diminishing stages. Were it not for the two-storeyed plinth and the fine setting of the lake it would, however, have been a somewhat huddled structure. Sher Shāh also destroyed Humāyūn's city of Delhi, named Dīn Panāh (Shelter of the Faith), and fortified the Purāna Qalʿa (Old Fort), in which he built a beautiful mosque.

Jaunpur, the capital of the Sharqī rulers, was known as 'the Shīrāz of India'. The screen before the prayer chamber of the Atāla mosque of Jaunpur is dominated by a massive arch forming a gateway over seventy-five feet high and fifty-five feet wide at the base; within it is a recessed arch containing a small entrance archway over which rise three rows of windows. Such imposing gateways are characteristic of all Sharqī mosques.

In Bengal brick was used by the ancient Indian monarchs and Muslims alike. Examples include the Eklakhī mausoleum at Pandua containing the remains of Sultan Jalāl ad-Dīn Muhammad Shāh (817–35/1414–32). The cornice of the flat roof is slightly curved, imitating the effect of a bamboo construction. A hemispherical dome covers the tomb chamber, unfortunately strangely ill-fitting in appearance, being considerably smaller in diameter than the building itself.

The restrained brick carving and tile work of the Eklakhī mausoleum contrasts with the riotous brilliance of the Lotan Mosque at Lakhnawti (Gaur), which was all but covered with gaudy glazed tiles. The Great Golden Mosque (Bara Sona Masjid) built by Nusrat Shāh (925–

39/1519–32) marks the culmination of the Bengali style. Of brick, faced with black basalt, its severe and massive bulk is broken by eleven pointed arches, and its austerity is relieved only by a few courses of plain moulding.

The Jāmiʿ Masjid in Ahmadābād, built by Sultan Ahmad Shāh of Gujerat (814–46/1411–42), was decorated by Hindu and Jain craftsmen. The prayer hall, 210 feet by 95 feet, is a jungle of slender stone pillars finished with ornamentation in the Jain style. The most famous of all Gujerati works of art are the three perforated screens in the small plain Mosque of Sidi Sayyid, built in the last quarter of the x/16th century. The decoration of walls with carved stone screens, filtering light and creating a pleasant chiaroscuro, had already reached a high degree of excellence and was to be eagerly adopted by the Mughuls; but these three screens are of a fineness never afterwards reproduced. The central screen shows a palm tree around which is entwined a luxuriant tropical parasite whose tendrils curve and writhe on each side of the tree, growing smaller and smaller until every inch of the screen is filled.

The Mālwa buildings show only a few traces of Hindu influence. They are generally built on high plinths reached by flights of steps, and are ornamented with marble, slate, coloured stone and glazed tiles.

Deccan buildings are predominantly Iranian in influence. The Jāmiʿ Masjid at Gulbarga, the early capital of the Bahmanī sultans (748–932/1347–1526), has no courtyard; the whole area is covered by domes, supported by massive square pillars from which spring sharply pointed arches. The arches of the monuments of the ʿĀdil Shāhī dynasty of Bijapur (895–1097/1490–1686) exhibit some Turkish influence, as well as Persian and Indian. The domes emerge from a band of a conventional petal design, bulging slightly as they rise. The mausoleum of Muhammad ʿĀdil Shāh (1036–67/1626–56) is the most remarkable monument of all. The great hemispherical dome from which the structure takes its name, Gol Gumbaz (Round Dome), covers an area of about five thousand square feet and is 144 feet in external diameter. The plain outline of the square structure which supports it is broken by a row of small arches surmounted by crenellations, and at each of the four corners stands a six-sided tower. The Chār Minār, a monumental doorway at the Qutbshāhī capital of Hyderabad, is dominated by four slender towers rising at its corners, which give it its name, meaning Four Minarets.

In Srinagar, Kashmir, the Mosque of Shāh Hamadān stands on the stone foundations of a demolished temple. It is a two-storeyed building with an imposing pyramidal tiered roof; and the bases and capitals of its pillars are covered with carved leaf patterns. The Jāmiʿ Mosque of Sultan Sikandar (796–819/1394–1416) was extended by Sultan Zayn al-ʿĀbidīn (823–75/1420–70). Although the mosque has been burned three times its style has generally been preserved. The lower portion of the walls is of brick, but the surrounding colonnades of huge wooden trunks stand on a stone plinth. Sultan Zayn al-ʿĀbidīn's tomb, likewise of brick, was also built on the stone foundation of a temple. The large central dome, with cupolas on four sides, and the use of glazed tiles, suggest both Persian and Delhi influences.

In the design of gardens Bābur introduced a formal pattern. At Agra remnants of his Ārām Bāgh (Rām Bāgh), dominated by a pavilion, still survive. The formal Mughul garden was square, and laid out with straight walks at right angles to a central pond or platform, hence the name Chārbāgh (Quadripartite Garden).

Nothing remains of Humāyūn's monuments; but Akbar's programme of systematically planned forts and towns has left many survivals. He designed the vast Agra fort in the trabeated style, which he also used for his palace buildings. The Agra fort contained about five hundred masonry buildings in the beautiful styles of Bengal and Gujerat; but now only the outer walls, the gateways and the famous Jahāngīrī Mahal (partly altered by Jahāngīr) are left. The inlay of the Delhi gate of the Agra fort exhibits a curious blending of the Assyrian gryphon, Indian elephants and birds. The deep eaves resting on twisted stone brackets are reminiscent of the palaces of the rock fort at Gwalior, known as Mān Mandir, built by Mahārājah Mān Singh (891–922/1486–1516) and seized by Bābur in 933/1527.

An expression of Akbar's synthesizing policies, and a landmark in the development of his ideas in town planning, is Fathpūr-Sīkrī, twenty-two miles from Agra. The most interesting group of buildings at Fathpūr-Sīkrī, and the ones which have always aroused most admiration, are the Jāmiʿ Mosque complex with its Chishtī monuments, the Buland Darwāza and the many palaces, baths and caravanserais. Their decorative elements are a curious mixture of Persian and indigenous styles; but the overall effect is unforgettable.

Humāyūn's widow, Hājjī Begum, supervised the building of Humāyūn's tomb at Delhi. A broad and lofty plinth with deep recessed arches all round supports the tomb, which is faced with red sandstone picked out with marble. Its double dome adds to the appearance of the inner hall by allowing the ceiling to be hemispherical. Akbar's own tomb at Sikandra in Agra was started by the Emperor himself and completed by Jahāngīr. Built on a high foundation, it is a structure of three diminishing arcaded galleries furnished with small pavilions, some with pyramid-shaped roofs.

Beside the River Jumna at Agra, Nūr Jahān, the beloved queen of Jahāngīr, completed the tomb of her father, Iʿtmād ad-Dawla. In form it is not unlike an Ottoman kiosk. Not only does the rich inlay of coloured stones give pleasure with its luxuriance but it mitigates the brilliant glare that would, under an Indian sun, be reflected from the unrelieved white marble. Jahāngīr's own tomb at Shāhadra near Lahore stands in a fine garden; but structurally it is disappointing.

When Shāhjahān began to build the famous Tāj Mahal on the left bank of the Jumna at Agra as a tomb for his beloved wife, Mumtāz Mahal (d. 1040/1631), all the essential features of a garden tomb had already been evolved, so that the stage was already set for a masterpiece. The white marble tomb stands in a fine garden, reflected in a long narrow pool of water. The Jumna flows behind the Tāj Mahal, which overlooks it from a high terrace. Four minarets, their marble revetments picked out with black stone, frame the tomb, which is dominated by a lofty dome rising from a broad plain band edged with a conventional petal design. The dome bulges gently before culminating in the gilded bronze finial which replaces the original gold one. The tomb itself is square, with chamfered corners into which open two broad arches. The finely cut marble cenotaphs of the Empress and her husband are surrounded by an elegant marble screen, some eight feet high. The hemispherical ceiling is in fact the interior of a second, inner dome. The outer walls, the cenotaphs and the screen around them, are decorated with traditional Indo-Persian foliage design in the finest *pietra dura* work.

Shāhjahān's Jāmiʿ Masjid, in the so-called seventh city of Delhi (Shāhjahānābād, now Old Delhi), also stands on a high platform. Massive piers support the prayer chamber, over which rise three splendid white domes. From behind, over the plain red wall panelled with en-grailed arches in low relief, the domes look most impressive. The Motī Masjid, also built for Shāhjahān, in the Agra fort, and completely of white marble, lacks the pleasing proportions of the Delhi mosque. A tiny marble mosque built by Awrangzīb in the Delhi fort is charming, but hints with the greater roundness of its dome at the impending decline of Mughul architecture.

In his new fort at Delhi, Shāhjahān was able to plan a very satisfactory ensemble by arranging the palace buildings along the eastern wall of the fort overlooking the Jumna. Awrangzīb, however, was no builder of palaces. In the XII/18th century the Jāts plundered the Agra palaces for building materials with which to construct their own palaces at Bharatpūr and Dīg. The architectural traditions of the Mughuls were revived by the courts of Oudh, at Faydābād and Lucknow, but in a less brilliant form. Using brick and mortar in place of stone and marble, the rulers of Oudh flooded Lucknow with interesting religious monuments and palaces.

The art of the miniature

None of the painting of the Delhi sultanate have survived but literary sources indicate that the Ghaznavids followed the traditions of the Umayyads, who adorned their palaces in outlying desert regions with wall paintings. Human and animal figures were painted on Iltutmish's palace walls, and paintings of this kind continued throughout the reigns of the Delhi sultans. The fresco tradition of Ajanta had never died completely. Dim outlines still survive on the walls of the pavilion in Rām Bāgh in Agra, in Akbar's bedroom and in Maryam's house at Fathpūr-Sīkrī.

The earliest surviving book of illustrations dates from the reign of an independent Sultan of Mālwa. Subsequently, Humāyūn was particularly interested in painting. Despite his slender resources he was able to attract to his court in Kabul several eminent Persian painters who had been trained in the style of the celebrated Bihzād. Although Akbar never learned to read and write, a miniature in the Gulistān Library in Tehran shows him as a young man presenting a picture he had painted himself to his father, Humāyūn.

About 975/1567 Akbar ordered his artists to prepare an illustrated copy of the *Hamza-nāma*, the story of the legendary deeds of the adventurer Hamza ibn ʿAbdallāh of Sīstān, who lived in the reign of Hārūn ar-Rashīd. A team of one hundred painters, gilders and binders were engaged in the task, under the supervision of the Persian painters Sayyid ʿAlī and ʿAbd as-Samad, also of Bihzād's

school. The twelve-volume work contained no less than 1,004 illustrated passages. The surviving pages, now preserved in various libraries throughout both the West and the East, measure 27 inches by 20 inches. The paintings were intended to imitate Bihzād's successors. Since the work took fifteen years to complete, the later sections, peculiarly Indian as far as costumes, buildings and plant life are concerned, represent a Mughul–Rajput synthesis. Other manuscripts illustrated in the first half of Akbar's reign are full of vivid representations of plants, flowers, animals and men.

The Persian style only served as a basis for Mughul miniature painting, which gained its distinctive character from the talented indigenous painters whom Akbar was so successful in discovering.

Among the most outstanding painters of Akbar's reign was Daswanth. The son of a potter, he used to paint figures on walls. Akbar found him promising and in about 983/1575 handed him over for tutelage to ʿAbd as-Samad. His work survives in illustrated manuscripts of the Persian version of the *Mahābhārata*, now owned by the Maharajah of Jaipur.

Equal in talent was Basāwan who, according to Abū 'l-Fadl, excelled 'in preparing backgrounds, drawing of features, distribution of colours, portrait painting and in several other branches'. Of more than one hundred painters employed by Akbar, Abū 'l-Fadl mentions the names of only thirteen Hindu and five Muslim artists; but the signatures on the illustrations of this period include many Hindu names, including some from Gujerat, Gwalior and Kashmir, which are not included in Abū'l-Fadl's list of court painters. These artists illustrated such works as the Persian translations of the *Mahābhārata* and the *Ramāyana, Kalīla wa-Dimna, Akbar-nāma*, etc., and were the founders of the Mughul school of painting.

Long before the end of Akbar's reign, court painters became aware of European miniature and portrait painting. The *Dāstān-i Ahwāl i-Hawāriyān*, a Persian version of the lives of the Apostles presented to Jahāngīr by Father Jerome Xavier in 1016/1607, was later illustrated in India in the Italian style. Jahāngīr encouraged his artists to copy European art. In 1024/1615, Sir Thomas Roe, the ambassador of King James I, presented the Emperor with a miniature portrait by Isaac Oliver, the greatest English exponent of the genre of this period. Jahāngīr ordered several copies to be made by his artists. European shading and chiaroscuro began to replace the flatness and formality of the figures of early Persian painters; and a sense of realism dominates Mughul painting of the late X/16th and early XI/17th centuries. Miskīn, who in 1004/1595 illustrated the story of the 'unfaithful wife' in the *Bahāristān* of Jāmī, appears strongly under the influence of the Italian painters of the mid-X/16th century.

In the beginning of the following century, Basāwan, Miskīn, Lāl, Kēsu, Mādhu and Ikhlās illustrated the *Akbar-nāma* manuscript, which is now in the Victoria and Albert Museum in London. One of its outstanding illustrations is the scene of Akbar swimming his elephant across the Ganges in 975/1567. Akbar also had portraits made of himself and his nobles. Several nobles employed their own artists, and the general interest in painting sharpened the talents of artists of lesser merit.

In Jahāngīr's reign, the synthesis of indigenous, Persian and European artistic trends bestowed a distinctive character on Mughul painting. Among the painters of this time, Abū 'l-Hasan, Manohar, Bishun Dās, Gowardhan, Mansūr and Dawlat were the most important. Jahāngīr claimed to be able to distinguish the work of each of his painters at a glance, even in a composite painting. The full-length portraits of Jahāngīr's time, featuring both profile and three-quarter face against a turquoise blue or dark green background, are very fine.

Portraits of rare animals and birds were the speciality of Mansūr. Pidārath and 'Ināyat painted the animal and vegetable world with great skill. Some thrilling moments in Jahāngīr's hunting adventures were also captured in illustrations with distant hills and animals in characteristic attitudes.

Some of the eminent painters of Jahāngīr's reign continued to serve Shāhjahān. The most important painters during the latter's rule were Chaturman, Manohar, Muhammad Nādir Samarqandī, Mīr Hāshim and Muhammad Faqīr Allāh Khān. The art of colouring was further improved; everyday themes such as groups of jovial servants, dancers, concerts and fireworks on a dark night were favoured. Emotional tension and noble sentiments are evident in many scenes portrayed by Shāhjahān's artists.

A painting of Awrangzīb depicts him on horseback with the typical halo surrounding his head, while a saint presents him with a sword. But stagnation is evident in the art of this period. About 1080/1669 Awrangzīb put an end to the imperial patronage of painters; and all the wall paintings in the imperial palaces and garden houses were covered with plaster.

A golden age of Islamic science

The great architectural monuments left by Indian Muslim rulers indicate an awareness of western Asian developments in the realms of engineering, mechanics, hydrostatics and technology. Both Delhi sultans and Mughuls were interested in improvising mechanical devices. Thirteen illustrations in the *Sīrat-i Fīrūz Shāhī*, written in Fīrūz Shāh's reign, explain the mechanical devices such as piers and pulleys used to transfer a huge stone pillar built by Aśoka from Topra, between Ambala and Sirsa, to Fīrūzābād. This great monolith was re-erected in Kotla Fīrūz Shāh (Delhi) at the summit of a huge stepped structure like a pyramid.

During the reign of Sultan Nāsir Shāh (906–17/1500–11) of Mālwa, Muhammad ibn Dā'ūd made a Persian translation of some Arabic works on mechanical devices, in which he explained several types of machines and included illustrations.

Father Monserrate saw Akbar personally working on machines and directing new mechanical inventions. Every New Year's Day and on other ceremonial occasions, Hakīm Fath Allāh (d. 997/1589), a leading astronomer, scientist and philosopher from Shīrāz, would display his new mechanical inventions. He also wrote books discussing mechanical inventions, mechanical concepts and the force of movement. At Fathpūr-Sīkrī and the Tāj Mahal water was raised mechanically to tanks more than a hundred yards higher than its source and then distributed to gardens.

Fīrūz Shāh, a sultan of the pre-Mughul Tughluq dynasty, transported an Aśokan pillar weighing 50 tons from Topra to his capital at Delhi. It was a considerable feat of engineering. This contemporary illustration shows the mechanism for taking down the pillar from its original position. (3)

Indian Muslims also followed the western Asian mathematical classification into numerical sciences, geometrical sciences and astronomy – although these were often mixed together. They translated Sanskrit works on all branches of mathematics, but found it difficult to successfully blend the different ideas contained in Sanskrit and Persian–Arabic works, although some original contributions were made in this respect.

Advanced mathematical texts included the Arabic translation of Euclid's *Elements* by Nasīr ad-Dīn Muhammad at-Tūsī (597–672/1201–74) and its Persian translation by his pupil, Qutb ad-Dīn Mahmūd Shīrāzī (d. 710/1311). Based on the above translations, and at-Tūsī's original works on mathematics, Hājjī 'Abd al-Hamīd Muharrir Ghaznavī began writing an advanced mathematical text, *Dastūr al-Albāb fī 'Ilm al-Hisāb*, which he completed about twenty-six years later, in 760/1358–9.

Faydī (954–1001/1547–92), Abū 'l-Fad'l's brother and Akbar's court poet, translated the Sanskrit work *Lilāvatī*, by Bhaskaracharya (508–56/1114–60), in 995/1587. It presents algebraical and arithmetical theorems as problems which were posed to a beautiful girl in terms of bees and flowers. The translation was a great success and stimulated 'Atā' Allāh Rushdī in 1044/1634-5 to translate the rest of Bhaskaracharya's works on algebra and mensuration.

Study of the works of Nasīr ad-Dīn at-Tūsī and Bahā' ad-Dīn Muhammad ibn Husayn al-'Āmilī (953-1030/1547-1621) and the above-mentioned Sanskrit translations, stimulated the production of some original treatises on mathematics by Ustād Ahmad Mi'mār-i Lāhawrī (d. 1059/1649) and his three sons, 'Atā' Allāh Rushdī, Lutf Allāh Muhandis and Nūr Allāh, and by his grandson, Imām ad-Dīn Riyādī ibn Lutf Allāh. Ustād Ahmad Mi'mār was the architect of the Tāj Mahal and the Red Fort. Inscriptions on the Jāmi' Masjid and Tāj Mahal were made from the drawings of Nūr Allāh. Ustād Ahmad's sons and grandsons were talented engineers and mathematicians. Their works are based on a deep knowledge of Greek, Persian and Sanskrit mathematics.

In the realm of astronomy, Muslims were unable to improve on the original contributions of al-Bīrūnī, who made a critical study of Ptolemy and of Persian and Sanskrit works. Indian Muslims studied the Arabic and Persian translations of Ptolemy's *Centiloquium* and were also much impressed by the importance of the Arabic translation of the *Megalē suntaxis*, which expounded a system of astronomy and trigonometry, called *al-Majistī* in its Arabic garb. The earliest astronomical table prepared under the Delhi sultans was the *Zīj-i Nāsirī*. The work of Mahmūd ibn 'Umar, it was dedicated to Sultan Nāsir ad-Dīn Mahmūd. In the reign of Fīrūz Shāh Tughluq the *Brihat-samhitā* of Varāha-mihra, which al-Bīrūnī had already translated into Arabic, was rendered into Persian, in a version that aroused considerable interest in Hindu astronomy.

The study of various types of *asturlāb* (astrolabe) was based on the *Bīst Bāb dar Asturlāb* by the mathematician and astronomer, Nasīr ad-Dīn at-Tūsī, and the works of Qutb ad-Dīn Mahmūd Shīrāzī. Bahā' ad-Dīn 'Āmilī's influence was also considerable. The interests of Ulugh Beg ibn Shāhrukh (850-53/1447-9), a Tīmūrid ruler of Samarqand, were far-reaching. He collected a galaxy of astronomers to help him to prepare astronomical tables. The Emperor Humāyūn inherited the traditions of his ancestors and invented some new models of *asturlāb*. Shāhjahān's astronomer, Farīd ad-Dīn Mas'ūd (d. 1039/1629), completed astronomical tables based on those of Ulugh Beg and in 1006/1597 wrote a treatise on astronomy called *Sirāj al-istikhrāj*. To Shāhjahān, Muhammad Fādil dedicated his *Majma' al-fadā'il*, which was completed in 1046/1636-7. The most important contribution to astronomy throughout this period was the *Zīj-i jadīd-i Muhammad Shāhī*, or astronomical tables, completed in 1140/1728, a project directed by Rajah Jai Singh Sawā'ī under the patronage of the Emperor Muhammad Shāh (1131-61/1719-48). Muslim, Brahman and European astronomers collaborated with Rajah Jai Singh, and several new astronomical instruments were devised. Abū 'l-Khayr, a son of Luft Allāh, acted as adviser to the Rajah in the construction of his observatory at Delhi. Some competent astronomers were sent to Europe with Padre Manoel and returned with Philippe de La Hire's tables for comparison with the results contained in the *Zīj-i jadīd-i Muhammad Shāhī*.

The theoretical basis of medicine, known as *Yūnānī* (Greek) in India, was contained in the works of the Persian, Abū Muhammad ibn Zakariyā' ar-Rāzī (d. 313/925), and in the *Qānūn fi 'l-tibb* ('Canon of Medicine') by Ibn Sīnā (Avicenna) (370-428/980-1037). These were deeply concerned with chemistry, pharmacology and even alchemy. The most popular handbook, and one which left an indelible mark on Indian medical practice between the VI/12th and IX/15th centuries, was the *Dhakhīra-i Khwarāzmshāhī* by Zayn ad-Dīn Abū Ibrāhīm Ismā'īl. The author lived during the time of the Seljuq governor of Khwārazm, known as Arslān Tegin (491-521/1098-1127). His work defines medicine and explains its utility, and deals with the structure and capacities of the human body; health and disease; causes, symptoms and diagnosis; fevers; localized diseases; tumours; ulcers; poisons and antidotes; and medicines. A more elaborate work by Zayn ad-Dīn was his *Aghrād at-tibb*. The *Ashāb wa'l-'alāmat*, written in Arabic by Najīb ad-Dīn Abū Hāmid of Samarqand (d. 619/1222), had an amplified translation, the *Tibb-i Akbarī*, made by Nafīs ibn 'Iwad Kirmānī in 827/1424. It was also very popular with Indian medical practitioners. The above works were the basic texts of the Muslim medical profession in India. A VIII/14th-century work on anatomy was written by Mansūr ibn Muhammad, a migrant from Fārs to Kashmir, where he wrote the *Kifāya-i mujāhidiyya*. A work containing prescriptions and remedies for all diseases was compiled by Yūsuf ibn Muhammad of Herat, Humāyūn's secretary.

Miyān Bhuwā ibn Khawāss Khān, one of Sultan Sikander Lodī's ministers, wrote the *Ma'dan ash-Shifā'-i Sikandarshāhī*, in which he blended knowledge obtained from Islamic and Sanskrit medical texts. Another mixture of indigenous Indian and Yūnānī medicine is found in *Dastūr al-atibbā'*, by the historian Muhammad Qāsim Hindūshāh, also known as Firishta (d. after 1033/1624). A nephew of Abū 'l-Fadl, Nūr ad-Dīn Muhammad 'Abdallāh, wrote a treatise on herbs and medicines, using terms borrowed from Greek, Arabic, Latin, Spanish, Hebrew, Syriac, Berber, Turkish, Persian and Sanskrit. It was given the title *Alfāz-i adwiya* and dedicated to Shāhjahān. General hygiene and maintenance of health was discussed by Muhammad Ridā of Shīrāz in his *Riyād-i 'Ālamgīrī*, which was dedicated to Awrangzīb.

The impact of the West

The most noticeable effect of the advent of the Portuguese was their influence on Indian languages in coastal areas. At a different level, Jesuit missionaries stimulated Akbar's interest in Portugal and in Christianity; but in their missionary zeal they frustrated Akbar's efforts to have Western philosophical works translated into Persian. Later, many nobles in the courts of Jahāngīr and Shāhjahān were able to discuss Western philosophy and religion with English and French merchants and adventurers.

While the loss of political power in Bengal was naturally a great shock to Muslims, the Calcutta Madrasa (college), founded by the Governor-General, Warren Hastings (1774-85), in 1781 attracted talented teachers and produced qualified Muslim officers for the judicial service. Muslims contributed articles to *Asiatick Re-*

India: sites, regions and natural features. (4)

searches, the official journal of the Asiatic Society founded by the orientalist, William Jones, in 1784. Under the patronage of the East India Company, many Muslim scholars wrote historical and mathematical works; and Muslims served in the army of the East India Company. Fort William College, established in 1800, was a rendezvous for some of the best Muslim scholars in India, and the dedications in the Urdu works published by the College were as extravagant in their praise of the expansionist Governor-General Lord Wellesley (1798–1805), as were the eulogies on Akbar or Shāhjahān. The prose literature published by the Fort William College, although officially said to be in Hindustani, came to be a landmark in Urdu prose and encouraged further Muslim literary contributions.

The 1793 Permanent Settlement of Bengal, devised by Lord Cornwallis (1786–93), confirmed the earlier displacement of the Muslim land-owning classes in favour of the Calcutta merchant community, which was basically Hindu. Though the Muslim upper classes gradually became impoverished and weak, able Muslim lawyers achieved superiority over their Hindu counterparts in the legal field at least. The myth of initial Muslim dissociation from British rule is unfounded. What relegated Muslims to the background in the second quarter of the nineteenth century was the lack of facilities for a higher English education for Muslims; the 1835 decision to spend public funds on Western education alone; and, three years later, the replacement of Persian by Sanskritized Bengali as the official language in Bengal.

The Indian Mutiny of 1857–8, led by dispossessed members of the Muslim and Hindu land-owning classes and adventurers from the two religious communities, was the last bid by the old medieval-style leadership to regain political power. During this abortive struggle the two communities fraternized with each other, but did not always cooperate. Their rustic weapons and methods of warfare were no match for the superior arms and discipline of the British, and the failure of the Mutiny was a foregone conclusion.

A new synthesis

After the suppression of the Mutiny, the British government in India began to conduct its affairs in the name of the British crown. The élite who had played a part in the rebellion were replaced by those who had remained loyal; and to them, as to the common Muslims, the name of the 'Sovereign of England' conjured up a royal mystique that had died with Shāhjahān.

This newly emerging class of Muslim élite considered the reformer Sayyid Ahmad Khān (1817–98) as their sincere friend and adviser. Originally a member of the decadent Mughul nobility, the Sayyid began his career by writing polemics on Sunnī–Shī'ī controversies. Contact with British officers of the East India Company, whom he had decided to serve in preference to the Mughuls, re-orientated his thinking. He began to write and edit works on Indian history. In the *Āthār as-Sanādīd*, which he produced in 1847, is preserved a vivid account of many Delhi buildings and inscriptions.

After the suppression of the Mutiny, Sayyid Ahmad Khān wrote two important works intended to clear up British misunderstandings with the Muslims. His first work was an analysis of the causes of the Mutiny, in which he attributed most of the blame to the missionaries for their short-sightedness in alienating the feelings of Indians against their masters. He also criticized the lack of any instrument by which the government could gauge public opinion. Sayyid Ahmad Khān's second book, *Loyal Muhammadans of India*, set out to prove Muslim loyalty to the British.

Sayyid Ahmad Khān's religious works and essays bitterly attacked the orthodox Muslim theory of *tashabbuh bi'l-kufr* (resembling an infidel). According to this theory anyone wearing Western dress or eating Western-style food with knives and forks was treated as an infidel. He stressed the necessity for a modern *kalām* based on Western ideas, at the same time underlining the fact that Islam was not hostile to science and that 'nature' and Islam were identical. In 1869–70 he visited England; and eight years later he established the Muhammadan Anglo-Oriental College at Aligarh. In 1878 he was appointed a member of the Viceregal Legislative Council and ten years later he was knighted. In 1886 Sayyid Ahmad Khān started a Muhammadan Educational Conference in order to stimulate the interest of the Muslim élite in problems of higher English education. From 1887 until his death he persistently struggled against the Indian National Congress, advising Muslims to keep themselves aloof from politics, obtain a higher English education and reap the advantages of unswerving loyalty to the British.

A galaxy of Muslim scholars and supporters from Urdu-speaking regions near Delhi and Aligarh gathered around Sayyid Ahmad Khān. However, advocates of the Indian National Congress, such as the great nationalist Badr ad-Dīn Tyabjī (1844–1906) of Bombay, were opposed to his views, believing him to be a reactionary. In Calcutta Sayyid Amīr 'Alī (1849–1928), who wrote the famous book, *The Spirit of Islam*, did not openly oppose the Sayyid, but favoured Muslims having their own political platform as opposed to the Indian National Congress.

Early in the 20th century the movement for greater Indian representation in the government made English-educated Muslims more politically aware. Nevertheless, the Muslim leadership remained in the hands of the landlords and moneyed classes of the Urdu-speaking regions. In December 1906 the foundations of the Muslim League were laid, and in 1908 the Nizārī Ismā'īlī Āghā Khān was elected its Permanent President. After considerable political vicissitudes, the Muslim League, led by Muhammad 'Alī Jinnah (1876–1948), another Ismā'īlī (from Bombay), succeeded in carving out an 'independent homeland for Indian Muslims' which was named Pakistan. The concept of Pakistan had first been outlined by the poet and philosopher Sir Muhammad Iqbāl (1876–1938) in his presidential address to the annual session of the Muslim League in 1930.

Iqbāl wrote in both Persian and Urdu. His Persian poetry was designed to convey his ideas to an educated Muslim public in both Iran and India. In 1915 he published the *Asrār-i Khudī* ('The Secrets of the Self') and three years later the *Rumūz-i bīkhudī* ('Mysteries of Selflessness'). His greatest work was the *Jāwīd-nāma* ('Pilgrimage to Eternity'). His Urdu *mathnawīs* and short poems were designed to stir up 'Islamic dynamism' among the non-Persian-speaking Muslim élite. A collection of his lectures in English, published under the title of *The Reconstruction of Religious Thought in Islam*, gives his personal interpretation of Islam and carries much weight with the educated élite of the sub-continent.

Iqbāl drew on both Islamic and Western sources. Being at once a poet and philosopher, he produced a writing that was unique. He believed that 'western republicanism and its constitutional bodies, reforms, privileges and rights' were not 'the fairies of liberty' but 'Kaiserism' in which 'the demon of exploitation danced in republican garb'. A large number of Muslims regard Iqbāl as the father of 'Islamic socialism'. His view of Russian Communism as a sort of secular equivalent of Islam was controversial at the time; and after the events of the last forty years it is perhaps even more controversial today. But it does raise the question of the future of Islam in the sub-continent, a question which presents itself unavoidably to everyone who has studied its thousand-year-old past.

As a monument to the victory of the Turks over India, Qutb ad-Dīn Aybak began the great Qutb Minār (opposite) about 588/1192, on the site of Delhi's Jain and Hindu temples. Made by local Hindu craftsmen, and combining Qur'ānic inscriptions with Indian floral designs, it supersedes other victory towers built in the Islamic world. It was also used as a *ma'dhana*, or the minaret from which the Muslims were called to prayer. (1)

The splendours of Mughul art reflect the wide range of the emperors' sympathies, which embraced Persia, Hindu India and even Europe. To the endlessly inventive use of flat pattern which is characteristic of all Islamic art was added a feeling for shadow and depth that is uniquely Indian. Perforated stone screens, exemplifying just this combination of qualities, had, at Gujerat by the early IX/15th century, reached a standard which they were never to surpass. Here the craftsmen were Hindu or Jain. Their art was eagerly taken up by the Mughuls, producing works such as the marble grille of the tomb at Fathpūr-Sīkrī of Salīm Chishtī (above), the holy man whose prayers Akbar believed were responsible for the birth of his son, Salīm (later Emperor Jahāngīr). The screen, which produces most beautiful shadow-patterns, defines the space of the verandahs enclosing the tomb and arrests the eye for its own sake, but also leads beyond itself to the mystery of farther spaces and volumes. (2)

As his own resting place Sultan Ghiyāth ad-Dīn Tughluq built a majestic tomb at Multan (right). Octagonal in plan, it is made of chiselled brick, the walls sloping inwards, with glazed tiles and bands of carved timber. In the end it received the body not of the Sultan but of the Sūfī shaykh Rukn ad-Dīn Multānī (d. 735/1334), whose grandfather founded the Suhrawardī order of the Sūfīs in the region. (4)

The Tāj Mahal (begun 1041/1631) is as outstanding for the details of its craftsmanship as for its overall conception. Shown here is a small part of the *pietra dura* work, with traditional Indo-Persian designs. (3)

A well-planned new capital was built by Akbar at Fathpūr-Sīkrī, twenty-two miles from Agra. Begun in 979/1571, the palaces were completed in one year. Carved brackets and beams were constructed off-site and assembled under the Emperor's personal supervision. Right: view from the Panch Mahal ('five-storeyed' tower) in the palace complex. (5)

The Mughul dynasty came to power in India in the early x/16th century, maintaining their position until the British conquest. In terms of wealth and cultural achievements it was the greatest of the Islamic dynasties to rule India, though these achievements fall almost entirely during the reigns of only three emperors – Akbar, Jahāngīr and Shāhjahān.

The founder was Bābur (left, a later miniature of about 1019/1610), descended on his father's side from Tamerlane and on his mother's from Chingiz Khān. Beginning from a small principality in the modern Tashkent region, he succeeded during his short life-time – he was only forty-seven when he died – in uniting under his rule the region from Kabul to Bihar. (6)

Jahāngīr succeeded Akbar in 1014/1605. Although he rebelled against his father during his lifetime, after his death he continued his policies unchanged. This miniature (above) shows Jahāngīr with a portrait of Akbar, who holds a globe. (7)

Akbar, Bābur's grandson, emerges as the key figure in the story of the Mughuls, and one of the great rulers of world history. His disappointment with the Muslim relious leadership prompted him to investigate the truth in all religions, including Christianity. These exercises culminated in the crystallization of his belief in universal concord. (8)

Friendship and friction between Mughuls and Persians is a recurring theme in their histories, perhaps because of the fact that culturally they had so much in common. The strategic and commercial significance of Kandahar made it a bone of contention between them. A miniature (left) featuring an imaginary permanent peace between the two countries shows Jahāngīr seated next to the Safavid Emperor Shāh 'Abbās I, attended by Āsaf Khān, the brother of the Emperor's queen, Nūr Jahān (left), and Khan-i 'Alam (right), the Mughul ambassador to Persia. (9)

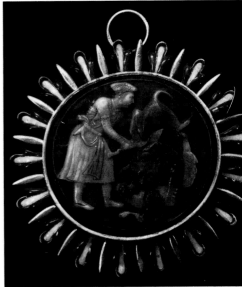

Shāhjāhan (above), depicted killing a lion, was the son of Jahāngīr and a far-sighted administrator and builder of monuments and cities. He founded a new city at Delhi, called Shāhjahānābād, as well as building the Tāj Mahal for his favourite wife. He ended his life as a prisoner of his son, Awrangzīb. (10)

Diplomats, missionaries and visitors flocked from all parts of the world to the Mughul court. This detail (left) shows the English ambassador, Sir Thomas Roe, among those being received by Jahāngīr. (11)

317

سپاه لشکرکز و فضل سنگ اندازیا بتمام مخلص حقیقت پوشند قاسم خان میر بر و حبه به فرنج

و فیروزی صورت و نقش اختتام کرفت

Miniature painting was virtually the creation of Akbar, who imported artists from Persia and encouraged his own subjects to imitate them. The resulting style, however, was quite distinct. Left: completion of the Fort at Agra, from the history of his reign, the *Akbar-nāma*. (12)

An artist at work, *c.* 1024/1615. At about this time Sir Thomas Roe presented Jahāngīr with a miniature by Isaac Oliver. European art soon had a decisive influence on Indian painting. (14)

Akbar crossing the Ganges– another illustration from the *Akbar-nāma*. It is one of Akbar's best-known exploits and occurred in 975/1567. (13)

Gardens were essential to the Mughul conception of the good life, as they were to all Islamic cultures. Exquisite compositions of flowers, trees and water, they are the settings from many court scenes shown in the miniatures. Here (right), in a work by Bichitr, a young prince talks with his advisers. (15)

Europe's conquest was the last of India's many defeats; the briefest, but perhaps the most profound. Mughul provincial power was broken at Plassey in 1171/1757, and Muslims found themselves placed much as the Hindus has been centuries earlier – bent on preserving their culture and religion but politically helpless. There was also from the first a certain mutual respect and fascination. Left: European ladies taking tea by a lake – an Indian idea of Europe rather than a representation of Europeans in India. Below: Mahādajī Sindhia of Gwalior, entertaining British officers to a party with dancing girls, about 1790. Although a Hindu Maratha leader, Mahādajī helped the Mughul Emperor Shāh 'Ālam II to abandon his life of exile and accede to the throne of his ancestors at Delhi in 1186/1772. (16, 17)

Chapter Thirteen

ISLAM TODAY

Elie Kedourie

This 19th-century hatchment of arms is carved in stone in the Topkapi Saray. It is a confident celebration of military power, as yet unproblematic and unselfconscious in adopting its European symbols. (1)

THE LAST TWO HUNDRED YEARS or so have not been kind either to Islam or to the Muslims. From the latter part of the XII/18th century their territories, whether in the centre or at the periphery, were simultaneously or successively under attack from non-Muslim Europeans. In Bengal, the British East India Company was becoming a fully-fledged government, gradually branching out into the rest of the Indian sub-continent and supplanting the authority of the Mughul emperor of Delhi. Similarly the Dutch government, taking over the properties and rights of the Dutch East India Company in 1800, had decisively established its authority in Java by the fourth decade of the XIII/19th century. In 1830, France invaded Algeria, and after almost two decades of war succeeded in conquering the country and opening it up to large-scale European colonization. During the same period, Russia too was steadily bringing into subjection ancient Muslim lands in the Caucasus and in Central Asia, and encouraging their settlement by large numbers of non-Muslims.

This process whereby large, immemorially Muslim territories came to be occupied or controlled by non-Muslims went on well into the XIV/20th century. Between 1865 and 1873 Tsarist Russia extinguished the independence of the Central Asian amirate of Khokand and established a protectorate over the two other amirates of Khiva and Bukhārā. France established a protectorate over Tunisia in 1881, and to all intents and purposes became its ruler. The British occupied Egypt in 1882, and remained its rulers, practically if not formally, until after World War I. The British occupation of Egypt led in due course to the establishment of an Anglo-Egyptian 'condominium' in the Sudan, in which the real power was unequivocally in the hands of the British. By the end of the XIII/19th century, also, the Dutch had conquered the native kingdoms of Sumatra and established a rich and extensive empire in the islands of the Indonesian archipelago. And by the 1880s, the Muslim rulers of neighbouring Malaya came to acknowledge Britain as the protecting power. In the first decade or so of the XIV/20th century, Italy invaded and conquered Tripolitania; and the French established a protectorate over the greater part of Morocco, while the Spaniards, as their junior partners, exercised their protectorate over the rest of the Sharīfian kingdom. As in Tunisia, in Morocco too the protecting Powers established a network of their own officials who in effect governed the country.

European power affected Muslim states in other, indirect, ways. By a natural development, the British empire in India led to British paramountcy in the Persian Gulf and to the control of Aden and Hadramawt. It also gave Britain a privileged position in southern Persia. Similarly, on the eve of World War I, the Ottoman empire had come to be divided into zones of influence between the European powers by means of informal, but nonetheless effective, understandings that allowed them to establish a preponderance of economic enterprise and, if they could, of political power. As a direct result of this expansion, and of the concomitant weakening of Ottoman power and prestige, the Christian populations of the Balkans began to aspire to political independence. These aspirations, supported more or less actively by one or other European power, led eventually to the independence of Greece, Serbia, Rumania and Bulgaria. All these territories contained sizable and old-established Muslim populations whose position was undermined, and whose possessions and lives were, in many cases, imperilled or destroyed.

The long period of European dominance reached its apogee during and after World War I, in which its Young Turk rulers led the Ottoman empire to defeat and eventual destruction. The end of the war saw Mesopotamia and the Levant under Allied occupation, with British troops in Baghdad and Damascus – cities which had been Muslim time out of mind, and which no Christian had ever conquered. The aftermath of war, and the Bolshevik Revolution which it occasioned, led, in 1920, to the final extinction of Khiva and Bukhārā as distinct entities, and the incorporation of their territories, in due course, within the USSR.

The term which is most frequently used to describe this European expansion into the Muslim world (and elsewhere) is imperialism. The term has now in fact become little more than a slogan or a catchword. Its origins, in any case, lie in European political and intellectual history, and it is only in the European context that it is at all intelligible. Muslims certainly would not have understood it or found it of much use in explaining their predicament. In their own traditional categories, the conflict with Europe, which issued in such a dismal series of political and military reverses, would have been seen as a clash between Islam and Christendom – as the latest phase of a conflict in which, over many centuries, two worlds, two militant faiths, had confronted and defied one another.

In this protracted confrontation, which dated from the beginnings of Islam, the Muslims had so far on the whole been conspicuously successful. Spain, it is true, had in the end been lost; but the other areas taken from the Christians became irreversibly Muslim, became indeed the heartlands of Islam. The Grand Duchy of Moscow, again, had liberated itself from Tatar domination; but, on the other hand, the Ottoman empire succeeded in annexing extensive Christian territories in the Balkans and in Central Europe, and its armies could threaten Vienna as late as the 1680s. This long record of military success and assured domination had for Muslims a transcendental significance. It served to prove that Muhammad's message was true, that God prospered those who believed in Him and hearkened to His revelation. Political success vindicated Islam, and the course of world history proved the truth of the religion. Muslims fought to extend the bounds of Islam and humble the unbelievers; the fight was holy, and the reward of those who fell was eternal bliss. Such a belief, which the history of Islam itself seemed to establish beyond doubt, inspired in Muslims self-confidence and powerful feelings of superiority. Hence, the long series of defeats at the hands of Christian Europe could not but undermine the self-respect of the Muslims, and result in a far-reaching moral and intellectual crisis. For military defeat was defeat not only in a worldly sense; it also brought into doubt the truth of the Muslim revelation itself.

Threat and resistance

The loss of self-confidence, the failure of nerve which a long series of setbacks and defeats induced took quite long to manifest itself. Even though there was great disproportion between European military and technical resources and those at the disposal of Muslim society, opposition to European encroachments was in many cases remarkably stout-hearted, resourceful and tenacious. The French landing in Algiers elicited native resistance which the conquerors found it by no means easy to overcome. The best known of those who organized and led this resistance was the famous 'Abd al-Qādir, who originated from Oran in western Algeria. In the course of fighting the French between 1833 and 1847, when he was finally defeated and taken prisoner, 'Abd al-Qādir amassed a large following of tribes and came to control a large territory not only in the west, but also in the centre and in the east of the country. The French certainly regarded him as more than a mere guerilla leader and more than once entered into agreements with him – agreements which in many ways resembled treaties between two sovereign states. 'Abd al-Qādir himself

certainly looked upon his role as much more than that of a tribal leader. From the start he and his supporters considered the movement as the setting up (or restoration) of an Islamic polity of which 'Abd al-Qādir was the imam who had received the suffrages *(bay'a)* of the faithful, whose duty was to uphold the faith, and protect the people of Islam. And 'Abd al-Qādir indeed attempted to set up a state which transcended tribal loyalties and rivalries, and to organize a modern army whose loyalty went to the imam and to the (embryonic) state which he had set up. For this army, 'Abd al-Qādir drew up a code which laid down the different ranks of the troops, their respective uniforms and pay and the discipline to which they were subject. The code ended with a description of 'Abd al-Qādir himself – an idealized picture, to be sure, but nonetheless significant in showing us precisely the ideal to which he himself looked up. The imam, the code declared,

cares not for this world, and withdraws from it as much as his avocations will permit. He despises wealth and riches. He lives with the greatest plainness and sobriety. He is always simply clad. He rises in the middle of the night to recommend his own soul and the soul of his followers to God. His chief pleasure is in praying to God with fasting, that his sins may be forgiven.

He is incorruptible. He never takes anything out of the public funds for himself. All the presents which are brought to him he sends to the public treasury; for he serves the State, not himself. He neither eats, nor drinks, nor dresses, but so as religion ordains. When he administers justice, he hears complaints with the greatest patience. A smile is always on his face for the encouragement of those who approach him. His decisions are conformable to the words of the sacred book. He hates the man who does not act uprightly; but honours him who strictly observes the precepts and practises the duties of religion.

From his boyhood he learned to mount the most fiery horse without a teacher. He never turns before an enemy; but awaits him firmly. In a retreat he fights like a common soldier, rallying his men by his words and example, and sharing all their dangers. Thus, brave, disinterested, and pious, when he preaches, his words bring tears into all eyes, and melt the hardest hearts. All who hear him become good Mussulmans.

He explains the most difficult passages of the Koran and of the Hadeeth (Traditions) without referring to books or Ulemahs. The most learned Arabs and the greatest Talebs acknowledge him as their master and teacher. May God increase his nobleness of character, his wisdom, his learning, his understanding, his honour, glory, and success, a thousandfold.

It is immaterial whether 'Abd al-Qādir was in reality exactly as he is described in this passage. What is more interesting to note here is that this is a deliberate harking back to the simple piety, the uprightness, the egalitarianism and the valour which the faithful believed to characterize Islam under the Prophet and the well-guided caliphs. 'Abd al-Qādir and his followers indeed took very seriously the parallel between Muhammad's foundation of the Islamic polity, and its restoration in Algeria by 'Abd al-Qādir. His son, in the voluminous biography which he devoted to his father, describes the occasion on which 'Abd al-Qādir was invested with office. It was 'Abd al-Qādir's own father who first proclaimed his allegiance to the new leader and gave him the title Nāsir ad-Dīn, Champion of Religion. The ceremony, we are told, took place under a tree, and thus was significantly similar to that earlier one when, in the sixth year of the *hijra*, also under a tree, the Muslims pledged themselves to Muhammad and a Qur'ānic verse (xlviii, 18) declared: 'God is pleased with the believers as they pledge themselves to you under the tree. He knows what is in their hearts and gives them peace, and rewards them with a forthcoming conquest.'

At the other end of the Muslim world, in Dāghistān, an equally tenacious resistance to the Russian conquest of the Caucasus manifested itself in the movement known as Murīdism. The leaders of this movement were followers, *murīds*, of the Naqshbandī religious brotherhood. They proclaimed the primacy of the *sharī'a* and the duty incumbent on all Muslims to uphold it, by fighting the unbelievers and resisting their rule. The core of Murīdism consisted of a select band of fighters who were organized as a religious brotherhood. This small band of warriors succeeded in overawing many Dāghistāni tribes, and inducing or forcing them to join in a *jihād* against the Russian conquerors. The Murīds succeeded in maintaining themselves from 1830 to 1859 against repeated assaults mounted by the Russians with all the military and technical resources available to a great power. It is of course true that the Murīds were fighting a mountain war in terrain with which they were familiar; but the length and tenacity of their resistance remains nonetheless remarkable. There can be no doubt that this is to be attributed to the solidarity, cohesion and self-confidence which Islam produced and maintained. This religious impulse was sufficiently powerful to endow the movement with a rudimentary political structure in which the leaders of the Murīds were recognized as imams by their followers, this politico-religious office being held in succession by three leaders of whom the last, Shāmil, became quite well known in the Europe of his day.

Resistance to European penetration took other, sometimes less sustained, but no less significant forms. The disturbance and the threat which this penetration represented would become manifest through the spread of millennial expectation focused and crystallized in the preaching of a leader who would claim to be the *mahdī* or *sāhib as-sā'a*, the 'rightly guided one', the 'master of the hour'; he who in Muslim tradition was to inaugurate, by means of prodigies or superhuman acts, the everlasting reign of truth and justice. Thus, about 1838 there appeared in Algeria someone who claimed to be a descendant of 'Abd al-Qādir al-Jīlānī, the founder of the Qādiriyya religious brotherhood, and to be called Muhammad ibn 'Abdullāh (i.e. to have the same name as the Prophet). He joined some tribes who were disaffected towards (the Algerian) 'Abd al-Qādir and began to preach against him. He declared that 'Abd al-Qādir was powerless to save the Muslims from the Europeans; that on the contrary he was their accomplice. He claimed that he, Muhammad ibn 'Abdullāh, was the awaited *mahdī* who would bring deliverance to the Muslims. 'Abd al-Qādir naturally resented this challenge to his authority.

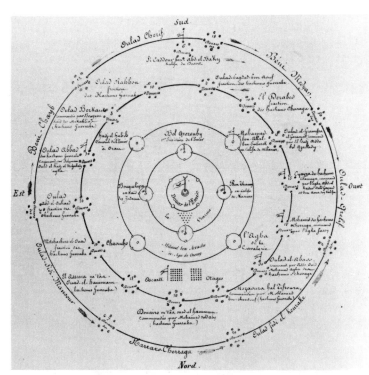

Resistance to French expansion in Algeria between 1833 and 1847 was led by 'Abd al-Qādir, who saw himself as reviving the piety and valour of early Islam. This schematic plan of his camp in 1843 was made by his French adversaries. 'Abd al-Qādir's standard is set up in the centre; around him are grouped his officers, picked troops and hostages; and on the outside of the circle are the Algerian tribes who have thrown in their lot with his cause. (2)

He organized an expedition against the supporters of the so-called *mahdī*, defeated them and thus put an end to his preaching. A few years later, in 1845, when 'Abd al-Qādir was no longer at the apogee of his power, another *mahdī* appeared. He also was a member of a religious brotherhood, the Darqāwa, and also called himself Muhammad ibn 'Abdullāh. Prophecies attributed to a Moroccan saint were applied to this *mahdī*, commonly known as Bū Ma'za, the Man with the Goat. According to these prophecies the man of the hour would eventually dominate all the Eastern countries, and all of Algeria would belong to him; but only after *banū 'l-asfar*, the yellow ones (i.e. the French), would have taken it: 'If you seize it now,' the prophecy went on, 'they will deprive you of your conquest; if, however, the French take this country first, the day will come when you will take it back from them.' The prophecy was not destined to be fulfilled in Bū Ma'za's day, for the French defeated his followers and took him captive to France. Decades later, at the beginning of the XIV/20th century, when Morocco was increasingly feeling the effects of European penetration, another member of the Darqāwa appeared there to proclaim the millennial hope. Bū Hamāra, the Man with the Donkey, who was active in Taza, to the east of Fez, between 1900 and 1909, preached against 'Abd al-'Azīz, the Sultan of Morocco. Bū Hamāra accused the Sultan of following Western ways and delivering his country over to Christians. He claimed to be in reality a brother of the Sultan and thus as a member of the Moroccan ruling house, a descendant of the Prophet. His followers proclaimed him sultan, and Bū Hamāra set up court at Taza as Mawlāy Muhammad and proceeded to organize an army and to increase his standing by war as well as by having begun his movement in 1881, the Mahdī succeeded, with the help of a tribal army, in occupying El Obeid in 1883 and the capital, Khartoum, in 1885, and in setting up a state which survived under his companion and successor ʿAbdullāh ibn Muhammad until 1898, when an expedition led by Kitchener finally destroyed the Mahdist state. Though the government against which the Mahdī and his supporters rebelled was Muslim, it was – and had been for some decades – profoundly influenced by Western ideas, and drew heavily on Western administrative techniques, so that the Mahdī's rejection of an Islamic government was to a large extent still really the rejection of Europe.

But it was rejection at one remove, rejection of ideas and methods which many Muslim governments in the XIII/19th and XIV/20th centuries adopted, whether enthusiastically, or only in sheer self-defence. And, along with direct or indirect European rule over Muslim territories, this spread of European ideas and techniques is the most significant and striking theme in the modern history of Islam.

'Necessary reforms'
In 1867, a well-known Muslim statesman, Khayr ad-Dīn at-Tūnisī, who was to become prime minister of Tunisia and grand vizier in Constantinople, published an Arabic work which set out to acquaint his readers with European civilization and the political arrangements associated with it. The work was prefaced by a long introduction in which Khayr ad-Dīn examined existing Muslim institutions. This introduction was shortly afterwards translated into French and published under the title, *Réformes nécessaires aux états musulmans*. This title indicates clearly enough that Khayr ad-Dīn was critical of the Muslim polities of his day, and was convinced that they should be 'reformed'. The 'reforms' he had in mind were unmistakably inspired by the example of a Europe which was powerful and prosperous, and in which the citizen enjoyed freedom under the law. He quotes with approval the words of a 'leading European' to the effect that 'the torrent of European civilization' was overflowing the world and that non-European countries were 'in danger from this current unless they imitate it'. By the time Khayr ad-Dīn had published his book, this opinion was in fact common currency in Europe, as well as among the intellectual and official classes of the Muslim world. And as time went on, those who held it became much more numerous than those who shared the attitudes of ʿAbd al-Qādir, Shāmil, Bū Maʿza or the Mahdī. Nor is this surprising, for there was nothing unreasonable in believing that the Muslim world could attain the power and prosperity of Europe by the same methods that Europe had used, and that this could be done without endangering any of the essential values of Islam.

This was at the outset merely a simple uncritical assumption. In any case, those who had the power to initiate changes on the European model, namely the rulers, had neither need nor leisure to worry about the compatibility of such changes with Islam. By the end of the XII/18th century, it was amply clear that the military threat posed by the European powers was formidable. Survival meant the quick adoption of European military methods and techniques. The earliest one among Islamic

The Caucasian leader Shāmil offers a parallel to ʿAbd al-Qādir at the other end of the Muslim world. He preached a holy war against Russian conquest and for twenty-five years (1834–59) was able to marshal support among Muslims threatened by absorption into the Tsarist empire. (3)

propaganda. Emissaries of his among the Berber tribes quoted alleged sayings of the Prophet, declaring that he was the awaited *mahdī* who would regenerate Islam and expel the Christians from the Maghrib. His defiance of the Moroccan government came to an end when the Sultan's forces captured him and exhibited him in a public garden in Fez locked up in a cage.

Bū Hamāra's movement was directed against a Muslim government, but his attack was justified by the allegation that this government was abandoning the Muslims into the hands of Christians. This reason, on the other hand, did not loom very large in the movement of the Sudanese *mahdī*, who in the modern history of Islam has come to be known as the Mahdī *par excellence*. The movement of the Sudanese Mahdī was directed against the Egyptian government headed by a descendant of Muhammad ʿAlī Pasha who had invaded the Sudan in 1820, and against the Ottoman sultan-caliph who was the nominal suzerain of Egypt. The Mahdī's movement, in other words, was directed primarily against a Muslim government. The Mahdī, Muhammad Ahmad ibn ʿAbdullāh, who claimed descent from the Prophet whose name he bore, and who had belonged to a religious brotherhood which was an offshoot of the Qādiriyya, preached the restoration of the Islamic *umma* as it had been in the Prophet's time, and the ending of Egyptian rule, which he looked upon as alien and inimical to Islam. As is well known, rulers systematically to translate this conclusion into practice was the Ottoman Sultan Selīm III (1789–1807). Shortly after his accession, Selīm embarked on a determined effort to create modern arsenals and military technical schools. He also began organizing new military formations in which European instructors tried to instil into the recruits the drill and discipline which were by then practised in the armies of the great European states. These methods greatly impressed Selīm and his advisers. As one of them wrote in a memorandum advocating the reforms, European troops 'keep in a compact body, pressing their feet together that their order of battle may not be broken; and their cannon being polished like one of Marcovich's watches they load twelve times in a minute and make the bullets rain like musket balls'.

Selīm's reforms aroused fear and antagonism among the Janissaries and other traditional formations. Recourse to European methods and instructors was demeaning and irreligious. And a military formation so directly fashioned and controlled by the Sultan, who had stationed it in the environs of Constantinople, not only offended the prejudices of the Janissaries; it also threatened their position and their vested interests. For however infirm the Janissaries were now in the face of foreign enemies, they had become a formidable power in the state, enjoying privilege and profit, and by their readiness to mutiny checking the sultan's power, and even on occasion deposing him. And, in fact, Selīm's *nizām-i jadīd*, or new order, so antagonized the Janissary heads and their supporters among the religious leaders that in May 1807 a revolt toppled the 'infidel Sultan' from the throne; and his successor, Mustafā IV, abolished Selīm's innovations within a few days of his accession. Mustafā was himself deposed the following year, and replaced by his brother (and Selīm's cousin) who reigned until his death in 1839 as Mahmūd II. The new Sultan resumed Selīm's military reforms, but only after a very long interval. In the meantime another Muslim ruler, Muhammad ʿAlī, Pasha of Egypt, tried (with what seemed a large measure of success) to fashion for himself a European-style army and navy with which to forward his very extensive ambitions.

Muhammad ʿAlī, an Albanian from Kavalla, was an officer in the Ottoman force which was sent to Egypt in pursuance of an Anglo-Ottoman scheme to dislodge the French who, led by Bonaparte, had occupied Egypt, nominally an Ottoman province, in 1798. A man of great ability and ruthlessness, he managed to ruin his superiors and his rivals and by 1805 to be recognized by the Sultan as governor of the province. Ottoman Egypt in the XI/17th and XII/18th centuries was very much under the control of military grandees, the mamlūks, who acted in virtual independence of Constantinople. When Muhammad ʿAlī became Pasha of Egypt they were still a powerful force in the land, and able to act as a check on the Ottoman governor in the same way as the Janissaries acted as a check on the sultan. In 1811 Muhammad ʿAlī managed by treacherous means to massacre most of the mamlūks and thus secure himself against any internal threat to his power. In 1815 he proceeded to train the forces at his disposal in European military methods. As in Selīm's case, European innovations aroused opposition, and there was a mutiny which obliged Muhammad ʿAlī to proceed cautiously. In any case, his ambitions required

the recruitment of a large army. To have the necessary reservoir of power he invaded the Sudan in 1820–21 and enslaved large numbers of its inhabitants, whom he sent to Egypt to be incorporated in his armies. Experience, however, showed that slaves did not make good or willing soldiers, and on the advice of his European experts he began conscripting Egyptian fellahs. However, conscription had to proceed by violent means, and the peasants reacted with flight, self-mutilation and occasional resistance. Military reform may thus be seen to have meant a great increase in the demands made by the state on the subject, and to have *ipso facto* enhanced the power of the state to make such demands. Muhammad ʿAlī, the modernizer, became literally the owner of Egypt. When he exterminated the mamlūks he had also confiscated their lands to his own benefit. He also, on various plausible pretexts, confiscated the lands which benefactors had over the centuries put in trust for the upkeep of mosques and other charitable purposes. The beneficiaries of these trusts, writes the chronicler al-Jabartī (who was a contemporary of Muhammad ʿAlī's),

> were greatly disturbed and many of them appealed to the sheikhs, who went off to speak to the pasha on this subject. They said to him that that would lead to the ruin of the mosques, whereupon he replied: 'Where are the flourishing mosques? If anyone is not satisfied with this arrangement let him raise his hands and I will restore the ruined mosques and provide them with the necessary means.' Their protests were of no avail and they returned to their homes.

Muhammad ʿAlī laid his hand not only on the property of the mamlūks and the charitable foundations. The title to all private property whatsoever became highly uncertain; and the owner was obliged to provide documents and title-deeds to the satisfaction of the Pasha's officials, whose interest and duty was precisely not to be easily satisfied: the more suspicious they were, the better they served the Pasha, and the greater the eagerness of the claimants to sweeten them with benevolences. Muhammad ʿAlī also had a new cadastral survey made, in which his officials used a measuring unit smaller than that previously employed:

> When this was done [al-Jabartī tells us] they reckoned the land in the new *faddān*, showing an increase in area, and proceeded to tax it at the rate of 15, or 14, or 12, or 11, or 10 *riyals* per *faddān*, according to the nature of the region and the quality of the soil. The result was an enormous increase: thus the village which had formerly paid 1,000 *riyals* in taxes – a sum that had given rise to complaints on the part of [tax farmers] and peasants and had resulted in uncollectable arrears – was now assessed at between 10,000 and 100,000 *riyals*, more or less.

Muhammad ʿAlī's centralized government machine was clearly more efficient than any of its ramshackle predecessors in extracting resources from the peasantry to cover his increased military expenditure. But terms like 'machine' and 'extraction' are here only metaphors. The reality to which they refer is simply that of compulsion by force or the threat of force. In his well-known work on *The Manners and Customs of the Modern Egyptians*, Edward

It is easy to illustrate the attitude of Europeans towards Muslims in the 19th century. Shown here are the capture of Adrianople (Edirne) by the Russians during the Russo-Turkish War of 1829–30 and the entry of General Berthézène into Algiers on 5 July 1830. More important than the military defeats themselves, however, was the fact that until 1914 great numbers of Muslims increasingly came to see themselves with the eyes of the West. (4,5)

William Lane has a chapter on 'Government' which, he tells us, was written in 1834 and 1835 during 'the best period' of Muhammad ʿAlī's reign. He includes in this chapter an episode involving the collection of taxes from a village which may serve to describe graphically what Muhammad ʿAlī's extractive activities involved. Lane tells us that a tax-collector demanded sixty *riyals* from a peasant, who was unable to find this sum. So, the tax-collector confiscated the peasant's only possession, a cow, which he ordered to be slaughtered and divided into sixty portions, the butcher receiving the head as his fee. Sixty villagers were then called together, and ordered each to buy for a *riyal* a portion of the cow. The peasant, however, complained to the tax-collector's superior, who ordered all the parties, including the butcher and the sixty villagers, to appear before him. They all confirmed the peasant's story, and the butcher declared that had he refused to kill the cow, the tax-collector would have beaten him and destroyed his house. The Qādī was then sent for and the tax-collector's actions put before him.

'He is [declared the Qādī] a cruel tyrant, who oppresses everyone under his authority. Is not a cow worth a hundred and twenty riyals or more? And he has sold this one for sixty riyals: This is tyranny towards the owner.' The Defterdār then said to some of his soldiers, 'Take the Nāzir [i.e. the tax-collector], and strip him, and bind him.' This done, he said to the butcher, 'Butcher, dost thou not fear God? Thou hast killed the cow unjustly.' The butcher again urged that he was obliged to obey the Nāzir. 'Then,' said the Defterdār, 'if I order thee to do a thing wilt thou do it?' 'I will do it,' answered the butcher. 'Slaughter the Nāzir,' said the Defterdār. Immediately, several of the soldiers present seized the Nāzir, and threw him down; and the butcher cut his throat, in the regular orthodox manner of killing animals for food. 'Now, cut him up,' said the Defterdār, 'into sixty pieces.' This was done: the people concerned in the affair, and many others, looking on; but none daring to speak. The sixty peasants who had bought the meat of the cow were then called forward, one after another, and each was made to take a piece of the flesh of the Nāzir, and to pay for it two riyals; so that a hundred and twenty riyals were obtained from these. They were then dismissed; but the butcher remained. The Kadee was asked what should be the reward of the butcher; and answered that he should be paid as he had been paid by the Nāzir. The Defterdār therefore ordered that the head of the Nāzir should be given to him; and the butcher went away with his worse than valueless burden, thanking God that he had not been more unfortunate, and scarcely believing himself to have so easily escaped until he arrived at his village. The money paid for the flesh of the Nāzir was given to the owner of the cow.

The unfortunate tax-collector, we may observe, was really victim not of his tyranny, which, in comparison with the oppression practised by his betters, was quite venial, but of his incompetence. Since Muhammad ʿAlī had decreed that communities were collectively liable for the unpaid taxes of their members, the tax-collector had no need to sell cow's meat in order to secure the Pasha's due. In any case, we may note, whatever happened, the Pasha's interests were in no way harmed. In an agricultural country like Egypt the bulk of the taxes naturally fell on the countryside. As a peasant in Upper Egypt said: 'Muhammad ʿAlī is jealous of the lice which eat up the fellah.' But it did not follow that the cities escaped the burden. On the contrary, all trades, however lowly, contributed their share. Even prostitutes had to pay a tax on their activities.

Muhammad ʿAlī was not content merely to centralize and improve the collection of taxes. He gave himself the monopoly of trade in, and export of, most agricultural produce. Also, after a French textile engineer, Alexandre Jumel, had discovered towards 1820 a superior variety of cotton native to Egypt, the cultivation and export of this cotton became one of the Pasha's most lucrative sources of revenue. But cotton cultivation was not favoured by the fellah; it therefore entailed strict regulation of agricultural activities, and led to a great increase in the control exercised by the state over the life and livelihood of the peasantry. The perennial irrigation which went together with cotton cultivation also required that canals should be regularly cleaned and kept in good repair, and thus greatly increased the burden of the corvée on the peasant. In bad times, the burden of taxes and corvée led to a flight from the countryside which the Pasha found inconvenient. He therefore decreed that villagers who had left their villages over a period of ten years had to return or suffer the death penalty.

It is quite clear that Muhammad ʿAlī was attempting to set up in Egypt a strictly centralized, 'planned' economy, the purpose of which was to extract from the inhabitants the maximum resources for use in the pursuit of political and military power. For it was not only agriculture which the Pasha minutely regulated; he arranged also to supply craftsmen with their raw materials and compelled them to sell all their products to him at a fixed price, which he re-sold at a great profit. He himself, or merchants he desig-nated, enjoyed a monopoly in the export of manufactures. And lastly, in an effort to industrialize the country, he set up state factories which his own employees managed.

In the end, Muhammad ʿAlī's centralized, all-embracing state proved short-lived. Eventually, his political schemes failed and his will flagged; again, he could not be literally all-seeing, and since the state he set up was rigorously centralized, no subordinate of his, whether prominent or humble, was willing to take upon himself decisions which could be for him a matter of life and death. The fate of the tax-collector is instructive not only in itself, but for its exemplary value in a state in which one man alone was free. Such a state of affairs, so Hegel said, characterizes the traditional Oriental despotism; but what we see in Muhammad ʿAlī's state is something more potent and more fearful. It is that European 18th-century absolutism which its partisans called 'enlightened' and which, equip-ped with the 'social science' and the *Kameralwissenschaft* of the day, aspired to fashion society in the likeness of a machine, the cogs of which were the subjects, the opera-tor of which was the ruler and the product of which was happiness rationally defined and scientifically appor-tioned by the government. And in fact we even see Muhammad ʿAlī adopting the rhetoric of this 'enlight-ened absolutism' – if only for the benefit of his European visitors. Thus, to a British visitor who suggested that the fellahs be allowed a greater latitude in what to cultivate, Muhammad ʿAlī replied: 'No! my peasantry are suffering from the disease of ignorance to their true interest, and I must act the part of the doctor. I must be severe when anything goes wrong.' These words show the Pasha of Egypt to be aware of the benefits not only of European scientific techniques, but also of the European rhetoric of 'enlightened' absolutism.

Tyrannies old and new

Muhammad ʿAlī's record shows that his professed tenderness for the 'true interest' of his subjects to be a cynical sham, and that his sole preoccupation was how to exploit them most efficiently. What distinguishes him from his predecessors is the greatly enlarged scope for intervention in social and economic activities which Europe suggested and justified, and in the extreme centralization which European methods made possible. The point is made in a striking passage by a Russian observer writing in 1875 about the impact of Russian methods and ideas (and in this context Russian and European are synonymous) on Muslim Central Asia:

As concerns the Mussulman despotism destroyed by Russian institutions [wrote N. Petrofsky], it would be difficult for us to guarantee that these institutions seem less arbitrary and despotic to the natives than did their former Mussulman ones. Under Mussulman sway tyranny and arbitrary rule indeed existed, but this tyranny was far from being without limits, and was as much a product of the country as were all its other institutions, morals, and customs. It was native there and it was understood there ... In consequence of their exclusively religious education of the same character as that of the whole mass of the population, and of the common character of their life, of their customs and of their habits, the Mussulman rulers confined their tyranny within certain well known and fixed limits, and their arbitrariness was considered as a necessary attribute of their power, without which the very existence of their rule would be inconceivable. On the other side, the people too looked on this arbitrariness with the eye of their ruler, seeing in him not a tyrant and a persecuting despot, but a lucky favourite of fortune, who had received the right to arbitrary and uncontrolled power ... In a word, the native was at home with Mussulman tyranny.

We may supplement and confirm what Petrofsky has to say by a remarkable statement which comes from the other side of the Muslim world, from Morocco. Its author, Raisuli, was one of those tribal chieftains who were able to defy the Moroccan sultan's decayed authority, and with tribal support carve out for themselves territorial enclaves which even the French and Spanish occupants of Morocco found difficult to subdue. At the end of his career (he died in 1925), when the Spaniards had been established for a decade and more in his part of Morocco, he expressed in a striking manner one reason why Euro-pean methods were felt to be so irksome by traditional Muslim society:

You give a man safety [he told a European interlocutor] but you take away hope. In the old days everything was possible. There was no limit to what a man might become. The slave might be a minister or a general, the scribe a Sultan. Now a man's life is safe, but for ever he is chained to his labour and his poverty.

In his discussion of the Russian impact over Central Asia, Petrofsky goes on to make another point which is also of wide application:

The natives [he wrote] were expected of themselves to understand the – for them – complicated organization of the Russian government, and to guess at the relations of the various branches of the administration which were quite new to them, and not easily intelligible ... Naturally these institutions appear to the natives to be far more arbitrary and far more tyrannical than those under which they formerly lived under Mussulman rulers, not because they are really arbitrary and tyran-nical, but because, seeing their frequent change, the native is not able to understand and to explain to him-self either the meaning of the frequent changes, or the existence of these institutions.

327

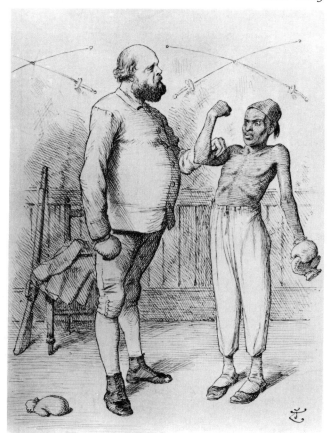

Ismāʿīl, Khedive of Egypt, was the grandson of the Pasha Muhammad ʿAlī. Under his rule Egypt sank deeper and deeper into debt to foreign creditors, and in 1876 he was forced to surrender his own estates and agree to a measure of control by Britain and France. Punch published a cartoon called 'Disgorging', showing a righteous John Bull reclaiming his money from the discomforted Khedive. This

financial dependence led eventually to the British (in fact though not in law) governing Egypt. How they saw themselves in this role is made clear by another Punch *cartoon, of 1891. A fatherly Lord Salisbury builds up the puny figure of Egypt, long starved by his old corrupt masters, until he is as fit and strong . . . as an Englishman. When Cromer ruled Egypt, this view of the British role was widely accepted. (6,7)*

Exactly similar reasons account for the widespread hostility with which European reforms undertaken by Islamic rulers like Muhammad ʿAlī were received by their subjects. There is, likewise, a significant similarity between Algerian resistance to the French, that of the Sudanese Mahdī to the Egyptian regime and that of various towns and villages in the Levant who in 1834 rose against the Egyptian forces, which had taken the area from the Ottomans a few years earlier.

In the modern history of the Islamic peoples, Muhammad ʿAlī stands as an archetype, because he shows with extreme clarity how, not so much European conquests, as European ideas and methods, affected these peoples. Of course, few if any Islamic rulers even attempted to do all that Muhammad ʿAlī did to Egypt. But those who were convinced of the necessity of 'reform', i.e. of emulating European ways – and they became the majority among Muslim leaders – embarked on policies similar in some way or another to Muhammad ʿAlī's which, whatever their ostensible aim, ended up by increasing enormously the power of the rulers over the ruled, widening the gap between them, and generating powerful tensions and strains in society. As we have seen, Selīm's attempt to modernize the Ottoman army evoked a very powerful opposition, and it eventually led to his downfall. His cousin Mahmūd II was naturally aware of the threat to himself which modernization policies represented, but as his actions showed, he was also clearly convinced of their necessity. He bided his time, and did not move until he

had a force in Constantinople of which he could be sure, and until he secured support for his policies from religious and military leaders. In May 1826 Mahmūd promulgated a rescript providing for the creation of a new force, to be drawn from the Janissary corps, and to be given new weapons and training, and to be subject to new regulations in respect of discipline, pay and promotion. The Janissaries were unwilling to allow this new formation to be set up, and some three weeks after the Sultan's rescript, on 15 June, they rose in rebellion. Mahmūd succeeded in putting down the rebellion. He promptly abolished the Janissary order, and killed all the Janissaries he could catch. He also shortly afterwards abolished the other traditional military formations of the Ottoman army. The way was now open for the creation of a modern conscript army, fully under the control of the Sultan, administered and directed by officials and officers entirely dependent on his favour, and thus utterly obedient to his command. The history of the so-called Eastern Question before 1914 shows that in spite of continued 'reforms', the Ottoman army never really became a match for the European armies which were its potential opponents. In fact, ironically enough, it was in the very period when the Ottoman army, as well as other Ottoman institutions, were undergoing modernization, that the empire came to be known as the 'Sick Man of Europe'. But the modernization of the Ottoman army enabled Mahmūd and his successors to establish the authority of Constantinople over provinces where nominally subordinate governors had to all intents and purposes become autonomous. Again, the very needs of the new army, financial and administrative, required the setting up of new centrally controlled departments which increased still further the power of the Sultan at the expense of his subjects. Such an expression is warranted, when we remember that like Muhammad ʿAlī in Egypt, Mahmūd laid his hand not only on the so-called 'military fiefs', which had been traditionally awarded to the 'feudal cavalry', but on the extensive resources of the *awqāf* or pious foundations on the pretext of improving and rationalizing their administration. The 'reform' which began with the army gradually but inexorably ended by involving everything in state and society. Some of the most serious of the proliferating consequences of 'reform' were prophetically described in 1830 by Captain Adolphus Slade, whom we may recognize as one of the most intelligent observers of the Ottoman empire in his day and later.

Hitherto [Slade pointed out] the Osmanley has enjoyed by custom some of the dearest privileges of freemen, for which Christian nations have so long struggled. He paid nothing to the government beyond a moderate land-tax, although liable, it is true, to extortions, which might be classed with assessed taxes. He paid no tithes, the vacouf [i.e. pious foundations] sufficing for the maintenance of the ministers of Islamism. He travelled where he pleased without passports; no custom-house officer intruded his eyes and dirty fingers among his baggage; no police watched his motions, or listened for his words. His house was sacred. His sons were never taken from his side to be soldiers, unless war called them. His views of ambition were not restricted by the barriers of birth and wealth: from the lowest origin he might aspire without presumption to the rank of pasha; if he could read, to that of grand vizir; and this consciousness, instilled and supported by numberless precedents, ennobled his mind, and enabled him to enter on the duties of high office without embarrassment . . . One more example, rather burlesque, however than correct. The Janizzaries of Constantinople somewhat resembled a chamber of deputies, for they often compelled their sovereign to change his ministers, and any talented, factious member among them, with the art of inflaming men's passions, was sure to obtain a good employment in order to appease him.

In Mahmūd's new model state, on the other hand,

The few are strengthened against the many, the powerful armed against the weak. The sovereign, who before found his power (despotic in name) circumscribed, because with all the will, he had not the real art of oppressing, by the aid of science finds himself a giant – his mace exchanged for a sword. In scanning over the riches of civilization, spread out before him for acceptance, he contemptuously rejects those calculated to benefit his people, and chooses the modern scientific governing machine, result of ages of experiment, with its patent screws for extracting blood and treasure – conscription and taxation. He hires foreign engineers to work it, and waits the promised result – absolute power. His subjects, who before had a thousand modes of avoiding tyranny, have not now a loop-hole to escape by: the operations of the uncorroding engine meet them at every turn, and, to increase their despair, its movement accelerates with use, and winds closer their chains.

'Enlightenment' versus tradition

But 'reform' acquired a momentum and dialectic of its own, and in due course those leaders who were convinced that Europe was the only model worth following, became equally convinced that 'reform', to be real and effective, had to mean more than the introduction of mere military techniques and administrative methods. We may perhaps gain a cursory but sufficient idea of the views of 'enlightened' Easterners if we look at the 'Discourse with a Governor-General or a Pasha' which Assaad Yacoob Kayat included in his phrase-book, *The Eastern Traveller's Interpreter*, the second edition of which appeared in London in 1846. In his discourse with the Pasha, Kayat's English traveller is made to instruct him in this wise:

This is a fine country.
It wants good roads.
All prosperity to the nation comes from good laws.
Good government is the foundation.
Every one ought to be equal in the sight of the law.
Schools will do your country much good.
Printing-presses will promote many blessings.

And it must be said that the pashas – or at any rate an influential party among them – were willing to be instructed. In his efforts at modernization, the Sultan was seconded by a number of high officials. Of these, the best known was Mustafā Rashīd Pasha, who was outstanding in helping to transform the empire into a European-style *Rechtstaat* in accordance with the maxims propounded in Kayat's phrase-book. In these attempts, the Noble Rescript of the Rose Chamber of 1839 undoubtedly stands as a landmark. The Rescript was promulgated shortly after the death of Mahmūd II, who was succeeded as sultan by his son ʿAbd al-Majīd. The empire was then seriously threatened by the Pasha of Egypt, whose armies had inflicted a crushing defeat on the Ottomans at Nezib (in south-western Anatolia) in June 1839. In this emergency, the empire was very much dependent on greatpower support, and particularly on the support of Great Britain. The Rescript of the Rose Chamber expresses not only the genuine beliefs of the reformers, but is a response to the similar beliefs about the Ottoman empire (and the Islamic world in general) which were widely prevalent in the West. The Noble Rescript promised 'to seek by new institutions to give to the provinces of the Ottoman empire the benefit of a good administration'. These new institutions related to:

1. The guarantees insuring to our subjects perfect security for life, honour, and fortune.
2. A regular system of assessing and levying taxes.
3. An equally regular system for the levying of troops and the duration of their service.

Yet another landmark in this reform movement is also associated with a wartime emergency: the Imperial Rescript of 1856 which was promulgated in the aftermath of the Crimean War, and the architects of which were two disciples of Rashīd Pasha, ʿAlī Pasha and Fuʾād Pasha. The new Rescript affirmed and amplified the provisions of the earlier document and insisted particularly on the equality which was to be accorded to all the Sultan's subjects whether Muslim, Christian or Jewish. It 'confirmed and consolidated' the rights which the Noble Rescript had granted 'to all the subjects of my empire, without distinction of classes or of religion'. The Crimean War had ostensibly broken out over the Russian claim to exercise a protectorate over the Greek Orthodox subjects of the Sultan, and it was no doubt to close the door on further similar claims, but also because the architects of reform genuinely believed in the necessity of such measures, that the Rescript was particularly emphatic on the equality of treatment for all the Sultan's subjects, regardless of their religion.

Intermittently, throughout the 1840s, the declarations of the Noble Rescript were translated into laws, regulations and institutions, and the same was the case with Imperial Rescript of 1856. The effects were not always – or even frequently – what might have been anticipated from these high-minded aspirations. Aimed at increasing the security, the liberty and the welfare of the subject, the new laws and institutions were in fact nothing less than a revolution in social, commercial and religious arrangements. The population did not take kindly to them, and they had therefore to be worked and enforced by the government. This, *ipso facto*, meant a further increase in the unchecked, centralized power of the government. This vicious circle meant in the end that government and the governed came to inhabit two distinct universes of discourse.

One feature in particular of the Ottoman legal and constitutional reforms seriously increased social tension and complicated the work of government. This was the provision, hinted at in 1839 and spelled out much more explicitly in 1856, whereby non-Muslims were to be treated by the state on an equality with Muslims. Such a policy could not but damage the cohesion of a state which, in the last resort, rested on Islamic feelings of pride and solidarity – feelings which, in the eyes of Muslims, were sanctioned alike by divine law and by the immemorial history of Islam. For a Muslim government to concede equality to non-Muslims seemed to the mass of its Muslim subjects a demoralizing humiliation. 'If the Jews and the Christians are our equals before the law,' asked an Ottoman official when the Noble Rescript of the Rose Chamber was publicly read in Cairo, 'what will become of us?' The Ottoman government was not alone in pursuing such a policy. When he invaded the Levant Muhammad ʿAlī, too, for various reasons, chose to show favour to the Christians in this way, and indeed went much further than the Ottomans. This aspect of his policy was a potent reason for the revolt against Egyptian rule which broke out in 1834. Muslim feelings are captured in the words of a Damascene clerk who wrote that 'The government has become a Christian government, the rule of Islam is ended.' An official British observer, Richard Wood, described the Pasha's policies which evoked this bitter comment. Ibrāhīm (Muhammad ʿAlī's son and commander of the Egyptian forces), wrote Wood in a letter of 1834,

respected neither [the Muslims'] prejudices or their rights but proclaimed Toleration, Equality and equal taxation with the enjoyment of equal privileges throughout Syria. These severe steps towards the annihilation of Mahommedan superiority broke the spirits of the followers of the Prophet, and gave confidence and energy to the Christians, who, long accustomed to consider themselves doomed to perpetual servility, now fondly clung to the least spark of hope, but never accustomed to sway the sceptre, they knew not the advantage of using with moderation their power, nor could they foresee that their present elevation may be but transient. Abusing therefore of their exalted state, they despised their former Masters, who on the other hand dreaded that it was now their turn to be roasted in ovens as were the Christians at the time of the notorious Djezzar Pasha the Butcher [governor of Acre 1775–1804] . . .

Wood went on:

The Turks finding that their hopes of deliverance were frustrated, and that they were destined to be governed by Egyptians, and above all resenting what they termed the insolence of the Christians, many Towns revolted: among the foremost were Sidon, Aleppo, Damascus, Nazareth; the present inhabitants of the country of Samaria, and the fellah Arabs of the Horan or Decapolis.

Less than three decades later, in 1860, the Levant, now once more under Ottoman rule, was again the scene of serious disturbances when Christian communities in Damascus and elsewhere were attacked and massacred. It is not to be doubted that this explosion was – among other things – an outcome of the Imperial Rescript of 1856, and the inter-communal tension its promises precipitated. Contemporary European observers, the majority of whom saw nothing but good in the reform policy, sarcastically remarked that the Rescript of 1856 'left nothing to be desired but its execution'. What is implicit in such a remark is that the reform was a mere paper reform, and that if only it had been implemented, the empire would have basked in peace and contentment. This was far from the truth. The very attempt to implement the promises of reform led to political and social tensions, by undermining the self-confidence of Muslims, rulers and subjects alike, and raising the expectations of the non-Muslims. Unlike most observers, the sagacious Slade, in a work published two years before the Rescript of the Rose Chamber, anticipated exactly this outcome. Removal of the disabilities of the non-Muslims was

not calculated to produce, as was fondly expected and is stoutly asserted by many, attachment to the Sultan's government, but, on the contrary, depression of the Mussulman interest, *on which alone his throne is based* . . . Touched on theoretically, concession is a lady's fan; practically handled, it became a double-edged sword: it sets loose the fell tide of party rancour, which spurns an equal participation of rights, and it rouses the spirit of revenge, which scorns any justice, save the fullest measure – which is, to rule where ruled, to scoff at by whom scoffed. Arms thus given to the oppressed cannot be resumed: the confidence of the ruling sect cannot be regained.

Reform, then, meant change. But change did not necessarily mean unqualified or universal improvement. It did not make for visibly better government, and it did not serve to strengthen the state against foreign encroachments. On the contrary, the erosion of Muslim superiority, and the concomitant increase in the self-assertiveness of the non-Muslims, gave increased opportunities for foreign powers to intervene. Again, reform worked, in unforeseen ways, to the advantage of some groups and to the detriment of others; and it is of course impossible to say whether the advantage or the detriment was the greater. Consider, for example, another piece of reform, the change in the land laws which was related to the abolition of 'feudal' tenures and tax-farming. A new, European-model land law was promulgated in 1858 which resulted in the transformation of customary tenures and of land in common or tribal ownership or use into state-registered, individually owned freeholds. This reform rode rough-shod over customary rights which, though not set down in official documents, yet had immemorially regulated agrarian relationships in large parts of the empire. The Land Code did not create a European-style small landed peasantry with a stake in the land. On the contrary, the small agriculturist, whether member of a settled village community, or of a tribe which had never known individual ownership of land, found his customary rights and interests squeezed and destroyed by a law, the operation of which was made even more vicious by the corruption and malpractices that a large, unwieldy, centralized bureaucracy naturally entailed. Was there, one wonders, any substantive difference between the conditions of the tribesman of southern Mesopotamia or the villager of the north Syrian plain whom the operation of a benevolent Land Code reduced to a kind of serf, and that of the Egyptian peasant who became Muhammad 'Ali's virtual property, or that of the Kazakh nomad whose tribal lands were expropriated in the latter half of the XIII/19th century to the benefit of Russian settlers, or that of the Algerian Kabyles whose land was likewise expropriated to the benefit of French settlers? We must of course not forget that Russian and French settlement looked even more injurious; for the victims were Muslims and the expropriators Christian conquerors. But it is significant that the results of modernization by a Muslim state should be so similar to those produced by European conquests.

Another aspect of reform deserves examination. The westernization of laws and the increase in the functions of government was accompanied by the setting up of provincial councils. These councils, composed of local notables elected by a complicated franchise, were deemed to represent the various communities of a province. To start with, as Rashīd Pasha set them up, they were given judicial as well as administrative functions and were supposed to act as a check on the governor. As the historian H. W. V. Temperley observed, the council system 'was absolutely bad'. Councillors were under no real check by their constituents, and were thus hardly representative. The councillors, then, proved to be an oligarchy of quasi-officials who exploited to their own benefit the increasing intricacy of laws and administrative regulations, and whose mutual jealousies seldom advanced the public interest or the welfare of the ordinary

subject. The evils of the council system were soon perceived, and both in 1852 and 1864 changes were made which diminished the powers of the councillors and, notably, removed judicial matters from their purview. But the councils never succeeded in becoming effective organs of local self-government or local representation.

One of the best works on the Ottoman empire written in English, Sir Charles Eliot's *Turkey in Europe*, opens with an imaginary conversation between a European businessman and an Ottoman pasha. At one point in their discussion the pasha is led to speak in metaphors:

> This country [he exclaims] is a dish of soup and no one has any real intention except to eat it. We eat it in the good old-fashioned way with a big spoon. You bore little holes in the bottom of the soup-bowl and draw it off with pipes. Then you propose that the practice of eating soup with spoons should be abolished as uncivilised, because you know we have no gimlets and don't understand this trick of drinking through pipes.

To use the pasha's arresting language, we may liken the European-inspired local councils to the scientific device whereby soup was sucked through the pipe, rather than eaten with an old-fashioned spoon. It is of course difficult, if not impossible, positively to say which was the more efficacious, but we may suspect at any rate that the more modern method caused in its victims the greater anguish, both because it was unfamiliar, and because a large number of small pipes had replaced the one big spoon. We may illustrate this by the reaction of the Tunisians to these reforms, similar to the Ottoman, which the Bey of Tunis (nominally a part of the empire) introduced at about the same time. Between 1857 and 1861 the Beys of Tunis introduced European-style laws, which aimed at ensuring security of the person, and equality in taxation and before the law. A centralized bureaucracy and a new network of tribunals were set up to carry out the reforms, and the edifice was crowned by a constitution promulgated in 1861. The constitution made provision for a grand council to which the ministers and the bey himself were made ostensibly responsible. The council was made up of officials and notables, partly appointed and partly co-opted, and was supposed to be the authority of last resort in matters of taxation and in judicial affairs. These reforms proved to be a great burden for the subject. Under the old order, administrative matters were decided by the governor and judicial cases determined by the *qādī*, subject in both cases to an appeal to the Bey. Thus, as a French observer put it, the ordinary Tunisian had hitherto been 'eaten' by two men, and no more. With the coming of the new tribunals,

> he is eaten by all the members of these tribunals. He used to accept the decision of the local judge because it was a prompt decision, and only in grave issues would he appeal to the Sovereign. Today, the inhabitant of Gabes, which is 80 leagues from Tunis, who wants to appeal a judgment rendered by the local tribunal, has to go to Tunis. And even after a journey so costly for him, he does not enjoy the privilege of personally rehearsing his grievances before the Bey. It is yet another committee issuing from the supreme Council, a number of these detested mamlūks transformed into a court of appeal, who will annul or confirm the first verdict.

331

The discontent which the Tunisian reforms aroused led to a tribal rebellion in 1864. The battle-cry of the rebels was: 'No more mamlūks, no more *mejba* [a tax greatly increased by the council], no more constitution.' Among the demands made by the leaders of the rebellion was that the new tribunals should be abolished, and the bey himself render justice according to the *sharī'a*. The rebellion was eventually put down; but the constitution was suspended, never to be activated again.

Khayr ad-Dīn at-Tūnisī, mentioned above, was one of those Tunisian officials who were, as has been seen, most persuaded of the necessity of European-style reforms, and he took a prominent part in carrying out the reforms of 1857–61. At one point, in fact, he became president of the grand council, the activities of which led to the rebellion of 1864. His work, *Réformes nécessaires aux états musulmans*, was written in the aftermath of this rebellion, and it contains a significant passage which seems to refer obliquely to the claims of the rebels. Khayr ad-Dīn enumerates four objections to reform advanced by those who believed that they were not suitable to Islamic society:

1. The Tanzīmāt [i.e. reforms] are contrary to the *sharī'a*.
2. They are inappropriate since there is no disposition on the part of the *umma* [i.e. the Muslim community] to accept the civilization upon which they are based.
3. They will almost certainly lead to the loss of rights given the long time needed to settle lawsuits, and identical delays will be seen throughout the administrative system.
4. The increased government employment required for various administrations will require an increase in taxation.

The Muslim intellect in search of progress
But it was not only traditionally minded tribal chieftains in an outlying part of the Muslim world who were finding European reforms irksome in their application and doubtful in their results. Disappointment or disenchantment with reforms was to be seen also among those who were most exposed to European ideas. They too thought the new-fangled administrative arrangements were both oppressive and inefficient. But they did not exactly hark back to or yearn for a restoration of traditional Islam. If the reforms had failed this was because they were the shadow rather than the substance of European civilization. The secret of European power and prosperity lay not in machines or administrative organization. It lay rather in the political and social habits prevalent among Europeans – habits which made for initiative, inventiveness and enterprise. The essence of these habits may be summed up by the expression, freedom under the law. This could be secured only by limited, representative, constitutional government. Such government, it was argued, would be no more than a return to the pure tradition of early Islam, before it had been adulterated by despotism and superstition. Such an argument had little historical value since, whatever political doctrine might be drawn out of or extrapolated from the Qur'ān, Islam almost from the beginning had known little else but autocratic rule, and was utterly unfamiliar with constitu-

tional and representative government. Again, the administrative and military reforms had greatly increased the ruler's power, and weakened such defences as had been traditionally available to the subject. And it is this greatly strengthened ruler, controlling a modernized army and a highly centralized administration, who was now bidden to transform himself into a constitutional monarch and allow his power to be regulated by a constitution and checked by the people's representatives.

There was of course little prospect of this coming to pass, and constitutional representative government could usually be established only by such action as would itself make more remote the successful operation of such a government. In 1876, when the Ottoman empire was in the throes of a military and financial crisis, a number of high officials conspired to depose the Sultan and establish a parliamentary government. They eventually put on the throne a young member of the Ottoman dynasty who seemed to agree with their views. And in fact, the new Sultan, 'Abd al-Hamīd II, did, shortly after his accession, grant a constitution and a parliament. What this meant in effect was a transfer of power from the Sultan himself to the ministers and other members of the official classes who understood these innovations and exploited them to their advantage. This was in many ways analogous to the situation in Tunisia after 1861, and to that in the Ottoman provinces after the introduction of local councils which had served only to increase the power and perquisites of the local notables. 'Abd al-Hamīd was naturally averse to any diminution of his power, and with shrewdness and good luck he succeeded in suspending both constitution and parliament after they had been operating for barely a year. His long reign, from 1876 to 1909, saw no abatement of the modernizing and centralizing tendencies which had become increasingly dominant in the xiii/19th century.

One consequence of this was an increase in the number of officials and officers influenced by European ideas and who, precisely owing to their European-style education, were disaffected towards the regime. They were convinced that only its transformation into a state governed by a constitution and a parliament would save the empire from ruin. A conspiracy by junior officers, the 'Young Turks', succeeded, in July 1908, and forced 'Abd al-Hamīd to restore the constitution of 1876. But parliamentary government in the Ottoman empire, and in its successor states after 1918, proved on the whole to be a mere façade: the reality was that of a centralized state endowed with a numerous and powerful bureaucracy run by an official class whose European-style education made it quite remote from the traditional-minded mass which it governed. In spite of ostensibly representative institutions, this official class was in reality little responsive to those whom it governed, because the latter were unfamiliar with elections and parliaments and because they were traditionally in awe of the rulers and, as the scope of government increased, progressively more dependent on it for their very livelihood. Political life consisted in rivalry and conflict between various groups within the official class; a conflict which, in the absence of constitutional checks and balances, was very often resolved by the military, who could not resist the temptation to take power into their own hands.

For the European doctrines which so influenced their thinking led to exaggerated hopes about political action and what it could accomplish. This kind of expectation may be described as, among other things, secular and humanist: secular in stressing that the world has no supernatural dimension or providential destiny; and humanist in emphasizing that man is his own master and makes himself. Such a vision is, of course, far removed from the traditional Islamic outlook, and its impact, gradual as it was, was in the end both pervasive and far reaching. We see it appear quite early in the contacts between European civilization and Islam. For instance, large parts of the Caucasus were conquered by Russia in the first three decades of the XIII/19th century, and educated Muslims of this region came into intimate contact with European ideas and institutions. One of the best known of these was Mīrzā Fath ʿAlī Ākhundzāda (1812–78). Beginning with a traditional religious education, Ākhundzāda soon abandoned it for the study of Russian language and literature. In Tiflis, where he became a Russian official, he came in close touch with Russian intellectuals, some of whom were actually exiles in Transcaucasia because of their advanced political ideas. Ākhundzāda became known particularly as a playwright, and his plays contributed in the Azeri- and Persian-speaking world to the spread of a secular and sceptical attitude if not to Islam itself, then to the men of religion – divines, *qādīs* and dervishes – who were portrayed as devious and corrupt, taking advantage of a credulous, respectful and superstitious public. Another comparable and significant figure in an out-of-the-way part of the Muslim world was the Bukhariot writer Ahmad Makhdūm Donish (1827–97). The Khān of Bukhārā was defeated by Russia and had to acquiesce in a Russian protectorate in 1868. It was then that he sent Donish as ambassador to St Petersburg. Donish came back profoundly impressed with Russian culture, with the fact that women were unveiled, that books and periodicals were published in large quantities, that educated men were numerous, and the country, compared with Bukhārā, prosperous. He became persuaded that these benefits were withheld from his fellow countrymen by the greed and corruption of the rulers and men of religion, and that the Bukhariots could take steps to end oppression, obscurantism and poverty. He did not mince his words:

The Emirs and the Vizirs [he wrote], the clergy and the aristocracy are all alike. You, reader, should find out what kind of man the Emir himself is, the sovereign of orthodox Muslims and your Sultan. Look around and you will see that he is a libertine and tyrant. His supreme Kazi is a glutton and hypocrite. Of the same kind are the Ra'is and the head of police. The latter is simply a perpetually drunk gambler and consort of brigands and thieves.

Donish also questioned the traditional Islamic beliefs. As one of his disciples wrote, the Muslim divines accused him of claiming to be able to predict the eclipse of the sun and the moon, which meant that he was impiously trying to put himself on a level with God, who alone can know the future.

The same disaffection towards Islamic institutions and practices may be seen among educated Indian Muslims who had come into contact with English thought and the British way of life. The famous writer Khwaja Altaf Husayn Hālī (1837–1914), who has been described as the most distinguished poet of his generation, writes bitter words about the decadence of Indian Islam, and leaves his reader in no doubt about those responsible, namely the mystics and the theologians who have killed all initiative and spirit in the Muslims, and fostered intolerance and fear:

They speak only to inflame men's hatred, write only to wound men's hearts. God's sinful servants they despise; their Muslim brethren they brand as infidels. These are the paths of the learned divines, these the methods of our guides.

If a man goes to lay a problem before them, he will come away with a yet heavier burden on his soul. And if he is so unfortunate as to feel doubt about their answer, they will brand him unerringly as one of the damned. Indeed if he gives voice to some objection he will be fortunate to escape whole from their hands . . .

They offer him no guidance in morality, produce in him no purity of heart; but have multiplied external observances to such a degree that not for a single moment can he escape them. That religion which was the source of gentleness and goodness they have degraded into a code of rules for baths and ablutions.

The most colourful and best known of these modern figures who have depreciated Islam and demanded its replacement by some modern ideology was the Persian Shīʿī who went under the name of Jamāl ad-Dīn al-Afghānī (1838–97). Afghānī's activities extended to all the central lands of Islam: Persia, India, the Ottoman empire, Egypt; and he preached a secret doctrine of infidelity and scepticism. His teaching may be summed up in the words of a disciple, Muhammad ʿAbduh, who, ironically, was to become Muftī of Egypt – one of the three highest religious dignitaries in the country. In a letter to Afghānī, ʿAbduh wrote: 'We regulate our conduct according to your sound rule: we do not cut the head of religion except with the sword of religion.' Afghānī's view of Islam comes out clearly in an exchange he had in Paris in 1883 with Ernest Renan. In a lecture at the Sorbonne Renan had attacked Islam as an engine of despotism, terror and persecution. In a commentary published in the *Journal des Débats*, Afghānī agreed with Renan's estimate of Islam and expressed the hope that Islamic society 'will succeed some day in breaking its bonds and marching resolutely in the path of civilization, after the manner of Western society'.

Islam and Communist Russia

The adventures and disappointments of the Muslim intellect in search of a valid amalgam between its native inheritance and 'the path of civilization, after the manner of Western society', as Afghānī put it, have taken many forms. In politics, there was the quest for constitutionalism which, in the Ottoman empire and its successor states, paradoxically inaugurated a period – by no means over yet – of military *coups d'état* and unrepresentative military regimes. In the Russian empire and in the Central Asian khanates under Russian protection, there was a vigorous movement to reform Muslim education, to do away with the intellectual and social tyranny of the men of religion, and the political tyranny of the Khāns. During the Russian Revolution of 1905 the modernizing leaders of the Tatars – those Muslims who had been under Russian rule since the XII/18th century and earlier – cast their lot with the Russian Kadets (Constitutional Democrats). The political programme which they formulated at a congress of 1906 demanded legal equality for all the peoples of Russia, and equal access by Muslims to civil and military posts, the equality of all religions with the Orthodox faith and the institution of local self-government controlled by democratically elected councils. As events proved, this constitutionalist dream was incompatible with the Russian autocracy, and was far removed from the realities of Russian politics. What is noteworthy about it is that a congress speaking in the name of a Muslim community was ready to envisage a society in which Muslims would take their place on an equality with other faiths which Islam had hitherto considered inferior. With the Bolshevik Revolution a decade or so later, the life of politics seemed to hold a new promise of fulfilment to Russian Muslim intellectuals. Thus, one of Stalin's first Muslim collaborators in the Commissariat for Nationalities, Mullanur Vahitov (1885–1918), was certain, according to a Tatar author writing in the 1920s, that

> the influence of ancient Arab culture on the universal culture which would emerge as a result of world-wide socialist reconstruction would be immense. In his dreams he pictured this Islamic culture – whose impact extended from Arab lands to the sacred river, Ganges – as great, beautiful and profound in its content. He could not conceive of its possible disintegration or disappearance and dreamed that in the future it would . . . illumine all humanity. Of this he was convinced.

Vahitov died before he could see how illusory such hopes were. It was otherwise with another Tatar, Sultan Galiev (1895–?1940), who served, between 1918 and 1923, as Stalin's colleague in the Commissariat of Nationalities. Sultan Galiev was a Marxist and a Communist, but in his eyes the class struggle was not so much one between capitalist and proletariat in an industrialized country, as between Europeans and the Eastern world which they exploited, colonized and oppressed. And the liberation of humanity was to come from a liberated East of which the vanguard were the Communist Tatars in the Soviet Union. This was not only a deviation from orthodox Marxism, but a threat to the power of Moscow. Sultan Galiev was dismissed from his official post, and up to 1928 occupied himself in organizing political and doctrinal resistance among Soviet Muslims to the dominant, European, element in the Communist Party of the Soviet Union. For these activities he was arrested in 1929 and sentenced to a long term of imprisonment. He is said to have been released in 1939, but when exactly or how he died remains unknown.

The same disappointments or disasters overtook the modernizers of Central Asia in their attempts to engage in politics, and to ameliorate by political action the life of their people. The *Jadīds* (i.e. modernizers) of Bukhārā began to be active towards the end of the XIII/19th and in the first decade of the XIV/20th century. Starting with a desire to introduce modern education and thus, as they

believed, do away at once with despotism and superstition, their horizon was suddenly widened by the Russian Revolution of 1917. Forming themselves as a Young Bukhariot party, they attempted to force the Khān to introduce in Bukhārā the reforms they believed desirable, and in pursuit of their aim they finally collaborated with a Communist force which marched from Tashkent on Bukhārā in 1920. The Khān was expelled and the Young Bukhariots proclaimed a seemingly independent Popular Republic. But the independence did not last long. It was terminated in 1924 when the ancient state of Bukhārā (the independence of which had survived the Tsarist regime) became a Socialist Republic and was absorbed in the Soviet Union; it is now a part of the Uzbek Soviet Socialist Republic. The dreams and ambitions of the *Jadīds* thus met with a failure that may be symbolized by the fate of their ideological mentor, ʿAbd ar-Raʾūf Fitrat. Born sometime in the last decades of the XIII/19th century, he was very active in educational and religious reform until World War I. In 1920 he took office as minister of education, and then of foreign affairs in the Popular Republic. When the Republic was suppressed he became a teacher in the university of Samarqand. In 1937 he was arrested, and his fate thereafter is unknown.

India: partition and paradox

The Muslim modernizers in India who, like their counterparts in Russia ended by becoming the leaders of their community, were scarcely more lucky in their encounter with politics. Hālī, whom we have quoted earlier, fervently believed that the welfare of the Muslims lay in adapting themselves to the modern world under the aegis of their British rulers:

> Your government has given you freedom. All the roads of advancement are wide open to you. From all sides comes the cry that, from prince to peasants, all men prosper. The rule of peace and prosperity is established in all lands, and caravans may travel in safety along every route.

It was a friend of Hālī, the famous Sir Sayyid Ahmad Khān (1817–98), who laboured most successfully to bring home to his fellow Muslims a realization of the possibilities offered by Western science, and strove to convince them that if Muslims were to fulfil their destiny – which was to prosper, to be powerful and to make a mark in the world – they had better accept modern education which, he insisted, was fully compatible with Islam. So far as Sir Sayyid Ahmad Khān and the men of his generation could see, the future of India and its Muslims was bound up with British rule. Muslims were a minority in India and thus all the more looked to the British to safeguard their interests. But the subsequent rise of Hindu nationalism, the political mobilization of the Hindu masses by figures like Tilak or Gandhi, aroused increasing disquiet among the Muslim leaders. The ensuing prospects were considered by Muslim leaders, foremost among whom was Muhammad ʿAlī Jinnāh (1876–1948), as dangerous and even desperate. If Muslims were to preserve themselves and safeguard their identity, it followed that they had to establish a state of their own. There were, he argued, two distinct nations in India. Hinduism and

A carved frieze outside the Officers' Club in Cairo makes a significant contrast to the Ottoman relief at the beginning of this chapter. This too is an assertion of power. It looks back to past military greatness. But the tone is strident and the connection with the past is self-conscious, contrived, and hence unconvincing. (8)

Islam 'are not religions in the strict sense of the word, but are, in fact, different and distinct social orders. . . . The Hindus and Muslims belong to two different religious philosophies, social customs, literatures. They neither intermarry nor interdine together and, indeed,' Jinnāh affirmed, 'they belong to two different civilizations which are based mainly on conflicting ideas and conceptions.'

Jinnāh was successful in obtaining such a state in Pakistan, which came into existence in 1947 when the British abandoned their empire in India. But Pakistan as the emanation of Indian Islam and its shield suffers from a double paradox. In the first place, Pakistan came into being as a result of the Muslims of India voting against a single state for the sub-continent. But Pakistan embraced nothing like the totality of the Indian Muslims; when it came into being Pakistan had about 65 million Muslims, while the new Hindu-dominated India contained no less than 35 million.

But the snares and disappointments of political action went even further. The whole *raison d'être* of Pakistan was Islam. This is what the 1956 constitution of Pakistan unequivocably shows. It ordains, in Part III, on 'Directive Principles of State Policy', that 'Steps shall be taken to enable the Muslims of Pakistan individually and collectively to order their lives in accordance with the Holy Qur'ān and Sunnah.' But nothing in the history of Pakistan since its inception indicates that these statements have become more than mere words, and the rulers of Pakistan have discovered that to live 'in accordance with the Holy Qur'ān and Sunnah' may not be compatible with the character of a modern state. Some six years after the birth of Pakistan, serious riots erupted in Lahore against the Ahmadīs, a sect which orthodox Muslim divines consider heretical. These divines claimed that if Pakistan was an Islamic state, then it ought to maintain the distinction between Muslims and non-Muslims and deny Ahmadīs (and by implication all non-Muslims) that equality of rights which modern civilized states recognize for all their citizens (and which the Pakistan constitution subsequently affirmed). The riots, in which *'ulamā'* in Lahore took a leading part, were investigated by a court of enquiry which produced a notable report. This report (known as the Munīr report) highlights the incompatibility between modern European-inspired constitutionalism and the Islamic notions of state which a state like Pakistan was supposed to put into practice. Pakistan, declared the report in a notable passage,

> is being taken by the common man, though it is not, as an Islamic State. This belief has been encouraged by the ceaseless clamour for Islam and Islamic State that is being heard from all quarters since the establishment of Pakistan. The phantom of an Islamic State has haunted the Musalman throughout the ages and is a result of the memory of the glorious past . . .

The modern Muslim, the report went on,

> finds himself standing on the crossroads, wrapped in the mantle of the past and with the dead weight of centuries on his back, frustrated and bewildered and hesitant to turn one corner or the other. The freshness and the simplicity of the faith, which gave determination to his mind and spring to his muscle, is now denied to him. He has neither the means nor the ability to conquer and there are no countries to conquer . . . He therefore finds himself in a state of helplessness, waiting for some one to come and help him out of this morass of uncertainty and confusion . . . Nothing but a bold re-orientation of Islam to separate the vital from the lifeless can preserve it as a World Idea and convert the Musalman into a citizen of the present and the future world from the archaic incongruity that he is today.

Almost a decade and a half after these words were written, we find Ayyūb Khān, President of Pakistan from 1962 to 1969, complaining of the same incongruity and incoherence between the claims of Islam and those of the modern world. In a book published in 1967, Ayyūb Khān remarked that Islam visualizes life as a unity in which all activity is determined by the same principle. But, he went on to add, 'The picture of our society, as I saw it, did not conform to this. In practice, our life was broken up into two distinct spheres and in each sphere we followed a different set of principles.' It was a problem which the setting up of Pakistan did by no means solve for the Indian Muslims. Moreover, less than a quarter of a century after the foundation of Pakistan, it seemed that Islam did not constitute a tie sufficiently strong to keep the state together. In 1971 the Muslims of East Pakistan manifestly preferred to take advantage of an Indian military intervention to secede and form an independent state of their own.

Islam—faith or social order?

It is apparent from Jinnāh's language that he considered Islam more a 'civilization' and a 'social order' than a faith. In this of course he was not alone, for westernized Muslims (and Jinnāh was one of them) had long learnt to do so; to transform Islam from an eternally true divine revelation independent of temporal changes and vicissitudes, into a product and agent of historical change, or into a social cement. In other words, one was a Muslim not because Islam was true, but because it served, by means of the solidarity which it instilled, to keep together and thus endow with political power the societies in which Islam had hitherto held sway. This in fact is the political doctrine of Afghānī, who, so we have seen, was a religious sceptic. A statement of his establishes with utter clarity the secular, humanist tendencies which he expressed and popularized:

> There are two kinds of philosophy in the world [he told a friend]. One of them is to the effect that there is nothing in the world which is ours, so we must remain content with a rug and a mouthful of food. The other is to the effect that everything in the world is beautiful and desirable, that it does and ought to belong to us. It is the second which should be our ideal, to be adopted as our motto.

To gain possession of the beautiful and desirable is, then, a feasible goal; it is the end of human activity, and specifically of political activity. Political activity harnesses the will of the multitude to the will of the political leader, who uses whatever captures the imagination of the mass. For the Muslim mass, the means is precisely Islam, and it is no surprise that Afghānī favoured the preaching of an Islamic messianism promising the faithful earthly salvation and the establishment of a reign of prosperity and justice. Afghānī, however, recognized that there were solidarity-producing beliefs other than religion. And these beliefs, along with this ambitious view of human abilities – namely to lay hold of all that is beautiful and desirable – became familiar and attractive to the westernized leaders of Islamic society. Two such European creeds promising liberation and salvation here on earth are nationalism and socialism. Nationalism is the belief that the good life cannot be lived except within a politically autonomous 'nation', in which all members of the nation are brothers; while socialism is the conviction that injustice, poverty and unhappiness can be abolished through the abolition of private property. The excessive hopes placed in politics, the expectation that public prosperity and private bliss will alike flow from it, the religious aura with which political action and political leaders are endowed – such seems the clearest outcome of a century and a half of westernization. An example may perhaps suffice to illustrate. In 1974 appeared a small volume of poetry by the Syrian poet Nizār Qabbānī (b. 1923), entitled *Political Works*. Most of the poems denounced the political impotence of the Arabs as the result of a feeble and corrupt leadership. In one poem, the speaker confesses having murdered an imam, i.e. a man of religion, for having so long lulled the faithful with mere words:

> In killing him I have killed
> All the weeds in the garden of Islam
> All who seek a living in the shop of Islam
> In killing him, honoured Sirs, I have killed
> All those who, for a thousand years,
> Have been fornicating with speech.

In another poem addressed to the Palestinian organization *Fatah*, the poet declares:

> Only bullets
> Not patience is the key to deliverance

In yet another poem the Egyptian leader Jamāl 'Abd an-Nāsir is commemorated, shortly after his death, with religious imagery the evocative power of which is here harnessed to the celebration of a secular political figure. Qabbānī says:

> We have filled the cups for you, O you with love of whom
> We have become drunk, as the Sūfī is drunk with God

And again:

> You are the Mahdī for us. You are the Liberator

The collection, however, ends with a poem celebrating the Egyptian crossing of the Suez Canal in October 1973. The poem is remarkable for the fusion between the public concerns of politics and the very private world of love, a fusion which is characteristic of the new outlook, at once unmistakably secular and fervently messianic, which seems to have captured the westernized élite. The poem, entitled 'Observations in time of love and war', is addressed by the poet to his love. The lovers are together when they hear the news of the crossing:

> Did you notice [the poet asks]
> How I overflowed all my banks
> How I covered you like the waters of rivers
> Did you notice how I abandoned myself to you
> As though I was seeing you for the first time.
> Did you notice how we fused together
> How we panted, how we sweated
> How we became ashes, and how we were resuscitated
> As though we were making love
> For the first time . . .

The high sexual ecstasy which the poet here celebrates in so strident a fashion is brought about by the news of a successful military action. But politics (which embraces war) cannot sustain such fervour for very long: wars are sometimes lost, if also sometimes won, and in politics is no salvation. Disappointment with politics is sure to come. Will the failure of such inordinate hopes set up intolerable pressures and threaten frightful explosions? It is with such a question that an observer must end his survey of a Muslim world which has lost its classical poise, and is now highly strung and deeply disturbed.

After a thousand years of virtually unchallenged supremacy, the power of Islam was clearly waning by the end of the XII/18th century. In the Balkans an ancient Muslim empire was yielding to Russia and Austria-Hungary, in India to the British. During the XIII/19th century, confronted by European material superiority, Muslim rulers had to choose between subservience and hopeless resistance. ʿAbd ar-Rahmān, Sultan of Morocco from 1822 to 1859, had to stand by while the French conquered his neighbour, Algeria – sympathizing with the rebel leader ʿAbd al-Qādir, but being finally forced to give up helping him. A diplomatic mission which visited his court in 1831 included Delacroix, who left this impressive painting of him with his entourage outside the walls of Meknès, arrayed in traditional splendour fast becoming meaningless. By a typical irony, Europe began to respond culturally to Islamic civilization only when about to crush it politically. (1)

European attitudes to Islam were also marked by a feeling of moral and cultural superiority. Two details of illustrations from a French history of Algeria published in 1843 typify these attitudes. On the left, *Conquest and Civilization*, a classical figure bestowing the blessing of civilization on a group of properly contrite and defeated Arabs. Right: the French consul insulted by the Dey of Algiers. M. Deval was struck on the face with a fly-whisk, an incident which was made the pretext for the French invasion of 1830. (2,3)

Through Russian eyes: Russia was expanding her power into Central Asia and the Caucasus. A colourful painting by V. V. Vereschagin of 1872 called *Celebration in Turkistan* (below) represents the barbarian Muslims celebrating a victory at the tomb of Tamerlane by sticking the heads of Russian officers on poles. (4)

Resistance to conquest revived the spirit of primitive Islam. 'Abd al-Qādir (below) certainly saw himself, and was seen by the French, as more than a guerilla leader. He was the imam of the Muslim community: 'His decisions are conformable to the words of the sacred book.' (5)

The holy war waged by the Mahdī and his followers in the Sudan was against a Muslim government, but it was a government which had adopted European values and which relied ultimately on European power to maintain them. Kitchener before the Mahdī's tomb at Omdurman in 1898 symbolizes the triumph of European military and administrative methods over traditional Islam. (6)

Allenby's entry into Jerusalem in 1917: yet another highlight marking the retreat of Islam. (7)

For Turkey Allied victory meant the end of the Ottoman dynasty and – apparently – of any hope of remaining a world power. The spectacle of the Allied fleet anchored in the Golden Horn (below) is a symbol of Islam's darkest hour. It was this humiliation which provoked Mustafā Kemal's revolution and the beginning of a new role for Turkey as a modern state aspiring to become a part of Europe. (8)

The dilemma of all Muslim governments in the 19th century was how to meet the challenge of Europe without delivering themselves into European hands. They could modernize only by asking for foreign help, which was usually the first step towards foreign interference and aroused determined opposition. Selīm III (below), Sultan of Turkey from 1789 to 1807, made a sustained effort to transform his administration, and especially his army, on modern lines. This offended the traditionalist Janissaries; he was overthrown in 1807 and killed the following year, though his programme was revived afterwards by his cousin Mahmūd II. (9)

The most successful Muslim leader to use European methods was Muhammad ʿAlī Pasha of Egypt. The changes that he introduced were aimed entirely at increasing his own power. He built factories, organized the fight against cholera, improved agriculture and constructed the first railway between Cairo and Alexandria, and thus began the modernization of Egypt. All this could only be done with the aid of foreign experts. In this lithograph (above) he is seen conferring with Colonel Patrick Campbell and French engineers. (10)

Turkey

Cavalry   Infantry.

Inevitably much that was most characteristic of the old Muslim way of life was lost with the change, a process which could be illustrated in numberless ways. Here are shown four uniforms in the Turkish army. Left: early 19th century. Right: cavalry and infantry in 1890. (11–14)

Turkey became a republic in 1923, with Mustafā Kemal as its president. Kemal pushed through a series of radical reforms in the teeth of widespread opposition – in law and religion, secularizing the state and suppressing the dervishes; in social conduct, encouraging Western dress, prohibiting polygamy and giving women equal status with men (he is seen, above left, with his wife); in education, replacing Arabic script by Latin, and having it taught in a network of new schools (demonstrations, above, by himself); and in many other fields. Such a programme was bound to produce dichotomies, which still exist in Turkey today. Women (left) can live in almost 19th-century seclusion or in up-to-the-minute emancipation. (15,16,17)

Egypt in crisis. In the wake of riot and revolution in 1952 (above) King Faruk was deposed by a military *coup d'etat*. The real power in the new government was Colonel Gamal ʿAbd al-Nasser. Nasser claimed the leadership of the Arab world and for a while a new pan-Arab spirit seemed to evoke enthusiastic response. In 1958 the proclamation of the United Arab Republic (Egypt and Syria) was received with rapture (above right), but was never a political reality. Nasser, however, remained the focus of Arab ambitions (below left), holding together disparate parties by his charisma. The 'socialism' on which Egypt embarked under his aegis greatly increased the scope of government and its centralizing tendencies. As such, it may be seen as the culmination of what Muhammad ʿAli had inaugurated. At his death in 1970, his grandiose plans seemed to lie in ruins; but his successor, Sadat, retrieved some of his losses. In October 1973 Egyptian troops crossed the Suez Canal (below right), regaining part of Sinai, in a war which could be claimed to have achieved a victory. (18–21)

Islam today still retains the staunch loyalty of the masses. But it is increasingly challenged by the values and assumptions of industrial civilization. Can the two co-exist, or will the secular world of the Cadillac and the Mirage drain Islam of its vitality, and confine it to the 'imaginary museum'?

EPILOGUE

Bernard Lewis

THE HISTORY OF ISLAM is punctuated by three great invasions. The first was that of the Muslim Arabs in the 1/7th and 11/8th centuries, which initiated the classical age of Islamic civilization, and created the Islamic heartlands from the Atlantic to the borders of India and China. The second was the invasion of the steppe peoples from the north, between the v/11th and viii/14th centuries, which directed Islamic culture and institutions into new paths, gained vast new territories and created political structures which endured until the dawn of the modern age. The third was the invasion or counter-attack of Christendom, beginning in the late ix/15th century, and reaching its peak in the 19th and 20th centuries. It is this third invasion which has been the dominant fact of modern times, and has posed the most important problems still confronting the Muslim peoples at the present day.

In the later Middle Ages, the grip which Islam had established on Europe at both ends was beginning to loosen. In Spain and Portugal the eight-centuries-long presence of Arab and Berber Islam was finally terminated by the Christian reconquest. At the other end of Europe the Russians freed themselves from the Islamicized Turks and Mongols who had conquered and dominated them. The Moors returned to Africa, the Tatars to Asia. At both ends, the reconquest did not stop with the recovery of the original homeland. In the west, the Spaniards and the Portuguese pursued their retreating Muslim adversaries across the sea, and established a series of outposts in North Africa, the last of which are still held by Spain on the Moroccan coast. The Portuguese went much farther, circumnavigated the African continent, and arrived in southern Asia where they inaugurated an era of Western European supremacy. The Russians followed their former masters across the steppe, gradually absorbed one after another of the Muslim khanates along the Volga, and in time reached the shores of the Caspian and the Black Sea and pressed against the great empires of Turkey and Iran. In the west the Portuguese were followed by the Dutch, the French and the English, all of whom participated in the great expansion of European commerce, culture and power. In the east, the Russians reigned alone and supreme, with the lesser Christian peoples of their empire as coadjutors.

For a time the growing power of Europe and the growing weakness of the Islamic world were concealed by the still imposing might of the surviving Islamic monarchies. The Mughuls in India were still expanding their sphere of influence at the expense of lesser Indian states. Iran, in the xii/18th century, produced a mighty conqueror in Nādir Shāh, who won vast new realms in Central Asia and for a brief period even in India, while farther west the Ottoman Turks were able to advance twice to the walls of Vienna and to maintain their hold over the greater part of South-East Europe.

But the vital changes in the real relationship of power had already taken place. Europe was stronger, technologically, economically, militarily and politically, and in time the Turkish, Persian and Indo-Muslim empires were compelled to retreat before the inexorable European advance. By the end of the xii/18th century, the great struggles of the Napoleonic Wars brought this advance into the very heartlands of Islam in the Middle East, with the invasion and occupation of Egypt by a French expedition led by General Bonaparte. In the course of the 19th century, while the Ottoman and Persian empires remained formally independent, they fell to an increasing extent under the influence of the European powers, and it was largely thanks to the disagreements between these powers that a few Muslim states were able to preserve their independence. Large areas of Islam were directly occupied by colonial powers, four in particular. The French established a vast Muslim empire in North Africa; the British in India with later extensions into the Middle East; the Dutch in South-East Asia; the Russians in the Caucasus, Transcaucasia and Central Asia. The heartlands remained to Turkey and Iran but even these were gravely and obviously threatened.

The retreat of Islam reached its culmination during World War I. Iran, though formally neutral, was overrun by warring armies from both sides, regular and irregular, fighting one another on Iranian soil as if Iranian sovereignty did not exist. The Ottoman empire fought its last war as a great power in alliance with Germany and Austria against the West and Russia. The Ottomans were defeated and lost the greater part of their Islamic territories, which were placed under British and French mandates, while the Turkish homeland in due course became a secular republic. The Muslim lands under Russian Imperial rule seemed for a short time about to achieve their independence, during the interval of liberty which resulted from the Russian Revolution and civil war. But with the ending of the civil war, the authority of Russia was once again imposed, and the Muslim states were reincorporated in the great Russian domain in a new form, as Soviet Socialist Federal Republics.

Between the two wars, Anglo-French supremacy in the Middle East seemed for a time secure and unshakable. The main threat to it came from the quarrels between the British and the French themselves and, from the early 1930s onwards, from the increasing challenge offered by two potential rival imperial powers, Nazi Germany and Fascist Italy.

But even before the threat of the Axis powers materialized in World War II, the position of the Anglo-French domination in the Islamic world was already fatally undermined. World War I, despite the victories and acquisitions which it brought, left a legacy of economic weakness and moral discouragement. Western Europeans in the 20th century no longer had the assurance or strength of will of their predecessors who had built the empires. They were no longer convinced of the basic rightness of their position – of their God-given duty to rule over other peoples, their mission to bring them a purer religion and a higher civilization. Instead, the mood of self-confidence had given place to one of self-criticism and self-doubt.

This was matched by a growing mood of revolt among the subject peoples of the European empires. At first, these had with few exceptions meekly submitted to imperial domination, transferring to their new masters a habit of acquiescence and obedience nurtured by centuries of autocratic rule. Such resistance as occurred was religiously inspired, and found expression in a series of religious revolts from the western to the eastern extremities of the Islamic world. These were in due course suppressed, and a period of intellectual and administrative westernization followed, during which a new élite arose within the empires, familiar with Western languages, with the ideas expressed in those languages and with the political institutions and aspirations of the home countries of their imperial masters. The subjects of the British, French and Dutch empires learned about parliamentary democracy, constitutional government and national freedom, and felt that they too should share in these blessings. Even in the vast territories of the Russian empire, where no comparable questions arose nor any comparable opportunity of discussing them, the ferment of revolutionary movements and ideas spread from the Russians and Ukrainians to the various Muslim subject peoples of the Tsars.

A major landmark was the victory of Japan over Russia in 1905 – the first occasion when an Asian country inflicted a military defeat on a European imperial power. The lesson was not lost upon the peoples of Asia, among whom it sent a wave of joy and exultation. In India, in South-East Asia, in Egypt, even in Turkey, nations beginning to chafe under the yoke of European rulers or the influence of European powers identified themselves with the victorious Japanese and shared with them in the joy of victory. Many perceived a further lesson, that the one Asian power which had been able to win such a victory was the one Asian power which had adopted constitutional and parliamentary government, while the one European imperial power which had suffered such a defeat was the one that still refused to accept this enlightened form of government.

The result of this was an immense upsurge of liberal and constitutional ideas in the Islamic world. These led to the Persian constitutional revolution in 1906 and to the constitutional revolution in Turkey in 1908, known as that of the Young Turks. The victory of the Allied and the associated powers over their somewhat less democratic adversaries in World War I seemed to provide final proof of the proposition that parliamentary democracy makes a country healthy, wealthy and strong. In the aftermath of World War I, liberal democracy was the pattern which most Muslim countries aspiring to any form of progress or modernity sought to imitate, and liberal constitutions spread like a rash across those parts of the Islamic world which still had some freedom to choose their own political way of life. In the countries under British and French mandate, the Mandatory Powers sought to impose their own image – constitutional monarchies in the British territories, parliamentary republics in the French.

The Japanese had shown some of the advantages of democracy and modernization. It was a Muslim nation, for long the leading nation of Islam, which demonstrated the strength of secular nationalism. Alone among the defeated powers of World War I, the Turks were able to confront the victors, reject the terms imposed on them, and create their own national state. Their victory, and the establishment of the Turkish republic, marked the first successful nationalist revolution, and awoke new hope among Muslim peoples who saw, for the first time, a way to defy and defeat their imperial rulers.

Towards the end of the 1930s the attractions of constitutionalism were beginning to wear thin. Not surprisingly, constitutional democracy was not working very well among peoples whose own political traditions and habits did not prepare them for this form of government and whose present situations imposed strains and stresses with which their imported parliamentary institutions were unable to cope. In the meantime, the militant radical nationalism of Fascist and Nazi Europe seemed to offer a seductive alternative. Both Germany and Italy were countries which had within fairly recent memory achieved their own unity by bringing together a number of small states, and their example had served to inspire the leaders of movements pursuing similar ideas of ethnic or religious unification.

With the defeat of the Axis powers in World War II, Fascism, at least as a name, was discredited, and new ideals came to the fore. Western Europe, though nominally victorious, was no longer seen as providing a major source of inspiration. There were now two others – the two new super-powers, the Soviet Union and the United States, each with its own political ideals and institutions, each offering its own distinctive way of life as a model to follow.

Since the end of World War II, these have been the two dominant influences in the Islamic world, and much of the course of Muslim history has been shaped by the confrontation between the Soviet and Western blocs, in which the Muslim world is willy-nilly involved. The course of events in the Muslim countries dependent on or affected by one or other of the two blocs has been vastly different. The Muslim territories of the Russian empire still remain incorporated in the Soviet Union; and there is little evidence of any relaxation of control from the centre. Indeed, of the four great European Islamic empires, the Russian is the only one which not only still exists, but appears to be advancing by what are often classical, imperial techniques. The Western colonial powers withdrew and returned home. The Dutch left the Indies, the French left North Africa, the British left India and the Middle East. Despite some rearguard actions and some unsuccessful attempts to maintain indirect influence, the countries of the former British, French and Dutch empires became politically independent.

Independence brought new opportunities and new dangers. While much of the world of Islam had fallen under foreign rule, the heartlands had remained under Muslim sovereignty, sheltered from attack and even in a

SELECT BIBLIOGRAPHY

Chapter One
The Faith and the Faithful

THE QUR'ĀN

ANDRAE, TOR *Mohammed, the Man and his Faith* (trans. from the German; London, 1936)
CAHEN, CLAUDE *L'Islam des origines au début de l'empire Ottoman* (Paris, 1970)
The Encyclopaedia of Islam (1st edn, Leiden, 1913–42; 2nd edn, Leiden and London, 1960–)
GIBB, H. A. R. *Mohammedanism* (New York, 1962)
GOLDZIHER, I. *Le dogme et la loi de l'Islam* (Paris, 1920; trans. from the German 1st edn, *Vorlesungen über den Islam*; Heidelburg, 1910)
VON GRUNEBAUM, G. E. (trans. Katherine Watson) *Classical Islam: A History 600–1258* (London, 1970)
— *Medieval Islam, A Study in Cultural Orientation* (Chicago, 1953)
HOLT, P. M.; LAMBTON, A. K. S.; LEWIS, BERNARD, eds. *The Cambridge History of Islam*, 2 vols. (Cambridge, 1970)
LEVY, R. *The Social Structure of Islam* (Cambridge, 1957)
LEWIS, BERNARD *Islam from the Prophet Muhammad to the Capture of Constantinople*, 2 vols. (New York, 1974)
— *Race and Color in Islam* (New York, 1971)
MACDONALD, D. B. *Development of Muslim Theology, Jurisprudence and Constitutional Theory* (New York, 1903; reprinted Lahore, 1960; Beirut, 1964)
MUHAMMAD ABDUL RAUF *Islam, Creed and Worship* (Washington D.C., 1974)
DE PLANHOL, XAVIER *The World of Islam* (Ithaca, N.Y., 1959; trans. from the French; *Le monde Islamique*, Paris, 1957)
RAHMAN, FAZLUR *Islam* (London, 1966)
SCHACHT, J. *An Introduction to Islamic Law* (Oxford, 1964)
SCHACHT, J., and BOSWORTH, C. E., eds. *The Legacy of Islam* (Oxford, 1974)
SOURDEL, D. and J. *La civilisation de l'Islam classique* (Paris, 1968)
WATT, W. MONTGOMERY *Muhammad, Prophet and Statesman* (London, 1961)

Chapter Two
The Man-Made Setting

General
ASLANAPA, OKTAY *Turkish Art and Architecture* (London, 1971)
POPE, ARTHUR UPHAM *A Survey of Persian Art from Pre-historic Times to the Present*, 6 vols. (London, 1938–9); reprinted, 12 vols. (Tokyo)
SOURDEL-THOMINE, JANINE, and SPULER, BERTOLD *Die Kunst des Islam* (Berlin, 1973)

Architecture
CRESWELL, K. A. C. *Early Muslim Architecture: Umayyads, early 'Abbāsids and Tūlūnids*, 2 vols. (Oxford, 1932–40); Vol. I, 2nd edn (1969)

— *The Muslim Architecture of Egypt*, 2 vols. (Oxford, 1958)
HILL, DEREK *Islamic Architecture and its Decoration AD 800–1500 (with an introductory text by Oleg Grabar)* (London, 1964)
MARÇAIS, GEORGES *L'Architecture musulman d'Occident: Tunisie, Algérie, Maroc, Espagne* (Paris, 1954)
SAUVAGET, JEAN *Alep. Essai sur le développement d'une grande ville syrienne des origines au milieu du XIXe siècle*, 2 vols. (Paris, 1941)
WILBER, D. N. *The Architecture of Islamic Iran. The Il Khānid Period* (New York, 1969)
— *Persian Gardens and Garden Pavilions* (Rutland, Vt, 1962)

Decorative Arts
BARRETT, DOUGLAS *Islamic Metalwork in the British Museum* (London, 1949)
ERDMANN, JURT (trans. Charles Grant Ellis) *Oriental Carpets: an account of their history* (London, 1960)
LANE, ARTHUR *Early Islamic Pottery (Mesopotamia, Egypt and Persia)* (London, 1947)
— *Later Islamic Pottery (Persia, Syria, Egypt, Turkey)* (London, 1957)
SARRE, FRIEDRICH *Islamische Bucheinbände* (Berlin, 1923)
WIEBEL, ADÈLE C. *Two Thousand Years of Textiles: the Figured Textiles of Europe and the Near East* (New York, 1952)

Calligraphy and Painting
BINYON, LAWRENCE, WILKINSON, J. V. S., and GRAY, BASIL *Persian Miniature Painting* (New York, 1971)
ETTINGHAUSEN, RICHARD *Arab painting* (Geneva, 1962)
SCHIMMEL, ANNEMARIE *Islamic Calligraphy* (Leiden, 1970)

Chapter Three
Cities and Citizens

BEAUDOUIN, EUGÈNE, and POPE, A. U. 'City Plans' in *A Survey of Persian Art*, ed. A. U. POPE, Vol. 2 (London 1938–9), pp. 1391–1410
CAHEN, CLAUDE 'Zur Geschichte der Städtischen Gesellschaft im Islamischen Orient des Mittelalters' in *Speculum*, Vol. 9 (1958), pp. 59–76
VON GRUNEBAUM, GUSTAVE 'The Structure of the Muslim Town' in *Islam: Essays in the Nature and Growth of a Cultural Tradition*, ed. G. von GRUNEBAUM, American Anthropological Assoc., Vol. 57, Memoir no. 81 (1955)
— 'The sacred character of Islamic cities' in *Mélanges Taha Hussein* (Cairo, 1962), pp. 25–37
LAPIDUS, I., ed. *Middle Eastern Cities: Ancient, Islamic and Contemporary. Middle Eastern Urbanism: A Symposium* (Berkeley, Calif., 1969)
LESTRANGE, GUY *The Lands of the Eastern Caliphate* (Cambridge, 1930)
LE TOURNEAU, ROGER *Les villes musulmanes de l'Afrique du Nord* (Algiers, 1957)

MARÇAIS, GEORGES 'La conception des villes dans l'Islam' in *Revue d'Alger*, Vol. 2 (1945), pp. 517–33
— *Mélanges d'Histoire et d'Archéologie de l'Occident musulmane*, Vol 1, 'Les jardins de l'Islam (Algiers, 1957), pp. 233–44
— *La Ville*, Vol 6, 'Considérations sur les villes musulmanes et notamment sur le rôle du Mohtasib' (Brussels, 1955), pp. 248–62
— *Comptes Rendus*, 'L'Islamisme et la vie urbaine', Académie des Inscriptions et Belles Lettres (1928), pp. 86–100

Chapter Four
The Mystic Path

ABUN-NASR, JAMIL M. *The Tijaniyya. A Sufi Order in the Modern World* (Oxford, 1965)
AFFIFI, A. E. *The Mystical Philosophy of Muhyid Din-Ibnul 'Arabi* (Cambridge, 1939)
ANAWATI, G.-C., and GARDET, LOUIS *Mystique musulmane* (Paris, 1961)
ARBERRY, ARTHUR J. *The Doctrine of the Sūfīs* (Cambridge, 1935)
— *Sufism. An Account of the Mystics of Islam* (London, 1950)
BOWEN in GIBB, H. A. R., and BOWEN, HAROLD *Islamic Society and the West*, Vol. 1, Part II (Oxford, 1957), pp. 179–206
CORBIN, HENRY *L'homme de lumière dans le soufisme iranien* (Paris, 1971)
— *En Islam iranien. Aspects spirituels et philosophiques*, 4 vols. (Paris, 1971–2)
GARDET, LOUIS *Etudes de philosophie et de mystique comparées* (Paris, 1972)
GRAMLICH, RICHARD 'Die schiitischen Derwischorden Persiens' in *Abhandlung für die Kunde des Morgenlandes*, XXXVI (Wiesbaden, 1965)
MASSIGNON, LOUIS *La passion d'al-Hosein-ibn-Mansour al-Hallaj* (Paris, 1922)
— *Essai sur les origines du lexique technique de la mystique musulmane* (Paris, 1954)
— *Akhbar al-Hallaj* (Paris, 1957)
MEIER, FRITZ *Eine Darstellung mystischer Erfahrungen im Islam aus der Zeit — Der meister von Mehana (357–440/967–1049)* (Louvain, forthcoming)
MICHON, JEAN-LOUIS *Le soufi marocain Ahmad Ibn 'Ajība (1746–1809) et son Mi'rāj* (Paris, 1973)
NICHOLSON, REYNOLD ALLEYNE *Studies in Islamic Mysticism* (Cambridge, 1967)
— *The Mathnawi of Jalalu'ddin Rumi*, Gibb Memorial Series, N. S. IV, 8 vols. (Leiden and London, 1925–40)
— *Rumi, Poet and Mystic 1207–1273* (London, 1964)
NWYIA, PAUL *Exégèse coranique et langage mystique* (Beirut, 1970)
REINERT, BENEDIKT *Die Lehre vom tawakkul in der klassischen Sufik* (Berlin, 1968)
RITTER, HELLMUT *Das meer der seele* (Leiden, 1955)
TRIMINGHAM, J. SPENCER *The Sufi Orders in Islam* (Oxford, 1971)

ZARRINKOOB, ABDOL-HOSEIN 'Persian Sufism in its Historical Perspective' in *Iranian Studies*, Vol. III, Nos. 3–4 (1970)

Chapter Five
Jewellers with Words

On Arabic Literature
BLACHÈRE, R. *Histoire de la littérature arabe des origines jusqu'à la fin du XVe siècle*, Vols. 1–3 (Paris, 1952–66)
BROCKLEMANN, C. *Geschichte der arabischen Litteratur* (Weimar and Berlin, 1898–1902)
GIBB, H. A. R. *Arabic Literature. An introduction* (London, 1963)
GONZÁLEZ PALENCIA, A. *Historia de la literatura arábigo-española* (Barcelona, 1945)
LANDAU, J. M. *Studies in the Arab theater and cinema* (Philadelphia, 1958)
NICHOLSON, R. A. *A literary history of the Arabs* (Cambridge, 1930)
PELLAT, CH. *Langue et littérature arabes* (Paris, 1970)
PÉRÈS, H. *La poésie andalouse, en arabe classique, au XIe siècle* (Paris, 1953)
SEZGIN, F. *Geschichte der arabischen Schrifttums* (Leiden, forthcoming)
WIET, G. *Introduction à la littérature arabe* (Paris, 1966)

On Persian Literature
ARBERRY, A. J. *Classical Persian literature* (London, 1958)
BROWNE, E. G. *A literary history of Persia*, 4 vols. (Cambridge, 1951–3)
RYPKA, J., et al. *History of Iranian Literature* (Dordrecht, 1968)
STOREY, C. A. *Persian Literature* (London, 1927–39)

Other Literatures
BOMBACCI, A. *Storia della letteratura turca* (Milan, 1956)
GRAHAM BAILEY, T. *A History of Urdu literature* (Calcutta, 1932)

Chapter Six
The Dimension of Sound

BARKECHLI, M. *La Musique traditionelle de l'Iran* (Tehran, 1964)
CAUSSIN DE PERCEVAL, A. P. 'Notices anecdotiques sur les principaux musiciens arabes des trois premiers siècles de l'Islamisme' in *Journal Asiatique* (1873)
CHOTTIN, A. *Tableau de la musique marocaine* (Paris, 1939)
COLLANGETTES, M. 'Etudes sur la musique arabe' in *Journal Asiatique* (1904), pp. 365–422; (1906) pp. 149–90
FARMER, H. G. *A History of Arabian Music* (London, 1929)
— *Historical Facts for the Arabian Musical Influence* (London, 1930)
— *The Organ of the Ancients from Eastern Sources* (London, 1930)

— *The Sources of Arabian Music* (Bearsden, 1940)
HICKMANN, H., and STAUDER, W. *Orientalische Musik* (Leiden and Cologne, 1970)
KIESEWETTER, R. G. *Die Musik der Araber* (Leipzig, 1842)
LAND, J. P. N. *Actes du sixième congrès international des Orientalistes,* 'Recherches sur l'histoire de la gamme arabe' (Leiden, 1883)
LANE, E. W. *An Account of the Manners and Customs of the Modern Egyptians* (5th edn, London, 1860; reprinted London, 1966)
REINHARD, KURT and URSULA *Les Traditions musicales: Turquie* (Paris, 1969)
REZVANI, M. *Le Théâtre et la danse en Iran* (Paris, 1962)
ROUANET, J. *Encyclopédie de la musique Lavignac,* Vol. V, 'La Musique arabe' (Paris, 1913–22), pp. 2676–2944
SALVADOR-DANIEL, F. *La musique arabe, ses rapports avec la musique grecque et le chant grégorien* (Algiers, 1879)
VILLOTEAU, G. A. *Description historique, technique et littéraire des instruments de musique des Orientaux* (Paris, 1823)
ZONIS, E. *Classical Persian Music: an Introduction* (Cambridge, Mass., 1973)

Chapter Seven
The Scientific Enterprise

ANAWATI, G. 'Science' in *The Cambridge History of Islam,* ed. P. M. Holt, A. K. S. Lambton, Bernard Lewis, Vol. II (Cambridge, 1970), pp. 741–79
ARNALDEZ, R., and MASSIGNON, L. 'Arabic science' in *History of Science,* ed. R. Taton, *Ancient and Medieval Science from the Beginning to 1450* (London, 1964), pp. 385–421
Encyclopaedia of Islam, 'Asturlāb', 'al-Djabr wa 'l-muqabāla', ''Ilm al-hay'a', ''Ilm al-hisab' (Leiden and London, 1960–)
AYDIN SAYILI *The Observatory in Islam and Its Place in the General History of the Observatory* (Ankara, 1960)
BROWNE, E. *Arabian Medicine* (Cambridge, 1921)
CAMPBELL, D. *Arabian Medicine and Its Influence on the Middle Ages,* 2 vols. (London, 1926)
ECHE, YOUSSEF *Les bibliothèques arabes publiques et semi-publique en Mésopotamie, en Syrie et en Egypte au Moyen Age* (Damascus, 1967)
GILLISPIE, C. C., ed. *Dictionary of Scientific Biography* (New York, 1970–)
HARTNER, WILLY *Oriens-Occidens* (Hildesheim, 1968)
JUSCHKEWITSCH, A. P. *Geschichte der Mathematik im Mittelalter* (Leipzig, 1964)
KENNEDY, E. S. 'Late medieval planetary theory' in *Isis,* LVII (1966), pp. 365–78
— 'The Arabic heritage in the exact sciences' in *al-Abḥāth,* XXIII (1970), pp. 327–44
— 'The exact sciences in medieval Iran' in *The Cambridge History of Iran* (Cambridge, 1975)
LECLERC, L. *Histoire de la médecine arabe* (Paris, 1876)
PINES, S. 'What was original in Arabic science?', in A. C. Crombie, ed., *Scientific Change* (New York, 1963), pp. 181–205
SARTON, GEORGE *Introduction to the History of Science,* 3 vols. (Baltimore, Md, 1927–48)
SCHACHT, J., and BOSWORTH, C. E. *The Legacy of Islam,* Ch. X (Oxford, 1974)
TEMKIN, OWSEI *Galenism, Rise and Decline of a Medical Philosophy* (Ithaca, N.Y., and London, 1973)

Chapter Eight
Armies of the Prophet

AYALON, D. *L'esclavage du Mamelouk* (Jerusalem, 1951)
— *Gunpowder and firearms in the Mamluk kingdom: a challenge to a mediaeval society* (London, 1956)
BOSWORTH, C. E. 'Ghaznevid military organisation' in *Der Islam,* XXXVI (1960)
— 'Military organisation under the Būyids of Persia and Iraq' in *Oriens,* XVIII–XIX (1965–6)
— 'The armies of the Saffārids' in *Bulletin of the School of Oriental and African Studies,* XXXI (1968)
BOUDOT DE LA MOTTE, A. *Contribution à l'étude de l'archerie musulmane* (Damascus, 1968)
CAHEN, CLAUDE 'Un traité d'armurerie composé pour Saladin' in *Bulletin d'Etudes Orientales,* XII (Damascus, 1947–8)
HUURI, K. *Zur Geschichte des mittelalterlichen Geschützwesens aus orientalischen Quellen* (Helsinki, 1941)
LATHAM, J. D., and PATERSON, W. F. *Saracen archery, an English version and exposition of a Mameluke work on archery (ca. A.D. 1368)* (London, 1970)
LEVY, R. *The social structure of Islam,* 'Military organization in Islam' (Cambridge, 1962)
MAYER, L. A. *Saracenic heraldry* (Oxford, 1933)
— *Islamic armourers and their work* (Geneva, 1962)
PARRY, V. J., and YAPP, M. E., eds. *War, technology and society in the Middle East* (London, 1975)
SCANLON, G. T. *A Muslim manual of war* (Cairo, 1961)

Chapter Nine
Moorish Spain

ASÍN, MIGUEL *Huellas del Islam* (Madrid, 1941)
CODERA, FRANCISCO *Tratado de Numismática arábigo-española* (Madrid, 1879)
CONDE, JOSÉ ANTONIO *Historia de la dominación de los Arabes en España*
DOZY, R. *Histoire des musulmans d'Espagne,* 3 vols. (Leiden, 1932)
GARCÍA GÓMEZ, EMILIO *Poemas arábigoandaluces,* Colection Austral no. 162 (Madrid, 1971)
— *Las jarchas romances de la serie árabe en su marco* (Madrid, 1965)
— *Todo Ben Quzmān,* 3 vols. (Madrid, 1972)
GÓMEZ-MORENO, MANUEL *Iglesias mozárabes (arte español de los siglos IX a XI)* (Madrid, 1919)
HOENERBACH, W. *Spanisch-Islamische Urkunden aus der Zeit der Nasriden und Moriscos* (Berkeley, Calif., 1965)
LÉVI-PROVENÇAL, E. *Histoire de l'Espagne musulmane,* 3 vols. (Paris, 1950–53)
MILES, G. C. *Coins of the Spanish Mulūk al-Tawā'if* (New York)
NICHOLSON, R. A. *A Literary History of the Arabs* (London, 1914)
RIBERA, JULIÁN *Disertaciones y Opúsculos,* 2 vols. (Madrid, 1928)
TERRASSE, H. *Art hispano-mauresque* (Paris, 1932)
TORRES, BALBÁS, L. 'Crónica arqueológica de la España musulmana' in *Al-Andalus*

Chapter Ten
Land of the Lion and the Sun

ARBERRY, A. J., ed. *The Legacy of Persia* (Oxford, 1953)
AVERY, PETER *Modern Iran* (London, 1965)
BENY, ROLOFF *Bridge of Turquoise* (London, 1975)

BROWNE, E. G. *A Literary History of Persia,* 4 vols. (Cambridge, 1902–24; reprinted 1964)
The Cambridge History of Iran (projected in 8 vols.; Vols. I and V, 1968; Vol. IV, 1975)
FRYE, R. N. *Persia* (New York, 1969)
— *The Heritage of Persia* (London, 1962)
HOLT, P. M.; LAMBTON, A. K. S.; LEWIS, BERNARD, eds. *The Cambridge History of Islam,* Vol. I (Cambridge, 1970): Part III/5, R. M. Savory 'Safavid Persia', pp. 394–429; Part III/6, A. K. S. Lambton 'Persia: The Breakdown of Society', pp. 430–67; Part IV/3, R. M. Savory 'Modern Persia', pp. 595–626
LAMBTON, A. K. S. *Landlord and Peasant in Persia* (London, 1953)
— *The Persian Land Reform 1962–1966* (Oxford, 1969)
MORRIS, JAMES; WOOD, ROGER; WRIGHT, SIR DENIS *Persia* (London, 1969)
H. I. M. MUHAMMAD RIZĀ SHĀH PAHLAVĪ *Mission for my country* (New York, 1961)
NASR, SAYYID HUSAYN 'Ithna 'Ashari Shi'ism and Iranian Islam' in *Religion in the Middle East,* ed. A. J. Arberry, Vol. 2 (Cambridge, 1969), pp. 96–118
OLMSTEAD, A. T. *History of the Persian Empire* (Chicago and London, 1966)
POPE, A. U. *A Survey of Persian Art from prehistoric times to the present,* 6 vols. (London, 1939)
WILBER, D. N. *Iran, Past and Present* (Princeton, N.J., 1958)
— *Riza Shah Pahlavi: the resurrection and reconstruction of Iran 1878–1944* (Hicksville, N.Y., 1975)

Chapter Eleven
The Ottoman Empire

General Works
HOLT, P. M., *et al.* *The Cambridge History of Islam,* 2 vols. (Cambridge, 1970)
VAUGHN, DOROTHY M. *Europe and the Turk: A Pattern of Alliances* (Liverpool, 1954)

Seljuqs and Early Ottomans
CAHEN, CLAUDE (trans. J. Jones-Williams) *Pre-Ottoman Turkey* (New York, 1968)
INALCIK, HALIL 'Ottoman Methods of Conquest' in *Studia Islamica,* Fas. II (1954), pp. 103–29
WITTEK, PAUL *The Rise of the Ottoman Empire* (London, 1938)

Ottoman Institutions
ANDRIC, IVO (trans. Lovett F. Edward) *The Bridge on the Drina* (New York, 1967)
GIBB, H. A. R., and BOWEN, HAROLD *Islamic Society and the West,* Vol. I, Parts 1 and 2 (London, 1950–57)
ITZKOWITZ, NORMAN *Ottoman Empire and Islamic Tradition* (New York, 1972)
LEWIS, BERNARD *Istanbul and the Civilization of the Ottoman Empire* (Norman, Okla., 1963)
WRIGHT JR, WALTER LIVINGSTON *Ottoman Statecraft: The Book of Counsel for Vezirs and Governors* (Princeton, N.J., 1935)

The Ottomans 1500–1800
ALLEN, W. E. D. *Problems of Turkish Power in the Sixteenth Century* (London, 1963)
INALCIK, HALIL (trans. Norman Itzkowitz and Colin Imber) *The Ottoman Empire: The Classical Age* (London, 1972)
ITZKOWITZ, NORMAN, and MOTE, MAX *Mubadele: An Ottoman-Russian Exchange of Ambassadors* (Chicago, 1970)

Chapter Twelve
Muslim India

'ABD AL-HAMID MUHARRIR *Dastūr al-Albāb fī 'Ilm al-Hisāb* (MS (Persian), Rida Library, Rampur, India)
ABŪ 'L-FADL (trans. H. Blockmann, Vol. I; H. S. Jarrett, Vols. II, III) *The A'in-i Akbarī* (Calcutta, 1873–94)
AHMAD I-MI'MAR *Risalah Ahmad i' Mimar* (Subhan Allah MSS (Persian), Aligarh University)
DE BARY, W. T., ed. *Sources of Indian Tradition* (New York, 1958)
BROWNE, P. *Indian Architecture,* The Islamic Period (Bombay, 1956)
— *Indian Painting under the Mughals, AD 1550 to AD 1750* (Oxford, 1924)
FAIDI *The Lilavati* (Persian) (Calcutta, 1827)
FERGUSON, J. *History of Indian and eastern architecture* (London, 1876; rev. edn J. Burges and R. P. Spiers, 2 vols., London, 1910)
GOETZ, H. *Arte dell' India Musulmana e Correnti moderne* (Rome, 1962)
IBN BATTŪTA *Rihla* (Arabic edn with French trans. C. Defremery and B. R. Sanguinetti, 4 vols., 1853–9); English trans. H. A. R. Gibb, *The Travels of Ibn Battuta* (Cambridge Hakluyt Society, 1958–)
JAI SINGH, SAWA'Ī *Zif i-Jadid i-Muhammad Shāhī* (British Museum MS. Add. 14, 373)
MIYAN BHUWA IBN KHAWASS KHĀN *Ma'dan al-Shifa'-i Sikandar-shahi* (Lucknow, 1877)
QURESHI, I. H. *The Muslim Community of the Indo-Pakistan Sub-Continent* (The Hague, 1962)
RIZVI, S. A. A. *Muslim Revivalist Movements in Northern India in the Sixteenth and Seventeenth Centuries* (Agra, 1965)
— *Religious and Intellectual History of the Muslims in Akbar's Reign* (Delhi, 1975)
RIZVI, S. A. A., and FLYNN, V. J. A. *Fathpur-Sikri* (Bombay, 1975)
TŪSĪ, NASĪR AD-DĪN *Bist Bāb dar Asturlāb* (Persian) (Tehran, 1859)
RIZVI, S. A. A., and FLYNN, V. J. A.

Chapter Thirteen
Islam Today

AVERY, PETER *Modern Iran* (London, 1965)
ELIOT, SIR CHARLES *Turkey in Europe* (London, 1965)
VON GRUNEBAUM, G. E. *Modern Islam: The Search for Cultural Identity* (Cambridge, 1962)
HAIM, SYLVIA G. *Arab Nationalism* (Cambridge, 1962)
HARDY, P. *The Muslims of British India* (Cambridge, 1972)
HOLT, P. M.; LAMBTON, A. K. S.; LEWIS, BERNARD, eds. *The Cambridge History of Islam* (Cambridge, 1970): Akdes Nimet Kurat 'Tsarist Russia and the Muslims of Central Asia' and 'Islam in the Soviet Union'; William R. Roff 'South-East Asian Islam in the Nineteenth Century'; Harry J. Benda 'South-East Asian Islam in the Twentieth Century'
KEDOURIE, ELIE *Afghani and 'Abduh: an Essay on Religious Unbelief and Political Activism in Modern Islam* (London, 1966)
— *Arabic Political Memoirs and Other Studies* (London, 1974)
LEWIS, BERNARD *The Emergence of Modern Turkey* (Oxford, 1961)
SMITH, WILFRED CANTWELL *Islam in Modern History* (Oxford, 1957)
VATIKIOTIS, P. J. *The Modern History of Egypt* (London, 1969)
WHEELER, GEOFFREY *The Modern History of Soviet Central Asia* (London, 1964)

SOURCES OF ILLUSTRATIONS

The page on which an illustration appears is shown by the first set of numerals in bold type, its plate or figure number by the second. Sources of photographs are given in italics. The following abbreviations have been used: P.B., Peter Bridgewater; Bib. Nat., Bibliothèque Nationale; B. L., British Library; B. M., British Museum.

Introduction

17 1. Mecca with orientation of the various Islamic countries; frontispiece to a portolan of the Mediterranean by 'Alī ibn Ahmad ibn Muhammad ash-Sharqī, of Sfax, 958/1551. MS. ar. 2278 f. 2v. *Bib. Nat., Paris*
18 2. Village in Morocco. *Bruno Barbey, Magnum*
3. Desert landscape near Mecca in Saudi Arabia. *G. Mandel*
19 4. Irrigated fields near Baghdad, Iraq. *Georg Gerster, Magnum*
20 5. Stucco head from the palace at Khirbat al-Mafjar, near Jericho, built by the Caliph al-Walīd II, first half of II/8th century. *Rockefeller Museum, Jerusalem*
6. Dancing girl; lustre painting from a fragment of a glass bowl, Syria, I/7th to II/8th century. *B. M., London*
7. Ruins of an Umayyad palace at Anjar in the Lebanon, I/7th to II/8th century. *Paul Almasy, Camera Press*
8. Armed horseman; ivory chess figure, Iran, II/8th to III/9th century. *L. A. Mayer Memorial Institute for Islamic Art, Jerusalem*
21 9–10. Stucco figures from Khirbat al-Mafjar, near Jericho, built by the Caliph al-Walīd II, first half of II/8th century. *Rockefeller Museum, Jerusalem*
11. Fragments of wall painting from the palace at Samarra, middle of III/9th century. *Museum für Islamische Kunst, Berlin*
12. Carved ivory panel with hunting scenes, from Egypt, V/11th to VI/12th century. *Museum für Islamische Kunst, Berlin*
22 13–14. An Arab prince and his court and a Turkish military official; details from the double frontispiece to al-Harīrī's *Maqāmāt*, manuscript executed by al-Wāsitī, signed and dated Baghdad 635/1237. MS. ar. 5847 f. 1 verso–2r. *Bib. Nat., Paris*
15. A boat crossing the Persian Gulf; illustration from the 39th *Maqāma* of al-Harīrī's *Maqāmāt* (see pls. 13–14), f. 119r. *Bib. Nat., Paris*
23 16. Indian prince of the Eastern Isles of the Indian Ocean; detail of illustration from the 39th *Maqāmā* of al-Harīrī's *Maqāmāt* (see pls. 13–14), f. 122v. *Bib. Nat., Paris*
17. The siege of Baghdad by the Mongols; from Rashīd ad-Dīn's *Universal History*, manuscript copied in Tabrīz, late VIII/14th century. MS. suppl. pers. 1113 f. 180v–181r. *Bib. Nat., Paris*
24 18. The Gur-i Emir mausoleum, the tomb of Tamerlane, Samarqand. *A. F. Kersting*
19. The Mongol ruler Tahmaras the 'fully armed', and an Arab scribe; detail of a miniature from Rashīd ad-Dīn's *Universal History*, manuscript dated 707–14/1307–14. MS. 20 f. 2v. *Edinburgh University Library*

Chapter One
The Faith and the Faithful

25 The name 'Muhammad' in stylized Arabic script from the mausoleum of Tamerlane, Samarqand. Drawn by P.B.

26 2. Symbol of the five precepts of the Qur'ān; keystone on the Puerta de la Justicia, Alhambra, Granada. Drawn by P.B.
27 3–4. Two drawings from a poem on the rites of pilgrimage, Persian, X/16th century. MS. Or. 343 f. 28r, 31v. *B. L., London*
28–29 5. Map of the Islamic world. Drawn by Shalom Schotten
31 6. Gold coin of 'Abd al-Malik. *Bib. Nat., Paris*. Drawn by P.B.
7. Silver dirham of the Caliph al-Muqtadir. *B. M., London*. Drawn by P.B.
32 8. Bronze fals of Salāh ad-Dīn. *B. M., London*. Drawn by P.B.
34 9. Fragment of pilgrimage certificate, VI/12th century. *Museum of Islamic Art, Istanbul*
38 10. Record of a pious foundation; pottery disc from Kāshān, 711/1312. Musée National de Céramique, Sèvres. *Dr Yolande Crowe*
41 1. The Archangel Gabriel; miniature from Syria or Egypt, VIII/14th century. *B. M., London*
42 2. Chingiz Khān proclaiming from the pulpit of the mosque to the people of Bukhārā; miniature from a manuscript of epics including the poetic history of the Mongols by Ahmad of Tabrīz, copied in Baghdad, 789–90/1387–8. MS. Or. 2780 f. 61r. *B. L., London*
3. The conversion of Abū Zayd in the mosque at Basra; illustration from al-Harīrī's *Maqāmāt*, manuscript executed by al-Wāsitī, signed and dated Baghdad 635/1237. MS. ar. 5847 f. 164v. *Bib. Nat., Paris*
4. The courtyard of the Great Mosque at Aleppo; photograph taken c. 1890. *Courtesy Max van Berchem Foundation, Geneva*
43 5–6. Two sides of a *qibla* indicator; wood, painted and gilded, Turkey, XII/18th century. *L. A. Mayer Memorial Institute for Islamic Art, Jerusalem*
7. Decoration on a house in Jerusalem to show that the occupants have made the pilgrimage to Mecca. *Dr Carolyn Elliott*
44 8. Plan of the Ka'ba at Mecca; Turkish pulpit tile, c. 1077/1666. Victoria and Albert Museum, London. *John Webb*
9. Inscription of the Muhammadan creed; Turkish pulpit tile, early XI/17th century. Victoria and Albert Museum, London. *John Webb*
10. Map of the Nile delta; from Idrīsī's atlas, 549/1154. MS. Pococke 375 f. 114v–115r. *Bodleian Library, Oxford*
45 11. Majnūn at the Ka'ba; miniature from a copy of *Khamseh* of Nizāmī; Herat, 846/1442. MS. Add. 25900 f. 114v. *B. L., London*
46 12. Arab scribes; detail from an illustration to Peter of Eboli's work celebrating the conquest of Sicily by the Emperor Henry VI in 591/1195. Cod. 120 f. 101v. *Burgerbibliothek, Bern*
13. Mongol soldier; detail from a brass basin, the so-called Baptistère de St Louis, Egypt or Syria, first half of VIII/14th century. *Louvre, Paris*

14. Abū Zayd and his daughter accuse each other before a *qādī*; illustration from the 8th *Maqāma* of al-Harīrī's *Maqāmāt*, manuscript illustrated in Baghdad, dated 620/1222. MS. ar. 6094 f. 24r. *Bib. Nat., Paris*
47 15. The Virgin and Child; illumination from a Gospel Lectionary, copied and illuminated in Mosul, Iraq, 613–17/1216–20. MS. Add. 7170 f. 24r. *B. L., London*
16. Passover service in a Jewish home in Spain; from a Hebrew manuscript of the Passover service written in a Spanish hand. MS. Or. 2884 f. 18v. *B. L., London*
17. Porters carrying sacks of grain; miniature, Baghdad school, first half VII/13th century. *Bib. Nat., Paris*
18. Porters carrying baskets. Illustration to the poem *Kalīla wa-Dimna*. Manuscript copied in Baghdad, about 751/1350. MS. arabe 3467 f. 26. *Bib. Nat., Paris*
19. Gold dinar from Syria, before 71/690, and silver dirham. B. M., London, *Ray Gardner*
49 20. Slave market in Zabīd in the Yemen; illustration from the 34th *Maqāma* of al Harīrī's *Maqāmāt* (see pl. 3), f. 105. *Bib. Nat., Paris*
21. Glass weight, Fātimid, Egypt. B. M., London. *Ray Gardner*
50 22. Enthroned figure with attendants surrounded by caravan; bowl from Ray, Iran, c. 579/1200. *Hetjens Museum, Düsseldorf*
23. A boat on the Euphrates; illustration from al-Harīrī's *Maqāmāt*, manuscript executed in Baghdad, 622–33/1225–35. *State Hermitage Museum, Leningrad*
24. Caravanserai at Wāsit; illustration from al-Harīrī's *Maqāmāt* (see pl. 3), f. 89. *Bib. Nat., Paris*
51 25. Caravanserai of As'ad Pasha in Damascus. *Courtesy Max van Berchem Foundation, Geneva*
26. Caravanserai at Mahyar, Iran. *Roger Wood*
52–3 27–36. Ploughing, pounding grain, churning, shaping a millstone, processing cotton (31–34), dyeing cloth, manufacturing gold wire; illustrations to a Persian glossary of rare words compiled in 873–4/1468–9, from a manuscript executed in early X/16th century, probably by a Persian artist working in western India. MS. Or. 3299. *B. L., London*
54 37. Silver dirham, Khurāsān, 64/683. B. M., London. *Ray Gardner*
38. Silver dirham, Bīshāpūr, 129/746. B. M., London. *Ray Gardner*
39. Gold dinar, Baghdad, 218–28/833–42. B. M., London. *Ray Gardner*
40. Reverse of gold dinar, Baghdad, 251–2/855–6. *Kunsthistorisches Museum, Vienna*
41. Gold dinar, from Ray, 387–420/997–1029. B. M., London. *Ray Gardner*
42. Quarter dinar, Sicily, 427–88/1036–94. B. M., London. *Ray Gardner*
43. Bronze coin, Mārdīn, 547–72/1152–76. B. M., London. *Ray Gardner*
44. Bronze coin, Mosul, 572–89/1176–93. B. M., London. *Ray Gardner*

45. Silver dirham of Chingiz Khān. B. M., London. *Ray Gardner*
46. Silver dirham, Tiflis. B. M., London. *Ray Gardner*
55 47. The Bazaar in Aleppo. *Werner Forman*
56 48. The physician Andromaches watching labourers at work; from an Arabic version of the *Book of Antidotes*, Pseudo-Galen, executed 595/1199. MS. ar. 2964. *Bib. Nat., Paris*

Chapter Two
The Man-Made Setting

57 1. Lustre plate from Iraq, IV/10th century. Freer Gallery of Art, Washington D.C. Drawn by P.B.
60 2. Detail of calligraphy from bronze bowl, late VII/13th century. Victoria and Albert Museum, London. Drawn by P.B.
61 3. Fātimid silk fragment. Museum of Islamic Art, Cairo. Drawn by P.B.
63 4. Lustre plate from Iran, c. 597/1200. Museum für Islamische Kunst, Berlin. Drawn by P.B.
73 1. Frontispiece to the ninth section of a thirty-volume Qur'ān, Egypt, end of VIII/14th century. MS. Or. 848 f. 1 verso. *B. L., London*
74 2. Detail from Kūfic inscription in mosaic around octagonal arcade in the Dome of the Rock, Jerusalem, built 72/691. *Middle East Archive*
3. Mosque lamp with Qur'ānic inscriptions, Syria, VIII/14th century. *Victoria and Albert Museum, London*
4. *Mihrāb* tile with Qur'ānic inscriptions, Kāshān, VII/13th century. *Gulbenkian Foundation, Lisbon*
75 5. Frieze of inscription in turquoise tiles on minaret of Jam, Iran, second half of VI/12th century. *Dr Yolande Crowe*
6. Calligraphic decoration from entrance façade of the *khanaqah* at Natanz, built 724–5/1324–5. *H. C. Seherr-Toss*
76 7. Engraved pattern from brass basin, Iran, beginning of VIII/14th century. *Bequest of Edward C. Moore, Metropolitan Museum of Art, New York*
8. Gold tooled leather book-binding, Morocco, 655/1256. *B. M., London*
9. Star pattern in stonework from main portal of the caravanserai of Sultan Han on Konya-Aksaray road; Seljuq, early VII/13th century. *Yan*
10. Hispano-Moresque tiles in imitation of the inlaid mosaic work in the Alhambra, Granada. *Victoria and Albert Museum, London*
77 11. Detail of wooden shutter from the Green Mosque (Yeshil Jāmi'), Bursa, built 818–27/1414–24. *Yan*
12. Door-knocker from Puerta del Perdón, Seville Cathedral, VI/12th century. *Mas*
13. Page from a Qur'ān in Maghribī script, VI/12th to VII/13th century. MS. Or. 12523 f. 39v. *B. L., London*
14. Bronze doors of the Sultan Hasan Madrasa, Cairo, 757/1356. *Islamic Museum, Cairo*
78 15. Interior of the Great Mosque at Qayrawān, Tunisia, I/7th century, rebuilt III/9th century. *Roger Wood*

16. Interior of the Alaeddin Mosque in Konya, Turkey, built 617/1220. *Sonia Halliday*
79 17. Courtyard of the al-Azhar Mosque, Cairo, founded 360/970, subsequently rebuilt. *Middle East Archive*
18. *Mihrāb* and *minbar* of the Mosque of Sultan Hasan, Cairo, *c.* 763/1361. *Wim Swaan, Camera Press*
80 19. Courtyard of the Friday Mosque at Isfahan, founded v/11th century. *Roger Wood*
20. Interior of the Great Mosque in Cordoba, founded 169–70/785–6. *Henri Bertault*
81 21. Iskele Jāmiʿ, Üsküdar, by Sinān, 954/1547. *Boudot-Lamotte*
82 22. Tiled portal of the Masjid-i Shāh, Isfahan, built 1010–28/1601–18. *Bruno Barbey, Magnum*
82–3 23. Carpet made for the mosque at Ardabīl, by order of Shāh Tahmāsp, signed and dated; Tabrīz, 946/1539. *Victoria and Albert Museum, London*
83 24. Safavid tents; detail from Persian-style miniature from the *Sulaymān-nāma*, manuscript copied in Istanbul in 964/1557. H. 1517 f. 374r. Topkapi Saray Museum, Istanbul. *Sonia Halliday*
25. Prayer-hall of the Masjid-i Shāh, Isfahan, built 1010–28/1601–18. *Roger Wood*
84 26. Bronze mosque lamp pierced with Kūfic inscription, iv/10th to v/11th century. *David Collection, Copenhagen*
27. Brass writing-box with copper and silver inlay, Mosul, early vii/13th century. *B. M., London*
85 28. Bronze incense-burner in the form of a lion, Iran, vi/12th century. *State Hermitage Museum, Leningrad*
29. Bronze griffin, Pisa Campo Santo, *c.* v/11th century. *Anderson/Mansell*
30. Brass ewer with bird design inlaid with copper, Iran, vi/12th century. *State Hermitage Museum, Leningrad*
31. The Bobrinski bucket; bronze with copper and silver inlay, signed by two artists, Herat, 559/1163. *State Hermitage Museum, Leningrad*
86 32. The garden of the Emperor Bābur; Mughul miniature painting from a copy of the *Bābur-nāma*. *Victoria and Albert Museum, London*
33. The Court of the Myrtles, Alhambra, Granada, viii/14th century. *Mas*
87 34. Garden carpet, southern Persia, xi/17th century. *Burrell Collection, Glasgow*
88 35. Tomb tower at Ahlāt, eastern Turkey, 799/1396. *Dr Yolande Crowe*
36. Mausoleum of the Sāmānids, Bukhārā, Transoxiana, first half of the iv/10th century. *Richard Harrington, Camera Press*
37. The Southern cemetery outside Cairo. *A. F. Kersting*

Chapter Three
Cities and Citizens

89 *1.* Bitlis; detail of a miniature from the *Itinerary* by Nāsūh al-Matrakī, Istanbul, *c.* 943/1536. T. 5964 f. 99r. Istanbul University Library. Drawn by P.B.
90 *2.* Kāshān; engraving from *Les Voyages*, by Chardin, Amsterdam 1123/1711. *J. R. Freeman*
92 *3.* House types in Egypt; from an engraving from *Description de l'Egypte*, Paris 1822–3
93 *4.* Carved wooden inscription from Fustāt, Egypt. Museum für Islamische Kunst, Berlin. Drawn by P.B.
95 *5.* *Sūq* at Isfahan; from P. Coste and E. Flandin, *Monuments modernes de la Perse*, Paris 1865
97 *6.* The Talisman gate of Baghdad (destroyed); after a photograph by P. Sarre and E. Herzfeld. Drawn by P.B.
98 *7.* Bread-stamps from Egypt. Victoria and Albert Museum, London. Drawn by P.B.
101 1. View of Aleppo; from Nāsūh al-Matrakī's *Itinerary*, a description of the campaign of Sultan Sulaymān the Magnificent to Iraq in 941–3/1534–6, at which the author, who also illustrated the manuscript, was present. T. 5964 f. 105r. *Istanbul University Library*
102–3 2. Aerial view of Jerusalem. *Georg Gerster, Magnum*
104–5 3. The bazaar in Ankara; detail from a painting by J. B. Van Mour, a French artist who lived in Istanbul, 1111–50/1699–1737. *Rijksmuseum, Amsterdam*
104 4. The interior of a bazaar; from the heroic love story of *Warqa and Gulsah*, beginning of vii/13th century. Hazine 841 f. 3v. *Topkapi Saray Museum, Istanbul*
105 5. Tannery in the *medina* of Fez, Morocco. *Bruno Barbey, Magnum*
106 6. Lustre plate from Ray, Iran, end of vi/12th century. *David Collection, Copenhagen*
7. Acquamanile in the form of a water buffalo suckling her calf; cast bronze with silver incrustation, signed by the artist; Khurāsān, 603/1206. *State Hermitage Museum, Leningrad*
8. Water-jar, unglazed earthenware, Mesopotamia, probably Mosul, vi/12th to vii/13th century. *Gift of Joan Palevsky, Nasli M. Heeramaneck Collection, Los Angeles County Museum of Art, Los Angeles*
107 9. The so-called 'Freer Canteen'; brass, inlaid with silver, Syria, mid vii/13th century. *Freer Gallery of Art, Washington D.C.*
10. Flask in the form of an animal; glass, from Aleppo, Syria, ii/8th to iii/9th century. *B. M., London*
11. Brass ewer inlaid with silver and copper, Mosul, Iraq, 630/1232. *B. M., London*
108 12. View of Sanʿāʾ, North Yemen. *Georg Gerster, Magnum*
13. Yazd, Iran. *Peter Fraenkel*
109 14. Souf El Oued, Algeria. *Georg Gerster, Magnum*
110 15. Giant water-wheel at Hama, Syria. *Bruno Barbey, Magnum*
16. Fountain of ʿAbd ar-Rahmān Katkhudā, Cairo. *Museum of Islamic Art, Cairo*
17. Najjārīn fountain, Fez, Morocco, xii/18th century. *Ormond Gigli, Camera Press*
111 18. Scene in a bath; miniature from a copy of the *Khamseh* of Nizāmī, Shīrāz, 935/1528. MS. 195 f. 33. *Chester Beatty Library, Dublin*
19. Courtyard of the caravanserai al-Ghūrī, Cairo, x/16th century. *Sophie Ebeid*
20. Interior of hospital at Divrigi, central Turkey, part of a mosque-hospital complex built under the Turkish Seljuqs in 626/1228. *Dr Yolande Crowe*
112 21. Scene in a mosque; illustration from the 7th *Maqāma* of al-Harīrī's *Maqāmāt*, manuscript copied and illustrated by al-Wāsitī, executed Baghdad 635/1237. MS. ar. 5847 f. 18v. *Bib. Nat., Paris*
22. A barber's shop; illustration to the 47th *Maqāma* of al-Harīrī's *Maqāmāt*, manuscript copied in Baghdad, 1222–3. MS. ar. 6094 f. 174. *Bib. Nat., Paris*
23. The public library at Hulwān, near Baghdad; illustration from the 2nd *Maqāma* of al-Harīrī's *Maqāmāt* (see pl. 21), f. 5. *Bib. Nat., Paris*
24. Disputation in a school in Aleppo; illustration from the 2nd *Maqāma* of al-Harīrī's *Maqāmāt* (see pl. 21), f. 148. *Bib. Nat., Paris*
113 25. The travellers, Abū Zayd and al-Hārith, arrive in a village; illustration from the 43rd *Maqāma* of al-Harīrī's *Maqāmāt* (see pl. 21), f. 138r. *Bib. Nat., Paris*
114 26. Courtyard of the Bādshāhī Mosque at Lahore, Pakistan. *Josephine Powell*
27. The minarets of the al-Azhar Mosque, Cairo, founded 360/970, subsequently rebuilt. *Museum of Islamic Art, Cairo*
28. Courtyard of the Great Mosque at Damascus, built 706–15/1306–15. *A. F. Kersting*
115 29. The Golden Mosque in Baghdad, founded iii/9th century, last rebuilt xiii/19th century. *Georg Gerster*
116 30. The early Tīmūrid mausoleums, the Shāh-i Zinda at Samarqand. *Josephine Powell*
31. Burial scene; illustration from the 11th *Maqāma* of al-Harīrī's *Maqāmāt* (see pl. 21), f. 29. *Bib. Nat., Paris*

Chapter Four
The Mystic Path

117 *1.* Sīmurgh; detail from a miniature of the conference of the birds, Turcoman, 899/1493. MS. Elliot 246 f. 25v. Bodleian Library, Oxford. Drawn by P.B.
119 *2.* A Sūfī warming his feet; Persian drawing, x/16th century. *B. M., London*
121 *3.* Inscription from the tomb of al-Ansārī at Gāzurgāh. Drawn by P.B.
122 *4.* Dervishes dancing in a *tekke* at Pera; drawing after J. B. Van Mour. *Searight Collection, London*
123 *5.* Dervish covered with stigmata; Persian drawing, x/16th century. *Bib. Nat., Paris*
124 *6.* Lion from a xiii/19th-century Turkish wall-hanging, from T. K. Burge, *The Bektashi Order of Dervishes*, London, 1952
127 *7.* Dervish carpet, Iran, xi/17th century. Atighetchi Collection, Paris. Drawn by P.B.
129 1. Dancing dervishes; from a manuscript of the *Dīwān* by Hāfiz, Herat school, 896/1490. *Rogers Fund, Metropolitan Museum of Art, New York*
130 2. A mystic preaching to a mixed congregation; from a manuscript of the *Madjālis al-ʿushshāk*, Persian, mid x/16th century. MS. Ouseley Add. 24 f. 55v. *Bodleian Library, Oxford*
3. Two dervishes meditating; Persian drawing, *c.* 1050/1640. *B. M., London*
4. Young dervish; drawing by Muhammadi, *c.* 986/1578. *India Office Library, London*
131 5. Dancing dervishes; miniature from a manuscript of the *Madjālis al-ʿushshāk* (see pl. 2), f. 119r. *Bodleian Library, Oxford*
6. Fakhr ad-Dīn ʿIrāqī travelling with devotees; miniature from a manuscript of the *Madjālis al-ʿushshāk* (see pl. 2), f. 79v. *Bodleian Library, Oxford*
7. Dervish bowl from Persia, xiii/19th century. Victoria and Albert Museum, London. *John Webb*
8. Portrait of a dervish, Tīmūrid, late ix/15th century. *Metropolitan Museum of Art, New York*
132 9. Dancing dervishes in India; Mughul miniature, xi/17th century. Victoria and Albert Museum, London. *J. R. Freeman*
10. Rūmī greeted by a cow; Turkish miniature, late x/16th century. *Topkapi Saray Museum, Istanbul*
133 11. Dervishes dancing at Saʿdī's tomb in Shīrāz; miniature from Saʿdī's *Gulistān*, Persian, Shīrāz style, copied in 974/1566. MS. Add. 24944. *B. L., London*
134 12. Mystical diagram from Ibn al-ʿArabī's *Futuhat*, manuscript copied 1003/1594. MS. Or. 1610. *B. L., London*
13. Medina; ceramic tile, xi/17th century. Museum of Islamic Art, Cairo. *Werner Forman*
14. The Muslim creed; from portal of the Mosque of Shaykh Malik Monayyad, Cairo, 816–23/1413–20. *Museum of Islamic Art, Cairo*
135 15. Lustre-painted plate from Iran, 607/1210. *Freer Gallery of Art, Washington D.C.*
136 16. 'The Travellers and the Elephant'; from a manuscript of Rūmī's *Mathnawī*, Tabrīz style, executed *c.* 937/1530. MS. Add. 27263 f. 134. *B. L., London*
17. Saʿdī travelling to Mecca; from his *Gulistān* (see pl. 11), f. 164v. *B. L., London*
137 18. The conference of the birds; Turcoman, 899/1493. MS. Elliott 246 f. 25v. *Bodleian Library, Oxford*
138 19. Ceiling of a cell in shrine of Shāh Niʿmatullāh Walī by Shāh ʿAbbās at Māhān. *Dr Yolande Crowe*
20. Dancing dervishes; painting by J. B. Van Mour, a French artist who lived in Istanbul, 1111–50/1699–1737. *Rijksmuseum, Amsterdam*
139 21. Shrine of al-Ansārī at Gāzurgāh, near Herat. *Dr Yolande Crowe*
22. The tomb of Baba Rukn ad-Dīn, Isfahan. *Professor F. Meier*
23. The tomb of Rūmī, Konya. *Sonia Halliday*
140 24. Monastery and shrine at Māhān. *Robert Harding*
25. Ceramic decoration from the shrine of al-Ansārī at Gāzurgāh, near Herat. *Dr Yolande Crowe*

Chapter Five
Jewellers with Words

141 *1.* Scribe; from a manuscript of al-Harīrī's *Maqāmāt*, executed by al-Wāsitī, signed and dated Baghdad 635/1237. MS. ar. 5847 f. 79. Bib. Nat., Paris. Drawn by P.B.
142 *2.* Colophon of a Qur'ān, Morocco, 976/1568. MS. Or. 1405 f. 399v–400r. *B. L., London*
144 *3.* Ink mortar, bronze, vi/12th century. B. M., London. Drawn by P.B.
149 *4.* A poet reading to a prince; miniature from Bukhārā, 968/1560. *Collection David Khalili*
151 *5.* The poet Hāfiz and courtier; Mughul miniature, *c.* 1019/1610. *Courtesy Sotheby's, London*
153 1. Plate with concentric bands of Kūfic inscription, Iran, iv/10th century. *Freer Gallery of Art, Washington D.C.*
154 2. Papyrus fragment of a manuscript of the stories of famous lovers, from al-Fustāt, Egypt, second half of iii/9th or early iv/10th century. Charter 25612. *Österreichische Nationalbibliothek, Vienna*
3. The lover faints at receiving bad news; miniature from the unique manuscript of the story of Bayād and Riyād, Spain or Morocco, early vii/13th century. MS. Arab 368. *Biblioteca Apostolica Vaticana*
155 4. Majnūn throws himself on Laylā's tomb; painting from a copy of Amīr Khusraw Divlavi's *Khamseh*, India, middle of ix/15th century. *Freer Gallery of Art, Washington D.C.*
5. The old woman brings Majnūn to Laylā's tent; Persian miniature, ix/15th century. *B. M., London*
156 6. Page from Qur'ān in Kūfic script, iii/9th century. MS. Or. 1397 f. 13r. *B. L., London*
7. Page from Qur'ān in Persian Kūfic, 466/1073. *Mashhad Shrine Library*

8. Page from Qur'ān in bent Kūfic, 361/972. MS. K/17/1 f. 2v. *Chester Beatty Library, Dublin*
9. Qur'ān stand in carved wood; Mongol, Iran, 762/1360. *Metropolitan Museum of Art, New York*
157 10. Page from Qur'ān in Naskhī, Baghdad, 391/1000. MS. K/16 f. 283v. *Chester Beatty Library, Dublin*
11. Page from Qur'ān in Maghribī script, North Africa, VI/12th to VII/13th century. MS. Or. 12523 f. 19r. *B. L., London*
12. Page from Qur'ān in Jalil script, Mamlūk, VII/13th century. MS. Or. 1009 f. 303v. *B. L., London*
13. Page from Qur'ān in Jalil script, Mosul, Iraq, 710/1310. MS. Or. 4945 f. 3. *B. L., London*
158 14. Illustration to *Kalīla wa-Dimna* (Arabic version by Ibn al-Maqaffaʿ), Baghdad, *c.* 617–28/1220–30. MS. ar. 3465 f. 33. *Bib. Nat., Paris*
15. Dimna and the lion; from *Kalīla wa-Dimna* (see pl. 14), f. 125. *Bib. Nat., Paris*
16. Frontispiece to a Persian version of *Kalīla wa-Dimna*, Persian, 705/1307. MS. Or. 13506. *B. L., London*
17. The owls attacking the crows; illustration to the *Humāyūn-nāma*, a free Turkish translation by ʿAlī Chelebi of the Persian version of the fables of Bidpay. MS. Add. 15153 f. 215r. *B. L., London*
159 18. A literary assembly in a garden of Baghdad; illustration from the 24th *Maqāma*, set in 'the quarters', of al-Harīrī's *Maqāmāt*, manuscript executed by al-Wāsitī, signed and dated Baghdad 635/1237. MS. ar. 5847 f. 69. *Bib. Nat., Paris*
160 19. An island of the Indian Ocean; illustration from the 39th *Maqāma*, set in Oman, of al-Harīrī's *Maqāmāt* (see pl. 18), f. 121. *Bib. Nat., Paris*
20. Al-Harīrī and his companions meet Abū Zayd; illustration from the 25th *Maqāma*, set in Kerej, of al-Harīrī's *Maqāmāt*, executed in Baghdad, second quarter of VII/13th century. MS. ar. 3929 f. 54v. *Bib. Nat., Paris*

Chapter Six

The Dimension of Sound

161 *1.* Musicians; detail from a brass ewer inlaid in silver and copper, Mosul, 630/1232. B. M., London. Drawn by P.B.
162 *2.* Women's song from a wedding ceremony
3. Introduction to a song
4. Excerpt from a *debka*
163–4 *5–6.* A *nuzha* and an *ʿūd*; from Safī ad-Dīn's *Kitāb al-adwar.* MS. Marsh 521 f. 157v–158r. *Bodleian Library, Oxford*
164 *7.* Tetrachord
165 *8.* Excerpt from a vocal improvisation
166–7 *9–16.* A *mizmār* and a *nāy*, three string instruments, two forms of cithar, two bowed instruments; illustrations from the *Kanz at-tuhaf*, Persian, mid VIII/14th century. MS. Or. 2361 f. 263r, 260v, 265r, 263v, 264r, 264v, 262r, 262v. *B. L., London*
170 *17.* Excerpt from a Mawlawi ceremony
18. Excerpt from music played at *zikr* ceremonies
171 *19–20.* Shepherd playing a *nāy*, and a harp and lute; illustrations from a Persian dictionary of rare words, X/16th century. MS. Or. 3299 f. 288r–289v. *B. L., London*
(Musical examples supplied by the author)
173 1–2. Dancer, lute and flute player; Fātimid ivory panels, V/11th to VI/12th century. Bargello, Florence. *Alinari/Mansell*
174 3. Muezzins calling to prayer; detail of a miniature showing the Kaʿba at Mecca from a copy of Saʿdī's *Gulistān*, made in Shīrāz, 974/1566. MS. Add. 24944 f. 150v. *B. L., London*
4. Musicians accompanying dancing dervishes; detail from a Mughul miniature, 1004/1595. Victoria and Albert Museum, London. *J. R. Freeman*
175 5. Pilgrim caravan going to Mecca; illustration from al-Harīrī's *Maqāmāt*, manuscript executed by al-Wāsitī, signed and dated Baghdad 635/1237. MS. ar. 5847 f. 94v. *Bib. Nat., Paris*
176 6. Lute player; Seljuq marble relief, *c.* 597/1200. *Staatliche Museen, Berlin*
7. Three musicians in a tavern scene; illustration from al-Harīrī's *Maqāmāt*, executed in Mosul, 654/1256. MS. Or. 1200 f. 34r. *B. L., London*
8. Harp player accompanying a game of chess; illustration from the *Libro de los juegos* of Alfonso the Wise, executed in Spain, VII/13th century. MS. T.j. 6. Escorial, Madrid. *Mas*
9–11. Harp, flute and lute players; details from a brass basin, inlaid with silver, Syria or Mesopotamia, VII/13th century. *Victoria and Albert Museum, London*
177 12. A shepherd(?) playing a horn; Persian album painting, *c.* 1036/1626. *B. M., London*
13. An elderly musician playing a flute; Persian album painting, Qazwin style, *c.* 968–78/1560–70. *Courtesy Sotheby's, London*
14–15. Trumpeters and a dancer with castanets; illustrations from a Persian glossary of rare words compiled in 870–71/1468–9, manuscript executed in early X/16th century, probably by a Persian artist working in western India. MS. Or. 3299 f. 184v, 100v. *B. L., London*
178 16. Turkish military band; detail of a miniature from the *Sebinsah-nāma*, describing events of the reign of Murād III, manuscript executed in 1001/1592. MS. B 200 f. 159v. Topkapi Saray Museum, Istanbul. *Sonia Halliday*
17. Military band from a water-clock; illustration from al-Jazarī's *Automata*, manuscript executed in 715/1315. *Museum of Fine Arts, Boston*
179 18. Scene with musicians and dancers at the marriage entertainment of Akbar's brother at Agra in 969/1561; one leaf of a two-page miniature, executed before 999/1590 by Lāl and Sanwalah. Victoria and Albert Museum, London. *J. R. Freeman*
180 19–21. Folk music instruments in use at village festivals. *Courtesy Professor A. Shiloah*
22–23. Folk music instruments at the Congrès de Musique Arabe, 1932. *Courtesy Professor I. Katz*

Chapter Seven

The Scientific Enterprise

181 *1.* Persian plate with signs of the Zodiac, 971/1563. Staatliche Museen, Berlin. Drawn by P.B.
182 *2.* Detail from first page of 'The book of the excellent Galen *On Medical Sects*'. MS. ar. 2859. *Bib. Nat., Paris*
185 *3.* Page from al-Uqlīdisī's *Kitāb al-Fusūl* showing the use of the decimal point. MS. Yeni Jāmiʿ 802 f. 61r. Istanbul
186 *4.* Page from Nasīr ad-Dīn at-Tūsī's *ar-Risāla ash-Shāfiya* showing parallelogram. MS. ar. 2467 f. 84v. *Bib. Nat., Paris*
187 *5–6.* Diagrams from Ibn ash-Shātir's *Nihāyat as-sūl* illustrating the motions of Mercury. MS. Marsh 139 f. 29r–29v. *Bodleian Library, Oxford*
188 *7.* Diagrams from the Arabic version of Ptolemy's *Planetary Hypotheses*, known in Arabic as *Kitāb al-Iqtisās*, 639/1242. MS. Add. 7473 f. 98v–99r. *B. L., London*
189 *8.* Diagram of the eye, from a manuscript of Ibn al-Haytham's *Optics*, 476/1083. Bk I, Aya Sofya 3212, Aya Sofya Library, Istanbul
9. Diagram from a Latin version of Ibn al-Haytham's *Optics*. MS. Royal 1267. *B. L., London*
10. Diagram illustrating the *camera obscura* from manuscript by Kamāl ad-Dīn al-Fārisī. Aya Sofya 2451, Aya Sofya Library, Istanbul
190 *11.* Diagram from al-Qazwīnī's *Wonders of Creation* illustrating Avicenna's theory of the rainbow. MS. Add. 7894 f. 115v. *B. L., London*
191 *12.* Page from Abū 'l'Qāsim az-Zahrāwī's *Kitāb at-Tasrīf* showing surgical instruments. MS. Hunt 156. *Bodleian Library, Oxford*
193 1. Astronomers; from an Ottoman manuscript of the *Shahinshāh-nāma*, second half of X/16th century. F. 1404 f. 56v. Istanbul University Library. *Courtesy Professor M. S. Ipsiroglu*
194 2. Celestial sphere, copper, Iran, 684/1285. *Louvre, Paris*
3. Spherical astrolabe, brass and silver, signed and dated 885/1480. *Museum of the History of Science, Oxford*
4. Hülegü Khān's astronomers in the observatory at Marāgha; miniature from a manuscript of the *Nusret-nāma* in Turkish, Bukhārā, X/16th century. MS. Or. 3222 f. 105v. *B. L., London*
5. Astronomical table for the rising points of the constellations of the Zodiac; from a manuscript of the *Il-Khānid zīj*, an astronomical work by Nasīr ad-Dīn at-Tūsī composed for Hülegü. MS. Add. 7698 f. 126r. *B. L., London*
195 6. Astrolabe dedicated to Djafar, son of the Caliph al-Muktafī, Iraq, III/9th century. *Bib. Nat., Paris*
7. The track of the observatory at Samarqand. *Richard Harrington, Camera Press*
8–9. Cepheus and Sagittarius; from a copy of the *Book of Fixed Stars*, by ʿUmar as-Sūfī, copied and illustrated in 400/1009. MS. Marsh 144 f. 61, f. 272. *Bodleian Library, Oxford*
10. Andromeda; from a copy of the *Book of Fixed Stars*, illustrated in Mosul, early VIII/14th century. MS. Or. 5323 f. 32v. *B. L., London*
196 11. Aristotle; from a manuscript of the *Description of Animals*, by Ibn Bakhtīshūʿ, early VII/13th century. MS. Or. 2784 f. 96. *B. L., London*
12. Saxifrage; from the Dioscorides Codex, executed in Constantinople, AD 512 (each herb is identified by a later Arabic hand). Codex Vindob. Med Gr I f. 290v. *Österreichische Nationalbibliothek, Vienna*
13. Coordinate table of the use of herbs; from an Arabic translation of the *Pseudo-Galen*, executed in 595/1199. MS. ar. 2964 f. 9. *Bib. Nat., Paris*
197 14. The anatomy of the eye; from a VII/13th-century copy of Hunayn ibn Ishāq's *Book of the Ten Treatises on the Eye*, 593/1197. National Library, Cairo. *A. Duncan, Middle East Archive*
15. Scene in a pharmacy; from an Arabic version of Dioscorides' *Materia Medica*, Baghdad, VII/13th century. Metropolitan Museum of Art, New York. *Werner Forman*
16. The circulation of the blood; drawing from a Persian *Medical Treasury*, XI/17th century. MS. Fraser 201 f. 104r. *Bodleian Library, Oxford*
198 17. World map, copied from al-Idrīsī's map of 549/1154. MS. Uri 887. *Bodleian Library, Oxford*
18. Map of Egypt; from a IV/10th-century copy of al-Istakhrī's *Book of Countries*. Cod. Arab 1521. *Forschungsbibliothek, Gotha*
19. World map; from al-Qazwīnī's *The Marvels of Nature*, written for the library of the Il-Khānid sovereign of Baghdad, 791/1388. MS. suppl. pers. 332 f. 50. *Bib. Nat., Paris*
20. Map of Persia (see pl. 18), f. 40. *Forschungsbibliothek, Gotha*
199 21. Machine for lifting water; illustration from al-Jazarī's *Automata*, manuscript of late VIII/14th century. MS. Graves 27 f. 101v. *Bodleian Library, Oxford*
22. Blood-letting device; illustration from al-Jazarī's *Automata*, 715/1315. *Freer Gallery of Art, Washington D.C.*
23. Hydraulic device in the form of a slave with a pitcher; illustration from al-Jazarī's *Automata*, 715/1315. *Freer Gallery of Art, Washington D.C.*
200 24. Astronomers; from an Ottoman manuscript of the *Shahinshāh-nāma* (see pl. 1), f. 57r. *Courtesy Professor M. S. Ipsiroglu*
25. Scene with an astrologer; from al-Harīrī's *Maqāmāt*, Baghdad, second quarter of VII/13th century. MS. ar. 3929 f. 178. *Bib. Nat., Paris*
26. Brass astrolabe, engraved and inlaid in silver and copper, Cairo, 634/1236. *B. M., London*

Chapter Eight

Armies of the Prophet

201 *1.* Detail from the so-called Baptistère de St Louis; bronze inlaid with silver and copper, Egypt or Syria, first half of VIII/14th century. Louvre, Paris. Drawn by P.B.
203 *2.* Turkish battle standard. *Topkapi Saray Museum, Istanbul*
205 *3.* Leather shadow-play figure, Egypt, IX/15th century. *Staatliche Museen, Berlin*
206 *4.* View of the Cairo Citadel; engraving from *Description de l'Egypte*, Paris, 1822–3. *J. R. Freeman*
207 *5.* Silver plate, Iran, IV/10th century. State Hermitage Museum, Leningrad. Drawn by P.B.
209 *6.* Ink drawing on paper, Fustāt, Egypt, V/11th century. *Museum of Islamic Art, Cairo*
210 *7–8.* Woodcuts by Melchior Lorich, 1576. B. M., London. *J. R. Freeman*
213 1. Large *minai* dish with representation of warriors attacking a fortress; Seljuq, Iran, early VII/13th century. *Freer Gallery of Art, Washington D.C.*
214 2. Battle scene; fragment of a miniature painting, Fātimid, Egypt, V/11th to VI/12th century. *B. M., London*
3. The Battle of the Rival Clans; illustration from the *Khamseh* of Nizāmī, Persian, 846/1442. MS. Add. 25900 f. 121v. *B. L., London*
214–15 4–9. Arms and war machines; illustrations from a treatise on arms and their manufacture written by Murdab ʿAlī for Saladin after the siege of Jerusalem in 583/1187. MS. Huntington 264 f. 134v–135r, 117v, 102v, 85v, 141v. *Bodleian Library, Oxford*
216 10–11. Attack on the fortress of Arg, and Mahmūd ibn Sebuktigin defeating the Ilig Khān; from Rashīd ad-Dīn's *Jami at-Tawarik* ('Universal History'), manuscript in Arabic copied at Rashidiyya, near Tabrīz, 706–14/1306–14. MS. 20 f. 124v, 127v. *Edinburgh University Library*

Islamic dynasties back to Adam; originally compiled during the reign of Sulaymān, this manuscript was executed in the XI/17th century. *Metropolitan Museum of Art, New York*

288-9 10–14. Osman I; Orhan; Murād I; Bāyazīd I; Mehmed I; portraits from a description of the Ottoman sultans, executed during the reign of Murād III (982–1004/1574–95). H. 1563. Topkapi Saray Museum, Istanbul. *Sonia Halliday*

288 15. Sulaymān; Ottoman miniature, x/16th century. Book No. 3109. Topkapi Saray Museum, Istanbul. *Sonia Halliday*

288-9 16–19. Murād II; Mehmed II; Bāyazīd II; Selīm I; portraits from a description of the Ottoman sultans, executed during the reign of Murād III (982–1004/1574–95). H. 1563. Topkapi Saray Museum, Istanbul. *Sonia Halliday*

290-1 20–29. A *qādī*; a Jewish doctor; a Janissary; a Turkish woman and her Moorish servant; a Sūfī; a Christian merchant; an Arab merchant; a Turkish prostitute; a woman in Syrian dress; a Moorish slave; from a series of coloured etchings by the Master L. D., illustrating *Les Quatre Premiers Livres des navigations et pérégrinations orientales*, by Nicolas de Nicolay, Lyons, 1568. B. L., London. *J. R. Freeman*

291 30. Sulaymān's signature. Topkapi Saray Library, Istanbul. *Sonia Halliday*

31. Sulaymān; woodcut by Jan Swaart, c. 933/1526. B. M., London. *J. R. Freeman*

292 32. Bāyazīd I at the siege of Nicopolis castle; miniature from a manuscript of the first volume of the *Hünernāma* ('The Book of Accomplishments'), a historical work by Sayyid Lokman describing the reign of the Ottoman sultans up to the reign of Selīm I, by Nakkas Osman, c. 992/1584. H. 1523 f. 170v. Topkapi Saray Library, Istanbul. *Sonia Halliday*

293 33. Selīm II and European taxpayers; illustration from a manuscript of the *Nuzhet ul-ahbar der Sefer-i Sigetvar*, a historical work by Ahmed Feridun Pasa describing the siege of Szigetvár, copied in 976–7/1568–9. H. 1339 f. 178r. Topkapi Saray Library, Istanbul. *Sonia Halliday*

34. The Second Courtyard of the Topkapi Saray; illustration from the *Hüner-nāma* (see pl. 32), f. 19r. Topkapi Saray Library, Istanbul. *Sonia Halliday*

294 35. The Gök *madrasa*, Sivas, built 670–71/1270–71. *Yan*

36. The Yeshil Jāmi', Iznik, VIII/14th century. *G. Goodwin*

37. The Üch Sherefeli Jāmi', Edirne, IX/15th century. *G. Goodwin*

38. The cenotaph of Mehmed II in the Green Turbe in Bursa, 816–27/1413–24. *Yan*

295 39. The Sultan Ahmed Jāmi', or Blue Mosque, Istanbul. *Wim Swaan, Camera Press*

296 40–41. Details from the panelling of a room made for a Christian Arab merchant of Aleppo, lacquer on wood, depicting Christian and Oriental scenes, 1009–12/1600–1603. *Staatliche Museen, Berlin*

297 42. Fanciful drawing of Aya Sofya, made by an Englishman taken captive by the Turks during Queen Elizabeth I's reign, in the fifteenth year of his captivity. MS. Sloane 5234 f. 92. B. L., London.

43. Selīm III receiving an ambassador at the Gate of Felicity in the Topkapi Saray; oil painting. Topkapi Saray Museum, Istanbul. *Sonia Halliday*

298 44. Dancing girl; album painting by Levni (d. 1145/1732). *Topkapi Saray Library, Istanbul*

45. A European gentleman; album painting by Levni. *B. M., London*

46. The interior of a room in Damascus, 1170/1756. *Victoria and Albert Museum, London*

299 47. Interior of the Qara Mustafā Pasha Kiosk, renovated by Ahmed III in 1116–17/1704–5, near the Baghdad Kiosk in the Topkapi Saray. *Boudot-Lamotte*

48. Fountain on the terrace adjoining the Baghdad Kiosk built in 1049/1639 in the Topkapi Saray. *Wim Swaan, Camera Press*

300 49. Mecca; panel of tiles in the harem, late XI/17th century. *Topkapi Saray Museum, Istanbul*

Chapter Twelve
Muslim India

301 1. Detail from *pietra dura* decoration in the Tāj Mahal. Drawn by P.B.

302 2. Kūfic inscription from the marble sacrophagus of Mahmūd of Ghazna, Ghazna, Afghanistan. Drawn by P.B.

309 3. Mechanism for taking down an Aśokan pillar; illustration from the *Sīrat-i Fīrūz Shāhī*. Khudabkhsh Library, Patna. *Courtesy Professor S. Nur al-Hasan*

311 4. Map of India. Drawn by Shalom Schotten

313 1. Qutb Minār, Delhi. *Courtesy S. A. A. Rizvi*

314 2. Fathpūr-Sīkrī, marble grille in the tomb of Salīm Chishtī. *J. Allan Cash*

315 3. Detail of inlaid marble from the Tāj Mahal. *Federico Borromeo*

4. Tomb of Shaykh Rukn ad-Dīn Multānī, d. 735/1334, Multan. *Courtesy Professor A. H. Dani and W. Wali Allah Khān*

5. Fathpūr-Sīkrī, from the Panch Mahal Pavilion. *J. Allan Cash*

316 6. The Emperor Bābur; Mughul miniature, c. 1019/1610. Kevarkion Foundation. *Courtesy Sotheby's, London*

7. Jahāngīr with a portrait of his father; Mughul illuminated manuscript, mostly by Abū 'l-Hasan, c. 1008–14/1599–1605. *Musée Guimet, Paris*

8. Akbar receiving divines; miniature by Nan Singh, from a copy of the *Akbar-nāma*, c. 1014/1605. *Chester Beatty Library, Dublin*

317 9. Jahāngīr and Shāh 'Abbās I attended by two courtiers; Mughul painting mounted on an album leaf (recto), colour and gold, c. 1030/1620. *Freer Gallery of Art, Washington D.C.*

10. Shāhjahān kills a lion; cameo, mid XI/17th century. *Bib. Nat., Paris*

11. The court of Jahāngīr with portrait of Sir Thomas Roe; Mughul miniature, 1025/1616. *B. M., London*

318 12. Work on the water-gate during building of the Red Fort at Agra; miniature from a copy of the *Akbar-nāma*; Mughul, c. 1004/1595. Victoria and Albert Museum, London. *J. R. Freeman*

13. Akbar crossing the Ganges; miniature from a copy of the *Akbar-nāma*, painted by Ikhlās (composition) and Mādhu (portraits), Mughul, c. 1009/1600. Victoria and Albert Museum, London. *J. R. Freeman*

14. An artist at work; Mughul, c. 1019–24/1610–15. Victoria and Albert Museum, London. *J. R. Freeman*

15. A young prince with sages in a garden; painting by Bichitr. Indian MS. 3 pl. 59. Chester Beatty Library, Dublin. *Pieterse Davison International Ltd*

320 16. Europeans taking tea beside a lake. *B. L., London*

17. Mahādajī Sindhia (ruled 1196–1209/1782–94) entertaining British officers to a *nautch* in his house in Delhi; painting by Delhi artist, c. 1820. *India Office Library, London*

Chapter Thirteen
Islam Today

321 1. Carved stone hatchment of arms in the Topkapi Saray, Istanbul, XIII/19th century. Drawn by P.B.

323 2. Plan of the camp of 'Abd al-Qādir in 1843; from M. Berbrugger, *Algérie historique*, Paris, 1843

324 3. Portrait of Shamīl; contemporary German woodcut. *Mary Evans Picture Library*

326 4. The Russian army entering Adrianople (Edirne), 1828–9; French popular woodcut. *Bib. Nat., Paris*

5. Entry of General Berthézène into Algiers, 5 July 1830; French popular woodcut. *Roger Viollet*

328 6. 'Disgorging'; drawing by Sir John Tenniel for *Punch*, 1878. *Searight Collection, London*

7. 'The Egyptian Pet'; drawing by Sir John Tenniel for *Punch*, 1891. *Searight Collection, London*

335 8. Frieze outside Officers' Club, Cairo. *Stuart Heydinger, Camera Press*

337 1. 'Abd ar-Rahmān, Sultan of Morocco, surrounded by his court; painting by Eugène Delacroix, 1845. Musée des Augustins, Toulouse. *Giraudon*

338 2. 'Conquest and Civilization'; detail of the frontispiece to L. A. Berbrugger, *Algérie historique*, Paris, 1843. *J. R. Freeman*

3. The French Consul insulted by the Dey of Algiers; detail of a lithograph from L. A. Berbrugger, *Algérie historique*, Paris, 1843. *J. R. Freeman*

4. Celebration in Turkistan; painting by V. V. Vereschagin, 1872. *Tretyakov Gallery, Moscow*

5. 'Abd al-Qādir; lithograph after L. Lassale. Bib. Nat., Paris. *Bulloz*

339 6. Sir Herbert Kitchener, later Earl Kitchener of Khartoum, at the Mahdi's tomb at Omdurman in 1898; watercolour by R. Caton Woodville. *Searight Collection, London*

7. The Allies entering Jerusalem, 11 December 1917; watercolour by James McBey. Imperial War Museum, London. *Eileen Tweedy*

8. The Allied fleet at Constantinople; watercolour by Frank H. Mason. Imperial War Museum, London. *Eileen Tweedy*

340 9. Selīm III; painting by Hippolite Berteaux. Topkapi Saray Museum, Istanbul. *Sonia Halliday*

340-1 10. Mehmed 'Ālī with Colonel Patrick Campbell and French engineers; coloured lithograph after D. Roberts. Victoria and Albert Museum, London. *A. C. Cooper*

340 11–13. Turkish military costume; watercolours, first half of XIII/19th century. Victoria and Albert Museum, London. *J. R. Freeman*

341 14. Turkish uniforms in 1890; coloured lithograph. B. L., London. *J. R. Freeman*

342 15. Mustafā Kemal with his wife in their garden. *Radio Times Hulton Picture Library*

16. Mustafā Kemal teaching the Roman alphabet. *Ministry of Information, Istanbul*

17. Turkish women's costumes of the 1920s. *Radio Times Hulton Picture Library*

343 18. Riots in Cairo in 1952. *Associated Press*

343 19. The reception of Nasser at Damascus. *Dalmas, Camera Press*

20. Nasser speaking to his people, 1962. *Camera Press*

21. Egyptian soldier in Sinai during the 1973 war. *Camera Press*

344 22. Prayer in Jordan. *Charles Harbutt, Magnum*

23. American cars for Kuwait. *René Burri, Magnum*

INDEX

Page numbers in *italic* refer to illustrations.

Look at the great anatomy and physiology study tools WCB/McGraw-Hill has to offer!

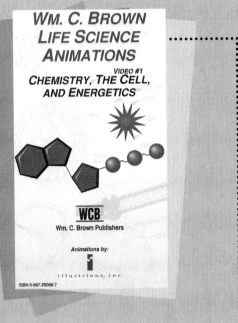

WCB Life Science Animations Videotapes

Series of six videotapes containing animations of complex physiological processes. These animations make challenging concepts easier to understand.

Tape 1 Chemistry, The Cell, and Energetics
ISBN: 0-697-25068-7

Tape 2 Cell Division, Heredity, Genetics, Reproduction, and Development
ISBN: 0-697-25069-5

Tape 3 Animal Biology #1
ISBN: 0-697-25070-9

Tape 4 Animal Biology #2
ISBN: 0-697-25071-7

Tape 5 Plant Biology, Evolution, and Ecology
ISBN: 0-697-26600-1

Tape 6 Physiological Concepts of Life Science Videotape
ISBN: 0-697-21512-1

Life Science Living Lexicon CD-ROM

by William Marchuk
ISBN: 0-697-29266-5

This interactive CD-ROM contains a complete lexicon of life science terminology. Conveniently assembled on an easy-to-use CD-ROM are components such as a glossary of common biological roots, prefixes, and suffixes; a categorized glossary of common biological terms; and a section describing the classification system.

To order any of these products, contact your bookstore manager or call our Customer Service Department at 800–338–3987.

QuickStudy:
Computerized Study Guide for
Human Anatomy
by Kent M. Van De Graaff

Focus study time only in the areas where you need the most help.

Available on diskette:
IBM: 0-697-34630-7
Macintosh: 0-697-34631-5

How does it work?

- Take the computerized test for each chapter.
- The program presents you with feedback for each answer.
- A page-referenced study plan is then created for all incorrect answers.
- Look up the answers to the questions you missed.
- This easy-to-use *QuickStudy* is not a duplicate of the printed study guide that accompanies your text. It's full of new study aids.

Four different review methods available.

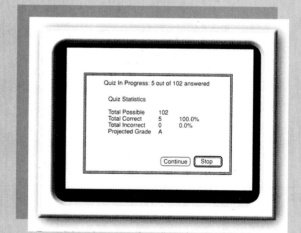

Provides instant feedback on quiz results.

- **Learning Objectives** outline the major points covered in each text chapter.
- **Key Terms** and their definitions are listed for each chapter.
- **Review** presents important concepts and facts in detail.
- **Take Quiz** allows testing on any combination of—or all—chapters.

To order any of these products, contact your bookstore manager or call our Customer Service Department at 800–338–3987.